ZAGATSURVEY®

2007

NEW YORK CITY RESTAURANTS

D0003181

Editors: Curt Gathje and Carol Diuguid

Coordinator: Larry Cohn

Published and distributed by
ZAGAT SURVEY, LLC
4 Columbus Circle
New York, New York 10019
Tel: 212 977 6000
E-mail: newyork@zagat.com
Web site: www.zagat.com

Acknowledgments

We thank Siobhan Burns, Caren Weiner Campbell, Daphne Dennis, Mikola De Roo, Lynn Hazlewood, Laura Mitchell, Bernard Onken, Blake Royer, Steven Shukow, Miranda Van Gelder, Laura Vogel and Barak Zimmerman, as well as the following members of our staff: Emily Parsons (associate editor), Rachel McConlogue (editorial assistant), Sean Beachell, Maryanne Bertollo, Reni Chin, David Downing, Victoria Elmacioglu, Andrew Eng, Jeff Freier, Shelley Gallagher, Randi Gollin, Jessica Grose, Karen Hudes, Natalie Lebert, Mike Liao, Dave Makulec, Josh Rogers, Becky Ruthenburg, Troy Segal, Robert Seixas, Thomas Sheehan, Carla Spartos, Kelly Stewart, Donna Marino Wilkins, Yoji Yamaguchi, Sharon Yates and Kyle Zolner.

Contents

About This Survey

Here are the results of our *2007 New York City Restaurant Survey* covering 2,014 establishments as rated and reviewed by 31,604 local restaurant-goers. To help you find NYC's best meals and best buys, we have prepared a number of lists. See Most Popular (page 10), Top Ratings (pages 11–21) and Best Buys (pages 22–25) as well as a total of 50 handy indexes (pages 240–315).

This marks the 28th year that Zagat Survey has reported on the shared experiences of diners like you. What started in 1979 as a hobby involving 200 of our friends rating NYC restaurants has come a long way. Today we have over 250,000 active surveyors and now cover dining, entertaining, golf, hotels, resorts, spas, movies, music, nightlife, shopping, theater and tourist attractions around the world. All of these guides are based on consumer surveys. They are also available by subscription at zagat.com, and for use on BlackBerry, Palm, Windows Mobile devices and mobile phones.

By regularly surveying large numbers of avid customers, we have achieved a uniquely current and reliable series of guides. More than a quarter-century of experience has verified this. In effect, these guides are the restaurant industry's report card, since each place's ratings and review are really a free market study of its own customers. Hopefully this customer feedback will enable the restaurants to improve their performance over time.

This year's 31,000-plus participants dined out an average of 3.4 times per week, bringing roughly 5.6 million meals' worth of experience to this *Survey*. Of these surveyors, 54% are women, 46% men; the breakdown by age is 15% in their 20s; 28%, 30s; 18%, 40s; 20%, 50s; and 19%, 60s or above. While these people are a diverse group, they share one thing in common – they are all restaurant lovers.

Our editors have done their best to synopsize our respondents' opinions, with specific comments shown in quotation marks. We sincerely thank each of these people; this book is really "theirs."

Finally, we invite you to join any of our upcoming *Surveys* – to do so, just register at zagat.com, where you can rate and review any restaurant at any time during the year. Each participant will receive a free copy of the resulting guide when it is published. Your comments and even criticisms of this guide are also solicited. There is always room for improvement with your help. You can contact us at newyork@zagat.com.

New York, NY
October 11, 2006

Nina and Tim Zagat

What's New

State of the Union: NYC dining continued its steady forward course over the last year. Although the top winners – Le Bernardin for Food, Daniel for Decor, per se for Service and Gramercy Tavern as Most Popular – are all repeats from our 2006 *Survey,* there were 222 noteworthy openings vs. only 102 closings last year.

Neighborhood Alert: Hot new restaurant rows arrived, most notably along a once-barren stretch of 10th Avenue between 14th and 23rd streets, where Anzu, Cookshop, Craftsteak, Del Posto, Morimoto and Trestle on Tenth debuted. Just off of 10th Avenue, 16th Street had its own revival with Buddakan and the relocated Frank's joining La Bottega and Matsuri. Elsewhere, TriBeCa's Greenwich Street is humming with newcomers Devin Tavern, Industria Argentina, Turks & Frogs and Wolfgang's Steakhouse. Similarly, the Madison Square Park area saw the debut of A Voce, Café at Country, Country and Ureña.

Up, Up and Away: The $39.43 average dinner cost was up nearly 5% from last year's $37.61, roughly double the inflation rate that we have seen over the last decade. At Gotham's 20 most expensive places, prices soared 14.5% to $128.79 a meal. Two years ago, this figure was $91.28!

Celeb Chefs on the Move: The roller-coaster world of celeb chefdom continues its dizzy pace with arrivals that included Mario Batali and Lidia Bastianich (Del Posto), Tom Colicchio (Craftsteak), Kurt Gutenbrunner (Blaue Gans), Thomas Keller (Bouchon Bakery), Masaharu Morimoto (Morimoto), François Payard (In Tent), Eric Ripert (Barça 18), Joël Robuchon (L'Atelier de Joël Robuchon), Bill Telepan (Telepan), Laurent Tourondel (Brasserie Ruhlmann), Alex Ureña (Ureña) and Geoffrey Zakarian (Country). Still, when we asked "do you seek out restaurants that have celebrity chefs?", 79% of our surveyors replied "no." Go figure.

Steakhouse Stampede: Continuing a long-term trend, the past year witnessed the opening of a number of first-rate steakhouses such as AJ Maxwell's, Alonso's, Blair Perrone, Craftsteak, Harry's Steak, Industria Argentina, Porter House NY, Quality Meats, Staghorn and Wolfgang's in TriBeCa. Giving this growth a little perspective, in 1993 we listed 28 NYC steakhouses; this year that number has risen to 93.

Chinese Invasion: The long-suffering Chinese segment made some high-end beachheads at Buddakan, Buddha Bar, Chinatown Brasserie, Mr. Chow TriBeCa and Philippe, all of which rolled out prices never before seen for the genre. On the horizon lies an important import from the renowned Alan Yau (London's Hakkasan, Wagamama, Yauatcha) that's scheduled to open this November. However, with 24 Japanese restaurants outscoring the No. 1 Chinese (Phoenix Garden) this year, Chinese dining has a long way to go.

Hotels Humming: Accelerating a recent trend, more hotels are importing top talent, to wit, Gordon Ramsay (at The London NYC, ex Rihga Royal), Joël Robuchon (Four Seasons), Laurent Tourondel (Ritz-Carlton), Alan Yau (Gramercy Park) and Geoffrey Zakarian (Carlton).

BBQ Burnouts: The recent rash of BBQ joints was reversed this year with the flame-outs of Pearson's, Rib, Smoked, Smoke Shack and the venerable Tennessee Mountain. Fortunately, the field remains strong thanks to such stalwarts as Blue Smoke, Daisy May's, Dinosaur and Virgil's, plus the recently opened Pioneer Bar-B-Q and Rack & Soul.

Decor Watch: In the ever more theatrical world of restaurant design, 'mega' was the word in 2006 with the arrival of Buddakan, Buddha Bar, Chinatown Brasserie, Craftsteak, Del Posto, Le Cirque, Megu Midtown, Morimoto and Porter House NY, all of which have upwards of 150 seats and no-expense-spared decor. Hip rusticity, a genre pioneered by taxidermy-heavy Freemans, showed up at Alonso's, Aspen and Lodge, while deco devotees were delighted by Brasserie Ruhlmann, fittingly found in Rockefeller Center.

Farewell: Gone to that Great Kitchen in the Sky were such notables as Bellini, Le Zinc, Mainland, Manhattan Ocean Club, Park Avalon, 71 Clinton Fresh Food and such vets as Bill Hong (born 1955), McHales (1953) and Second Avenue Deli (1954 – though it's rumored that it will come back, just not on Second Avenue).

Random Notes: Restaurateur of the Year award went to Philadelphia's Stephen Starr, who imported both Buddakan and Morimoto to West Chelsea . . . Noise levels increasingly vexed diners – 26% report it's the most irritating thing about dining out, in comparison to 18% two years ago . . . The average tip continued to rise, this year to a reported 18.9% . . . Rating the city's current overall dining scene, surveyors gave NYC's culinary diversity a 28 on the Zagat 30-point scale and creativity a 25; hospitality and table availability did not fare as well, with respective scores of 15 and 13 . . . Union Square Hospitality Group was the city's most popular restaurant consortium, with five eateries in the Top 20: Gramercy Tavern (rated No. 1), Union Square Cafe (No. 2), Eleven Madison Park (No. 12), The Modern (No. 16) and Tabla (No. 18) . . . Department store dining, a too limited genre, welcomed BG in Bergdorf Goodman as well as David Burke at Bloomingdale's . . . The automat, that glass-windowed, coin-operated marvel of yesteryear, came back with a bang at Bamn!, only with dollar tokens replacing the original's nickels.

New York, NY
October 11, 2006

Nina and Tim Zagat

Ratings & Symbols

Zagat Ratings

Hours & Credit Cards

F	D	S	C
▽ 23	7	16	$15

Tim & Nina's ◐ ⋐ ⇗

4 Columbus Circle (8th Ave.), 212-977-6000;
www.zagat.com

Open 24/7, this "deep dive" in Columbus Circle's subway station offers "Chinese-German dining" where an "hour after you eat you're hungry for more sweet-and-sour schnitzel"; fans blast its "Bauhaus meets Mao's house" look and the staff's "yin-yang" uniforms (lederhosen for men, cheongsam for women) and say it's "some cheap trip", even if you must "shout to order when the A train comes in."

Review, with surveyors' comments in quotes

Top Spots: Places with the highest overall ratings, popularity and importance are listed in BLOCK CAPITAL LETTERS.

Hours: ◐ serves after 11 PM
⋐ closed on Sunday
Ⓜ closed on Monday

Credit Cards: ⇗ no credit cards accepted

Ratings are on a scale of **0** to **30**.

F	Food	D	Decor	S	Service	C	Cost
23		7		16		$15	

0–9 poor to fair
10–15 fair to good
16–19 good to very good

20–25 very good to excellent
26–30 extraordinary to perfection
▽ low response/less reliable

Cost (C): Reflects our surveyors' average estimate of the price of a dinner with one drink and tip and is a benchmark only. Lunch is usually 25% less.

For newcomers or survey write-ins listed without ratings, the price range is indicated as follows:

I	$25 and below	E	$41 to $65
M	$26 to $40	VE	$66 or more

Key Newcomers

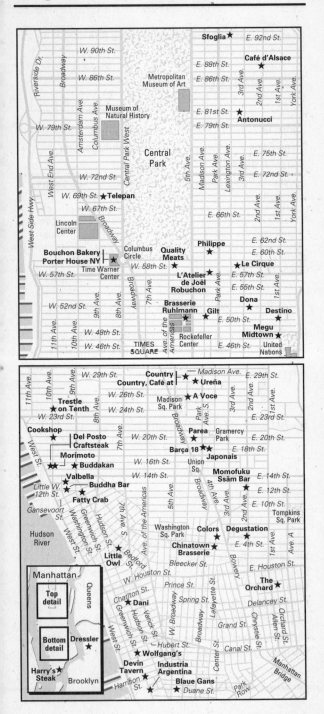

Sfoglia ★
E. 92nd St.
E. 88th St.
Café d'Alsace ★
E. 86th St.
W. 90th St.
W. 86th St.
Metropolitan Museum of Art
E. 81st St. ★
Antonucci ■
Museum of Natural History
W. 79th St.
E. 79th St.
E. 75th St.
Central Park
E. 72nd St.
W. 72nd St.
W. 69th St. ★ Telepan
W. 67th St.
E. 66th St.
Lincoln Center
E. 62nd St.
Columbus Circle
Philippe ★
E. 60th St.
Quality Meats ★
Bouchon Bakery
Porter House NY ★
W. 58th St.
Le Cirque ★
Time Warner Center
L'Atelier de Joël Robuchon ★
E. 57th St.
W. 57th St.
E. 55th St.
Dona ★
W. 52nd St.
Brasserie Ruhlmann ★
Gilt ★
Destino ★
W. 48th St.
Rockefeller Center
E. 50th St.
Megu Midtown ★
W. 46th St.
TIMES SQUARE
E. 46th St.
United Nations

W. 29th St.
Country ★
Madison Ave.
E. 29th St.
Country, Café at ★
Ureña ★
Trestle on Tenth ★
W. 26th St.
Madison Sq. Park
A Voce ★
W. 24th St.
W. 23rd St.
E. 23rd St.
Cookshop ★
Del Posto ★
W. 20th St.
Parea ★
Gramercy Park
Craftsteak ★
E. 20th St.
Morimoto ★
Barça 18 ★★
E. 18th St.
Buddakan ■
W. 16th St.
Japonais ★
Valbella ★
Union Sq.
Momofuku Ssäm Bar ★
E. 14th St.
Buddha Bar ★
W. 14th St.
E. 12th St.
Little W. 12th St.
E. 10th St.
Gansevoort St.
Fatty Crab ★
Tompkins Sq. Park
Hudson River
Washington Sq. Park
Colors ★
Degustation ★
E. 4th St.
Chinatown Brasserie ★
Manhattan
Little Owl ★
Bleecker St.
E. Houston St.
Top detail
Prince St.
The Orchard ★
Bottom detail
Dressler ★
Dani ★
Spring St.
Harry's Steak ★
Brooklyn
Wolfgang's ★
Devin Tavern ★
Industria Argentina ★
Blaue Gans ★
Harrison St.
Duane St.

8
subscribe to zagat.com

Key Newcomers

If New York is The City That Never Sleeps, the same can be said of its hyperactive dining scene. Here is our take on the past year's most notable arrivals. (For a full list, see page 299.)

Antonucci	Fatty Crab
A Voce	Gilt
Barça 18	Harry's Steak
Blaue Gans	Industria Argentina
Bouchon Bakery	Japonais
Brasserie Ruhlmann	L'Atelier/Joël Robuchon
Buddakan	Le Cirque
Buddha Bar	Little Owl
Café d'Alsace	Megu Midtown
Chinatown Brasserie	Momofuku Ssäm Bar
Colors	Morimoto
Cookshop	Orchard, The
Country	Parea
Country, Café at	Philippe
Craftsteak	Porter House NY
Dani	Quality Meats
Degustation	Sfoglia
Del Posto	Telepan
Destino	Trestle on Tenth
Devin Tavern	Ureña
Dona	Valbella
Dressler	Wolfgang's (TriBeCa)

The Year to Come shows plenty of potential with a number of high-profile projects in the works: **BLT Market,** the latest entry in Laurent Tourondel's empire set in the former Atelier space in the Ritz-Carlton Central Park; **Gordon Ramsay at the London,** the *Hell's Kitchen* TV show chef's first American beachhead in the London NYC Hotel (fka Rihga Royal); **Grayz,** Gray Kunz's take on finger food in the old Aquavit digs; **Kobe Club,** a Jeffrey Chodorow steakhouse in his former Mix space; **Morandi,** a new Village Italian from Keith McNally; **Park Chinois,** London star Alan Yau's haute Chinese in the refurbished Gramercy Park Hotel; and the return of the **Russian Tea Room,** helmed by Gary Robins (ex Biltmore Room).

Most Popular

This list reflects our surveyors' favorite restaurants followed in parentheses by last year's rankings. They are plotted on the map at the back of the book.

1. Gramercy Tavern (1)
2. Union Square Cafe (2)
3. Le Bernardin (5)
4. Babbo (3)
5. Peter Luger (9)
6. Bouley (8)
7. Gotham Bar & Grill (6)
8. Daniel (4)
9. Jean Georges (11)
10. Blue Water Grill (7)
11. Nobu (10)
12. Eleven Madison Park (14)
13. per se (13)
14. Rosa Mexicano (20)
15. Balthazar (12)
16. Modern, The (–)
17. Chanterelle (19)
18. Tabla (18)
19. Atlantic Grill (28)
20. Four Seasons (15)
21. Aquavit (22)
22. Artisanal (21)
23. davidburke/donatella (41)
24. Café des Artistes (42)
25. Aquagrill (29)
26. Aureole (17)
27. Spice Market (16)
28. Il Mulino (23)
29. Café Boulud (25)
30. Carmine's (24)
31. Ouest (31)
32. Picholine (26)
33. Palm (38)
34. Saigon Grill (44)
35. L'Impero (37)
36. Craft (27)
37. Lupa (42)
38. Blue Ribbon (38)
39. Café Gray (–)
40. Blue Hill (–)
41. One if by Land (33)
42. Blue Smoke (36)
43. Pastis (32)
44. Sparks (47)
45. Asia de Cuba (38)
46. Del Frisco's (45)
47. Tao (35)
48. Mesa Grill (49)
49. Felidia (30)
50. Becco (46)

If popularity were calibrated to price, many other restaurants would join the above ranks. Therefore we have added several lists to help navigate NYC's Best Buys on pages 22–25. These are restaurants that give real quality at extremely reasonable prices or offer inexpensive prix fixe menus. Bear in mind that lunches cost 25 to 30% less than dinners and the Bronx, Brooklyn, Queens and Staten Island have abundant dining bargains.

Top Ratings

Excluding places with low voting.

Food

28 Le Bernardin
    Daniel
    Sushi Yasuda
    per se
    Peter Luger (Brooklyn)
    Gramercy Tavern
    Café Boulud
    Bouley
    Jean Georges
27 Annisa
    Chanterelle
    Masa
    Gotham Bar & Grill
    Roberto's (Bronx)
    Alain Ducasse
    Veritas
    Aureole
    Sushi Seki
    Sushi of Gari
    Nobu
    Tomoe Sushi
    Babbo
    Grocery, The (Brooklyn)
    Saul (Brooklyn)
    La Grenouille

    Trattoria L'incontro (Queens)
    Garden Cafe (Brooklyn)
    Tasting Room
    Sripraphai (Queens)
    Union Square Cafe
    Il Mulino
26 Di Fara (Brooklyn)
    Jewel Bako
    Al Di La (Brooklyn)
    L'Impero
    Blue Hill
    Wallsé
    Pearl Oyster
    Picholine
    Aquagrill
    Oceana
    Grimaldi's (Brooklyn)
    Scalini Fedeli
    Danube
    River Café (Brooklyn)
    Il Giglio
    March
    Blue Ribbon Sushi
    Craft
    Nobu 57

By Category

American
28 per se
    Gramercy Tavern
27 Annisa
    Gotham Bar & Grill
    Veritas
    Aureole

American (Regional)
26 Pearl Oyster/*NE*
24 Roy's NY/*Hawaii Fusion*
22 Carl's Steaks/*Philly*
21 Michael's/*CA*
    Tropica/*FL*
20 Great Jones Cafe/*Cajun*

Barbecue
23 Daisy May's
22 Dinosaur BBQ
21 Blue Smoke
20 Virgil's Real BBQ
19 RUB BBQ
16 Brother Jimmy's

Caribbean/West Indies
22 Café Habana/*Cuban*
    A/*Caribbean*
21 Cuba/*Cuban*
    Victor's Cafe/*Cuban*
    Havana Alma/*Cuban*
    El Malecon/*Dominican*

Chinese
24 Phoenix Garden
    Mr. K's
    Oriental Garden
    Tse Yang
23 Shun Lee Palace
22 Shun Lee West

Coffeehouses
22 Ferrara
    Once Upon a Tart
20 Le Pain Quotidien
19 71 Irving Pl.
18 Omonia Cafe
15 French Roast

Top Food

Delis
23 Barney Greengrass
   Katz's Deli
21 Mill Basin Deli
   Carnegie Deli
19 Sarge's Deli
   Liebman's

Dessert
25 ChikaLicious
24 Chocolate Room
   Payard Bistro
23 La Bergamote
   Veniero's
   Sweet Melissa

Dim Sum
24 Oriental Garden
22 Mandarin Court
21 Ping's Seafood
20 Dim Sum Go Go
   Shun Lee Cafe
   Golden Unicorn

French
28 Le Bernardin
   Daniel
   Café Boulud
   Bouley
   Jean Georges
27 Chanterelle
   Alain Ducasse
   La Grenouille
26 Tocqueville
25 Fleur de Sel
   Modern, The
   L'Ecole
   Montrachet

French (Bistro)
25 db Bistro Moderne
   Le Gigot
24 JoJo
   Payard Bistro
23 Le Tableau
   Tournesol

Greek
26 Milos
25 Onera
24 Agnanti
   Taverna Kyclades
23 Periyali
   Pylos

Hamburgers
24 burger joint/Parker M.
23 DuMont Burger
   Shake Shack
   Corner Bistro
21 Island Burgers
   Rare B&G

Hotel Dining
28 Café Boulud
   Surrey Hotel
   Jean Georges
   Trump Int'l Hotel
27 Alain Ducasse
   Jumeirah Essex Hse.
25 Norma's
   Le Parker Meridien
   db Bistro Moderne
   City Club Hotel
24 Town
   Chambers Hotel

Indian
24 Tamarind
   dévi
   Chola
23 Amma
   Dawat
   Indus Valley

Italian
27 Roberto's
   Babbo
   Trattoria L'incontro
   Il Mulino
26 Al Di La
   L'Impero
   Scalini Fedeli
   Il Giglio
25 Erminia
   Fiamma Osteria
   Lupa
   Alto
   Pó

Japanese/Sushi
28 Sushi Yasuda
   Sugiyama
27 Masa
   Sushi Seki
   Sushi of Gari
   Nobu
   Tomoe Sushi
26 Jewel Bako
   Donguri
   Blue Ribbon Sushi
   Nobu 57
   Gari
   Honmura An

Korean
24 Hangawi
23 Woo Lae Oak
   Gahm Mi Oak
22 Cho Dang Gol
   Kum Gang San
21 Dok Suni's

Kosher
22 Prime Grill
21 Mill Basin Deli
   Chennai Garden
   Pongal
   Le Marais
20 Abigael's

Mediterranean
26 Picholine
25 Cru
   Il Buco
   Convivium Osteria
24 Red Cat
   Tempo

Mexican
25 Mexicana Mama
24 Pampano
   Itzocan
   Hell's Kitchen
23 Mercadito
   Maya

Middle Eastern
23 Taboon
22 Moustache
   Miriam
   Zaytoons
21 Al Bustan
19 Persepolis

Newcomers/Top Rated
25 Telepan
   Orchard, The
   Ureña
24 A Voce
23 Morimoto
   Country
   Del Posto
   Cookshop
   Buddakan
   Bouchon Bakery
22 Café d'Alsace
   Antonucci
   Philippe

Noodle Shops
26 Honmura An
23 Soba-ya
22 Momofuku Noodle
   Great NY Noodle
   New Bo-Ky
21 Pho Bang

Pizza
26 Di Fara
   Grimaldi's
24 Lombardi's
   Denino's
   Adrienne's Pizza
   Una Pizza

Raw Bars
26 Aquagrill
23 Blue Water Grill
   Ocean Grill
   Balthazar
   BLT Fish
   Mermaid Inn

Seafood
28 Le Bernardin
26 Pearl Oyster
   Aquagrill
   Oceana
   Milos
24 Mary's Fish Camp

Small Plates
24 Stanton Social
   Perbacco
23 Mercadito
   Frankies Spuntino
22 Bellavitae
   Alta

South American
23 Caracas
   Pio Pio
22 Churrascaria
   Chimichurri Grill
   Pampa
   Calle Ocho

Southern/Soul
22 Amy Ruth's
   Miss Mamie's/Maude's
   Ida Mae
21 Maroons
   Pink Tea Cup
   Mo-Bay

Southwestern
24 Mesa Grill
20 Canyon Road
19 Agave
18 Miracle Grill
   Santa Fe
   Los Dos Molinos

Spanish/Tapas
25 Casa Mono
   Ureña
23 Tía Pol
   Bolo
22 Sevilla
   El Pote

Steakhouses
28 Peter Luger
25 Strip House
   Sparks
   Del Frisco's
   MarkJoseph
   Wolfgang's

Top Food

Thai
27 Sripraphai
25 Joya
24 Pam Real Thai
23 Song
   Erawan
   Kittichai

Turkish
23 Turkish Kitchen
22 Ali Baba
   Sahara
21 Akdeniz
   Turkish Cuisine
   Beyoglu

Vegetarian
24 Candle 79
   Hangawi
22 Gobo
   Candle Cafe
   Counter
21 Pure Food & Wine

Vietnamese
24 O Mai
23 Nicky's Viet.
   Saigon Grill
   Nam
22 Boi
   Sapa

By Special Feature

Breakfast
   Annie's
   Balthazar
   Bubby's
   City Hall
   EJ's Luncheonette
   Good Enough to Eat
   Jean Georges
   Le Pain Quotidien
   Norma's
   Payard Bistro
   Regency
   Sarabeth's

Brunch Scenes/Downtown
   Balthazar
   Bubby's
   Clinton St. Baking
   Essex
   Félix
   Five Points
   Jerry's
   Odeon
   Pastis
   Pink Tea Cup
   Prune
   Schiller's

Brunch Scenes/Midtown
   Aquavit
   Beacon
   Cafeteria
   Cafe Un Deux Trois
   Eatery
   elmo
   L'Express
   Mayrose
   Norma's
   Penelope
   Rainbow Room
   Water Club

Brunch Scenes/Uptown
   Annie's
   Arté Café
   Billie's Black
   Carlyle
   Good Enough to Eat
   Isabella's
   JoJo
   Miss Mamie's/Maude's
   Ocean Grill
   Ouest
   Popover Cafe
   Sarabeth's

Business Lunch/Downtown
   Bobby Van's
   Bouley
   City Hall
   Da Silvano
   Duane Park Cafe
   Gotham Bar & Grill
   Les Halles
   MarkJoseph
   Megu
   Roy's NY
   Salaam Bombay
   Wolfgang's (TriBeCa)

Business Lunch/Midtown
   Aquavit
   Café Gray
   Dawat
   db Bistro Moderne
   Del Frisco's
   Four Seasons
   Jean Georges
   Le Bernardin
   Milos
   Nobu 57
   Palm
   Sushi Yasuda

Special Features

Celebrations
Bouley
Daniel
FireBird
Four Seasons
Le Bernardin
Le Cirque
Megu
Rainbow Room
River Café
River Room
Tavern on the Green
Water's Edge

Child-Friendly
Carmine's
Chat 'n Chew
Cowgirl
EJ's Luncheonette
Fetch
Googie's
Hard Rock Cafe
Jackson Hole
Nice
Peanut Butter & Co.
Serendipity 3
Shake Shack

Dining at the Bar
Aquagrill
Babbo
Bar Masa
Del Posto
Four Seasons (lunchtime)
Gotham Bar & Grill
Gramercy Tavern
Hearth
Picholine
Red Cat
Tabla (Bread Bar)
Union Square Cafe

Group Dining
Asia de Cuba
Carmine's
China Grill
Churrascaria Plataforma
English is Italian
Otto
Rosa Mexicano
Ruby Foo's
Sambuca
Stanton Social
Tao
Tony's Di Napoli

Hottest Servers
Asia de Cuba
Blue Water Grill
Bond Street
Brother Jimmy's
Cafeteria
Coffee Shop
Food Bar
44 & X Hell's Kit.
Indochine
Pastis
Spice Market
Tao

Late Dining
Balthazar
Baraonda
Blue Ribbon
Blue Ribbon Sushi
Frank
'ino
Mas
Pastis
Raoul's
Spotted Pig
West Bank Cafe
Wollensky's

Meet for a Drink/Downtown
Balthazar
Bond Street
Brouwers/Stone St.
Buddha Bar
City Hall
Gotham Bar & Grill
Harry's
Mo Pitkin's
Odeon
Spice Market
Stanton Social
Thor

Meet for a Drink/Midtown
Barbounia
Blue Fin
Country, Café at
Django
Houston's
Koi
Michael Jordan's
Modern, The
Nobu 57
Parea
Piano Due
Town

Special Features

Meet for a Drink/Uptown
Atlantic Grill
Café Gray
Cafe Luxembourg
Compass
Daniel
Demarchelier
Geisha
Jean Georges
Lenox Room
Mark's
Ouest
212

Milestone Anniversaries
120th   Peter Luger
100th   Gargiulo's
90th   Café des Artistes
25th   Ben Benson's
       Erminia
       Lusardi's
       Sapporo East
20th   Aquavit
       Bice
       China Grill
       Two Boots
       Zarela

People-watching: Celebs
Angus McIndoe
Balthazar
Bette
Cipriani Downtown
Da Silvano
Elaine's
Fresco by Scotto
Joe Allen
Nobu
Perry Street
Rao's
Spotted Pig

People-watching: Hipsters
Cafe Gitane
Employees Only
Five Points
Freemans
La Esquina
Orchard, The
Public
Schiller's
Stanton Social
Thor
wd-50
Zum Schneider

People-watching: Movers & Shakers
Bayard's
Café Boulud
Coco Pazzo
Elio's
Four Seasons
Jean Georges
Le Bernardin
Lever House
Michael's
Regency
Smith & Wollensky
21 Club

Singles Scenes
Baraonda
Buddakan
Buddha Bar
Butter
Chinatown Brasserie
Coffee Shop
'inoteca
La Esquina
Pre:Post
SushiSamba
Tao
Thor

24-Hour
Bereket
Cafeteria
Cozy Soup/Burger
Empire Diner
Florent
Gahm Mi Oak
Gray's Papaya
Kum Gang San
L'Express
Maison
Sarge's Deli
Won Jo

Winning Wine Lists
Alain Ducasse
Babbo
Bayard's
Blue Hill
Cru
Daniel
Landmarc
Montrachet
per se
21 Club
Union Square Cafe
Veritas

By Location

Chelsea
- 24 Red Cat
- Da Umberto
- O Mai
- 23 Morimoto
- Tía Pol
- Del Posto

Chinatown
- 24 Oriental Garden
- 22 New Green Bo
- Big Wong
- Peking Duck
- Great NY Noodle
- Nha Trang

East 40s
- 28 Sushi Yasuda
- 26 L'Impero
- 25 Sparks
- 24 Pampano
- Phoenix Garden
- Palm

East 50s
- 27 La Grenouille
- 26 Oceana
- March
- Four Seasons
- 25 Alto
- Aquavit

East 60s
- 28 Daniel
- 27 Aureole
- Sushi Seki
- 25 davidburke/donatella
- Kai
- Scalinatella

East 70s
- 28 Café Boulud
- 27 Sushi of Gari
- 24 Campagnola
- Candle 79
- Payard Bistro
- 23 Lusardi's

East 80s
- 26 Donguri
- 25 Erminia
- Etats-Unis
- Poke
- Sushi Sen-nin
- Spigolo

East 90s & East 100s
- 24 Itzocan
- 23 El Paso Taqueria
- Pio Pio
- 22 Nick's
- 21 Don Pedro's
- Zebú Grill

East Village
- 26 Jewel Bako
- 25 ChikaLicious
- Hearth
- 24 Prune
- Itzocan
- Lavagna

Financial District
- 25 MarkJoseph
- 24 Roy's NY
- Bayard's
- Adrienne's Pizza
- 22 Bobby Van's
- Delmonico's

Flatiron/Union Square
- 28 Gramercy Tavern
- 27 Veritas
- Union Square Cafe
- 26 Craft
- Tocqueville
- 25 Fleur de Sel

Garment District
- 24 Osteria Gelsi
- Uncle Jack's
- Keens
- 23 Gahm Mi Oak
- 22 Ida Mae
- Cho Dang Gol

Gramercy/Madison Park
- 26 Eleven Madison Park
- 25 Tabla
- Casa Mono
- Ureña
- 24 Yama
- BLT Prime

Greenwich Village
- 27 Annisa
- Gotham Bar & Grill
- Tomoe Sushi
- Babbo
- Il Mulino
- 26 Blue Hill

Top Food

Harlem
22 Amy Ruth's
   Miss Mamie's/Maude's
   Dinosaur BBQ
21 Rao's
   Mo-Bay
20 Patsy's Pizzeria

Little Italy
23 Nyonya
   Angelo's of Mulberry
   Il Fornaio
   Il Cortile
22 Pellegrino's
   Ferrara

Lower East Side
25 Orchard, The
24 Stanton Social
   Falai
   ápizz
   Clinton St. Baking
   Cube 63

Meatpacking District
23 Old Homestead
22 Spice Market
20 Pastis
   Ono
   Son Cubano
   Sascha

Murray Hill
25 Sushi Sen-nin
   Wolfgang's
24 Hangawi
23 Asia de Cuba
   Artisanal
   Mishima

NoHo
25 Bond Street
   Il Buco
23 Bianca
22 Five Points
21 Sala
   Quartino

NoLita
24 Lombardi's
23 Public
22 Café Habana
   Peasant
21 La Esquina
20 Le Jardin Bistro

SoHo
26 Aquagrill
   Blue Ribbon Sushi
   Honmura An
25 Fiamma Osteria
   L'Ecole
   Blue Ribbon

TriBeCa
28 Bouley
27 Chanterelle
   Nobu
26 Scalini Fedeli
   Danube
   Il Giglio

West 40s
25 Sushi Zen
   db Bistro Moderne
   Del Frisco's
24 Esca
   Pam Real Thai
   Hell's Kitchen

West 50s
28 Le Bernardin
   Sugiyama
27 Alain Ducasse
26 Nobu 57
   Milos
   Piano Due

West 60s
28 per se
   Jean Georges
27 Masa
26 Picholine
25 Telepan
   Café Gray

West 70s
26 Gari
25 Onera
23 Ocean Grill
   'Cesca
   Tenzan
   Swagat Indian

West 80s
25 Ouest
24 Celeste
23 Barney Greengrass
   Nëo Sushi
22 Neptune Room
   Calle Ocho

West 90s & Up
24 Gennaro
23 Indus Valley
   Pisticci
   Saigon Grill
22 Max SoHa
   Terrace in the Sky

West Village
26 Wallsé
25 Mexicana Mama
   Perry Street
24 Piccolo Angolo
   Mary's Fish Camp
23 Mercadito

Outer Boroughs

Bronx
27 Roberto's
24 Riverdale Garden
    Enzo's
    Jake's
22 Dominick's
    Mario's

Brooklyn: Bay Ridge
25 Areo
24 Agnanti
22 Tuscany Grill
    Chianti
    Pearl Room
    Chadwick's

Brooklyn: Heights/Dumbo
26 Grimaldi's
    River Café
25 Noodle Pudding
    Henry's End
24 Queen
21 Five Front

**Brooklyn: Carroll Gardens/
Boerum Hill/Cobble Hill**
27 Grocery, The
    Saul
25 Joya
    Osaka
24 Cube 63
23 Chestnut

Brooklyn: Park Slope
26 Al Di La
    Blue Ribbon Sushi
25 Rose Water
    applewood
    Blue Ribbon
    Convivium Osteria

Brooklyn: Williamsburg
28 Peter Luger
23 DuMont
22 Diner
    Bamonte's
21 SEA
    Relish

Brooklyn: Other
27 Garden Cafe
26 Di Fara
23 L & B Spumoni
    Franny's
    Nyonya
    360

Queens: Astoria/L.I.C.
27 Trattoria L'incontro
25 Piccola Venezia
24 Agnanti
    Taverna Kyclades
23 Tournesol (LIC)
22 Manducatis (LIC)

Queens: Other
27 Sripraphai
24 Park Side
    Don Peppe
    Sapori D'Ischia
    Uncle Jack's
23 Erawan

Staten Island
24 Denino's
    Trattoria Romana
23 Da Noi
    Carol's Cafe
22 Angelina's
    Aesop's Tables

Top Decor

28 Daniel	Aureole
Asiate	Jean Georges
Rainbow Room	Eleven Madison Park
27 River Café	Del Posto
Buddakan	View, The
per se	Country
Four Seasons	**25** Sapa
La Grenouille	Morimoto
Megu	Scalini Fedeli
Alain Ducasse	Public
Tao	EN Japanese
One if By Land	Kings' Carriage Hse.
Le Bernardin	Terrace in the Sky
Danube	Battery Gardens
Kittichai	Suba
26 Café des Artistes	Nobu 57
Spice Market	Water Club
Carlyle	Gotham Bar & Grill
Bouley	Hangawi
Chanterelle	Town
FireBird	Cávo
Gramercy Tavern	Tabla
Matsuri	Masa
Boathouse	Asia de Cuba
Modern, The	Perry Street

Gardens

Barbetta	Jolie
Battery Gardens	L & B Spumoni
Bottino	Le Jardin Bistro
Cávo	Osaka
Da Nico	Paradou
Five Front	Park, The
Fragole	Patois
Gascogne	Pure Food & Wine
Gnoccho Caffe	Relish
Grocery, The	Riverdale Garden
Home	Sripraphai
I Coppi	Surya
I Trulli	Tavern on the Green

Private Parties
(min./max. capacity)

Alain Ducasse (14/30)	Fiamma Osteria (65/80)
Barbetta (12/120)	Four Seasons (14/390)
Bayard's (10/200)	Le Cirque (25/80)
Beacon (25/300)	Oceana (24/60)
Blue Smoke (34/310)	per se (10/75)
Buddakan (30/320)	Picholine (8/24)
Café Gray (12/64)	River Café (50/125)
City Hall (32/110)	Spice Market (11/30)
Country (15/60)	Tavern on the Green (50/1,000)
Del Frisco's (22/75)	Thalassa (60/120)
Del Posto (24/200)	21 Club (16/400)

Romance

Alain Ducasse
Aureole
Café des Artistes
Café Pierre
Chanterelle
Convivium Osteria
Country
Danube
Erminia
Gascogne
Il Buco
JoJo
Kings' Carriage Hse.
La Grenouille
Le Gigot

Le Refuge
L'Impero
March
Mark's
One if by Land
Periyali
Petrossian
Piccola Venezia
Primavera
Rainbow Room
River Café
Scalini Fedeli
Suba
Terrace in the Sky
Water's Edge

Views

Asiate
Battery Gardens
Boathouse
Café Gray
Foley's Fish
Gigino (Wagner Park)
Liberty View
per se
Pete's Downtown

Porter House NY
River Café
River Room
Sea Grill
Terrace in the Sky
Top of the Tower
View, The
Water Club
Water's Edge

Top Service

28 per se
Le Bernardin
Daniel
Alain Ducasse
27 Gramercy Tavern
Chanterelle
Jean Georges
Bouley
Garden Cafe
La Grenouille
26 Four Seasons
Annisa
Aureole
Gotham Bar & Grill
Union Square Cafe
Café Boulud
Masa
Alto
Tasting Room
25 River Café
Oceana
Veritas
March
Blue Hill
Eleven Madison Park

Erminia
Danube
Grocery, The
Carlyle
Picholine
Babbo
Tocqueville
Scalini Fedeli
24 Le Perigord
Mas
Trattoria L'incontro
Saul
Acappella
Asiate
One if by Land
Tabla
Craft
Sushi Yasuda
Wallsé
Mr. K's
Fiamma Osteria
Jewel Bako
L'Impero
Montrachet
Honmura An

Best Buys

Everyone loves a bargain, and fortunately, NYC offers plenty of places that fill the bill. There are three general rules: 1) The outer boroughs are less costly than Manhattan; 2) Lunch typically totals 25% to 30% less than dinner; and 3) More than 200 top places offer bargain prix fixe menus as part of the city's biannual Restaurant Week promotion (usually in January and June). Following are listings of some of the city's best bangs for the buck.

All You Can Eat
24 Chola
23 Turkish Kitchen
22 Churrascaria
     Yuka
21 Becco
     Diwan
     Chennai Garden
20 Vatan
     Sapphire Indian
19 Green Field Churr.
18 English is Italian
17 Delegates' Dining Rm.

Bargain Prix Fixe Lunch
28 Bouley ($38)
     Jean Georges ($24)
27 Gotham Bar & Grill ($24)
     Aureole ($35)
26 Milos ($35)
     Honmura An ($19)
     Tocqueville ($25)
25 davidburke/donatella ($24)
     Fleur de Sel ($25)
     db Bistro Moderne ($32)
     Perry Street ($24)
     Tabla ($35)

Bargain Prix Fixe Dinner
28 Sushi Yasuda ($21)
27 Saul ($30)
     Garden Cafe ($30)
26 Caviar Russe ($35)
25 L'Ecole ($40)
24 Petrossian ($37)
     Hangawi ($38)
23 Brasserie LBC ($35)
     Artisanal ($34)
     Vong ($35)
21 Becco ($22)
20 Kitchen 22 ($29)

Buffets
25 Aquavit
24 Roy's NY
     Chola
23 Turkish Kitchen
     Surya
22 Churrascaria
     Jackson Diner
     Brick Lane Curry
21 Diwan
     Bukhara Grill
     Utsav
19 East Buffet

BYO
26 Di Fara
25 Poke
24 Phoenix Garden
     Cube 63 (LES)
23 Sweet Melissa
22 A
     Tartine
     Zaytoons
21 Nook
20 Angelica Kitchen
18 Afghan Kebab
17 Olive Vine Cafe

Family-Style
24 Piccolo Angolo
     Don Peppe
     Phoenix Garden
     Oriental Garden
23 Pisticci
     Frank
22 Dominick's
     China Grill
20 Carmine's
19 Tony's Di Napoli
18 English is Italian
     La Mela

Full-Menu Restaurants

Alice's Tea Cup/*Eclectic*
Bereket/*Turkish*
Big Wong/*Chinese*
Brennan & Carr/*American*
Cubana Café/*Cuban*
Doyers/*Vietnamese*
DuMont/*American*
El Malecon/*Dominican*
Energy Kitchen/*health food*
Excellent Dumpling/*Chinese*
Fresco on the Go/*Italian*
Friendhouse/*Asian*
Gahm Mi Oak/*Korean*
Goodies/*Chinese*
Great NY Noodle/*Chinese*
Joya/*Thai*
L & B Spumoni/*Italian*
La Taza de Oro/*Puerto Rican*
Mama's Food/*American*
Mill/*Korean*
Mill Basin Deli/*kosher*
Momofuku/*noodles*
New Bo-Ky/*Vietnamese*
Nha Trang/*Vietnamese*
Nyonya/*Malaysian*

Old Devil Moon/*Southern*
Olive Vine/*Middle Eastern*
Penelope/*American*
Pepe . . . To Go/*Italian*
Pho Bang/*Vietnamese*
Pho Pasteur/*Vietnamese*
Pho Viet Huong/*Vietnamese*
Pukk/*Thai*
Pump/*health food*
Republic/*Asian*
Rice/*Eclectic*
Saigon Grill/*Vietnamese*
SEA/*Thai*
Song/*Thai*
Sparky's/*American*
Sripraphai/*Thai*
Sweet-n-Tart/*Chinese*
Thai Pavilion/*Thai*
Thai Son/*Vietnamese*
Tierras/*Colombian*
Tuk Tuk/*Thai*
Whole Foods/*Eclectic*
Wo Hop/*Chinese*
X.O./*Chinese*
Zaytoons/*Middle Eastern*

Specialty Shops

Amy's Bread/*baked goods*
Better Burger/*burgers*
Blue 9 Burger/*burgers*
burger joint/P.M./*burgers*
Burritoville/*Mexican*
Caracas/*arepas*
Carl's/*cheese steaks*
ChikaLicious/*desserts*
Chipotle/*Mexican*
Chocolate Room/*desserts*
Chop't Creative/*salads*
Coals/*pizza*
Corner Bistro/*burgers*
Cosmic Cantina/*burritos*
Cozy Soup/*burgers*
Di Fara/*pizza*
Dishes/*sandwiches*
Dumpling Man/*dumplings*
Emack & Bolio's/*ice cream*
Empanada Mama/*S. American*
Ess-a-Bagel/*deli*
F & B/*European hot dogs*
Ferrara/*Italian pastry*
goodburger/*burgers*
Gray's Papaya/*hot dogs*

Grimaldi's/*pizza*
Hale & Hearty/*soup*
Hampton Chutney/*Indian*
Island Burgers/*burgers*
Joe's Pizza/*pizza*
Kati Roll Co./*Indian*
La Bergamote/*bakery*
Mother's Bake Shop/*bakery*
Nicky's/*Vietnamese*
99 Miles to Philly/*cheese steaks*
Once Upon a Tart/*sandwiches*
Papaya King/*hot dogs*
Peanut Butter/*sandwiches*
Philly Slim's/*cheese steaks*
Pizza Gruppo/*pizza*
Pizza 33/*pizza*
Press 195/*sandwiches*
Rickshaw/*dumplings*
Roll-n-Roaster/*sandwiches*
71 Irving Pl./*coffeehouse*
Shake Shack/*burgers*
Sweet Melissa/*pastry*
Tony Luke's/*cheese steaks*
Two Boots/*pizza*
Veniero's/*Italian pastry*

Best Buys

Prix Fixe Lunch

Abboccato	$24	L'Ecole	27
Adä	16	Le Colonial	35
Agave	13	Lenox Room	24
Alcala	26	Le Perigord	32
Amarone	17	Le Rivage	20
Artisanal	20	Levana	30
Asiate	35	Le Zie 2000	15
Atlantic Grill	24	L'Impero	35
Aureole	35	Madison Bistro	23
Avra	27	Mercer Kitchen	24
Baldoria	28	Michael Jordan's	23
Basta Pasta	15	Milos	35
Beacon	28	Molyvos	25
Becco	17	Montparnasse	23
Bistro du Nord	19	Montrachet (Fri.)	20
Blue Water Grill	24	Mr. K's	25
Bolo	24	Ocean Grill	24
Bouley	38	Odeon	24
Brasserie LCB	26	Park Ave. Cafe	20
Café Botanica	19	Park Bistro	25
Café des Artistes	25	Patsy's	32
Cafe Luxembourg	30	Perry Street	24
Capsouto Frères	24	Petrossian	25
Centolire	25	Philippe	20
Chiam	21	Pó	32
Chin Chin	24	Portofino Grille	13
Churrascaria	31	Queen	24
Cibo	27	René Pujol	24
Copper Chimney	11	Roc	20
Crema	17	Salaam Bombay	14
davidburke/donatella	24	San Domenico	30
Dawat	15	Sapphire Indian	13
db Bistro Moderne	32	Sardi's	30
Delegates Dining Rm.	25	Scarlatto	15
Diwan	14	Sette	15
Django	24	Shun Lee Palace	20
Dona	38	Solera	22
Duane Park Cafe	24	Spice Market	24
Ecco	20	Sushi Yasuda	21
Felidia	30	Tamarind	24
FireBird	29	Tao	24
Fleur de Sel	25	Tartine	14
Frankie & Johnnie	29	Tavern on the Green	35
fresh	20	Terrace in the Sky	25
Gallagher's	24	Thalia	17
Gascogne	20	Tocqueville	25
Giambelli	29	Trata Estiatorio	20
Giorgio's/Gramercy	24	Tse Yang	28
Gotham Bar & Grill	24	Turkish Kitchen	14
Hangawi	20	21 Club	33
Honmura An	19	Utsav	16
Il Bastardo	15	Vong	20
Jean Georges	24	Water Club	24
JoJo	24	Water's Edge	26
La Palapa	11	Zarela	25
La Petite Auberge	17	Zoë	24

Prix Fixe Dinner

PT = pre-theater only; where two prices are listed, the first is pre-theater and the second for normal dinner hours.

Abboccato	$35	La Baraka	25/36
Akdeniz	19	La Boîte en Bois/PT	34
Aki/PT	26	La Giara/PT	20
Alcala	40	La Mangeoire	24/31
Alouette/PT	24	La Mediterranée/PT	20
A.O.C. Bedford/PT	32	La Petite Auberge	26
Artisanal	34	Le Boeuf/Mode	38
Atlantic Grill/PT	28	L'Ecole	40
Avra/PT	35	Le Madeleine/PT	32
Baldoria/PT	38	Lenox Room/PT	30
Bay Leaf/PT	21	Le Singe Vert/PT	30
Becco	22	Levana	30
Bistro du Nord/PT	19	Luca	22
Bistro Les Amis/PT	22	Luxia/PT	29
Bistro 61/PT	25	Madison Bistro	29
Bistro Ten 18	26	Mamlouk	40
Bombay Palace	20/30	Métisse/PT	25
Brasserie Julien/PT	25	Metrazur	35
Brasserie LCB	35	Michael Jordan's/PT	24
Bryant Park Grill/PT	30	Molyvos	35
Café Botanica/PT	40	Montparnasse/PT	23
Cafe Centro	35	Ocean Grill/PT	28
Cafe Un Deux	29	Odeon/PT	32
Candela/PT	20	Osteria del Circo	34
Capsouto Frères	35	Ouest/PT	29
Cascina/PT	25	Park Bistro/PT	25
Caviar Russe	35	Pascalou/PT	22
Cebu/PT	19	Payard Bistro/PT	34
Chelsea Bistro	30	Petrossian	37
Chez Napoléon	25	Remi/PT	35
Chin Chin	35	Roth's Westside/PT	23
Cibo	30	San Domenico/PT	33
Compass	35	Saul	30
Del Frisco's/PT	40	Savann/PT	19
Dervish Turkish/PT	23	Scottadito	15/25
dominic	38	Sharz Cafe/PT	20
English is Italian	39	Siam Inn	20
etcetera etcetera	35	Sorrel	25
44/PT	36	Sushi Yasuda	21
Garden Cafe	30	Table d'Hôte/PT	24
Gascogne/PT	27	Tavern on the Green/PT	38
Gavroche/PT	19	Thalia/PT	35
Gigino	28	360	25
Giorgio's/Gramercy	35	Trata Estiatorio/PT	24
Hangawi	38	21 Club/PT	38
Henry's End/PT	23	Utsav/PT	25
Indochine/PT	28	Vatan	24
Jacques/PT	22	ViceVersa	35
Jarnac	34	Village	29
Jewel of India/PT	22	Vincent's	26
Kitchen 22	29	Vivolo/PT	26
Kittichai/PT	35	Vong	35
Korea Palace	39	Water Club/PT	40

Restaurant Directory

A ⌧Ⓜ⌐

22 | 11 | 19 | $23

947 Columbus Ave. (bet. 106th & 107th Sts.), 212-531-1643
"Adventuresome", all-organic French-Carib food emerges from the "tiniest kitchen" imaginable at this "offbeat" Morningside Heights BYO; the dining room is "as small as its name", but the "quality", "unbeatable value" and overall "can-do" spirit keep it crowded.

Abboccato

23 | 20 | 21 | $61

Blakely Hotel, 136 W. 55th St. (bet. 6th & 7th Aves.), 212-265-4000; www.abboccato.com
Fast becoming a Midtown "favorite", this yearling sibling of Oceana and Molyvos delivers "delicious", "dressed-up" Italian dishes with "imaginative tweaks"; a "genial" staff, "handsome room" and "convenience to City Center" make it "perfect" pre-theater, but "bring your rich daddy-o."

Abigael's

20 | 16 | 18 | $45

1407 Broadway (bet. 38th & 39th Sts.), 212-575-1407; www.abigaels.com
"Designer kosher" fare is dished out in "you-won't-leave-hungry"-size portions at this "reliable" Garment District New American (with Pan-Asian items including sushi offered upstairs); so-so decor is counterbalanced by an "upbeat ambiance."

Above

18 | 19 | 18 | $50

Hilton Times Sq., 234 W. 42nd St., 21st fl. (bet. 7th & 8th Aves.), 212-642-2626
Handy for theatergoers, this "quiet sanctuary" 21 floors above Times Square offers "above-average" New American eats and "pleasant" service; a "hotel lobby" setting with a "view of nothing in particular" may explain why it "never seems very busy."

Aburiya Kinnosuke NEW

∇ 25 | 21 | 21 | $51

213 E. 45th St. (bet. 2nd & 3rd Aves.), 212-867-5454
It's "such fun" trying "dishes you've never heard of" at this "different" East Midtown Japanese where many of the "delicately flavored" items come off a robata grill; it's a lot "like going to Tokyo", so "don't expect to hear much English."

Acappella ⌧

24 | 21 | 24 | $67

1 Hudson St. (Chambers St.), 212-240-0163; www.acappella-restaurant.com
"Romance is in the air" at this "dark" TriBeCa Northern Italian where "delicious" food is served by waiters who put on a "great show"; be sure to "finish the night" with the "gratis homemade grappa" – it'll "help dull the shock of the bill."

Acqua Pazza ⌧

21 | 19 | 20 | $51

36 W. 52nd St. (bet. 5th & 6th Aves.), 212-582-6900; www.acquapazzanyc.com
"Civilized" and "centrally located", this "upscale" Midtowner features a "tasty", "well-prepared" Italian menu emphasizing seafood; "suits" making deals keep it "hopping at lunch", though come suppertime it's much more "serene."

Adä

∇ 24 | 21 | 22 | $49

208 E. 58th St. (bet. 2nd & 3rd Aves.), 212-371-6060; www.adanyc.com
To savor "gourmet" Indian cooking, try this "quiet" East Midtowner where "lovely service" and "haute presentation" keep everything "a notch above"; despite tabs fit for a "mogul's court", it's "worth every rupee", while the $16 prix fixe lunch thrills bargain-hunters.

Adrienne's Pizzabar ●NEW

24 | 17 | 17 | $23

87 Pearl St. (bet. Coenties Slip & William St.), 212-248-3838
This Italian newcomer purveys "innovative", "crispy" pizzas (both round and square) in the Financial District "wasteland"; be prepared

to "fight the crowds at lunch", though there's more room at the "outside tables" on "historic Stone Street" at the dinner hour.

Aesop's Tables Ⓜ   22 | 18 | 20 | $44
1233 Bay St. (Maryland Ave.), Staten Island, 718-720-2005
A "quaint" respite hidden away on Staten Island, this "intimate" Med–New American bistro is fabled for its "fine" food, "cozy" ambiance and "responsive" service; a "wonderful garden" perfect for "balmy summer nights" seals the moderately priced deal.

Afghan Kebab House   18 | 10 | 16 | $23
764 Ninth Ave. (bet. 51st & 52nd Sts.), 212-307-1612
1345 Second Ave. (bet. 70th & 71st Sts.), 212-517-2776
74-16 37th Ave. (bet. 74th & 75th Sts.), Queens, 718-565-0471
"Expertly made" kebabs lead the parade of "aromatic" items at this "cheap" Afghan trio where the "warm" hospitality overcomes the dilapidated decor; the BYO policy makes them "real bargains."

Agata & Valentina Food Bar NEW   18 | 16 | 14 | $32
1513 First Ave. (79th St.), 212-452-0691
Spun off from its famed gourmet-shop parent across the street, this new UES Sicilian offers "creative" buffet breakfasts and full-service lunches and dinners; but many say it's "still working out the kinks", citing "awkward seating", "slow service" and "overpricing."

Agave   19 | 19 | 18 | $36
140 Seventh Ave. S. (bet. Charles & W. 10th Sts.), 212-989-2100;
www.agaveny.com
Set in "dressed-up adobe" digs, this modestly priced "new wave" Village Southwesterner draws "young" types with a "decent", rather "fancy-pants" menu; but few "can remember the food" (or the "spotty" service) after sampling from its "extensive tequila list."

Agnanti ◑   24 | 15 | 19 | $34
7802 Fifth Ave. (78th St.), Brooklyn, 718-833-7033 NEW
19-06 Ditmars Blvd. (19th St.), Queens, 718-545-4554
www.agnantimeze.com
"True tavernas", these outer-borough Greeks are as "authentic as it gets", serving "excellent appetizers" as a prelude to their "homestyle" entrees and "just-off-the-boat" fish; while both are "remarkable values", the Astoria Park original boasts bonus "outdoor seating."

Aix Brasserie   21 | 21 | 20 | $59
2398 Broadway (88th St.), 212-874-7400; www.aixnyc.com
Chef Didier Virot's "Gallic charm" remains, but his "revamped" menu is "more down to earth" at this French Upper Westsider that's been "remade into a brasserie"; problem is, this "much-needed" spot is "still very expensive" for the neighborhood.

Aja ◑   20 | 23 | 20 | $43
1068 First Ave. (58th St.), 212-888-8008
An "innovative" menu including "delish sushi" draws locals to this "hip" Asian near the Queensboro Bridge; it's renowned as a "great date place" thanks to "fab cocktails", "thumping rock music" and "exotic" decor (a "fish-tank floor" and a "giant Buddha").

Aji Sushi NEW   ▽ 21 | 14 | 20 | $26
519 Third Ave. (bet. 34th & 35th Sts.), 212-686-2055
This "tiny, squeeze-'em-in" sushi yearling in Murray Hill impresses with "inspired" specialty rolls "made with brown rice" as well as "great bento lunch specials"; "decent prices" and "good service" lead locals to label it a "keeper."

AJ Maxwell's Steakhouse NEW

| | | | E |

57 W. 48th St. (bet. 5th & 6th Aves.), 212-262-6200; www.ajmaxwells.com
Rock Center's latest comer is this new steakhouse offering pricey prime beef in the former site of the legendary Forum of the Twelve Caesars; the standard-issue digs are jazzed up by a Roman mosaic mural behind the bar, salvaged from its illustrious predecessor.

Akdeniz ☒

| 21 | 13 | 20 | $30 |

19 W. 46th St. (bet. 5th & 6th Aves.), 212-575-2307; www.akdenizturkishusa.com
"Appetizers can make a meal" at this "tasty" Turkish Midtowner where the "flavorful" fare is both "well-spiced" and well-priced (notably the $18.95 prix fixe dinner); devotees "go early or late to avoid the crush" caused by the "narrow space and squeezed tables."

Aki Ⓜ

| 26 | 13 | 22 | $41 |

181 W. Fourth St. (bet. Barrow & Jones Sts.), 212-989-5440
"Japan meets Jamaica" on the menu of this "memorable" Village sushi "original" with a "distinctive" mix of flavors; since the "minuscule" space can be a serious "squeeze", many opt for "takeout."

Aki Sushi

| 18 | 11 | 16 | $30 |

121 E. 27th St. (bet. Lexington Ave. & Park Ave. S.), 212-213-9888
366 W. 52nd St. (bet. 8th & 9th Aves.), 212-262-2888
128 W. 36th St. (bet. B'way & 7th Ave.), 212-868-8091 NEW
1425 York Ave. (bet. 75th & 76th Sts.), 212-628-8885
"Dependable" is the word on these "no-frills", "no-lines" sushi sites with "lots of specials" to keep prices "decent"; what "they lack in ambiance", they make up for with "super-fast delivery."

ALAIN DUCASSE ☒

| 27 | 27 | 28 | $215 |

Jumeirah Essex House, 155 W. 58th St. (bet. 6th & 7th Aves.), 212-265-7300; www.alain-ducasse.com
Everything's "extraordinary" at Alain Ducasse's Central Park South "temple to modern French food", where "sublime", "sophisticated" flavors (via exec chef Tony Esnault), "cosseting" service and "old-style opulence" make for a "gastronome's paradise"; yes, it's "big bucks" for a "pageant" staged "for a select few", so bring your banker along for this "once-in-a-lifetime experience"; N.B. the status of the restaurant is in question – it is rumored to be relocating.

Alamo, The ☒ NEW

| 18 | 15 | 16 | $34 |

304 E. 48th St. (bet. 1st & 2nd Aves.), 212-759-0590; www.thealamorestaurant.com
Back after a siesta, this U.N.-area Mexican "fixture" has amigos applauding its "plentiful", modestly tabbed plates, though fun seekers say "it's all about the drinks" ("amazing margaritas"); either way, the mood's "festive" and the tableside-made guacamole's a "good show."

Al Bustan

| 21 | 15 | 18 | $43 |

827 Third Ave. (bet. 50th & 51st Sts.), 212-759-5933; www.albustanny.com
"Meze fit for a king" draws loyalists to this longstanding Midtown Lebanese "bastion" proffering "traditional", "like-my-grandmother-used-to-make" dishes; "attentive" service keeps it a "good alternative" for "easy business lunches", even if a "face-lift" is overdue.

Alcala

| ▽ 22 | 18 | 21 | $50 |

342 E. 46th St. (bet. 1st & 2nd Aves.), 212-370-1866; www.alcalarestaurant.com
A "U.N. crowd" tucks into "enjoyable", if pricey, Basque fare and "tapas par excellence" at this East Midtown "gem"; expect "relaxed, unhurried" dining, a "wide range of Spanish wines" and a "back garden" that doubles as a "romantic hideaway."

AL DI LA

| 26 | 18 | 21 | $43 |

248 Fifth Ave. (Carroll St.), Brooklyn, 718-783-4565; www.aldilatrattoria.com
"Success hasn't spoiled the luster" of this Park Slope Venetian that offers "exquisite" meals and "gracious" service in "intimate" digs; if "no reserving" and "gentle prices" result in "killer" lines, the "wine bar around the corner" makes the wait "tolerable."

Aleo

| 19 | 17 | 19 | $40 |

7 W. 20th St. (5th Ave.), 212-691-8136; www.aleorestaurant.com
"Pleasant all around", this "unassuming" Med-Italian "sleeper" serves "savory", affordable fare in an "off-the-beaten-path" Flatiron address; decor may be somewhat "lacking" (except in the "charming garden"), but the staff's "caring" and it's "quiet enough to have a conversation."

Alexandra ●∅⇄

| ▽ 22 | 18 | 18 | $41 |

455 Hudson St. (bet. Barrow & Morton Sts.), 212-255-3838
Striving for a "balance between creativity and comfort", this "low-key", cash-only West Village yearling purveys "wonderful" American bistro eats in "intimate" digs; it's a "best-kept secret" in these parts.

Alfama

| 21 | 20 | 21 | $47 |

551 Hudson St. (Perry St.), 212-645-2500; www.alfamarestaurant.com
"Classy" yet "easygoing", this West Village Portuguese "standout" evokes a "Lisbon-on-the-Hudson" vibe via "succulent" provender and a "treasure trove" of ports and Madeiras served by "attentive" staffers; "Wednesday night fado" singers add to the authenticity.

Al Forno Pizzeria

| 19 | 12 | 17 | $22 |

1484 Second Ave. (bet. 77th & 78th Sts.), 212-249-5103
Upper Eastsiders report "terrific, thin-crust" brick-oven pies with a "large selection of tasty toppings" at this "standby" pizzeria with a "family-friendly" ambiance; fans say there's "less of a wait" and none of the "hype" of its archrival, Totonno's.

Alfredo of Rome

| 19 | 19 | 18 | $47 |

4 W. 49th St. (bet. 5th & 6th Aves.), 212-397-0100; www.alfredos.com
The "namesake" fettuccine is "worth the trip" to this "midpriced" Rock Center Italian chainlet (with branches in "Rome and Disney World"); both the room and the staff are "pretty", however some say the "food doesn't live up to its billing" and is "aimed at tourists."

Algonquin Hotel Round Table

| 16 | 22 | 18 | $54 |

Algonquin Hotel, 59 W. 44th St. (bet. 5th & 6th Aves.), 212-840-6800; www.algonquinhotel.com
You'll enter "another time zone" at this Theater District "literary landmark" where the "tranquil", "old-world" mood is somewhat diminished by "pedestrian", "overpriced" American eats; savvy sorts "go for the cabaret" in the adjoining Oak Room, "not for the food", or to enjoy the drinks in the wood-paneled lobby.

Alias

| 22 | 16 | 20 | $37 |

76 Clinton St. (Rivington St.), 212-505-5011; www.aliasrestaurant.com
A "funky crowd" noshes on "novel spins" of "top-notch" American comfort chow at this "unpretentious" LES storefront; the "hip atmosphere" and "nice staff" have made it a "neighborhood hit", and Sunday's "$25 prix fixe supper" is "quite a deal."

Ali Baba

| 22 | 14 | 17 | $28 |

212 E. 34th St. (bet. 2nd & 3rd Aves.), 212-683-9206; www.alibabaturkishcuisine.com
"Sumptuous kebabs" and other "tangy" treats "fit for a sultan" but "priced for a commoner" turn up at this "popular" Murray Hill Turk

that's more "spacious" after recently relocating; despite the added room, this "local favorite" is perpetually "packed."

Alice's Tea Cup
19 | 21 | 17 | $25

102 W. 73rd St. (bet. Amsterdam & Columbus Aves.), 212-799-3006
156 E. 64th St. (Lexington Ave.), 212-486-9200 **NEW**
www.alicesteacup.com
"Mostly populated by mothers and daughters", this "whimsical" West Side tearoom is known for its "terrific" brews, "out-of-this-world" scones, "limited hours" and "maddening" waits; N.B. the "charming" new East Side spin-off offers a full American menu and stays open later.

Aliseo Osteria del Borgo ▽ 21 | 19 | 21 | $42

665 Vanderbilt Ave. (bet. Park & Prospect Pls.), Brooklyn, 718-783-3400
A "personable" chef-owner's "imaginative" specialties, "excellent artisanal cheeses" and "wonderful wines" from Italy's Marche region ensure that this Prospect Heights spot is "not your usual Italian"; trade-offs are "limited seating" and "less-than-gentle" prices.

Alma
20 | 22 | 18 | $32

187 Columbia St., 2nd fl. (Degraw St.), Brooklyn, 718-643-5400;
www.almarestaurant.com
The "original", "upscale" Mexican fare and "strong margaritas" taste even better when on the "romantic" roof deck of this Carroll Gardens spot; toss in "million-dollar" harbor views and "you'd pay twice as much in Manhattan."

Alma Grill **NEW**
– | – | – | E

Radisson Lexington Hotel, 134 E. 48th St. (bet. Lexington & 3rd Aves.), 212-593-5900
East Midtown's Radisson Lexington Hotel has received a shot in the arm via this intimate New American from Latin music impresario Ralph Mercado; it's open from the crack of dawn till 11 PM, when things at his downstairs dance club, LQ, start heating up.

Alonso's Steakhouse **NEW**
– | – | – | M

265 W. 20th St. (bet. 7th & 8th Aves.), 212-675-7749; www.chelseadining.com
If you like stuffed animal heads and photos of cows, this new hunting lodge–like Chelsea chop shop will have appeal; if the setting isn't to your taste, just close your eyes because its budget-minded lineup of steaks and sides plus fish and raw-bar options are likely to please.

Alouette ☾
19 | 16 | 18 | $44

2588 Broadway (bet. 97th & 98th Sts.), 212-222-6808; www.alouettenyc.com
Upper Westsiders head to this "unpretentious" "haven from trendiness" for "well-prepared" French bistro dishes served in "weathered" digs; a little "more breathing room" would help, but pleased penny-pinchers praise the $24 early-bird prix fixe.

Alta
22 | 23 | 18 | $43

64 W. 10th St. (bet. 5th & 6th Aves.), 212-505-7777
You'll "never get bored" at this Village Mediterranean given the "abundance" of "flavorful" small plates paired with an "impressive wine list"; "balcony" seating and a "cozy fireplace" compensate for having to "pay a lot to fill up" on those "tiny portions."

ALTO ☒
25 | 24 | 26 | $84

11 E. 53rd St. (bet. 5th & Madison Aves.), 212-308-1099;
www.altorestaurant.com
"Don't expect anything familiar" at Scott Conant's "high-style", "shoot-for-the-stars" Midtown Italian, just "astonishing cuisine"

"brilliantly executed" and "impeccably served" in an "über-cool", wall-of-bottles setting (with a "better-than-first-rate" wine list as a bonus); it's a bit "formal" (jackets suggested) with a "price tag to match", but the whole experience is nothing short of "memorable."

Ama
| 22 | 18 | 17 | $49 |

48 MacDougal St. (bet. King & Prince Sts.), 212-358-1707; www.amanyc.com
The "fashion-white decor" may be "slick" and "trendy", but the "delicious" Puglian cuisine is "clean and light" at this "uncommon" SoHo Southern Italian; too bad "dining diva" Donatella Arpaia has moved on, leaving "hit-or-miss" service in her wake.

Amaranth ●
| 19 | 16 | 18 | $52 |

21 E. 62nd St. (bet. 5th & Madison Aves.), 212-980-6700;
www.amaranthrestaurant.com
"Good-looking girls" and "Eurotrash men" exchange air "kisses" at this "very UES" Mediterranean bistro where the "tasty", "reliable" fare plays second fiddle to the "hopping" scene; it "helps to be a regular" – "everyone seems to know each other" here.

Amarone ●
| 19 | 14 | 18 | $37 |

686 Ninth Ave. (bet. 47th & 48th Sts.), 212-245-6060;
www.amaronenyc.com
"Tried-and-true", this "busy, busy, busy" Hell's Kitchen Italian not only boasts "consistently good" "homemade pastas", but will also "get you to the show on time"; even better, it's "very affordable."

American Grill
| 19 | 17 | 18 | $42 |

1180 Victory Blvd. (Clove Rd.), Staten Island, 718-442-4742
"More upscale than most Staten Island eateries", this American is "popular" with local "bigwigs" accustomed to "fine food" and "pricey" tabs; a change of owners and a recent move to "larger" digs draw mixed reviews: "slipped" vs. "hooray."

Amici Amore I
| ∇ 20 | 18 | 20 | $37 |

29-35 Newtown Ave. (30th St.), Queens, 718-267-2771; www.amiciamore1.com
A "warm welcome" awaits at this Astoria Italian offering "consistently good" pasta and "excellent wines"; an "attached steakhouse" lends a "two-for-one" vibe, as does the option to stay "cozy" indoors or "sit outside in the summer."

Amma
| 23 | 16 | 20 | $39 |

246 E. 51st St. (bet. 2nd & 3rd Aves.), 212-644-8330; www.ammanyc.com
The "refined sauces" alone will make you "rethink what to expect from Indian cuisine" at this "distinctive" East Midtowner; a "personable" staff and "interesting" Southern Indian wines make up for the "uninspiring" decor.

Ammos
| ∇ 22 | 21 | 19 | $50 |

52 Vanderbilt Ave. (bet. 44th & 45th Sts.), 212-922-9999 NEW
20-30 Steinway St. (bet. 20th Ave. & 20th Rd.), Queens, 718-726-7900 ● M
www.ammosnewyork.com
Greek standards are "elevated" by "skillful chefs" at these "high-end" Hellenics, but the "superb" seafood nets the most superlatives; both the Astoria and Grand Central outposts are "beautifully designed", so the "pricey" tabs are no surprise.

Amorina M⇌ NEW
| ∇ 22 | 12 | 17 | $22 |

624 Vanderbilt Ave. (Prospect Pl.), Brooklyn, 718-230-3030
This Prospect Heights focacceria purveys "dependable" pastas and "savory" panini, but is best known for its perfect Roman-style pizzas; fair pricing and a "pleasant" ambiance make it a "good family option."

Amy Ruth's

22 | 12 | 17 | $22

113 W. 116th St. (bet. Lenox & 7th Aves.), 212-280-8779

"Gi-normous" portions of "killer" fried chicken, ribs and the like are the appeal of Carl Redding's "finger-licking", "hip-sticking" Harlem soul fooder ("sometimes you have to go north to get down south"); despite the "nothing" decor and "slow-as-molasses" service, you're bound to feel "festive" when you see the bill.

Amy's Bread

23 | 11 | 16 | $12

250 Bleecker St. (bet. Carmine & Leroy Sts.), 212-675-7802
Chelsea Mkt., 75 Ninth Ave. (bet. 15th & 16th Sts.), 212-462-4338
672 Ninth Ave. (bet. 46th & 47th Sts.), 212-977-2670
www.amysbread.com

"Savory aromas" of "leavened heaven" draw fans to these "superior" bakeries' "divine" breads, pastries and sandwiches; since seating's "tight" and service "clueless", they're recommended for "quick bites."

Angelica Kitchen ⊘

20 | 15 | 16 | $23

300 E. 12th St. (bet. 1st & 2nd Aves.), 212-228-2909; www.angelicakitchen.com

"Still truckin' after all these years", this "mellow" East Village vegan "virtuoso" draws the "Birkenstock-and-granola" set for "soul-healing" chow "done right"; still, the "hippie-dippy service" and "needs-a-spruce-up" decor are "not everyone's cup of green tea."

Angelina's

22 | 19 | 19 | $54

26 Jefferson Blvd. (Annadale Rd.), Staten Island, 718-227-7100;
www.angelinasristorante.com

Fans say the "surefire" fare found at this "old-world" Staten Island Italian can "rival Manhattan's best", ditto its "romantic" setting and "service without attitude"; yet skeptics say it sure seems "costly" in this "unimpressive" strip-mall locale.

Angelo & Maxie's ◑

21 | 18 | 18 | $52

233 Park Ave. S. (19th St.), 212-220-9200; www.angelo-maxies.com

"Beefcake" meets "beefsteak" at this "frenetic" Flatiron "power scene for suits", where "everything's big", from the "monster steaks" to the "fishbowl martinis"; it's "more of a scene" than others in the genre, but so "noisy" you may be "texting across the table."

Angelo's of Mulberry Street ◑ Ⓜ

23 | 15 | 19 | $43

146 Mulberry St. (bet. Grand & Hester Sts.), 212-966-1277;
www.angelomulberry.com

In the "heart of Little Italy", this "venerable" 105-year-old Neapolitan is ever "crowded" thanks to its "on-the-mark", "*O Sole Mio*" standards; the "tired" decor and "rushed" service don't deter diehards who declare it's "like grandma's – just a lot noisier"; P.S. if Ronald Reagan liked it, who are we to argue?

Angelo's Pizzeria

21 | 13 | 15 | $23

1697 Broadway (bet. 53rd & 54th Sts.), 212-245-8811
1043 Second Ave. (55th St.), 212-521-3600
117 W. 57th St. (bet. 6th & 7th Aves.), 212-333-4333
www.angelospizzany.com

"Super-duper" thin-crust pizzas with "generous toppings" and "zesty sauce" make this trio a natural for the "Midtown lunch" bunch; "fair prices" overcome the "ditzy staff" and "lousy decor."

Angon on the Sixth ◑ Ⓜ

▽ 21 | 14 | 19 | $28

320 E. Sixth St. (bet. 1st & 2nd Aves.), 212-260-8229; www.angon.biz

"Head and shoulders above" its Curry Row competition, this "wonderful" East Village Indian offers highly "authentic" fare for "low" dough; a "helpful staff" and brick-walled, Christmas light–free environs make fans "feel at home."

Angus McIndoe ❶   17 | 14 | 18 | $39
258 W. 44th St. (bet. B'way & 8th Ave.), 212-221-9222;
www.angusmcindoe.com
Stargazers rub elbows with "off-the-clock" show folk at this "informal", tri-level Theater District American where the "celeb spotting" outshines grub that's just "a step above pubby"; though the staff's "courteous", "don't be surprised if the waiter hands you his résumé."

Anh   21 | 17 | 18 | $26
363 Third Ave. (bet. 26th & 27th Sts.), 212-532-2858
It's "surprisingly" anh-crowded at this "pleasant" Gramercy Vietnamese offering "real-deal" dishes done with a "delicate touch"; a "tranquil" setting, "low-key service" and "budget" pricing make it "serenity personified."

Annie's ❶   18 | 14 | 15 | $28
1381 Third Ave. (bet. 78th & 79th Sts.), 212-327-4853
There are always "long waits" for the popular brunch at this "homey", "hopping" UES American where "serious", reasonably priced comfort grub is served by an "absent-minded" crew; even though strollers are banned, it still draws lots of "moms and tots."

ANNISA   27 | 22 | 26 | $70
13 Barrow St. (bet. 7th Ave. S. & W. 4th St.), 212-741-6699;
www.annisarestaurant.com
An "oasis of civility in rambunctious Greenwich Village", Anita Lo's "other-worldly" New American "labor of love" serves "exquisite", "beautifully presented" food (including a "ticket-to-heaven" tasting menu) served by a "solicitous" staff in a "minimalist", "Zen-like" setting; it "doesn't come cheap", but "stellar experiences" seldom do.

Anthony's NEW   ▽ 20 | 15 | 20 | $22
426A Seventh Ave. (bet. 14th & 15th Sts.), Brooklyn, 718-369-8315
Park Slopers pronounce this "family-run" Italian newcomer a "blessing" for its "super-tasty" standards and "very light" brick-oven pizzas (whole pies only, no slices); a "lively", "neighborhoody" vibe and "inexpensive" tabs ice the cake.

Antica Venezia   ▽ 23 | 23 | 25 | $45
396 West St. (W. 10th St.), 212-229-0606;
www.anticaveneziany.com
Although out-of-the-way, this West Village Italian boasts a "cozy", "rustic" setting with a "toasty fireplace" and "sunset" Hudson views; given the "impeccable service" and "delicious" food (often "prepared tableside"), its days as a "sleeper" seem limited.

Antonucci NEW   22 | 16 | 19 | $52
170 E. 81st St. (bet. Lexington & 3rd Aves.), 212-570-5100
"Immediately popular", this not inexpensive UES newcomer features "interesting", "well-executed" Italian dishes delivered by "helpful" (if sometimes "slow") servers; a "warm" storefront setting adds to the overall "pleasurable experience."

Anzu ❶ Ⓢ NEW   – | – | – | M
207 10th Ave. (bet. 22nd & 23rd Sts.), 212-627-7777
Operating out of a slim West Chelsea space, this new Japanese restaurant (fka D'or Ahn) offers a serene ambiance for its modestly priced sushi and other traditional fare; the early word is lots of laidback locals like it.

A.O.C. ◐

19 | 16 | 16 | $35

314 Bleecker St. (Grove St.), 212-675-9463; www.aocnyc.com

"Honest" French bistro fare turns up in the West Village at this "quintessential neighborhood joint" enhanced by a "pleasant" garden; it "opens early, closes late", and if service can be "typically Gallic", at least the tabs are "cheap and cheerful."

A.O.C. Bedford

23 | 21 | 21 | $51

14 Bedford St. (bet. Downing & Houston Sts.), 212-414-4764; www.aocbedford.com

"Wonderfully flavorful" Southern European fare, a "sophisticated wine list", "friendly service" and "romantic" albeit "snug" digs combine to make this "well-hidden" West Village retreat "AOK"; the Sunday/Monday BYO policy is a bonus.

ápizz ☒

24 | 21 | 21 | $44

217 Eldridge St. (bet. Rivington & Stanton Sts.), 212-253-9199; www.apizz.com

This "tiny" Lower East Side "hideaway" purveys "stupendous" pizza and "light takes on Italian favorites", fresh from a huge wood-fired brick oven; don't mind the bland exterior and "shady locale", there's plenty of "homey warmth" within, and "decent prices" to boot.

applewood Ⓜ

25 | 20 | 22 | $46

501 11th St. (bet. 7th & 8th Aves.), Brooklyn, 718-768-2044; www.applewoodny.com

"Socially conscious Park Slopers" like this "earnest" New American yearling offering dishes "cooked with care" using "first-tier" seasonal organic ingredients; service is "charming" and the farmhouse-style room exudes a "pleasant", "earth-mother vibe", leaving the "small portions"/"big bills" ratio as the only downside.

AQ Cafe ☒

▽ 22 | 16 | 15 | $21

Scandinavia House, 58 Park Ave. (bet. 37th & 38th Sts.), 212-847-9745; www.aquavit.org

Those seeking to "satisfy their Scandinavian food jones" head for Marcus Samuelsson's lunch-only cafeteria in Murray Hill; despite "spartan surroundings" and "surly" service, the "steal" of a smorgasbord and other "tasty tidbits" provide "Aquavit flair without the cost."

AQUAGRILL

26 | 19 | 23 | $55

210 Spring St. (6th Ave.), 212-274-0505; www.aquagrill.com

"Seafood is an art" at this SoHo piscatory "mecca" famed for "flapping-fresh" fish and a "sweet" raw bar smoothly served in "casual", "airy" digs; ok, it's "packed" and "noisy" at peak times and the tab can "set you back" a few clams, but overall "you can't go wrong here."

Aquamarine NEW

– | – | – | M

713 Second Ave. (bet. 38th & 39th Sts.), 212-297-1880

Offering reasonably priced sushi and sizzling platters, this new Murray Hill Japanese fusion practitioner is keeping up with the current vogue for splashy Asian decor: its modern design employs the liberal use of pebbles, seashells and birch with a soothing water wall as its centerpiece.

Aquaterra NEW

▽ 20 | 17 | 17 | $53

209 E. 56th St. (bet. 2nd & 3rd Aves.), 212-644-4447; www.aquaterrany.com

"Pleasant" is the vibe at this new Midtown Italian that features both a working fireplace and waterfall in its "comfortably rustic" digs; the ingredient-driven "homestyle" cooking is similarly "satisfying", if a bit on the "pricey" side.

AQUAVIT

25 24 24 $70

65 E. 55th St. (bet. Madison & Park Aves.), 212-307-7311; www.aquavit.org
"Glorious", "polished" Scandinavian fare, "choreographed" service and a "minimalist luxe" setting "dazzles diners" at Marcus Samuelsson's "classy" Eastsider, now in its 20th year; the "memorable" meals do require "deep pockets" when the check comes, but the more "casual" front cafe is "less expensive and equally delicious."

Arabelle

23 26 26 $69

Plaza Athénée Hotel, 37 E. 64th St. (Madison Ave.), 212-606-4647; www.arabellerestaurant.com
This "elegant dowager" in the Plaza Athénée is "lovely" and "formal", the "way things used to be", with fine French-American food and "treat-you-like-royalty" service; however, it's a "little stuffy" and more than a little "expensive", so it has never attracted much of a following despite its "high standards."

Areo ●Ⓜ

25 20 21 $48

8424 Third Ave. (bet. 84th & 85th Sts.), Brooklyn, 718-238-0079
At this "consistently excellent" Bay Ridge Italian, the "wonderful" "old-world" fare is prepared with an "artistic touch" for a "dressed-to-impress" grown-up crowd; in short, it's quite a "scene" and not too expensive either.

Arezzo Ⓢ

22 18 19 $50

46 W. 22nd St. (bet. 5th & 6th Aves.), 212-206-0555; www.arezzo-nyc.com
"Quiet" enough to do double duty for either a "biz lunch or a romantic dinner", this "straightforward", "underappreciated" Flatiron Tuscan dishes out "delicious" dishes that transcend the "pleasant but unengaging" room; still, even well-wishers "wish it were cheaper."

Arqua

24 21 23 $51

281 Church St. (White St.), 212-334-1888
"Still going strong" after 20 years, this "outstanding" TriBeCa "pioneer" provides perennially pleased patrons with "perfecto" Northern Italian cuisine in an "airy", "elegant" setting reminiscent of a late afternoon in a Tuscan hill town; "welcoming" service and plenty of "space between tables" complete the "solid" package.

Arté Café

17 16 17 $34

106 W. 73rd St. (bet. Amsterdam & Columbus Aves.), 212-501-7014; www.artecafenyc.com
"Perfectly serviceable" Italian eats at "bargain" tabs make this "pleasant, spacious" Westsider a "neighborhood favorite"; service may be "artless", but a $12.95 prix fixe dinner and an "unlimited-mimosa" Sunday brunch keep 'em coming.

Artie's Deli

18 10 14 $22

2290 Broadway (bet. 82nd & 83rd Sts.), 212-579-5959; www.arties.com
"Stuffed sandwiches rule" at this "blast-from-the-past" UWS "dilly of a deli" where "piles of pastrami" and "heaping portions" of all the old heartthrobs are "rushed" to your table in "fluorescent-lit" digs; "bring your appetite" and earplugs too, since it's "overrun by babies in strollers."

ARTISANAL

23 20 19 $51

2 Park Ave. (enter on 32nd St., bet. Madison & Park Aves.), 212-725-8585
Terrance Brennan's handsome, high-ceilinged Murray Hill French brasserie is a "temple to cheese" with "knowledgeable" servers guiding devotees; though extremely popular, some find the "huge" space too "echoey" and opt for its retail counter instead.

Arturo's Pizzeria ◐
21 | 12 | 16 | $24

106 W. Houston St. (Thompson St.), 212-677-3820
"Nothing ever changes" at this 50-year-old Village Italian "dive" where the "old NY vibe" enhances the "superior" thin-crust pies made in "real coal-fired ovens"; it scores "extra points for the jazz combo", "cheap wine" and "tacky yet lovable" artwork.

A Salt & Battery
19 | 9 | 14 | $15

112 Greenwich Ave. (bet. 12th & 13th Sts.), 212-691-2713;
www.asaltandbattery.com
"Lovely" fish 'n' chips lead the "fried-food frenzy" at this "no-fuss" West Villager where even Mars bars go into the deep fryer; but most Anglophiles say the "spartan" setup suggests taking out.

ASIA DE CUBA
23 | 25 | 20 | $56

Morgans Hotel, 237 Madison Ave. (bet. 37th & 38th Sts.), 212-726-7755;
www.chinagrillmgt.com
"Stunning", "white-on-white" Philippe Starck design sets the "fancy" tone at this forever hip Murray Hill Asian-Cuban known for its "intriguing" eats and "roaming mobs of skinny folk"; a "place to be seen but not heard", it can be "a bit pretentious" and is certainly "not cheap", but "worth putting up with" for the "killer calamari salad and lobster mashed potatoes" alone.

ASIATE
23 | 28 | 24 | $84

Mandarin Oriental Hotel, 80 Columbus Circle, 35th fl. (60th St. at B'way),
212-805-8881; www.mandarinoriental.com
It's all "so glamorous" at this Japanese-French "aerie" in the Mandarin Oriental Hotel, with its "peerless views" and chef Nori Sugie's equally "memorable" Japanese-French cuisine that looks as "gorgeous" as the "serene" room; a "fantastic" wine list and seamless service "make any meal a special occasion", as do the fittingly "sky-high prices."

Aspen ◐ Ⓢ NEW
▽ 18 | 24 | 15 | $44

30 W. 22nd St. (bet. 5th & 6th Aves.), 212-645-5040; www.aspen-nyc.com
"More about the scene than the food", this "trendy" Flatiron new-comer boasts "cool" "après-ski" decor (i.e. "Lucite deer heads") that thrills its young, "good-looking crowd"; not so thrilling is the "rude" service and "small-portioned" New Americana at "hefty prices."

ATLANTIC GRILL ◐
22 | 19 | 20 | $48

1341 Third Ave. (bet. 76th & 77th Sts.), 212-988-9200;
www.brguestrestaurants.com
The mood is always "upbeat" at Steve Hanson's "crazy-popular" "up-scale" Upper Eastsider whose "staying power" is due to "consistently delicious", fairly fared fin fare; alright, it's "not a place for intimate conversation" at prime times, but it compensates with "sixth-sense" service and first-rate people-watching.

August
22 | 19 | 19 | $44

359 Bleecker St. (bet. Charles & W. 10th Sts.), 212-929-4774;
www.augustny.com
Those "flavorful" regional European dishes taste "even better" when prepared in the "open hearth" brick oven at this "rustic" West Villager; its "no-reservations policy is a bummer" and "more elbow room would help", but the glassed-in garden is a "year-round luxury."

Au Mandarin
19 | 14 | 18 | $31

World Financial Ctr., 200-250 Vesey St. (West St.), 212-385-0313;
www.aumandarin.com
"Consistent" and "convenient" are the watchwords at this "upscale" if "mall-ish" WFC Chinese that's a popular "business" lunch spot and

a "default delivery" choice for those "late nights at the office"; word is the chow "tastes good – until you get the bill."

AUREOLE Ⓢ
27 26 26 $83

34 E. 61st St. (bet. Madison & Park Aves.), 212-319-1660;
www.charliepalmer.com

"Wonderful from start to finish", Charlie Palmer's East Side New American "treasure" is "still aglow" thanks to chef Dante Boccuzzi's "impeccable" food (and "heavenly desserts") "artfully presented" by a "classy" staff in an "opulent", flower-bedecked townhouse; for those without a "full wallet", the $35 prix fixe lunch is the ticket.

Aurora ⌷
▽ 25 22 20 $35

70 Grand St. (Wythe Ave.), Brooklyn, 718-388-5100; www.aurorabk.com

Fans say a "true Italian rules the kitchen" at this "off-the-beaten-path" Williamsburg trattoria where "sophisticated" Piedmontese dishes are served "without attitude" in "rustic" environs; "reasonable" pricing and a "wonderful garden" make it "worth a trek."

Austin's Steakhouse
▽ 23 20 22 $57

8915 Fifth Ave. (90th St.), Brooklyn, 718-439-5000;
www.austinssteakhouseny.com

"Juicy", "taste-of-Texas" steaks await at this "neighborhood" Bay Ridge chophouse with a "warm ambiance" and "friendly" staffers; still, the "give-me-Peter-Luger" crowd says the kitchen's "inconsistent" and the tabs too "expensive for Brooklyn."

A Voce 🆕
24 22 21 $61

41 Madison Ave. (26th St.), 212-545-8555; www.avocerestaurant.com

A "deceptively rustic" Italian menu gets some "sophisticated" twists at Andrew Carmellini's "approachable" newcomer that's a player in the "increasingly happening Madison Square Park" scene; the "airy", "modern" layout and "exuberant" service make up for noise levels "louder than U2 at the Garden."

Avra ◗
23 20 20 $53

141 E. 48th St. (bet. Lexington & 3rd Aves.), 212-759-8550; www.avrany.com

The "fish is so fresh" that you can "smell the ocean" at this "fail-safe" Midtown Greek seafooder whose patio adds to the "vacationing-in-Mykonos" air; sure, it can be a "madhouse" and the per-pound pricing is "a little crazy" too, but ultimately "everyone has a good time."

Awash Ethiopian
22 12 16 $23

947 Amsterdam Ave. (bet. 106th & 107th Sts.), 212-961-1416
338 E. Sixth St. (bet. 1st & 2nd Aves.), 212-982-9589 ◗
www.awashnyc.com

"Unusual" eats in "plentiful" portions compensate for the "oblivious staff" and "desolate" decor at this "cheap" Ethiopian duo; it's a no-forks, "eat-with-your-hands" experience that's most "fun with friends."

Azafran ◗Ⓜ
21 17 19 $45

77 Warren St. (bet. Greenwich St. & W. B'way), 212-284-0578;
www.azafrannyc.com

"Delish morsels" make up the menu of this "buzzy" TriBeCa tapas dispenser where an array of "tasty", if "pricey", Spanish tidbits are supported by "sublime sangria"; "harried servers", "fashionista sightings" and "tables about an inch apart" come with the territory.

Azucar ◗
19 16 17 $35

939 Eighth Ave. (bet. 55th & 56th Sts.), 212-262-5354; www.azucarnyc.com

For a "pre-theater change of pace", this "festive" Hell's Kitchen yearling supplies "hearty" "homestyle" Cuban chow at "bargain" tabs;

the live music can be "deafening" and service "inattentive", but for those who still smoke, there's a free "freshly rolled cigar" at the end of the meal.

Azul Bistro ◑

21 | 16 | 18 | $39

152 Stanton St. (Suffolk St.), 646-602-2004

"Fantasteak" slabs of beef at "kind prices" keep the trade brisk at this "authentic" Lower East Side Argentine "carnivores' extravaganza"; despite the "intimate" setting and off-the-beaten-track address, it's too "noisy" for some, though others like the "party feel."

Azuri Cafe ⊅

∇ 24 | 4 | 8 | $13

465 W. 51st St. (bet. 9th & 10th Aves.), 212-262-2920

"Excellent Israeli street food" is the draw at this West Side "hole-in-the-wall" where the "delicious" "cheap eats" include some of "NYC's best falafel"; since there's "no decor", "nowhere to sit" and a famously "grouchy proprietor", most "go for takeout."

BABBO ◑

27 | 23 | 25 | $74

110 Waverly Pl. (bet. MacDougal St. & 6th Ave.), 212-777-0303;
www.babbonyc.com

"Every bit as fabulous as you've heard", Mario Batali and Joe Bastianich's "masterful" Village Italian is *numero uno* for pairing "inspired" food with an "encyclopedic" wine list; those snaring an "impossible" reservation find the service "smart", the carriage house setting "surprisingly relaxed" and being "bombarded with a big bill" bearable for a dinner that's "last-meal-on-earth good"; by the way, "upstairs is better if you want to talk."

Baci & Abbracci ◑⊅ NEW

– | – | – | M

204 Grand St. (bet. Bedford & Driggs Aves.), Brooklyn, 718-599-6599;
www.baciabbracciny.com

Italian for 'kisses and hugs', this modern Williamsburg trattoria teams a Tuscan chef with a Neapolitan pizza maker, and the result is a modestly priced intersection of north and south; as plenty of diners have already discovered, either region is best enjoyed in the spacious courtyard.

Baldoria

21 | 16 | 20 | $54

249 W. 49th St. (bet. B'way & 8th Ave.), 212-582-0460;
www.baldoriamo.com

Aka "Rao's South", Frank Pellegrino Jr.'s "quality" Theater District Italian is "accessible to all comers" hankering for "toothsome" "traditional" fare served in an "upbeat", "ring-a-ding-ding" atmosphere; the "retro" digs can get "noisy", but at least the staff is "personable."

BALTHAZAR ◑

23 | 23 | 19 | $52

80 Spring St. (bet. B'way & Crosby St.), 212-965-1414;
www.balthazarny.com

The "never-ending bustle" is part of the "unflagging charm" of Keith McNally's "piping hot" SoHo brasserie where "delightful" French food is served by a "convivial" crew in a setting that accurately recalls "Paris in the 1920s"; it's hard to beat for "stargazing grazing" amid "fabulous" folk, "shoppers" and "tourists", and hard to believe it's now celebrating its 10th anniversary, without slowing down or missing a beat.

Baluchi's

18 | 14 | 16 | $26

224 E. 53rd St. (bet. 2nd & 3rd Aves.), 212-750-5515
111 E. 29th St. (bet. Lexington Ave. & Park Ave. S.), 212-481-3861
1149 First Ave. (63rd St.), 212-371-3535
275 Greenwich St. (Warren St.), 212-571-5343
104 Second Ave. (6th St.), 212-780-6000

(continued)
Baluchi's

1565 Second Ave. (bet. 81st & 82nd Sts.), 212-288-4810
1724 Second Ave. (bet. 89th & 90th Sts.), 212-996-2600
193 Spring St. (bet. Sullivan & Thompson Sts.), 212-226-2828
240 W. 56th St. (bet. B'way & 8th Ave.), 212-397-0707
8321 Third Ave. (84th St.), Brooklyn, 718-238-6998
www.baluchis.com
Additional locations throughout the NY area
"Consistency is the byword" at this "ubiquitous" chain offering "savory" if "not very exciting" Indian items at "rock-bottom" rates that dip further for the "50 percent off lunch special"; critics of the "no-frills" digs and "not-reliable service" tout the "ultrafast" delivery.

Bamn! ◑⇌ NEW
| – | – | – | I |

37 St. Marks Pl. (bet. 2nd & 3rd Aves.), 212-358-7685;
www.bamnfood.com
The long-gone automat concept is reborn at this new 24/7 East Villager, a phone booth–size spot that makes up for its diminutive stature with hot-pink, Hello-Kitty decor; the comfort food choices (think sliders, croquettes, hot dogs) may not cost a quarter anymore, but they're still so economical that there's already a line out the door.

Bamonte's
| 22 | 16 | 19 | $40 |

32 Withers St. (bet. Lorimer St. & Union Ave.), Brooklyn, 718-384-8831
For a "welcome refuge from Williamsburg hipsters", try this 107-year-old Italian "red-sauce joint" (with matching "red-velvet decor") lures the "family" trade with its *molto delicioso* dishes and *molto bene* pricing; though "dressed better than you are", the "grumpy" waiters "look like they've been here since it opened."

Bandol Bistro
| 17 | 16 | 18 | $43 |

181 E. 78th St. (bet. Lexington & 3rd Aves.), 212-744-1800;
www.bandolbistro.com
Exuding a "neighborly" vibe, this "sleepy little" UES French bistro is a local "favorite" for its "limited" but "well-done" menu of "standards"; a "broad wine selection" and "reasonable prices" complete the "pleasant" picture.

Banjara ◑
| 22 | 14 | 17 | $29 |

97 First Ave. (6th St.), 212-477-5956
A "grown-up" version of "Sixth Street's continuous kitchen", this East Village Indian offers "fresh", "zesty" takes on "traditional dishes" that are well "worth the extra couple bucks"; still, some say both the service and setting need work.

Bann
| ∇ 22 | 24 | 21 | $47 |

Worldwide Plaza, 350 W. 50th St. (bet. 8th & 9th Aves.), 212-582-4446;
www.bannrestaurant.com
"Hidden" in Worldwide Plaza, this "progressive" Korean provides a "serene"-verging-on-"swanky" setting for sampling "full-flavored" fare enhanced by "super" cocktails and "charming" service; "cook-it-yourself" options lend an "interesting twist" to the otherwise "high-end" experience.

Bann Thai
| 21 | 18 | 19 | $29 |

69-12 Austin St. (Yellowstone Blvd.), Queens, 718-544-9999;
www.bannthairestaurant.com
There's "zeal in the spicing" at this Forest Hills Thai "favorite" where the dishes' heat varies from "safe" to "outer space"; it's a bit "off the strip" but "worth seeking out" for its "pretty" room, "thoughtful" service and "decent prices."

Bao Noodles
20 | 13 | 16 | $26

391 Second Ave. (bet. 22nd & 23rd Sts.), 212-725-7770
Admirers "slurp their way through" the menu of this Gramercy "neighborhood" noodle shop known for serving "really tasty" Vietnamese food "for not a lot of money"; despite an "indifferent" staff and "downscale" decor, most surveyors say it "never disappoints."

Bao 111 ●
22 | 19 | 19 | $39

111 Ave. C (bet. 7th & 8th Sts.), 212-254-7773; www.bao111.com
"Exotic drinks" and a "stylish" room fit for a "candlelit date" supply the "good vibes" at this "hip" East Villager, but it's the "original" "nouveau Vietnamese" cuisine that keeps the place "packed"; minor downsides include "puny" portions and "tight confines."

Bar Americain
23 | 23 | 21 | $60

152 W. 52nd St. (bet. 6th & 7th Aves.), 212-265-9700; www.baramericain.com
"Bold flay-vors" emerge from the "open kitchen" of Bobby Flay's "bustling" Midtown American; set in a grand, "soaring" space, it seamlessly serves suits seeking a soigné business lunch or a smoothly flowing liquid soiree; no surprise, it's best enjoyed "on the company dime."

Baraonda ●
19 | 18 | 15 | $46

1439 Second Ave. (75th St.), 212-288-8555; www.baraondany.com
It's "quite a scene" at this "packed" UES Italian that's "more party than restaurant" thanks to a "beautiful Euro" following prone to "late-night table dancing"; the "food ain't bad either", though service veers from "flirtatious" to "snooty."

Barbès ●
21 | 18 | 20 | $40

21 E. 36th St. (bet. 5th & Madison Aves.), 212-684-0215
A "haven" in Murray Hill's "gastronomic wasteland", this "tiny" place delivers an "artful blend" of French-Moroccan cuisine in quarters that "feel like Marrakech"; the service is "solicitous" and the value's "hard to beat", so fans abide the "crowded" conditions.

Barbetta ● Ⓜ
20 | 23 | 21 | $58

321 W. 46th St. (bet. 8th & 9th Aves.), 212-246-9171; www.barbettarestaurant.com
Ever "civilized" at 101 years old, this Restaurant Row Northern Italian set in a "luxe townhouse" remains "endearing" for its "old-world style", "flavorful" fare and "cordial service"; some say it "needs updating", but for the majority it's just fine, especially in the "spectacular" garden.

Barbone ● Ⓜ NEW
– | – | – | M

186 Ave. B (bet. 11th & 12th Sts.), 212-254-6047
This new East Village Italian enoteca has a rather formal ambiance and an ambitious, midpriced menu of seasonal classic dishes; it's most memorable for its all-Italian wine list and backyard patio, one of the most spacious in these parts.

Barbounia NEW
20 | 24 | 18 | $55

250 Park Ave. S. (20th St.), 212-995-0242; www.barbounia.com
"Pillow-lined banquettes" and a "vaulted ceiling" with a "feathered chandelier" make for a "sexy" mood at this "airy" new Flatiron Mediterranean; the "expensive" eats are "tasty" enough, but the "loud" acoustics and "spacey service" need work.

Barbuto
21 | 17 | 17 | $47

775 Washington St. (bet. Jane & W. 12th Sts.), 212-924-9700; www.barbutonyc.com
Jonathan Waxman's "bustling" Village Italian puts forth "elegant" fare (with "ingredients straight from the fields") that works well with the

"renovated garage" setting; its "trendy" crowd says service is "haphazard", adding that one diner's "cacophony" is another's "fabulous buzz."

Barça 18 ● NEW 19 | 20 | 18 | $48
225 Park Ave. S. (bet. 18th & 19th Sts.), 212-533-2500;
www.brguestrestaurants.com
New to the "Flatiron feeding grounds" comes this "hip" Spaniard where Eric Ripert and Steve Hanson's "take on tapas" gets mixed marks ("delicious" vs. "Spanglish"); some say the "swank", "seductive" room, "noisy" crowd and "ditzy" service make it "feel like a nightclub."

Barking Dog 16 | 13 | 15 | $23
Afinia Dumont, 150 E. 34th St. (bet. Lexington & 3rd Aves.), 212-871-3900 ●
1678 Third Ave. (94th St.), 212-831-1800 ⇱
1453 York Ave. (77th St.), 212-861-3600 ⇱
"Sit, stay" and "sink your canines" into "cheap" American diner chow at these pooch- and "stroller-friendly" Eastsiders with mutt-motif decor; you may have to bark to "wake up the waiters", but what's really "for the dogs" is that "cash-only policy."

barmarché ● 18 | 19 | 17 | $36
14 Spring St. (Elizabeth St.), 212-219-2399; www.barmarche.com
"Hipsters" and "trendinistas" are drawn to this "unsung" NoLita "neighborhood" bistro by the "solid" New American eats and decent pricing, not the "flighty, Mohawked" staff; the room is "pleasant" enough in a "laid-back" Downtown kind of way.

Bar Masa ● 🅐 23 | 20 | 21 | $69
Time Warner Ctr., 10 Columbus Circle, 4th fl. (60th St. at B'way),
212-823-9800; www.masanyc.com
Those who "can't afford Masa" like its adjacent sibling where the sushi and other Japanese dishes are "less pricey" than next door but still "expensive"; however, given the "minuscule" portions and middling "quality-to-cost ratio", some suggest you "save up for the main show."

Barney Greengrass 🅜⇱ 23 | 7 | 13 | $25
541 Amsterdam Ave. (bet. 86th & 87th Sts.), 212-724-4707;
www.barneygreengrass.com
Our surveyors' No. 1 deli, this UWS "time capsule" is a "madhouse" on weekends, drawing crowds craving "real-deal" bagels topped with the "perfect schmear"; for folks who "plotz" over the "divey" digs, "surly" servers and "interminable waits", there's always "takeout."

Barolo ● 18 | 21 | 19 | $51
398 W. Broadway (bet. Broome & Spring Sts.), 212-226-1102;
www.nybarolo.com
Everyone "loves the garden" at this "upscale" SoHo Italian where the food, though good enough, is "secondary to the great outdoor space"; but even indoors, it's a "civilized" experience with a "happy vibe" that makes it a "good place for a date."

Bar Pitti ●⇱ 22 | 14 | 16 | $36
268 Sixth Ave. (bet. Bleecker & Houston Sts.), 212-982-3300
"If you can't get into Da Silvano", this nearby Village Italian is a good stand-in thanks to its sidewalk seating and "stellar" celeb-spotting; toss in "unbeatable" pastas at "honest" prices, and the "long waits" and "hurry-up-and-finish attitude" are more tolerable.

BarTabac ● 18 | 19 | 16 | $28
128 Smith St. (Dean St.), Brooklyn, 718-923-0918
"Breezy young" types frequent this "rustic" Boerum Hill bistro for "simple, well-prepared" Gallic fare presented in a "laid-back"

setting; sure, service can be "lackluster", but no one's complaining given the pricing.

Basilica ◑
| 20 | 14 | 20 | $28 |

676 Ninth Ave. (bet. 46th & 47th Sts.), 212-489-0051
"Hearty, unpretentious" Italian cooking is offered at this "cramped" Hell's Kitchen "hole-in-the-wall" that "knows how to get you to the theater on time"; it's "cheap" to begin with, but that $21.95 "prix fixe with a bottle of wine" is an "amazing value."

Basso Est ◑
| ∇ 23 | 16 | 24 | $36 |

198 Orchard St. (Houston St.), 212-358-9469; www.bassoest.com
"Small and spunky", this Lower Eastsider produces "rich" Italian dishes with "lots of flavor" in "intimate" but "not claustrophobic" digs; the "knowing" staff "works hard to please", and prices are "affordable" to boot.

Basta Pasta
| 21 | 16 | 20 | $39 |

37 W. 17th St. (bet. 5th & 6th Aves.), 212-366-0888; www.bastapastanyc.com
Diners "with open minds" are in for a "pleasant surprise" at this "unique" Flatiron Italian where "perfectly prepared pastas" from an "airy open kitchen" are given a "Japanese twist"; "lovely" service and presentation enliven the otherwise "minimalist" experience.

Battery Gardens
| 18 | 25 | 19 | $47 |

SW corner of Battery Park (State St.), 212-809-5508; www.batterygardens.com
"It's all about the view" at this "relaxing", midpriced American-Continental where the "good quality" food tastes better on the "sprawling" patio overlooking the harbor and Lady Liberty; it's "a little hard to find", hidden within Battery Park, but worth seeking out.

BAYARD'S ▣
| 24 | 24 | 23 | $64 |

1 Hanover Sq. (bet. Pearl & Stone Sts.), 212-514-9454; www.bayards.com
Full of ship models and paintings, this "special place" in the Financial District's "historic India House" embodies the "grace and style of a bygone era" – beginning with the "exquisitely prepared" French-American cuisine of chef Eberhard Müller (ex Lutèce, Le Bernardin), and buoyed by an "extraordinary" wine list and service that's "polished without being pretentious"; it all adds up to a "refined" reminder of the days "when dinner was an occasion"; P.S. it also has lots of private rooms for parties of all sizes.

Bay Leaf
| 19 | 16 | 17 | $35 |

49 W. 56th St. (bet. 5th & 6th Aves.), 212-957-1818; www.bayleafny.com
"All your favorites" are up for grabs at this "reliable", "white-tablecloth" Indian best known for its "can't-be-beat" $13.95 lunch buffet; critics complain about "erratic" service and "high-end" dinner pricing, but like its "convenience to City Center and Carnegie Hall."

Beacon
| 22 | 21 | 20 | $58 |

25 W. 56th St. (bet. 5th & 6th Aves.), 212-332-0500; www.beaconnyc.com
Grill "wizard" Waldy Malouf serves up "succulent", "wood-roasted" fare at this "handsome", multi-tiered Midtown New American that's a "bright spot" for either "business or pleasure"; it may be "on the expensive side" unless you opt for the "reasonable" prix fixes.

Beast
| ∇ 19 | 15 | 19 | $32 |

638 Bergen St. (Vanderbilt Ave.), Brooklyn, 718-399-6855
This "friendly" "neighborhood" retreat for Prospect Heights locals serves an "interesting" menu of Mediterranean items, including an

assortment of "delicious" small plates; an "upscale pub atmosphere" and reasonable tabs complete the picture.

BECCO ◗ | 21 | 17 | 20 | $42 |

355 W. 46th St. (bet. 8th & 9th Aves.), 212-397-7597; www.becconyc.com
Famed for its $21.95 prix fixe all-you-can-eat "pasta orgy", Joe Bastianich's Restaurant Row Italian adds further value with a *"bellissimo"* list of $20 wines and solid service; this "winning combination" naturally makes for "daunting crowds" pre-theater.

Beccofino NEW ∇ | 24 | 19 | 21 | $29 |

5704 Mosholu Ave. (bet. Fieldston Rd. & Spencer Ave.), Bronx, 718-432-2604
Though new on the Riverdale scene, this "homey" Italian "already feels long-established" thanks to its "stylish", "on-the-money" dishes and "accommodating" crew; "reasonable" pricing, a "small" setting and "no reserving" are already producing "lengthy waits."

Bella Blu | 19 | 16 | 18 | $47 |

967 Lexington Ave. (bet. 70th & 71st Sts.), 212-988-4624
"Young", "eye-pleasing" types turn up for "uncomplicated" pastas and "designer pizzas" out of the brick oven at this "festive" UES Northern Italian; "saucy waiters", "tired" decor and "pricey" specials aside, it's a "jumping" joint that's "all about hanging out."

Bella Via | 21 | 17 | 19 | $29 |

47-46 Vernon Blvd. (48th Ave.), Queens, 718-361-7510; www.bellaviarestaurant.com
Some "serious pizza" emerges from the "coal-fired brick oven" at this LIC "neighborhood" Italian that also offers "terrific pastas" in "Queens-size" portions; it's a "welcome change" in an otherwise "lackluster" area, and "moderate" prices ice the cake.

Bellavitae ◗ | 22 | 18 | 19 | $49 |

24 Minetta Ln. (bet. MacDougal St. & 6th Ave.), 212-473-5121; www.bellavitae.com
"Small plates are a big deal" at this "outstanding" Village Italian wine bar known for the "purity of the ingredients" in its "simple" yet "sophisticated" dishes; though the servers may "take themselves too seriously" and the "bill adds up quickly", this just could be the "poor man's Babbo."

Belleville | 18 | 20 | 16 | $35 |

350 Fifth Ave. (5th St.), Brooklyn, 718-832-9777
"Direct-from-Paris" decor (including a "transporting" zinc bar) and "consistently good" food make "hanging out a pleasure" at this "amiable" Park Slope French bistro; *"quel dommage"* that the "Parisian" service is so "laid-back."

Bello ⌧ | 19 | 16 | 19 | $45 |

863 Ninth Ave. (56th St.), 212-246-6773; www.bellorestaurant.com
"They deliver what they promise" at this Hell's Kitchen "time warp": "basic" Italian fare, "well-done" at "fair prices"; there are "plenty of regulars" thanks to a "courteous" staff, "pleasantly quiet" room and the "real bonus" of free parking at the dinner hour.

Bello Sguardo | 19 | 16 | 18 | $37 |

410 Amsterdam Ave. (bet. 79th & 80th Sts.), 212-873-6252
A "wonderful mix" of Mediterranean small plates for "prices that seem more old-world than new" is the draw at this "different" Upper Westsider; it's a "perfect place for a group of friends to share" a variety of dishes and let the time while away.

Ben & Jack's Steak House

| 24 | 17 | 22 | $65 |

219 E. 44th St. (bet. 2nd & 3rd Aves.), 212-682-5678;
www.benandjackssteakhouse.com

Another "spawn of Peter Luger", this Grand Central–area steakhouse features the same "crackling" chops, along with owners who "actually wait on tables"; maybe the surroundings are "underwhelming", but at least "you can use your credit card" here.

Ben Benson's

| 23 | 18 | 21 | $63 |

123 W. 52nd St. (bet. 6th & 7th Aves.), 212-581-8888;
www.benbensons.com

"Huge hunks" of beef and "bucket"-size martinis draw desk jockeys armed with "hefty expense accounts" to this "tried-and-true" Midtown chop shop; it's a "guy's place if ever there was one", what with the "butch" setting, "gruff" waiters and "general hubbub."

Ben's Kosher Deli

| 18 | 11 | 14 | $22 |

209 W. 38th St. (bet. 7th & 8th Aves.), 212-398-2367
Bay Terrace, 211-37 26th Ave. (211th St.), Queens, 718-229-2367
www.bensdeli.net

Giving new meaning to "tongue in cheek", this "busy" kosher deli duo is known for its "vast menu" and "mile-high sandwiches"; "nonexistent" decor and "abrupt service" to the contrary, these "relics" of a "dying breed" are "keeping tradition alive."

Beppe ⊠

| 23 | 20 | 21 | $53 |

45 E. 22nd St. (bet. B'way & Park Ave. S.), 212-982-8422; www.beppenyc.com

Despite losing its founding chef, this Flatiron Northern Italian is "holding its own" with "earthy" food dispensed by a "cordial" crew in "understated", "rustic" digs; most say everything's *molto bene* here, except for the "high cost."

Bereket ●⊄

| 20 | 4 | 12 | $12 |

187 E. Houston St. (Orchard St.), 212-475-7700

"After a night of drinking and partying", this "no fuss, no muss" LES Turk is a 24/7 savior for "satisfying" kebabs and other "Turkish roadside food" on the "cheap"; "dumpy" looks, "surly" service and a "million cabbies" in the crowd come with the territory.

Beso

| 20 | 14 | 17 | $25 |

210 Fifth Ave. (Union St.), Brooklyn, 718-783-4902

"For a place that looks so hip", this Park Slope Nuevo Latino is "shockingly family-friendly", drawing droves of "stroller"-pushers with its "deliciously different", "modestly priced" dishes; it's usually "very crowded" for brunch, but oddly underpopulated at suppertime.

Bette

| 19 | 22 | 18 | $59 |

461 W. 23rd St. (bet. 9th & 10th Aves.), 212-366-0404; www.betterestaurant.com

There's "lots of buzz" in the air at Amy Sacco's "sceney" West Chelsea yearling where "unsung" yet "chicly done" European eats play second fiddle to random "star sightings"; foes find "no bang for the buck" here, but admit the afternoon tea is "really special."

Better Burger

| 15 | 10 | 14 | $13 |

178 Eighth Ave. (19th St.), 212-989-6688 ●
587 Ninth Ave. (bet. 42nd & 43rd Sts.), 212-629-6622
1614 Second Ave. (84th St.), 212-734-6644
561 Third Ave. (37th St.), 212-949-7528
www.betterburgernyc.com

"Not your typical fast-food joints", this "healthy" chainlet offers organic hamburgers and air-baked fries for guilt-ridden types craving "naughty food"; partisans tart them up with "unusually good condiments", though wags tag them "blah burger."

Bettola ◐ | 21 | 17 | 19 | $35

412 Amsterdam Ave. (bet. 79th & 80th Sts.), 212-787-1660;
www.bettolanyc.com

A "low-key" UWS "favorite", this "cozy", "brick-lined" Italian features a pizza oven that puts forth "fantastic" thin-crust pies as well as other "delectable" dishes; further assets include a "happy staff" and sidewalk seating.

Beyoglu ◐ | 21 | 17 | 18 | $34

1431 Third Ave. (81st St.), 212-650-0850

Regulars "make a meal" of the "terrific" tapas at this "meze-focused" UES "Turkish delight"; the "staff works hard" and the "price is right", so no one cares that the "cheerful" surroundings "aren't fancy."

BG NEW | ▽ 19 | 24 | 19 | $46

Bergdorf Goodman, 754 Fifth Ave., 7th fl. (bet. 57th & 58th Sts.),
212-872-8977

"Ladies who lunch" like this "chic" new arrival on Bergdorf's seventh floor as a "nice diversion" from "deciding which Chanel bag to buy"; "solid" New Americana and a "gilded-cage ambiance" (plus Central Park views) complete the "expensive" picture.

Bianca ⇥ | 23 | 17 | 20 | $33

5 Bleecker St. (bet. Bowery & Elizabeth St.), 212-260-4666;
www.biancarestaurantnyc.com

"Perfect for a match.com outing", this "intimate", "all-cash" NoHo Italian emits a "lovely, cozy" vibe, following up with a "limited menu" of "spot-on" Emilia-Romagnan dishes (notably a "to-die-for lasagna"); service is "warm" and "prices low."

Bice ◐ | 20 | 19 | 19 | $57

7 E. 54th St. (bet. 5th & Madison Aves.), 212-688-1999

"Beautiful people", "Eurogentry" and other "complacently elite" types frequent this Midtown Northern Italian for its "pretty darn good" cooking and "power" sidewalk seating – not the "high decibels", "hefty tabs" and service that's "nice if they know you, spotty if they don't."

Big John NEW | – | – | – | M

199 Orchard St. (bet. Houston & Stanton Sts.), 212-353-2731;
www.bigjohnles.com

Hearty, greasy grub lies in store at this new, ultracasual LES American specializing in dishes like the 'White Trash-a-Role' (their take on a sloppy joe); it works well for the younger set looking for a cheap stomach-lining before a night of Downtown drinking and carousing.

Big Nick's Burger Joint ◐ | 18 | 5 | 13 | $15

2175 Broadway (77th St.), 212-362-9238
70 W. 71st St. (Columbus Ave.), 212-799-4444

Burgers the "size of manhole covers" head up the "huge menus" of these separately owned UWS joints vending "cheap", "classic greasy spoon" grub; the 24/7 Broadway outpost may have longer hours, but both share "don't-judge-a-book-by-its-cover" decor.

Big Wong ⇥ | 22 | 4 | 11 | $12

67 Mott St. (bet. Bayard & Canal Sts.), 212-964-0540

Despite its "unfortunate name", this "lowbrow" Chinese "classic" offers an "authentic" "C-town experience" at "no damage to your wallet", provided you can abide "surly" service and "no atmosphere"; P.S. it's "mecca for congee fans."

Billie's Black Ⓜ NEW
– | – | – | M
*271 W. 119th St. (bet. Frederick Douglass Blvd. & St. Nicholas Ave.),
212-280-2248; www.billiesblack.com*
Set on a quiet Harlem block, this cozy nook turns out upscale soul food
and soulful cocktails at moderate prices; in addition to lunch and dinner, there's also a Sunday gospel brunch as the high point of its week.

Biricchino Ⓩ
18 | 11 | 18 | $38
260 W. 29th St. (8th Ave.), 212-695-6690
"Great homemade sausages" are the stars of the show at this "welcome" Northern Italian "oasis" in the otherwise "frumpy" area
around Madison Square Garden; it's "not expensive", so its "lacking"
looks and "not-so-solid service" are easier to stomach.

Bistro Cassis
21 | 18 | 18 | $42
*225 Columbus Ave. (bet. 70th & 71st Sts.), 212-579-3966;
www.bistrocassisnyc.com*
"Downtown's loss is the West Side's gain" at this newly transplanted
French bistro where "good value" Gallic grub is served by "heavily
accented" waiters in "Left Bank"–like quarters; given the "napkin-
size tables" and "no-reservations" policy, it's "already crowded."

Bistro Citron NEW
– | – | – | M
*473 Columbus Ave. (bet. 82nd & 83rd Sts.), 212-400-9401;
www.bistrocitronnyc.com*
Affordable French fare with a seafood emphasis lands on the UWS at
this charming new bistro equipped with the tin signs and distressed
mirrors that are de rigueur for the genre; umbrella-covered sidewalk
tables lend Left Bank appeal.

Bistro du Nord
18 | 15 | 17 | $44
1312 Madison Ave. (93rd St.), 212-289-0997
"Hearty, simply prepared" French fare with "super value" prix fixes
keep this tiny Carnegie Hill bistro "tightly packed" (hint: the "upstairs
balcony tables" offer more "breathing room"); "spotty" service and
"tired" decor are the downsides.

Bistro Les Amis ◑
20 | 16 | 20 | $38
180 Spring St. (Thompson St.), 212-226-8645; www.bistrolesamis.com
Just "as friendly as the name suggests", this "tiny" Gallic "respite"
from SoHo's "hustle-bustle" proffers "trusted standbys" for "inexpensive" tabs, mostly for the "locals"; with "no aspiring actors" on board,
service is genuinely "charming."

Bistro Le Steak ◑
18 | 14 | 16 | $44
1309 Third Ave. (75th St.), 212-517-3800; www.bistrolesteak.com
"Excellent value" is the name of the game at this UES French bistro–
steakhouse serving "decent" food at the "right price" in "publike"
environs; the "generic" decor and "European service" are more
palatable when dining in the "glassed-in sidewalk seats."

Bistro 61 ◑
19 | 16 | 20 | $37
1113 First Ave. (61st St.), 212-223-6220; www.bistro61.com
"Parisian" decor, "attentive" servers and "decent prices" make this
"old-school" French bistro near the Queensboro Bridge the "platonic
ideal" of a neighborhood hangout; fans wish it were "a bit larger", but
few find fault with the "sit-down-and-relax" mood.

Bistro Ten 18
19 | 18 | 19 | $38
1018 Amsterdam Ave. (110th St.), 212-662-7600; www.bistroten18.com
A "godsend" to Morningside Heights, this New American bistro offers
"delicious", "relatively inexpensive" eats in "congenial" digs with a

"working fireplace" and a view of St. John the Divine; "small but comfortable", it's a hit with both "locals" and the "Columbia crowd."

Blair Perrone Steakhouse ☒ NEW · 21 | 23 | 22 | $70

885 Second Ave. (bet. 47th & 48th Sts.), 212-796-8000;
www.blairperrone.com

"Another entry in the steakhouse wars", this "classy" new Midtowner from Peter Luger/MarkJoseph alums offers a "straightforward", "old-school" menu in a "spacious", "tall-ceilinged" room; all agree it's "pricey", but whether it's "excellent" or just "average" is debatable.

Blaue Gans ● NEW · 21 | 17 | 19 | $44

139 Duane St. (bet. Church St. & W. B'way), 212-571-8880;
www.wallse.com

The latest from Kurt Gutenbrunner (Wallsé), this TriBeCa Austro-German offers "easygoing" dining via "hearty", "*gasthaus*-style" cooking at "affordable" prices; not as pleasing is the no-reserving policy and "bare-bones" decor (left over from its predecessor, Le Zinc).

Bliss ☒ · ▽ 21 | 16 | 18 | $34

45-20 Skillman Ave. (46th St.), Queens, 718-729-0778;
www.blissgardens.com

"So far, so good" is the word on this "trying hard" New American yearling, an "upscale" affair that's "brought style to Sunnyside"; despite "sluggish service", the food's "tasty", the decor "simple and cheerful", and the $25 prix fixe "bliss on the budget."

Blockhead's Burritos · 17 | 10 | 15 | $17

954 Second Ave. (bet. 50th & 51st Sts.), 212-750-2020
1563 Second Ave. (bet. 81st & 82nd Sts.), 212-879-1999
499 Third Ave. (bet. 33rd & 34th Sts.), 212-213-3332
Worldwide Plaza, 322 W. 50th St. (bet. 8th & 9th Aves.), 212-307-7029
www.blockheads.com

"Gigantic burritos" are the name of the game at this Mexican chainlet famed for "stick-to-your-ribs" grub and "killer" drinks at "*muy cheapo*" rates; given the "slacker" service and "tasteless" quarters, you may "want to order in."

Blossom NEW · ▽ 24 | 20 | 22 | $36

187 Ninth Ave. (bet. 21st & 22nd Sts.), 212-627-1144

All-vegan, all-organic takes on international recipes define the "original" menu of this Chelsea newcomer that's made for those "willing to try something different"; "pretty" surroundings add to the "upscale" air, even if a few say it's "too expensive for what it is."

BLT Fish ☒ · 23 | 20 | 20 | $60

21 W. 17th St. (bet. 5th & 6th Aves.), 212-691-8888; www.bltfish.com

Upstairs at Laurent Tourondel's Flatiron seafooder, priviledged pescavores "construct their own meals" from an "inventive" slate (seafood plus sauces plus sides), while younger bottom-feeders dive down to the "laid-back" street-level clam shack featuring more "casual", "beachy" items; although "sharkingly expensive", dining on either floor is a "treat."

BLT Prime · 24 | 22 | 22 | $73

111 E. 22nd St. (bet. Lexington Ave. & Park Ave. S.), 212-995-8500;
www.bltprime.com

"Holy cow!", the chow's "delish" at this Gramercy chophouse where Laurent Tourondel's "everything-à-la-carte" New American menu centers on "tender" steaks, paired with a "something-for-everyone" wine list and served by a "cordial" crew; add "chic" environs, and it's no surprise that it especially appeals to a prime "expense-account crowd."

BLT Steak ⌧

24 | 21 | 21 | $69

106 E. 57th St. (bet. Lexington & Park Aves.), 212-752-7470; www.bltsteak.com
The BLT brand's flagship, this "posh" East Midtowner feeds its "good-looking" clientele "killer steaks" with some "fabulous" à la carte accompaniments and "outstanding" wines; penny-pinchers protest "those sides add up", but proponents prepared to "splurge" simply shrug "power scene, power prices" and join the crowd trying to snag a table.

bluechili ✷

19 | 20 | 18 | $40

251 W. 51st St. (bet. B'way & 8th Ave.), 212-246-3330; www.bluechilinyc.com
Cultivating a "Downtown vibe in a Midtown location", this Theater District Pan-Asian pulls in "young" folk with "exotic drinks", "disco music" and "ever-changing" colored lighting; though generally well-rated, critics say it's "inconsistent."

Blue Fin ✷

22 | 22 | 18 | $53

W Times Sq., 1567 Broadway (47th St.), 212-918-1400;
www.brguestrestaurants.com
Steve Hanson's "buzzing" Theater District seafooder has "tourists and residents alike" hooked on its "delish fish", "substantial wine list" and "sleek", bi-level setting; "mega-noise" and service "hiccups" aside, all agree it's "better than you'd expect to find in Times Square."

Blue/Green NEW

∇ 20 | 15 | 15 | $25

203 E. 74th St. (bet. 2nd & 3rd Aves.), 212-744-0940
248 Mott St. (bet. Houston & Prince Sts.), 212-334-0805
The Plant, 25 Jay St. (bet. John & Plymouth Sts.), Brooklyn, 718-722-7541
www.bluegreenjuice.com
Raw-food dude Matthew Kenney (ex Pure Food and Wine) is behind this vegan chainlet where the "super-healthy", "super-fresh" eats are all organic; while it's definitely "better than your normal juice bar", cynics nix the "small portions" and "super-slow" service.

BLUE HILL

26 | 22 | 25 | $68

75 Washington Pl. (bet. MacDougal St. & 6th Ave.), 212-539-1776;
www.bluehillnyc.com
A "little bit of foodie heaven" off Washington Square, Dan Barber's "haute organic" New American employs "superb" local ingredients in its "quietly inventive" preparations, paired with "stellar" wines; "gracious" staffers and an "understated" yet "lovely" setting "increase the enjoyment" while road-trippers recommend their upstate outlet, Blue Hill at Stone Barns.

Blue 9 Burger ✷≠

19 | 6 | 11 | $9

92 Third Ave. (bet. 12th & 13th Sts.), 212-979-0053; www.blue9burger.com
An "East Coast version of In-N-Out Burger", this East Village patty purveyor "scores big on taste" with "juicy, double-fisted" specimens served till the wee hours; given the low prices, its "college-students-on-the-go" crowd could care less about the "tepid" service and "no-frills" decor.

BLUE RIBBON ✷

25 | 19 | 22 | $48

97 Sullivan St. (bet. Prince & Spring Sts.), 212-274-0404
280 Fifth Ave. (bet. 1st St. & Garfield Pl.), Brooklyn, 718-840-0404
www.blueribbonrestaurants.com
"Beloved" by gastronomes, party people and insomniacs, these "unpretentious", "late-night" New American "scenes" in SoHo and Park Slope offer "high-end comfort food" from a "menu as eclectic as NYC"; they're "pricey" and you may have to "camp out for a table", but ultimately they're "worth every penny every time."

Blue Ribbon Bakery ⦿
23 | 18 | 20 | $40

33 Downing St. (Bedford St.), 212-337-0404; www.blueribbonrestaurants.com
"Carb lovers' dreams come true" at this "rustic" Villager that bakes
its own "fantastic breads", then serves them with a "genial" flourish
alongside "diverse" New American eats and "top-tier" wines; brunch
is "terrific" too, so "get there early" or plan to wait.

BLUE RIBBON SUSHI ⦿
26 | 19 | 22 | $51

119 Sullivan St. (bet. Prince & Spring Sts.), 212-343-0404
278 Fifth Ave. (bet. 1st St. & Garfield Pl.), Brooklyn, 718-840-0408
www.blueribbonrestaurants.com
"Only a shark eats fresher" fish than the "buttery" sushi and sashimi
served at these SoHo/Park Slope siblings; "exceptional cooked
dishes" and "wonderful sakes" round out the meal as staffers "make
you feel welcome" amid "serene", "minimalist" environs – even if the
treat may "cost you a fin and a tail."

BLUE SMOKE
21 | 17 | 19 | $39

116 E. 27th St. (bet. Lexington Ave. & Park Ave. S.), 212-447-7733;
www.bluesmoke.com
Barbecue meets "industrial chic" at Danny Meyer's "high-energy"
Gramercy smokehouse serving up "succulent" ribs, "outrageous"
sides and "smooth grooves" in the downstairs jazz club; though purists
protest the "upscale-downscale" experience, true-blue types say this
proves "you don't need sawdust underfoot to get good 'cue."

BLUE WATER GRILL ⦿
23 | 22 | 20 | $51

31 Union Sq. W. (16th St.), 212-675-9500;
www.brguestrestaurants.com
Steve Hanson's Union Square seafood standby serves the "freshest
fish" in a "cool" former bank setting at "citified" prices; fin fans flip
for the "upbeat" brunches, "mellow jazz" downstairs or dining on the
deck "with hot dates and cold martinis" – but warn that the "airy"
main room's "marble walls" make for "high noise levels."

Boathouse
16 | 26 | 16 | $50

Central Park, enter on E. 72nd St. (Central Park Dr. N.), 212-517-2233;
www.thecentralparkboathouse.com
It's all about that "breathtaking" view at this "idyllic" spot overlooking
Central Park's boat pond; maybe it's "overpriced" with "bland" New
American fare and "indifferent" service, but given the "romantic"
possibilities, "who comes here for the food?"; N.B. it's also a popular
site for parties.

Bobby Van's Grill ⦿ NEW
22 | 18 | 21 | $62

135 W. 50th St. (bet. 6th & 7th Aves.), 212-957-5050

Bobby Van's Steakhouse
25 Broad St. (Exchange Pl.), 212-344-8463 ⑤ NEW
131 E. 54th St. (bet. Lexington & Park Aves.), 212-207-8050
230 Park Ave. (46th St.), 212-867-5490 ⑤
www.bobbyvans.com
These "dependable" chophouses keep bobbing along, adding two
branches (in the Financial District and West Midtown) in the past
year; their "thick, chewy" steaks, mega–wine lists and "no-attitude"
service make for "serviceable" dining, with one unexpected bonus:
Downtown's "magnificent" bank-vault room.

Boca Chica
19 | 15 | 16 | $28

13 First Ave. (1st St.), 212-473-0108
At this "jammed" East Village "converted dive bar" what most *chicas*
put into their *bocas* are the "murderous margaritas" – hence the

"loud" "fiesta vibe"; still, folks focusing on the Pan-Latin fare find it "savory" and "reliable", "especially for the price."

Bocca
▽ 19 | 18 | 19 | $52

1435 Hylan Blvd. (Bath Ave.), Staten Island, 718-980-4470
Displaying a "superb", 2,000-label wine collection, this Staten Islander is no "run-of-the-mill" Italian but rather a "romantic" spot where "delicious" *piatti* are proffered by an "attentive staff"; the only drawback is that "this place thinks it's in Manhattan and charges accordingly."

Bocca Lupo NEW
– | – | – | M

391 Henry St. (Warren St.), Brooklyn, 718-243-2522
Reasonably priced wines abet a roster of Italian small plates at this casually stylish Cobble Hill newcomer that emits a friendly neighborhood vibe; granted, it's a few blocks from the Smith Street dining hub, but the early word is that it's worth a detour.

Bocelli
▽ 24 | 21 | 22 | $47

1250 Hylan Blvd. (bet. Clove & Old Town Rds.), Staten Island, 718-420-6150; www.bocellirest.com
Favored for "excellent traditional" Italian fare (including "great homemade pasta"), this Staten Island ristorante also scores well for its "professional" servers and attractive Tuscan-style room; to further enhance the mood, "Italian music fills the air" on weekends and prices are under control.

Bogota Latin Bistro
20 | 19 | 19 | $29

141 Fifth Ave. (bet. Lincoln & St. Johns Pls.), Brooklyn, 718-230-3805; www.bogotabistro.com
"Colorful" and "welcoming", this Park Slope yearling attracts amigos with "authentic" Pan-Latin dishes, "excellent" cocktails and a "jovial staff"; even those bugged by "inconsistency" agree that the patio is perfect for a "festive" "group night out."

Boi ☒
22 | 17 | 20 | $40

246 E. 44th St. (bet. 2nd & 3rd Aves.), 212-681-6541; www.boi-restaurant.com
"Hanoi meets the East Side" at this "calming" Midtown Vietnamese near Grand Central where folks "feel international" sampling its "novel", "mouthwatering" specialties; if the cooking seems too "unfamiliar", the "friendly" staffers are happy to guide you.

Bolo
23 | 20 | 21 | $54

23 E. 22nd St. (bet. B'way & Park Ave. S.), 212-228-2200; www.bolorestaurant.com
A "steady favorite", this Flatiron Iberian presents Bobby Flay's "imaginative" cooking paired with "top-notch" Spanish wines, all proffered by a "knowledgeable" team; amigos applaud the "festive yet sophisticated" experience, though a few say both the decor and menu "need freshening."

Bombay Palace
20 | 18 | 20 | $35

30 W. 52nd St. (bet. 5th & 6th Aves.), 212-541-7777; www.bombay-palace.com
"Rich" regional repasts and "attentive" service are yours at this "quiet, relaxing" Indian, a Midtown "mainstay" near MoMA; the wide-ranging buffet lunch – a spectacular "bargain" at $13.95 – is "popular with businessmen" who want to "get back to the office in under an hour" well fed.

Bombay Talkie
20 | 19 | 16 | $36

189 Ninth Ave. (bet. 21st & 22nd Sts.), 212-242-1900; www.bombaytalkie.com
Chelsea cinephiles can't agree on this bi-level Bollywood-themed boîte: fans say it's boffo for "authentic", "delectable" Indian street food

in a "campy, fun" setting, while bashers pan a "gimmicky" scene, "perfunctory" staff and munchies that are "overpriced and underspiced."

Bond 45 ❷
18	18	18	$49

154 W. 45th St. (bet. 6th & 7th Aves.), 212-869-4545; www.bond45.com
Set in a former Times Square "men's clothing store", this Shelly Fireman production draws applause for its "dependable" Italian surf 'n' turf served in a "big", "1940s"-style room; but it's not unanimous, as critics complain "too much noise, too little help" and "too costly."

Bondi Road NEW
–	–	–	M

153 Rivington St. (bet. Clinton & Suffolk Sts.), 212-253-5311
Fish 'n' chips plus South Pacific seafood are highlights of this diminutive, beach shack–esque Aussie newcomer; whether it's due to the prime location on the Rivington Street bar crawl or the high quality at modest prices, it's become an instant hit.

Bond Street ❷
25	23	19	$60

6 Bond St. (bet. B'way & Lafayette St.), 212-777-2500
Sushi lovers are in "paradise" at this "intimate" NoHo nouvelle Japanese serving "heavenly" rolls to "beautiful" types who head for the downstairs lounge after dinner to be "seen and not heard"; though "aloof" servers and "over-the-top" pricing get demerits, most surveyors consider it "worth every penny" and then some.

Bonita ❷
▽ 22	17	18	$21

338 Bedford Ave. (bet. S. 2nd & 3rd Sts.), Brooklyn, 718-384-9500
"Enjoyable Mexican" eats at prices that leave "money to spare for more sangria" make for a "bustling" scene at this Williamsburg cantina; the exterior may not "look like much", but the cool "retro" interior and "laid-back service" fit the casual mood.

Bonjoo ❷NEW
–	–	–	M

107 First Ave. (bet. 6th & 7th Sts.), 212-505-7974
Red accents, muted lighting and a solicitous staff set the mellow tone at this East Village Korean parked just off Curry Row; look for traditional fare with some fusion twists (think Asian nachos) served in a casual, comfy neighborhood setting.

Boom ❷
▽ 20	17	18	$37

152 Spring St. (bet. W. B'way & Wooster St.), 212-431-3663
Most get a bang out of the "good value" at this "quality" SoHo bistro where "delightful, fresh" Southern Italian plates arrive at "affordable prices" via "friendly" staffers; the muted decor may be "nothing fancy" but live weeknight jazz adds some pizzazz.

Boqueria ❷NEW
–	–	–	M

53 W. 19th St. (bet. 5th & 6th Aves.), 212-255-4160;
www.boquerianyc.com
Finding inspiration in the bars that surround the Barcelona food market, this Flatiron taperia neatly captures Spain's bold, modern spirit while remaining firmly rooted in tradition; as a result, crowds are already squeezing into the chic space that was once relaxed and is now often bustling.

Borgo Antico ❷
17	16	19	$40

22 E. 13th St. (bet. 5th Ave. & University Pl.), 212-807-1313;
www.borgoanticonyc.com
"Convivial" hosts and a staff that "really tries hard" make this "spacious" double-decker Village Italian a "local refuge"; the cooking may set off "no fireworks", but cronies call it quite suitable for a "lunch meeting" or a "quiet dinner."

Bottega del Vino
22 | 21 | 21 | $61

7 E. 59th St. (bet. 5th & Madison Aves.), 212-223-3028;
www.bottegadelvinonyc.com
Oenophiles endorse the "superb" vino selection and housemade pastas at this "high-class" (read: "expensive") Midtown Italian wine
bar – but the real "revelation" is its Alpine "chalet ambiance", similar
to the original in Verona; however, despite its many good qualities,
some wonder if it can overcome a jinxed location.

Bottino
18 | 17 | 17 | $44

246 10th Ave. (bet. 24th & 25th Sts.), 212-206-6766;
www.bottinonyc.com
"Packing them in" since the West Chelsea "gallery scene exploded",
this "solid standby" lures its "hip" clientele with "reliable" Tuscan
fare; outdoorsy types tout the "divine" back garden for "unsurpassed
art-world people-watching", but rap the "snobby" staff and bland decor.

Bouchon Bakery NEW
23 | 13 | 19 | $29

Time Warner Ctr., 10 Columbus Circle, 3rd fl. (60th St. at B'way),
212-823-9366; www.bouchonbakery.com
Though not a full-fledged restaurant per se, Thomas Keller's cafe/
patisserie on the Time Warner Center's third floor does offer "taste-
fully simple" New American takes on French boulangerie classics,
notably "delicious sandwiches" and "ethereal pastries"; despite the
"odd", "upscale food court" ambiance and "disorganized but friendly"
service", it's a "jaunty little stopover" best enjoyed before or after
the lunch rush.

Bouillabaisse 126
22 | 15 | 19 | $39

126 Union St. (bet. Columbia & Hicks Sts.), Brooklyn, 718-855-4405;
www.bouillabaisse126.com
The namesake soup is still "great", as are the other "carefully prepared" Gallic goodies at this seafood-focused Carroll Gardens bistro;
its new home may be "on the wrong side of the BQE", but its prices
are so "reasonable" "you can splurge on a car service."

BOULEY ◗
28 | 26 | 27 | $91

120 W. Broadway (Duane St.), 212-964-2525; www.davidbouley.com
"Food heaven from the first glance to the last dab of the napkin", David
Bouley's "rarefied" TriBeCa New French is "quintessential Manhattan
dining", pairing "sumptuous" cuisine with "memorably wonderful"
wines; the "swank", vaulted-ceiling setting "oozes romance", the
"mind-reading" staffers "serve with élan" and the offerings are "so
exquisite, they don't seem so expensive."

Bouley, Upstairs ⌧
25 | 16 | 18 | $46

Bouley Bakery & Mkt., 130 W. Broadway, 2nd fl. (Duane St.), 212-608-5829;
www.davidbouley.com
At this TriBeCa newcomer, you "feel like you're in David Bouley's home
kitchen" as the often-present maestro whips up "exquisite, nervy"
Eclectic eats to match his sushi chefs' "unbelievably fresh" morsels;
ok, it's "tiny" with little decor, service can be "spotty" and you can't
reserve in advance, but most insist the food's more than worth it.

Bouterin
19 | 21 | 21 | $62

420 E. 59th St. (bet. 1st Ave. & Sutton Pl.), 212-758-0323;
www.bouterin.com
A visit to this "hidden" Sutton Place French-Med is "like going to
grandma's house in Provence"; it's a "flower-filled" place that's a
Mother's Day and "bridal shower" magnet, with "friendly" service
and reliably good cooking.

Brasserie ◐   19 | 21 | 19 | $49
100 E. 53rd St. (bet. Lexington & Park Aves.), 212-751-4840;
www.restaurantassociates.com
"Not for the stodgy", this "dramatic", "uptempo" East Midtowner attracts architecture buffs with its "ultramod" "Space Age" design and
"corporate" types with its "upscale" brasserie fare and "busy, busy"
bar; still, dreamers wish the "food matched the sexy decor."

Brasserie 8½   21 | 23 | 21 | $55
9 W. 57th St. (bet. 5th & 6th Aves.), 212-829-0812;
www.restaurantassociates.com
Habitués of this "hopping" Midtowner make a "Hollywood entrance"
down a "winding staircase" into a subterranean "Fifth-Avenue-
meets-SoHo" expanse; fortunately the kitchen "delivers" as well,
with "delectable" French dishes served by an "attentive" staff.

Brasserie Julien   17 | 18 | 16 | $42
1422 Third Ave. (bet. 80th & 81st Sts.), 212-744-6327; www.brasseriejulien.com
"When you feel like Paris" but live in Yorkville, there's always this
"dim" deco bistro putting out moderately priced "French food in
American portions"; despite "inattentive" service, the "cool" weekend
jazz can make for a "romantic evening" – "even with your spouse."

Brasserie LCB   23 | 22 | 23 | $63
60 W. 55th St. (bet. 5th & 6th Aves.), 212-688-6525
At his "upscale" – and expensive – Midtown brasserie, Jean-Jacques
Rachou "preserves the French traditions" of his late La Côte Basque
via "terrific cassoulet, quenelles" and other "hearty" classics served by
"solicitous" staffers; even though this "scaled-down" "reincarnation"
is more "relaxed", the greying group of loyal customers will always
"mourn for the murals."

Brasserie Ruhlmann NEW   ▽ 19 | 23 | 19 | $61
45 Rockefeller Plaza (enter on 50th St., bet. 5th & 6th Aves.), 212-974-2020;
www.brasserieruhlmann.com
Named after a renowned French interior designer, this pricey new
Rock Center brasserie boasts "beautifully done" deco decor and
"trying-hard" staffers; in response to huffs that the "food needs more
attention", to the rescue comes everywhere-man Laurent Tourondel,
recently appointed executive chef.

Bravo Gianni ◐   22 | 15 | 21 | $61
230 E. 63rd St. (bet. 2nd & 3rd Aves.), 212-752-7272
No Gianni-come-lately, the "friendly" chef-owner of this UES longtimer
keeps his well-heeled clientele "loyal" with "generous portions" of
first-rate Northern Italiana; ok, the "Bee Gees–era" interiors "could
use sprucing up", but most customers like everything just the way it is.

Brawta Caribbean Café   ▽ 20 | 13 | 14 | $24
347 Atlantic Ave. (Hoyt St.), Brooklyn, 718-855-5515;
www.brawtacafe.com
Boerum Hill locals laud the "delicious", "super-affordable" dishes at
this "homey" Caribbean BYO; just "don't be in a hurry" – the "casual"
service keeps time with the "Bob Marley tunes on the stereo."

Bread Tribeca   19 | 16 | 16 | $34
301 Church St. (Walker St.), 212-334-8282; www.breadtribeca.com
Bread ◑
20 Spring St. (bet. Elizabeth & Mott Sts.), 212-334-1015
Sara Jenkins is now behind the burners of this "unpretentious"
TriBeCa Italian featuring "tasty", moderately priced dinners and

"work lunches with a surreptitious glass of wine"; an "airy", high-ceilinged interior helps offset the "tight seating" and "random" service; P.S. the considerably smaller NoLita affiliate specializes in panini.

Breeze
∇ | 21 | 16 | 17 | $34

661 Ninth Ave. (bet. 45th & 46th Sts.), 212-262-7777; www.breezenyc.com
Serving "inventive", affordably priced Thai-French fusion fare, this Hell's Kitchen sophomore also boasts "slick", "modern" digs; the problem is, there may be "too much concept" going on – "surreal neon", "overloud music", "Madonna videos" – leading some to beg "just let us eat."

Brennan & Carr ●≠
20 | 9 | 16 | $16

3432 Nostrand Ave. (Ave. U), Brooklyn, 718-646-9559
"Generations of Brooklynites" patronize this inexpensive family-run Sheepshead Bay sandwich shop renowned for double-dipped "roast beef the way you wish grandma made it"; "old shack" decor and "only fair" service hardly matter when "licking the gravy off your fingers."

Bricco
19 | 16 | 18 | $42

304 W. 56th St. (bet. 8th & 9th Aves.), 212-245-7160; www.bricconyc.com
"Solid" pastas and "satisfying" brick-oven pizzas lead off the menu at this "comfortable" Hell's Kitchen Italian overseen by a "friendly owner"; ladies are encouraged to "leave their lip prints on the ceiling", but given the "reasonable prices" you won't have to "kiss your wallet goodbye."

Brick Cafe
20 | 20 | 19 | $32

30-95 33rd St. (31st Ave.), Queens, 718-267-2735; www.brickcafe.com
A "bit of arty bohemia" in Astoria, this "shabby-chic" spot features a "consistent" Franco-Italian menu in "relaxed" environs that work equally well for "lively conversation" or as a "romantic rendezvous"; sidewalk tables are "superb for lounging day and night."

Brick Lane Curry House
22 | 16 | 17 | $29

306-308 E. Sixth St. (2nd Ave.), 212-979-2900; www.bricklanecurryhouse.com
"You'll think you're in London" at this Sixth Street Indian whose "genuine", "seriously good" British curries "blow away" its competitors (the "sluggish" service is another story); but "bring a fire extinguisher" – "when they say 'spicy', they mean it."

Bridge Cafe
21 | 16 | 20 | $42

279 Water St. (Dover St.), 212-227-3344
Although this circa-1794 brick-walled tavern "hidden under the Brooklyn Bridge" exudes "historic" charm, its menu is New American, featuring "delicious" seasonal fare; look for "friendly" personnel and the occasional pol from City Hall.

Bright Food Shop
20 | 10 | 16 | $26

216 Eighth Ave. (21st St.), 212-243-4433
Specializing in "Mexican-Asian comfort food" ("who knew?"), this "funky" "glorified diner" remains a "bright spot" in Chelsea, particularly "if price is important"; though service moves at a "snail's pace", patrons pass the time ogling "boys aplenty."

Brio
19 | 13 | 17 | $38

137 E. 61st St. (Lexington Ave.), 212-980-2300; www.brionyc.com
After retail therapy at Bloomie's, one can bag an "excellent gourmet pizza" at this "reliable" Italian "find" for "relaxed, easy" dining; recent renovations may help the Decor score, though service still seems "spotty" to some shoppers.

Brooklyn Diner USA ●
16 | 14 | 15 | $30

*212 W. 57th St. (bet. B'way & 7th Ave.), 212-977-2280;
www.brooklyndiner.com*

At Shelly Fireman's "upscale" "diner-themed diner" near Carnegie Hall, patrons take "guilty pleasure" from "mountainous portions" of good-old "artery-clogging" American eats; the service is "folksy" enough, but some say it's pure "NYC kitsch" that's designed for "tourists" who can't make it to the real Brooklyn.

Brooklyn Fish Camp Ⓢ
22 | 16 | 19 | $40

*162 Fifth Ave. (Degraw St.), Brooklyn, 718-783-3264;
www.brooklynfishcamp.com*

Afishionados assert this "friendly" Park Slope spin-off of Mary's Fish Camp "delivers exactly what it's supposed to": "simple", "immaculately fresh" seafood with flavors "highlighted, not masked" (e.g. the "spectacular lobster rolls"); a "loud", "bland" interior leads insiders to "thank goodness for the garden."

Brother Jimmy's BBQ
16 | 10 | 14 | $23

*428 Amsterdam Ave. (bet. 80th & 81st Sts.), 212-501-7515 ●
Grand Central, lower level (42nd St. & Vanderbilt Ave.), 212-661-4022
1485 Second Ave. (bet. 77th & 78th Sts.), 212-288-0999 ●
1644 Third Ave. (93rd St.), 212-426-2020 ●
www.brotherjimmys.com*

There's a "perpetual fratmosphere" at this smokehouse–cum–sports bar quartet that lures young post-collegians with "cheap beer", "falling-off-the-bone ribs" and "babelicious servers"; "sticky floors", "deafening" decibels and "white-trash" decor come with the territory.

Brouwers of Stone Street Ⓢ NEW
– | – | – | M

45 Stone St. (bet. Pearl & S. William Sts.), 212-785-5400

Parked off a historic cobblestoned lane, this Financial District newcomer is fitted out with antique mirrors and a huge 19th-century oak bar; in contrast, the cuisine (seafood-heavy Americana) and the crowd (Stone Street's swinging singles scene) are totally contemporary; N.B. closed weekends.

Bruckner Bar & Grill ●
▽ 22 | 21 | 19 | $20

*1 Bruckner Blvd. (3rd Ave.), Bronx, 718-665-2001;
www.brucknerbar.com*

"Beer and hipsters flow freely" at this "no-pretensions" Mott Haven "hangout" where SoBro's "growing artist population" chows down on "simple" but "tasty" New American eats; "cool booths" and a pool table distract from the occasionally "lackluster service."

Bruno Jamais ●Ⓢ
▽ 21 | 26 | 24 | $71

*24 E. 81st St. (Madison Ave.), 212-396-3444;
www.brunojamais.com*

Once a "private club", now open to all, this wood-paneled UES Contemporary French offers "delectable" vittles to the tune of "great music" via DJs or live performers; *bien sûr*, it's *très cher* but the chance to mingle with "socialites sipping straight-up martinis" is priceless.

Bryant Park Grill/Cafe
16 | 21 | 16 | $43

*behind NY Public Library, 25 W. 40th St. (bet. 5th & 6th Aves.),
212-840-6500; www.arkrestaurants.com*

Bryant Park's "serene" green "oasis" is the main draw at this "decent" American duo where the more formal Grill offers a "spacious" indoor setting and roof-deck seating, while the alfresco Cafe is a flat-out "pickup scene"; what with the "rushed" service and "overpriced", "uninspired" grub, many label them "missed opportunities."

B. Smith's Restaurant Row
18 | 18 | 18 | $45

320 W. 46th St. (bet. 8th & 9th Aves.), 212-315-1100; www.bsmith.com
A "bit of class" in the Theater District, TV personality Barbara Smith's "upbeat" Restaurant Row Eclectic is particularly "attractive to tourists" given the "welcoming" service and "solid" Southern cooking; still, critics say it's "lost some of its charm" and "needs an overhaul."

Bubby's
18 | 14 | 15 | $26

120 Hudson St. (N. Moore St.), 212-219-0666
1 Main St. (bet. Plymouth & Water Sts.), Brooklyn, 718-222-0666
www.bubbys.com
"Homey" and "relaxed", these low-budget American "headquarters" in TriBeCa and Dumbo are best known for their "quintessential brunches" garnished with "celeb sightings"; downsides include "banal" cooking, "erratic service" and "stroller obstacle courses."

BUDDAKAN ● NEW
23 | 27 | 22 | $63

75 Ninth Ave. (16th St.), 212-989-6699; www.buddakannyc.com
Philadelphia restaurateur Stephen Starr's "huge", "happening" contender in Chelsea Market purveys a "delicious" Asian fusion menu served by a "precise, helpful" team; still, as good as it is, the food is outshone by the "incredible", "goes-on-forever" theatrical setting that's centered around a "jaw-dropping" main dining hall; it's already so crowded that a woman could get pregnant going to the bar.

BUDDHA BAR ● NEW
∇ 19 | 26 | 16 | $53

25 Little W. 12th St. (bet. 9th Ave. & Washington St.), 212-647-7314;
www.buddhabarnyc.com
Spun-off from the Paris original, this "enormous" Meatpacking District newcomer features a "Vegas"-like interior incorporating a 17-ft. Buddha, private pagodas and jellyfish-stocked aquariums; but given the "awesome bar scene" incorporating lots of long legs and short skirts, dining isn't necessarily the top priority – what with the "standard", pricey Asian fusion items and staffers who "don't seem to care."

Buenos Aires ● NEW
∇ 19 | 16 | 17 | $38

513 E. Sixth St. (bet. Aves. A & B), 212-228-2775
A "classy new addition" to the East Village, this *pequeño* Argentinean proffers "hefty" servings of "flavorful" grilled meats and "enticing empanadas" paired with "affordable Malbecs"; a "genial owner" and overall "reasonable" pricing keep the mood "convivial."

Bukhara Grill
21 | 15 | 18 | $37

217 E. 49th St. (bet. 2nd & 3rd Aves.), 212-888-2839; www.bukharany.com
"Good-deal" $13.95 buffets keep the lunch trade brisk at this East Midtown Indian near the U.N. that's also known for its "great grills", "well-done" tandoori dishes and sizable wine list; the secret second-floor terrace is a "must in good weather."

Bull and Bear ●
20 | 21 | 22 | $58

Waldorf-Astoria, 570 Lexington Ave. (49th St.), 212-872-4900;
www.waldorfastoria.com
As "civilized" as its Waldorf-Astoria setting, this "clubby" steakhouse attracts mature "power brokers" accustomed to "polished" service from a "pro" staff; just as "old-school" are the "delicious" chops and "perfect drinks", though prices skew to bulls, not bears.

Bull Run
19 | 17 | 18 | $41

Club Quarters Hotel, 52 William St. (Pine St.), 212-859-2200;
www.bullrunwallstreet.com
Somehow "undiscovered", this "quiet, white-tablecloth" Financial District "oasis" serves "solid" New American cookery "in relative

privacy"; no surprise, it appeals to Wall Streeters who don't seem to mind the "Holiday Inn" decor and bullish pricing.

Burger Heaven
16 | 8 | 14 | $17

9 E. 53rd St. (bet. 5th & Madison Aves.), 212-752-0340
20 E. 49th St. (bet. 5th & Madison Aves.), 212-755-2166
804 Lexington Ave. (62nd St.), 212-838-3580
291 Madison Ave. (bet. 40th & 41st Sts.), 212-685-6250
536 Madison Ave. (bet. 54th & 55th Sts.), 212-753-4214
1534 Third Ave. (bet. 86th & 87th Sts.), 212-722-8292
www.burgerheaven.com

"Real NYers" go for the burgers at these chain "fallbacks" known for their juicy patties and "coffee-shop" settings; "overcrowding" and "brusque", hair-net service are readily forgiven given the "cheap" tabs.

Burger Joint ●≠
20 | 7 | 11 | $10

241 Third Ave. (bet. 19th & 20th Sts.), 212-228-1219

Folks on a "tiny budget" like the "cute", "bite-size" burgers and "can't-be-beat" prices at this "zero-decor" Gramercy patty purveyor; just be aware that the "menu is limited" and those "delicious little suckers" can be "dangerous in large quantities."

burger joint at
Le Parker Meridien ●≠
24 | 9 | 12 | $13

Le Parker Meridien, 119 W. 56th St. (bet. 6th & 7th Aves.), 212-708-7414;
www.newyork.lemeridien.com

A "secret no more", this Midtowner incongruously "hidden behind a curtain" in a fancy hotel lobby is always "jam-packed" owing to its "first-rate" grilled burgers; "out-the-door lines", "no table service", "no decor" and little seating make it like a "scene from *Seinfeld*."

Burgers & Cupcakes NEW
– | – | – | I

458 Ninth Ave. (bet. 35th & 36th Sts.), 212-643-1200;
www.burgersandcupcakes.us

Maybe it sounds like an eight-year-old's dream come true, but this meats-and-sweets Garment District venue has adult appeal thanks to proprietor Mitchel London, whose catering business occupies most of its large, unadorned space; despite the name, the menu also includes breakfast items.

Burritoville
17 | 7 | 12 | $12

298 Bleecker St. (7th Ave. S.), 212-633-9249 ●
116 Chambers St. (Church St.), 212-566-2300
625 Ninth Ave. (44th St.), 212-333-5352 ●
141 Second Ave. (bet. 8th & 9th Sts.), 212-260-3300 ●
1487 Second Ave. (bet. 77th & 78th Sts.), 212-472-8800 ●
866 Third Ave. (52nd St.), 212-980-4111
36 Water St. (Broad St.), 212-747-1100
166 W. 72nd St. (bet. Amsterdam & Columbus Aves.), 212-580-7700 ●
352 W. 39th St. (9th Ave.), 212-563-9088
264 W. 23rd St. (bet. 7th & 8th Aves.), 212-367-9844 ●
www.burritoville.com
Additional locations throughout the NY area

"Big-to-bursting burritos" served "without fanfare" bring amigos back to these "not-fancy", cheap counter-service chain links where the Tex-Mex eats "can actually be healthy" – if you order "carefully."

Butai
▽ 20 | 23 | 20 | $42

115 E. 18th St. (bet. Irving Pl. & Park Ave. S.), 212-387-8885; www.butai.us

It's possible to "hear your companions speak" at this "calm", "ethereal" Gramercy Japanese where the midpriced menu "spans a range" of culinary styles, including "hard-to-find robata" items; since portions are "tiny", veterans advise "be prepared to order a lot."

Butter ●Ⱬ⒵   19 | 23 | 18 | $56
415 Lafayette St. (bet. Astor Pl. & 4th St.), 212-253-2828; www.butterrestaurant.com
"Handy" for Public Theatergoers, this East Villager is also known for its "ultrahip scene", "woodsy" decor and churning downstairs bar; but some find the "upscale" New American eats (served with a side of "attitude") "too expensive" and suggest you "take your bread elsewhere."

Buzina Pop ●NEW   – | – | – | M
1022A Lexington Ave. (73rd St.), 212-879-6190
Named after the Brazilian clown who has become a pop icon, this vibrant new French-Brazilian brings some verve to the UES with an airy, bi-level dining room combining decorative tilework with exposed brick and weathered wooden floors; sidewalk seats are a bonus.

Cabana ●   20 | 18 | 17 | $34
South Street Seaport, Pier 17, 89 South St. (Fulton St.), 212-406-1155
1022 Third Ave. (bet. 60th & 61st Sts.), 212-980-5678
107-10 70th Rd. (bet. Austin St. & Queens Blvd.), Queens, 718-263-3600
www.cabanarestaurant.com
"Full of life", this Nuevo Latino trio scores with "flavorful" fare at very good prices; the Seaport branch provides a "mini-vacation" with "fantastic water views", but all three are "wildly popular", despite "inconsistent" service and "tight", "*chico-a-chico*" quarters.

Cacio e Pepe   22 | 17 | 21 | $39
182 Second Ave. (bet. 11th & 12th Sts.), 212-505-5931; www.cacioepepe.com
The "shortest way to Rome" may be via this rustic Italian East Villager where the "authentic", modestly priced cookery includes an "addictive" namesake dish, pasta presented in a wheel of Parmesan; service is "as warm as the food", and there's a "lovely" bonus back garden.

Cafe Asean ≠   20 | 14 | 18 | $27
117 W. 10th St. (bet. Greenwich & 6th Aves.), 212-633-0348
"Wonderfully spicy" Southeast Asian eats "with a bent toward Thai and Vietnamese" items please patrons of this "inexpensive", "unfussy" Villager where service is as "casual" as the vibe; regulars prefer the "delightful" backyard over the "tight" interior.

Cafe Bar ●   ▽ 19 | 19 | 10 | $22
32-90 36th St. (34th Ave.), Queens, 718-204-5273; www.cafebarastoria.com
"Bohemian and slick at the same time", this Astoria Greek-Med has a "hip Salvation Army" aesthetic updated with WiFi access and big-screen TVs; the food's "decent" enough and cheap enough, but given the "almost nonexistent service", most show up "for the scene."

Café Botanica   21 | 26 | 22 | $60
Jumeirah Essex House, 160 Central Park S. (bet. 6th & 7th Aves.), 212-484-5120
"Out-of-towners who want a little serenity" unwind at this "garden"-style Med–New American in the Jumeirah Essex House "overlooking Central Park"; despite "delicious" food and "impeccable" service, many say the "view is the main attraction."

CAFÉ BOULUD   28 | 23 | 26 | $77
Surrey Hotel, 20 E. 76th St. (bet. 5th & Madison Aves.), 212-772-2600; www.danielnyc.com
Bertrand Chemel is behind the burners at this UES sibling of Daniel, and he's up to the challenge, creating "stunning" French cuisine

"with finesse and depth" paired with one of NYC's "most thoughtful wine lists"; "sophisticated" service, "handsome yet unfussy" decor and a chic, designer-dressed crowd make the place feel like your typical "neighborhood bistro for billionaires."

Cafe Centro ⊠   19 18 18 $45
MetLife Bldg., 200 Park Ave. (45th St. & Vanderbilt Ave.), 212-818-1222;
www.restaurantassociates.com
Offering a "convenient" Grand Central location and "satisfying" Med fare at moderate prices, this "bustling" brasserie is a midday magnet for "recruiter meetings" given its "intentionally corporate" mien; "unwinding" commuters aside, it's even more appealing and a lot less crowded at dinner.

Cafecito ⊘   ▽ 22 15 18 $23
185 Ave. C (bet. 11th & 12th Sts.), 212-253-9966
Castronomes congregate at this "quaint", "laid-back" East Village Cuban for "moist and meaty" pressed sandwiches, the "best cafe con leche" and other "authentic" *comida* at "reasonable prices"; "spotty" service and a "remote" location don't keep habitués from havana good time.

Cafe Colonial   19 16 15 $33
276 Elizabeth St. (Houston St.), 212-274-0044; www.cafecolonialny.com
NoLita "boulevardistes" dig this "unpretentious" Brazilian for its "comfortable, cafe-society" vibe jazzed up with "Latin flair" and "interesting" people-watching; the "fantastic" breakfasts and "simple", "authentic" dinners are marred by "service with attitude", but at these prices few care.

Cafe Condesa ◖ NEW   – – – I
183 W. 10th St. (bet. 7th Ave. S. & W. 4th St.), 212-352-0050;
www.cafecondesa.com
Serving standard breakfast and brunch items in the morning and simple, Latin-accented New Americana the rest of the day, this new West Village cafe is already winning public attention; the vibe is laid-back and the space rustic, in sync with the low price tags.

Cafe Con Leche   17 11 15 $23
424 Amsterdam Ave. (bet. 80th & 81st Sts.), 212-595-7000
726 Amsterdam Ave. (bet. 95th & 96th Sts.), 212-678-7000
The combination of an "addictive" namesake beverage that "beats Starbucks hands down" and "tasty", "inexpensive" Cuban-Dominican chow keeps this UWS duo "crowded", despite "uninspired" interiors and "*Fawlty Towers*" service"; P.S. the "hearty" brunches are the "real deal."

Café d'Alsace ◖ NEW   22 19 19 $45
1695 Second Ave. (88th St.), 212-722-5133; www.cafedalsace.com
A "flashback" to Yorkville's "European roots", this "cheerful" new brasserie (from the team behind Nice Matin and Marseille) provides "savory" Alsatian specialties washed down with an "endless beer list"; it's already "crowded and noisy", proving the neighborhood "needed this place."

Café de Bruxelles ◖   21 16 18 $41
118 Greenwich Ave. (13th St.), 212-206-1830
Mussel-bound types are relieved that this tiny, "tried-and-true" Village Belgian (now in its 25th year) "never changes", serving up "excellent" moules, "unmatchable" frites and "superior beers" with "cordial charm"; though trendies find the "old-school" interior "drab", traditionalists say it's "so unhip it's cool."

CAFÉ DES ARTISTES ❶

22 | 26 | 23 | $66

1 W. 67th St. (bet. Columbus Ave. & CPW), 212-877-3500; www.cafenyc.com
"Très romantique", festooned with a "riot of flowers" and Howard Chandler Christy's "magical" murals of gamboling nymphs, this "sumptuous" Lincoln Center–area "grande dame" via George and Jenifer Lang is one of NYC's "most beautiful" dining rooms; equally "lovely" is the French cuisine presented by a "thoughtful staff" – no wonder this 90-year-old remains a consistent "crowd-pleaser" – as well as a favorite place for proposing.

Café du Soleil

20 | 18 | 15 | $39

2723 Broadway (104th St.), 212-316-5000
Appropriately "bright and sunny", this Columbia-area French-Med lures "university types" with "oh-so-good" cooking and a "cheerful" vibe, not the "lax service" or "noisy" decibels; its "pre-theater dinner is an excellent value, even though there's no theater nearby."

Cafe Español ❶

19 | 13 | 18 | $32

172 Bleecker St. (bet. MacDougal & Sullivan Sts.), 212-505-0657; www.cafeespanol.com
78 Carmine St. (bet. Bedford St. & 7th Ave. S.), 212-675-3312
Amigos aver these "authentic", separately owned Village Spaniards "never disappoint" with "plentiful", "relatively cheap" cuisine (particularly Monday night's lobster special) and "dull-your-senses" sangria; regulars "sit outside" to avoid the "dreary" interiors.

Café Evergreen

19 | 13 | 17 | $30

1288 First Ave. (bet. 69th & 70th Sts.), 212-744-3266; www.cafeevergreenat69.com
Oenophiles take oenterest in this "pleasant" UES Chinese for its sizable, "well-priced wine list" paired with "authentic" dim sum and other "tasty" Cantonese chow; since the decor's "a bit tired", aesthetes opt for the "fast delivery."

Café Fiorello ❶

20 | 16 | 18 | $47

1900 Broadway (bet. 63rd & 64th Sts.), 212-595-5330; www.cafefiorello.com
"Always bustling pre-concert", this "convenient" Italian opposite Lincoln Center "transcends its tourist location" with "paper-thin" pizza and a "stellar antipasto bar"; never mind the "crowding" and "stadium" acoustics: they always "get you out on time", and in summer there's great outdoor seating.

Café Frida

20 | 16 | 16 | $37

368 Columbus Ave. (bet. 77th & 78th Sts.), 212-712-2929; www.cafefrida.com
The "killer guacamole" and other "high-class", yet midpriced, Mexican fare is even more enjoyable when you "keep those margaritas coming" at this "reliable" Upper Westsider; it's also "convenient" for Natural History Museumgoers, though Frida fighters fret about "cramped" digs and "mediocre" service.

Cafe Gitane ❶≠

19 | 16 | 14 | $23

242 Mott St. (Prince St.), 212-334-9552
You can look forward to "good people-watching" at this "sceney" NoLita "eye-candy" magnet where "beautiful girls and strong coffee" collide; the "cheap", "tasty" French-Moroccan eats are "worth the wait", the "squeeze" and the "slow" service.

CAFÉ GRAY

25 | 23 | 23 | $78

Time Warner Ctr., 10 Columbus Circle, 3rd fl. (60th St. at B'way), 212-823-6338; www.cafegray.com
Gray Kunz's "adult" French brasserie up in the Time Warner Center purveys "brilliant" Asian-accented fare along with "assured service";

some say it's "too expensive" and the menu never changes, others debate David Rockwell's decor ("glittering" vs. "grandiose") but all agree lunch is an economical way to try it out.

Café Habana ●
22 | 12 | 14 | $23

17 Prince St. (Elizabeth St.), 212-625-2001
At this "ever-so-trendy" NoLita nook, hipsters are hep to the "heaven-on-a-stick" grilled corn and other "spicy" Cuban-Mexican eats, and undeterred by "snooty" service and a setting that's strictly "luncheonette"; insiders "avoid the wait" by going to the take-out shop around the corner.

Cafe Joul
18 | 13 | 16 | $42

1070 First Ave. (bet. 58th & 59th Sts.), 212-759-3131
"Homey and pleasant", this "low-key" bistro near the Queensboro Bridge lures "Sutton Place regulars" with "reliable" Gallic "standards" and "unusual" wines; though some find it "too pricey for what it is", most consider it an "easy place to dine" and have a good time.

Cafe Loup ●
19 | 17 | 20 | $41

105 W. 13th St. (bet. 6th Ave. & 7th Ave. S.), 212-255-4746
Regulars report this "unpretentious" French stalwart is "still surviving" despite years of "chronic construction" on its Greenwich Village block; "tasty" bistro standards and "accommodating" service create such a "comforting aura" that surveyors feel that a meal here is like "visiting an old friend."

Cafe Luluc ●⊘
19 | 16 | 18 | $26

214 Smith St. (Baltic St.), Brooklyn, 718-625-3815
All-around "pleasant", this "no-frills" Cobble Hill bistro offers "simple" French fare "done well" and served by a "wonderful" crew; even those who say its "limited" menu is "not particularly inspired" have to admit "the price is right."

Cafe Luxembourg ●
19 | 17 | 17 | $49

200 W. 70th St. (bet. Amsterdam & West End Aves.), 212-873-7411
Starting in 1983, this "hardy" Lincoln Center "perennial" brought "something cool" to the UWS, namely "classic" French bistro eats, an "irresistibly European" vibe and the possibility of "A-listers chowing down" beside you; no one cares that it's "*très* noisy" and "cheek-to-jowl crowded", since this neighborhood "staple" is always "kicking."

Cafe Mogador ●
22 | 16 | 17 | $24

101 St. Marks Pl. (bet. Ave. A & 1st Ave.), 212-677-2226;
www.cafemogador.com
"Savory", "authentic" tagines lead off the menu at this longtime East Village Moroccan known for its low tabs and high quality, and especially for its "unconventional brunches"; service is "absent-minded" and seating "cramped", yet the final verdict is "totally worthwhile."

Café Opaline
▽ 19 | 20 | 20 | $34

Dahesh Museum, 580 Madison Ave., 2nd fl. (bet. 56th & 57th Sts.),
212-521-8155; www.daheshmuseum.org
For a "leisurely lunch" or a "wonderful afternoon tea", check out this "chic" second-floor "hideaway" in the Dahesh Museum, whose assets include "creative" Med–New Americana, an "attentive" staff and spectacular Mad Ave people-watching through "floor-to-ceiling windows."

Café Pierre
▽ 20 | 25 | 22 | $76

Pierre Hotel, 2 E. 61st St. (5th Ave.), 212-940-8195
"Old-world elegance" is yours at this French-Continental in the Pierre Hotel where the ambiance is "quiet enough for conversation" and the

well-heeled crowd "well-dressed" (jacket required); "delectable"
cuisine and an extensive wine list add up to an "expensive" "special-
occasion treat", though it can be enjoyed more economically over
cocktails and the music of pianist Kathleen Landis.

Cafe Ronda

19 17 16 $33

249-251 Columbus Ave. (bet. 71st & 72nd Sts.), 212-579-9929;
www.caferonda.com
"Tasty" Med–South American cooking transports fans to "empanada
heaven" at this "relaxed" Upper Westsider known for its "delicious
brunches" and even tastier sidewalk seat "people-watching"; it may
be "noisy and crowded", but the "buzz" reminds you of Buenos Aires.

Café Sabarsky/Café Fledermaus

21 23 18 $39

Neue Galerie, 1048 Fifth Ave. (86th St.), 212-288-0665;
www.wallse.com
"1900 Vienna meets Central Park" at Kurt Gutenbrunner's Austrian
"charmer" in Ronald Lauder's Neue Galerie, where the "dark-wood
salon" look sets the stage for "savory soups", "superb" pastries and
coffee that "will spoil you for anything else"; to avoid "off-putting
waits", head downstairs to Fledermaus ("same food, more calm").

Cafe S.F.A.

17 16 15 $31

Saks Fifth Ave., 611 Fifth Ave., 8th fl. (bet. 49th & 50th Sts.),
212-940-4080
"Ready-to-drop" shoppers appreciate this "convenient refuge" on
Saks' eighth floor for a "civilized" New American lunch or afternoon
tea; "slow" service and "pricey" tabs are more tolerable if you "hold
out for a window table" overlooking Rock Center or St. Pat's.

Café Soleil ●NEW

– – – E

1016 Second Ave. (bet. 53rd & 54th Sts.), 212-758-1351
Set in a high-ceilinged space, this casual East Side Med is already
winning a place in the sun thanks to a grill-heavy menu backed up
with an array of raw-bar options; alfresco tables offer primo Second
Avenue people-watching.

Cafe Spice

18 13 15 $26

Grand Central, lower level (42nd St. & Vanderbilt Ave.),
646-227-1300
72 University Pl. (bet. 10th & 11th Sts.), 212-253-6999
54 W. 55th St. (bet. 5th & 6th Aves.), 212-489-7444
www.cafespice.com
"Flavorful", "satisfying" subcontinental eats keep fans cumin back to
this "colorful" Indian chainlet where most overlook the "slow" service given the "good value"; the takeout-only Grand Central offshoot
is perfect for a "grab-and-go" "curry fix" on the way home.

Café St. Bart's

16 21 16 $34

109 E. 50th St. (Park Ave.), 212-888-2664; www.cafestbarts.com
It's all about the "tranquil" terrace of this indoor/outdoor "sleeper" on
the steps of St. Bartholomew's Church; believers laud its "simple,
well-prepared" New Americana, though doubters confess the "passable" grub and "glacial" service are less than divine.

Cafeteria ●

18 16 13 $30

119 Seventh Ave. (17th St.), 212-414-1717; www.cafeteria247.com
"Be sure to look fabulous" before showing up at this "minimalist", 24/7
Chelsea American favored by "fashionistas" and "club kids"; boosters like the "updated comfort-food menu", "decent prices" and the
"energy", but foes fret over "monster waits", "pounding disco beats"
and "apathetic" servers who'd be happier if you served yourself.

Cafe Un Deux Trois ◐

16 15 17 $41

123 W. 44th St. (bet. B'way & 6th Ave.), 212-354-4148; www.cafeundeuxtrois.biz
"They've got pre-theater dining down to a science" – and lunch too –
at this 30-year-old Times Square French bistro where the room's
"big", the cooking "decent", the service "rushed" and the acoustics
"loud"; though cynics call it "touristy", parents report the "lively"
mood is "good for kids."

Caffe Bondi

∇ 23 19 21 $38

1816 Hylan Blvd. (Dongan Hills Ave.), Staten Island, 718-668-0100
Staten Islanders tout this "unobtrusive" Sicilian for its "tasty pastas"
and "creative" daily specials at prices that are "more than fair"; "accommodating" service and a "neighborhood feel" make it a "standout."

Caffe Buon Gusto

17 14 17 $30

236 E. 77th St. (bet. 2nd & 3rd Aves.), 212-535-6884
1009 Second Ave. (bet. 53rd & 54th Sts.), 212-755-1476
151 Montague St. (bet. Clinton & Henry Sts.), Brooklyn, 718-624-3838
"Dependable, no-frills" cooking at "moderate prices" explains
why this "friendly" Italian chainlet is a "major local favorite" for families or "first dates"; given their "modest" interiors, you may want
to consider takeout.

Caffe Cielo ◐

19 16 19 $42

881 Eighth Ave. (bet. 52nd & 53rd Sts.), 212-246-9555
A "find" in Hell's Kitchen, this oft-"overlooked" but "always reliable"
Northern Italian ingratiates itself with "well-prepared" "*paesano*-
style" standards served "quickly"; while it's "popular" for "casual" pre-
theater dinners, matinee-goers applaud the $10.95 prix fixe brunch.

Caffe Grazie

18 16 19 $45

26 E. 84th St. (bet. 5th & Madison Aves.), 212-717-4407;
www.caffegrazie.com
Museumgoers are grateful for this "close-to-the-Met" Italian offering "flavorful" fare, "efficient" service and a "comfortable"
townhouse setting; contrarians say thanks but no thanks, citing
"pricey", "pedestrian" eats.

Caffe Linda ⊠

19 12 18 $31

145 E. 49th St. (bet. Lexington & 3rd Aves.), 646-497-1818
"Delicious" pastas and other Italian basics highlight this "homey"
East Midtown Italian that's a "great lunch joint" for nearby desk jockeys; penny-pinchers praise the "affordable" tabs and advise "come
early, come often" – but "not for the atmosphere."

Caffé on the Green Ⓜ

21 22 22 $47

201-10 Cross Island Pkwy. (bet. Clearview Expwy. & Utopia Pkwy.),
Queens, 718-423-7272; www.caffeonthegreen.com
Set in a 1919 manse once owned by Rudolph Valentino, this "romantic"
Bayside Italian boasts bonus "beautiful views" of the Throgs Neck
Bridge; "delicious" cuisine and "attentive" service usually insure that
repasts here will hit all the high notes, but with many "special occa-
sions" going on, "it can get noisy."

Calle Ocho

22 22 19 $45

446 Columbus Ave. (bet. 81st & 82nd Sts.), 212-873-5025;
www.calleochonyc.com
"Miami meets Manhattan" at this "hot, hot, hot" UWS Nuevo Latino
where the "zesty decor matches the fusion dishes" – though the
food's "intriguing flavor combinations" may be muted by "seriously
potent mojitos"; just be warned, at prime times "it can be hard to hear
yourself think over the din."

CamaJe ⦿
                                                    21 | 15 | 17 | $34
85 MacDougal St. (bet. Bleecker & Houston Sts.), 212-673-8184;
www.camaje.com
"Quirky" yet "*très charmant*", this Village bistro delivers "inventive"
Franco-American cookery from "superwoman" chef-owner Abigail
Hitchcock, who also "gives cooking lessons"; it may be "tiny", but the
"great value" justifies "being a little crushed."

Cambalache
                                                  ▽ 21 | 15 | 18 | $40
406 E. 64th St. (bet. 1st & York Aves.), 212-223-2229;
www.cambalachenyc.com
Folks who've found this "friendly" UES Argentinean steakhouse are
bullish on its "delicious grilled meats, empanadas" and "good
wines", all "perfect for the appetite and wallet"; the colorful venue
also has a "killer back garden."

Camino Sur NEW
                                                  ▽ 23 | 19 | 21 | $42
336 W. 37th St. (bet. 8th & 9th Aves.), 212-695-4600;
www.caminosur.com
Parked on a "bleak" "industrial" block, this Garment District "find"
purveys "creative", "meat-heavy" South American specialties served
by "warm" staffers in "intimate", "stylish" digs; all agree it's a "much-
needed" option in an underserved area.

Campagnola ⦿
                                                    24 | 18 | 22 | $63
1382 First Ave. (bet. 73rd & 74th Sts.), 212-861-1102
"Delectable", if "expensive", Italian food and "NYC characters"
abound at this "always jammed" UES "scene" where "attentive"
staffers "with personality" minister to regulars sporting "suits and
heavy jewelry"; despite a pianist, it's too busy to be really romantic.

Canaletto
                                                    21 | 16 | 22 | $51
208 E. 60th St. (bet. 2nd & 3rd Aves.), 212-317-9192
"Reliably fine" *cucina* and a "welcoming" staff that "knows how to
treat regulars" make this "nothing-fancy" UES Northern Italian a "local favorite"; at lunch, it's "lovely and quiet", after work "crowded
and crazy" – but whatever the hour, it's "not cheap."

Candela
                                                    18 | 21 | 18 | $41
116 E. 16th St. (bet. Irving Pl. & Park Ave. S.), 212-254-1600;
www.candelarestaurant.com
The "beautifully candlelit room" works like an aphrodisiac at this
"romantic-as-hell" Union Square New American, a "dark-as-night"
"date place" done up like the "set of *Phantom*"; while food, service
and prices are all "good enough", they don't hold a candle to
the "sexy ambiance."

Candle Cafe
                                                    22 | 14 | 19 | $28
1307 Third Ave. (bet. 74th & 75th Sts.), 212-472-0970;
www.candlecafe.com
"Tofu is your friend" at this "ingenious", inexpensive UES vegan sibling
of Candle 79 where "true believers" feel "saintly" and "politically cor-
rect"; it's a "buzzing" place to "wear your Birks" and "veg out", with
"commitment and warmth" compensating for the "modest" quarters.

Candle 79
                                                    24 | 21 | 23 | $40
154 E. 79th St. (bet. Lexington & 3rd Aves.), 212-537-7179;
www.candlecafe.com
"Healthy never tasted as good" as it does at this "chic", "guilt-free"
UES vegan that some say is the "classiest in the city"; "ingredient-
conscious" types praise its "innovation" and say it's "worth every
penny – and they charge lots of them."

Canyon Road
20 | 17 | 17 | $34

1470 First Ave. (bet. 76th & 77th Sts.), 212-734-1600; www.arkrestaurants.com
This "spunky" UES Southwesterner lures in "younger" types with "solid", "well-priced" eats washed down with "dangerous", "send-you-over-the-edge" margaritas; the "adobe-walled" digs may get "jammed" and "noisy", but "consistent" quality keeps it a "first-date" favorite.

Capital Grille
23 | 23 | 22 | $62

155 E. 42nd St. (bet. Lexington & 3rd Aves.), 212-953-2000; www.thecapitalgrille.com
Philip Johnson's "dramatic" glass pyramid adjacent to the Chrysler Building is home to this "top-shelf" link of a national chop shop chain that draws "power wallet" types with "splendid" steaks and "attentive" service; it's a "truly prime" time, until you get the bill.

Capsouto Frères
23 | 22 | 23 | $53

451 Washington St. (Watts St.), 212-966-4900; www.capsoutofreres.com
A "hidden treasure", this "mercifully untrendy" Way West TriBeCa "pioneer" is "old-fashioned in the best sense"; "timeless" French bistro fare ("*vive le soufflé!*"), "warm", "witty service" and a "charming", "spacious" brick-walled setting make it worth the drive, and thankfully there's plenty of parking space.

Caracas Arepa Bar Ⓜ
23 | 13 | 16 | $15

93½ E. Seventh St. (bet. Ave. A & 1st Ave.), 212-529-2314
Caracas to Go Ⓜ
91 E. Seventh St. (1st Ave.), 212-228-5062
www.caracasarepabar.com
It "feels like South America" at this East Village "Venezuelan street food" vendor specializing in "*muy delicioso*" arepas with "fresh" fixings; given its "bargain" tabs, it's always "crowded", so regulars often "get it to go" from its nearby take-out sibling.

Cara Mia
19 | 15 | 17 | $35

654 Ninth Ave. (bet. 45th & 46th Sts.), 212-262-6767; www.nycrg.com
There's "big taste in a small place" at this Hell's Kitchen Italian "nook" serving "authentic", "traditional" dishes when you need a "fast pre-theater fix"; sure, it's a "hole-in-the-wall", but the prices "won't put a hole in your pocket."

Carbone Ⓢ NEW
– | – | – | M

331 W. 38th St. (bet. 8th & 9th Aves.), 212-290-2625
Set in a low-profile storefront on an unassuming Garment District block, this Southern Italian is already garnering a rep for its coal oven–fired pizza; the tiny, narrow interior can get crowded, but fortunately there's extra space in the back garden.

Carino
20 | 12 | 20 | $33

1710 Second Ave. (bet. 88th & 89th Sts.), 212-860-0566
"Like eating in your mother's kitchen", this "tiny" but "homey" UES Southern Italian provides "warm" hospitality along with "simple yet well-done" cooking, fairly priced; though "ordinary" to the eye, it's much "beloved" to the neighbors.

Carl's Steaks
22 | 6 | 14 | $10

79 Chambers St. (bet. B'way & Church St.), 212-566-2828
507 Third Ave. (34th St.), 212-696-5336 ◑
www.carlssteaks.com
Cheese steak buffs who "can't make it to Philly" show "brotherly love" for this Murray Hill/TriBeCa duo's "sloppy", "real-deal" sandwiches

that also work as "grease-laden hangover cures"; "cramped", divey digs with scarce stools lead most takers to "take it out."

CARLYLE RESTAURANT
22 | 26 | 25 | $78

Carlyle Hotel, 35 E. 76th St. (Madison Ave.), 212-744-1600; www.thecarlyle.com
Flaunting "luxury", this "fancy" UES hotel dining room attracts "mature", "dressed-up" folk with "excellent" New French fare "served with elegance" in a "velvety", "old-world" environment; it's just the place to "celebrate anything" so long as you "wear a jacket" and bring your platinum card.

CARMINE'S
20 | 15 | 17 | $37

2450 Broadway (bet. 90th & 91st Sts.), 212-362-2200
200 W. 44th St. (bet. B'way & 8th Ave.), 212-221-3800 ◐
www.carminesnyc.com
"Real eaters" participate in "gluttonous binges" and still need doggy bags at these "brash", low-budget Southern Italians famed for "heaping", family-style platters buried in "red sauce" and "garlic galore"; designed to replicate circa-1900 Little Italy, they're filled with "rowdy" groups who are "noisier than a Yankees game."

Carne
18 | 16 | 16 | $36

2737 Broadway (105th St.), 212-663-7010; www.carnenyc.com
This "roomy" UWS steakhouse with a coolly "austere" "Downtown feel" maintains a "mainstream" menu of "pretty decent" beef; "budget" pricing makes it a boon for the "Columbia date scene", despite a staff that "would rather be at an audition."

Carnegie Deli ◐⊄
21 | 8 | 12 | $26

854 Seventh Ave. (55th St.), 212-757-2245; www.carnegiedeli.com
You can "feel your arteries swell" simply by reading the menu at this "fabled" Midtown deli where "jaw-dislocating sandwiches" make for world-class "cholestofests"; "chaotic" quarters, a quintessential "NY tableau" crowd (hey, there's Woody) and "mouthy", "Ice Age"-era servers add up to a "must experience" that "never gets old."

Carne Vale ◐ NEW
– | – | – | M

46 Ave. B (bet. 3rd & 4th Sts.), 212-777-4686
The Le Souk folks have opened this new East Village churrascaria where the dim lights and Brazilian dancers transport you far from Avenue B; there's no menu, just a salad bar and all the carne you can consume for a $35 set price.

Carol's Cafe ⊠ M
23 | 17 | 19 | $54

1571 Richmond Rd. (bet. Four Corners Rd. & Seaview Ave.), Staten Island, 718-979-5600; www.carolscafe.com
An "eye-pleasing array" of "imaginative" Eclectic dishes awaits at this "upscale" Staten Islander helmed by chef Carol Frazzetta; granted, it's "on the expensive side" by SI standards, but "well worth it" for the "closest thing to Manhattan fine dining" you'll find in these parts.

Casa ⊠
∇ 20 | 17 | 18 | $41

72 Bedford St. (Commerce St.), 212-366-9410; www.casarestaurant.com
As "homey" as can be, this "tiny" Brazilian set on a "charming Village corner" provides an "outstanding" lineup of "hearty" dishes enhanced by "welcoming" service and "killer" caipirinhas; for a "real" taste of Rio "that isn't a churrascaria" and isn't too expensive, it's a "find."

Casa La Femme North ◐
∇ 19 | 23 | 15 | $54

1076 First Ave. (bet. 58th & 59th Sts.), 212-223-2322; www.casalafemme.com
Like a Nile "getaway" in East Midtown, this Egyptian oasis exudes "exotic" vibes via "veiled tents" and "random belly dancers"; the

"pricey" offerings are equally "tasty" ("they know their seasonings"), even if things head south with "inconsistent service."

Casa Mono ◑
25 18 20 $47

52 Irving Pl. (17th St.), 212-253-2773
"Adventurous eaters" shout *olé* over Mario Batali's "upbeat" Gramercy Spaniard where the small plates "blow you away" with "exquisite" flavors that "transcend tapas"; the "shoebox-snug" space is often "mosh-pit" packed, so "expect to wait" around the corner in Bar Jamón – in the end, it's "worth the hassle" and the pricey tabs.

Cascina ◑
18 16 17 $39

647 Ninth Ave. (bet. 45th & 46th Sts.), 212-245-4422; www.cascina.com
For theatergoers seeking "well-prepared" pastas and pizzas for "reasonable" dough, this "welcoming" Hell's Kitchen Italian "fits the bill"; a wood stove and wines from its "family-owned vineyard" boost the overall "agreeable" mood.

Casimir ◑
19 18 14 $34

103-105 Ave. B (bet. 6th & 7th Sts.), 212-358-9683
Besides a "film noir atmosphere", this "sepia-lit" Alphabet City French bistro supplies "*très bon*" eats to a "hip" crowd who all seem to be on "first dates"; it's also a "good buy", with "authentic" Gallic "attitude" tossed in for free.

Caviar Russe
▽ 26 24 23 $85

538 Madison Ave., 2nd fl. (bet. 54th & 55th Sts.), 212-980-5908; www.caviarrusse.com
Among the "finer things in life", this Midtown mezzanine New American dispenses "divine" caviar, seafood and now sushi in a "Fabergé egg" setting; it's the "perfect hideaway" for well-funded folks who feel they "should have been a tsar" and are prepared for the resulting bill.

Cávo ◑
19 25 18 $39

42-18 31st Ave. (bet. 42nd & 43rd Sts.), Queens, 718-721-1001; www.cavocafelounge.com
"One of the coolest" sites in Astoria, this "barn-size" Greek is best known for its "stunning" outdoor "piazza" that sets the "upscale" tone for its "quality" modern menu; "almost always filled to capacity", it morphs into a "nightclub" in the wee hours.

Cebu ◑
▽ 23 19 19 $33

8801 Third Ave. (88th St.), Brooklyn, 718-492-5095
"Late-night" noshing is the thing at this "top-notch" "neighborhood" Bay Ridge Continental that serves till 3 AM; separated into a "lively" bar and a "cozy", fireplace-equipped dining room, it offers a brunch "deal" that draws daylight types on weekends

Celeste ⌽
24 12 17 $32

502 Amsterdam Ave. (bet. 84th & 85th Sts.), 212-874-4559
"Get ready to fight the crowds" at this "too popular" UWS Neapolitan where "best-deal" pricing and a "no-reservations policy" often leads to "unbearable waits"; the "hectic", "closet"-size space is not much to look at, but is usually so crowded that you can't see it anyway.

Cellini ⊠
21 17 21 $52

65 E. 54th St. (bet. Madison & Park Aves.), 212-751-1555; www.cellinirestaurant.com
To seal "a deal" with "a touch of class", try this Midtown Northern Italian where the "corporate lunch" trade flourishes thanks to "solid" cooking and "obliging" staffers; it's "not flashy", but always "reliable" and enjoys a rep as a dinnertime "sleeper" with romantic possibilities.

Cendrillon Ⓜ

| 22 | 18 | 20 | $39 |

45 Mercer St. (bet. Broome & Grand Sts.), 212-343-9012;
www.cendrillon.com
For a "most original" "change of pace", this "inviting" SoHo "treat"
specializes in "inspired" Filipino-Asian food prepared with "finesse"
and "warmly" served; given that followers "feel at home" at this "labor of love", its "undiscovered" status is pretty "surprising."

Centolire

| 20 | 21 | 19 | $57 |

1167 Madison Ave. (bet. 85th & 86th Sts.), 212-734-7711
"Not your everyday" Italian, Pino Luongo's "beguiling" townhouse is
a "civilized retreat" for elegant Eastsiders who gravitate to its "stylish" second floor; though the "refined" Tuscan fare and "personal attention" are "not cheap", the $24.50 prix fixe lunch allows for an
"economical" right of passage.

Centrico

| 18 | 18 | 18 | $45 |

211 W. Broadway (Franklin St.), 212-431-0700;
www.myriadrestaurantgroup.com
Chef Aarón Sanchez's "flavorful", "high-end" Mexican fare has the
"flair" to set "tongues tingling" at this "airy" TriBeCan from Drew
Nieporent; throw in "awesome margaritas" and it's a "fun night out",
though "given the talent" involved, any "kinks" can be "disappointing."

Cercle Rouge ☉ NEW

| 15 | 19 | 16 | $46 |

241 W. Broadway (bet. Beach & White Sts.), 212-226-6252;
www.cerclerougeresto.com
This new French TriBeCan sure "looks the part", but unfortunately its
"serviceable" brasserie fare doesn't always taste the part; that's why
some see rouge over the high prices and "clueless" service.

'Cesca

| 23 | 21 | 21 | $57 |

164 W. 75th St. (Amsterdam Ave.), 212-787-6300; www.cescanyc.com
Despite founding chef Tom Valenti's departure, Westsiders report that
the "warmth and gusto" remain at this "top-flight" Southern Italian
where the "memorable" menu's "earthy", "unfussy excellence" is a
"perfect match" for the "appealing" space and "cordial" staff; "deservedly popular", it's "worth every penny."

Chadwick's

| 22 | 17 | 21 | $40 |

8822 Third Ave. (89th St.), Brooklyn, 718-833-9855; www.chadwicksny.com
By now a "Bay Ridge staple", this 20-year-old "pub-type" eatery supplies "really good steaks" and other "basic" Americana for "reasonable" prices; no kidding, it's "not fancy", but it is "comfortable", and
the "jovial hosts" do "aim to please."

Chance

▽ | 21 | 21 | 21 | $29 |

223 Smith St. (Butler St.), Brooklyn, 718-242-1515;
www.chancecuisine.com
Luckily, this Boerum Hill hideaway maintains "high standards" via its
"creative mix" of Pan-Asian items served in an "ultramodern",
"loungey" space; it's "trendier" than its neighbors, starting with the
scene at its "snazzy" "waterfall bar."

CHANTERELLE Ⓢ

| 27 | 26 | 27 | $93 |

2 Harrison St. (Hudson St.), 212-966-6960; www.chanterellenyc.com
"Simplicity reigns supreme" at David and Karen Waltuck's 28-year-old
TriBeCa "treasure", a "paragon" of "luxurious dining" with "knockout"
French cooking, "graceful" service that "never skips a beat" and a
"lovely", understated room with "pin-drop quiet" and "ample table
spacing"; all this "joy" comes with a "premium price tag", leading
bargain-hunters to tout the "unbeatable" $42 prix fixe lunch.

Chanto NEW · · · E
133 Seventh Ave. S. (bet. Charles & W. 10th Sts.), 212-463-8686;
www.chantonyc.com
You'd never guess from the outside that this upscale new Village
Japanese is arranged over four labyrinthine levels, but scenesters
will remember the layout from the days when it was Moomba; it's the
50th outpost of an Osaka-based chain, and its first U.S. foray.

Charles' Southern-Style Kitchen ⓜ ▽ 23 5 16 $16
2839 Frederick Douglass Blvd. (151st St.), 212-926-4313
"Addictive" Southern-fried chicken leads the lineup of "high-calorie"
soul food found at this Harlem "hole-in-the-wall" where you "serve
yourself and eat till you drop"; despite the painfully "plain" digs, it's
the "real thing" for cheap, "authentic" grub.

Chat 'n Chew ❶ 17 13 15 $22
10 E. 16th St. (bet. 5th Ave. & Union Sq. W.), 212-243-1616;
www.chatnchewnyc.com
Check out "affordable" "greasy-spoon" American chow, notably
a "mean mac 'n' cheese", at this "low-down", "kitschy" kitchen in
Union Square that "hits the spot"; despite "hokey", "garage-sale"
decor and "inept" service, it's a "kid-friendly" "crowd-pleaser"
that's most always "busy."

Chef Ho's Peking Duck Grill 20 13 18 $28
1720 Second Ave. (bet. 89th & 90th Sts.), 212-348-9444
"Terrific" Peking duck is the "main attraction" at this UES Chinese
that's bedecked with "white tablecloths" but "priced like Chinatown";
it's a "consistent favorite" with locals pleased to find something
"down-to-earth" just "around the corner."

Chelsea Bistro 20 18 19 $46
358 W. 23rd St. (bet. 8th & 9th Aves.), 212-727-2026
For a "real bistro experience", this "old-style" Chelsea venue
"holds its own" with "basic" French "comfort food" served either
in a warm, "homey" dining room or a glassed-in back terrace; the
overall atmosphere gets mixed marks: what's "tired" to some is
"unpretentious" to others.

Chennai Garden ⓜ 21 10 15 $22
129 E. 27th St. (bet. Lexington Ave. & Park Ave. S.), 212-689-1999
When vegetarians and kosher diners need a dose of dosas, this Curry
Hill Indian's "bountiful" array has "just the right amount of spice"; the
"brightly lit" digs lead some to opt for "takeout", though penny-pinchers
pop up for the "bargain" $6.95 lunch buffet.

Chestnut ⓜ 23 18 22 $39
271 Smith St. (bet. Degraw & Sackett Sts.), Brooklyn, 718-243-0049;
www.chestnutonsmith.com
"Undernoticed" albeit "ambitious", this Carroll Gardens New
American is "dedicated to securing the best seasonal ingredients"
for its "delectable", "creative" menu; set in a "simple room" that's
brightened by "easygoing" service, it's a "standout on Smith Street."

Chez Jacqueline 18 17 18 $45
72 MacDougal St. (bet. Bleecker & Houston Sts.), 212-505-0727
An "intimate" "bit o' Provence" tucked away in the Village, this "long-
lasting", midpriced bistro is known for "dependable", if "predictable",
French home cooking; with its "sweet" service and "old-world" style,
it's the kind of place "every neighborhood should have."

Chez Josephine ●Ⓜ

| 20 | 21 | 21 | $49 |

414 W. 42nd St. (bet. 9th & 10th Aves.), 212-594-1925;
www.chezjosephine.com
"Solid", reliable French bistro fare is served at this "flamboyant"
Theater District "ode to the great Josephine Baker" overseen by her
charming adoptive son, Jean-Claude; but it's the "campy", "plush-
velvet" decor and wannabe "Liberace at the piano" that make dining
here such a "hoot."

Chez Napoléon Ⓢ

| 19 | 13 | 20 | $42 |

365 W. 50th St. (bet. 8th & 9th Aves.), 212-265-6980;
www.cheznapoleon.com
Those "*nostalgique*" for "old-fashioned" dining and "value" salute
this circa-1959 Theater District "throwback" for its "reliable" lineup
of "familiar" French bistro dishes; *oui*, it's rather "fusty" and "faded",
but "friendliness" and "convenience" keep customers coming.

Chez Oskar ●

| 19 | 18 | 16 | $29 |

211 DeKalb Ave. (Adelphi St.), Brooklyn, 718-852-6250;
www.chezoskar.com
"Fort Greene hipsters" feel at home at this "lively" bistro, a "funky
haunt" where the "tasty" French cooking comes at an attractive tab;
sure, some zap the "slow service", but with "outside" seating and occasional live music, the scene still "holds up" well.

Chiam Chinese Cuisine

| 21 | 17 | 20 | $44 |

160 E. 48th St. (bet. Lexington & 3rd Aves.), 212-371-2323
Cantonese is "kicked up a notch" for the corporate crowd at this "sophisticated" Midtown Chinese, a "soothing" retreat for "excellent"
food paired with an "amazing" wine list; "courteous service" caps a "pro"
routine that's "Westernized" right down to the "upscale prices."

Chianti Ⓜ

| 22 | 17 | 20 | $40 |

8530 Third Ave. (86th St.), Brooklyn, 718-921-6300
"You'll leave stuffed" from this "popular" Bay Ridge Italian, which delivers the "delicious" "garlicky" goods on either "individual plates" or
"gigantic", "family-style platters"; locals tout it when you're in the
mood for "lotsa food and lotsa fun."

ChikaLicious ●

| 25 | 19 | 23 | $21 |

203 E. 10th St. (bet. 1st & 2nd Aves.), 212-995-9511;
www.chikalicious.com
Sweet tooths are "sugar high" on this "diminutive" East Villager offering "designer" dessert and wine pairings served as three-course,
fixed-price spreads; the portions are "minuscule" but "crafted with
love", and "service is so warm you can skip psychotherapy."

Chimichurri Grill ●

| 22 | 14 | 21 | $45 |

606 Ninth Ave. (bet. 43rd & 44th Sts.), 212-586-8655; www.chimichurrigrill.com
"Carnivorous theatergoers" like this Hell's Kitchen "hole-in-the-wall"
for its "top-notch" Argentinean steaks, "efficiently served" and slath-
ered with its "tasty" namesake sauce; outside of the "cramped"
quarters, it's so "authentic" you could be "in the pampas."

China Grill

| 22 | 20 | 19 | $52 |

60 W. 53rd St. (bet. 5th & 6th Aves.), 212-333-7788;
www.chinagrillmgt.com
"Big" and "brash", this sprawling, modern Midtown Asian remains
"quite a scene" offering "jumbo portions" of "fantastic fusion" chow
served amid "power-broker" bustle; it's "great for groups", but the
"lofty space" does reach "maximum noise levels" and pricing can be
equally high if you're not careful about what you order.

Chinatown Brasserie ● NEW   ▽ 21 | 24 | 19 | $49

380 Lafayette St. (Great Jones St.), 212-533-7000;
www.chinatownbrasserie.com

Already nicknamed the 'Chinese Balthazar', this "trendy" NoHo newcomer features "opulent" decor with an "oriental gloss" plus a menu
that runs the gamut from Sino standbys like Peking duck and BBQ ribs
to all-day dim sum; the wide-open setting also includes a "cool downstairs lounge" complete with its very own koi pond.

Chin Chin ●   22 | 17 | 21 | $46

216 E. 49th St. (bet. 2nd & 3rd Aves.), 212-888-4555;
www.chinchinny.com

"Not your ordinary Chinese", this "sophisticated" Midtowner is a 20-
year-old "favorite" that has reliably fine cuisine and service; sure, it's
"a bit pricey", but you can "throw darts at the menu and come up with
a fantastic meal" every time.

Chino's   20 | 15 | 17 | $29

173 Third Ave. (bet. 16th & 17th Sts.), 212-598-1200;
www.chinosnyc.com

"Mixing and matching" is the idea behind this "novel" Gramercy
Asian where an "imaginative", "affordable" menu of "big-flavored"
small plates is paired with a variety of "exotic drinks"; decorwise,
your chinos might rate better.

Chipotle   18 | 10 | 14 | $11

2 Broadway (Whitehall St.), 212-344-0941
55 E. Eighth St. (bet. B'way & University Pl.), 212-982-3081
150 E. 52nd St. (bet. Lexington & 3rd Aves.), 212-755-9754
150 E. 44th St. (bet. Lexington & 3rd Aves.), 212-682-9860
680 Sixth Ave. (bet. 21st & 22nd Sts.), 212-206-3781
19 St. Marks Pl. (bet. 2nd & 3rd Aves.), 212-529-4502
200 Varick St. (bet. Houston & King Sts.), 646-336-6264
9 W. 42nd St. (bet. 5th & 6th Aves.), 212-354-6760
304 W. 34th St. (8th Ave.), 212-268-4197
185 Montague St. (Court St.), Brooklyn, 718-243-9109
www.chipotle.com
Additional locations throughout the NY area

"McDonald's must be proud" of this "minimal-guilt" McMexican fran-
chise that offers "big, fat" "custom-made" burritos from a "speedy
assembly line" at south-of-the-border prices; the only drawback
is those "crazy lunchtime" waits – "if only people would line up like
this to vote."

ChipShop   20 | 15 | 17 | $19

129 Atlantic Ave. (bet. Clinton & Henry Sts.), Brooklyn,
718-855-7775

ChipShop/CurryShop ⊟

381-383 Fifth Ave. (bet. 6th & 7th Sts.), Brooklyn, 718-832-7701
www.chipshopnyc.com

"Homesick Brits" get a "fix of Anglophilia" at this Brooklyn pub pair
that presents "traditional" favorites like fish 'n' chips (as well as curries in Park Slope); the "high-fat" fare may require "pulmonary care",
but a "fantastic beer selection" keeps things chipper.

Chiyono ● M NEW   ▽ 21 | 17 | 21 | $29

328 E. Sixth St. (bet. 1st & 2nd Aves.), 212-673-3984

"Authentic Japanese homestyle cooking" makes for an "interesting
alternative" at this Curry Row "jewel" run by a "gregarious chef" who
takes "great pride" in her "delicious", sushi-free menu; happily, the
petite space comes with a petite bill.

Chocolate Room Ⓜ NEW
24 | 18 | 21 | $16

86 Fifth Ave. (bet. St. Marks Pl. & Warren St.), Brooklyn, 718-783-2900;
www.thechocolateroombrooklyn.com
It's almost impossible not to "overindulge" at this "intimate" Park Slope shrine to the "wonders of chocolate"; it's "perfect after BAM", but be prepared for a "tight squeeze" when you get dressed the next day.

Cho Dang Gol
22 | 15 | 16 | $28

55 W. 35th St. (bet. 5th & 6th Aves.), 212-695-8222; www.chodanggolny.com
If you want "authentic", "old-style" Seoul food, this Garment District Korean proffers "subtly flavored" fare that's highlighted by "killer" tofu and barbecue; a "calm" setting and "attentive" service make it dang easy to "just point and eat."

Chola
24 | 17 | 20 | $37

232 E. 58th St. (bet. 2nd & 3rd Aves.), 212-688-4619
For a "more interesting" Indian experience, this Eastsider proves it's got the "authentic stuff" with an "exhaustive" selection of "delicious", "perfectly spiced" food; service is "pleasant", and bargain-hunters tout its "amazing" $13.95 lunchtime buffet.

Chop't Creative Salad
21 | 9 | 14 | $12

165 E. 52nd St. (bet. Lexington & 3rd Aves.), 212-421-2300 Ⓢ NEW
60 E. 56th St. (bet. Madison & Park Aves.), 212-750-2467 Ⓢ
24 E. 17th St. (bet. B'way & 5th Ave.), 646-336-5523
www.choptsalad.com
"Rabbit food" fanciers like these "grab 'n' go" salad bars where the "mean mixed greens" are "custom" chopped with a "dizzying" variety of "super-fresh fixin's" and dressings; "ridiculous" lunch lines suggest they're "habit forming."

Chow Bar
21 | 17 | 18 | $38

230 W. Fourth St. (W. 10th St.), 212-633-2212
An "upbeat" magnet for young folk, this "festive" West Villager weds "reliable Asian fusion" fare with an "inventive" cocktail list; the clientele is more into the "hip" scenery than chowing down, and it's best to "go with a group and share."

Christos Steak House
∇ 23 | 19 | 21 | $51

41-08 23rd Ave. (41st St.), Queens, 718-777-8400
The "latest incarnation" of this "old-school" Astoria chop shop trades in its "Greek flair" for a "more traditional" feel but still supplies "terrific" surf 'n' turf; tabs are hefty for Queens but "economical by 212 standards", so beef eaters have incentive to "schlep."

Chubo Ⓜ
∇ 21 | 17 | 21 | $46

6 Clinton St. (bet. Houston & Stanton Sts.), 212-674-6300; www.chubo.com
"Highly innovative" dishes turn up on the "challenging" menu of this LES Eclectic set in a "shoebox"-size space; though the "minimal" room "manages to be cozy without feeling cramped", what's on the plate is sure to be more eye-catching.

Churrascaria Plataforma ◑
22 | 18 | 21 | $58

316 W. 49th St. (bet. 8th & 9th Aves.), 212-245-0505;
www.churrascariaplataforma.com

Churrascaria TriBeCa ◑
221 W. Broadway (bet. Franklin & White Sts.), 212-925-6969;
www.churrascariatribeca.com
They really "bring it on" at these Brazilian beef "bacchanals" where, after loading up at a huge salad bar, you're faced with an "endless parade" of "roaming waiters" slicing and serving "all-you-can-eat"

skewered meats; a roomful of "high-energy" carnivores bent on a "food orgy" ensures a "lively" experience.

Cibo
20 | 19 | 20 | $46

767 Second Ave. (41st St.), 212-681-1616
Operating from an "off-the-beaten-path" East Midtown address, this "upscale" Tuscan–New American is a good bet for "quiet, informal" dining; "flavorful" fare, "hospitable" service and "warm", "comfortable" quarters make this a "pleasant surprise."

Cilantro ❂
17 | 15 | 16 | $28

1321 First Ave. (71st St.), 212-537-4040
1712 Second Ave. (bet. 88th & 89th Sts.), 212-722-4242
www.cilantronyc.com
"Young" compadres fueled by "potent margaritas" keep this UES Southwestern duo "hopping"; they're also a "pretty cheap" fix for "tantalizing chips" and otherwise "decent" grub plated in "large portions."

Cipriani Dolci ❂
19 | 18 | 18 | $50

Grand Central, West Balcony (42nd St. & Vanderbilt Ave.), 212-973-0999;
www.cipriani.com
That "awesome vista" of Grand Central Station is a big draw at this "balcony eatery" that also comes across with "perfectly fine" Italian fare and blissful Bellinis; it's especially "fun for non-NYers", and even more enjoyable "when someone else is paying."

Cipriani Downtown ❂
20 | 19 | 18 | $62

376 W. Broadway (bet. Broome & Spring Sts.), 212-343-0999;
www.cipriani.com
"Watching is more important than eating" at this "kiss-kiss" SoHo Italian where "the young, the thin and the rich" toy with "great food" and sip "fab Bellinis"; "the old, the fat and the poor" think it's a "joke", starting with those "national debt"–worthy tabs.

Circus
19 | 18 | 19 | $49

132 E. 61st St. (bet. Lexington & Park Aves.), 212-223-2965;
www.circusrestaurante.com
"Fanciful" circus trappings add "flair" to this "welcoming" Midtowner's "distinctive" menu of "serious" Brazilian specialties and "great caipirinhas"; regulars wonder why such a "refreshing" change of pace "still hasn't been discovered."

Cité ❂
21 | 20 | 21 | $61

120 W. 51st St. (bet. 6th & 7th Aves.), 212-956-7100; www.citerestaurant.com
The "unparalleled" wine dinner with "unlimited refills" is an "oenophile's dream come true" at this "handy" French-accented New American in Midtown; its "tasty" food and "accommodating" staff earn it strong support from the law, media and banking sectors.

Cité Grill ❂ ⌧
20 | 18 | 20 | $50

120 W. 51st St. (bet. 6th & 7th Aves.), 212-956-7262; www.citerestaurant.com
Adjacent to the big Cité, this "pleasant" grill offers comparably "high quality" food in a "more casual" style, making it a "competent standby" for "pre-show" eats or cocktails with "Midtown bankers"; expect "no surprises", and it's a "satisfying" stop.

Citrus Bar & Grill
20 | 19 | 17 | $38

320 Amsterdam Ave. (75th St.), 212-595-0500; www.citrusnyc.com
"Best early if you value your hearing", this "groovy" UWS Latin-Asian lures "loud" "young" types who can create "quite a din" after a couple of the "amazing drinks"; though the food served is "above expectations", the "sexy" scene gets more attention as the evening progresses.

City Bakery
21 | 12 | 13 | $19

3 W. 18th St. (bet. 5th & 6th Aves.), 212-366-1414;
www.thecitybakery.com
A "treasure trove" of "indulgences" awaits at Maury Rubin's Flatiron bakery, from the "tempting buffet" and salad bar to the "sinfully sweet" baked goods; still, it's "expensive" for a "cafeteria-style", "serve-yourself" setup that's typically "totally swamped."

City Crab & Seafood Co.
17 | 14 | 15 | $42

235 Park Ave. S. (19th St.), 212-529-3800
You "rip whole crustaceans apart" at this "raucous" Flatiron fishfest, a "staple" for "keep-it-simple" seafood at "reasonable" prices; the house is "always full" with "young" types despite "uneven" service and a "run-down" setting – "Martha's Vineyard it's not."

City Hall ☒
21 | 21 | 20 | $54

131 Duane St. (bet. Church St. & W. B'way), 212-227-7777;
www.cityhallnyc.com
For a "Downtown power lunch supreme", check out Henry Meer's "vibrant" TriBeCan where "politicos", "bureaucrats", bankers and their lawyers congregate over "outstanding" surf 'n' turf amid "grand old Gotham" decor; despite "steep" prices, it's "grown-up dining at its best" with great party spaces to boot.

City Lobster & Crab Co.
17 | 15 | 16 | $49

121 W. 49th St. (bet. 6th & 7th Aves.), 212-354-1717;
www.citylobster.com
Though the enterprise feels "a bit commercial", the "basic seafood" at this "convenient" harbor near Radio City is "passable" for a "client lunch" or "pre-theater" fill-up – even if caustic critics carp at "over-pricing" and "flighty" service.

Clinton St. Baking Co.
24 | 14 | 18 | $25

4 Clinton St. (bet. Houston & Stanton Sts.), 646-602-6263;
www.greatbiscuits.com
"Fluffy", "Frisbee-size" flapjacks and "killer muffins" make for "crazy waits" at this "friendly" Lower East Side "glorified diner" known for its "phenomenal" weekend brunches; then again, the New American "comfort food" at the "much more laid-back" dinner is also "pretty darn good."

Coals ☒Ⓜ
▽ 25 | 17 | 19 | $19

1888 Eastchester Rd. (Morris Park Ave.), Bronx, 718-823-7002;
www.coalspizza.com
Maybe it's "quirky sounding", but this "out-of-the-way" Bronx joint produces "excellent", "unique" *grilled* pizzas with "light", "nicely charred" crusts and "superior" toppings, "served up quick and informal"; it also offers easily affordable soups, salads and panini.

Coco Pazzo
22 | 21 | 22 | $65

23 E. 74th St. (bet. 5th & Madison Aves.), 212-794-0205
Fans of "old-world style" like this "urbane" UES Northern Italian where "big hitters" savor "first-rate" food and service in "comforting" but crowded quarters; sure, it's "pricey" and "a bit haughty", but you'll mingle with an "elegant clientele" spiced with "celebs."

Coco Roco
20 | 14 | 15 | $25

392 Fifth Ave. (bet. 6th & 7th Sts.), Brooklyn, 718-965-3376
Locals are loco for this "economical" Park Slope "real Peruvian" that's "justly famous" for its rotisserie chicken; the "hectic" atmosphere and "turtle-speed" service are "nothing to brag about", but it's "still going strong" – "and they deliver."

Cocotte Ⓜ
21 | 20 | 18 | $36

337 Fifth Ave. (4th St.), Brooklyn, 718-832-6848
"Solid" French–New American eats served "without attitude" are yours at this "sweet", "intimate" bistro parked in "trendy Park Slope"; it's "what a neighborhood restaurant should be", with modest prices and an "excellent brunch" as a weekend bonus.

Coffee Shop Ⓓ
15 | 13 | 11 | $28

29 Union Sq. W. (16th St.), 212-243-7969
The "most popular dishes are the waitresses" at this affordable Union Square "fixture" that provides "decent" Brazilian-American chow to a young crowd; despite "dated" decor and "snippy" service from "modeling school" moonlighters, it hangs in there thanks to "late, late hours" and a great "location."

Col Legno Ⓓ Ⓜ
▽ 19 | 13 | 19 | $36

231 E. Ninth St. (bet. 2nd & 3rd Aves.), 212-777-4650
For a "satisfying" meal with "little fuss", check out this "unassuming", "relaxed" East Village Tuscan serving "straight-up" fare, notably a "wonderful brick-oven pizza"; there's "no ambiance, but who cares?" – it's so "affordable."

Colors NEW
▽ 21 | 22 | 21 | $53

417 Lafayette St. (bet. Astor Pl. & 4th St.), 212-777-8443; www.colors-nyc.com
Owned by a team of former Windows on the World employees, this "winning" East Village Eclectic purveys a "truly international" slate of "original" dishes "based on family recipes" served in a "global-themed" space; the "earnest" service alone is a tribute to its "spirit of survival and entrepreneurship."

Columbus Bakery
18 | 13 | 11 | $17

474 Columbus Ave. (bet. 82nd & 83rd Sts.), 212-724-6880
957 First Ave. (bet. 52nd & 53rd Sts.), 212-421-0334
www.arkrestaurants.com
"Always hopping", these "casual" bakery/cafes offer a variety of "high-quality" baked treats and light bites; if you can withstand the "surly service", "cutthroat" lines and "momzillas" with "double-wide strollers", they're a "real port in a storm."

Comfort Diner
16 | 11 | 15 | $21

214 E. 45th St. (bet. 2nd & 3rd Aves.), 212-867-4555
25 W. 23rd St. (bet. 5th & 6th Aves.), 212-741-1010
www.comfortdiner.com
There's "comfort in every bite" at these "throwback" diners featuring a "huge" selection of low-budget, "stick-to-your-ribs", "taste-of-yesterday" grub; if you can abide the "'50s shtick", there are "lots of healthy options" too.

COMPASS
22 | 22 | 21 | $57

208 W. 70th St. (bet. Amsterdam & West End Aves.), 212-875-8600; www.compassrestaurant.com
It's been "spun around" by all those "rotating chefs", but this "civilized" Westsider has gotten its bearings with an "intriguing" New American menu that works well with its "snazzy" quarters and "courteous" service; given its "swanky" aspirations (and prices), rooters are relieved it's finally back "on an upswing."

Convivium Osteria
25 | 23 | 21 | $48

68 Fifth Ave. (bet. Bergen St. & St. Marks Ave.), Brooklyn, 718-857-1833
"Are we really in Brooklyn?" ask the "transported" fans of this "very special" Park Slope Mediterranean serving "earthy", "belly-warming" fare in a "rustic", "softly lit" space, replete with a "garden

oasis"; indeed, everything's "consistently satisfying" here, except those "Manhattan prices."

Cookshop ●NEW   23 | 20 | 21 | $52
156 10th Ave. (20th St.), 212-924-4440; www.cookshopny.com
Making West Chelsea a "destination", this "hip 'n' happening" new "hot spot" "really cooks" with a "robust", "ever-changing menu" of "mouthwatering", "market-driven" Americana; throw in "polished" service, and it's no surprise that it has developed so much "buzz."

Copper Chimney   ▽ 20 | 18 | 18 | $36
126 E. 28th St. (bet. Lexington Ave. & Park Ave. S.), 212-213-5742; www.copperchimney.com
"Chicer than average", this Gramercy Indian shows its mettle with "fine", "creative" cooking and a "modern" setting that includes an "active" upstairs lounge; "you pay more than on Sixth Street", but it pays back with an experience that's "above the ordinary."

Coppola's ●   19 | 15 | 17 | $35
378 Third Ave. (bet. 27th & 28th Sts.), 212-679-0070
206 W. 79th St. (bet. Amsterdam Ave. & B'way), 212-877-3840
www.coppolas-nyc.com
Locals count on this coupla "standbys" for "hearty", "moderately priced" Italian food that's "as good as home-cooked", served with "no surprises"; those who can't cope with the "crowded" settings go the "delivery" route.

Cornelia Street Cafe ●   18 | 16 | 17 | $34
29 Cornelia St. (bet. Bleecker & W. 4th Sts.), 212-989-9319; www.corneliastreetcafe.com
It's easy to "linger" at this "very Village" French-American where the "enjoyable" food and "cheerful" "boho" ambiance "hit the spot" "without breaking the bank"; sidewalk seating and downstairs entertainment make this 30-year-old a local "staple."

Corner Bistro ●⊘   23 | 9 | 11 | $15
331 W. Fourth St. (Jane St.), 212-242-9502
Best known for its "legendary" "big fat juicy" burgers, "cheap beers" and "rock-bottom" prices, this "seedy" Villager is definitely not for the effete; it draws mobs of scruffy "young" types, who come prepared to "stand in line."

Cortina   ▽ 19 | 14 | 18 | $34
1448 Second Ave. (bet. 75th & 76th Sts.), 212-517-2066; www.ristorantecortina.com
Like your "own dining room", this "cozy" UES Northern Italian turns out "high-quality" food in a "pleasantly laid-back" room; maybe the "decor could use an upgrade" and service runs "slow", but it's still an appealing bang for the buck.

Cosette   19 | 13 | 20 | $37
163 E. 33rd St. (bet. Lexington & 3rd Aves.), 212-889-5489
A *très* "Parisian" bistro with a "personal touch", this "petite" in size and price but "big on flavor" Murray Hill French "secret" specializes in "*cuisine grand-mère*"; it's "minimally decorated", but cosseting from its "caring" staff pleases "homesick Francophiles."

Cosí   16 | 10 | 11 | $13
841 Broadway (13th St.), 212-614-8544 ●
2160 Broadway (76th St.), 212-595-5616
60 E. 56th St. (bet. Madison & Park Aves.), 212-588-1225
Paramount Plaza, 1633 Broadway (51st St.), 212-397-9838

(continued)
Cosí
257 Park Ave. S. (21st St.), 212-598-4070
498 Seventh Ave. (bet. 36th & 37th Sts.), 212-947-1005
504 Sixth Ave. (13th St.), 212-462-4188 ◐
700 Sixth Ave. (bet. 22nd & 23rd Sts.), 212-645-0223
11 W. 42nd St. (bet. 5th & 6th Aves.), 212-398-6662
World Financial Ctr., 200 Vesey St. (West St.), 212-571-2001
www.getcosi.com
Additional locations throughout the NY area
It's all about the "crackly" goodness of the "hearth-baked flatbread" and "versatile" stuffings at this "serviceable" sandwich chain; even though it's "not the cheapest" and the "assembly-line" service can be "bumbling", the daily "lunch stampedes" speak for themselves.

Cosmic Cantina ◐≠   19 | 8 | 13 | $12
101 Third Ave. (bet. 12th & 13th Sts.), 212-420-0975
A "college student's paradise", this East Village Mexican vends "organic" yet "oh-so-tasty" burritos in an "unspectacular" setting; its "beer-pong crowd" shows up because it's open "late" and costwise is "practically free by NYC standards."

Counter ◐   22 | 21 | 20 | $33
105 First Ave. (bet. 6th & 7th Sts.), 212-982-5870; www.counternyc.com
Counter to expectations, this "stylish" East Villager's "unique", "lovingly prepared" vegetarian cuisine is "actually filling" enough to satisfy even "dedicated omnivores"; the "surprisingly sexy" setting, "chill" staff and "all-organic" wine list are further proof that natural can be "pleasurable."

COUNTRY ⑤ NEW   23 | 26 | 21 | VE
Carlton Hotel, 90 Madison Ave., 2nd fl. (29th St.), 212-889-7100
CAFÉ AT COUNTRY ◐ NEW
Carlton Hotel, 90 Madison Ave. (29th St.), 212-889-7100
www.countryinnewyork.com
"Sophistication" is in the air at Geoffrey Zakarian's "sublime" new "splurge" in Gramercy's Carlton Hotel, a place that's certainly "more city than country" with its elegant New American fare, "luxe" looks and "civilized" service; downstairs, the Cafe at Country is a "less formal", more "bustling" option for similarly "upmarket" (but lower-priced) dishes.

Country Café Ⓜ   ▽ 20 | 16 | 20 | $35
69 Thompson St. (bet. Broome & Spring Sts.), 212-966-5417; www.countrycafesoho.com
For an "anti-trendy" SoHo alternative, this "small", "undiscovered" place plies "tasty", "traditional" French–North African plates served by a "smiling" staff; it's "bohemian" and "nothing fancy", but the prices aren't fancy either.

Cowgirl   16 | 18 | 16 | $25
519 Hudson St. (W. 10th St.), 212-633-1133; www.cowgirlnyc.com
"Loosen your belt" for some "good ol' home cooking" at this "cheap and cheerful" Village Southwesterner done up like a "tacky" "honky-tonk"; by day, it's kid central, but sundown brings on a "bawdy" singles scene fueled by "Mason jar margaritas" – "yee haw!"

Cozy Soup & Burger ◐   18 | 8 | 14 | $16
739 Broadway (Astor Pl.), 212-477-5566
"Juicy burgers" "as big as your head", "fantastic split-pea soup" and other "three-napkin staples" make this 24/7 Village diner a "main-

stay" for "midnight munchies"; it's a "no-fuss" joint, though, so try to ignore the "curt" staff and minimal decor.

CRAFT
26 | 24 | 24 | $72

43 E. 19th St. (bet. B'way & Park Ave. S.), 212-780-0880;
www.craftrestaurant.com

"It all comes together" at Tom Colicchio's Flatiron "triumph" where an "inspired", "do-it-yourself menu" of "impeccably crafted" New American choices are served by a "smooth", "informed staff"; the setting is "stylish" (but "not too-too"), and while it requires "ample credit", those who appreciate "food as an art form" consider this one a "sheer joy."

Craftbar
21 | 19 | 20 | $50

900 Broadway (bet. 19th & 20th Sts.), 212-461-4300;
www.craftrestaurant.com

As Craft's "more relaxed" sibling, this Flatiron New American supplies food that's almost as good for a lot less; a "hip" (albeit "hangarlike") setting and "pleasant" service round out an "impressive" performance, even if some say its "old location was better."

Craftsteak NEW
▽ 24 | 26 | 23 | $98

85 10th Ave. (bet. 15th & 16th Sts.), 212-400-6699;
www.craftsteaknyc.com

Tom Colicchio brings his take on steaks to the burgeoning restaurant row on lower 10th Avenue; look for a "large selection" of "expensive" pedigreed chops (whose breed-and-feed provenance is detailed on the menu) served in an "amazing", "high-ceilinged" main room dominated by a towering wine vault; a raw bar, large private room and views of the Hudson River ice the cake.

Crema M NEW
▽ 23 | 21 | 18 | $46

111 W. 17th St. (bet. 6th & 7th Aves.), 212-691-4477;
www.cremarestaurante.com

Julieta Ballesteros' "exciting" Nuevo Mexican cooking "grabs your attention" at this "hot" Chelsea newcomer; its colorful digs are "a far cry" from the typical taqueria, and with margaritas to "fuel the fun", it's becoming a "real destination."

Crispo ●
22 | 18 | 19 | $44

240 W. 14th St. (bet. 7th Ave. S. & 8th Ave.), 212-229-1818;
www.crisporestaurant.com

This "busy" West Village Northern Italian "delivers across the board" with "top-drawer" food served in "rustic" digs enhanced by "welcoming" service and a "piazza"-like, year-round garden; regulars protest it's "getting too popular."

Cru ☒
25 | 22 | 23 | $86

24 Fifth Ave. (9th St.), 212-529-1700; www.cru-nyc.com

Besides a "daunting wine list", this "first-class" Villager also features "superlative" Mediterranean food served by a highly "professional" crew; the "handsome" setting and "intimidating prices" ($85 prix fixe) are no surprise, but "blown-away" boosters just "save up and go"; P.S. a less formal, no-reserving front room is à la carte.

Cuba
21 | 18 | 18 | $35

222 Thompson St. (bet. Bleecker & W. 3rd Sts.), 212-420-7878;
www.cubanyc.com

Devotees dub this Cuban Villager an "island of quality" for its "genuine" "home cooking" and "jumping" "party atmosphere", fueled by "potent mojitos" and live "Latin jazz"; just be prepared for "dark", "loud", "crowded" digs.

Cuba Cafe

18 | 15 | 17 | $32

200 Eighth Ave. (bet. 20th & 21st Sts.), 212-633-1570; www.chelseadining.com
"You're in the tropics" at this "casual" Chelsea Cuban thanks to "satisfying" food, "magic mojitos" and "kitschy", "colorful" decor; though it's "no frills", it does the trick for an authentic, "upbeat" bite "until the embargo is lifted" – and the "price is right."

Cubana Café ●≠

19 | 15 | 18 | $23

110 Thompson St. (bet. Prince & Spring Sts.), 212-966-5366
272 Smith St. (Degraw St.), Brooklyn, 718-858-3980
www.cubanacafeelchulo.com
You get a "taste of old Havana" at these Village/Carroll Gardens Cuban "hangouts" that are "lively" stops for filling up "on the cheap"; "smiling" staffers add to the "cheerful" vibe, though some find the "tight" setups "a little too cozy."

Cube 63 ●

24 | 15 | 17 | $33

63 Clinton St. (bet. Rivington & Stanton Sts.), 212-228-6751 Ⓜ
234 Court St. (bet. Baltic & Warren Sts.), Brooklyn, 718-243-2208 **NEW**
www.cube63.com
It's just a "minimal" "shoebox", but the "scrumptious sushi" at this "green-lit" LES Japanese (and its roomier Cobble Hill spin-off) is a square deal for those seeking "delish" fish "on a budget"; the original's BYO policy "keeps the bill low", while in Brooklyn there's a sake bar.

Cub Room ●

17 | 18 | 16 | $44

131 Sullivan St. (Prince St.), 212-677-4100; www.cubroom.com
A "neighborhood joint" with "lots of energy", this "clubby" SoHo New American is known for its "happening bar" scene and "unassuming", "pretty good" eats; but some growl that the "expensive" tabs and "wayward service" are harder to bear.

Cucina di Pesce ●

17 | 14 | 17 | $27

87 E. Fourth St. (bet. Bowery & 2nd Ave.), 212-260-6800;
www.cucinadipesce.com
Vending "solid" "basic" Italian cooking, this "handy" 20-year-old East Villager is an "incredible value", especially the $11.95 early-bird; still, some say both the cooking and milieu are "pedestrian", but don't tell the "younger" crowd that comes here to stretch a buck.

Curry Leaf

19 | 10 | 15 | $25

99 Lexington Ave. (27th St.), 212-725-5558
151 Remsen St. (bet. Clinton & Court Sts.), Brooklyn, 718-222-3900
www.curryleafnyc.com
"More authentic than many" thanks to "spices by Kalustyan", these "homey" interborough Indians are "easy" options for "reliable" eating "without breaking the bank"; sure, the "tatty" decor could turn over a new leaf, but overall the experience curries most folks' favor.

Da Andrea

23 | 15 | 21 | $33

557 Hudson St. (bet. Perry & W. 11th Sts.), 212-367-1979;
www.biassanot.com
Deemed "dependable" for da-lightful regional dishes and service that "couldn't be any friendlier", this Village Northern Italian is "hard to beat" for "high-end" quality at "'70s prices"; since it's "not so secret" anymore, expect a "tight fit."

Da Antonio ⊠

20 | 16 | 20 | $53

157 E. 55th St. (bet. Lexington & 3rd Aves.), 212-588-1545; www.daantonio.com
The "enticing" specials list "goes on forever" at this "clubby" East Midtowner where "old-world" Italian fare from the "Sinatra" era is

paired with "warm service" and "lively tunes" from a house pianist; it's a "worthy" "sleeper", but no bargain.

Da Ciro
21 | 16 | 19 | $41

229 Lexington Ave. (bet. 33rd & 34th Sts.), 212-532-1636; www.daciro.com

Brick-oven "specialty pizzas" that may be "better than sex" lead a "surprisingly delicious" lineup of "rustic Italian" dishes at this longtime Murray Hill "favorite"; even though it's "on the pricey side", regulars just "can't get enough of it."

Da Dong ●⊠
19 | 14 | 16 | $29

17 W. 32nd St. (bet. B'way & 5th Ave.), 212-967-1900
220-15 Northern Blvd. (220th St.), Queens, 718-631-7100

When "Korean cravings" strike, this low-budget Bayside/Garment District duo saves the dae with "BBQ done right", providing a "spicy medley" "grilled right at the table" (as well as random Japanese items); the wild card is service that's "sometimes great, sometimes not."

Da Filippo
21 | 16 | 21 | $54

1315 Second Ave. (bet. 69th & 70th Sts.), 212-472-6688; www.dafilipporestaurant.com

A "warm welcome" awaits at this "worthwhile" Eastsider where "charmer" owner Carlo Meconi and his "attentive" team offer "traditional" Northern Italiana of "notable quality"; it's "a tad expensive" for a "neighborhoody" place, but then again "you'll never leave hungry."

DAISY MAY'S BBQ USA
23 | 4 | 14 | $19

623 11th Ave. (46th St.), 212-977-1500; www.daisymaysbbq.com

There's now indoor seating at this cafeteria-style Hell's Kitchen joint, dubbed the "real McCoy" (and once again voted NYC's best BBQ) for its L'il Abner–size portions of "lip-smacking" ribs, pork and brisket with "all the fixin's"; if 11th Avenue's not so handy, alternatives include "prompt delivery" and a super street-cart fleet.

Dakshin Indian Bistro
▽ 22 | 11 | 20 | $24

1713 First Ave. (bet. 88th & 89th Sts.), 212-987-9839

"Perfect spicing" makes this "tiny" UES storefront a "find" for "superb Indian food" served with "no attitude" and for "not much money" (its $7.95 buffet "lures in the lunch crowd"); despite an "upgraded interior", many still opt for "takeout."

Dallas BBQ ●
15 | 9 | 13 | $20

3956 Broadway (166th St.), 212-568-3700
261 Eighth Ave. (23rd St.), 212-462-0001
132 Second Ave. (St. Marks Pl.), 212-777-5574
1265 Third Ave. (bet. 72nd & 73rd Sts.), 212-772-9393
241 W. 42nd St. (bet. 7th & 8th Aves.), 212-221-9000 **NEW**
27 W. 72nd St. (bet. Columbus Ave. & CPW), 212-873-2004
180 Livingston St. (bet. Hoyt & Smith Sts.), Brooklyn, 718-643-5700
www.dallasbbq.com

For "utilitarian" BBQ binging, these chain "chicken-and-rib mills" do the trick with "extreme" helpings of "greasy grub" and "Texas-size" drinks served up "fast"; the "chaotic" settings may have "little charm", but hey, they're "so cheap it's almost free."

Danal
21 | 21 | 19 | $37

90 E. 10th St. (bet. 3rd & 4th Aves.), 212-982-6930

"Simple pleasures" are the signature of this "idiosyncratic" East Villager serving "fine" French-Med food at "sensible" prices; the "country-shabby" interior and "pretty" garden are as "comfy" as a "favorite sweater", and it's a "perennial brunch favorite" too.

F	D	S	C

Dani NEW
▽ 20 | 20 | 17 | $49

333 Hudson St. (Charlton St.), 212-633-9333; www.danirestaurant.com
"Sicilian style" enlivens the "high-end" cooking at this affordable new West SoHo Med from ex–Tribeca Grill chef Don Pintabona, who sure "knows his stuff"; the "airy" space attracts a "convivial" crowd that feels it's "much needed" but suggests curbing the "noise level."

Da Nico
20 | 17 | 18 | $35

164 Mulberry St. (bet. Broome & Grand Sts.), 212-343-1212;
www.danicoristorante.com
Popular with "tourists" and the "family set", this Little Italy Italian is a "solid bet" for "generous portions" of "old-school" dishes doused with "plenty of red sauce"; "amusing waiters" add appeal, but in warm weather the "real draw" is that "wonderful" large garden.

DANIEL ⧄
28 | 28 | 28 | $112

60 E. 65th St. (bet. Madison & Park Aves.), 212-288-0033; www.danielnyc.com
A "total experience for the senses", Daniel Boulud's East Side "tour de force" (voted No. 2 for Food and No. 1 for Decor) inspires "awe" with its "incomparable" New French menu, "exceptional wine list", "read-your-mind" service and "opulent" room; epicures who feel "like a million bucks" put their money where their mouth is, trading in their "retirement savings" for the "phenomenal tasting menu."

Da Noi
23 | 19 | 22 | $43

4358 Victory Blvd. (Westshore Expwy.), Staten Island, 718-982-5040
Ok, it's way out "in the boonies", but this "congenial" Staten Islander is "more than just a standard" Northern Italian given its modest prices for "ample helpings" of "outstanding" grub; "inviting" but "busy", it draws brickbats for da noise and the wearying "weekend waits."

DANUBE ◑⧄
26 | 27 | 25 | $86

30 Hudson St. (bet. Duane & Reade Sts.), 212-791-3771; www.davidbouley.com
To "dine like a Hapsburg", try David Bouley's "august" Austrian "fantasy" in TriBeCa, a "culinary marvel" for "sumptuous, smart" Viennese dining with a French twist topped off with "heavenly" desserts; the "gracious" service and "enchanting", Klimt-esque backdrop make the "fin de siècle" "come to life", so the "élan" is "worth the money", especially if you waltz in early for a warm-up in the "sexy" bar.

Darna
▽ 21 | 19 | 17 | $37

600 Columbus Ave. (89th St.), 212-721-9123
It's "no small achievement" to turn out "worthy" kosher fare, but this "attractive" Upper West Side French-Moroccan manages to keep the observant "satisfied" for a "reasonable price"; "somewhat inattentive" service aside, there's darn "little to kvetch about" here.

Da Silvano ◑
20 | 15 | 17 | $60

260 Sixth Ave. (bet. Bleecker & Houston Sts.), 212-982-2343;
www.dasilvano.com
"Page Six"–ready types packed "fork-to-fork" exchange "*ciao bellas*" at Silvano Marchetto's "sceney" Villager where the "memorable" Tuscan fare and "prime outdoor cafe" seating justify the "buzz"; if you "need resuscitation when they bring the check", the "more casual" Bar Pitti next door offers "better value."

Da Tommaso ◑
20 | 13 | 20 | $44

903 Eighth Ave. (bet. 53rd & 54th Sts.), 212-265-1890
Sure, the style's "low-key", but this Theater District stalwart is "unexpectedly charming" thanks to a "welcoming" owner and "well-prepared" Northern Italian "classics"; maybe the "dated" decor "could stand a face-lift", but the otherwise "comforting" routine "satisfies."

Da Umberto ☒   24 | 18 | 22 | $57
107 W. 17th St. (bet. 6th & 7th Aves.), 212-989-0303
"Grown-up" diners dub this "refined" Chelsea Tuscan a "mini-vacation"
for "delectable" food and "superlative service" that are both "finely
tuned" to "make sure that you're happy"; it's "pitiless on the wallet"
and the "old-fashioned" ambiance may be a bit "sleepy", but most
are "duly impressed" that the formula "still works" infallibly.

DAVIDBURKE & DONATELLA   25 | 23 | 23 | $73
133 E. 61st St. (bet. Lexington & Park Aves.), 212-813-2121;
www.dbdrestaurant.com
"Food as art" sums up chef David Burke's "brilliance" at this East
Side "powerhouse" where the "memorable" New American fare and
"divine" desserts are an "embarrassment of delights"; a "tricked-up"
townhouse setting and "meticulous service" under dreamboat
Donatella Arpaia's guidance help ease the "sticker shock", while the
$24 prix fixe lunch is a way to feel "privileged" for less.

David Burke at Bloomingdale's NEW   19 | 15 | 14 | $30
Bloomingdale's, 150 E. 59th St. (bet. Lexington & 3rd Aves.), 212-705-3800;
www.burkeinthebox.com
Another "reason to go shopping", this "snappy" new stop in
Bloomie's features a conjoined cafe and a "fast-food" self-seater
both offering David Burke's "playful" New American fare; despite
"narrow" dimensions and "disorganized" service, many buy into
this "promising concept."

Dawat   23 | 18 | 20 | $45
210 E. 58th St. (bet. 2nd & 3rd Aves.), 212-355-7555
"Gourmet" Indian dining is alive and well at this East Midtown standby
from actress/chef Madhur Jaffrey, which tenders a "marvelous"
array of "full-bodied" dishes; "pro service" ups da "crowd-pleaser"
wattage, even if the decor and prices dim some diners' delight.

DB BISTRO MODERNE   25 | 21 | 23 | $62
City Club Hotel, 55 W. 44th St. (bet. 5th & 6th Aves.), 212-391-2400;
www.danielnyc.com
Daniel Boulud's bustling Theater District French bistro "lives up to
its billing" with "superlative" cuisine (including the "much-hyped"
$29 "designer burger") that's enhanced by "urbane" environs and
"smooth service"; it's a "popular", "high-energy" scene and "you do
pay for it", but the $42 prix fixe early-bird is bargain-basement Boulud.

Deborah Ⓜ   22 | 15 | 21 | $34
43 Carmine St. (bet. Bedford & Bleecker Sts.), 212-242-2606;
www.deborahlifelovefood.com
"Restaurants don't come much smaller – or much friendlier" –
than this Village "shoebox" where chef Deborah Stanton prepares
"delish", "super-fresh" New Americana; fans wonder why it's
still such a "secret" given the "cute" back garden and "big bang
for the buck."

Dee's Brick Oven Pizza   22 | 19 | 20 | $26
107-23 Metropolitan Ave. (74th Ave.), Queens, 718-793-7553;
www.deesnyc.com
It's "easy to become a regular" at this "agreeable" Forest Hills pizzeria given its "fantastic" thin-crust pies and "consistent" Med-style
pastas; the premises are now "more spacious" following a move,
though the "family" crowds, drawn by the excellent quality-to-price
ratio, keep the volume "loud."

DeGrezia ☒
23 20 24 $55

231 E. 50th St. (bet. 2nd & 3rd Aves.), 212-750-5353
Despite its sub–street level site, this East Side Italian is worth seeking out for "terrific", "traditional" fare and "gracious" service in an "old-world" setting; its "middle-aged" crowd calls it "first-class" all the way – so long as "money isn't an obstacle."

Degustation ☒ NEW
▽ 25 22 26 $48

239 E. Fifth St. (bet. 2nd & 3rd Aves.), 212-979-1012
"Another hit" for Jewel Bako's Jack and Grace Lamb, this "tiny" new East Villager stations patrons at a 16-seat bar built around an open kitchen that puts out a variety of "fascinating" French and Spanish small plates that "make sense of the strangest combinations"; add "attentive" servers and you're assured of a "personalized treat."

Delegates' Dining Room ☒
17 20 17 $38

United Nations, 4th fl. (1st Ave. & 45th St.), 212-963-7626
The East River "views are spectacular" and the clientele "fascinating" at this sprawling U.N. Eclectic where "ambassadors of all nations" feast on "lavish" $25 lunch buffets (weekdays only); despite the "lack-luster" eats, the "experience" is worth the "security drama."

DEL FRISCO'S ❶
25 22 23 $66

1221 Sixth Ave. (49th St.), 212-575-5129; www.delfriscos.com
As a "splashy", "testosterone-charged" "biz scene", this Midtown mega–steak palace draws lots of "suits" hungry for "top-shelf", "Texas-size steaks" and "prime service"; those not on an "expense account" should "start saving up" or opt for the "cheapie" $39.95 pre-theater menu; P.S. check out those spectacular party rooms.

Delhi Palace
▽ 21 13 16 $22

37-33 74th St. (bet. 37th Ave. & 37th Rd.), Queens, 718-507-0666
You'll "eat like a rajah" for not a lot of rupees at this Jackson Heights Indian known for its "excellent" $7.95 lunch buffet and "splendid" regional specialties topped off by the "best sweets"; a "pleasant" atmosphere (i.e. "without the Jackson Diner crowds") seals the deal.

Delmonico's ☒
22 21 22 $58

56 Beaver St. (S. William St.), 212-509-1144;
www.delmonicosny.com
"It's not hard to imagine robber barons" supping at this circa-1827 Financial District "legend" known for its "superior steaks", "excellent" service and "old-world" setting; it's "best when someone else is paying", but young turks tout the "affordable bar menu."

DEL POSTO NEW
23 26 23 $90

85 10th Ave. (16th St.), 212-497-8090; www.delposto.com
The Batali-Bastianich juggernaut takes an ultra-"civilized" turn (think "Babbo meets Bouley") with the arrival of this "grand" new Way West Chelsea powerhouse, a "peaceful" marble-and-mahogany extravaganza that's one of the year's best newcomers with "nice spacing between tables" and "upscale" touches like valet parking and a piano player; the modern Italian menu is "haute", tabs are "stiff" and "head mama" Lidia Bastianich is on board, so there's a more "formal" approach; P.S. check out the primo private rooms.

Delta Grill ❶
19 15 17 $31

700 Ninth Ave. (48th St.), 212-956-0934; www.thedeltagrill.com
NOLA natives "leave smiling" from this "ragin'" Cajun-Creole in Hell's Kitchen, where the "enormous" dishes are both "consistently good" and cheap; come weekends, the "excellent" brunch and live music ratchet up an "eat-drink-and-be-merry" vibe.

Demarchelier

17	16	16	$45

50 E. 86th St. (bet. Madison & Park Aves.), 212-249-6300;
www.demarchelierrestaurant.com
Carnegie Hill regulars call this comfortable French standby near
Museum Mile "Uptown's answer to Raoul's"; "snooty" service and
"frayed" decor are offset by "tasty" cooking and prices that "aren't
bad for the neighborhood."

Demetris ●

∇	24	17	21	$34

32-11 Broadway (bet. 32nd & 33rd Sts.), Queens, 718-278-1877
"You can't go wrong" with the "wonderful seafood" specialties at this
"top-notch", moderately priced Astoria Hellenic; fans say the
"taverna-style" setting, "attentive" service and "good" live music will
"whisk you to the Greek isles."

Denino's Pizzeria ≠

24	8	16	$18

524 Port Richmond Ave. (bet. Hooker Pl. & Walker St.), Staten Island,
718-442-9401
Loyal subjects crown this "family-friendly" 70-year-old Staten Islander
the "king of pizzerias" for its "perpetually perfect" pies washed down
with "cold brews"; "long" waits and "loud patrons" notwithstanding,
it's "worth the tolls and traffic" for the "exceptional" ciao.

Dervish Turkish ●

19	15	19	$35

146 W. 47th St. (bet. 6th & 7th Aves.), 212-997-0070;
www.dervishrestaurant.com
An "unbeatable" $22.95 early-bird dinner caps this "dependable"
Turkish "delight" that adds a "touch of exotica" to the Theater
District; with "delicious" dishes, "accommodating" service and a
"comfortable" (albeit "not elegant") setting, it's a "great alternative"
for "bargain-hunters."

Destino NEW

∇	17	18	17	$58

891 First Ave. (50th St.), 212-751-0700; www.destinony.com
With Justin Timberlake as an investor and a former Rao's chef at
the stove, it's no wonder this "energetic" red-sauce Italian has
brought a "happening" vibe to sleepy Sutton Place; still, surveyors
split on the food ("tasty" vs. "nothing special") and hope they can fix
the "frazzled" service.

Deux Amis

19	15	19	$46

356 E. 51st St. (bet. 1st & 2nd Aves.), 212-230-1117
Locals laud this "old-fashioned" East Side bistro for its "solid" French
fare, "charming" owner and "pleasant" setting that includes an "excellent" outdoor terrace; parvenus protest it's "typical" with "*comme
ci, comme ça*" cuisine.

dévi

24	22	21	$55

8 E. 18th St. (bet. B'way & 5th Ave.), 212-691-1300; www.devinyc.com
"Culinary wizards" Suvir Saran and Hemant Mathur are behind this
"serious" Flatiron Indian serving "sumptuous" yet "refined" dishes that
"match the best in London"; "lush", "pretty-as-a-picture" decor and
"knowledgeable" service add to the "high-end", "high-priced" mood.

Devin Tavern NEW

–	–	–	E

363 Greenwich St. (bet. Franklin & Harrison Sts.), 212-334-7337;
www.devintavern.com
Purveying a mix of upscale and casual fare – from seafood and steaks
to sandwiches and ribs – this roomy new TriBeCa New American is
set in elegantly spare digs that juxtapose exposed brick with blonde
wood; the spacious, bi-level setting also includes a downstairs
lounge and a pair of private rooms.

Diablo Royale ◑
18 | 17 | 16 | $36

189 W. 10th St. (bet. Bleecker & W. 4th Sts.), 212-620-0223;
www.diabloroyale.com
A "new hot spot with a cool vibe", this "saloon"-like Villager supplies
"tasty, refined" Mexicana accompanied by "margaritas that make
everything go down easy"; drawbacks include "careless" service
and occasional "overpricing."

DI FARA ⊐
26 | 4 | 10 | $12

1424 Ave. J (15th St.), Brooklyn, 718-258-1367
"Maestro" Dominic De Marco "works magic" at this circa-1963
Midwood pizzeria offering "handcrafted", "epiphany"-producing
pies made with "totally fresh ingredients"; despite "seedy" decor,
"painfully long" waits and a "middle-of-nowhere" address, it's got
"da best pizza in Noo Yawk."

Dim Sum Go Go
20 | 12 | 14 | $21

5 E. Broadway (Chatham Sq.), 212-732-0797
The "delightful" dim sum is ordered off a menu and served "all day"
at this "modern" Chinatown joint; though traditionalists "miss
the carts", far more tout the "fresh" offerings, "speedy" service
and "great prices."

Diner ◑
22 | 18 | 17 | $27

85 Broadway (Berry St.), Brooklyn, 718-486-3077;
www.dinernyc.com
Williamsburg's "first and best" renovated diner is "always hopping",
a "perfect hipster date spot" where "tattooed and pierced servers"
deliver "inventive" New Americana and "unforgettable burgers";
brunch is a "hot scene with lines to match."

Dinosaur Bar-B-Que Ⓜ
22 | 16 | 18 | $28

646 W. 131st St. (12th Ave.), 212-694-1777;
www.dinosaurbarbque.com
To "release your inner carnivore", try this big, "raucous" BBQ joint
that's "worth the trek" to West Harlem for "addictive" pulled pork,
ribs and sides served in a "Disney Frontierland" setting; be sure to
"make a reservation" as it "gets packed on weekends."

Dirty Bird to-go ⊠ NEW
∇ 17 | 6 | 9 | $15

204 W. 14th St. (bet. 7th Ave. S. & 8th Ave.), 212-620-4836;
www.dirtybirdtogo.com
This tiny new Village take-out spot from Jack's Luxury Oyster Bar alums
Allison Vines-Rushing and Slade Rushing offers free-range chicken
that's brined and double-dipped, then fried or rotisseried; despite the
unfortunate name, early word is "they're trying hard"; stay tuned.

Dishes
22 | 11 | 12 | $16

6 E. 45th St. (bet. 5th & Madison Aves.), 212-687-5511 ⊠
Grand Central, lower level (42nd St. & Vanderbilt Ave.), 212-808-5511
Devotion to these "high-end" Midtown lunch joints "verges on the re-
ligious" thanks to their "huge variety" of "attractive" soups, sandwiches and salads; though the prices "add up", they are typically
"mobbed" at peak hours, so "expect to wait."

District
19 | 19 | 20 | $54

Muse Hotel, 130 W. 46th St. (bet. 6th & 7th Aves.), 212-485-2999;
www.themusehotel.com
"Hidden" in Times Square's Muse Hotel, this "romantic" New American
offers a "tasty" pre-theater prix fixe presented in an "ultramodern",
David Rockwell–designed setting; service is "attentive" though "variable", and fans love the after-dinner "treat bags."

Ditch Plains ●🆕   ▽ 17 | 16 | 17 | $40

29 Bedford St. (Downing St.), 212-633-0202; www.ditch-plains.com
Named for a "Montauk surfer beach", Marc Murphy's latest is a "casual" yet stylish Village "clam shack" where you can order "lovingly prepared" seafood from an all-day "mix-and-match menu"; hodads dig the lobster rolls and low wine markup, yet warn that it's still "working out the kinks."

Divino   19 | 15 | 20 | $39

1556 Second Ave. (bet. 80th & 81st Sts.), 212-861-1096;
www.divinoristorante.net
The "owner greets you" and the staff is similarly "welcoming" at this "old-school" Upper Eastsider where they've been dishing out "*delicioso*", "modestly priced" Northern Italian food for 30 years; despite rather "tired" decor, the live "piano music is a delight."

Diwan   21 | 17 | 17 | $33

Helmsley Middletowne, 148 E. 48th St. (bet. Lexington & 3rd Aves.),
212-593-5425; www.diwanrestaurant.com
A favorite of the corporate crowd (and consequently "very busy" midday), this East Midtown Indian supplies "authentic" subcontinental fare that's "very good for the price"; indeed, its all-you-can-eat $13.95 lunch buffet is a "steal."

Django 🅩   21 | 23 | 20 | $51

480 Lexington Ave. (46th St.), 212-871-6600; www.djangorestaurant.com
This bi-level Midtown "oasis" offers an "unusual" mix of French-Med dishes in a "lush", "genie-bottle" setting djazzed up with "sexy" tented areas; the "cool" ground-floor bar exudes "pizzazz", while the upstairs boasts "business-friendly acoustics."

Docks Oyster Bar   19 | 16 | 17 | $46

2427 Broadway (bet. 89th & 90th Sts.), 212-724-5588
633 Third Ave. (40th St.), 212-986-8080
www.docksoysterbar.com
Whether you're casting for the "freshest" fish or martinis "you can swim in", these "crowded" seafooders are "reliable if not inspired" places to drop anchor; sure, service can be "hit-or-miss", but tabs are "reasonable", the mood "convivial" and the femme fishing is fine.

Do Hwa   21 | 18 | 17 | $39

55 Carmine St. (bet. Bedford St. & 7th Ave. S.), 212-414-1224;
www.dohwanyc.com
For the "next best thing" to K-town, try this "upscale" Village Korean, a "chic" spot popular for its "clubby" vibe and weekend DJ; despite "North Korean portions at South Korean prices", the food's "delish" and the DIY BBQ a "must."

Dok Suni's ●⇄   21 | 15 | 17 | $28

119 First Ave. (bet. 7th St. & St. Marks Pl.), 212-477-9506
"Flavors that really pop" keep this "well-seasoned" East Village Korean "packed to the rafters" nightly with "hipsters"; it's also a "good date place" thanks to a "casually sexy" vibe and "light-on-the-wallet" pricing, but bear in mind it's cash only.

dominic 🅩   ▽ 21 | 19 | 18 | $44

349 Greenwich St. (bet. Harrison & Jay Sts.), 212-343-0700;
www.dominicnyc.com
Despite solid ratings, this TriBeCa Italian–New American has "never taken off"; though it may "lack personality and ambiance", at least the "kitchen's competent" as reflected by its "worth-the-trip" pig roast.

Dominick's ⊜
`22` `9` `17` `$35`

2335 Arthur Ave. (bet. Crescent Ave. & E. 187th St.), Bronx, 718-733-2807
You must "come hungry and patient" to enjoy this "no-reservations"
Bronx Italian landmark's "huge" portions of "red-sauce" fare at
"communal tables"; despite "no menus" and "no check" (the waiters
tell you "what you want" and what you pay), this "cash-only" joint
makes for such "soul-satisfying" meals that there are always long
lines at prime times.

Dona NEW
▽ `24` `26` `24` `$67`

208 E. 52nd St. (bet. 2nd & 3rd Aves.), 212-308-0830; www.donanyc.com
Hostess with the mostest Donatella Arpaia (davidburke & donatella)
has remade the former Bellini into this "beautiful" newcomer purveying a "creative" mix of Mediterranean items at prices geared to moneyed Midtowners; "fantastic" service comes naturally given
its "perfectionist" owner.

Don Giovanni ●
`18` `11` `15` `$24`

214 10th Ave. (bet. 22nd & 23rd Sts.), 212-242-9054
358 W. 44th St. (bet. 8th & 9th Aves.), 212-581-4939
www.dongiovanni-ny.com
Fans dig the "sublime" brick-oven pizza at these "solid" West Side
Italians where "generous" pasta portions and "good outdoor people-
watching" trump the "flaky" service and "no-frills", "time-warp" decor.

Donguri Ⓜ
`26` `16` `26` `$54`

309 E. 83rd St. (bet. 1st & 2nd Aves.), 212-737-5656; www.itoen.com
Following a "change in ownership", this UES Japanese "still shines",
serving "traditional", "delicate" dishes (but "no sushi") in a "tiny
shoebox" setting; even though "portions are infinitesimal" and prices
"large", fans say it's the "real thing" for "sublime" dining.

Don Pedro's
`21` `17` `20` `$34`

1865 Second Ave. (96th St.), 212-996-3274; www.donpedros.net
"Get your Latin groove on" at this "interesting" UES Caribbean–South
American, a "memorable" retreat in an "underserved area" thanks to
its "unusual combo" of Hispanic dishes; "gracious service" and "affordable" pricing make for good "bang for the buck."

Don Peppe Ⓜ⊜
`24` `11` `19` `$44`

135-58 Lefferts Blvd. (149th Ave.), Queens, 718-845-7587
"Everyone reeks of garlic" at this "old-school", cash-only Italian in
Ozone Park, where the "heavenly", "family-style" food is "plentiful"
and the decor "nonexistent"; you gotta "tuck your napkin in your shirt
collar" to blend in with the "*Sopranos*"-esque crowd.

Dos Caminos
`20` `21` `18` `$43`

373 Park Ave. S. (bet. 26th & 27th Sts.), 212-294-1000 ●
825 Third Ave. (50th St.), 212-336-5400 ● NEW
475 W. Broadway (Houston St.), 212-277-4300
www.brguestrestaurants.com
Usually "jam-packed", Steve Hanson's "party" Mexicans host "major
bar scenes" that can overwhelm the "solid" enough eats; they're renowned for "killer" guacamole made tableside, "*muy excellente*"
margaritas and a "slow" but "exceptionally attractive" staff; P.S. an
East Midtown branch is in the works.

Downtown Atlantic Ⓜ
`20` `17` `20` `$31`

364 Atlantic Ave. (bet. Bond & Hoyt Sts.), Brooklyn, 718-852-9945;
www.downtownatlantic.com
"All-around good", this "charming" Boerum Hill New American dishes
out "ample portions" of "tasty", "well-priced" chow in "warm",

"comfy" digs; "outstanding" cupcakes and other "fab" baked goods from its "attached bakery" enhance the "nice surprise."

Doyers Vietnamese
21 | 5 | 13 | $17

11-13 Doyers St., downstairs (Chatham Sq.), 212-513-1521

On a Chinatown "street that time forgot" lies this "hidden" basement Vietnamese where the "flavorful, well-spiced" food is served for "hard-to-beat" prices; given the year-round "Christmas decorations", fans either "close their eyes and eat", or opt for the "incredibly fast" delivery.

Dressler NEW
– | – | – | E

149 Broadway (bet. Bedford & Driggs Aves.), Brooklyn, 718-384-6343; www.dresslernyc.com

Williamsburg grows up a little with the arrival of this "classy" New American opposite Peter Luger, where the "inventive plates" are already producing "long waits"; the "beautiful" retro digs complement the "excellent" kitchen, so even though it's "expensive" for the area, it couldn't be more "welcome."

Duane Park Cafe
23 | 18 | 23 | $50

157 Duane St. (bet. Hudson St. & W. B'way), 212-732-5555; www.duaneparkcafe.com

"Thoroughly underrated" and "overshadowed by its glitzier neighbors", this "hype-free" TriBeCa New American is such a "sleeper" that "you can actually hear yourself speak"; "simple yet sumptuous" dishes and a "caring" staff compensate for its "somewhat sterile" looks.

Dublin 6 Wine & Dine NEW
– | – | – | M

575 Hudson St. (bet. Bank & W. 11th Sts.), 646-638-2900; www.dublin6nyc.com

Replacing a low-key Irish bar, this spruced-up West Village newcomer turns out a diverse, midpriced New American menu in the main dining area or in an adjacent wine bar; a cozy fireplace and breezy sidewalk seats lend seasonal appeal.

Due ◑
21 | 16 | 20 | $42

1396 Third Ave. (bet. 79th & 80th Sts.), 212-772-3331

"Casual dining still manages to impress" at this "popular" UES Northern Italian, an "unpretentious" "neighborhood" hangout that draws "older" types with "reliable" grub at "get-your-money's-worth" prices; news flash: they now accept plastic.

DuMont
23 | 20 | 19 | $27

432 Union Ave. (bet. Devoe St. & Metropolitan Ave.), Brooklyn, 718-486-7717

DuMont Burger ◑NEW

314 Bedford Ave. (bet. S. 1st & 2nd Sts.), Brooklyn, 718-384-6127 www.dumontrestaurant.com

"Dine with hipsters" on "dressed-up comfort food" (think "amazing" burgers, "divine" mac 'n' cheese) at this Williamsburg New American where the "cramped quarters" are more bearable when the back garden is open; P.S. the new Bedford Avenue branch offers an abbreviated sandwich menu.

Dumpling Man ◑⇗
19 | 9 | 14 | $11

100 St. Marks Pl. (bet. Ave. A & 1st Ave.), 212-505-2121; www.dumplingman.com

"Heaven on a budget" for "starving students", this "tiny" East Villager vends "addictive", "handmade" steamed dumplings; the "simple", "nothing-special" setup ("basically a deli counter without the deli") makes it a natural for "takeout."

Dylan Prime
24 | 23 | 22 | $61

62 Laight St. (Greenwich St.), 212-334-4783; www.dylanprime.com
A "great alternative to New York's aged steakhouses", this "darkly handsome" TriBeCan draws a crowd of "Downtown movers and shakers" with a "sexy interior" and "lively" mood; its "simple pleasures" menu and "phenomenal bar scene" make up for those "expense-account" prices.

East Buffet
19 | 13 | 13 | $26

42-07 Main St. (Maple Ave.), Queens, 718-353-6333; www.eastusa.com
This Flushing "eating orgy" is "how an all-you-can-eat buffet should be": "fresh", "well presented" and a "great value", with over 200 Eclectic-Asian dishes up for grabs; despite the "rude" service and especially "chaotic throngs" on Sundays and holidays, it's "fun for the family."

East Manor
▽ 18 | 14 | 14 | $25

46-45 Kissena Blvd. (Laburnum Ave.), Queens, 718-888-8998
The buffet is "fresh" and the variety "fabulous" at this "crazy" Flushing Chinese where "dim sum mania" at lunch and on weekends can lead to "long waits"; drawbacks include "tacky" "catering hall" decor, "lacking" service and "chaotic" takeout.

East of Eighth ◐
16 | 16 | 18 | $30

254 W. 23rd St. (bet. 7th & 8th Aves.), 212-352-0075;
www.eastofeighth.com
Both "families and Chelsea boys" patronize this Eclectic neighborhood "staple" for its "decent", "something-for-everyone" menu that's "modestly" priced; a "terrific" back garden and lots of "eye candy" at the bar are respites from the "drab" interior.

E.A.T.
19 | 11 | 13 | $38

1064 Madison Ave. (bet. 80th & 81st Sts.), 212-772-0022;
www.elizabar.com
Eli Zabar's "dependable" UES diner may be a no-brainer for a "post-museum lunch", but even those who say "scrumptious" are abashed by the "eye-popping" tabs; "bored servers" and "air-travel" seating don't help matters, but "great people-watching" and "devilishly good" bread do.

Eatery ◐
19 | 17 | 16 | $30

798 Ninth Ave. (53rd St.), 212-765-7080; www.eaterynyc.com
"Hip and fun", this "stylish" Hell's Kitchen New American serves "upscale" comfort food (including a "rock-the-house mac 'n' cheese") to a "loud young" crowd; but rappers knock the "too-tight" tables, "hipper-than-thou" servers and waits for the "fine brunch."

Ecco ☒
22 | 17 | 20 | $51

124 Chambers St. (bet. Church St. & W. B'way), 212-227-7074
"Even Don Corleone would be pleased" by this "old-fashioned" TriBeCa Italian where the tile floors, tin ceiling and "awesome" ancient bar give off a "historic", saloonlike vibe; despite "attentive" service and "nuanced" red-sauce fare, it's "rarely crowded."

Edison Cafe ⋈
14 | 8 | 12 | $20

Edison Hotel, 228 W. 47th St. (bet. B'way & 8th Ave.), 212-840-5000
There's "nothing canned or phony" about this "faded" Theater District coffee shop where authentically "surly" waiters serve "heavy", "cheap" Jewish grub to show folk and tourists; so long as you don't mind the "total lack of decor", the "Polish Tea Room always satisfies", and you may get a glimpse of the chorus line of the show you just saw.

EJ's Luncheonette ⌺
16 | 10 | 14 | $21

447 Amsterdam Ave. (bet. 81st & 82nd Sts.), 212-873-3444
1271 Third Ave. (73rd St.), 212-472-0600
These "bustling faux-diners" may be "*too* kid-friendly", but are still "dependable" for "big plates" of "basic" Americana, notably the all-day "killer breakfasts"; however, given the "rushed" service and "cramped tables", it's "comfort food without the comfort."

Elaine's ◖
12 | 13 | 13 | $50

1703 Second Ave. (bet. 88th & 89th Sts.), 212-534-8103
Still channeling "'70s NY", Elaine Kaufman's longtime UES Italian-American is "more about famous people–watching" than the "adequate" food and "indifferent" service; but even though "you can't eat celebrity", the joint is still "packed every night" – go figure.

El Centro ◖NEW
▽ 17 | 18 | 16 | $27

824 Ninth Ave. (54th St.), 646-763-6585
A "nice addition to the barrio", this new Hell's Kitchen Mexican set in the "old Vynl space" purveys "cheap" traditional street food in "small but filling" portions; the "crafty", "folkloric" furnishings (e.g. the Corona bottle chandelier) make for a "cheery" vibe.

El Charro Español
▽ 23 | 14 | 22 | $40

4 Charles St. (bet. Greenwich Ave. & 7th Ave. S.), 212-242-9547;
www.el-charro-espanol.com
This "garlicky" Greenwich Villager has somehow remained "under the radar" despite serving "delicious, unpretentious" Spanish food and "underpriced" steaks since 1925; the "hole-in-the-wall" basement setting "could use a face-lift", but ultimately fans "hope it never changes."

El Cid Ⓜ
22 | 11 | 19 | $36

322 W. 15th St. (bet. 8th & 9th Aves.), 212-929-9332
Known for "tapas before tapas was fashionable", this longtime Chelsea Spaniard serves "traditional" dishes that are truly "authentic"; it may be "smaller than your apartment" with "pure schlock" decor, but it's "great for a group that wants to get drunk."

Elephant, The ◖
21 | 17 | 15 | $33

58 E. First St. (bet. 1st & 2nd Aves.), 212-505-7739;
www.elephantrestaurant.com
Even though folks are "packed in like sardines" at this ironically named, ultra-"tiny" East Villager, the "unusual" Thai-French cooking is still "worth checking out"; "great drinks" come in handy since you "can't hear a word of conversation."

Elephant & Castle ◖
17 | 14 | 17 | $25

68 Greenwich Ave. (7th Ave. S. & W. 11th St.), 212-243-1400;
www.elephantandcastle.com
As "comfortable as an old shoe", this "cheap and cheerful" Villager can be counted on for "tasty" American diner classics, served by a "friendly" staff; "always crowded", it's a particularly "tight squeeze" for its "fantastic" brunch.

ELEVEN MADISON PARK
26 | 26 | 25 | $66

11 Madison Ave. (24th St.), 212-889-0905;
www.elevenmadisonpark.com
"Sublime" food, "impeccable" service and a "swank", high-ceilinged deco setting "all come together" at Danny Meyer's "touch-of-class" New American off Madison Square Park; it "hasn't skipped a beat" under new exec chef Daniel Humm, remaining "reliable" for a "special occasion" that's "expensive but worth it."

El Faro ● Ⓜ
21 | 10 | 17 | $37

823 Greenwich St. (Horatio St.), 212-929-8210; www.elfaronyc.com
Talk about a "blast from the past" – this "been-around-forever"
Village Spaniard stays "packed" thanks to its "classic" paella,
sangria and just about anything with green sauce on it; sure, it's
"shabby" verging on "grungy", but diehards declare "if it ain't broke,
don't fix it."

Eliá Ⓜ
▽ 25 | 20 | 22 | $46

8611 Third Ave. (bet. 86th & 87th Sts.), Brooklyn, 718-748-9891
It may be Bay Ridge, but "you'll think you're in Santorini" at this "unpretentious", family-run taverna supplying "serious Greek cuisine"
and "warm service" in "relaxing" digs; regulars say the "sensational"
fish tastes best at a table in the garden.

Elias Corner ● ⇄
21 | 8 | 14 | $35

24-02 31st St. (24th Ave.), Queens, 718-932-1510
The seafood is "straight off the boat, and so are the waiters" at this
"bustling" Astoria Greek renowned for its "brilliant grilled fish"; fans
applaud the "huge" portions, but settle for "no menus, no decor", no
credit cards and "nonexistent" service.

Elio's
23 | 16 | 19 | $58

1621 Second Ave. (bet. 84th & 85th Sts.), 212-772-2242
"Celebs" and "blue bloods" are always welcome at this "clubby,
classy" UES Italian, though mere mortals should "go with a regular"
to avoid a "long wait" and a "table in the back"; devotees dig the
"simple, amazingly good" food, and write off the "expensive" tabs.

El Malecon
21 | 8 | 15 | $17

764 Amsterdam Ave. (bet. 97th & 98th Sts.), 212-864-5648
4141 Broadway (175th St.), 212-927-3812 ●
5592 Broadway (231st St.), Bronx, 718-432-5155 ●
www.maleconrestaurants.com
"Totally satisfying, rib-sticking" grub (highlighted by an "addictive rotisserie chicken") at "ridiculously low" prices makes this Dominican
trio a no-brainer for bargain-hunters; since there's "no atmosphere"
and "little English" spoken, many opt for "fast delivery."

elmo ●
16 | 19 | 15 | $32

156 Seventh Ave. (bet. 19th & 20th Sts.), 212-337-8000;
www.elmorestaurant.com
"Go for the visuals, not the victuals" at this affordable Chelsea New
American where the '50s "airport lounge" decor serves as a "cruis-
ing" ground for "beautiful boys" (and random girls); brunch and the
"bar scene" get high marks, not the "loud" acoustics.

El Parador Cafe
22 | 16 | 22 | $41

325 E. 34th St. (bet. 1st & 2nd Aves.), 212-679-6812;
www.elparadorcafe.com
This Murray Hill Mexican "has been there forever for a good reason":
its "authentic", "richly flavored" cooking jazzed up with "dynamite
margaritas"; given its "welcoming" mien, fans don't mind the "iso-
lated location" and '50s "time-warp" setting.

El Paso Taqueria
23 | 10 | 16 | $22

64 E. 97th St. (Park Ave.), 212-996-1739
1642 Lexington Ave. (104th St.), 212-831-9831 ●
"*Muy autentico*", these UES Mexicans offer dishes brimming with
"amazingly complex flavors" at good "bang-for-the-buck" tabs;
locals and "Mt. Sinai students" keep them busy, even if service and
decor "need improvement."

El Pote ⊠

22 | 13 | 21 | $39

718 Second Ave. (bet. 38th & 39th Sts.), 212-889-6680

After 30 years, the staff "treats everyone like family" at this "cozy", "old-world" Murray Hill Spaniard; ok, it's a little "sleepy", with an "uninviting exterior" and "generic" decor, but the moderately priced cuisine is "classic" and the paella "fabulous."

El Quijote ●

19 | 14 | 17 | $38

226 W. 23rd St. (bet. 7th & 8th Aves.), 212-929-1855

"Lobster, garlic and cocktails – that's all you need to know" about this "nostalgic" Chelsea Spaniard "original" with "tired yet seductively retro" decor; fans love the "mammoth" helpings, "happy mood" and good "value", if not the "frenetic" service.

Emack & Bolio's ∇

25 | 10 | 17 | $7

389 Amsterdam Ave. (bet. 78th & 79th Sts.), 212-362-2747 ●
1564A First Ave. (bet. 81st & 82nd Sts.), 212-734-0105 ●
56 Seventh Ave. S. (bet. 13th & 14th Sts.), 212-727-1198 ●
73 W. Houston St. (W. B'way), 212-533-5610 ●
21-50 31st St. (bet. Ditmars Blvd. & 21st Ave.), Queens, 718-278-5380
www.emackandbolios.com

For "creamy", "dreamy" ice cream and "incredible" frozen yogurt in "every flavor imaginable", check out this Boston-based mini-chain; although fairly "expensive" for what it is, analysts advise it's "cheaper by the pint."

Embers

21 | 14 | 17 | $41

9519 Third Ave. (bet. 95th & 96th Sts.), Brooklyn, 718-745-3700

Some call this Bay Ridge "slabatorium" the "poor man's Peter Luger" thanks to its "really fine" but "moderately priced" steaks; still, cynics nix the "pinky ring" crowd and "tight" tables – "if I wanted to eat my neighbor's food, I would have ordered it."

Empanada Mama ● NEW

∇ 21 | 11 | 15 | $11

763 Ninth Ave. (bet. 51st & 52nd Sts.), 212-698-9008

Hell's Kitchen's latest "fad joint", this "small" South American offers 20-plus "creative" varieties of empanadas (including dessert versions) for less than your mama charges; just be careful: "no one can eat just one", 'cause they're so darn "addictive."

Empire Diner ●

15 | 14 | 14 | $23

210 10th Ave. (22nd St.), 212-243-2736

A bona fide "Chelsea icon", this circa-1929 "retro classic" dishes out "diner food in a real diner" (or on "wonderful" sidewalk seats) 24/7; granted, service can be "iffy", but "what do you expect in the middle of the night?"

Empire Szechuan

15 | 9 | 13 | $21

2642 Broadway (100th St.), 212-662-9404 ●
4041 Broadway (bet. 170th & 171st Sts.), 212-568-1600 ●
193 Columbus Ave. (bet. 68th & 69th Sts.), 212-496-8778 ●
15 Greenwich Ave. (bet. Christopher & W. 10th Sts.), 212-691-1535 ●
173 Seventh Ave. S. (bet. Perry & W. 11th Sts.), 212-243-6046 ●
251 W. 72nd St. (bet. B'way & West End Ave.), 212-873-2151

This "omnipresent" chain is best known for its "adequate", "bargain"-priced Chinese cooking featuring "lots of variety"; while its all-over-town locations "differ in quality" and some serve sushi, most avoid the "indifferent" service and "fluorescent" interiors by calling for "fast" delivery.

Employees Only ◑   17 | 19 | 17 | $44

510 Hudson St. (bet. Christopher & W. 10th Sts.), 212-242-3021;
www.employeesonlynyc.com
The "food is good, but the vibe is better" at this "hip" West Village
European best known for its "amazing" mixology and "speakeasy"
sensibility; indeed, many feel it's "more bar than dining venue", even
though regulars report "impeccably prepared" grub.

Energy Kitchen   17 | 7 | 15 | $12

82 Christopher St. (bet. Bleecker St. & 7th Ave. S.), 212-414-8880
364 Second Ave. (41st St.), 212-687-1200 **NEW**
1089 Second Ave. (bet. 57th & 58th Sts.), 212-888-9300
417 W. 47th St. (bet. 9th & 10th Aves.), 212-333-3500 **NEW**
307 W. 17th St. (bet. 8th & 9th Aves.), 212-645-5200
www.energykitchen.com
"Fast food meets health food" at this fitness-focused mini-chain
where "post-workout" "gym bunnies" flock for "quick, guiltless"
wraps, smoothies and bison burgers; there's "zero decor" and "low
levels of service", but devotees declare it's "great for what it is."

English is Italian   18 | 21 | 18 | $53

622 Third Ave. (40th St.), 212-404-1700; www.chinagrillmgt.com
Todd English's "cavernous" Midtown Italian offers a "family-style"
all-you-can-eat menu that's a "good value" at $39; even if some dis-
miss the experience as "gimmicky", regulars report getting plenty to
eat and the "buffalo mozzarella made tableside" is a must.

EN Japanese Brasserie   21 | 25 | 20 | $55

435 Hudson St. (Leroy St.), 212-647-9196; www.enjb.com
"There's more to Japanese food than raw fish" at this "huge", "sleek"
West Villager where the "sophisticated" tapas-style offerings include
"amazing homemade tofu"; it may be a bit "overpriced" and set "on
the fringes of nowhere", but the overall word is simple – "go."

Ennio & Michael   19 | 16 | 21 | $44

539 La Guardia Pl. (bet. Bleecker & W. 3rd Sts.), 212-677-8577;
www.enniomichael.com
This Village Italian "home-away-from-home" exudes "old-world style"
with "delicious" dishes and a staff that's "been there forever"; it attracts
"flocks of regulars", though some say it needs an "update."

En Plo   22 | 15 | 19 | $43

103 W. 77th St. (Columbus Ave.), 212-579-7777; www.enplonyc.com
"Fabulous fresh fish" and other "authentic" items jazz up the menu of
this "tranquil" Greek seafooder that feels like a "vacation" for Upper
West Side locals; it's "reasonably priced" with "friendly" service,
leading some to wonder "where the crowds are."

Enzo's   24 | 13 | 20 | $34

1998 Williamsbridge Rd. (Neill Ave.), Bronx, 718-409-3828 Ⓜ
2339 Arthur Ave. (bet. Crescent Ave. & 186th St.), Bronx, 718-733-4455 **NEW**
Owner-chef Enzo "greets you himself" at this "real find" in the Bronx
featuring "old-fashioned Italian comfort food" served by a "wonderful"
staff; "no reservations" are taken and there's "not much atmosphere", but it's still a "neighborhood destination"; N.B. the Arthur
Avenue branch opened post-*Survey*.

Epices du Traiteur   20 | 15 | 19 | $40

103 W. 70th St. (Columbus Ave.), 212-579-5904
A "not-so-well-kept secret", this "distinctive" Med-Tunisian near
Lincoln Center is "getting more popular by the minute", hence the "too-

snug" setting; reasons for its success include a "decently priced", "refreshingly different" menu and a "secret garden" out back.

Erawan
23 | 20 | 20 | $34

42-31 Bell Blvd. (bet. 43rd Ave. & Northern Blvd.), Queens, 718-428-2112
213-41 39th Ave. (Bell Blvd.), Queens, 718-229-1620
www.erawan-seafoodandsteak.com
At these "terrific" Bayside "hot spots", the "haute Thai" offerings have such a "Manhattan" taste that they're usually "too crowded for their own good"; the newer 39th Avenue branch offers Siamese twists on steaks and seafood.

Erminia ☒
25 | 23 | 25 | $63

250 E. 83rd St. (bet. 2nd & 3rd Aves.), 212-879-4284
"Romance is the word" at this "tiny", "couples-oriented" UES Italian where "inspired" Roman cuisine, "impeccable" service and a "first-rate" wine list make for "special candlelit occasions"; it's "not cheap" and may have "NY's smallest kitchen", but it's certainly a "memory maker"; P.S. try not to trip over all those guys down on one knee proposing.

Esca ◐
24 | 19 | 21 | $64

402 W. 43rd St. (9th Ave.), 212-564-7272; www.esca-nyc.com
For the "finest fruits of the sea" and al dente pasta "simply prepared", look no further than this Theater District Italian seafooder brought to you by the Batali-Bastianich team; it may be "expensive, but you get what you pay for", so start "hitting redial" now.

Esperanto ◐
21 | 18 | 17 | $30

145 Ave. C (9th St.), 212-505-6559
"Hugely popular", this "festive" East Village Nuevo Latino offers "delectable" eats for the "right price", but it's the "no-joke mojitos" and "live music" that fuel the "party" atmosphere; as for the "beautiful" but slow servers, they're "oblivious to the usual NY rush."

ESPN Zone
12 | 19 | 13 | $29

1472 Broadway (42nd St.), 212-921-3776; www.espnzone.com
"Sports TV addicts unite" at this Times Square athletic-themed triplex that's an "infield hit" with jocks, "hordes of tourists" and "10-year-old boys"; the "indifferent, chain-type service" and "standard" American fare draw penalties here.

Ess-a-Bagel
23 | 6 | 14 | $10

359 First Ave. (21st St.), 212-260-2252
831 Third Ave. (bet. 50th & 51st Sts.), 212-980-1010
www.ess-a-bagel.com
"Load up on those carbs" at this East Side deli duo batting out "Barry Bonds"–size bagels backed up with "dee-lish" spreads and a "schmear of attitude" from the theatrically "surly" schtaff; even the no-decor decor can't dampen these "comfort-food banquets."

Essex ◐ Ⓜ
19 | 18 | 16 | $29

120 Essex St. (Rivington St.), 212-533-9616; www.essexnyc.com
"Young Manhattanites" dig the "urbane vibe" at this "cool" Lower Eastsider, but it's the "boozy", three-drink brunch special that leads many to "skip church"; overall, the Jewish/Latin takes on American grub are "interesting" enough to blot out the "harried" service.

Etats-Unis
25 | 16 | 23 | $56

242 E. 81st St. (bet. 2nd & 3rd Aves.), 212-517-8826
"Cramped" seating and a "limited menu" don't keep fans from flocking to this UES "sleeper keeper" known for "seamlessly prepared" New

Americana and "careful service"; since it carries a "big price tag for such a tiny place", budget-conscious types head across the street to its "charming", less *cher* wine bar.

etcetera etcetera ● Ⓜ

22	20	22	$48

352 W. 44th St. (bet. 8th & 9th Aves.), 212-399-4141; www.etcrestaurant.com

"From the owners of ViceVersa" comes this "unexpectedly chic" Theater District Italian where the "imaginative" menu matches the "monochromatic", "ultramodern" look; "way too loud" acoustics seem to be the only misstep in this otherwise appealing package.

Ethiopian Restaurant

17	12	18	$25

1582 York Ave. (bet. 83rd & 84th Sts.), 212-717-7311

Your "bread's the utensil" at this "casual" Ethiopian set in an "unassuming storefront" on an "off-the-beaten" York Avenue path; it's "cheaper than a safari", and whether the food's "tasty" or "bland", it's always an "unusual experience."

Ethos ●

21	16	19	$37

495 Third Ave. (bet. 33rd & 34th Sts.), 212-252-1972

To save the "trip to Piraeus", just try this "authentic" Murray Hill Hellenic purveying a selection of "fresh whole fish" on ice at an "affordable" price; ok, service is "spotty" and the "casual" quarters "cramped", but the "plentiful" portions offset any complaints.

Euzkadi

20	18	16	$34

108 E. Fourth St. (bet. 1st & 2nd Aves.), 212-982-9788; www.euzkadirestaurant.com

Some show up for the "tasty" Basque eats, others for the "dark", "sexy" setting, but either way it's a "sensual feast" at this East Village Spaniard; "affordable" pricing, a "party" atmosphere and Monday night flamenco make it a magnet for "recently graduated" types.

Evergreen Shanghai

19	11	14	$23

10 E. 38th St. (bet. 5th & Madison Aves.), 212-448-1199
63 Mott St. (bet. Bayard & Canal Sts.), 212-571-3339 ⊄

"Sublime" soup dumplings and dim sum raise these "authentic", Shanghai-style sisters a "chopstick above the rest"; both suffer from "so-so" service and "dismal" settings, though there's rarely a wait at the "huge" Murray Hill outpost.

Excellent Dumpling House ⊄

20	4	11	$14

111 Lafayette St. (bet. Canal & Walker Sts.), 212-219-0212

This longtime "down 'n' dirty" C-towner may put the "dump" in dumpling, but "jury duty" types still convene for its "inexpensive" Shanghainese lunches; regulars stay focused on the "top-notch" namesake specialty – "that's all you really need to know."

Extra Virgin

22	17	17	$40

259 W. Fourth St. (bet. Charles & Perry Sts.), 212-691-9359

Despite a "recent expansion", this "fashionable" West Village Med remains as "snug" as ever, drawing in droves of "beautiful" folk with its "exceptionally well-prepared" cooking, not-bad pricing and "fashion model" staff; the "secret's out", so gird yourself for an "overwhelmingly busy brunch."

Fairway Cafe

19	8	12	$30

2127 Broadway, 2nd fl. (74th St.), 212-595-1888

"Honest" breakfasts and lunches give way to "reliable" steakhouse fare for dinner at this UWS "canteen" above the renowned grocer; sure, the decor's "early diner" and service "consistently inconsistent", but where else can you so affordably "park your cart", eat, then "shop till you drop"?

Falai Ⓜ

| 24 | 18 | 21 | $48 |

68 Clinton St. (bet. Rivington & Stanton Sts.), 212-253-1960; www.falainyc.com

Falai Panetteria Ⓜ NEW

79 Clinton St. (Rivington St.), 212-777-8956

Fans tout the "knockout" menu of this "modernist" Lower East Side Italian, even if both the room and portions are on the "small" side; an equally tiny satellite – serving breakfast, lunch and dinner – just landed across the street and is already garnering praise for its "sure-handed" cuisine.

F & B

| 18 | 10 | 13 | $11 |

150 E. 52nd St. (bet. Lexington & 3rd Aves.), 212-421-8600 Ⓢ
269 W. 23rd St. (bet. 7th & 8th Aves.), 646-486-4441
www.gudtfood.com

"*Gudt* fast food" is dispatched by this "Ikea"-esque "snack-shop" duo whose "European street" eats (frites, beignets, "haute dogs") can be washed down with champagne splits; they're best for takeout since the counter-service setups offer limited seating.

F & J Pine Restaurant ❶≠

| 22 | 19 | 20 | $31 |

1913 Bronxdale Ave. (bet. Morris Park Ave. & White Plains Rd.), Bronx, 718-792-5956

"You get lots of food for the money" at this "red-sauce" Bronx Italian where the "slugger"-size portions work well with the "Yankee memorabilia" and "sports celeb sightings"; not surprisingly, "long waits" and "crowds" are part of the bargain.

Farm on Adderley NEW

| – | – | – | M |

1108 Cortelyou Rd. (bet. Stratford & Westminster Rds.), Brooklyn, 718-287-3101; www.thefarmonadderley.com

Like the name suggests, this low-key New American is bringing farm-inspired dinners to up-and-coming Ditmas Park via a priced-to-move menu made from fresh local ingredients; a friendly vibe and casually intimate setting have made it an instant neighborhood hit.

Fatty Crab ❶ NEW

| 21 | 13 | 15 | $37 |

643 Hudson St. (bet. Gansevoort & Horatio Sts.), 212-352-3590; www.fattycrab.com

"Intense", tapas-style" Malaysian street food can be savored for not much money at Zak Pelaccio's West Village "exotic adventure"; just be prepared to deal with "sardine-can" digs, "deafening music" and a "tragically hip", "air guitar–playing" staff.

FELIDIA

| 25 | 21 | 23 | $69 |

243 E. 58th St. (bet. 2nd & 3rd Aves.), 212-758-1479; www.lidiasitaly.com

TV "matriarch" Lidia Bastianich "continues to inspire" at this "lush" East Side Italian where "mouthwatering pastas" and other "superb" dishes are paired with "out-of-this-world" wines in a "comfortable" townhouse setting; it's "worth the high price of admission" since the black-tie staff really "rolls out the red carpet."

Félix ❶

| 17 | 17 | 14 | $37 |

340 W. Broadway (Grand St.), 212-431-0021; www.felixnyc.com

It's a "never-ending party" at this "vibrant" French bistro, particularly when hordes of "boisterous Euros" turn up for "SoHo's sexiest brunch"; the "just ok" food plays second fiddle to all the "air kissing", "random hookups" and "dancing on tables" here.

Ferdinando's Focacceria ⬛⊅   22 | 11 | 16 | $22

151 Union St. (bet. Columbia & Hicks Sts.), Brooklyn, 718-855-1545
This circa-1904 Carroll Gardens "restaurant that time forgot" provides a "glimpse of Brooklyn of yore" via "unique Sicilian specialties" served in "huge portions"; there's not much decor or service and it's "often closed", so "call ahead" before showing up.

Ferrara ◕   22 | 15 | 15 | $18

195 Grand St. (bet. Mott & Mulberry Sts.), 212-226-6150; www.ferraracafe.com
A "stellar selection" of pastries and espresso awaits at this "stuffa-yo-face" Little Italy pasticceria, on the scene since 1892; despite garish decor and "dismissive" service, it still attracts nostalgic locals as well as "elbow-to-elbow tourists."

Fetch   17 | 17 | 16 | $26

1649 Third Ave. (bet. 92nd & 93rd Sts.), 212-289-2700; www.fetchbarandgrill.com
It helps to "love dogs" at this canine-themed UES American serving "typical" comfort chow in an "easygoing", "kid-friendly" setting; a doggy "wall of fame" (as well as photos of adoptable pooches) passes for decor here, and fortunately the tab won't bite.

FIAMMA OSTERIA   25 | 24 | 24 | $65

206 Spring St. (bet. 6th Ave. & Sullivan St.), 212-653-0100; www.brguestrestaurants.com
Steve Hanson's "high-profile" Italian set in a "chic" SoHo triplex remains "right on the money" thanks to its "richly flavored" fare, "luxe" digs and "exceptional" service; with the "epicurean bliss" extending to the "interesting" wine list, it's no wonder surveyors don't mind "spending quite a bit" here.

50 Carmine ◕   20 | 15 | 18 | $43

50 Carmine St. (bet. Bedford & Bleecker Sts.), 212-206-9134
"Romantic on the right night", "cramped" on the wrong one, this Village Northern Italian exudes a "homey neighborhood" vibe starting with the "warm welcome" at the door; its "authentic flavors" and "swoon"-worthy pastas trump the "boring decor."

Fig & Olive ◕   19 | 17 | 17 | $39

808 Lexington Ave. (bet. 62nd & 63rd Sts.), 212-207-4555; www.figandolive.com
"They really know their olive oil" at this "upscale" Upper Eastsider where the extra-virgin stuff is paired with "inventive" Med dishes served in small and large plates; the "loud", "trendy" crowd ignores the "slow" service, noting that it's "better at lunch."

F.illi Ponte ⬛   22 | 19 | 20 | $58

39 Desbrosses St. (West St.), 212-226-4621; www.filliponte.com
Set on the fringe of TriBeCa "off the West Side Highway", this "old-world" Italian boasts "beautiful sunsets" that complement its "consistently good" cooking; "Tony Sopranos" in the crowd don't mind the "oh-so-expensive" tabs given the "comfortable" atmosphere.

Fillip's NEW   ▽ 21 | 16 | 20 | $40

202 Seventh Ave. (bet. 21st & 22nd Sts.), 212-242-4787; www.fillipsnyc.com
French-American food prepared "*avec coeur*" is yours at this new Chelsea "charmer" offering "simple", "no-frills" dining in a "sliver of a room"; "pleasant" service and "good-value wines" add to its appeal.

Finestra   ▽ 18 | 15 | 18 | $35

1370 York Ave. (73rd St.), 212-717-8594
"Out of the way" and thus "not too crowded", this "unassuming" Yorkville Italian boasts "above-average", "attractively priced" stan-

dards served by a "hardworking" crew; maybe the "decor lacks style", but the weekend guitarist has plenty of it.

Fino ⬧
20 | 16 | 20 | $47

4 E. 36th St. (bet. 5th & Madison Aves.), 212-689-8040; www.finon36.com
1 Wall Street Ct. (Pearl St.), 212-825-1924
From the "reliable" eats to the "tries-hard-to-please" service, this "classic" Italian duo pleases fans of "old-world charm"; the Murray Hill branch is "plain" while Downtown is roomier, but either way, they're best enjoyed on the "corporate card."

Fiorentino's
21 | 13 | 19 | $31

311 Ave. U (bet. McDonald Ave. & West St.), Brooklyn, 718-372-1445
"Garlic-laden" "red-sauce" dishes keep this "cheap" Gravesend Neapolitan "busy" with a crowd that knows the difference between "good gravy and the stuff in a jar"; "nothing has changed" in decades, and that's "a good thing."

FireBird Ⓜ
21 | 26 | 21 | $64

365 W. 46th St. (bet. 8th & 9th Aves.), 212-586-0244;
www.firebirdrestaurant.com
It's "too bad the czars aren't around to enjoy" the "ambitious" Russian menu and "unobtrusive" service at this "lavish" Restaurant Row duplex that gleams like the "imperial palace on a cold winter night"; if the "addictive" honey-infused vodka doesn't "numb the reaction" to the bill, try the $40 EarlyBird instead.

Firenze ⬤
20 | 17 | 20 | $46

1594 Second Ave. (bet. 82nd & 83rd Sts.), 212-861-9368; www.firenzenyc.com
"Real-deal" Tuscan dishes arrive in "intimate", "candlelit" environs at this Upper East Side trattoria that's memorable for the "great homemade grappa" served at the end of the meal; It's a little "cramped" and "a little pricey", but "perfect for romantics."

Fish
19 | 12 | 16 | $37

280 Bleecker St. (Jones St.), 212-727-2879
"Excellent seafood with just-caught freshness" is the hook at this faux "New England fish shack" parked on "touristy" Bleecker Street turf; alright, the "stark" decor "could be improved" (ditto the "slow" service), but no one minds much given such "great prices."

Five Front
21 | 19 | 19 | $38

5 Front St. (Old Fulton St.), Brooklyn, 718-625-5559;
www.fivefrontrestaurant.com
At the "forefront" of Dumbo dining, this fairly "unknown" New American offers "delicious comfort food with contemporary twists" at "moderate prices"; most memorable is its "lovely" bamboo garden nestled "under the Brooklyn Bridge."

5 Ninth ⬤
20 | 22 | 17 | $57

5 Ninth Ave. (bet. Gansevoort & W. 12th Sts.), 212-929-9460;
www.5ninth.com
Set in a "cozy" Meatpacking District townhouse, this "standout" Eclectic showcases the "adventurous" cooking of chef Zak Pelaccio in a duplex setting enhanced by a "charming garden"; but "cramped seating", "glacially slow" service and "high pricing" leave a "bad taste" in some mouths.

Five Points ⬤
22 | 21 | 20 | $46

31 Great Jones St. (bet. Bowery & Lafayette St.), 212-253-5700
Weeknights, it's easy to be "transported" by the "sophisticated" Med–New American food and "dedicated service" at this "quietly

beautiful" NoHo "classic"; but come the weekend, its "killer brunch" draws "trendy" types resulting in "long waits" and much "noise."

Fives

▽ 23 22 24 $69

Peninsula Hotel, 700 Fifth Ave. (55th St.), 212-903-3918; www.peninsula.com
Though "little known", this "exceptional" French–New American in Midtown's Peninsula Hotel gets high fives across the board; despite "bloated prices" and a somewhat "stodgy" atmosphere, most call it an "elegant, understated" experience augmented by "dedicated service."

Flea Market Cafe ●

19 18 15 $28

131 Ave. A (bet. 9th St. & St. Marks Pl.), 212-358-9282
The "decor lives up to the name" at this "funky" East Village bistro serving "reliable", "inexpensive" Gallic grub in "tight", "chaotic" quarters; "floor-to-ceiling windows overlooking Tompkins Square Park" compensate for "rude", "authentically French" service.

Fleur de Sel

25 20 23 $69

5 E. 20th St. (bet. B'way & 5th Ave.), 212-460-9100; www.fleurdeselnyc.com
"Exquisite", "authentic" Bretagne cooking, a "romantic", "flower-filled" room and "impeccable" service show that chef Cyril Renaud has put "his heart and soul" into this Flatiron "gem"; for those who find it a bit "expensive", the $25 prix fixe lunch is the answer.

Flor de Mayo ●

20 9 16 $20

484 Amsterdam Ave. (bet. 83rd & 84th Sts.), 212-787-3388
2651 Broadway (101st St.), 212-663-5520
"Asia meets the Andes" at this UWS Peruvian-Chinese pair that's famed for "ambrosial" roast chicken served in "enormous portions" at "rock-bottom prices"; "nonexistent", "fluorescent-lit" decor and a "no lingering" mood make a strong case for their "speedy delivery."

Flor de Sol ☒

21 22 19 $42

361 Greenwich St. (bet. Franklin & Harrison Sts.), 212-366-1640;
www.flordesolnyc.com
There's a "smoking hot" vibe at this "sexy" TriBeCa Spaniard buoyed by "killer sangria", "candles galore" and "absolutely delicious" tapas (served by an equally "delicious staff"); sure, it can get "cramped", but no one minds rubbing elbows with this "beautiful" crowd.

Florent ●⇎

19 14 16 $30

69 Gansevoort St. (bet. Greenwich & Washington Sts.), 212-989-5779;
www.restaurantflorent.com
"Good at 2 PM *and* 2 AM", this "bohemian" 24/7 French bistro has been a Meatpacking District pioneer for over 20 years; despite "dodgy" decor and "intermittent" service, its "satisfying", "hangover-curing" grub still draws everyone "from grannies to trannies."

Flor's Kitchen

19 13 16 $23

149 First Ave. (bet. 9th & 10th Sts.), 212-387-8949
170 Waverly Pl. (bet. 6th Ave. & 7th Ave. S.), 212-229-9926
www.florskitchen.com
Folks "craving something different" head for these "no-frills" Venezuelans specializing in "outstanding" arepas and other "incredibly cheap" dishes; the "roomier" West Village outpost may be a "better date location", but its "tiny" Alphabet City sibling "has more character."

Foley's Fish House

20 23 21 $54

Renaissance NY Hotel, 714 Seventh Ave., 2nd fl. (bet. 47th & 48th Sts.),
212-261-5200; www.foleysfishhouse.com
"Electric" views of the "neon signs of Times Square" wow "even jaded NYers" at this "center-of-the-universe" seafooder that's natu-

rally "great for out-of-towners"; while the "expensive" fish is "fresh and tasty", it's definitely "secondary to the skyline scenery."

Food Bar ◐ 　　　17 | 16 | 16 | $30
149 Eighth Ave. (bet. 17th & 18th Sts.), 212-243-2020
"Better for boy-watching than food", this "gay-friendly" Chelsea New American is a magnet for types who "look like Tarzan but talk like Jane"; expect "ok", low-priced grub along with waiters "so cute" that some "don't know whether they're service or decor."

Fornino 　　　▽ 22 | 14 | 18 | $21
187 Bedford Ave. (N. 7th St.), Brooklyn, 718-384-6004
"Innovative", "artisanal" pies topped with "mouthwatering ingredients" are the bait at this Williamsburg pizzeria where patrons can "dine amongst homegrown herbs" in the back garden; despite only "so-so" inside decor, surveyors say "they have the goods" here.

44 　　　20 | 22 | 18 | $52
Royalton Hotel, 44 W. 44th St. (bet. 5th & 6th Aves.), 212-944-8844; www.royaltonhotel.com
"Formerly trendy", this "snazzy" Theater District hotel restaurant may be better known for its "designed-to-impress washrooms" than for its "good" (albeit "expensive") French–New American menu; the "blasé" service is a carryover from its "past glory" days.

44 & X Hell's Kitchen ◐ 　　　21 | 18 | 19 | $43
622 10th Ave. (44th St.), 212-977-1170; www.44andX.com
A "bustling scene" in a "lacking neighborhood", this moderately priced Hell's Kitchen "pioneer" serves New American fare "kicked up a notch"; the "fetching" waiters help distract from the "noise" and the "view of the Hess service station" across the street.

41 Greenwich Avenue Ⓜ 　　　▽ 18 | 18 | 19 | $35
41 Greenwich Ave. (bet. Charles & Perry Sts.), 212-255-3606
For "quintessential neighborhood" dining, Villagers head to this "best-kept secret" (fka Jones), a "small, pleasant" respite offering "upscale" American comfort chow for not much dough; a "beautiful garden" and "great brunch" add to its allure.

FOUR SEASONS Ⓧ 　　　26 | 27 | 26 | $86
99 E. 52nd St. (bet. Lexington & Park Aves.), 212-754-9494; www.fourseasonsrestaurant.com
"Whatever the season", there's "unparalleled" cuisine and "sophisticated" service under the aegis of Alex von Bidder and Julian Niccolini at this "superb" Midtown Continental, a "modernist beauty" that's the "epitome of luxurious decadence"; it's best in the Grill Room for the super "power-broker" lunch or the Pool Room for a simply "memorable occasion", but the overall "ambiance reminds you why you came to NYC" – and why you brought all those "C-notes to burn."

Fragole 　　　▽ 23 | 19 | 22 | $30
394 Court St. (bet. Carroll St. & 1st Pl.), Brooklyn, 718-522-7133; www.fragoleny.com
"Hearty" homemade pastas and other "tasty" standards "anchor the menu" at this "small" but "welcoming" Carroll Gardens Italian; a "cozy" garden adds to its allure, while frequent "wine specials" help produce those "easy-on-the-wallet" tabs.

Franchia 　　　▽ 24 | 23 | 23 | $33
12 Park Ave. (bet. 34th & 35th Sts.), 212-213-1001; www.franchia.com
All is "cool and calm" at this "transporting" Murray Hill teahouse, a "Zen respite from NY's frenetic pace" that also offers a "tasty", all-

vegetarian Korean menu; its "pretty multilevel setting" and modest prices encourage patrons to "linger" and "leave refreshed."

Francisco's Centro Vasco ◐

21	11	18	$42

159 W. 23rd St. (bet. 6th & 7th Aves.), 212-645-6224
"King Kong–size lobsters" are served for "Fay Wray–size" bucks at this "old-fashioned" Chelsea Spaniard, a "loud, boisterous" joint that's been on the scene for 30 years; even if the decor is "stale" and the mood "hectic", the "value is unbeatable."

Frank ◑≠

23	14	16	$30

88 Second Ave. (bet. 5th & 6th Sts.), 212-420-0202; www.frankrestaurant.com
"More crowded than the rush-hour subway", this "funky little" East Villager rolls out "terrific" "homestyle" Italiana in "elbow-to-elbow" digs; tabs are "cheap" and the portions could "fill Pavarotti's belly", so no wonder "waits can be a killer" here.

Frankie & Johnnie's Steakhouse ☒

21	14	18	$55

269 W. 45th St. (bet. B'way & 8th Ave.), 212-997-9494 ◐
32 W. 37th St. (bet. 5th & 6th Aves.), 212-947-8940
www.frankieandjohnnies.com
"Old-style steaks" (at new-style prices) arrive via "ancient waiters" at this chophouse duo, a "tight" 1926 "time capsule" in Times Square or its roomier Garment District sibling (set in John Barrymore's former townhouse); foes feel they're "coasting on their reputation."

Frankies Spuntino

23	20	19	$30

457 Court St. (bet. 4th Pl. & Luquer St.), Brooklyn, 718-403-0033 ≠
17 Clinton St. (bet. Houston & Stanton Sts.), 212-253-2303 ◐ NEW
www.frankiesspuntino.com
"Delicious" small plates + a "charming" back garden + "excellent" pricing = "long waits" at this Carroll Gardens Italian that ices the cake with a "restored carriage house" for private parties; a tinier Lower East Side spin-off opened recently.

Frank's

20	15	19	$53

410 W. 16th St. (bet. 9th & 10th Aves.), 212-243-1349; www.franksnyc.com
They "keep moving", and loyals "keep following" this "solid, old-time" Italian steakhouse, now based in Chelsea Market and still serving "consistent", "expense account"–priced beef; expect a crowd of "suited law-enforcement types" relaxing in "barnlike", "pool hall"–ish digs.

Franny's Ⓜ

23	16	19	$33

295 Flatbush Ave. (bet. Prospect Pl. & St. Marks Ave.), Brooklyn, 718-230-0221; www.frannysbrooklyn.com
"High-concept", "grown-up pizza" is the idea at this Prospect Heights pie purveyor employing "ecologically sound" ingredients in their "sublime", "paper-thin" product; but slightly high-side pricing makes some save it "for special occasions" only.

Fraunces Tavern ☒

16	21	18	$42

54 Pearl St. (Broad St.), 212-968-1776; www.frauncestavern.com
This circa-1762 Downtown "NY survivor" is sure "historic", with a "Colonial museum upstairs" that attracts lots of "tourists"; the problem is, its "uninspiring" American menu is so "hit-or-miss" that "George Washington may have had the last decent meal here."

Frederick's Madison

▽ 19	18	16	$60

768 Madison Ave. (bet. 65th & 66th Sts.), 212-737-7300;
www.fredericksnyc.com
There's plenty of "snob appeal" at this Madison Avenue Med that sometimes focuses on its "chichi", "good-looking" regulars more

than its "overpriced" food and "holier-than-thou" service; on the other hand, it's "hard to beat" for a "good sidewalk lunch."

Fred's at Barneys NY

| 20 | 18 | 17 | $45 |

Barneys NY, 660 Madison Ave., 9th fl. (60th St.), 212-833-2200
"People-watching is the point" at this Midtown Tuscan–New American where "media moguls", "trophy wives" and "shopaholics" convene to toy with "satisfying", "super-expensive" grub ferried by "rushed" waiters; ok, it's "too noisy" at lunch, but "great for a low-key dinner."

Freemans ◑

| 21 | 21 | 17 | $40 |

Freeman Alley (off Rivington St., bet. Bowery & Chrystie St.), 212-420-0012; www.freemansrestaurant.com
Finding this "clandestine" LES New American hidden "down an alley" is "half the fun", though its "hipster" crowd comes back for the "solid home cooking" and "European hunting lodge" look; a recent expansion hopefully will ease the "long waits."

French Roast ◑

| 15 | 14 | 13 | $26 |

2340 Broadway (85th St.), 212-799-1533
78 W. 11th St. (6th Ave.), 212-533-2233
www.frenchroastny.com
"Reliable if unexciting", this low-budget, "faux-French" duo is better remembered for its "24-hour" open-door policy than its *comme ci, comme ça* bistro offerings or "ersatz Left Bank décor"; "nonexistent" service is probably the most authentic thing about it.

Fresco by Scotto ⊠

| 22 | 19 | 21 | $57 |

34 E. 52nd St. (bet. Madison & Park Aves.), 212-935-3434;
www.frescobyscotto.com
There's "great energy" in the air at the Scotto family's "consistently popular" Midtown Tuscan (aka the 'NBC commissary') where "industry folks" appreciate the "wonderful food" and "impeccable service"; "big price tags" and frequent "air kissing" come with the see-and-be-seen territory.

Fresco on the Go ⊠

| 20 | 10 | 15 | $17 |

40 E. 52nd St. (bet. Madison & Park Aves.), 212-754-2700;
www.frescobyscotto.com
"Upscale takeout" is the hallmark of this Midtown Fresco adjunct that sates "on-the-run" biz types with "tasty" Italian offerings (many report it's "best for Caesar wraps"); though it can be a "madhouse" at lunchtime, it's a "great break from the company cafeteria."

fresh

| 23 | 20 | 21 | $56 |

105 Reade St. (bet. Church St. & W. B'way), 212-406-1900;
www.freshrestaurantnyc.com
"True to its name", this TriBeCa "catch" offers a "constantly changing", "just-off-the-boat" selection of seafood served in a "formal" room that's the "epitome of low-key elegance"; given its "earnest" service and overall quality, the "pricey" tabs are more than merited.

Friendhouse

| 20 | 17 | 18 | $24 |

225 E. 14th St. (bet. 2nd & 3rd Aves.), 212-614-8814 **NEW**
99 Third Ave. (bet. 12th & 13th Sts.), 212-388-1838 ◑
www.friendhouse2.com
Featuring "something for everyone", these East Village "multi-Asians" offer Chinese and Japanese items on Third Avenue and Thai plus sushi on 14th Street; "speedy takeout" and "cheap" prices keep them popular, though they do offer "more ambiance for the money" than you'd expect.

Friend of a Farmer   18 | 17 | 16 | $28
77 Irving Pl. (bet. 18th & 19th Sts.), 212-477-2188
A "ray of sunshine in the winter", this "alternate universe" Gramercy American recalls a "Vermont inn" with its "comforting menu", "delightful fireplace" and "farmhand"-size portions; relatively "poor service" and "epic waits for brunch" are the Maine downsides.

Fuleen Seafood ●   ∇ 23 | 8 | 15 | $25
11 Division St. (bet. Bowery & E. B'way), 212-941-6888
"They're not fuleen around" at this "cheap" Chinatown fish palace where the "outstanding" Hong Kong–style seafood is "extremely fresh" and "authentic"; late-night hours (till 3 AM) compensate for a "staff that knows very little English."

Fushimi   ∇ 25 | 23 | 23 | $42
2110 Richmond Rd. (Lincoln Ave.), Staten Island, 718-980-5300
"Manhattan meets Staten Island" at this Japanese "hot spot" where "fresh-off-the-boat sushi" is sliced in "upscale", "lounge"-like digs; acoustics-wise, it's "loud" and the "prices echo Nobu", yet it's "always crowded", so "go early or go somewhere else."

Futura ● NEW   ∇ 19 | 19 | 22 | $29
287 Ninth St. (bet. 4th & 5th Aves.), Brooklyn, 718-832-0085;
www.futurabm.com
This "wonderful addition" to Park Slope features "mighty tasty", plenty affordable Italian-Argentine grub served in cozy, brick-lined digs; it's still somewhat "undiscovered" given an off-the-beaten-track address, but admirers insist it's yet another "reason to travel to Brooklyn."

Gabriela's NEW   – | – | – | M
688 Columbus Ave. (bet. 93rd & 94th Sts.), 212-961-0574;
www.gabrielas.com
Habitués remain loyal to this midpriced Mexican, now in new UWS digs 20 blocks north of its original home; although the kitchen is as good as ever, with hardly any noticeable change, they've added a brand-new tequila bar and an outdoor patio perfect for summer sousing.

Gabriel's ⊠   22 | 18 | 21 | $57
11 W. 60th St. (bet. B'way & Columbus Ave.), 212-956-4600;
www.gabrielsbarandrest.com
"Perfectly located" near Lincoln Center and the Time Warner colossus, Gabriel Aiello's "well-run", celeb-studded Tuscan features a menu "cooked and seasoned to perfection" delivered by an "unfailingly courteous" staff that has "curtain-time service down pat"; true, it's a tad "pricey", but cheaper (and "quieter") at lunchtime.

Gahm Mi Oak ●   23 | 14 | 16 | $22
43 W. 32nd St. (bet. B'way & 5th Ave.), 212-695-4113
"Always open" and "always reliable", this 24/7 Garment District Korean dispenses "authentic", "hearty" Seoul food for "cheap"; it's also renowned for its *sollongtang* beef soup, a "soothing" concoction that "will cure you of anything."

Gallagher's Steak House ●   21 | 17 | 18 | $58
228 W. 52nd St. (bet. B'way & 8th Ave.), 212-245-5336;
www.gallaghersnysteakhouse.com
With its "manly", wood-paneled "boys' club" air and "great slabs of beef" displayed under glass, this "never-changing", 80-year-old Theater District warhorse is the "granddaddy of NY steakhouses"; "ancient waiters" and "very expensive" tabs burnish its "old-school", checkered-tablecloth allure.

GARDEN CAFE 🖼Ⓜ️ — 27 | 20 | 27 | $51

620 Vanderbilt Ave. (Prospect Pl.), Brooklyn, 718-857-8863
Thanks to John Policastro's "memorable" New American cooking, this "little place with a big heart" in Prospect Heights "only gets better with age"; add in a "romantic", "jewel-box" setting and a "welcoming", "accommodating" staff and it's obvious that this is a "labor of love" where prices should be irrelevant.

Gargiulo's — 21 | 18 | 21 | $42

2911 W. 15th St. (bet. Mermaid & Surf Aves.), Brooklyn, 718-266-4891; www.gargiulos.com
For a "quintessential Brooklyn experience", nostalgists revere this 100-year-old Coney Island Southern Italian where "basic", "red-sauce" fare is served by "tuxedoed waiters" to a "Scorsese"-esque crowd; after your meal, you can even "roll the dice" for a chance at a "free dinner."

Gari — 26 | 17 | 19 | $74

370 Columbus Ave. (bet. 77th & 78th Sts.), 212-362-4816
"Nothing else in the area rivals" this "avant-garde", "mega-expensive" West Side sushi specialist spun off from chef Gari Sugio's crosstown original; though "service and decor are just ok", it's the "amazing", "worth-the-hype" omakase that keeps regulars regular, even if it "costs an arm and a leg."

Gascogne — 23 | 20 | 21 | $49

158 Eighth Ave. (bet. 17th & 18th Sts.), 212-675-6564; www.gascognenyc.com
"Avoid the long flight to Paris" and stop instead at this "Chelsea favorite" that specializes in "hearty" Southwestern French fare; fans say this "delicious" bistro has "gotten better with time", and especially like its "magic" garden out back.

Gavroche — 19 | 16 | 19 | $43

212 W. 14th St. (bet. 7th Ave. S. & 8th Ave.), 212-647-8553; www.gavroche-ny.com
"Straightforward French comfort food" is yours at this "*c'est-si-bon*" West Village bistro boasting the "deal of the neighborhood", a renowned $19 early-bird special; a back garden that doubles as a "little piece of heaven" ices the cake.

Geisha ●🖼 — 22 | 21 | 18 | $61

33 E. 61st St. (bet. Madison & Park Aves.), 212-813-1112; www.geisharestaurant.com
"Euros", "plastic surgery addicts" and their escorts frequent this "über"-the-top East Side "designer restaurant" offering "distinctive" French-inflected Japanese food in a "showy" setting; the downstairs lounge is "trendy", the upstairs dining room more adult, but either way is "expensive."

Gennaro ≠ — 24 | 14 | 16 | $37

665 Amsterdam Ave. (bet. 92nd & 93rd Sts.), 212-665-5348
"Extremely tasty" Italian food, an "excellent price point" and "no reservations" result in "endless waits" at this "outstanding" Upper Westsider; "rushed" service and an "inconvenient" cash-only policy come with the always crowded territory.

Ghenet — ∇ 21 | 13 | 17 | $29

284 Mulberry St. (bet. Houston & Prince Sts.), 212-343-1888; www.ghenet.com
Eating is a hands-on experience at this "finger-licking good" NoLita Ethiopian where the "designed-to-share" entrees arrive sans utensils, so enthusiasts "dig in" with their digits or the "spongy injera bread"; it's a guaranteed "good time with a group of friends."

Giambelli ◐
20 | 15 | 20 | $54

46 E. 50th St. (bet. Madison & Park Aves.), 212-688-2760;
www.giambelli50th.com
Fans of this 50-year-old Midtowner say it "only gets better with age", starting with an "old-school" menu that's like an "encyclopedia of Italian standards"; but foes fret it's gotten "stale" and "expensive."

Gigino at Wagner Park
21 | 19 | 18 | $41

20 Battery Pl. (West St.), 212-528-2228; www.gigino-wagnerpark.com

Gigino Trattoria
323 Greenwich St. (bet. Duane & Reade Sts.), 212-431-1112;
www.gigino-trattoria.com
"Upbeat and charming", this "rustic" TriBeCa Italian offers "abundant choices" of "above-average" fixings along with "great brick-oven pizza"; its nearby sibling off Wagner Park is equally "delicious", but better known for its alfresco seating with "smashing harbor views."

Gilt ⊠ⓂNEW
– | 27 | 28 | $142

NY Palace Hotel, 455 Madison Ave. (bet. 50th & 51st Sts.), 212-891-8100;
www.giltnewyork.com
Bring plenty of "gelt" to this "opulent" newcomer set in the former Le Cirque 2000 space in Midtown's Palace Hotel; the departure of chef Paul Liebrandt negates its Food score, but the foodies in the movers-and-shakers crowd are pleased to hear of the arrival of Christopher Lee (ex Philly's Striped Bass), who's planning a New American menu.

Ginger NEW
▽ 20 | 19 | 18 | $31

1400 Fifth Ave. (116th St.), 212-423-1111; www.gingerexpress.com
A "refreshing addition" to the East Harlem scene, this "delightful" newcomer gives a "fresh", "health-conscious" spin to Chinese food, using mostly organic ingredients with nothing fried; "inexpensive" tabs, "attractive" digs and all-day hours contribute to its popularity.

Gin Lane ◐⊠NEW
– | – | – | E

355 W. 14th St. (bet. 8th & 9th Aves.), 212-691-0555; www.ginlanenyc.com
On the fringe of the frenetic Meatpacking District comes this rather sedate newcomer, a retro salute to old NY featuring classic Continental cuisine paired with vintage cocktails in clubby digs (think flocked wallpaper); up front a roomy lounge has nightlife potential.

Gino ≠
19 | 13 | 19 | $46

780 Lexington Ave. (bet. 60th & 61st Sts.), 212-758-4466
"Time travelers" tout this "been-around-forever" Italian "warhorse" near Bloomie's as a "classic", citing its "reliable red-sauce" eats and that "so-bad-it's-good" zebra wallpaper; but even regulars admit the "cash-only rule" and "gruff service" are "tired out."

Giorgione
21 | 18 | 18 | $49

307 Spring St. (bet. Greenwich & Hudson Sts.), 212-352-2269

Giorgione 508 NEW
508 Greenwich St. (bet. Canal & Spring Sts.), 212-219-2444
"Well-executed" Italian dishes fill out the menu of this "chic" Way West SoHo trattoria (and its new, 'round-the-corner spin-off) from celeb grocer Giorgio DeLuca; expect a "well-heeled, damn good-looking" crowd, making so much "noise" that it's "hard to hear yourself chew."

Giorgio's of Gramercy
23 | 18 | 22 | $45

27 E. 21st St. (bet. B'way & Park Ave. S.), 212-477-0007;
www.giorgiosofgramercy.com
"Often overlooked", this Flatiron New American is a "good local spot" for "consistently wonderful" food served in "peaceful, unhurried" en-

virons; despite somewhat "cramped" conditions, it's still a "relative bargain" in these parts.

Girasole ❶
21 | 17 | 20 | $55

151 E. 82nd St. (bet. Lexington & 3rd Aves.), 212-772-6690
A "real old-world feel" sets the "gracious" mood at this longtime UES Italian, a "comfortably predictable" place where the food's "dependable" and the staff "warm"; its "older" following doesn't mind that it's rather "expensive", but the acoustics are another story.

Gnocco Caffe ❶
23 | 18 | 18 | $35

337 E. 10th St. (bet. Aves. A & B), 212-677-1913; www.gnocco.com
The eponymous, "piping hot" fried dough appetizer hints at the "delicious", "serious" Emilian fare to come at this "inexpensive" East Village Italian offering "Roman holiday" dining; a "delightful" garden makes up for "so-so decor" and "not-the-best" service.

Gobo
22 | 19 | 19 | $31

401 Sixth Ave. (bet. 8th St. & Waverly Pl.), 212-255-3242 ❶
1426 Third Ave. (81st St.), 212-288-5099
www.goborestaurant.com
As these "inspiring" spots prove, vegan grazing "doesn't have to be a sacrifice" and with food this good, even your "scoffing carnivore friends" will happily "go green"; "serene" settings and "inexpensive" tabs add to the feeling of "guilt-free indulgence."

Golden Unicorn
20 | 11 | 13 | $23

18 E. Broadway, 2nd fl. (Catherine St.), 212-941-0911
"Still the grande dame of dim sum", this "stadium"-size C-towner may be a "madhouse" on weekends but is worth braving the "crush" and chancy service for its "really cheap", "real McCoy" food; indeed, the toughest decision is "to figure out when to stop eating."

Gonzo
22 | 17 | 18 | $41

140 W. 13th St. (bet. 6th Ave. & 7th Ave. S.), 212-645-4606
Pie-eyed proponents praise the "amazing", "must-try" grilled pizza at this Village Italian helmed by "hands-on chef" Vincent Scotto; sure, it can be "deafening" ("don't go with anyone you want to talk to"), but the mood is certainly "congenial" at this "overachiever."

good
20 | 14 | 18 | $32

89 Greenwich Ave. (bet. Bank & W. 12th Sts.), 212-691-8080;
www.goodrestaurantnyc.com
"Brunch is the way to travel" at this West Village New American where the "long" weekend waits are "not so good"; ultimately, the space is "comfortable", prices "moderate" and the "simply prepared" food turns out to be "better than good."

goodburger NEW
18 | 8 | 11 | $12

800 Second Ave. (43rd St.), 212-922-1700; www.goodburgerny.com
The burger wars have a new contender in this "real-deal" Tudor City patty palace vending a "small, juicy" version served old-school style in a wax-paper wrapper; despite "slow" service, most agree "the name fits."

Good Enough to Eat
20 | 15 | 17 | $25

483 Amsterdam Ave. (bet. 83rd & 84th Sts.), 212-496-0163;
www.goodenoughtoeat.com
"Comfort food done to a T" makes for weekend brunch "lines around the corner" at this UWS "escape to Vermont", where the "farm-style" Americana is "old-fashioned" (ditto the prices) and the decor is like "grandma's country kitchen gone wild."

Good Fork Ⓜ NEW

391 Van Brunt St. (bet. Coffey & Van Dyke Sts.), Brooklyn, 718-643-6636;
www.goodfork.com

In up-and-coming Red Hook, this midpriced Eclectic newcomer is already drawing foodies eager to sample a diverse variety of hearty fare; in contrast to the area's gritty, industrial character, its pleasant room glows with dim lighting and warm wood accents.

Goodies

1 E. Broadway (bet. Catherine & Oliver Sts.), 212-577-2922

"Heavenly" soup dumplings that "rival Joe's Shanghai" are the draw at this "genuine" C-towner; regulars "close their eyes" to the "unattractive" space and focus instead on the "succulent" flavors.

Googie's ●

1491 Second Ave. (78th St.), 212-717-1122

Brace yourself for "strollers galore" at this UES Italian diner that's best known for its "nuts brunches" and "outstanding shoestring fries", and best forgotten for its "worn-out" looks; just don't forget "your doogie bag" – portions are "humongous" here, prices are not.

GOTHAM BAR & GRILL

12 E. 12th St. (bet. 5th Ave. & University Pl.), 212-620-4020;
www.gothambarandgrill.com

"Superb", "soaring" dishes by chef Alfred Portale "continue to amaze" at this "chic yet approachable" New American "perennial" in the Village, also known for its "high ceilings" and "gracious", "on-point" service; all agree the overall "celebratory" mood will make "you feel like a million bucks" and even though the check may "break the bank", the $25 prix fixe lunch is a "flat-out steal."

Grace's Trattoria

201 E. 71st St. (bet. 2nd & 3rd Aves.), 212-452-2323;
www.gracesmarketplace.com

"Reliable and civilized", this "low-key" UES adjunct to Grace's Marketplace draws a "neighborhood crowd" with its "creative" Pugliese cooking; but critics slam the "stuffy service" and think the food should be better "considering the quality of the retail store."

Gradisca

126 W. 13th St. (bet. 6th Ave. & 7th Ave. S.), 212-691-4886;
www.gradiscanyc.com

What's too "dark" to some is *molto* "sexy" to others at this "cavelike" Village Italian known for its variety of "toothsome pastas"; though service turns "flighty" when the room "bustles", most call it a "keeper."

GRAMERCY TAVERN

42 E. 20th St. (bet. B'way & Park Ave. S.), 212-477-0777;
www.gramercytavern.com

Again voted No. 1 for Popularity, this Flatiron "standard bearer" via Danny Meyer "seems to get better every year", offering an "extraordinary" New American menu, "comfortably elegant" surroundings and "impeccable service"; in short, it's a "fabulous place to spend a bundle", though regulars report you'll find the "same quality" for less dough in the walk-in–friendly front room; N.B. Michael Anthony (ex Blue Hill at Stone Barns) is now overseeing the kitchen following the departure of founding chef Tom Colicchio.

Gramercy 24

Marcel Hotel, 323 Third Ave. (24th St.), 212-532-1766; www.gramercy24.com

They're "trying really hard "at this "underrated", midpriced American seafood yearling where the "quiet atmosphere" suits a "meal with the family" or dining alone at the "friendly" bar; despite "inconsistent" service, it's a "pleasant" break from the area's raft of "kiddie bars."

Grand Sichuan
22 | 8 | 13 | $23

125 Canal St. (Bowery), 212-625-9212
227 Lexington Ave. (bet. 33rd & 34th Sts.), 212-679-9770
229 Ninth Ave. (24th St.), 212-620-5200
745 Ninth Ave. (bet. 50th & 51st Sts.), 212-582-2288
1049 Second Ave. (bet. 55th & 56th Sts.), 212-355-5855
19-23 St. Marks Pl. (bet. 2nd & 3rd Aves.), 212-529-4800
www.thegrandsichuan.com

"If you like it hot", brace yourself for the "tongue-numbing", "whoa-mama" Szechuan dishes offered on the "telephone book"–size menu of this "easy-on-the-wallet" mini-chain; "dull" decor and "haphazard" service make a strong case for "takeout."

Grand Tier Restaurant
18 | 24 | 23 | $75

Metropolitan Opera House, Lincoln Center Plaza, 2nd fl. (bet. 63rd & 65th Sts.), 212-799-3400

Fortify yourself for "four hours of *Aida*" at this "magnificent"-looking Metropolitan Opera venue that caters to a "captive audience" (i.e. ticket-holders) with a "reliable" American-Continental menu served with "laserlike precision"; sure, it's "silly expensive", but having "dessert during intermission" is a "treat" that even Carmen would enjoy.

Gray's Papaya
20 | 4 | 13 | $5

2090 Broadway (72nd St.), 212-799-0243
539 Eighth Ave. (37th St.), 212-904-1588
402 Sixth Ave. (8th St.), 212-260-3532

Irresistible "guilty pleasures", these "classic" wiener wonderlands vend the "best darn dogs" washed down with "fresh" tropical drinks 24/7; what with the "insanely cheap" tabs, no one cares that there's no place to sit – you're having one of those "quintessential" NY experiences, so shut up and eat!

Great Jones Cafe
20 | 11 | 15 | $25

54 Great Jones St. (bet. Bowery & Lafayette St.), 212-674-9304;
www.greatjones.com

Alright, it's "cramped" and "seedy", but this "no-frills", low-budget NoHo Cajun oozes enough "Southern comfort" to make it "tough to get a table" (especially for that "boisterous" brunch); the "spicy" grub goes down easy thanks to a "surprisingly good beer selection."

Great NY Noodle Town
22 | 5 | 12 | $16

28½ Bowery (Bayard St.), 212-349-0923

Insiders opt for "anything salt-baked" at this C-town vet that also gets raves for its "terrific" noodle soups, all priced so low they're "almost free"; "sloppy service" and "subway-car ambiance" notwithstanding, it's a longtime "late-night" staple.

Greek Kitchen
20 | 14 | 18 | $30

889 10th Ave. (58th St.), 212-581-4300

"Worth the detour", this West Hell's Kitchen Hellenic is a "welcome diversion" from the "usual Italian and Japanese joints"; although the "traditional" chow is "well prepared" and "reasonably priced", the "nothing-fancy" decor is another matter.

Green Field Churrascaria
19 | 14 | 18 | $36

108-01 Northern Blvd. (108th St.), Queens, 718-672-5202;
www.greenfieldchurrascaria.com

"Especially good if you're still on Atkins", this Corona Brazilian BBQ bonanza offers a $26, "eat-till-you-drop" "meat parade" served by "roving waiters" in "football field–size" digs (there's also a "huge salad bar", if anyone cares); for best results, "wear loose pants" and "pack an extra artery."

Gribouille NEW

| – | – | – | M |

2 Hope St. (Roebling St.), Brooklyn, 718-384-3100; www.gribouillenewyork.com

Young French expats in Williamsburg have opened this comfy new cafe/patisserie where fresh-baked baguettes lead off the affordable French comfort-food offerings; the name means 'scribble', and the neighborhood's budding draftsmen do just that over afternoon tartines, omelets and *chocolat chaud*.

Grifone ☒

| 23 | 17 | 23 | $57 |

244 E. 46th St. (bet. 2nd & 3rd Aves.), 212-490-7275; www.grifonenyc.com

A "real sleeper" in the "sleepy U.N. area", this venerable Northern Italian deserves greater attention for its "top-notch, top-dollar" meals and "crisp, professional service"; while too "old-fashioned" and "boys' club"–ish for some, they strive for "excellence, not sizzle" here.

Grill Room ☒

| 18 | 22 | 19 | $50 |

World Financial Ctr., 225 Liberty St. (West St.), 212-945-9400; www.arkrestaurants.com

An "ideal location" – featuring "to-die-for" Hudson River views and handsome, airy quarters – is the trump card of this WFC surf 'n' turfer where the "pretty good" chops taste best on an "expense account"; the underwhelmed find everything here "extremely average", except for the price.

GRIMALDI'S ⊘

| 26 | 11 | 15 | $20 |

19 Old Fulton St. (bet. Front & Water Sts.), Brooklyn, 718-858-4300; www.grimaldis.com

"So thin, so crunchy", so "coal-charred", the "classic" pies at this Dumbo pizzeria "institution" are definitely "worth crossing the bridge for"; no one minds the "apathetic service" and "no-frills" decor, but "consider the weather since you'll likely be waiting in line."

GROCERY, THE ☒

| 27 | 17 | 25 | $55 |

288 Smith St. (bet. Sackett & Union Sts.), Brooklyn, 718-596-3335

It's "all about the food" at this upmarket Carroll Gardens New American where "delightful" chef-owners Charles Kiely and Sharon Pachter purvey "artfully crafted" seasonal fare that shines with "fresh, pure flavors"; "flawless service" and a "delightful garden" in back add to its allure, but it's so "tiny" (and popular) that "reservations are hard to come by."

Grotta Azzurra ◗

| 17 | 16 | 16 | $47 |

177 Mulberry St. (Broome St.), 212-925-8775; www.grottaazzurrany.com

Reworking the "long-gone" 1908 original, this reborn Little Italy Southern Italian divides voters: fans like its "gracious dining room" and "wholesome" offerings, but foes blast the "small portions", "chancy" service and "touristy" crowd, wondering "where's Tony Soprano when we need him?"

Gusto

| 21 | 20 | 18 | $52 |

60 Greenwich Ave. (Perry St.), 212-924-8000; www.gustonyc.com

Off to an "auspicious start", this "talked-about" Village Italian yearling is already "enormously popular" thanks to a "creative", "ever-changing" menu served in "Euro-chic" digs; the "cool scene" includes lots of "good-lookers" who report "everything works" with gusto here; P.S. a recent chef change puts its Food score in question.

Gyu-Kaku

| 23 | 20 | 21 | $42 |

34 Cooper Sq. (bet. Astor Pl. & 4th St.), 212-475-2989; www.gyu-kaku.com
"Great for groups" and "dates", this East Village link of the international Japanese BBQ chain offers "fun, do-it-yourself grilling" on charcoal roasters; the "meats are tender and nicely seasoned", but a "big appetite can quickly inflate the tab."

Hacienda de Argentina ●

| 20 | 20 | 17 | $50 |

339 E. 75th St. (bet. 1st & 2nd Aves.), 212-472-5300;
www.haciendadeargentina.com
"Dark and seductive", this UES Argentinean steakhouse purveying grass-fed beef is more "woman-friendly" than the norm thanks to "candlelight" and comfortably upholstered chairs; though service is "spotty" and tabs "pricey", the empanadas are a "must-try."

Hakata Grill

| 20 | 15 | 17 | $33 |

230 W. 48th St. (bet. B'way & 8th Ave.), 212-245-1020; www.hakatagrill.com
"Fresh, quick sushi" and "dependable" service make this Theater District Japanese a "find" for both locals and tourists; thanks to its being "extremely affordable", regulars don't mind that there's "no decor."

Hale & Hearty Soups ⌀

| 19 | 7 | 12 | $11 |

55 Broad St. (Beaver St.), 212-509-4100 ⑤
Chelsea Mkt., 75 Ninth Ave. (bet. 15th & 16th Sts.), 212-255-2400
Grand Central, lower level (42nd St. & Vanderbilt Ave.), 212-983-2845
849 Lexington Ave. (bet. 64th & 65th Sts.), 212-517-7600
Rockefeller Plaza, 30 Rockefeller Plaza (49th St.), 212-265-2117 ⑤
462 Seventh Ave. (35th St.), 212-971-0605 ⑤
685 Third Ave. (43rd St.), 212-681-6460 ⑤
55 W. 56th St. (bet. 5th & 6th Aves.), 212-245-9200 ⑤
49 W. 42nd St. (bet. 5th & 6th Aves.), 212-575-9090 ⑤
32 Court St. (Remsen St.), Brooklyn, 718-596-5600 ⑤
www.haleandhearty.com
Additional locations throughout the NY area
Soup, salad and sandwich lovers like this affordable, "assembly-line" chain that vends a "rather nice" daily lunch; they're "worth the price", despite "long lines" midday and the lack of "any vibe at all."

Hallo Berlin

| 18 | 8 | 12 | $23 |

626 10th Ave. (bet. 44th & 45th Sts.), 212-977-1944
For an "Oktoberfest atmosphere year-round", hit this "cheap" Hell's Kitchen German *brauhaus* where a "sausage-manic" menu is paired with "beer in steins"; a "pleasant" patio distracts from the "no-frills, no-thrills" digs and "unfriendly" staffers.

Hampton Chutney Co.

| 21 | 11 | 15 | $15 |

464 Amsterdam Ave. (bet. 82nd & 83rd Sts.), 212-362-5050 **NEW**
68 Prince St. (bet. Crosby & Lafayette Sts.), 212-226-9996
www.hamptonchutney.com
"Inventive", "New-Age" dosas stuffed with "delicious fillings" draw "yoga-hipster" types to these "mellow" SoHo/UWS Indian fusion specialists; they may "hit the spot" for a "quick, healthy lunch", but at these bargain prices, "good luck finding a seat."

Hangawi

| 24 | 25 | 24 | $43 |

12 E. 32nd St. (bet. 5th & Madison Aves.), 212-213-0077;
www.hangawirestaurant.com
"You won't miss the meat" at this Murray Hill Korean "vegetarian paradise" where the "interesting" offerings "could convert the hardiest carnivore"; the "soothing", "otherworldly" setting comes complete with a "no-shoes policy" and prices that add to the "Zen-like bliss."

Harbour Lights ◐
16 | 21 | 17 | $42

South Street Seaport, Pier 17, 3rd fl. (Fulton St.), 212-227-2800; www.harbourlts.com
A "breathtaking" water's edge "view of the bridges" makes this Seaport seafooder a "great place to take visitors" and especially "romantic on summer nights"; too bad the "priceless" panorama completely "overshadows" the "ordinary food."

Hard Rock Cafe ◐
13 | 20 | 14 | $30

1501 Broadway (43rd St.), 212-343-3355; www.hardrock.com
"Food isn't the point" of this Times Square rock 'n' roll–themed "memorabilia" megaplex where most advise "stick with the burgers"; on the other hand, it's "festive" enough if you're a "tourist", a "teenager" or want to "get up close to Clapton's guitar."

Harrison, The
24 | 21 | 22 | $57

355 Greenwich St. (Harrison St.), 212-274-9310; www.beanstalkrestaurants.com
The "fresh, innovative" cooking "just sings" at Jimmy Bradley's "top-notch" TriBeCa New American that's all the more "memorable" thanks to "crisp", "seamless" service and serious, but "fair", pricing; the "civilized" room "hums" "without being deafening" and also offers bonus "stargazing."

Harry's Cafe ◐ NEW
− | − | − | E

1 Hanover Sq. (bet. Pearl & Stone Sts.), 212-785-9200
Harry's Steak NEW
97 Pearl St. (bet. Broad St. & Hanover Sq.), 212-785-9200 www.harrysnyc.com
Two distinct eateries make up host Harry Poulakakos' return to the red-meat biz in the landmark India House: first, an atmospheric Eclectic cafe, and second, a clubby steakhouse; either way, you can expect first-rate food and wine, an old-NY setting and a big swinging crowd of bankers, lawyers and traders.

Haru
21 | 17 | 17 | $38

433 Amsterdam Ave. (bet. 80th & 81st Sts.), 212-579-5655 ◐
220 Park Ave. S. (18th St.), 646-428-0989 ◐
280 Park Ave. (48th St.), 212-490-9680
1327 Third Ave. (76th St.), 212-452-1028 ◐
1329 Third Ave. (76th St.), 212-452-2230 ◐
205 W. 43rd St. (bet. B'way & 8th Ave.), 212-398-9810 ◐
www.harusushi.com
"Humongous pieces" of sushi and sashimi plump up the menu of this all-over-town Japanese chainlet where "mind-numbing noise levels" can evoke a "nightclub" vibe; they're good for a "quick in-and-out" given the "rushed" service.

Hasaki ◐
24 | 15 | 19 | $39

210 E. Ninth St. (bet. 2nd & 3rd Aves.), 212-473-3327; www.hasakinyc.com
"Straight-up bang for the buck" keeps this longtime East Village Japanese "crowded but cozy" with folks seeking "pristine" sushi and "attentive service"; since there's almost "always a wait", early birds chirp "go for the $20 twilight special."

Hatsuhana ⌧
24 | 15 | 19 | $50

17 E. 48th St. (bet. 5th & Madison Aves.), 212-355-3345
237 Park Ave. (46th St.), 212-661-3400
www.hatsuhana.com
"Tokyo-quality chefs" prepare "impeccable" sushi and other Japanese delicacies for "business" types at these "respectable" vet-

erans that "pioneered" the cuisine in Midtown; maybe they "need better digs" – and pricing – but admirers say they "still shine" despite "lots of competition."

Havana Alma de Cuba
21 | 18 | 20 | $33

94 Christopher St. (bet. Bedford & Bleecker Sts.), 212-242-3800; www.havanavillagenyc.com
One of the "best Cubano sandwiches around" lights up the menu of this "lively" Village Cuban where "robust" grub and *delicioso* sangria is served by a "hospitable" staff; sure, it's "a bit cramped", but in clement weather there's always the "large garden."

Havana Central
18 | 16 | 16 | $29

22 E. 17th St. (bet. B'way & 5th Ave.), 212-414-2298
151 W. 46th St. (bet. 6th & 7th Aves.), 212-398-7440 ◐
www.havanacentral.com
For a "taste of old Cuba", try this "reasonably priced" duo dishing out "hearty" island fare; at Union Square the mood is "informal" and "fast-foody" while the "airy" Restaurant Row outpost is "more upscale with a hot bar scene"; sadly, both suffer from "poor service."

Havana Chelsea ⊅
19 | 8 | 13 | $22

190 Eighth Ave. (bet. 19th & 20th Sts.), 212-243-9421
"Cheap", "down-home" Cuban chow in "plentiful" portions has kept this "blue-collar" Chelsea joint on the scene for 25 years; forget the "distracted" service and "fluorescent"-lit "luncheonette" setting – it's the real deal for a "quick, hearty food fix."

Haveli ◐
20 | 17 | 19 | $30

100 Second Ave. (bet. 5th & 6th Sts.), 212-982-0533; www.haveli.citysearch.com
Curry connoisseurs claim this "consistently good" East Village Indian is "worlds better" than its nearby Sixth Street competitors, citing "subtly flavored" dishes, "customer-sensitive" service and a "classier ambiance"; in return, plan to pay a "few extra dollars.."

Hearth
25 | 20 | 23 | $60

403 E. 12th St. (1st Ave.), 646-602-1300; www.restauranthearth.com
Though the room is "casual", everything else is "first-class" at this East Village Tuscan-American where the "best seats" are the barstools opposite the open kitchen where chef Marco Canora "works his magic"; maybe it's "a bit pricey", but the payoff is a truly "wonderful eating experience."

Heartland Brewery
14 | 14 | 14 | $27

Empire State Bldg., 350 Fifth Ave. (34th St.), 212-563-3433
1285 Sixth Ave. (51st St.), 212-582-8244
South Street Seaport, 93 South St. (Fulton St.), 646-572-2337
35 Union Sq. W. (bet. 16th & 17th Sts.), 212-645-3400
127 W. 43rd St. (bet. B'way & 6th Ave.), 646-366-0235 ◐
www.heartlandbrewery.com
"Boisterous" and "bustling", this "popular" microbrewery chain is particularly popular "after work" and on weekends according to hard-core hopsheads; the "basic" pub grub, though satisfying, plays second fiddle to the vast list of "brewskis."

Hedeh ◐☒
▽ 24 | 21 | 21 | $48

57 Great Jones St. (bet. Bowery & Lafayette St.), 212-473-8458; www.hedeh.com
"Out of the way" and "under the radar screen", this "brilliant" NoHo Japanese "hasn't caught on yet" despite its "jewel"-like sushi and

other "out-and-out tasty" dishes; granted, it's "not cheap" but "delightful experiences" seldom are.

Heidelberg

17 15 16 $33

1648 Second Ave. (bet. 85th & 86th Sts.), 212-628-2332;
www.heidelbergrestaurant.com
Yorkville's "last surviving German *haus*", this "blast from the past" keeps Deutschland devotees "stuffed and happy" with "a lot of food" including "authentic Wiener schnitzel" and "boots of beer"; "waiters in lederhosen" enhance the "Bavarian-kitsch" scheme.

Hell's Kitchen

24 16 18 $41

679 Ninth Ave. (bet. 46th & 47th Sts.), 212-977-1588;
www.hellskitchen-nyc.com
There's a "nice burn level" underlying the "provocative" fare served at this "upscale", "high-energy" Clinton Mexicano; thanks to good bang for the buck, it's often overcrowded and is best "after the theater crowd departs."

Henry's End

25 14 24 $43

44 Henry St. (Cranberry St.), Brooklyn, 718-834-1776; www.henrysend.com
Long renowned for its "exotic" wild game, this "cheery" Brooklyn Heights New American "shoebox" offers a "wide-ranging", "flawlessly executed" menu year-round paired with "impeccable" wines; the setting may be "tight" and "plain", but the "small-town" vibe and prices prevail.

Highline ●

20 23 18 $36

835 Washington St. (Little W. 12th St.), 212-243-3339; www.nychighline.com
No surprise, the "hyper-mod design" and "happening" scene overwhelm the "dependable" Thai grub at this "trendy" Meatpacking District triplex; more astonishing is finding "affordable" pricing in an otherwise "bargain-free neighborhood."

Hispaniola ●

20 19 17 $39

839 W. 181st St. (Cabrini Blvd.), 212-740-5222
"Tasty Dominican" chow with an Asian twist draws fusion fans to this "SoHo-like" rarity in Washington Heights; though nitpickers nix the "inexperienced help", the "upstairs view of the GW Bridge at sunset" seals the deal for most.

HK ●

17 17 15 $30

523 Ninth Ave. (39th St.), 212-947-4208
"In the middle of the nothingness" behind Port Authority, this "trendy" American comfort fooder comes across with "decent" eats in a "sleek", all-white setting; its "cool vibe" and "pretty cheap" tabs offset the "snooty service."

Holy Basil ●

22 19 19 $29

149 Second Ave., 2nd fl. (bet. 9th & 10th Sts.), 212-460-5557
The local faithful "worship" daily at the altar of this "upscale" East Village Thai "stalwart" known for "fresh, clean-tasting" food served in "dark, sexy" digs by a "prompt" team; low prices make it a touch "too popular" for some.

Home

21 16 19 $40

20 Cornelia St. (bet. Bleecker & W. 4th Sts.), 212-243-9579;
www.recipesfromhome.com
Talk about a "real charmer": this "down-home" Village "neighborhood place" offers "deceptively simple" American comfort chow in a "convivial atmosphere" ("if only mom cooked this well"); given the "tight" quarters, claustrophobes tout the "wonderful" garden.

Honmura An 🅜

26 | 23 | 24 | $53

170 Mercer St., 2nd fl. (bet. Houston & Prince Sts.), 212-334-5253

"Tokyo"-class "homemade soba" stars at this "marvelous" SoHo Japanese noodle specialist once again rated No. 1 for the genre; indeed, its "Zen setting" is so "serene" you'll "want to float home" – though "the prices will bring you back to reality."

Houston's

20 | 18 | 19 | $35

Citigroup Ctr., 153 E. 53rd St. (enter at 54th St. & 3rd Ave.), 212-888-3828
NY Life Bldg., 378 Park Ave. S. (27th St.), 212-689-1090
www.houstons.com

"Brutal waits" come with the territory at these "solid" Americans, but it's all "worth it when your chip hits the spinach dip", the "must-have" house specialty; the "dependable" menu is amazingly "good for a chain" and buttressed by "congenial" service and "decent pricing."

Hq NEW

▽ 22 | 21 | 24 | $38

90 Thompson St. (bet. Prince & Spring Sts.), 212-966-2755;
www.hqrestaurant.com

SoHo's latest bistro is this stylish "little" New American, a "cozy", "romantic" lair that makes the most of its exposed-brick walls and stamped-tin ceilings; its modestly priced menu smartly showcases organic, farm-raised ingredients, and as a bonus, it serves brunch seven days a week.

HSF

18 | 9 | 11 | $22

46 Bowery (bet. Bayard & Canal Sts.), 212-374-1319

"Dim sum is the specialty" of this venerable Chinatown Cantonese, a "large, noisy" place where "hard-working" cart-pushers "peddle their wares"; just "don't expect luxury", and bring a "translator" for best results; P.S. the "bathrooms are an adventure" in themselves.

Hudson Cafeteria ⦿

19 | 23 | 18 | $46

Hudson Hotel, 356 W. 58th St. (bet. 8th & 9th Aves.), 212-554-6000;
www.chinagrillmgt.com

"Fancy comfort food" arrives from an open kitchen at this rather Gothic Hudson Hotel American-Eclectic that's "not as hip" as it used to be, but still attracts plenty of pretty young things; its "Harry Potter library" look – "high ceilings", "baronial" chairs, "communal" tables – distracts from the "snooty" staff.

Hunan Park ⦿

19 | 9 | 17 | $23

235 Columbus Ave. (bet. 70th & 71st Sts.), 212-724-4411

"Old-style" Chinese food at "bargain" tabs has kept this "deservedly popular" Upper Westsider a longtime neighborhood "staple"; what with the "spartan decor" and "rushed service", regulars recommend their "speed-of-light" delivery.

Ichiro ⦿

21 | 14 | 18 | $30

1694 Second Ave. (bet. 87th & 88th Sts.), 212-369-6300; www.ichi-ro.com

"Unusual sushi rolls" employing "super-fresh" fish may be the reason this UES Japanese "gets more crowded every time we go"; "reasonable" tabs are another reason, but surely not the decorless decor.

Ici 🅜

22 | 20 | 19 | $39

246 DeKalb Ave. (bet. Clermont & Vanderbilt Aves.), Brooklyn, 718-789-2778; www.icirestaurant.com

"Great care" and "organic", "locally grown" ingredients go into the "simple", "high-caliber" preparations at this moderately priced Fort Greene Franco-American; if it seems "cramped", don't forget the "delightful garden" and food that's the "equivalent of a massage."

I Coppi

22 21 20 $45

432 E. Ninth St. (bet. Ave. A & 1st Ave.), 212-254-2263;
www.icoppinyc.com

The "ambiance is worth the price" at this East Village Tuscan where they gracefully dish up "heaven-on-a-plate" items in "charming", "rustic" environs; an "enchanting", year-round garden helps ease the crush up front.

Ida Mae

22 19 17 $46

111 W. 38th St. (bet. B'way & 6th Ave.), 212-704-0038

Bringing a "bit of style" to the Garment District, this "upscale" Southerner serves "brightly flavored", "unexpectedly delicious" fare; but those who sigh "Jezebel wannabe" fault its "slow pace" and high pricing.

Ideya

∇ 21 16 18 $35

349 W. Broadway (bet. Broome & Grand Sts.), 212-625-1441;
www.ideya.net

"Something different" in SoHo, this "laid-back" Caribbean comes as a "surprise in such a trendy neighborhood" (ditto the "reasonable prices"); the food is "authentic", the mojitos "awesome" and the staff "flirtatious", ergo it's a "fun place to go with the girls."

Il Bagatto ●Ⓜ

22 16 15 $34

192 E. Second St. (bet. Aves. A & B), 212-228-0977

They're obviously "passionate" in the kitchen of this "inspired" East Village Italian, but the same passion doesn't apply in the front of the house where you'll face a "humorless" staff and "endless waits" "even with a reservation"; still, the place is "always packed" because the food quality is so high and rates so low.

Il Bastardo ●

18 18 18 $37

191 Seventh Ave. (bet. 21st & 22nd Sts.), 212-675-5980;
www.ilbastardonyc.com

Expect a "clubby" feel at this "spacious" Chelsea yearling, a former nightspot that still features "loud music" and a vaguely "Euro vibe"; its "delicious" Tuscan steakhouse cooking is "varied" and prices "moderate", but some say service still "needs more polish."

Il Buco ●

25 24 22 $56

47 Bond St. (bet. Bowery & Lafayette St.), 212-533-1932;
www.ilbuco.com

"Beautiful people" and "beautifully prepared" dishes meet at this "out-of-this-world" NoHo Med-Italian famed for its "seasonal", "market-driven" menu and "hefty price tags"; its "antiques-filled" interior radiates so much "farmhouse charm" that you'll feel transported to another place and time.

Il Cantinori

22 21 22 $59

32 E. 10th St. (bet. B'way & University Pl.), 212-673-6044;
www.ilcantinori.com

"Uptown style" comes Downtown at this airy Village vet that attracts both "celebs" and locals with its "delectable", "simply prepared" Northern Italiana; it's "expensive" and "elite" but "not stuffy", so it makes some "feel like a star."

Il Corallo Trattoria ●

22 12 19 $24

176 Prince St. (bet. Sullivan & Thompson Sts.), 212-941-7119

Famed for its "endless selection of fresh pasta", this "simple" SoHo Italian follows through with an "amazing quality-to-price ratio" that makes for great "bang for the buck"; downsides include "cramped" seating and virtually "no atmosphere at all."

Il Cortile ◐

23 | 20 | 19 | $50

125 Mulberry St. (bet. Canal & Hester Sts.), 212-226-6060; www.ilcortile.com

A longtime "shrine to red sauce", this justifiably popular "old-school" Mulberry Street Italian puts out "plentiful portions" of *"bellissimo"*, "ambitiously priced" chow; romeos recommend its "pretty" garden room – "if you can't close the deal there, something's wrong."

Il Fornaio

23 | 14 | 19 | $30

132A Mulberry St. (bet. Grand & Hester Sts.), 212-226-8306

"Not designed for San Gennaro visitors", this "vintage" Little Italy "hole-in-the-wall" has been serving "great meatballs and spaghetti" and the like at "fair prices" for 20 years; just "don't let its size fool you" – though rather "cramped", fans say it feels "like home."

Il Gattopardo ◐

23 | 18 | 23 | $60

33 W. 54th St. (bet. 5th & 6th Aves.), 212-246-0412; www.ilgattopardonyc.com

Somehow "undiscovered" despite being "across from MoMA", this Midtown Neapolitan is a "real find" for first-class formal dining; while its decor divides diners ("civilized" vs. "sparse"), there's agreement on the "professional, nonintrusive" service and "expense-account" prices.

IL GIGLIO ☒

26 | 18 | 23 | $68

81 Warren St. (bet. Greenwich St. & W. B'way), 212-571-5555; www.ilgigliorestaurant.com

There's so much "excellent", "old-style" Tuscan food served at this "formal" TriBeCa "favorite" that "freebie appetizers" arrive "the minute you sit down" (try "not to eat the day before"); it's also renowned for "corporate-card" pricing, "plain" decor and "impeccable" service from a "tuxedoed" team.

Il Mattone ☒

▽ 20 | 13 | 18 | $29

413 Greenwich St. (Hubert St.), 212-343-0030

"Savory" brick-oven pizza and "divine pastas" at "low prices" make some wonder why this "reliable" Italian remains one of "TriBeCa's best-kept secrets"; still, "spartan surroundings" and "limited seating" make a strong case for "delivery."

IL MULINO ☒

27 | 18 | 23 | $83

86 W. Third St. (bet. Sullivan & Thompson Sts.), 212-673-3783; www.ilmulinonewyork.com

"You're showered with food from the moment you sit down" at this "classic" Village "experience" that's still the "gold standard" for "old-school Italian dining"; sure, "tables are tight" and it's "difficult" – verging on "impossible" – to get a table, but the 'in' crowd says "unbuckle your belt and take out a loan" (or "rob a bank") – it's "worth it"; N.B. lunch is more casual, less expensive and easier to book.

Il Nido ☒

23 | 18 | 22 | $63

251 E. 53rd St. (bet. 2nd & 3rd Aves.), 212-753-8450; www.ilnidonyc.com

"Nothing's changed in 25 years" – and "that's fine" – at this "genteel" Midtown Northern Italian "throwback" praised for its "first-class" fare and "formal" service; its "older" clientele says it's best enjoyed if you "don't worry about money."

Il Palazzo

21 | 17 | 20 | $42

151 Mulberry St. (bet. Grand & Hester Sts.), 212-343-7000

"Managing to stay authentic", this Little Italy trattoria "holds its own" with a "well-prepared", midpriced, seafood-heavy menu; alright, it's "no palazzo", but it does offer a "charming", glass-roofed garden festooned with "twinkly lights."

Il Postino ⬤
23 | 19 | 22 | $63

337 E. 49th St. (bet. 1st & 2nd Aves.), 212-688-0033
"Bring a tape recorder": the "old-school" waiters "recite the menu by heart" at this U.N.-area Italian where the food is "excellent" and the "day's specials outnumber the entrees"; it attracts "business" types who don't mind the "hard sell", but is "not for the faint of credit card."

Il Riccio ⬤
20 | 14 | 18 | $53

152 E. 79th St. (bet. Lexington & 3rd Aves.), 212-639-9111
Ok, it "would help if it were bigger", but this "tight" UES "neighborhood resource" has "lots of repeaters" thanks to its "consistently good" Southern Italian cooking; regulars "request the back room" where you just might bump into Ralph Lauren or Mayor Bloomberg.

Il Tinello ⊠
24 | 20 | 24 | $63

16 W. 56th St. (bet. 5th & 6th Aves.), 212-245-4388
"Excellent" food "sends spirits soaring" at this Midtown Northern Italian that lures "decorous", "monied" folk with its "civilized" air, "spacious seating" and "white-glove" service; it's good for "special occasions" (and "Regis sightings"), and surprisingly little known.

Il Vagabondo ⬤
18 | 14 | 17 | $40

351 E. 62nd St. (bet. 1st & 2nd Aves.), 212-832-9221; www.ilvagabondo.com
"Still going strong", this "been-there-forever" East Side Italian rolls out an "all-red-sauce-all-the-time" menu for "reasonable" tabs; it's famed for its indoor bocce ball court (a "great digestif" after dinner), but the "bland" setting and mood are not as memorable.

Inagiku
23 | 19 | 20 | $59

Waldorf-Astoria, 111 E. 49th St. (bet. Lexington & Park Aves.), 212-355-0440; www.inagiku.com
"Sushi, Waldorf-Astoria–style" is the idea behind this "quiet, civilized" Midtowner where the "artistic preparations" and "gracious, kimono-garbed staff" draw kudos; though it's far from cheap, the "wonderful lunch special" is an economical alternative.

Indochine ⬤
21 | 20 | 17 | $49

430 Lafayette St. (bet. Astor Pl. & 4th St.), 212-505-5111; www.indochinenyc.com
"Chic" without "taking itself too seriously", this East Village "throwback to '80s glam" always works for nibbling "tempting" French-Vietnamese fare, sipping tropical cocktails and eyeballing "beautiful people"; the "colonial" decor distracts from the "expressionless" staff.

Industria Argentina ⬤ NEW
∇ 20 | 17 | 19 | $49

329 Greenwich St. (bet. Duane & Jay Sts.), 212-965-8560
Buenos Aires lands in TriBeCa via this new "modern" Argentinean; the menu emphasizes "delicious" steaks from "grass-fed" cattle along with a few Italian dishes, and the coolly "minimalist" decor is a perfect match for its sleek customer base.

Indus Valley
23 | 15 | 20 | $30

2636 Broadway (100th St.), 212-222-9222
The "best thing to happen to the UWS in a while" is this "delicate" Indian offering "top-notch", "not ordinary" fare – and "they're not afraid to make it hot"; "attentive service" and "affordable" pricing offset the "standard-issue decor."

'ino ⬤
24 | 14 | 18 | $25

21 Bedford St. (bet. Downing St. & 6th Ave.), 212-989-5769; www.cafeino.com
Sure, it's "broom closet–size" with "tables so close together you have to make sure you take the right napkin", but the payoff at this low-

budget Village Italian wine bar is "heavenly panini" paired with "reasonably priced wine"; less celestial are the "long lines" and "no-decor" decor.

'inoteca ●   23 18 20 $37
98 Rivington St. (Ludlow St.), 212-614-0473; www.inotecanyc.com
A "nibbler's delight", this "energetic" LES panini-and-vino vendor matches "fabulous small plates" with "to-die-for wines"; although considerably larger than its sibling, 'ino, it's just as "loud and crowded", and unless you can read Italian, the menu gives "no clue what's what."

Inside   ▽ 22 17 20 $45
9 Jones St. (bet. Bleecker & W. 4th Sts.), 212-229-9999
"Upscale comfort food" makes up the "innovative", "always-changing" menu at this "undiscovered", "ought-to-be-busier" Village New American; though the "lackluster name" may be reflected in the "bland" decor, service is "kind" and the tabs "moderate."

In Tent Ⓜ NEW   – – – M
231 Mott St. (bet. Prince & Spring Sts.), 212-966-6310; www.intentny.com
François Payard and Philippe Bertineau are the talents behind this smart new NoLita Mediterranean serving innovative regional fare; a small front lounge is the prelude to the main event, a tented back dining area lined with banquettes that's focused around a cascading wall of water; given the owners' track record at Payard Bistro, this seems a good bet.

Intermezzo ●   19 16 17 $31
202 Eighth Ave. (bet. 20th & 21st Sts.), 212-929-3433; www.intermezzony.com
"Slightly upscale" yet "without pretension", this "go-to" Chelsea Italian is just the ticket for an "unfettered pasta meal" among "gym bunnies" and other "trendy" types; though its "sleek", "totally renovated" space recalls a "dance club", it remains quite "affordable."

Iron Sushi   20 14 18 $29
355 E. 78th St. (bet. 1st & 2nd Aves.), 212-772-7680
440 Third Ave. (bet. 30th & 31st Sts.), 212-447-5822
"Respectable sushi" at low prices is the lure at these "standard", "no-wait" Japanese Eastsiders where you can "just walk in and be served"; an "attentive" staff and "lavish portions" distract from the "nothing-special" decor.

Isabella's ●   19 18 18 $41
359 Columbus Ave. (77th St.), 212-724-2100; www.brguestrestaurants.com
"Busy and buzzy", Steve Hanson's "long-running" Med–New American draws "stylish yuppies" with its "consistent" food, "cheerful" vibe and "eavesdropping" possibilities; it's *the* place for Sunday brunch" on the UWS, and best when you can "snag an outside table" to people-watch.

Island Burgers & Shakes ⊭   21 9 13 $15
766 Ninth Ave. (bet. 51st & 52nd Sts.), 212-307-7934
A "helluva variety" of "monster burgers" (with an "insane list of toppings") washed down with "tasty shakes" keeps the trade brisk at this Hell's Kitchen "hole-in-the-wall"; "low" tabs take the edge off the "harried" service and "almost criminal" lack of fries.

Isle   ▽ 19 17 19 $25
282 Bleecker St. (bet. Jones St. & 7th Ave. S.), 212-929-5699; www.islethai.com
"Stylish" and "calming", this Village Thai vends "agreeable if not transcendent" dishes in "lovely" digs dominated by a large

tropical mural; "service is quick and friendly", and thanks to a location on "touristy" Bleecker Street and very modest prices, it's often "jam-packed."

Ithaka
20 | 17 | 19 | $43

308 E. 86th St. (bet. 1st & 2nd Aves.), 212-628-9100; www.ithakarestaurant.com
"Quite good for the money", this "homey" UES Greek seafooder is known for its "good grilled fish" and "hospitable" crew; its "airy" space reminds some of a "seaside taverna", a feeling reinforced by a "live guitarist" strumming Hellenic harmonies.

I Tre Merli ●
18 | 18 | 16 | $43

463 W. Broadway (bet. Houston & Prince Sts.), 212-254-8699
183 W. 10th St. (W. 4th St.), 212-929-2221
www.itremerli.com
There's some "major bar action" going on at this lofty SoHo trattoria that's particularly "pleasant when the doors are open" to the street; its Village sibling is similarly "pretty, but tinier", with the same "lazy" service and "reliable", "reasonably priced" Northern Italian grub.

I Trulli
23 | 21 | 21 | $55

122 E. 27th St. (bet. Lexington Ave. & Park Ave. S.), 212-481-7372
"Everything clicks" at this "grown-up" Gramercy Italian where the "soulful" Pugliese cuisine and "la dolce vita" vibe are burnished by a "romantic garden" for summer and "cozy fireplace" for winter; an "impressive wine list" (also decanted at the next-door enoteca) helps soften the rather "costly" tabs.

Itzocan ⊭
24 | 10 | 18 | $31

438 E. Ninth St. (bet. Ave. A & 1st Ave.), 212-677-5856 ●
1575 Lexington Ave. (101st St.), 212-423-0255
Picture a "tiny studio apartment with an amazing chef" to get the gist of this East Village Mexican known for "high-quality", French-accented cooking at an "incredibly cheap price"; its Upper Upper East Side offshoot is a bit bigger, with the same "private kitchen" feel.

Ivo & Lulu ⊭
▽ 23 | 12 | 20 | $26

558 Broome St. (bet. 6th Ave. & Varick St.), 212-226-4399
"That magical acronym – BYO" – keeps prices "dirt-cheap" at this "tiny" SoHo "hideaway" where the "French-Caribbean comfort food" is "genuine", "spicy" and largely organic; optimists find the beyond-"tiny" quarters to be "very, um, romantic."

Ivy's Cafe ●
▽ 19 | 9 | 18 | $23

154 W. 72nd St. (bet. B'way & Columbus Ave.), 212-787-3333
"Decent Chinese food and better-than-that sushi" meet up at this something-for-everyone UWS eatery; habitués say the cheap "eclectic" menu "deserves a better setting" than this drab", "uninviting" space, and recommend the "super-fast delivery."

Ixta
20 | 16 | 17 | $41

48 E. 29th St. (bet. Madison Ave. & Park Ave. S.), 212-683-4833;
www.ixtarestaurant.com
"Imaginative" dishes and a long tequila list pair well with the "cool", Miami-esque decor and energetic vibe at this "trendy" Gramercy Mexican; it's one of the few "chic spots" in a "cuisine-bereft neighborhood", so the "noise" and "loud music" are more forgivable.

Jack ● NEW
▽ 17 | 17 | 19 | $35

80 University Pl. (11th St.), 212-620-5544
Village locals call this French bistro a "promising newcomer" given its "reliable food", "fair" pricing and overall "easy comfort"; even

those who report an "unimpressive beginning" think it's "slowly improving"; stay tuned.

Jack's Luxury Oyster Bar ⊠
24 | – | 22 | $73

101 Second Ave. (bet. 5th & 6th Sts.), 212-979-1012
"Every detail is perfect" at this "eccentric" East Villager where "exquisite" French-Continental fare plus "one-on-one personal service" equal a "great date restaurant for serious foodies"; P.S. it recently moved to the former Jewel Bako Makimono space, invalidating its Decor score.

Jackson Diner ⊅
22 | 11 | 14 | $22

37-47 74th St. (bet. Roosevelt Ave. & 37th Rd.), Queens, 718-672-1232
It's "worth the trip from any borough" to sample the wonderful dishes at this Jackson Heights Indian that's famed for its "dirt-cheap" $8.95 buffet brunch; given the "rushed" service, "spartan decor" and "tiresome crowds", regulars recommend "close your eyes and eat."

Jackson Hole
16 | 9 | 13 | $19

517 Columbus Ave. (85th St.), 212-362-5177
232 E. 64th St. (bet. 2nd & 3rd Aves.), 212-371-7187 ☾
1270 Madison Ave. (91st St.), 212-427-2820
1611 Second Ave. (bet. 83rd & 84th Sts.), 212-737-8788 ☾
521 Third Ave. (35th St.), 212-679-3264 ☾
69-35 Astoria Blvd. (70th St.), Queens, 718-204-7070 ☾
35-01 Bell Blvd. (35th Ave.), Queens, 718-281-0330 ☾
www.jacksonholeburgers.com
"Burgers too big to wrap your mouth around" have boosters "busting their buttons" (and "soaking up their hangovers") at this American mini-chain; parents abide the "shaky service", "glorified diner" decor and pervasive "grease smell" since it "hits the spot with kids."

Jacques
19 | 16 | 17 | $41

204-206 E. 85th St. (bet. 2nd & 3rd Aves.), 212-327-2272
20 Prince St. (bet. Elizabeth & Mott Sts.), 212-966-8886 ☾ **NEW**
www.jacquesnyc.com
Everything's "French to the bones" at these "charming" brasseries where the "solid" cooking is proudly "old-fashioned"; the new NoLita branch brings a North African spin to the mix, while both locations are beloved for their "extraordinary" weekly moules/frites/beer deals.

Jacques-Imo's NYC
16 | 14 | 15 | $33

366 Columbus Ave. (77th St.), 212-799-0150
Grand Central, lower level (42nd St. & Vanderbilt Ave.), 212-661-4022
www.jacquesimosnyc.com
Maybe it "doesn't live up to the N'Awlins original", but this UWS Cajun-Creole does serve "better-than-average" grub (including a "to-die-for fried chicken") enhanced by a reasonably authentic "frat-house-during-Mardi-Gras" vibe; P.S. the Grand Central location is a food court counter.

Jaiya Thai ☾
21 | 9 | 13 | $28

396 Third Ave. (28th St.), 212-889-1330; www.jaiya.com
"They don't kid around" with the spices at this "fiery" Gramercy Thai that's really "delicious – if you can handle the sweating"; "nonexistent" decor and "ragged-around-the-edges" service make a strong case for takeout or delivery.

Jake's Steakhouse
24 | 19 | 22 | $47

6031 Broadway (242nd St.), Bronx, 718-581-0182; www.jakessteakhouse.com
A "Manhattan restaurant in the Bronx", this reasonable, bi-level Riverdale steakhouse is run by meat wholesalers so you can antici-

pate "awesome" chops "in the Peter Luger fashion"; insiders request an upstairs table featuring splendid "views of Van Cortlandt Park."

Jane ●
21 | 17 | 20 | $39

100 W. Houston St. (bet. La Guardia Pl. & Thompson St.), 212-254-7000; www.janerestaurant.com

It's "easy to like" this "consistent", "unpretentious" American bistro parked on the Village-SoHo border, where the food is "simple but elegant" and the pricing "easy on the budget"; the generally "nice buzz" can really hum during the "popular" weekend brunch.

JAPONAIS NEW
– | – | – | E

111 E. 18th St. (bet. Irving Pl. & Park Ave. S.), 212-260-2020; www.japonaisnewyork.com

Just blown into Gramercy from the Windy City, this highly anticipated French-accented Japanese offers a pricey menu prepared by dueling chefs, one responsible for hot fare, the other cold dishes; supported by Jeffrey Beers' swank, red-lacquered room and bracketed by two sexy lounges, the place is living up to its advance hype.

Japonica
22 | 14 | 19 | $42

100 University Pl. (12th St.), 212-243-7752; www.japonicanyc.com

One of NY's "original sushi destinations", this longtime Village Japanese still "holds its own against the newer upstarts" by offering "superbly fresh", "jumbo"-size rolls; less pleasing is the "somewhat tired" decor and "not cheap" prices.

Jarnac Ⓜ
21 | 18 | 22 | $50

328 W. 12th St. (Greenwich St.), 212-924-3413; www.jarnacny.com

"You'll think you're in France, except they're nice to you" at this "homey" West Village "neighborhood favorite" where the owners routinely "chat with patrons"; the French bistro menu is prepared with "nuance and panache", though it's a "little pricey for what it is."

Jasmine
20 | 16 | 17 | $25

1619 Second Ave. (84th St.), 212-517-8854

"Consistently tasty", this "better-than-average" UES "neighborhood" Thai is "always packed" thanks to its "heaping" portions and "modest prices"; "crowds" and "bland" looks lead some to suggest "takeout."

Jean Claude ⊄
22 | 16 | 20 | $41

137 Sullivan St. (bet. Houston & Prince Sts.), 212-475-9232

"True Gallic charm" emanates from this SoHo French bistro that "looks as if was transplanted from a Provençal town square"; *la cuisine* is "always excellent" and the tariffs "decent", though what's "intimate" to some is "small" to others.

JEAN GEORGES ⊠
28 | 26 | 27 | $98

Trump Int'l Hotel, 1 Central Park W. (bet. 60th & 61st Sts.), 212-299-3900; www.jean-georges.com

An "absolutely ethereal" experience, Jean-Georges Vongerichten's New French flagship in Columbus Circle offers always "inventive" food in a "chicly understated", Adam Tihany–designed setting; it's "heavenly" dining, prices included, but the "royal-treatment" service alone will make you "feel important just being there", so "break the piggy bank and go for it" – or try the $24 prix fixe lunch on the terrace or in the "more casual" Nougatine Room.

Jerry's
18 | 13 | 16 | $31

101 Prince St. (bet. Greene & Mercer Sts.), 212-966-9464; www.jerrysnyc.com

"Arty" folk toy with "well-executed comfort food" at this 20-year-old SoHo "diner with standards to maintain"; ok, it's "not what you'd call pretty" and service can be as "slow" as grass growing, but it's "just the thing" for "casual" grazing – and "you can't beat the prices."

JEWEL BAKO ⬛

26	22	24	$77

239 E. Fifth St. (bet. 2nd & 3rd Aves.), 212-979-1012
"High expectations" are met at this "impeccable" East Village Japanese purveying "exotic sushi" that's "fresher than anything the Great Whites eat" served in a "super-stylish", bamboo-lined sliver of a space; the "amazing attention to detail" extends to the "solicitous" service and "incredibly warm" hosts Jack and Grace Lamb, who even make the jewelry-store pricing palatable.

Jewel of India

21	18	19	$38

15 W. 44th St. (bet. 5th & 6th Aves.), 212-869-5544;
www.jewelofindiarestaurant.com
"Winning cuisine" is served by a "courtly" staff at this Midtown Indian that's "reliable", "relaxed" and best known for its "bargain" lunch buffet; still, those who see more of a "zircon" find things "a bit stale" and suggest "updating the decor."

Jezebel ⬛ Ⓜ

19	24	18	$50

630 Ninth Ave. (45th St.), 212-582-1045; www.jezebelny.com
"Blanche DuBois would feel at home" at this "transporting" Theater District Southern belle best remembered for its theatrical "Biloxi bordello" setting complete with potted palms and porch-swing seating; too bad the "tasty" food is "not as memorable as the decor."

J.G. Melon ◐ ⧸

21	12	15	$24

1291 Third Ave. (74th St.), 212-744-0585
This "enduring" UES "institution" is renowned for its "consistently good" burgers and "delicious cottage fries"; its "slumming prepster" crowd digs the "summer-in-the-Hamptons" vibe, not the "run-of-the-mill" decor and "cash-only" policy.

Jing Fong

19	13	13	$20

20 Elizabeth St. (bet. Bayard & Canal Sts.), 212-964-5256
"Like dining inside Madison Square Garden", this "gargantuan" Chinatown dim sum palace–cum–party space vends "Hong Kong–style" grub in "gaudy", as in very gaudy, digs; it's "cheap", it's "manic" and it's all about "pointing", since the "staff's command of English is as thin as a rice noodle."

JivamukTea Cafe NEW

–	–	–	I

Jivamukti Yoga School, 841 Broadway, 2nd fl. (13th St.), 212-353-2487;
www.jivamuktiyoga.com
Chef Matthew Kenney sticks to his roots and shoots at this casual, low-budget vegan/raw-food cafe serving salads, sandwiches and desserts, washed down with smoothies and organic coffee; just off Union Square in the new Jivamukti Yoga School, it features stained-glass panels and a soothing soundtrack.

Joe Allen ◐

17	16	18	$40

326 W. 46th St. (bet. 8th & 9th Aves.), 212-581-6464;
www.joeallenrestaurant.com
An old "reliable on Restaurant Row", this "classy saloon" serves "familiar" American comfort chow in a "congenial" if slightly "shabby" setting; "B'way personality" sightings compensate for the "disengaged" service, while habitués hint it's "better after theater than before."

Joe's Ginger ⧸

22	8	13	$23

113 Mott St. (bet. Canal & Hester Sts.), 212-966-6613
25 Pell St. (Doyers St.), 212-285-0333

(continued)

Joe's Shanghai

9 Pell St. (bet. Bowery & Mott St.), 212-233-8888 ●⊟
24 W. 56th St. (bet. 5th & 6th Aves.), 212-333-3868
136-21 37th Ave. (bet. Main & Union Sts.), Queens, 718-539-3838 ⊟

You'll "believe the soup dumpling hype" at this Shanghai-style Chinese chain where the justifiably "famous buns" and "really cheap" tabs triumph over the "long lines", "zero decor", "gruff service" and "elbow-to-elbow" seating.

Joe's Pizza
| 23 | 5 | 12 | $8 |

7 Carmine St. (bet. Bleecker St. & 6th Ave.), 212-255-3946 ●
137 Seventh Ave. (bet. Carroll St. & Garfield Pl.), Brooklyn, 718-499-9198

"Setting the standard for slices in Manhattan", these cross-borough "stand-up" joints feature "non-designer" pizzas that meld "thin, slightly charred crusts" with an "incredible sauce-to-cheese consistency"; thanks to high quality and low prices, they're "always buzzing" – till 5 AM at the Village branch.

John's of 12th Street ⊟
| 19 | 13 | 18 | $32 |

302 E. 12th St. (2nd Ave.), 212-475-9531

Featuring "dripping-candle" decor right out of "*Lady and the Tramp*", this circa-1908 East Village Italian follows up with "beyond-huge" portions of "garlic-laden" "red-sauce" fare; maybe it's a bit "worn out", but it still has plenty of "throwback" appeal.

John's Pizzeria ●
| 22 | 12 | 15 | $21 |

278 Bleecker St. (bet. 6th Ave. & 7th Ave. S.), 212-243-1680 ⊟
408 E. 64th St. (bet. 1st & York Aves.), 212-935-2895
260 W. 44th St. (bet. B'way & 8th Ave.), 212-391-7560
www.johnspizzerianyc.com

For "pizza as pizza should be" – made in coal-fired brick ovens, its crust "cracker-thin" – try this "fabulous" trio famed for serving "no slices"; the circa-1929 Village original with its wooden booths has "more character", though Times Square's "renovated church" setting is said to be "heavenly."

JoJo
| 24 | 22 | 23 | $66 |

160 E. 64th St. (bet. Lexington & 3rd Aves.), 212-223-5656;
www.jean-georges.com

Jean-Georges Vongerichten's "first place", this haute French bistro "never disappoints" thanks to its "subtle, elegant" cuisine, "polished" service and that "romantic jewel box" setting in an East Side townhouse; sure, it's "pricey", but the $24 prix fixe lunch is a "great buy"; diners debate whether "upstairs is nicer than downstairs."

Jolie
| 21 | 21 | 21 | $37 |

320 Atlantic Ave. (bet. Hoyt & Smith Sts.), Brooklyn, 718-488-0777;
www.jolierestaurant.com

"*Jolie* indeed" say supporters smitten by this "sexy", "sophisticated" French settler in Boerum Hill, where the food's "terrific" and the service "lovely"; the "great vibe" and easy pricing make it a "good choice for special occasions" – especially in the "gorgeous garden."

Josephina ●
| 18 | 16 | 17 | $44 |

1900 Broadway (bet. 63rd & 64th Sts.), 212-799-1000;
www.josephinanyc.com

"As popular as *La Bohème*", this "big, bustling" American-Eclectic "standby" opposite Lincoln Center offers "fine if not special" repasts served by an "efficient" crew; despite the "frenetic" pre-theater scene, it "will get you to the opera on time", and for an "affordable" price.

Josie's
19 | 15 | 16 | $32

300 Amsterdam Ave. (74th St.), 212-769-1212 ◑
565 Third Ave. (37th St.), 212-490-1558
www.josiesnyc.com

"Virtuous eaters" love these "wholesome" crosstown Eclectics known for their organic, "karma-enriching" meals; they "attract lots of chicks" who like "eating healthy while feeling spoiled", even if noise levels may make it "difficult to have a conversation."

Jovia NEW
– | 23 | 22 | $63

135 E. 62nd St. (bet. Lexington & Park Aves.), 212-752-6000; www.jovianyc.com

"Comfortable and relaxing", this "upscale" UES Italian-American newcomer from the owners of SoHo's Zoë is set in a "pretty townhouse" with casual ground-floor dining and a more formal feel upstairs; many report "cerebral", "innovative" cooking, but the loss of chef Josh DeChellis negates its Food score.

Joya ⊖
25 | 19 | 20 | $21

215 Court St. (Warren St.), Brooklyn, 718-222-3484

The setting may be "minimalist", but the food is not at this "trendy" Cobble Hill Thai where "spicy means spicy"; it's always "crazy crowded" because it's so "crazy cheap", so those hoping to escape the "clublike" hubbub take refuge in its "sublime garden."

Jubilee
22 | 16 | 19 | $46

347 E. 54th St. (bet. 1st & 2nd Aves.), 212-888-3569; www.jubileeny.com

"Totally charming" and "unpretentious", this Sutton Place French bistro draws a "lovely mature crowd" with "solid" cooking highlighted by "wonderful" signature mussels; despite "cheek-to-jowl" seating, it's a "good value" and "always crowded."

Junior's
18 | 11 | 14 | $21

386 Flatbush Ave. (DeKalb Ave.), Brooklyn, 718-852-5257 ◑
Grand Central, lower level (42nd St. & Vanderbilt Ave.), 212-983-5257
Shubert Alley, 1515 Broadway (enter on 45th St., bet. B'way & 8th Ave.), 212-302-2000 ◑ NEW
www.juniorscheesecake.com

"Legendary cheesecake" is the star of this Downtown Brooklyn "institution" where "old pro" waiters serve "huge" plates of "imitation NY deli" food in "memorabilia"-laden digs; the Grand Central and Shubert Alley outposts are "junior varsity" versions of the original, but still enjoyable for their modest tabs.

Kai ⊠Ⓜ
25 | 25 | 26 | $79

Ito En, 822 Madison Ave., 2nd fl. (bet. 68th & 69th Sts.), 212-988-7277; www.itoen.com

Proving that "food can be art", this "serene" UES Japanese provides "exquisite" kaiseki cuisine via a chef who "composes the meal like a symphony"; "portions are small" and the "sticker shock" large, but "transcendental experiences" rarely come cheap.

Kam Chueh ◑
∇ 23 | 8 | 16 | $24

40 Bowery (bet. Bayard & Canal Sts.), 212-791-6868

Pick your dinner "fresh from the tanks by the entrance" of this C-town Cantonese known for "spectacular" fish and "imaginative dim sum"; it's hard to beat for "authenticity", so it helps to "order in Mandarin."

Kang Suh ◑
21 | 13 | 17 | $32

1250 Broadway (32nd St.), 212-564-6845

For a "meal and an adventure", try this 24/7 Garment District Korean featuring "flavorful", do-it-yourself BBQ plus a host of other items, sushi included; though "the waiters' English is limited", it's still "foreigner-friendly" and "great fun" to boot.

Kanoyama ◉

▽ 27 | 17 | 22 | $42

175 Second Ave. (11th St.), 212-777-5266
"Still a secret", this East Village Japanese is "one of Manhattan's best sushi options" with an "unparalleled" selection of "fish you never heard of"; the "minimalist" space matches its "midrange" pricing.

Kapadokya

▽ 20 | 16 | 17 | $26

142 Montague St., 2nd fl. (bet. Clinton & Henry Sts.), Brooklyn, 718-875-2211
Those seeking an "exotic escape" in Brooklyn Heights head for this "creative" Turk offering "original variations on familiar Mideast themes" plus a patio and weekend belly dancers; a "nice change of pace", it's especially "good for a jury duty lunch."

Kati Roll Co.

22 | 6 | 12 | $10

99 MacDougal St. (bet. Bleecker & W. 3rd Sts.), 212-420-6517 ◉
140 W. 46th St. (bet. 6th & 7th Aves.), 212-730-4280 NEW
"Cheap little bites" don't get much better than the kati rolls (aka "Indian burritos") at these Midtown/Village storefronts, but beware: "one is not enough" and service is "slow" for so-called "fast food."

Katsu-Hama

24 | 11 | 16 | $23

11 E. 47th St. (bet. 5th & Madison Aves.), 212-758-5909; www.katsuhama.com
For a "Japanese restaurant sans sushi", try this "engaging" Midtown katsu parlor specializing in "delicious" fried cutlets; it's "hard to go wrong here when you're not looking to spend much money", but be aware there's "always a wait for lunch."

Katz's Delicatessen

23 | 9 | 11 | $20

205 E. Houston St. (Ludlow St.), 212-254-2246; www.katzdeli.com
An "authentic NYC experience", this LES "trip-back-in-time" deli where Harry met Sally is famed for its "oy"-inducing corned beef, pastrami and latkes, along with grungy cafeteria decor, a "Byzantine ordering system" and waiters specially schooled in the "art of rudeness"; it can be hard to get a seat or the counterman's attention (tipping helps), but it's "worth every belch."

Keens Steakhouse

24 | 22 | 21 | $60

72 W. 36th St. (bet. 5th & 6th Aves.), 212-947-3636; www.keens.com
"Meat and testosterone" collide at this "steeped-in-history" Midtown steakhouse where 88,000 – yes 88,000 – "clay pipes line the ceiling" and the "signature mutton chop" is the thing to order; "prompt" service and a handsome setting filled with a museum's worth of American memorabilia add to its allure, while the upstairs private rooms are perfect for a party of any size.

Kellari Taverna ◉ NEW

▽ 21 | 24 | 19 | $52

19 W. 44th St. (bet. 5th & 6th Aves.), 212-221-0144; www.kellari.us
"Sleek and sophisticated", this new "high-end" Theater District Greek specializes in "fresh grilled fish" and serves it in airy, "high-ceilinged" digs meant to invoke a wine cellar; while it's still "getting the kinks out", the "very reasonable" pre-theater prix fixe needs no adjustments.

Kelley & Ping

16 | 14 | 13 | $24

325 Bowery (2nd St.), 212-475-8600
127 Greene St. (bet. Houston & Prince Sts.), 212-228-1212
These "no-frills", "assembly-line" Downtown Pan-Asian noodle shops offer cafeteria-style lunches and full-service dinners, but either way they're "cheap" and "tasty"; too bad about the "bland" decor and "hit-or-miss" staffers.

Killmeyer's Old Bavaria Inn
19 | 20 | 20 | $30

4254 Arthur Kill Rd. (Sharrotts Rd.), Staten Island, 718-984-1202; www.killmeyers.com

There's "nothing like a brat in the biergarten" of this "casual" German renowned for its "great beer selection"; while its Staten Island location may be "remote", the moderately priced food is reasonably "authentic", so it's an "asset" when you seek "something different."

Kings' Carriage House
21 | 25 | 23 | $55

251 E. 82nd St. (bet. 2nd & 3rd Aves.), 212-734-5490; www.kingscarriagehouse.com

"Charm" is the watchword at this "romantic" UES New American where a "traditional", "country-mansion" setting is burnished by "go-out-of-their-way" service and "delicious" food that's priced for a well-heeled "older generation"; insiders say the "real treat here is afternoon tea."

King Yum ●
▽ 17 | 13 | 17 | $27

181-08 Union Tpke. (181st St.), Queens, 718-380-1918

On the Fresh Meadows scene since 1953, this Cantonese "institution" serves an "old-fashioned" mix of Chinese and Polynesian items "of the pupu platter variety"; the "tacky" thatched-hut decor and "weekend karaoke" still "draw crowds" – and it seems like they "haven't raised their prices in 20 years."

Kin Khao
21 | 17 | 17 | $36

171 Spring St. (bet. Thompson St. & W. B'way), 212-966-3939

Still "rolling along" after 15 years, this SoHo Thai owes its "staying power" to "better-than-average" cooking and a dark, "sexy" setting; economists figure you "can't beat it for the price", even if the "no-reservations policy" is rather "frustrating."

KitchenBar ● NEW
– | – | – | I

687 Sixth Ave. (20th St.), Brooklyn, 718-499-5623; www.kitchenbarny.com

Ever gentrifying South Park Slope is home to this arty new gastropub dispensing low-priced Med-American vittles in a funky space festooned with local artwork that's also for sale; the tapas-size plates also come in family-size portions, à la the one-pound cheeseburger.

Kitchen Club
▽ 20 | 18 | 19 | $43

30 Prince St. (Mott St.), 212-274-0025; www.thekitchenclub.com

The "eccentric owner" and Chibi, her "enchanting" pup, are both "very present" at this "quirky" NoLita French-Japanese purveying "eclectic" dishes in "cozy" digs; it's the "definition of a neighborhood joint", with an adjacent sake bar as an "unexpected bonus."

Kitchenette
20 | 12 | 15 | $22

1272 Amsterdam Ave. (bet. 122nd & 123rd Sts.), 212-531-7600
156 Chambers St. (bet. Greenwich St. & W. B'way), 212-267-6740

"Millions of calories" are consumed hourly at these "kitschy" "hangover helpers" slinging "ridiculous amounts" of all your Southern "comfort favorites", although "slow-as-molasses service" and "sloppy settings" are part of the package; N.B. the TriBeCa outpost has moved to larger Chambers Street digs.

Kitchen 22 ⊠
20 | 17 | 18 | $36

36 E. 22nd St. (bet. B'way & Park Ave. S.), 212-228-4399; www.charliepalmer.com

"Upscale" food for "lowscale" prices is the appealing formula at Charlie Palmer's Flatiron New American that offers $29 three-course meals (as well as à la carte options); the "limited menu" and "no-reservations" policy to the contrary, this one's a good bet.

KITTICHAI

23 27 20 $56

*60 Thompson Hotel, 60 Thompson St. (bet. Broome & Spring Sts.),
212-219-2000; www.kittichairestaurant.com*

"Darkly atmospheric", this "trendy" SoHo Thai set in an "über-groovy" hotel offers "advanced", "creative" fare and "perfect cocktails" in "Bangkok chic" quarters complete with a "lily-pad pool" and "orchids galore"; given its "hostesses out of *Vogue*" and "models-bankers-fashionistas" clientele, many say it's "more about the scene than the food."

Klong ❿

21 19 17 $22

*7 St. Marks Pl. (bet. 2nd & 3rd Aves.), 212-505-9955;
www.klongnyc.com*

An East Village block "known more for tattoos and body shots" gets the "feng-shui" treatment via this "chic" Thai serving "delicious" "Bangkok street food" in a "modern-cool" setting; "absolute bargain" pricing is increasing the traffic on this "already busy sidewalk."

Knickerbocker Bar & Grill ❿

20 17 19 $44

*33 University Pl. (bet. 8th & 9th Sts.), 212-228-8490;
www.knickerbockerbarandgrill.com*

A "Village institution" for 30 years, this "no-pretensions" place attracts "NYU students and their parents" with its "classic" New American steakhouse menu; maybe it's "old-fashioned" in a "handsomely frumpy" way, but touches like "live weekend jazz" keep it "vibrant."

Knife + Fork Ⓜ NEW

– – – M

*108 E. Fourth St. (bet. 1st & 2nd Aves.), 212-228-4885;
www.knife-fork-nyc.com*

There's a rustic farmhouse feel at this petite new East Villager thanks to its 100-year-old pine tables, white-washed walls and candlelit bar; the modestly priced, thoughtfully composed Modern European menu comes either à la carte or via a $45, six-course tasting option.

Kodama ❿

20 11 18 $30

301 W. 45th St. (bet. 8th & 9th Aves.), 212-582-8065

"When you're in a hurry to make the curtain", this Theater District Japanese "does the job" with "first-rate" sushi served by a "quick" staff for a fair price; despite "austere" decor, it's a "dependable" "value."

Koi

23 23 18 $62

*Bryant Park Hotel, 40 W. 40th St. (bet. 5th & 6th Aves.), 212-921-3330;
www.koirestaurant.com*

"Sleek and elegant", this "trendy LA import" in the Bryant Park Hotel is a magnet for "twentysomethings" and other "beautiful" types who graze on "fresh", "flavorful" sushi and Japanese fusion fare that taste even "better on an expense account."

Korea Palace Ⓢ

20 15 18 $34

*127 E. 54th St. (bet. Lexington & Park Aves.), 212-832-2350;
www.koreapalace.com*

"Excellent" Korean BBQ (plus sushi for "the less adventurous") and a "large menu" of traditional dishes that the staff "will patiently explain" are draws at this "value"-oriented Midtown "lunch favorite"; at dinner "live piano music" softens its "big, bright" space.

Kori Ⓢ

∇ 21 19 21 $34

253 Church St. (bet. Franklin & Leonard Sts.), 212-334-4598

Though relatively "unknown", this "upscale" TriBeCa Korean dispenses "fantastic cocktails" and "tasty" dishes "stylized" "for the American palate"; "attentive" staffers man the "relaxed" quarters that are "intimate" enough to be a "date spot."

Ko Sushi
20 | 15 | 19 | $31

1329 Second Ave. (70th St.), 212-439-1678
1619 York Ave. (85th St.), 212-772-8838
www.newkosushi.com
In a "neighborhood jammed with Japanese" restaurants, these separately owned East Side sushi dens "hold their own" with fish that's "as fresh as fresh can be" and "affordably priced" too; besides having "quick", "efficient" service, they're also "decent take-out" options.

Kuma Inn ● Ⓜ ⇄
∇ 23 | 15 | 19 | $34

113 Ludlow St., 2nd fl. (bet. Delancey & Rivington Sts.), 212-353-8866;
www.kumainn.com
"Hidden" in a "secret upstairs" LES location, this "small" Filipino-Thai is worth seeking out for its "inventive, delicious" small plates that "you won't find anywhere else"; it looks a little "like someone's apartment", so it's apt that the "kind" staff makes you "feel like a guest in their home."

Kum Gang San ●
22 | 15 | 16 | $31

49 W. 32nd St. (bet. B'way & 5th Ave.), 212-967-0909
138-28 Northern Blvd. (bet. Bowne & Union Sts.), Queens, 718-461-0909
"Korean soul food at its best" – including "heavenly" BBQ – keeps this 24/7 Garment District–Flushing duo "bustling with happy families"; its "cavernous" digs are "so cheesy it's great", and though service "isn't perfect", it's "solicitous."

KURUMA ZUSHI Ⓢ
∇ 28 | 15 | 23 | $109

7 E. 47th St., 2nd fl. (bet. 5th & Madison Aves.), 212-317-2802
"Serious" sushi-philes feel this "stellar" Midtown Japanese must have been blessed by the "fish gods", if not a decor deity; "sit at the sushi bar" and take your pick from the "rare selection", or go "omakase all the way" – but just "be prepared" for a substantial tab.

Kyma ●
18 | 15 | 16 | $40

300 W. 46th St. (8th Ave.), 212-957-8830
Theatergoers seeking a "Greek alternative" pre-show head to this "pleasant" Midtowner for "good grilled fish" and other "dependable" Hellenic classics; no one minds much if the "light, airy" space is a bit "frayed" or the service seems "rushed" – they "get you out in time!"

La Baraka
21 | 16 | 23 | $40

255-09 Northern Blvd. (Little Neck Pkwy.), Queens, 718-428-1461;
www.labarakarest.com
"Graciousness is the name of the game" at this "family-run" Little Neck Gallic, a "cozy" "local gem" serving "homestyle" classics at "modest prices"; maybe the decor needs "sprucing up", but not "sweet" owner-hostess Lucette, who's a "unique French experience unto herself."

La Bergamote ⇄
23 | 13 | 14 | $13

169 Ninth Ave. (20th St.), 212-627-9010
"Phenomenal French pastries, breads, sandwiches" – there are "temptations everywhere" at this "low-key", "Paris-in-Chelsea" bakery/cafe; "mundane" quarters and "variable" service aside, most find it just the "place to enjoy a coffee and the Sunday *Times*."

La Boîte en Bois
21 | 15 | 20 | $47

75 W. 68th St. (bet. Columbus Ave. & CPW), 212-874-2705;
www.laboitenyc.com
You're sure to "meet your fellow diners" at this "phone booth"–size, yet still "civilized", Lincoln Center "standby" dispensing "first-rate French food" via a "polite" staff; though the quarters are "slightly down-at-the-heel", its $34 pre-theater prix fixe is simply "*charmante*."

La Bonne Soupe
18 14 15 $29

48 W. 55th St. (bet. 5th & 6th Aves.), 212-586-7650; www.labonnesoupe.com

"Delicious" onion soup "shines" among other "souper" "satisfying bistro" items at this "down-to-earth" Midtown "reminder of France"; regulars love the "low-budget" rates, but warn of "acerbic French wit" from the "harried" staff, and wish for just "a bit more elbow room."

La Bottega ◑
17 20 14 $41

Maritime Hotel, 88 Ninth Ave. (17th St.), 212-243-8400; www.themaritimehotel.com

It's "not your father's pizza for sure", but the "solid" Italian fare at this "big", "star-studded" Chelsea trattoria isn't really the point anyway; the "main attraction" is the "fabulous" patio where "pretty" "scenesters" "people-watch" while wondering "how long the staff can ignore" them.

L'Absinthe
22 22 20 $62

227 E. 67th St. (bet. 2nd & 3rd Aves.), 212-794-4950; www.labsinthe.com

"Blink and you're in Paris" at this "glamorous" Eastsider that "captures the essence of a French brasserie" with its handsome "art nouveau decor" and "remarkably fine" food; "snooty" "pro" service and a "posh" clientele "dressed to impress" are also "*classique*", as are the "prices that truly evoke Europe."

La Cantina Toscana
▽ 24 13 22 $48

1109 First Ave. (bet. 60th & 61st Sts.), 212-754-5454

Something of an "undiscovered jewel", this "rustic" East Side Tuscan's "ambitious" menu features "fabulous game dishes" plus a "long list of superb specials"; "affordable wines" and "engaging" service offset any deficits in its decor.

Lady Mendl's Ⓜ
21 26 26 $42

Inn at Irving Pl., 56 Irving Pl. (bet. 17th & 18th Sts.), 212-533-4466; www.ladymendls.com

You feel "grown-up" and "civilized" nibbling on the "lovely little sandwiches and cakes" amid the "Victorian splendor" at this Gramercy "tea parlor"; it's perfect for "mother-daughter bonding" or a "girlie afternoon" enjoying the feel of "a different century", even if the pricing is up-to-date.

La Esquina ◑
21 20 16 $38

106 Kenmare St. (bet. Cleveland & Lafayette Sts.), 646-613-7100; www.esquinanyc.com

At this "beyond-hip" Mexican, those "in-the-loop" use the "secret entrance" to an "underground" grotto where "NoLita society" nibbles "delicious" bites by "candlelight"; it's a "three-tiered" affair, though, so if you can't take the "catacomb" room's "reservation hassle" and "too-cool-for-you attitude" try the cafe or taco stand upstairs.

La Flor Bakery & Cafe ⊄
▽ 24 14 18 $23

53-02 Roosevelt Ave. (53rd St.), Queens, 718-426-8023

An "inspired" "mix of cuisines" plus "seriously good desserts" make this "small" Mexican-Eclectic "under the elevated 7 train" in Woodside "worth the trek"; though the setup is "sparse" and service sometimes "lacking", you "can't help but like the place" – especially when you see the modest bill.

La Focaccia
19 18 18 $36

51 Bank St. (W. 4th St.), 212-675-3754

"As expected, the focaccia is super" at this "cute" West Village Italian, but the "fresh" brick oven–fired meat and fish dishes ensure carbophobes can chow down without "scrapping the diet"; the prices are "a fair bargain" and service "friendly", so no surprise it's typically "crowded."

La Giara

20	16	20	$36

501 Third Ave. (bet. 33rd & 34th Sts.), 212-726-9855; www.lagiara.com
A "cozy" "oasis" on a "tawdry stretch of Third", this "dependable" Murray Hill Italian proffers a "simple" menu with "homemade pastas" in the "starring" role; locals "love the sidewalk seating" and the "$19.95 early-bird prix fixe."

La Gioconda

21	15	19	$38

226 E. 53rd St. (bet. 2nd & 3rd Aves.), 212-371-3536; www.lagiocondany.com
You'll find "no paparazzi" at this "unpretentious" Midtown "hideaway", just "really good", "flavorful" Italian food served in quarters so snug the "friendly" staff should "seat you with a shoehorn"; still, it's "calm, relaxed" and "affordable", so you'll likely "leave smiling."

La Goulue ●

19	19	16	$61

746 Madison Ave. (bet. 64th & 65th Sts.), 212-988-8169
"Perfect for the leisure class" and "ladies who shop", this UES "real French bistro" offers "quality" classics and "great people-watching", especially in the "prime outside seats"; it's *très cher* and sometimes the staffers "forget they're working", but it's "always an experience."

LA GRENOUILLE ⊠ Ⓜ

27	27	27	$94

3 E. 52nd St. (bet. 5th & Madison Aves.), 212-752-1495; www.la-grenouille.com
Among the last of the city's "old guard", this justly renowned Midtown French restaurant "serves up dreams" via "sublime" classic "haute cuisine" and "perfectly pitched service" in a "stunning", "serene" space abloom with "famously" "gorgeous flowers"; *oui*, such "glamorous" repasts "come dear", but you'll leave "feeling like a million bucks"; N.B. check out the second-floor party room.

La Grolla

20	13	19	$42

413 Amsterdam Ave. (bet. 79th & 80th Sts.), 212-496-0890; www.lagrolla.us
Focus on the "rich", "unusual" "Alpine Italian" specialties at this "mellow" UWS "stalwart" and it's easy to ignore its "tight" "grungy" interior; another endearment is that the staff is so "friendly", "your first visit feels like your 10th."

Lake Club

20	24	20	$43

1150 Clove Rd. (Victory Blvd.), Staten Island, 718-442-3600; www.lake-club.com
The "sylvan setting" complete with "beautiful lake view" is as "amazing" as ever at this SI Continental seafooder, and word is the food has "greatly improved" thanks to a new chef and "revamped" menu; meanwhile, a "recent redo" has upped the "romance" factor.

La Lanterna di Vittorio ●

▽ 19	20	16	$27

129 MacDougal St. (bet. W. 3rd & 4th Sts.), 212-529-5945; www.lalanternacaffe.com
"Talk about romantic", this "moody" Village Italian offers "oodles of atmosphere" ("cozy" fireplaces, live jazz) to go with its "lovingly crafted pizzas" and "delectable" desserts; the service "could use shoring up", but that can't spoil those "close, quiet conversations" over a glass of vino.

La Locanda dei Vini

21	15	20	$45

737 Ninth Ave. (bet. 49th & 50th Sts.), 212-258-2900; www.lalocandadeivinirestaurant.com
Outside, it may look like a "hovel", but that only adds to the sense that "you've discovered a secret" once inside this "rustic" midpriced

Hell's Kitchen Italian that "gets all the basics right" and is often "fabulous"; "terrific" service makes it a "reliable" pre-theater option too.

La Lunchonette
21 | 15 | 19 | $40

130 10th Ave. (18th St.), 212-675-0342
"Charming in a run-down way", this "easygoing" Chelsea "favorite" dispenses "well-prepared","real-as-it-gets" French bistro fare with "no hassles and no attitude" from "attentive", if "eccentric", staffers; all in all it's a "welcome relief" from the neighborhood's "trendiness."

La Mangeoire
19 | 19 | 19 | $46

1008 Second Ave. (bet. 53rd & 54th Sts.), 212-759-7086; www.lamangeoire.com
Like a trip to "Provence on the cheap", this "upscale" yet "semi-casual" East Side French bistro's "pretty" quarters are elevated by "standout flower arrangements"; it's been "serving the same dishes for 30-plus years", meaning the "classic" "hearty" fare is as "reliable" as the "friendly" service.

Lamarca ⊠
18 | 8 | 16 | $21

161 E. 22nd St. (3rd Ave.), 212-674-6363
For "good, cheap" "homemade pastas" and such with "reasonable" wines to match, this "simple" Gramercy Sicilian "can't be beat"; although the "no-frills" setup may suggest "takeout or delivery", really "the only bummer" is that "they close on weekends."

La Masseria ●
22 | 19 | 21 | $52

235 W. 48th St. (bet. B'way & 8th Ave.), 212-582-2111; www.lamasserianyc.com
A "favorite Theater District haunt" thanks to its "unexpectedly excellent" Southern Italian food and "pleasant" "farmhouse" setting, this "winner" boasts a "pro" staff that's "attentive" even amid "pre-show pandemonium"; the only rub: it's on the "pricey" side.

La Méditerranée
18 | 16 | 18 | $45

947 Second Ave. (bet. 50th & 51st Sts.), 212-755-4155; www.lamediterraneeny.com
The "friendly" "new bar" at this "old-style" Midtown French bistro attracts an "upbeat crowd", but longtimers can still snare "fine" "comfort food" at "decent prices"; "veteran waiters" and a "delightful piano player" further boost the "charm" factor.

La Mela ●
18 | 11 | 17 | $35

167 Mulberry St. (bet. Broome & Grand Sts.), 212-431-9493; www.lamelarestaurant.com
"Raucous, hungry groups" who like their Italian "family-style, in a circus atmosphere" find this Little Italy "experience" a "hoot"; some say it's best for "the tourist crowd", but it's hard to argue with the "no-menu" $32 prix fixe because "the food just keeps coming."

La Mirabelle
21 | 17 | 22 | $47

102 W. 86th St. (bet. Amsterdam & Columbus Aves.), 212-496-0458
It's "totally unhip", and that's the way the "mature", "enthusiastic regulars" like it at this "unfailingly pleasant" UWS French standby; it maintains its "reliable" rep with "delicious" "old-style" dishes, "warm greetings" and "charming", "homey-lace-curtains" decor.

Lan ●
23 | 18 | 20 | $42

56 Third Ave. (bet. 10th & 11th Sts.), 212-254-1959
At this "stylish" East Village Japanese, a "sophisticated" midpriced menu that goes beyond the "sushi-tempura-teriyaki–bento box" formula (including the "best shabu-shabu") pleases its "cool Downtown" demographic; "attentive" service adds to the overall "pleasant" experience.

Land
22 | 17 | 18 | $26

450 Amsterdam Ave. (bet. 81st & 82nd Sts.), 212-501-8121;
www.landthaikitchen.com
"Lines are out the door" at this "cute" but "teeny-tiny" UWS Thai that's become a local "favorite" for "delicious", "wonderfully seasoned" dishes; "pleasant" servers and "inexpensive" tabs are other reasons why it's worth the "squeeze."

L & B Spumoni Gardens
23 | 11 | 15 | $20

2725 86th St. (bet. 10th & 11th Sts.), Brooklyn, 718-449-6921;
www.spumonigardens.com
"It screams Brooklyn" at this Bensonhurst pizzeria/ice cream parlor "icon", where "crowds have gathered" "since the earth cooled" for "perfect squares" of "legendary Sicilian pie" chased with "decadent" Italian ices; in summer, there's also a lively "picnic table scene."

Landmarc ●
23 | 19 | 21 | $49

179 W. Broadway (bet. Leonard & Worth Sts.), 212-343-3883;
www.landmarc-restaurant.com
Fast becoming a "TriBeCa landmark", Marc Murphy's "stylish" yet "family-friendly" bistro purveys "enticing" French fare with "a touch of Italian"; yes, the "no-reservations policy is a drag", but it's offset by "genuinely nice" service and a "fantastic", "almost-at-cost" wine list.

La Paella
20 | 19 | 17 | $33

214 E. Ninth St. (bet. 2nd & 3rd Aves.), 212-598-4321
Every night's "date night" at this "dark, romantic", "reasonable" East Village Spaniard, where "excellent" paella for two, "tasty tapas" and "delicious sangria" make it easy to overlook "aloof" waiters and "cramped seating" and focus on the "hot atmosphere."

La Palapa ●
20 | 18 | 18 | $34

359 Sixth Ave. (bet. Washington Pl. & W. 4th St.), 212-243-6870
77 St. Marks Pl. (bet. 1st & 2nd Aves.), 212-777-2537
www.lapalapa.com
"Exotic margaritas" meet "well-flavored" "upscale" (but not up-priced) Mexican at this "sexy" cross-Village twosome; with "enthusiastic" staffers and a "festive, casual" vibe it's a "step up from the usual", though "always-crowded" conditions mean the "noise" level is elevated too.

La Petite Auberge
19 | 15 | 21 | $44

116 Lexington Ave. (bet. 27th & 28th Sts.), 212-689-5003;
www.lapetiteaubergeny.com
"Suspended in time, in a good way", this Gramercy "staple" presents "traditional" French cuisine in a "Breton cottage"–like space presided over by "authentic waiters, not aspiring actors"; maybe it's a bit "stale", but it's "affordable" and "no one rushes you."

La Pizza Fresca Ristorante
22 | 16 | 17 | $37

31 E. 20th St. (bet. B'way & Park Ave. S.), 212-598-0141;
www.lapizzafrescaristorante.com
"Good any time", this "easygoing" Flatiron Italian dishes up "terrific" thin-crust pizzas and other classics "presented simply" and backed by an "enormous wine list"; service is "slow" and tabs "a little pricey", but still it's a "happy spot."

La Ripaille ●
∇ 19 | 19 | 20 | $48

605 Hudson St. (bet. Bethune & W. 12th Sts.), 212-255-4406
A "proprietor who loves his job" sets the tone at this "longtime" Village bistro that has stood the test of time thanks to its "consistent

country-style" cooking, "low-key" "French farmhouse" vibe and "lovely staff"; "bargain prices" are another reason it would be an "asset" in any neighborhood.

La Rivista ●☒
19 | 16 | 20 | $44

313 W. 46th St. (bet. 8th & 9th Aves.), 212-245-1707; www.larivistanyc.com
An "efficient" "pre-show" "niche" player, this "old-style" Theater District Italian dispenses "ample" servings of "decent" eats and then "gets you out in time" for the curtain; nightly piano music offsets otherwise "lacking ambiance", and the discounted parking is "a deal."

Las Ramblas ●NEW
▽ 19 | 17 | 24 | $34

170 W. Fourth St. (bet. Cornelia & Jones Sts.), 646-415-7924
"Authentic" tapas and "terrific sangria" "straight outta" Barcelona help this "friendly", "affordable" Village Spaniard do a "lively" business; its "sooo-small" digs offer "not much sitting room", but luckily it's "new and not overcrowded" – for now.

La Taza de Oro ☒⇗
18 | 6 | 16 | $14

96 Eighth Ave. (bet. 14th & 15th Sts.), 212-243-9946
"Divey" it may be, but this "friendly" Chelsea coffee shop is a "staple" for "blue-collar workers" and others looking for "heaping plates" of "genuine" "homestyle" Puerto Rican cooking and "the best cafe con leche"; better still, it costs "next to nothing."

L'Atelier de Joël Robuchon ●NEW
– | – | – | VE

Four Seasons Hotel, 57 E. 57th St. (bet. Madison & Park Aves.), 212-350-6658; www.fourseasons.com
Legendary chef Joël Robuchon makes his NYC debut with this sleek New French cafe on the 58th Street side of the I.M. Pei–designed Four Seasons Hotel; besides featuring an open kitchen, sushi bar–like counter seating and a handful of comfortable tables, the restaurant features a pared-down menu that emphasizes small plates and tasting options that come at Paris price levels – i.e. eating $20 bills is cheaper.

Lattanzi ●☒
22 | 19 | 21 | $52

361 W. 46th St. (bet. 8th & 9th Aves.), 212-315-0980; www.lattanzinyc.com
A "fine pre-theater choice", this "charming", but "not cheap", Restaurant Row standby plies "delightful" Italian classics in a "big", "comfortable" space; however, it really takes the spotlight "after curtain time" when "interesting Jewish-Roman" dishes are available – with "divine fried artichokes" in the starring role.

Lavagna
24 | 17 | 21 | $41

545 E. Fifth St. (bet. Aves. A & B), 212-979-1005; www.lavagnanyc.com
East Villagers in search of "more polished" Italian head for this "tiny", "off-the-beaten-path" entry whose "inspired" dishes are matched with a "fab wine list" and served by "caring" staffers; a "warm", "neighborly" vibe and "fair prices" are other reasons it's "always packed."

La Vela
18 | 15 | 19 | $34

373 Amsterdam Ave. (bet. 77th & 78th Sts.), 212-877-7818
"Regulars" file into this "wonderful neighborhood" Westsider in a "steady stream" for "satisfying", "down-to-earth" Tuscan *cucina*; "sweet" service, a "leisurely" ambiance and "reasonable" rates mean few quibble with the "nondescript" digs.

La Villa Pizzeria
21 | 15 | 17 | $25

261 Fifth Ave. (bet. 1st St. & Garfield Pl.), Brooklyn, 718-499-9888; www.lavillaparkslope.com

(continued)

(continued)

La Villa Pizzeria

Key Food Shopping Ctr., 6610 Ave. U (bet. 66th & 67th Sts.), Brooklyn, 718-251-8030
Lindenwood Shopping Ctr., 82-07 153rd Ave. (bet. 82nd & 83rd Sts.), Queens, 718-641-8259

Perfect for an "affordable family outing", this "red-sauce" trio plies "outstanding thin-crust" pizzas "from wood-burning ovens" plus other "uncomplicated" Italian classics; add "pleasant" (if "suburban-feeling") interiors, and, no surprise, they're "always crowded."

La Vineria

▽ **21** **16** **20** **$43**

21 W. 55th St. (bet. 5th & 6th Aves.), 212-247-3400; www.lavineriarestaurant.com

A Midtown "find", this "tiny" Italian's setup supplies "sardine" squeezes that are "made up for" by "heavenly" wood-oven pizzas and other "delicious" dishes; "caring" service and tabs "light on the wallet" are further endearments.

LE BERNARDIN ⊠

28 **27** **28** **$106**

155 W. 51st St. (bet. 6th & 7th Aves.), 212-554-1515; www.le-bernardin.com

"All superlatives are warranted" when it comes to the "celestial experiences" at Maguy LeCoze's French Midtown "temple to seafood"; the "stellar service" and "serene", "luxurious" quarters alone place it in a "league of its own", but chef Eric Ripert "approaches perfection" with his "stunningly well-executed" and "beautifully presented" cuisine that "takes your breath away" (and is once again voted No. 1 for Food in NYC); yes, it's "very expensive", but if you can swing it "by all means, go"; P.S. the $55 prix fixe lunch is "a steal."

Le Bilboquet

20 **15** **15** **$54**

25 E. 63rd St. (bet. Madison & Park Aves.), 212-751-3036

"Beautiful people" "jam-packed" in a "terrifically noisy boîte" is the normal "scene" at this "clubby" East Side "Euro-favorite" bistro; those able to focus on what's on the plate report "tasty", "*très française*" cuisine delivered with a side of "attitude."

Le Boeuf à la Mode

21 **18** **21** **$52**

539 E. 81st St. (bet. East End & York Aves.), 212-249-1473

This "classy" Yorkville French "throwback" maintains a loyal following for its "classic bistro" fare, "pretty" quarters and "real pro" service; though it's "expensive", it's "getting better with age", and the prix fixe is a "bargain."

LE CIRQUE NEW

▽ **24** **25** **21** **$93**

One Beacon Court, 151 E. 58th St. (bet. Lexington & 3rd Aves.), 212-644-0202; www.lecirque.com

Sirio Maccioni's roving three-ring circus is back, now in a "knockout", Adam Tihany—designed room on the ground floor of Midtown's Bloomberg Building, where it attracts a full house of the bold, the beautiful and the Botoxed, all enjoying Pierre Schaedelin's "exquisite" French cooking; gawkers who can't get a ticket to the main show should try squeezing into the cheaper, more casual cafe, where reservations and jackets aren't required.

L'Ecole ⊠

25 **20** **22** **$45**

French Culinary Institute, 462 Broadway (Grand St.), 212-219-3300; www.frenchculinary.com

The "energetic" chefs-in-training get an "A for effort" from surveyors "glad to be guinea pigs" at the French Culinary Institute's "student-run" restaurant in SoHo; "diligent service" and "bargain prices" win high marks too, so "go before they're too famous" to afford.

Le Colonial

19 | 22 | 18 | $50

149 E. 57th St. (bet. Lexington & 3rd Aves.), 212-752-0808;
www.lecolonialnyc.com
Think "Indochine fantasia" and you've got this "mysterious, sexy" Eastsider where the "tasty", "complex" French-Vietnamese flavors come in "exotic" environs ("especially upstairs"); to a few it's "becoming a little corny", but romeos rely on it as a "fabulous" "date place."

Leela Lounge

▽ 26 | 22 | 21 | $32

1 W. Third St. (bet. B'way & Mercer St.), 212-529-2059;
www.leelalounge.com
Early visitors to this Village newcomer find "real flair" in its "delicious" Indian dishes with "some unconventional" elements (fig chutney, corn salsa); "sweet" service and a "fun", stylish space complete with an adjoining lounge place it "a class" up from the usual.

Le Gamin

19 | 15 | 14 | $24

536 E. Fifth St. (bet. Aves. A & B), 212-254-8409 ◐
522 Hudson St. (bet. Charles & W. 10th Sts.), 212-807-7357 ◐ **NEW**
258 W. 15th St. (bet. 7th & 8th Aves.), 212-929-3270 ◐
132 W. Houston St. (bet. MacDougal & Sullivan Sts.), 212-475-1543 ⊟
556 Vanderbilt Ave. (bet. Bergen & Dean Sts.), Brooklyn,
718-789-5171
www.legamin.com
"Laid-back, easy bistro grub" dished up with "friendly" "bohemian attitude" makes these "cheap", "cute", "cozy" crêperies a welcome "diversion from the city's harried pace"; just plan on a "leisurely" experience because the service is "slow."

Le Gigot Ⓜ

25 | 19 | 23 | $50

18 Cornelia St. (bet. Bleecker & W. 4th Sts.), 212-627-3737
A "little Gallic paradise" that "holds its own" on a Village block "crammed with dining options", this "tiny, charming" bistro's "pricey" Provençal specialties are "prepared with care and élan" and delivered by a "super staff"; yes, it's "tightly packed", but that's just because it does so many things right.

Le Grainne Café ❶ **NEW**

▽ 20 | 16 | 14 | $23

183 Ninth Ave. (21st St.), 646-486-3000; www.legrainnecafe.com
"Soup bowl–size" café au lait and a "relaxed atmosphere" still reign at this cheap Chelsea French cafe that serves the same "delicious crêpes" and such as when it was a branch of Le Gamin; they've "brightened up" the space, but "haphazard service" and weekend "lines" for brunch live on.

Le Jardin Bistro

20 | 18 | 19 | $42

25 Cleveland Pl. (bet. Lafayette & Spring Sts.), 212-343-9599;
www.lejardinbistro.com
"All the old bistro favorites" are in bloom at this NoLita French "charmer"; it's ideal in "warm weather" when you can "eat under the grape vines" in the "enchanting" garden, but its "unpretentious", "real-deal" style and "reasonable" prices make it a "favorite" standby "all year" long.

Le Madeleine

20 | 18 | 19 | $45

403 W. 43rd St. (bet. 9th & 10th Aves.), 212-246-2993;
www.lemadeleine.com
For "satisfying", "well-turned-out" pre-theater meals, this "hospitable" Hell's Kitchen French bistro is "a sure thing", with a seasoned staff to steer you through the "tight" quarters and get you "out on time"; the "lovely" "indoor garden room" is another plus.

Le Marais
21 | 15 | 16 | $50

150 W. 46th St. (bet. 6th & 7th Aves.), 212-869-0900
A "special find" for pre- or post-show dining, this kosher French steakhouse "won't disappoint" declare devotees of its "top-notch" meat and frites; maybe it's "noisy beyond belief" and unredeemed by "perfunctory service", but "if you want kosher in the Theater District", "this is the place."

Le Miu ●Ⓜ NEW
▽ 24 | 17 | 19 | $59

107 Ave. A (bet. 6th & 7th Sts.), 212-473-3100
Among the "unique surprises" at this "small", "relaxed" new Alphabet City Japanese, admirers cite both the "superb" sushi and the "creative" cooked dishes that are definitely "not the usual suspects"; maybe it's "pricey for the neighborhood", but given such "outstanding" quality, "the value's there."

Le Monde ●
17 | 18 | 15 | $31

2885 Broadway (bet. 112th & 113th Sts.), 212-531-3939; www.lemondenyc.com
"Get a sidewalk seat" and "order something simple" to best enjoy this "bustling" Morningside Heights French brasserie–cum–"Columbia hangout"; considering the "reasonable" prices for "ample" portions of "reliable favorites" and "capacious" digs, no one minds much that service is "lackadaisical."

Lemongrass Grill
17 | 12 | 15 | $22

2534 Broadway (bet. 94th & 95th Sts.), 212-666-0888
9 E. 13th St. (bet. 5th Ave. & University Pl.), 646-486-7313 ●
138 E. 34th St. (bet. Lexington & 3rd Aves.), 212-213-3317
84 William St. (Maiden Ln.), 212-809-8038
156 Court St. (bet. Dean & Pacific Sts.), Brooklyn, 718-522-9728
61A Seventh Ave. (bet. Berkeley & Lincoln Pls.), Brooklyn, 718-399-7100
www.lemongrassgrill.com
It "won't bowl you over", but the "serviceable Thai" from this "always crowded" mini-chain "hits the spot" when "pennies are tight"; if "hurry-hurry service" and "plain" digs don't appeal, "have them bring it to you" via "Road Runner"–speed delivery.

Lenox Room
19 | 20 | 19 | $52

1278 Third Ave. (bet. 73rd & 74th Sts.), 212-772-0404; www.lenoxroom.com
Owner Tony Fortuna ("a prize") sets the "courteous" tone at this East Side New American that's a "favorite" of the "chic" set; "older patrons" appreciate "top-notch" repasts and tables spaced "for civilized conversation", while the "jumpin' bar" is "popular" with the next generation.

Le Pain Quotidien
20 | 15 | 14 | $21

ABC Carpet & Home, 38 E. 19th St. (bet. B'way & Park Ave. S.), 212-673-7900
494 Amsterdam Ave. (84th St.), 212-877-1200
252 E. 77th St. (bet. 2nd & 3rd Aves.), 212-249-8600
10 Fifth Ave. (8th St.), 212-253-2324
100 Grand St. (bet. Greene & Mercer Sts.), 212-625-9009
833 Lexington Ave. (bet. 63rd & 64th Sts.), 212-755-5810
1131 Madison Ave. (bet. 84th & 85th Sts.), 212-327-4900
922 Seventh Ave. (58th St.), 212-757-0775
50 W. 72nd St. (bet. Columbus Ave. & CPW), 212-712-9700
60 W. 65th St. (bet. B'way & CPW), 212-721-4001 NEW
www.painquotidien.com
The "go-to place" for a "quick bite" or "relaxed lunch", this Belgian bakery-cafe chain proffers "fabulous" breads, sandwiches and other "fresh" "organic goodies" amid "Euro *rustique*" environs; service ranges from "cheerful" to "surly", but communal tables and a "casual, welcoming" vibe are constants.

Le Père Pinard ☕

▽ | 19 | 19 | 16 | $35

175 Ludlow St. (bet. Houston & Stanton Sts.), 212-777-4917
"Dark" and "moody", this "authentic" French bistro has become a LES "standard" for "good", "basic" food at "reasonable prices"; its "rowdy twentysomething" fan base finds it "more fun when packed", and don't mind service that's just "ok."

Le Perigord

24 | 21 | 24 | $76

405 E. 52nd St. (bet. FDR Dr. & 1st Ave.), 212-755-6244;
www.leperigord.com
"Still holding its own" after 40-plus years as a "delightfully formal" French, this Sutton Place "classic" excels at "elegant", "mouth-watering" cuisine enjoyed by "upscale" regulars who "don't look at prices"; "consummate host" Georges Briguet sets the tone for the "gracious service" in "ageless" surroundings evoking the "glamour days of Truman and Jackie O."

Le Refuge

21 | 21 | 20 | $54

166 E. 82nd St. (bet. Lexington & 3rd Aves.), 212-861-4505;
www.lerefugenyc.com
"Truly a refuge" from the "clatter of the city", this "civilized" UES bistro's "pro" staff delivers "fine" French fare in – just "squint your eyes" – a "romantic" "French country house"; if "steep prices throw you", go for the "bargain early-bird prix fixe."

Le Refuge Inn Ⓜ ⌂

▽ | 26 | 24 | 23 | $53

Le Refuge Inn, 586 City Island Ave. (bet. Beach & Cross Sts.), Bronx,
718-885-2478; www.lerefugeinn.com
French cuisine "done to perfection", "top-rate service" and a "charming" "country inn" setting combine to make meals at this City Islander "like taking a short vacation"; it's "pricey for the Bronx" but "worth it", so "book a room and make a night of it."

Le Rivage

20 | 17 | 21 | $43

340 W. 46th St. (bet. 8th & 9th Aves.), 212-765-7374; www.lerivagenyc.com
They'll "whisk you out before curtain call" at this "cramped but pleasant" Restaurant Row French that's a "pre-theater favorite" thanks to its "tasty" standards and "friendly" staff; "excellent prix fixe values" also boost its standing as an area "must."

Le Sans Souci Ⓜ

▽ | 22 | 20 | 20 | $35

44-09 Broadway (bet. 44th & 45th Sts.), Queens, 718-728-2733;
www.lesanssouci.net
This "charming" French "find" in Astoria offers "reasonably priced" "hearty" Breton-style bistro dishes and "friendly service" in "charming countrified" quarters; it gets even more bucolic out in the "especially lovely garden."

Les Enfants Terribles ☕

19 | 20 | 16 | $36

37 Canal St. (Ludlow St.), 212-777-7518; www.lesenfantsterriblesnyc.com
A "casual, late-night kinda place", this LES French-African's "hip" "safari vibe" is abetted by "ceiling fans" and nightly DJs; its "original" fare's "tasty" and delivered by "friendly" (if "slightly inept") staffers, but some only "go for the drinks" and a "change of scenery."

Les Halles ☕

20 | 16 | 15 | $42

15 John St. (bet. B'way & Nassau St.), 212-285-8585
411 Park Ave. S. (bet. 28th & 29th Sts.), 212-679-4111
www.leshalles.net
"Fantabulous" steaks and frites "still draw crowds" to this "boisterous" French bistro duo that's celeb chef Anthony Bourdain's "home base" – though cynics suspect "Tony has left the building"; service is

"spotty" and noise levels "deafening", yet these "reasonably priced" "classics" deliver "what a night out in NYC ought to be."

Le Singe Vert ●   19 16 17 $36
160 Seventh Ave. (bet. 19th & 20th Sts.), 212-366-4100
Good "noisy" "fun" is had by all at this Chelsea French bistro that's "seriously Parisian" from the "solid" "standard" eats to the "inattentive" service and "elbow-to-elbow" seating; in warmer months there's also "great people-watching" from the sidewalk tables.

Le Tableau   23 16 21 $41
511 E. Fifth St. (bet. Aves. A & B), 212-260-1333;
www.letableau.citysearch.com
"Always a delight", this East Village "brick-walled hideaway" makes a choice "date place" thanks to its "meticulously prepared" French bistro fare, "romantic vibe" and staffers who "go out of their way to please"; the "quaint" quarters are so "tiny" that devoted regulars hope "word won't get out."

Levana   ▽ 21 17 19 $58
141 W. 69th St. (bet. B'way & Columbus Ave.), 212-877-8457; www.levana.com
"Kosher and classy", this Lincoln Center–area Med is the place to "take your orthodox friends" for a "solid" "high-end" meal with a "creative" twist ("the venison alone is worth the trip"); overall, the "pleasant experiences" here transcend "dated" decor and "expensive" tabs.

Le Veau d'Or ⊠   ▽ 21 17 21 $52
129 E. 60th St. (bet. Lexington & Park Aves.), 212-838-8133
An East Side "landmark" for nearly 70 years, this vintage French bistro offers a chance to "dine like *grand-mère*" on "delicious" "traditional" dishes; it's "a gracious retreat from faddish Manhattan" complete with good "old-fashioned" service, so who cares if it's "a little faded" and a little *cher.*

Lever House   22 23 21 $71
390 Park Ave. (enter on 53rd St., bet. Madison & Park Aves.),
212-888-2700; www.leverhouse.com
"Sleek and unique", this "trendy" Midtown "expense-account" pick offers a "retro-mod" setting for chef Dan Silverman's "creative yet classic" New American cuisine that's fodder for many a "power lunch" or "special-occasion" dinner; regulars know to "ask for a booth" to beat the "acoustics."

L'Express ●   17 14 13 $29
249 Park Ave. S. (20th St.), 212-254-5858; www.lexpressnyc.com
Open 24/7, this "basic", "fast-paced, funky" French bistro in the Flatiron draws the most applause for its "consistent", "cheap" "late-night eats"; its setup is "cafeteria-like" and the staff "doesn't seem to care if you stay or go", but the fact that it's "packed" "wall-to-wall" at prime times speaks for itself.

Le Zie 2000 ●   21 14 18 $36
172 Seventh Ave. (bet. 20th & 21st Sts.), 212-206-8686; www.lezie.com
This "cozy" Chelsea Italian is "popular among locals" thanks to its "marvelous" Venetian-style cuisine, "amazing prices" and service "without fanfare"; waits can now be spent in a "new bar", but for those averse to "cramped" digs that "need sprucing up", "two words: they deliver."

Liberty View NEW   ▽ 20 17 17 $25
21 South End Ave. (bet. 3rd Pl. & W. Thames St.), 212-786-1888
"Stellar" Statue of Liberty views are the backdrop for this Battery Park City Chinese's "authentic", "better-than-average" eats; quite

"decent" prices and a "super-polite" staff mean it's "a godsend" for area office workers.

Liebman's
19 | 9 | 16 | $20

552 W. 235th St. (Johnson Ave.), Bronx, 718-548-4534;
www.liebmansdeli.com
"One of the last" of "a dying breed", this "old-fashioned" Bronx "classic" kosher deli delivers just "what you expect": Jewish "comfort food done well", from "quality" sandwiches to "chicken soup like mama's"; some kvetch "there's "no decor", but hey, delis aren't supposed to be pretty.

Lil' Frankie's Pizza ●⊄
22 | 15 | 15 | $25

19-21 First Ave. (bet. 1st & 2nd Sts.), 212-420-4900;
www.lilfrankies.com
Be prepared to encounter "crowds of cool kids" in pursuit of "top-notch" "crisp-crust" pizzas "loaded" with "fresh toppings" at this "homey", "cheap" East Village Italian kid brother to nearby Frank; it's a prime "hangout" that's apparently not hurt by "spacey" service and "incredibly loud" music.

Lili's Noodle Shop & Grill
17 | 13 | 15 | $22

Embassy Suites, 102 North End Ave. (Vesey St.), 212-786-1300;
www.lilisnoodle.com
1500 Third Ave. (bet. 84th & 85th Sts.), 212-639-1313
200 W. 57th St. (enter on 7th Ave., bet. 56th & 57th Sts.), 212-586-5333;
www.lilis57.com
Maybe these Chinese slurp specialists "won't rock your world", but they "hit the spot" for a "huge delicious" bowl of noodles or another "quick", "reliable", "cheap" fix; those troubled by "assembly-line" ambiance or "robotic service" tout the "lightning-fast delivery."

Lima's Taste ●
∇ 22 | 15 | 15 | $36

122 Christopher St. (Bedford St.), 212-242-0010;
www.limastaste.com
Now that its original East Village location has closed, all the "true" flavor of this "fabulous Peruvian" is concentrated in its "fancier" West Village digs; the focus is on "cheap", "fresh" ceviche and other "tasty, spicy" dishes, with "amazing drinks" as chasers.

L'IMPERO ☒
26 | 24 | 24 | $71

45 Tudor City Pl. (bet. 42nd & 43rd Sts.), 212-599-5045;
www.limpero.com
Scott Conant is the "magician in the kitchen" at this "swank", "seductive" Tudor City Italian, a "soothing" "hideaway" where "solicitous" staffers convey "memorable", "simply divine" meals that "explode with flavor"; though it's undeniably a "splurge", the prix fixe options are a "fantastic bargain", at least "by NY standards."

Lisca
19 | 16 | 19 | $42

660 Amsterdam Ave. (bet. 92nd & 93rd Sts.), 212-799-3987
"Personable service", "hearty" fare and "generous pours" from a "nice wine list" are helping this UWS Tuscan gain a following; its relatively "serene" setting is another reason "it's a good choice" if you can't get into "Gennaro across the street."

Little Bistro 🆕
∇ 20 | 19 | 20 | $33

158 Court St. (Pacific St.), Brooklyn, 718-797-5655; www.littlebistro.net
"Busy since the doors opened", this New American is a "hip" new addition to Cobble Hill; while its "trendy, sleek interior", "sociable" staff and "eclectic mix" of "interesting" Asian-inflected "comfort food" bodes well for its future, a few feel it's "not consistent" yet.

Little Charlie's Clam Bar ⏺

▽ 22 | 7 | 14 | $30

19 Kenmare St. (bet. Bowery & Elizabeth St.), 212-431-6443;
www.littlecharliesclambar.com

Sure, its "traditional red sauce" comes in "mild and medium", but it's the five-alarm "hot" version that this circa-1926 NoLita Italian is known for, not to mention "the best seafood"; nothing-fancy digs and a non-touristy "clientele straight out of the movies" complete the "authentic" picture.

Little D Eatery Ⓜ NEW

▽ 24 | 17 | 23 | $36

434 Seventh Ave. (bet. 14th & 15th Sts.), Brooklyn, 718-369-3144;
www.littled-eatery.com

"Share" is the concept at this popular Park Slope newcomer whose "thoughtful, simple" New American–Eclectic small plates reflect "amazing attention to detail"; "always packed", its bite-size space is presided over by a "charming, helpful" staff that abets the "lovely" neighborhood vibe.

Little Giant

23 | 18 | 19 | $42

85 Orchard St. (Broome St.), 212-226-5047; www.littlegiantnyc.com

"Hipsters and yupsters alike" wolf "witty" New American dishes at this "little" Lower Eastsider where the "high-quality artisanal eats" include some "adventurous" choices; you'll "sit awfully close to your neighbors" in its "cool" digs, but that's just part of the "charm."

Little Owl NEW

– | – | – | M

90 Bedford St. (Grove St.), 212-741-4695; www.thelittleowlnyc.com

This diminutive West Village Med–New American is already packing in neighborhood types with a moderately priced menu emphasizing fish and seasonal produce; happily, the dining room feels more spacious than it is thanks to windowed walls and a semi-open kitchen.

Lobster Box ⏺

19 | 17 | 18 | $40

34 City Island Ave. (Belden St.), Bronx, 718-885-1952; www.lobsterbox.com

The "decor needs help" so just keep your eyes on the "beautiful view of the Sound" at this "City Island landmark" for "quality seafood" including "lobster over 20 ways"; fans say it makes a fine "family restaurant" with "fair prices", but crabs call it "tired."

Locanda Vini & Olii Ⓜ

▽ 23 | 23 | 22 | $44

129 Gates Ave. (Cambridge Pl.), Brooklyn, 718-622-9202;
www.locandany.com

Set in a "gorgeous" renovated "old pharmacy", this midpriced Clinton Hill Tuscan dispenses "delicious", "unique" regional specialties via "superb" staffers; to those who gripe about "microscopic portions", insiders explain "that's the deal" – just "order more."

Lodge ⏺

▽ 16 | 20 | 14 | $23

318 Grand St. (Havemeyer St.), Brooklyn, 718-486-9400;
www.lodgenyc.com

"Bark-laden tables", "elk antlers" and "drinks in jelly jars" bring "campy" Adirondack style to this Williamsburg "hipster"; the "inexpensive" American food is deemed "folksy" and the service "erratic", but all agree that the "outdoor seating is a draw."

Loft ⏺ NEW

18 | 22 | 15 | $45

505 Columbus Ave. (bet. 84th & 85th Sts.), 212-362-6440;
www.loftnyc.net

"Downtown comes to the Upper West Side" via this "swanky" new duplex Med that brings a "clublike" feel to its "beautiful" loft-style space; "delicious" tapas and tagines get the nod from early patrons, but a few wonder if someone "forgot to hire waiters."

Lombardi's 🚫

24 | 11 | 15 | $21

32 Spring St. (bet. Mott & Mulberry Sts.), 212-941-7994

A candidate for NYC's "pizza hall of fame", this "reasonable" NoLita "institution" remains a beloved provider of "perfectly charred" "coal-fired" pies with "terrific toppings"; despite an expansion of its "generic" digs not long ago, there's "always a queue" of folks seeking their "slice of history."

Londel's Supper Club Ⓜ

▽ 22 | 20 | 20 | $33

2620 Frederick Douglass Blvd. (bet. 139th & 140th Sts.), 212-234-6114; www.londelsrestaurant.com

"Charming" owner Londel Davis ensures this "sharp", "classy" Harlem Southerner's always "a fun place to be"; other endearments are "good" "down-home soul food", "friendly service" and "fabulous ambiance" – especially on "fun" weekend jazz nights when you may even "end up dancing."

London Lennie's

21 | 17 | 17 | $40

63-88 Woodhaven Blvd. (bet. Fleet Ct. & Penelope Ave.), Queens, 718-894-8084; www.londonlennies.com

"Delicious fresh fish" at "fair prices" "and plenty of it" are what made this "big", "bustling", nearly 50-year-old Rego Park seafooder an "institution", though "long waits" for a table are also notorious; "so-so service" and decor in need of a "freshen-up" don't deter devotees.

Long Tan ◑

20 | 19 | 19 | $27

196 Fifth Ave. (bet. Berkeley Pl. & Union St.), Brooklyn, 718-622-8444; www.long-tan.com

The "funky fusion" flavors found at this "lively" Park Sloper place it "a cut above the usual Thai"; "affordable" tabs, "creative mixed drinks" and "stylish" digs, complete with a "romantic garden", make it a contender for "best way to wow a date" or "chill with a group" on the strip.

Lorenzo's

▽ 23 | 22 | 22 | $49

Hilton Garden Inn, 1100 South Ave. (off Staten Island Expwy.), Staten Island, 718-477-2400; www.sihilton.com

This "lovely" Italian-accented American remains an "overlooked" "jewel" in Staten Island's Hilton Garden Inn; yes, the "pleasing" cuisine is a bit "expensive", but given the "thoughtful" service and "elegantly renovated" space, you'll get your money's worth.

Los Dos Molinos ⓈⓂ

18 | 15 | 16 | $32

119 E. 18th St. (bet. Irving Pl. & Park Ave. S.), 212-505-1574

"Heat"-seekers gravitate to this "low-key" Gramercy Southwestern for "spicy" eats served without "hoopla", and then "cool down" with "gigantic margaritas"; "dumpy" Arizona-flavored decor doesn't dispel the "loud" "party atmosphere."

Loulou

▽ 22 | 18 | 19 | $33

222 DeKalb Ave. (bet. Adelphi St. & Clermont Ave.), Brooklyn, 718-246-0633

Fort Greene dwellers jonesing for a "French bistro fix" find relief at this "ever so charming" source of "wonderful", "rustic" Brittany-style fare served "*sans* attitude"; if the "modest" setting can get "a bit cramped", there's always the "magical" garden.

Luca

20 | 15 | 20 | $39

1712 First Ave. (bet. 88th & 89th Sts.), 212-987-9260; www.lucatogo.com

"Congenial" chef-owner Luca Marcato and his "nice staff" present "reliably good" Italian "priced right" at this "comforting" Yorkville "neighborhood favorite"; maybe it "needs soundproofing", but its "plain" room's "pleasant" air makes it a local "home away from home."

Lucien ●   21 16 18 $40

14 First Ave. (1st St.), 212-260-6481; www.luciennyc.com
A "mix of families, singles, older people" and "trendier" types "later on" populate this "hopping" East Village bistro proffering "genuine" classics; it's "authentic" down to the "shabby", "dollhouse"-scale digs, sometimes "aloof" service and "warm host" Lucien's "Gallic humor" ("shrug, sigh, smile").

Lucy Latin Kitchen   22 22 19 $47

ABC Carpet & Home, 35 E. 18th St. (bet. B'way & Park Ave. S.),
212-475-5829; www.lucylatinkitchen.com
At this Flatiron "sexy Mexi", an "exotically lovely" space serves as backdrop for "delicious", slightly pricey "south-of-the-border fusion" fare and "luscious libations"; later, the "lively" vibe takes on a "hip lounge" feel (and there's "salsa dancing" on Sundays), leading devotees to declare "I love Lucy."

Luna Piena   18 15 17 $38

243 E. 53rd St. (bet. 2nd & 3rd Aves.), 212-308-8882; www.lunapienanyc.com
Appreciated as a "respite" from fancier Midtown choices, this "low-key", "no-nonsense" Italian's "fresh, simple" fare, "friendly staff" and "inexpensive" tabs make it a solid "safe bet"; what's more, a meal on its "lovely terrace" is a "treat in warm weather."

LUPA ●   25 18 21 $50

170 Thompson St. (bet. Bleecker & Houston Sts.), 212-982-5089;
www.luparestaurant.com
Think "Babbo on a budget" and you've got this "polished" Village trattoria from the Batali-Bastianich-Denton team, which "deserves all its praise" for "rich, earthy", *verismo* Roman dishes, "classy" staffers and an overall "easygoing" atmosphere despite "tight", "chaotic" quarters; just plan to "pitch a tent on the sidewalk" because it's nearly "impossible" to "snag a table."

Lupe's East L.A. Kitchen ⊄   ▽ 18   8 17 $20

110 Sixth Ave. (Watts St.), 212-966-1326
"Solo or con amigos", you'll be "comfortable" at this West SoHo "hole-in-the-wall" dishing up "fresh, delicious" "diner-style Mexican grub"; it's all "fast", "cheap and cheerful" so expect "no frills"; N.B. check out the weekend brunch.

Lure Fishbar   – – – E

142 Mercer St., downstairs (Prince St.), 212-431-7676; www.lurefishbar.com
Newly reconstructed after a fire last year, this SoHo seafooder's subterranean space has been restored to its former luxury yacht–like glory, and now has a new sushi bar to boot; its upscale fin fare and pro service have lured back well-heeled types who don't flinch at the pricey tabs.

Lusardi's ●   23 18 22 $57

1494 Second Ave. (bet. 77th & 78th Sts.), 212-249-2020; www.lusardis.com
An "East Side fixture" for "25 years and counting", this Northern Italian pleases its "mature", "more conservative" fan base with "excellent" "classic" dishes and "thoughtful" service; ok, it's "pricey", "a bit stodgy" and often "crowded", but its "regulars" "love it just as it is."

Luxia ●   19 17 18 $42

315 W. 48th St. (bet. 8th & 9th Aves.), 212-957-0800; www.luxianyc.com
"Tasty organic cuisine" at not-bad prices and "out-of-this-world martinis" make this "gracious" "off-the-beaten-path" Italian a "real find"

in the Theater District; those who feel the "decor needs shaking out" gravitate to the "gorgeous" "secret garden in back."

Luz

▽ 24 | 20 | 21 | $32

177 Vanderbilt Ave. (bet. Myrtle Ave. & Willoughby St.), Brooklyn, 718-246-4000; www.luzrestaurant.com

Inhabiting a "forlorn stretch of Vanderbilt", this Fort Greene Nuevo Latino looks somewhat "garage"-like from the outside, but its interior is "dim, mysterious and hip"; "amazing" cuisine redolent with "bold flavors" is drawing an "eclectic clientele" who call it a "star in the making."

Luzia's

18 | 13 | 17 | $33

429 Amsterdam Ave. (bet. 80th & 81st Sts.), 212-595-2000

Upper Westsiders find "a certain charm" in this "simple Portuguese place", where the pace is Lisboa-"leisurely" and the "homestyle cooking" is matched with "homey" decor; insiders suggest "order lots of tapas" to soak up the "fabulous sangria"; P.S. brunch is "a steal" at $10.95.

Macelleria ◗

19 | 17 | 17 | $49

48 Gansevoort St. (bet. Greenwich & Washington Sts.), 212-741-2555; www.macelleriarestaurant.com

"Italian comfort food for carnivores" is the forte of this "bustling" Meatpacking District steakhouse whose faux "butcher shop" digs include a "wine cellar right out of Tuscany"; it's a "fun" "respite from cooler-than-thou" neighbors, with the only "negatives" being "uneven service" and "high prices."

Madiba ◗

▽ 18 | 20 | 18 | $32

195 DeKalb Ave. (Carlton Ave.), Brooklyn, 718-855-9190; www.madibarestaurant.com

"Get your funk on" at Fort Greene's South African "study in hipness", a "unique dining experience" that for some is "an acquired taste" ("ostrich tartare", anyone?); critics carp about "slow" service and "more hype than quality", but for most it makes an enjoyable night out.

Madison Bistro

19 | 16 | 17 | $44

238 Madison Ave. (bet. 37th & 38th Sts.), 212-447-1919; www.madisonbistro.com

A "comfortable" "neighborhood meeting place" such as you'd find "on any Paris corner", this "quiet, cozy" Murray Hill French bistro plies "consistently fine" classics delivered by an "attentive", "no-attitude" staff; lunch and dinner prix fixes are "terrific on the pocketbook and in the tummy."

Madison's

20 | 19 | 20 | $37

5686 Riverdale Ave. (259th St.), Bronx, 718-543-3850

When looking for a "meal that's a little more special", Riverdale residents head for this "warm" Italian marrying "Manhattan style" with a "delightfully varied menu", "interesting, snazzy" specials and "good service"; if "noise levels" get too high, just eat in the "big, friendly bar."

Maggie Brown ⊟

▽ 19 | 18 | 14 | $23

455 Myrtle Ave. (bet. Washington & Waverly Aves.), Brooklyn, 718-643-7001

"Velvet all over the place" contributes to the "happy" "bohemian" vibe at this cheap Clinton Hill Eclectic–New American known for its "reimagined" "home cooking" and "mobbed" weekend brunch; "highly questionable" service doesn't even register with those swilling "Bloody Marys that could wake the dead."

Magnolia
18 | 16 | 16 | $29

486 Sixth Ave. (12th St.), Brooklyn, 718-369-4814;
www.magnoliabrooklyn.com

Mahogany and "mood lighting" set a "warm, inviting" tone at this "comfy" Park Slope New American overseen by an "accommodating" staff; the kitchen is "a little slow" but turns out "solid" fare with "gourmet touches", leading locals to call it "ye olde standby."

Mai Ⓜ⊅ NEW
▽ 23 | 20 | 22 | $22

497 Atlantic Ave. (bet. Nevins St. & 3rd Ave.), Brooklyn, 718-797-3880

Getting early "raves" for its "good range" of "fresh" Pan-Asian fare with a "creative twist", this "quiet" "little" Boerum Hill newcomer also benefits fom a "beautiful garden" and staffers who "go out of their way" to please; a few who "want it to remain their secret" plead "don't tell anyone about this place!"

Maison ●
▽ 22 | 18 | 17 | $33

1700 Broadway (enter on 7th Ave., bet. 53rd & 54th Sts.), 212-757-2233

In a "great location" for hungry "tourists, local workers or theater"-goers, this "adorable" Midtown French brasserie offers "tasty", pleasingly "predictable" fare at the "right price" 24/7; also, its all-weather "garden seating" is a prime "people-watching" perch.

Malagueta Ⓜ
▽ 27 | 16 | 22 | $28

25-35 36th Ave. (28th St.), Queens, 718-937-4821

A "refreshing surprise" in Astoria, this "cute, laid-back" "little place" offers a "well-rounded" lineup of "excellent", "authentic" Brazilian dishes that are priced "affordably" and served by a "simply lovely" staff; who's going to quibble about "so-so" decor?

Malatesta Trattoria ●⊅
▽ 21 | 16 | 19 | $34

649 Washington St. (Christopher St.), 212-741-1207

Customers "aren't sure what's more delicious" at this "far West Village" trattoria, the "fresh" Northern Italian dishes and "cheap wine" or the "adorable" expat waiters; it boasts a "fun atmosphere", "charming outdoor" seating and seriously "good bang for the buck" to boot.

Maloney & Porcelli ●
22 | 19 | 21 | $61

37 E. 50th St. (bet. Madison & Park Aves.), 212-750-2233;
www.maloneyandporcelli.com

"An easy pick" for "Midtown business meals" on the "expense ac-count", this "good ol' steak joint" offers "two-fisted drinks" and "suc-culent" meats including the "awesome" "signature" crackling pork shank; "Fred Flintstone"–worthy portions, "pro" service, "great" pri-vate party rooms and a "buzzing bar" are other appeals.

Mamá Mexico ●
19 | 17 | 17 | $33

2672 Broadway (102nd St.), 212-864-2323
214 E. 49th St. (bet. 2nd & 3rd Aves.), 212-935-1316
www.mamamexico.com

"*Muy festivo*", these "frenetic" Mexicans bring on "sensory overload" via "wandering mariachis", "cacophonous" crowds, "carnival lighting" and "lethal margaritas"; those able to focus on the "flavorful" food (don't miss the "guacamole made tableside") declare it "*delicioso.*"

Mama's Food Shop �⊅
21 | 10 | 13 | $14

200 E. Third St. (bet. Aves. A & B), 212-777-4425;
www.mamasfoodshop.com

"Heaping plates of grandma's cooking" (think "heavenly" meatloaf or mac 'n' cheese) are "dished out by hipsters" at this "bare-bones", "cafeteria-style" East Village American; "hungry folk" report having "lots of leftovers" and appreciate getting it all "for a song."

Mamlouk ●Ⓜ
▽ | 22 | 19 | 19 | $41

211 E. Fourth St. (bet. Aves. A & B), 212-529-3477
"Go with a group" to best enjoy this East Villager's "fit-for-a-sultan" Middle Eastern cuisine, offered in a "menu-free", six-course $40 prix fixe format and served "family-style"; its "dark", "exotic" room is "relaxing", but revs up on weekends when the belly dancing begins.

Mancora ●
22 | 16 | 21 | $26

99 First Ave. (6th St.), 212-253-1011
176 Smith St. (bet. Warren & Wyckoff Sts.), Brooklyn, 718-643-2629
Maybe the "simple" digs are "not much to look at", but that's beside the point at these "perfect" Peruvians proffering "excellent" eats (including rotisserie chicken that "not much can top"); it's all "competently served" by a "jovial" staff and comes at "bargain" rates.

Mandarin Court
22 | 9 | 15 | $21

61 Mott St. (bet. Bayard & Canal Sts.), 212-608-3838
Carts bearing "endless varieties" of "phenomenal dim sum" roll "non-stop" at this "hectic" Chinatown "favorite" also known for its "fresh seafood dishes"; "brusque" service and "dumpy" decor do nothing to deter "crowds" intent on "well-priced", "tasty" eats.

Mandoo Bar
19 | 11 | 15 | $21

2 W. 32nd St. (bet. B'way & 5th Ave.), 212-279-3075
"Fabulous" namesake "multicolored dumplings" and "delicious hot pots" are among the Korean "comfort" classics available at this "spartan" Garment District "joint"; "speedy service" and "dirt-cheap prices" have admirers asserting it's "fast food like it oughta be."

Manducatis
22 | 13 | 20 | $43

13-27 Jackson Ave. (47th Ave.), Queens, 718-729-4602
"If you want Italian" of the "delicious, old-fashioned", "red-sauce" variety, this "family-run" Long Island City "favorite" is "the place to go"; wash it down with something from the "rich cellar", bask in the staff's "warm attention" and you won't care about the "beyond-dated" decor.

Manetta's 🅂
▽ | 22 | 17 | 20 | $34

10-76 Jackson Ave. (49th Ave.), Queens, 718-786-6171
It's "like your favorite aunt's house" at this "comfortable", "friendly" Long Island City Italian, assuming she offers "excellent brick-oven pizza" and other "*delicioso*" dishes served by an "accommodating pro staff"; "sane prices" make it easy to "return again and again."

Mangia 🅂
20 | 13 | 13 | $19

16 E. 48th St. (bet. 5th & Madison Aves.), 212-754-7600
Trump Bldg., 40 Wall St. (bet. Nassau & William Sts.), 212-425-4040
50 W. 57th St. (bet. 5th & 6th Aves.), 212-582-5554
22 W. 23rd St. (bet. 5th & 6th Aves.), 212-647-0200
www.mangiatogo.com
"Packed" with members of the "working set" in search of "stellar" "grab 'n' go" lunches, this Med quartet offers a "multitude" of options including "superior" salads, sandwiches and "snack bites"; staffers can be "snooty" and prices "high", but still it's "about as good as takeout gets."

Mangiarini
19 | 12 | 18 | $35

1593 Second Ave. (bet. 82nd & 83rd Sts.), 212-734-5500;
www.mangiarini.com
"Blink and you'll miss" this "tiny" UES Italian, a "minimalist" purveyor of "delicious pasta dishes" from a "value"-packed menu; "casual" and "friendly", it sports a "downtown feel" and makes a "great date place" – either because of the "tight quarters" or despite them.

Mara's Homemade

19 | 8 | 19 | $30

342 E. Sixth St. (bet. 1st & 2nd Aves.), 212-598-1110;
www.marashomemade.com

The digs may be "desperate-looking" but still "everyone's all smiles" at this "real-deal" Cajun-Creole on the East Village's Curry Row; it "does New Orleans proud", from "tasty" "crawfish and po' boys" to "draft Abita" beer and "gracious" hospitality.

Marbella ● NEW

▽ 19 | 21 | 19 | $37

162 E. 33rd St. (bet. Lexington & 3rd Aves.), 212-725-4499;
www.marbellanycity.com

Early-goers rate the room "sexy" and the tapas "imaginative" at this new Murray Hill Spaniard, where on weekends "spirited" flamenco dancers boost the "festive" vibe; dining at a marble-topped bar and "great Latin music" have most saying it shows much "potential."

MARCH

26 | 24 | 25 | $91

405 E. 58th St. (bet. 1st Ave. & Sutton Pl.), 212-754-6272;
www.marchrestaurant.com

Set in an "enchanting" East Side townhouse, this New American is considered "romance central" thanks to the "magical" meeting of chef Wayne Nish's "ever-changing, ever-wonderful" cuisine and "gracious" pro staffers who make you "feel like an honored guest"; a few find it all a little "too la di da" and have trouble stomaching the "hefty price tag", but for most, it's the ultimate "special-occasion" destination.

Marco Polo Ristorante

21 | 17 | 22 | $41

345 Court St. (Union St.), Brooklyn, 718-852-5015;
www.marcopoloristorante.com

This "popular" Carroll Gardens "traditional Italian" offers a "gaudy, loud" "movie-set" backdrop for its lusty "red-sauce" classics; "old-world waiters" who "know how to make you feel welcome" are another reason "everyone just loves" this "neighborhood staple."

Maremma ● ⌧

19 | 17 | 19 | $51

228 W. 10th St. (bet. Bleecker & Hudson Sts.), 212-645-0200;
www.maremmanyc.com

Following a "Tuscan cowboy" theme, Cesare Casella's "informal" West Village newcomer is tricked out in "funky" "spaghetti western" decor, while the kitchen turns out "excellent housemade pastas" and other Italian dishes; still a work in progress, it's "definitely a must-try."

Maria Pia

21 | 18 | 20 | $37

319 W. 51st St. (bet. 8th & 9th Aves.), 212-765-6463; www.mariapianyc.com

A "solid performer" in the Theater District, this "terrific little" Italian's "warm" staff and "quality" cuisine at "fair prices" (especially the $21.95 dinner prix fixe) will "leave you satisfied"; decorwise it "isn't fancy", but "aah, the garden!"

Marina Cafe

20 | 23 | 19 | $44

154 Mansion Ave. (Hillside Terrace), Staten Island, 718-967-3077;
www.marinacafegrand.com

After an "extreme makeover", this "friendly" Staten Island seafooder's new "cruise ship"–like quarters "take full advantage" of "gorgeous" Great Kills Harbor views; surveyors say the fin fare's "tasty" and the "dockside tiki bar" "can't be beat", but the setting "alone" is "worth the money."

Marinella

▽ 23 | 16 | 23 | $41

49 Carmine St. (Bedford St.), 212-807-7472

"Untouched by development fever", this West Village "valued antique" is a "quiet little" provider of "reasonable" "old-world Italian at its finest", boosted by a "chalkboard full of specials"; the pace is "relaxed" and the staff "couldn't be nicer", so, no surprise, locals "love it."

Mario's Ⓜ
22 | 17 | 20 | $39

2342 Arthur Ave. (bet. 184th & 186th Sts.), Bronx, 718-584-1188
"They're always happy to see you" at this circa-1919 Bronx "throwback" "run by a wonderful family"; given its "delicious" "red-sauce Southern Italian" doled out in digs reminiscent of a "vintage" "ballroom", it's not hard to see why the place "factors into Arthur Avenue folklore"; P.S. the "appetizer pizzas" are a "must."

MarkJoseph Steakhouse Ⓢ
25 | 17 | 23 | $63

261 Water St. (off Peck Slip), 212-277-0020; www.markjosephsteakhouse.com
The "three-piece-suit crowd" and other "old-boy network" members gather at this "riotous" Financial District steakhouse for "mouthwatering" "perfectly charred" beef; "efficient service" overcomes "ho-hum ambiance", and helps justify the "amazingly" "dear prices."

Mark's
22 | 25 | 25 | $68

Mark Hotel, 25 E. 77th St. (Madison Ave.), 212-879-1864;
www.mandarinoriental.com
A "quiet", "genteel" Edwardian-style setting makes this "classy" East Sider "a fine place" to take "high tea" or "unwind" over "sumptuous" French–New American fare "perfectly served"; though you may need "eye shades to look at the tab", if you want to see how the other half lives, "splurge."

Markt ☻
19 | 19 | 17 | $42

401 W. 14th St. (9th Ave.), 212-727-3314; www.marktrestaurant.com
"Beautiful people" and "wannabes" alike down "fantastic Belgian beers" and "mussels galore" at this "big", "hopping" Belgian brasserie; though service is "harried" and decibels "deafening", the sidewalk seating's a Meatpacking District "people-watching paradise" where "everyone has a good time."

Maroons
21 | 15 | 18 | $34

244 W. 16th St. (bet. 7th & 8th Aves.), 212-206-8640; www.maroonsnyc.com
Hyperbolic habitués of this "lively" Chelsea Jamaican-Southern declare its "flavorful", "rib-sticking", low-budget fare the best "this side of the mighty Mississippi" and "north of the Mason-Dixon line"; no wonder they take the "Caribbean-speed" service and "cramped" setup in stride.

Marseille ☻
20 | 19 | 18 | $48

630 Ninth Ave. (44th St.), 212-333-3410; www.marseillenyc.com
This "well-run" Hell's Kitchen French-Med brasserie "continues to please" with "interesting", "well-executed" meals in "spacious" art deco digs sporting a "convincing" "you're-in-Paris" feel; it "gets noisy" and tabs tend to be a tad "pricey", but all is forgiven because "you'll get to the theater on time."

Maruzzella ☻
21 | 16 | 21 | $40

1483 First Ave. (bet. 77th & 78th Sts.), 212-988-8877
"The right combination" of "dependable, often memorable" Italian standards and "gracious" "personal attention" has made this "quaint" Eastsider a "neighborhood" "favorite" for almost a decade; now hopefully a post-*Survey* expansion will shorten the "waits for a table" without affecting the "reasonable" prices.

Mary Ann's
15 | 11 | 14 | $25

2452 Broadway (bet. 90th & 91st Sts.), 212-877-0132

(continued)

(continued)

Mary Ann's
116 Eighth Ave. (16th St.), 212-633-0877 ⊟
80 Second Ave. (5th St.), 212-475-5939 ⊟
1503 Second Ave. (bet. 78th & 79th Sts.), 212-249-6165 ◐
107 W. Broadway (bet. Chambers & Reade Sts.), 212-766-0911 ◐
Hit these "cheap and cheerful" Tex-Mexers for an "instant party"; "potent margaritas" "soaked up" by "decent" eats help you ignore "olé-fiesta" decor that's "not much to look at" and servers with "a huge tortilla chip on their shoulders."

Mary's Fish Camp ⊠   24 | 12 | 18 | $39
64 Charles St. (W. 4th St.), 646-486-2185; www.marysfishcamp.com
"Simple but extraordinary" is the skinny on the "fresh-off-the-boat" catch at this "sunny" West Village "seafood shack"; legions of fans gladly face "annoying waits" to snare an "uncomfortable seat" in its "tiny", "cramped" space just to get their "claws into" its trademark "platonic ideal of a lobster roll."

Mas ◐⊠   26 | 25 | 24 | $74
39 Downing St. (bet. Bedford & Varick Sts.), 212-255-1790;
www.masfarmhouse.com
"Complex, wonderful" cuisine and "killer wines" are enjoyed in "gorgeous" "sexy farmhouse" digs at this Village New American manned by a "phenomenally pleasant" "pro" staff; acolytes who would "build a shrine" to "superb" chef Galen Zamarra are not daunted by "quite high" tabs.

MASA ⊠   27 | 25 | 26 | $446
Time Warner Ctr., 10 Columbus Circle, 4th fl. (60th St. at B'way),
212-823-9800; www.masanyc.com
To fully savor the "once-in-a-lifetime" "evening of theater and sensations" presented by legendary chef Masayoshi Takayama, just "check your guilt at the door" of this Zen-like Japanese – a "model of simple, tranquil excellence" – and don't even try to "justify" the "insane" $350 kaiseki-style prix fixe that makes it NYC's most costly eatery; just be warned that after sampling these "perfect morsels" you may be "spoiled for any other sushi."

Matsuri ◐   23 | 26 | 20 | $60
Maritime Hotel, 369 W. 16th St. (9th Ave.), 212-243-6400;
www.themaritimehotel.com
Those who descend into this "cavernous subterranean" Chelsea Japanese "extravaganza" find "breathtaking decor" that sets the scene for chef Tadashi Ono's "superb" sushi and an "unsurpassed sake selection"; the "good-looking crowd" with "lots of celebs" is unfazed by "steep prices", although a few skeptics scoff "all scene, no substance."

Maurizio Trattoria   ▽ 20 | 16 | 19 | $46
35 W. 13th St. (bet. 5th & 6th Aves.), 212-206-6474;
www.mauriziotrattoria.com
Locals label this "traditional" Village Tuscan a "perfect neighborhood Italian" citing its "excellent", "hearty" dishes and "relaxing", "homey" environs; "attentive" service and a location that's handy "after a movie" at the Quad are other virtues.

Max ◐⊟   23 | 16 | 15 | $26
51 Ave. B (bet. 3rd & 4th Sts.), 212-539-0111; www.max-ny.com
"Nobody leaves hungry" from this "popular" "pint-sized" East Village "red-sauce" Italian where the "hearty, fresh" dishes "cost less than it would be to make" them at home; that explains the "long lines" to get in and "cramped" conditions once you do.

Max Brenner ⦿ NEW
`— | — | — | I`

841 Broadway (bet. 13th & 14th Sts.), 212-388-0030;
www.maxbrenner.com

The eponymous international chain chocolatier has landed in NY at this affordable new Union Square bistro that's one part Viennese cafe, one part candy store; though the limited, French-accented menu is solid enough, the whimsical desserts are the main event here.

Max SoHa ⦿⇗
`22 | 14 | 16 | $27`

1274 Amsterdam Ave. (123rd St.), 212-531-2221; www.max-ny.com

A "haven" in Morningside Heights, this "cozy", if "impossibly noisy", Southern Italian is "jammed" with "hordes" of "starving" Columbia students who "squeeze" into its "tiny tables" for "well-flavored" pastas and such; "churlish service" is easier to bear given the "rock-bottom" rates.

Maya
`23 | 19 | 19 | $50`

1191 First Ave. (bet. 64th & 65th Sts.), 212-585-1818;
www.modernmexican.com

Amigos attest there's "much to ad-maya" at this "high-end" East Side "Margaritaville" dishing up "inventive", "first-class" Mexican via a "gracious" staff; a "vibrant", tequila-fueled "Santa Fe" ambiance means you'll need "earplugs" – and "mucho pesos to cover the bill."

Mayrose
`16 | 10 | 14 | $22`

920 Broadway (21st St.), 212-533-3663; www.mayrose-nyc.com

American "comfort food with style" is the draw at this "energetic", "ever-so-slightly upscale diner" in the Flatiron District, beloved for its "amazing" but "very crowded" weekend brunch; "reasonable prices" help make up for "long waits" and "scatterbrained" service.

Maz Mezcal
`21 | 17 | 18 | $36`

316 E. 86th St. (bet. 1st & 2nd Aves.), 212-472-1599;
www.mazmezcal.com

"Marvelous mole" and other "real" Mexican dishes "done right" plus "margaritas that pack a punch" keep this "colorful", "affordable" Eastsider "really busy"; "smiling servers" and a "family-friendly back room" offset the "echo chamber" acoustics and "awful waits."

McCormick & Schmick's
`19 | 18 | 19 | $49`

1285 Sixth Ave. (enter on 52nd St., bet. 6th & 7th Aves.), 212-459-1222;
www.mccormickandschmicks.com

"Not bad as chains go", this "generic" Midtown seafooder reels 'em in with an "extensive menu" of "fresh, simple" fin fare backed up by a "big and friendly bar"; critics citing a "formulaic" feel crab it's "nothing exceptional."

Mediterraneo ⦿
`19 | 16 | 16 | $36`

1260 Second Ave. (66th St.), 212-734-7407;
www.mediterraneonyc.com

Surveyors "wish they owned stock" in this "busy" Eastside trattoria, a "reliable" standby for "simple", "fresh" pastas and thin-crust pizzas at "fair prices"; "staffers from Italy" make it all "feel real", and the "place-to-be" sidewalk tables provide "perfect people-watching."

Mee Noodle Shop
`18 | 4 | 13 | $15`

795 Ninth Ave. (53rd St.), 212-765-2929
547 Second Ave. (bet. 30th & 31st Sts.), 212-779-1596
922 Second Ave. (49th St.), 212-888-0027

"Eat your body weight for $10" should be the tagline at this Chinese noodle trio whose "tasty", "bountiful" bowls at "can't-be-beat" prices make it a lunchtime "mainstay"; those deterred by "testy" service and "unappealing" interiors rely on the "hang-up-the-phone-and-it's-there" delivery.

MEGU
25 | 27 | 21 | $95

62 Thomas St. (bet. Church St. & W. B'way), 212-964-7777;
www.megunyc.com

"Spectacle"-seekers flock to this "absolutely gorgeous" TriBeCa Japanese, where a "gigantic" "Buddha ice sculpture" presides over the "circus-like" "scene"; the food's "fabulous", but simply "deciphering the menu is an achievement", so consider "letting the staff order for you" – and bring "Megu-bucks" to cover the tab.

Megu Midtown NEW
– | – | – | VE

Trump World Tower, 845 United Nations Plaza (1st Ave. & 47th St.),
212-964-7777; www.megunyc.com

Though not as sprawling as its TriBeCa sire, this ultra-pricey Japanese spin-off in Midtown's Trump World Tower still offers plenty of decorative zip via a tiger mural, signature Buddha ice sculpture and what may be the largest lampshades on earth; the food is served on two levels, but foodies prefer the downstairs banquettes around the open kitchen.

Melba's M
∇ 19 | 21 | 18 | $32

300 W. 114th St. (Frederick Douglass Blvd.), 212-864-7777;
www.melbasrestaurant.com

Owner Melba Wilson "makes you feel like family" at her "grown-up", retro-style Traditional American yearling in Harlem; some say the "fancy" Southern-accented fare is "uneven", but insiders suggest "order the comfort-food items and you'll be happy."

Melteml
19 | 13 | 18 | $46

905 First Ave. (51st St.), 212-355-4040

"Fresh", "old-school Greek" seafood and "attentive" service render this East 50s taverna a "neighborhood staple" for "U.N. folk" and "Sutton seniors"; ok, there's "no ambiance to speak of", but regulars report the "pleasant, relaxed" atmosphere "feels like home."

Menchanko-tei ●
19 | 11 | 15 | $21

131 E. 45th St. (bet. Lexington & 3rd Aves.), 212-986-6805
43-45 W. 55th St. (bet. 5th & 6th Aves.), 212-247-1585
www.menchankotei.com

"Slurp to your heart's content" at this "absolutely authentic" Japanese ramen duo in Midtown; the "savory noodles" and "steaming", "flavor-packed" broth are served "without fanfare" and the decor is "no-frills", but nobody minds much given the "good value."

Mercadito ●
23 | 17 | 17 | $38

179 Ave. B (bet. 11th & 12th Sts.), 212-529-6490
100 Seventh Ave. S. (Grove St.), 212-647-0410

"Not for the Taco Bell crowd", these "ambitious" cross-Village Mexicans entice amigos with "addictive" small plates and margaritas; "spotty service" and "macro prices for micro portions" don't dispel the "festive" mood.

Mercer Kitchen ●
21 | 22 | 18 | $54

Mercer Hotel, 99 Prince St. (Mercer St.), 212-966-5454;
www.jean-georges.com

"Natives, tourists" and "hip" "jet-setter" types alike gravitate to this "sleek subterranean" SoHo French–New American whose "sexy vibe" and "wonderful", "expensive" food have won it perpetual "scenester" status; it hardly matters if service can be "blasé" and the "dim" digs demand "night-vision goggles."

Mermaid Inn
23 | 18 | 20 | $42

96 Second Ave. (bet. 5th & 6th Sts.), 212-674-5870;
www.beanstalkrestaurants.com

Pescavores are hooked on this East Village "New England–style fish house" whose "amazing lobster rolls" and other "superbly fresh" catch come via a "friendly" crew in "comfortable, easy" quarters (try for the "cool back garden"); if a few carp "prices are a bit high", most find reel "value" here.

MESA GRILL
24 | 20 | 21 | $53

102 Fifth Ave. (bet. 15th & 16th Sts.), 212-807-7400; www.mesagrill.com

Bobby Flay's Flatiron "flagship" "still packs 'em in" thanks to the "vibrant" Southwestern cooking that "surprises even jaded palates", especially at "terrific" weekend brunch; despite "deafening" acoustics and "splashy" decor that some find "dated", the mood remains "festive", due in part to staffers who "serve with verve."

Meskerem
19 | 8 | 14 | $24

124 MacDougal St. (bet. Bleecker & W. 3rd Sts.), 212-777-8111
468 W. 47th St. (bet. 9th & 10th Aves.), 212-664-0520 ◑

"Adventurous" eaters find "forkless fun" at these Ethiopians serving "delicious", "sometimes fiery" stews scooped up with injera flatbread; the "dirt-cheap" tabs have most discounting the "drab" interiors and "absentminded – or just plain absent" staff.

Métisse
19 | 17 | 19 | $40

239 W. 105th St. (bet. Amsterdam Ave. & B'way), 212-666-8825;
www.metisserestaurant.com

"Don't be put off by" the new "cheesy-looking awning" outside, because inside it's as "romantic" as ever at this "friendly" UWS French that's a "favorite" of "Columbia" types seeking "quiet conversation" and "reasonable", "reliable" repasts; regulars report a recent management change has left this vet's "solid rep" intact.

Metrazur ☒
19 | 20 | 17 | $49

Grand Central, East Balcony (42nd St. & Park Ave.), 212-687-4600;
www.charliepalmer.com

Charlie Palmer's "buzzing" New American with an "amazing location" overlooking Grand Central Concourse is ideal if you're "waiting for a train" or have "out-of-town guests" in tow; the "creative" food is "satisfying", if "pricey", but service is so "slow", it "must be run by Amtrak."

Metsovo
18 | 19 | 18 | $39

65 W. 70th St. (bet. Columbus Ave. & CPW), 212-873-2300

With a "homey" mountain-lodge look – complete with "appealing" fireplace – that's "unusual" among its Aegean-toned peers, this "gracious" UWS Greek offers "rare specialties" from the Hellenic highlands; for a pre- or postprandial tipple, hit the downstairs lounge, Shalel.

Mexicana Mama Ⓜ ⌿
25 | 11 | 18 | $31

47 E. 12th St. (bet. B'way & University Pl.), 212-253-7594 **NEW**
525 Hudson St. (bet. Charles & W. 10th Sts.), 212-924-4119

"Top-quality ingredients and preparations" elevate the "creative" cuisine at this "funky" Village Mexican to "best-in-city" status; service is "good-natured" to boot, but given the "tiny, cramped" quarters, some prefer to visit the roomier new offshoot on East 12th Street.

Mexican Radio ◑
18 | 15 | 16 | $31

19 Cleveland Pl. (bet. Kenmare & Spring Sts.), 212-343-0140;
www.mexrad.com

You don't need a radio to hear the "lively" reactions to this "relaxed" NoLita cantina's "awesomely strong" margaritas and "spicy", "reasonable" Mexican eats; however, some diners are turned off by the "nothing-special" decor and "not-great" service, and wish someone would lower the "noisy" volume.

Meze NEW
— | — | — | M

7204 Third Ave. (72nd St.), Brooklyn, 718-567-8300

Bay Ridge is home to this new Turk featuring feta-laden fare and a variety of kebabs in transporting digs complete with clouds painted on the ceiling; a solicitous staff distracts from the sporting events broadcast over the giant flat-screen above the bar.

Mezzaluna ●
19 | 13 | 16 | $41

1295 Third Ave. (bet. 74th & 75th Sts.), 212-535-9600; www.mezzalunany.com

"Solid", "real-deal" pizzas and pastas keep the UES locals loyal to this "casual" "little" "neighborhood Italian"; never mind if it can be "noisy" and the tables are so "tight" they're nearly "communal."

Mezzogiorno ●
20 | 17 | 18 | $42

195 Spring St. (Sullivan St.), 212-334-2112; www.mezzogiorno.com

Befitting its name ('noon'), this "reliable" SoHo Tuscan is a "shoppers' lunch" standby offering "above-average" pastas, wood-fired pizzas and the like; it's "a little pricey" and service can falter, but its "charm" (try the sidewalk tables) "ultimately wins out."

Michael Jordan's The Steak House NYC
20 | 20 | 18 | $62

Grand Central, West Balcony (42nd St. & Vanderbilt Ave.), 212-655-2300; www.theglaziergroup.com

"Score one" for "Air Jordan" – this "spectacularly" situated "carnivorium" in Grand Central offers a "soaring view of the main concourse" to go with its "solid" steaks and wine list; opponents call foul on uneven service and "top-line pricing", but the "great" prix fixe deals are a slam dunk.

Michael's ☒
21 | 20 | 22 | $65

24 W. 55th St. (bet. 5th & 6th Aves.), 212-767-0555; www.michaelsnewyork.com

"Publishing and entertainment celebs" "eat, meet and greet" here, but "you don't have to be a media maven to enjoy" this "stylish" Midtown Californian where "attentive" servers proffer "sophisticated" but "accessible" cuisine; though you pay a "premium to be seen here", most maintain it's worth it just to admire the "beautiful" modern art "on every wall."

Mi Cocina
22 | 17 | 19 | $43

57 Jane St. (Hudson St.), 212-627-8273

"Creative", "fancy Mexican" that "rises above" the usual standards keeps this West Villager's "perennial favorite" status in tact – as do "all those tequilas" at the bar; factor in an "inviting", "colorful" interior and "hospitable" staff, and most don't mind that it's "a little pricey."

Mill Basin Kosher Deli
21 | 14 | 17 | $22

5823 Ave. T (59th St.), Brooklyn, 718-241-4910; www.millbasindeli.com

"Bring on the pastrami!" – this Mill Basin kosher Jewish deli "can't be beat" for its "overstuffed sandwiches" sized for "superhuman" appetites; "as sides" there are "original artworks" by the likes of Erté and Lichtenstein, all for sale, and the staff and customers "right out of central casting" add local "color."

Mill Korean
19 | 14 | 17 | $21

2895 Broadway (bet. 112th & 113th Sts.), 212-666-7653

"Only in NYC" would you find a place like this "converted malt shop" now selling "authentic Korean" eats along with "fabulous" lime rickeys and egg creams; it's become a "Columbia fixture" thanks to "student-friendly" prices and "speedy" servers.

MILOS, ESTIATORIO ◑

26 | 23 | 22 | $72

125 W. 55th St. (bet. 6th & 7th Aves.), 212-245-7400; www.milos.ca
At this Midtown "piscine Parthenon" plan on "impeccable" "Greek cooking for the Aristotle Onassis crowd" – namely, fish "just pulled from the sea" and "vegetables so crisp they echo when you bite them"; a "knowledgeable" crew and "airy" quarters evocative of a Mykonos "marketplace" help justify the "hefty bill", and those less rich than Croesus opt for "bargain" prix fixe menus.

Minetta Tavern ◑

18 | 16 | 17 | $41

113 MacDougal St. (bet. Bleecker & W. 3rd Sts.), 212-475-3850
Now entering its eighth decade, this "unassuming", "unchanging" Greenwich Village Northern Italian gratifies "nostalgists" seeking "classic" "comfort *cucina*" delivered via staffers who "work hard for their tips"; insiders suggest visiting this dim, "old-school" spot "after dark for best effect."

Mingala Burmese

20 | 10 | 17 | $23

21-23 E. Seventh St. (bet. 2nd & 3rd Aves.), 212-529-3656
1393-B Second Ave. (bet. 72nd & 73rd Sts.), 212-744-8008
Burmese food – a "flavorful" "crossroads cuisine" combining Indian, Thai and Chinese elements – gets its due at this "cheap", "satisfying" duo; "kind" service and a "soothing atmosphere" trump the "cramped", sorta "shabby" settings.

Minnow

20 | 17 | 19 | $37

442 Ninth St. (bet. 6th & 7th Aves.), Brooklyn, 718-832-5500
"Hands-on" chef-owner Aaron Bashy turns out "imaginative dishes using the freshest ingredients" at this "convivial" Park Slope sea-fooder, recently renovated and now sharing a menu with its "more casual" neighbor, Bar Minnow; "nimble", "obliging" service and "great brunch" are but two of the reasons it's a local "favorite."

Mint NEW

▽ 23 | 21 | 19 | $42

San Carlos Hotel, 150 E. 50th St. (bet. Lexington & 3rd Aves.),
212-644-8888; www.mintny.com
This new Midtown establish-mint serves "delicious variations on traditional Indian" to "pretty people in an even prettier space"; the "trendy", modern room is manned by a "charming" crew, but its "distracting" greenish lighting "makes people look ghostly" and leaves a few feeling blue.

Miracle Grill

18 | 15 | 17 | $33

415 Bleecker St. (bet. Bank & W. 11th Sts.), 212-924-1900
222 Seventh Ave. (4th St.), Brooklyn, 718-369-4541
"Comfortable", "casual" and "no-fuss", these West Village–Park Slope Southwesterns are known for "can't-be-beat" brunches and other "tasty" repasts at "reasonable prices"; despite gripes about "inconsistent" service, their performance as "reliable" local "staples" "makes a believer" of most everyone.

Miriam

22 | 18 | 20 | $32

79 Fifth Ave. (Prospect Pl.), Brooklyn, 718-622-2250;
www.miriamrestaurant.com
At this Park Slope Israeli-Mediterranean yearling, "surprisingly sophisticated" meals at "bargain prices" are matched with an "appealing list" of "affordable wines"; its "bohemian" setting is as "relaxed" as the "always-friendly" servers; P.S. the "killer brunch" is an "excellent value."

Mishima
23 | 13 | 19 | $35

164 Lexington Ave. (bet. 30th & 31st Sts.), 212-532-9596;
www.mishimany.com
Murray Hill maki mavens report "quality sushi at quality prices" and an "outstanding" sake selection at this bi-level Japanese "neighborhood choice"; still, the "gracious" staff can be "disorganized" and the "pristine" interior is strictly "no-frills."

Miss Mamie's
22 | 12 | 15 | $24

366 W. 110th St. (bet. Columbus & Manhattan Aves.), 212-865-6744

Miss Maude's
547 Lenox Ave. (bet. 137th & 138th Sts.), 212-690-3100
www.spoonbreadinc.com
Perfect "for brunch right after church", these casual Harlem twins serve up "heavenly" "home-cooked" Southern "for the soul and the stomach"; as for decor, expect settings that "look like your grandma's kitchen" in rural North Carolina.

Miss Saigon
18 | 10 | 14 | $25

1425 Third Ave. (bet. 80th & 81st Sts.), 212-988-8828
"Crowded" conditions are "a testament" to the "huge following" of this UES Vietnamese known for its "authentic, simple" victuals at "the right price"; given the "harried" service and "dark", "noisy" conditions, plenty prefer the "speedy delivery."

Mizu Sushi ⌧
24 | 14 | 19 | $34

29 E. 20th St. (bet. B'way & Park Ave. S.), 212-505-6688
No longer a "secret", this "cute" Flatiron Japanese is now "packed" with "recent grads" and other seekers of "reasonable", "delicious" sushi; conversationalists should expect to "yell" over "bumping hip-hop" as servers bustle to "increase turnover."

Mo-Bay
21 | 18 | 15 | $27

17 W. 125th St. (bet. 5th & Lenox Aves.), 212-876-9300 ◑
112 DeKalb Ave. (bet. Ashland Pl. & St. Felix St.), Brooklyn,
718-246-2800
www.mobayrestaurant.com
These "friendly" siblings dish a "delicious" mix of "down-home" soul food and "authentic" Caribbean at "reasonable" rates; the Harlem branch, with live jazz and works by local artists, is "swankier" than the 22-seat Fort Greene original, but both suffer from "sketchy, sporadic" service.

MODERN, THE ⌧
25 | 26 | 23 | $75

Museum of Modern Art, 9 W. 53rd St. (bet. 5th & 6th Aves.),
212-333-1220; www.themodernnyc.com
"Living up to" its "spectacular" setting overlooking MoMA's sculpture garden, Danny Meyer's "divine" French–New American makes a "sleek" showcase for Gabriel Kreuther's "phenomenal" prix fixe dinners that are "a rare treat" – at "rarefied prices", while the larger front bar area's "more casual" Alsatian bites are "equally delicious" and "half the cost"; either way, it's the "perfect finish" to a day at the museum – in fact, perfect any day!

Molyvos ◑
22 | 19 | 20 | $51

871 Seventh Ave. (bet. 55th & 56th Sts.), 212-582-7500;
www.molyvos.com
A "pre–Carnegie Hall reliable" that's also "perfect for a business lunch", this "upscale" West 50s Greek proffers "delectable", "hearty" fare in a "warm", "spacious" setting; the "polite" servers are almost too "efficient", but at least you'll "make the curtain."

Momofuku Noodle Bar
22 | 14 | 17 | $24

163 First Ave. (bet. 10th & 11th Sts.), 212-475-7899; www.eatmomofuku.com
Its name sounds profane (it actually means 'lucky peach') but it's the "obscenely delicious", affordable Japanese fusion dishes employing "superior" "seasonal" ingredients that make this "tiny" East Village noodle shop provocative; "mesmerizing" "chaos" in the open kitchen distracts from "tight" counter seating.

Momofuku Ssäm Bar NEW
_ | _ | _ | I

207 Second Ave. (13th St.), 212-254-3500; www.eatmomofuku.com
The East Village's wildly popular Momofuku Noodle Bar has been joined by this nearby New American–Korean fusion sibling specializing in burritolike *ssäm* wraps and other small plates made with top-quality seasonal ingredients; its dark wood–and–stainless steel space follows the same counter-service setup as the original, and soon may boast a raw bar.

Momoya ⊠
22 | 21 | 19 | $38

185 Seventh Ave. (21st St.), 212-989-4466
Chelsea dwellers cheer this "casually" "hip" Japanese sake-sushi specialist as just "what the neighborhood needed"; "succulent" fish and other "upscale" items come via a "friendly" staff "without the attitude found elsewhere."

Monkey Bar ⊠
19 | 21 | 19 | $52

Elysée Hotel, 60 E. 54th St. (bet. Madison & Park Aves.), 212-838-2600; www.theglaziergroup.com
Gibbon credit where it's due, boosters go bananas over the art deco "flair" at this "sophisticated" Midtown New American; "relax" over "pricey" cocktails and "dependably" "delicious" steaks while "listening to the piano player" (Saturday nights), but expect service to "suffer" when its front bar gets "crowded."

Monkey Town ●NEW
▽ 19 | 23 | 23 | $32

58 N. Third St. (bet. Kent & Wythe Aves.), Brooklyn, 718-384-1369; www.monkeytownhq.com
"Surreal" and "ultrahip", this Williamsburg newcomer offers up an "interesting take on dinner theater": "flipped-out" flicks and "performance events" backed by a "creative" Eclectic menu; while the cooking may be "inconsistent" and concept "gimmicky", "when it's good, it rocks."

Mon Petit Cafe
18 | 16 | 18 | $36

801 Lexington Ave. (62nd St.), 212-355-2233; www.monpetitcafe.com
"Not fancy" but "genteel", this "anxious-to-please" East Side French bistro remains "popular" for brunch or "after shopping at Bloomie's"; though some find the "small" room "tight", alfresco tables compensate.

Monster Sushi
18 | 10 | 15 | $30

535 Hudson St. (Charles St.), 646-336-1833
22 W. 46th St. (bet. 5th & 6th Aves.), 212-398-7707
158 W. 23rd St. (bet. 6th & 7th Aves.), 212-620-9131 ●
www.monstersushi.com
Fish fiends claim "chopsticks can't handle" this Japanese trio's "Godzilla-size portions" of "fresh", "reliable" sushi; the modestly priced "monster" helpings "make up" for "minimal" decor, a "franchiselike feel" and "rushed" service.

Monte's
▽ 19 | 14 | 19 | $37

97 MacDougal St. (bet. Bleecker & W. 3rd Sts.), 212-228-9194; www.montes1918.com
At this NYU-area Italian – a "hardy perennial" since 1918 – they'll "make you happy" with "satisfying" classics served in a "back-in-

the-day" setting; a few say it's "not the same" since "changing hands" recently, but for most it's "still satisfying."

Montparnasse ◐   20 | 18 | 17 | $42
Pickwick Arms, 230 E. 51st St. (bet. 2nd & 3rd Aves.), 212-758-6633; www.montparnasseny.com
Habitués of this "unsung" East Midtown hotel French profess "*amour*" for its "solid" bistro "favorites" and "tremendous-value" prix fixe lunches; its Gallic interior has "charm" too but service is *comme ci, comme ça.*

Montrachet ⊠   25 | 20 | 24 | $70
239 W. Broadway (bet. Walker & White Sts.), 212-219-2777; www.myriadrestaurantgroup.com
"Consistently fabulous" "high-end" French cuisine matched with "one of New York City's best wine lists" and served "seamlessly" by a pro staff keeps Drew Nieporent's TriBeCa "class act" "going strong"; complaints about "tired" surroundings are being addressed by a post-*Survey* renovation.

Mo Pitkin's ◐   17 | 17 | 18 | $28
34 Ave. A (bet. 2nd & 3rd Sts.), 212-777-5660; www.mopitkins.com
"Paying homage to its neighborhood's ethnic roots", this "original" East Villager serves a Judeo-Latino menu (think Cuban Reubens) washed down with signature "Manischevetinis"; the "kitschy", '50s-style setting draws everyone from "families" to "hipsters", and there are "strange live shows upstairs" to boot.

Moran's Chelsea   18 | 19 | 19 | $45
146 10th Ave. (19th St.), 212-627-3030; www.moranschelsea.com
An "oasis of comfort" in "increasingly chic" West Chelsea, this vintage Irish surf 'n' turfer entices neighbors "on wintry nights" with its "cozy" period interiors and a "warm, personable" crew; the "classic" cookery elicits mixed reviews, but all agree that the "great bar" is a "mainstay."

Morgan, The NEW   – | – | – | M
The Morgan Library & Museum, 225 Madison Ave. (bet. 36th & 37th Sts.), 212-683-2130; www.themorgan.org
Set in the newly reopened Morgan Library, this lunch specialist offers casual dining in a glass-enclosed atrium or more stately supping in J.P. Morgan's former dining room; the menu similarly mixes the à la mode with the old-fashioned, with New American dishes served alongside relish trays and champagne cocktails.

MORIMOTO ◐ NEW   23 | 25 | 22 | $88
88 10th Ave. (16th St.), 212-989-8883; www.morimotonyc.com
"Destined to become a destination", this "over-the-top" West Chelsea Japanese is already a "scene" thanks to "genius" architect Tadao Ando's "sophisticated" setting and the "wonderful textures and flavors" of Iron Chef Masaharu Morimoto's "impressive" (and "eye-wateringly expensive") omakase dinners; still, the "friendly" servers "need training", and critics carp that the cuisine is "not always on the mark."

Morton's, The Steakhouse   23 | 19 | 22 | $66
551 Fifth Ave. (45th St.), 212-972-3315; www.mortons.com
Ok, it's "formulaic", but this East Midtown steakhouse chain link comes through with "delicious" "slabs" and "football-size potatoes" ("share or risk exploding"); frequent feeders fault the "plastic-wrapped" show-and-tell menu presentation as well as "exorbitant" "expense-account" tabs, but put their stake there nonetheless.

Mother's Bake Shop ⊄
▽ 21 | 7 | 16 | $9

548 W. 235th St. (Oxford Ave.), Bronx, 718-796-5676
Since 1954 this "old-line Riverdale bakery", though "not a restaurant.
per se", has offered breads and "old-world" confections of which
fans could happily "make a meal"; basic surroundings and "lackadaisical" personnel don't deter "nostalgic" noshers.

Moustache ◕⊄
22 | 11 | 15 | $22

90 Bedford St. (bet. Barrow & Grove Sts.), 212-229-2220
265 E. 10th St. (bet. Ave. A & 1st Ave.), 212-228-2022
Cross-Village groupies swoon over the "delicious hummus" and other
"fresh" Middle Eastern eats on offer at these "low-key" siblings;
"sketchy" service and "cramped" confines ensure "you'll wait" – but
the "authentic" flavors are deemed "well worth it."

Moutarde
18 | 19 | 17 | $37

239 Fifth Ave. (Carroll St.), Brooklyn, 718-623-3600;
www.restaurantmoutarde.com
Diners divide over this Park Slope French bistro; partisans praise its
"quaint" 1930s style and "tasty cooking", but critics cite a "spotty"
kitchen, "overly leisurely" pace and decor "straight out of Epcot" –
choose your side.

Mr. Chow ◕
22 | 19 | 19 | $72

324 E. 57th St. (bet. 1st & 2nd Aves.), 212-751-9030;
www.mrchow.com
"Music moguls" and other glitterati do their "stargrazing" at this
"clubby" black-and-silver art deco East Midtowner where the "high-
class" Chinese chow is "worth the attitude on the side"; detractors
dislike the occasional "obnoxious" vibes and say given the "inordi-
nate" prices it "should be called Mr. Ouch."

Mr. Chow Tribeca ◕ NEW
– | – | – | VE

121 Hudson St. (N. Moore St.), 212-965-9500; www.mrchow.com
Michael Chow has added to his Chinese empire with this new TriBeCa
spin-off where the drop-dead chic setting includes enough celebs
in the crowd to compensate for the high-end tabs; whether the formula that has succeeded so well Uptown can make it Downtown
is anyone's guess.

MR. K'S
24 | 24 | 24 | $53

570 Lexington Ave. (51st St.), 212-583-1668; www.mrks.com
The "overall feeling is one of luxury" at this "palatial" East Midtown
Sino showplace, a "staid but classy" venue for "quiet conversation"
along with "excellent" "upscale" Chinese cuisine and "first-class
service"; generally it's "expense-account-required", but the prix fixe
lunch is "a steal."

Mr. Tang
20 | 13 | 16 | $25

50 Mott St. (Bayard St.), 212-233-8898
2650 Coney Island Ave. (Ave. X), Brooklyn, 718-769-9444 ⊄
7523 Third Ave. (76th St.), Brooklyn, 718-748-0400
When dining at these "old-fashioned" Chinese siblings in Bay Ridge
and Chinatown, aficionados advise opting for "anything that swims";
most dishes are prepared "simply" and "without too much spice", or
too much price, so never mind the no-frills settings.

Mughlai ◕
20 | 14 | 17 | $32

320 Columbus Ave. (75th St.), 212-724-6363
A "wide-ranging menu" featuring some "hard-to-find" specialties
has made this comparatively "upscale", yet affordable, UWS Indian a
"fine neighborhood staple"; regulars report it's remained almost "un-

changed through the years", providing an "overall pleasant experience" despite service that can be "uneven."

My Moon NEW

▽ | 18 | 26 | 16 | $31

184 N. 10th St. (bet. Bedford & Driggs Aves.), Brooklyn, 718-599-7007; www.mymoonnyc.com

Besides inhabiting an "extremely cool", "cavernous" space inside a converted Williamsburg factory, this art-filled Mediterranean also boasts a "wonderful tiled outdoor seating area"; critics claim the fare's "forgettable" and the service "glacial", but to most the ambiance alone "is worth" checking out.

My Most Favorite Dessert Co.

18 | 14 | 16 | $37

120 W. 45th St. (bet. B'way & 6th Ave.), 212-997-5130; www.mymostfavorite.com

"True to its name", this kosher New American in Times Square concocts "celestial desserts" – "worth the extra hour of cardio" – to chase its "solid" savories; despite often "harried" service, theatergoers find it a "pleasant" (if "pricey") place "for coffee and cake" or a "pre-matinee lunch."

Ñ ●◗≠

▽ | 19 | 19 | 17 | $31

33 Crosby St. (bet. Broome & Grand Sts.), 212-219-8856

Think "tasty" "tapas for trendies" and you'll comprehend this "candlelit, cosmopolitan" SoHo Spaniard where the "loud", "packed" scene is fueled by "inexpensive sangria" and flamenco (Wednesdays); maybe there are "closets bigger than this place", but none with such an "intimate", "sexy" mood.

Nam

23 | 20 | 18 | $38

110 Reade St. (W. B'way), 212-267-1777; www.namnyc.com

"Light, yet deeply satisfying" Vietnamese fare is the draw at this "tightly packed", "chic" TriBeCa "favorite"; service that's alternately "helpful" and "snooty" is outweighed by "reasonable prices."

Nana ≠

20 | 17 | 18 | $29

155 Fifth Ave. (bet. Lincoln & St. Johns Pls.), Brooklyn, 718-230-3749

The "versatile" Asian fusion menu at this Park Slope "bargain" has "something for everyone" from sushi to Thai; party people call its room "relaxed" and "jovial", but others overpowered by the sound system's "incessant beat" head for the "terrific garden" instead.

Nanni ⊠

23 | 15 | 22 | $52

146 E. 46th St. (bet. Lexington & 3rd Aves.), 212-697-4161

"Year in, year out" this little Northern Italian "hidden" near Grand Central comes through with "excellent" "traditional" dishes; the "efficient" "elderly" waiters "make you feel at home", but given the "high prices" maybe they could stand to "update" the "old-school" decor.

Naples 45 ⊠

17 | 14 | 15 | $32

MetLife Bldg., 200 Park Ave. (45th St.), 212-972-7001; www.naples45.com

"Location, location, location" – just North of Grand Central – and "solid", "reasonably priced" pizzas and pastas mean this sizable Southern Italian is always "busy" at weekday lunch; post-work a "young crowd" packs in, undeterred by "inconsistent service" and "loud noise"; N.B. closed weekends.

Neary's ◐

15 | 11 | 18 | $39

358 E. 57th St. (1st Ave.), 212-751-1434

"Consummate host" Jimmy Neary, the nearest NYC comes to having its own "leprechaun", makes "everyone feel important" at this East Midtown Irish pub; it's a "fixture" for "writers, bankers, attorneys" and politicos who rely on its "basic" "comfort food", but really it's all about the "general air of conviviality" here.

Negril ⏺
21 17 16 $33

70 W. Third St. (bet. La Guardia Pl. & Thompson St.), 212-477-2804
362 W. 23rd St. (bet. 8th & 9th Aves.), 212-807-6411
www.negrilvillage.com
"Yeah, mon", for "authentic" Caribbean "home cooking" and a "great island vibe", head for this lively Jamaican duo; the Village branch is larger, more upscale and offers live reggae on Wednesdays, but the staff at both "couldn't be nicer" – though they also "couldn't be slower."

Nello ⏺
18 16 15 $77

696 Madison Ave. (bet. 62nd & 63rd Sts.), 212-980-9099
"You're sure to see someone famous" at this East Side Northern Italian "scene" where "jet-setters" and "glitterati" come to "air-kiss" and nibble "surprisingly good" fare; but the "pompous" service and "unconscionable prices" have mere mortals wondering "why?"

Nëo Sushi ⏺
23 17 19 $58

2298 Broadway (83rd St.), 212-769-1003; www.neosushi.com
"If you can't get down to Nobu" try this "modern" UWS Japanese where the "imaginative", "delicious" sushi comes "with a welcoming smile"; still, a few në-sayers report that it's "way too pricey" for portions "too small to satisfy your cat."

Neptune Room
22 19 20 $50

511 Amsterdam Ave. (bet. 84th & 85th Sts.), 212-496-4100;
www.theneptuneroom.com
Nautical by nature, this "pricey" UWS seafooder's hook is "sparkling fresh" Med-accented fish; the "unpretentious" staff adds to its "fashionable easygoing vibe", leading locals to laud it as most "welcome" in an "area with few high-level" eateries.

New Bo-Ky ⇗
22 5 11 $11

80 Bayard St. (bet. Mott & Mulberry Sts.), 212-406-2292
"Stomach-filling, soul-satisfying" Chinese and Vietnamese soups ladled out "steaming hot" are the stock in trade at this Chinatown noodle specialist; "brusque service" and "nada" ambiance aside, it delivers "consistent" "value" – no wonder it's "packed every day."

New Green Bo ⏺⇗
22 5 11 $17

66 Bayard St. (bet. Elizabeth & Mott Sts.), 212-625-2359
Yes, this "busy" Chinatowner is "famous for its soup dumplings", but cognoscenti also commend its other "delicious, cheap" Shanghai dishes; few fret about the "perfunctory" service or "tiny", "zero-atmosphere" setting – "be prepared to share your table" or "wait."

New Leaf Cafe Ⓜ
20 22 17 $37

Fort Tryon Park, 1 Margaret Corbin Dr. (190th St.), 212-568-5323; www.nyrp.org
Though just blocks from the A train, this "sophisticated" New American in a "charming", "rustic" stone building in Fort Tryon Park feels like an "exquisite escape to the country"; while a new chef has taken the "reasonable" menu up a notch, service remains the same – "pleasant" but "disorganized."

New York Burger Co.
17 8 11 $13

303 Park Ave. S. (bet. 23rd & 24th Sts.), 212-254-2727
678 Sixth Ave. (bet. 21st & 22nd Sts.), 212-229-1404 NEW
www.newyorkburgerco.com
"Fabulous" "organic" burgers "cooked precisely to order" "in front of your eyes" and adorned with a "wide array" of "fresh, tasty" toppings

are the specialty of this "solid" Flatiron District patty pair; just don't be surprised if lines at the counter "get slow" at midday.

Nha Trang
22 | 7 | 15 | $16

87 Baxter St. (bet. Bayard & Canal Sts.), 212-233-5948
148 Centre St. (bet. Walker & White Sts.), 212-941-9292
"Who cares" about "tacky lighting", "tight quarters" and "sparse decor" when you can "eat like a king and pay like a pauper" at this Chinatown Vietnamese duo; "hustle-you-in-and-out" service ensures the inevitable "crowds" are "quickly" accommodated.

Nice
20 | 11 | 15 | $24

35 E. Broadway (bet. Catherine & Market Sts.), 212-406-9510
"Push-cart dim sum" "at its best" and other "dependable", "reasonable" Cantonese dishes are the province of this "chaotic" Chinatown "banquet hall"; it may look "shopworn", but the "din" makes it easy to "take the kids" – as does the "friendly" staff.

Nice Matin ◐
20 | 18 | 17 | $46

201 W. 79th St. (Amsterdam Ave.), 212-873-6423; www.nicematinnyc.com
"Real Parisian bistro" looks, "reliable" (if "pricey") standards and the "perfect not-too-sceney scene" keep this "breezy" UWS French-Med "bustling", especially at "wonderful brunch"; still, doubters dis the "indifferent" service as "not commensurate with its popularity."

Nick & Stef's Steakhouse Ⓢ
21 | 17 | 20 | $57

9 Penn Plaza (enter on 33rd St., bet. 7th & 8th Aves.), 212-563-4444; www.restaurantassociates.com
Most appreciated for its "proximity to Madison Square Garden" (complete with "back door" into the arena), this "casual" chophouse does "delicious steaks" supplemented by some 400 wines; better still, the "pleasant" staff "gets you to the game on time" even when things are "crowded" and "chaotic."

Nick and Toni's Cafe
17 | 14 | 17 | $47

100 W. 67th St. (bet. B'way & Columbus Ave.), 212-496-4000; www.nickandtoniscafe.com
For "convenience" to Lincoln Center, this "reliable", "straightforward" Mediterranean offshoot of the East Hampton original makes a "charming" choice; foes find it "a little tired", with "indifferent" service, though everyone appreciates that they're "mindful of your curtain."

Nick's
22 | 13 | 16 | $23

1814 Second Ave. (94th St.), 212-987-5700 ◐
108-26 Ascan Ave. (bet. Austin & Burns Sts.), Queens, 718-263-1126 ⇄
Pie-sanos praise the "divine", "crispy-crusted", "wood-fired" pizzas at this Italian twosome; however, they advise you to "disregard the noise" and "surly" service and just "mangia, mangia, mangia."

Nicky's Vietnamese Sandwiches ⇄
23 | 6 | 17 | $8

150 E. Second St. (Ave. A), 212-388-1088
311 Atlantic Ave. (bet. Hoyt & Smith Sts.), Brooklyn, 718-855-8838 **NEW**
There's an "explosion of taste sensations" – "crunchy, tangy, savory, spicy" – in every "unbelievably delicious" bite of made-to-order *banh mi* sandwich at this East Village Vietnamese "hole-in-the-wall"; "amazingly low prices" offset serious "dive" decor; N.B. the Boerum Hill outpost has yet to be surveyed.

Nicola's ◐
22 | 16 | 20 | $57

146 E. 84th St. (Lexington Ave.), 212-249-9850
"Top-notch" "traditional" fare and a "wonderfully clubby" feel keep things copacetic for the "old-money" set at this "pricey" Yorkville

Italian "fixture"; though it is "terrifically welcoming if you're a regular", outsiders are left wondering where the "members only" sign is posted.

99 Miles to Philly ⏱≠ NEW   19 | 8 | 15 | $10
94 Third Ave. (bet. 12th & 13th Sts.), 212-253-2700
Many "Philly transplants" claim that the "sloppy" cheese steaks at this "tiny, no-frills" East Villager are "damn close" to the original, given their "heft" alone; but "nice-try" types vow to head south and return only after "a few more years of grease build-up on the grill."

Ninja   ▽ 18 | 21 | 21 | $79
25 Hudson St. (bet. Duane & Reade Sts.), 212-274-8500;
www.ninjanewyork.com
This "movie set"–like, theatrically priced TriBeCa Japanese is done up in a faux mountain village theme with diners downing elaborate fusion dishes ferried by waiters in "kitschy Ninja" drag; to many the focus is too much on "the show" and not enough on substance, but still the experience can be "fun" – if you take "a sense of humor and an expense account."

Nino's ⏱   21 | 19 | 22 | $53
1354 First Ave. (bet. 72nd & 73rd Sts.), 212-988-0002
Nino's Positano
890 Second Ave. (bet. 47th & 48th Sts.), 212-355-5540
Nino's Tuscany
117 W. 58th St. (bet. 6th & 7th Aves.), 212-757-8630;
www.ninostuscany.com
"Sporty guys bring their arm candy" to these "all-around-pleasurable" Italians for "delectable" "old-school" meals delivered by "personality-filled" "pro" staffers; while the slightly more affordable Positano is quiet enough for talking, Tuscany's "live piano" makes it "fun for an older crowd."

Nippon ▣   ▽ 22 | 16 | 19 | $49
155 E. 52nd St. (bet. Lexington & 3rd Aves.), 212-758-0226;
www.restaurantnippon.com
Since 1963 this "old-school" East Midtown Japanese has been turning out "quality" sushi and cooked dishes "attentively" served in simple surroundings; modernists may find the scene "so traditional it hurts", but partisans prefer to "call it timeless."

Nisos ⏱   18 | 15 | 17 | $37
176 Eighth Ave. (19th St.), 646-336-8121; www.nisos-ny.com
Chelsea-goers like this "decent" Mediterranean for "delish" fish dishes "before the Joyce", or for prime boy watching over "great drinks" at a sidewalk table; on the other hand, skeptics say the food's "variable" and service "not so quick."

NOBU   27 | 22 | 23 | $76
105 Hudson St. (Franklin St.), 212-219-0500
NOBU, NEXT DOOR ⏱
105 Hudson St. (bet. Franklin & N. Moore Sts.), 212-334-4445
www.myriadrestaurantgroup.com
Nobu Matsuhisa's "celebrity-gawker's paradise" in TriBeCa remains a "true classic" where the "transcendent" Japanese fusion fare with Peruvian touches will "set you back a month's rent" but is "well worth" the splurge – and the "monthlong wait for a reservation"; N.B. the "more accessible" Next Door adjunct offers "equally compelling" dining at slightly lower rates, and is "easier to get into" since it's first come, first served.

NOBU 57 ●🅩   26 | 25 | 22 | $77

40 W. 57th St. (bet. 5th & 6th Aves.), 212-757-3000;
www.myriadrestaurantgroup.com
Nobu's "super-sized Midtown brother" boasts a "stunning" David
Rockwell–designed interior featuring "undulating wave"–like walls and
plenty of "stargazing" via its "celeb and corporate mogul" clientele; as
for the Peruvian-accented Japanese cuisine, it's "every bit as" "sublime" as the original's, and is served up by a "super" staff; the tough
part is "getting a reservation" and footing the "mind-boggling" bill.

Nocello   21 | 17 | 20 | $48

257 W. 55th St. (bet. B'way & 8th Ave.), 212-713-0224
"Convenient to Carnegie Hall", this "tried-and-true" Tuscan pleases
with "flavorful", "down-to-earth" fare, a "genial host" and "courteous"
service; its "small" space "packed with tables" gets "hectic pre-
theater" so come "off peak."

NoHo Star ●   17 | 14 | 15 | $31

330 Lafayette St. (Bleecker St.), 212-925-0070; www.nohostar.com
Favored for its "great hearty breakfasts", this "casual" NoHo "staple"
"adds a bit of pizzazz" to its "extensive", "affordable" New American
dinner menu by adding Chinese choices; despite "slowish" service and
"noisy", less-than-pristine quarters, locals simply "love this place."

Nomad NEW   – | – | – | M

78 Second Ave. (4th St.), 212-253-5410; www.nomadny.com
Evoking Marrakech, this affordable East Village North African newcomer offers an atmospheric setting and aromatic tagines that have
locals hoping this nomad will put down permanent roots.

Nonna   17 | 15 | 16 | $34

520 Columbus Ave. (85th St.), 212-579-3194; www.nonnarestaurant.com
At this "great neighborhood" Italian, "simple" pastas, "bargain" prix fixe
menus and "welcoming" vibes have Westsiders "bringing the family";
still, a few claim it's no slam dunk, citing "uneven" experiences.

Nooch   15 | 18 | 14 | $24

143 Eighth Ave. (17th St.), 212-691-8600
A "groovy" "Starship Enterprise"–like interior and "blaring club music"
create a "cool techno vibe" at this "filling" Chelsea Thai-Japanese
noodle bar; it's "cheap enough", but still a "disappointed" cadre contend that the food and service "don't live up to" the atmosphere.

Noodle Bar ⇗ NEW   ▽ 21 | 17 | 20 | $24

26 Carmine St. (bet. Bedford & Bleecker Sts.), 212-524-6800
It's fun to "watch the chefs" create "nouveau" Pan-Asian "street
food" in the open kitchen of this "cute" new Villager; locals who want
an "inexpensive lunch" they can "slurp down in no time" find it a
"great addition to Carmine Street's Restaurant Row."

Noodle Pudding Ⓜ⇗   25 | 18 | 22 | $34

38 Henry St. (bet. Cranberry & Middagh Sts.), Brooklyn,
718-625-3737
"I'd eat here once a week" rave regulars of this "homey" Brooklyn
Heights Italian beloved for its "modest prices" and "expert" rendering
of "super-fresh ingredients" into "bright sauces and hearty specials";
it's always "bustling", but the staffers are always "gracious."

Nook ●⇗   21 | 12 | 16 | $29

746 Ninth Ave. (50th St.), 212-247-5500; www.nynook.com
This "thimble-size" Hell's Kitchen Eclectic has mavens marveling at
its "home cooking" with "haute" touches as well as its "reasonable"

prices; service is occasionally "abrupt", and decor is nonexistent, but the bottom line is this nook is always booked.

Norma's
25 | 20 | 21 | $37

Le Parker Meridien, 118 W. 57th St. (bet. 6th & 7th Aves.), 212-708-7460; www.parkermeridien.com
At this Midtown New American, the "savory" morning menu is among "NYC's best" and reads "like brunch porn" ("$1,000 caviar omelet", anyone?); its "glamorous" setting is "ideal for business", and service is "prompt", so for most it's "worth the prices" and "tedious waits."

North Square ●
23 | 19 | 20 | $43

Washington Square Hotel, 103 Waverly Pl. (MacDougal St.), 212-254-1200; www.northsquareny.com
Despite a "great location", this subterranean "sleeper" "doesn't get the attention it deserves" per Villagers who vaunt its "inventive" seasonal New American fare and "user-friendly" prices; a "helpful", "efficient" staff sustains the "informal" vibe that's ideal for "quiet chatting."

Novecento ●
20 | 16 | 17 | $42

343 W. Broadway (bet. Broome & Grand Sts.), 212-925-4706; www.novecentogroup.com
"Specializing in two of Argentina's best exports: beef and wine", this "sexy" SoHo steakhouse serves "tasty" provender from the pampas in a "fun" setting that's "loud" and "crowded" into the wee hours; it's a "great value" in an area where "looks" often "prevail over substance."

Novitá
23 | 18 | 22 | $51

102 E. 22nd St. (bet. Lexington Ave. & Park Ave. S.), 212-677-2222; www.novitanyc.com
The "secret" is out about this "wonderful" Gramercy Northern Italian that "year after year" maintains "top-flight" fare and "congenial" service; word has spread so far that there's almost "never an empty seat."

Novo ⊠ NEW
∇ 21 | 19 | 20 | $38

290 Hudson St. (bet. Dominick & Spring Sts.), 212-989-6410; www.novonyc.com
Chef Alex Garcia (ex Calle Ocho) whips up "tasty" Nuevo Latino flavors at this SoHo "bargain" small-plate specialist; the long, narrow room with its communal table turns loungey on weekends when a DJ spins, and "fresh" infusion drinks may spin you too.

Nurnberger Bierhaus NEW
∇ 19 | 18 | 19 | $29

817 Castleton Ave. (Davis Ave.), Staten Island, 718-816-7461
"Delivering what it promises", this "lively" new Staten Islander pours "a great selection" of ales to go with its "hearty" German standards; "efficient, friendly" "waitresses in costume" tend to the "cozy" room bedecked with cuckoo clocks, vintage steins and the like.

Nyonya ●⊄
23 | 12 | 15 | $20

194 Grand St. (bet. Mott & Mulberry Sts.), 212-334-3669
5323 Eighth Ave. (54th St.), Brooklyn, 718-633-0808
Eats "about as close to authentic Malaysian" as you'll get "outside of Kuala Lumpur" draw "crowds" to this "inexpensive" Little Italy–Sunset Park duo; the "unique" dishes redolent with "complex spices" mean most find no fault with having "not much" decor and "rushed" service.

OCEANA ⊠
26 | 24 | 25 | $77

55 E. 54th St. (bet. Madison & Park Aves.), 212-759-5941; www.oceanarestaurant.com
This "sublime", prix fixe–only East Midtown New American does "fearless and fantastic things" with "boat-fresh" seafood in "delight-

ful" "luxury liner"–like quarters, while the "caring" crew "treats every diner like an admiral"; N.B. the post-*Survey* departure of chef Cornelius Gallagher places the above Food rating in question.

Ocean Grill ● | 23 | 20 | 20 | $49 |

384 Columbus Ave. (bet. 78th & 79th Sts.), 212-579-2300;
www.brguestrestaurants.com
It's "steady as she goes" at Steve Hanson's portholed pescatorium, an UWS "mainstay" for "fresh" fin fare (including a "wonderful raw bar"), "solid" weekend brunch, "serious" service and "addictive" prix fixe "bargains"; still, "tight quarters" and "loud" acoustics cause sensitive sorts to "deep-six it" at peak times.

Odeon ● | 18 | 17 | 17 | $44 |

145 W. Broadway (bet. Duane & Thomas Sts.), 212-233-0507;
www.theodeonrestaurant.com
"Still hip after all these years", TriBeCa's Franco-American "pioneer" remains a beloved "institution" where "a great mix of people" downs "reliable" bistro fare in "classic" deco digs; true, it's "no longer as inexpensive", but it "satisfies" for everything from a "mean brunch" with the "munchkins" to a "late-night" "nosh" with would-be kins.

O.G. ● ▽ | 23 | 15 | 22 | $34 |

507 E. Sixth St. (bet. Aves. A & B), 212-477-4649;
www.ogrestaurant.com
The chef at this oft-"overlooked" East Village Pan-Asian "must stay up nights thinking of flavor combos" because his "creative", "not-too-fussy" menu reflects a "masterful fusion" approach; despite somewhat "dated" decor, it has a "cozy" vibe that's enhanced by "warm, knowledgeable" service.

Old Devil Moon | 19 | 16 | 15 | $21 |

511 E. 12th St. (bet. Aves. A & B), 212-475-4357; www.olddevilmoon.com
"Down-home" "Southern comfort food" for "hipsters", "yuppies", "meat eaters and vegheads" alike is dished out at this affordable East Villager, where the "happily kitschy" quarters "border on bizarre"; service is "friendly" but "lax", so "don't be in a hurry."

Old Homestead | 23 | 17 | 20 | $63 |

56 Ninth Ave. (bet. 14th & 15th Sts.), 212-242-9040;
www.theoldhomesteadsteakhouse.com
An "unpretentious" "reminder that the Meatpacking District used to pack meat", this circa-1868 "granddaddy of steakhouses" challenges carnivores to "bring an appetite" for slabs so "huge", "only the head, tail and hooves are missing"; its "classic" cow-palace decor was refreshed recently (post-*Survey*), but some suggest the service still "could be nicer" at these prices.

Olea NEW ▽ | 22 | 20 | 19 | $34 |

171 Lafayette Ave. (Adelphi St.), Brooklyn, 718-643-7003
From the owners of nearby Maggie Brown comes this "beguilingly laid-back" Med in Fort Greene, whose "cute" corner space is the backdrop for "ingenious, creative" cuisine (including tapas) and "interesting", "affordable" wines; add an "amazing brunch" and there's no wonder that the locals are turning into regulars.

Oliva ● ▽ | 21 | 18 | 17 | $36 |

161 E. Houston St. (Allen St.), 212-228-4143; www.olivanyc.com
It's a "relaxed Spanish party" every night at this Lower East Side Basque where the "festive" scene is fueled by "fun live music" and "delicious" tapas and sangria, all at "the right price"; as for its 45-seat space, one person's "cramped" cantina is another's "sexy date place."

Olives

23 | 21 | 21 | $54

W Union Sq., 201 Park Ave. S. (17th St.), 212-353-8345;
www.toddenglish.com

At Todd English's "happening" Mediterranean off Union Square, "unusual combinations" yield "delicious, sometimes edgy" results, well matched by a "superb, idiosyncratic" cellar; a "snazzy" setting and "pro" service make it easier to tune out the "noise" from the adjacent "pickup haven" bar.

Olive Vine Cafe ⊅

17 | 9 | 15 | $17

362 15th St. (7th Ave.), Brooklyn, 718-499-0555
54 Seventh Ave. (bet. Lincoln & St. Johns Pls.), Brooklyn, 718-622-2626

"Reliable", well-spiced Middle Eastern standards make this "welcoming" Park Slope duo a "neighborhood staple", while the BYO policy "makes it a great deal"; "uninteresting" interiors lead many to opt for "can't-be-beat takeout" – or the North Slope branch's nifty back garden.

Ollie's ●

16 | 9 | 13 | $21

1991 Broadway (bet. 67th & 68th Sts.), 212-595-8181
2315 Broadway (84th St.), 212-362-3111
2957 Broadway (116th St.), 212-932-3300
200B W. 44th St. (bet. B'way & 8th Ave.), 212-921-5988

"Tasty", "basic dishes" priced "unbelievably low" and served "at warp speed" mean this West Side Chinese quartet achieves that "elusive sweet spot" at the "intersection of good-cheap-fast"; still, "nonexistent ambiance" and "eat-it-and-beat-it" service have some saying "pass it by."

O Mai

24 | 17 | 20 | $37

158 Ninth Ave. (bet. 19th & 20th Sts.), 212-633-0550; www.omainyc.com

"Oh my" sigh surveyors swooning over the "superlative" "updated" Vietnamese cuisine at this Chelsea "charmer" whose "small" but "peaceful" space is manned by a "personable" team; factor in "reasonable" prices and you've got "value" enough to have tables "tightly packed" most nights.

Omen ●

24 | 18 | 21 | $54

113 Thompson St. (bet. Prince & Spring Sts.), 212-925-8923

Here's a "wonderful omen": the "excellent" "traditional" Kyoto-style dishes at this "serene", "quietly chic" SoHo Japanese set it apart from NYC's "million sushi joints"; "lovely" service rounds out the "pricey-but-worth-it" experience – no wonder it's favored by "low-key" "celebs" and "in-the-know" Japanophiles.

Omonia Cafe ●

18 | 13 | 14 | $18

7612-14 Third Ave. (bet. 76th & 77th Sts.), Brooklyn, 718-491-1435
32-20 Broadway (33rd St.), Queens, 718-274-6650

"Sugar fix" seekers make a beeline for the "mouthwatering desserts" at these Hellenic coffeehouses in Astoria and Bay Ridge; forget those "tacky" interiors and "slow" service – just "have an espresso" and some "to-die-for baklava", listen to the regulars "speaking Greek" and you'll feel like you've had a vacation in Athens.

Once Upon a Tart . . .

22 | 13 | 14 | $15

135 Sullivan St. (bet. Houston & Prince Sts.), 212-387-8869;
www.onceuponatart.com

"On your way to wherever", this affordable SoHo cafe supplies "scrumptious" sweets and sandwiches over the counter in a cubbyhole space that's "quaint" but "not too comfortable" when "crowded"; as to the service, some tartly term it "so low-key, there's almost none at all."

One ◐

18 | 22 | 15 | $49

1 Little W. 12th St. (9th Ave.), 212-255-9717; www.onelw12.com
One "fashionable" "young crowd" assembles "after dark" at this "trendy" Meatpacking District lounge/eatery for "tempting drinks" and "pricey" "people-watching"; the "not bad" New American small plates tend to get "overlooked" since so few guests "go for the food."

O'Neals' ◐

16 | 16 | 18 | $43

49 W. 64th St. (bet. B'way & CPW), 212-787-4663; www.onealsny.com
A "standby for Lincoln Center–goers", this "lively" "overgrown pub" provides "no-nonsense" American "grub" and "prompt, pleasant service" to see that "you'll make the curtain"; the "accommodating" style and "pleasant" quarters explain its "Teflon" rep.

One 83

19 | 20 | 19 | $47

1608 First Ave. (bet. 83rd & 84th Sts.), 212-327-4700;
www.one83restaurant.com
Though "unprepossessing", this UES Northern Italian "aims to please" with "decent" "straightforward" food in a "spacious" interior harboring a "pretty" "covered back patio"; "civilized" sorts note its "undiscovered" status facilitates "audible conversation."

ONE IF BY LAND, TWO IF BY SEA

23 | 27 | 24 | $73

17 Barrow St. (bet. 7th Ave. S. & W. 4th St.), 212-228-0822;
www.oneifbyland.com
"Seal the deal" with "that special someone" at this "breathtaking" Village New American, transforming Aaron's Burr's "Colonial" carriage house into the "apex of romance" with its "wonderful" prix fixe menu, "formal" service and "over-the-top" atmospherics; "gorgeously appointed" with flowers, candles and lilting piano music, it commands "quite a price", but she'll "say 'I do'" – or you can "give up."

101

20 | 18 | 17 | $38

10018 Fourth Ave. (bet. 100th & 101st Sts.), Brooklyn, 718-833-1313 ◐
3900 Richmond Ave. (Amboy Rd.), Staten Island, 718-227-3286
Now with "two locations", this Italian–New American tag team in Bay Ridge and Staten Island offers "consistent" cooking, "friendly" staffing and "happening" bar scenes; "good value" ensures better than passing grades.

107 West

17 | 13 | 16 | $28

2787 Broadway (bet. 107th & 108th Sts.), 212-864-1555
811 W. 187th St. (bet. Ft. Washington & Pinehurst Aves.), 212-923-3311
"Serviceable" is the word on these Cajun–Tex-Mex "standbys" where regulars recommend "anything blackened" on the "uneven menu"; though kind of "dullsville" ("mundane decor", "ho-hum service"), there's "not much to choose from" in these parts.

Onera

25 | 20 | 22 | $57

222 W. 79th St. (bet. Amsterdam Ave. & B'way), 212-873-0200;
www.oneranyc.com
With its "deliciously inventive", "updated" Greek fare, this UWS "find" rises to "a different class than most" and follows through with a "fine wine list" and "expert" service; "impressed" diners "don't mind paying a little more" despite the "homey" room's "close" quarters.

Ono

20 | 24 | 17 | $64

Gansevoort Hotel, 18 Ninth Ave. (enter on 13th St.), 212-660-6766;
www.chinagrillmgt.com
"Stargazers" at Jeffrey Chodorow's "dark", "dramatic" Meatpacking District Japanese claim the "sexy" surroundings (including the "place-to-be" garden) can overshadow the "imaginative sushi" and

robata-grill choices; just beware of "attitude" and prepare to "say 'oh no' when they bring the check."

Orchard, The ⬛NEW

25 | 22 | 20 | $48

162 Orchard St. (bet. Rivington & Stanton Sts.), 212-353-3570
"Stimulus for the jaded palate" awaits at this Lower East Side sapling from John LaFemina (Peasant, ápizz), which is "starting out strong" with "delectable", Italian-accented New American fare matched with "informative service" and a "stylishly austere setting"; now that it has finally acquired a liquor license, it may well be "unstoppable."

Oriental Garden

24 | 11 | 16 | $29

14 Elizabeth St. (bet. Bayard & Canal Sts.), 212-619-0085
You can't do better for fresh fish than the seafood "from the tanks" at this taste of "Chinatown's high end", a surefire source of "superior" "Cantonese-style seafood" that also features "top-notch" dim sum; if the "brusque" service and "institutional" setting is "standard"-issue, the high quality and modest prices are anything but.

Orsay ☻

17 | 20 | 16 | $54

1057 Lexington Ave. (75th St.), 212-517-6400;
www.orsayrestaurant.com
"Keep your chin up", 'cause this UES "social X-ray" brasserie is "bustling" with "overly maintained" types who find its "belle epoque" looks and "pleasing", "*très cher*" French food "convincing enough"; just be prepared for "snooty service", except when everyone is away in the Hamptons or Palm Beach.

Orso ☻

22 | 17 | 21 | $54

322 W. 46th St. (bet. 8th & 9th Aves.), 212-489-7212;
www.orsorestaurant.com
If you want to get "in the mood for Broadway", try this "refined" Theater District Northern Italian, which reliably "delivers" with "superb" food, "warm service" and the occasional "celeb" encounter; the house is "always full", so "book very early" or opt for lunch and save some bucks.

Osaka

25 | 17 | 20 | $30

272 Court St. (bet. Degraw & Kane Sts.), Brooklyn, 718-643-0044;
www.osakany.com
"Gigantic" "hunks" of "dreamy", "artfully prepared" sushi signal that this "often-packed" Cobble Hill entry is "not your average Japanese"; add "polite" service, a "Zen-like garden" and "reasonable" prices, and locals boast it's the kind of place "Manhattan wishes it had."

Osso Buco

17 | 14 | 17 | $35

1662 Third Ave. (93rd St.), 212-426-5422
88 University Pl. (bet. 11th & 12th Sts.), 212-645-4525
www.ossobuco2go.com
You can "relax and shovel in" the pasta at these "family-style foodfests" providing "overflowing" platters of "Italian staples" at prices that "won't break the bank"; though the "tawdry" setups offer "nothing new", they're sure "popular" among "friends who want to share."

Osteria al Doge ☻

20 | 17 | 18 | $46

142 W. 44th St. (bet. B'way & 6th Ave.), 212-944-3643;
www.osteria-doge.com
By now a Times Square "fixture", this "welcoming" Italian "works" as a "fail-safe pre-theater stop" specializing in "hearty" "Venetian delights" served by an "efficient" team; it's "enjoyable" overall, but to dodge the "loud", "frenetic" mob, "sit upstairs if you can."

Osteria del Circo ◑
22 | 23 | 22 | $58

120 W. 55th St. (bet. 6th & 7th Aves.), 212-265-3636; www.osteriadelcirco.com
If you can't get into the new Le Cirque, "spoil yourself" instead at the Maccioni family's other "vibrant" Midtowner, where the "circus motif" is a "fanciful" side show to the "enjoyable" Northern Italian cuisine and "gracious" service; yes, it's "kinda pricey", but it's sure to improve your day.

Osteria del Sole ◑
21 | 17 | 18 | $45

267 W. Fourth St. (Perry St.), 212-620-6840
It's just an "unpretentious" Village Italian, but this "upbeat" spot "really delivers" with "ambitious Sardinian" dishes that furnish "tons of flavor"; add "personable" service and most say the sole drawback is the "overpriced wine list."

Osteria Gelsi
24 | 18 | 21 | $44

507 Ninth Ave. (38th St.), 212-244-0088; www.gelsinyc.com
Italian minus "the usual clichés" makes this "civilized" Garment District "outpost" near the Port Authority a "star" in a "tough" area; cognoscenti hail the "tempting menu" of "top-quality" cuisine from Puglia and the "warm" "hospitality", saying they only regret that it's a "find" that more and more are "finding out" about.

Osteria Laguna ◑
22 | 19 | 19 | $45

209 E. 42nd St. (bet. 2nd & 3rd Aves.), 212-557-0001; www.osteria-laguna.com
A "safe" haven for "business lunch" folks and "U.N. types", this "respectable" Midtowner proffers a "solid", "not-too-pricey" selection of "core Italian dishes" in "inviting" surroundings; it's "noisy" at peak times, but most praise a "professionally run" show.

Ota-Ya
21 | 16 | 20 | $33

1572 Second Ave. (bet. 81st & 82nd Sts.), 212-988-1188; www.ota-ya.com
"Yummy fresh sushi" "at regular prices" qualifies this UES "neighborhood" Japanese as a "keeper"; despite the "standout" fare, the "comfortable" digs are on the "quieter" side since it's more "unknown" than it ota be.

Otto ◑
21 | 19 | 19 | $37

1 Fifth Ave. (enter on 8th St.), 212-995-9559; www.ottopizzeria.com
"All aboard" cry celebrants "piling in" to the Batali-Bastianich team's "energetic" Village enoteca/pizzeria to devour "awesome" "gourmet" pies with "unique" (sometimes "bizarro") toppings and a "deep" Italian vino list; the "rail station"–inspired setting's "a little crazed", but "populist" pricing makes this an otto-matic "winner."

OUEST
25 | 22 | 22 | $60

2315 Broadway (bet. 83rd & 84th Sts.), 212-580-8700; www.ouestny.com
"It's all here" gush Upper Westsiders who "relish" this "first-class" "wonder" where "brilliant" chef Tom Valenti blends "haute" with "homestyle" to craft "uniformly" "exceptional" New American cuisine; with "unobtrusive" service and a "sumptuous" yet "unstuffy" setting ("get a red booth"), the "humming" scene's a "tough" reservation but well "worth the try."

Our Place
21 | 15 | 20 | $32

141 E. 55th St. (bet. Lexington & 3rd Aves.), 212-753-3900
1444 Third Ave. (82nd St.), 212-288-4888
www.ourplaceuptown.com
Eastsiders know this "upscale" duo as "a safe place" for "top-tier" "midpriced" Chinese with some "genuine" Shanghai surprises in the mix; with "calming decor", "attentive service" and "on-time delivery", they're "consistently" "worth the extra few bucks."

Outback Steakhouse

15 | 13 | 16 | $32

919 Third Ave. (enter on 56th St., bet. 2nd & 3rd Aves.), 212-935-6400
60 W. 23rd St. (bet. 5th & 6th Aves.), 212-989-3122
1475 86th St. (15th Ave.), Brooklyn, 718-837-7200
Bay Terrace, 23-48 Bell Blvd. (26th Ave.), Queens, 718-819-0908
Queens Pl., 88-01 Queens Blvd. (56th Ave.), Queens, 718-760-7200
www.outback.com
"Don't knock it", mate – this "cookie-cutter" chain of "corny Aussie" steakhouses has the "greasy" "good eats" to satiate a "ravenous meat hunger"; sure, they're "tacky" and favored by "bloomin' tourists", but the "value" has fans "boomeranging back for more."

OYSTER BAR ☒

21 | 17 | 16 | $45

Grand Central, lower level (42nd St. & Vanderbilt Ave.), 212-490-6650;
www.oysterbarny.com
"The one and only", Grand Central's "cavernous" "underground" seafooder has been a source of "delectable" "bivalve beauties" ("who needs Viagra?"), pan roasts and "wonderfully fresh" fish since 1913; never mind the "gruff" service and "echo chamber" "din", it's a "quintessential NY" experience that would be a bargain at any price.

Pair of 8's ●NEW

21 | 16 | 19 | $49

568 Amsterdam Ave. (bet. 87th & 88th Sts.), 212-874-2742; www.pairof8s.com
Locals "welcome" this new UWS wine bar/eatery for its "honest", "lip-smacking" New American eats, paired with "wonderful" pours and "amiable" service; despite "thisclose" seating, the setting's deemed a "diamond in the rough", and most gladly chip in the "pricey" ante to back this winning hand.

Palà ●NEW

▽ 21 | 17 | 20 | $27

198 Allen St. (Stanton St.), 212-614-7252
To satisfy "pizza cravings" "as the Romans do" check out this new LES Italian, where "awesome" pies sold "by the slice or foot" showcase "light", "crunchy crusts" and "flavorful" "gourmet" toppings; it's "casual", but the "rustic" feel and "quality wines" make it a success.

Paladar ●

20 | 15 | 17 | $35

161 Ludlow St. (bet. Houston & Stanton Sts.), 212-473-3535;
www.paladarrestaurant.com
"Que bueno!" exclaim amigos of this "very satisfactory" Lower Eastsider from Aarón Sanchez, serving "well-executed Nuevo Latino" fare that's priced for "value"; also, the "festive" setting makes it a "cool place" to palaver over "potent mojitos."

PALM

24 | 17 | 21 | $64

837 Second Ave. (bet. 44th & 45th Sts.), 212-687-2953 ☒
840 Second Ave. (bet. 44th & 45th Sts.), 212-697-5198
250 W. 50th St. (bet. B'way & 8th Ave.), 212-333-7256 ●
www.thepalm.com
These "warhorse" chophouses are "the real deal" for "man-size" "slabs" of beef and "monster lobsters", along with "old-fashioned" "surly" service and plenty of "bustle"; they're "hard on the wallet" and seem "stodgy" to some, but "you can't knock" a "NY icon"; P.S. the founding site on the west side of Second Avenue with all the "entertaining celebrity caricatures" is "where you want to be."

Pampa ●⇸

22 | 15 | 16 | $36

768 Amsterdam Ave. (bet. 97th & 98th Sts.), 212-865-2929;
www.pamparestaurant.com
"Meat eaters" "on a budget" attest that this "authentic" Upper West Side Argentinean steakhouse "holds its own", serving "generous

portions" of "delicious" "garlicky beef" "without the ridiculous prices"; the garden's "wonderful" too, though the "cash-only" routine is "getting old."

Pampano
24 | 22 | 21 | $52

209 E. 49th St. (bet. 2nd & 3rd Aves.), 212-751-4545; www.modernmexican.com
Co-owned by Placido Domingo and chef Richard Sandoval, this "classy" Midtown Mexican "hits the high notes" with an "exceptional" "coastal" menu displaying a "mastery" of "creative seafood"; with a "chic", "airy" space and "attentive" service, it elicits many a "*gracias*" as a "distinctive" "change of pace."

Pam Real Thai Food ♯
24 | 7 | 15 | $21

404 W. 49th St. (bet. 9th & 10th Aves.), 212-333-7500
402 W. 47th St. (bet. 9th & 10th Aves.), 212-315-4441 ● Ⓜ NEW
www.pamrealthai.com
You "can't get more authentic" than this Hell's Kitchen Thai duo, where the "reliably first-rate" food is "a real delight", especially if "you like it spicy"; though the "barren decor" detracts, it's balanced by "rock-bottom prices"; N.B. the new 47th Street branch has outdoor seating.

Panino'teca 275 Ⓜ
▽ 24 | 18 | 21 | $23

275 Smith St. (bet. Degraw & Sackett Sts.), Brooklyn, 718-237-2728;
www.paninoteca275.com
A "varied", "panini-centric" lineup of "mouthwatering" "Italian munchies" makes this Carroll Gardens "neighborhood joint" a "favorite" for casual sipping and "nibbling"; the "cozy" interior is augmented by a "lovely" back garden, and "easygoing" vibes prevail throughout.

Paola's
22 | 19 | 21 | $48

245 E. 84th St. (bet. 2nd & 3rd Aves.), 212-794-1890;
www.paolasrestaurant.com
"Fabulous food without all the hype" marks "wonderful hostess" Paola Bottero's UES Italian, a "quietly elegant" "charmer" where the "traditional" food is "consistently" "satisfying"; "efficient service" and a "warm", flower-filled room reinforce its "romantic" rep among "impressed" admirers.

Papaya King
20 | 3 | 11 | $6

179 E. 86th St. (3rd Ave.), 212-369-0648 ● ♯
200 W. 14th St. (7th Ave. S.), 212-367-8090 ●
121 W. 125th St. (bet. Lenox & 7th Aves.), 212-665-5732 ♯
www.papayaking.com
"What a wiener" exclaim locals who feel "no shame" washing down "classic", "snappy" hot dogs with "sweet" fruit drinks at these "renowned" "standing room–only" frankfests; they're less than "no-frills", but unbelievably "cheap" tabs ensure that they remain "one of NY's institutions."

Paper Moon Milano Ⓩ
20 | 17 | 19 | $49

39 E. 58th St. (bet. Madison & Park Aves.), 212-758-8600;
www.papermoonrestaurant.com
"Handy" if you're in Midtown, this Northern Italian is "nothing too fancy" but it "works" for "solid" cooking via Milan served in "well-maintained" digs; it's been "steady" for many moons, though a few fret that the "noise level" and cost can climb "too high" in the nighttime sky.

Pappardella ●
19 | 16 | 18 | $38

316 Columbus Ave. (75th St.), 212-595-7996
They "aim to please" at this "comforting" West Side Italian, a long-time "local" favorite specializing in "tasty pastas" including the "namesake" noodle; it's pappular as an "affordable", if "workman-

like", "standby", and the "outside seating" is "a big plus" for those who want to watch the Columbus Avenue parade.

Paradou ◐
19 | 17 | 16 | $42

8 Little W. 12th St. (bet. Greenwich & Washington Sts.), 212-463-8345; www.paradounyc.com
An "unexpected" "retreat" from the Meatpacking District "madness", this "quaint" "little" French bistro supplies "quality" cuisine with a "real Provençal" flavor; the atmosphere and "pretty" year-round garden are "so relaxing" that only a few note the service is "*comme ci, comme ça.*"

Parea NEW
– | – | – | E

36 E. 20th St. (bet. B'way & Park Ave. S.), 212-777-8448; www.parea-ny.com
The name of this sleek new Gramercy Park Greek translates as 'a gathering of friends', and there's plenty to share with them on its wide-ranging haute menu; meanwhile, the cool subterranean cocktail lounge is made for postprandial imbibing.

Paris Commune
19 | 19 | 17 | $39

99 Bank St. (Greenwich St.), 212-929-0509; www.pariscommune.net
Keeping its knack for "solid", "not-too-expensive" "French bistro fare", this "casual" Village "favorite" remains "worth the visit" to its "spruced-up" second home; "lines are still long" for the "amazing" brunch, even if service "can be touch and go."

Paris Match ◐
∇ 18 | 19 | 16 | $45

29 E. 65th St. (bet. Madison & Park Aves.), 212-737-4400
Worldly types appreciate this "attractive" Eastsider's "intriguing combo of French and sushi" items as a pleasant, midpriced change of pace in an "authentic bistro" setting; skeptics say it's "no match for Paris", but the "chic" "young Euro crowd" "could stay all night."

Park, The ◐
15 | 24 | 14 | $41

118 10th Ave. (bet. 17th & 18th Sts.), 212-352-3313; www.theparknyc.com
"Go for the scenery" – including the walking kind – at this West Chelsea "party" central, a "happenin'" playground with a "luscious" look incorporating "skylights", "greenery" and a "wonderful garden"; as for the merely "adequate" Med menu and "absent-minded" service, after "lots of drinks" "who cares?"

Park Avenue Cafe
23 | 22 | 22 | $66

100 E. 63rd St. (bet. Lexington & Park Aves.), 212-644-1900; www.parkavenuecafe.com
Dine with "your co-op board" at this "tony" Eastsider, where chef Neil Murphy's "splendid" menu showcases "Americana at its best" in a handsome "Americana"-filled setting that balances "class" with "comfort"; it's certainly "not cheap", but by any standard it's a "winner" – especially for the chef's table's "chosen few."

Park Bistro
20 | 16 | 19 | $48

414 Park Ave. S. (bet. 28th & 29th Sts.), 212-689-1360
"Truly French" with "no pretense", this "longtime" Gramercy bistro is a "neighborhood delight" thanks to "excellent" "country" cookery served by an "efficient" team "without the attitude"; "welcoming" vibes sustain it as a place for a "loyal following" to park.

Park East Grill
∇ 20 | 17 | 17 | $56

1564 Second Ave. (bet. 81st & 82nd Sts.), 212-717-8400; www.parkeastgrill.com
"Solid" steaks lead the lineup of "fine kosher" fare at this UES meatery, an "enjoyable" "upscale" affiliate of the butcher shop next door;

however, critics kvetch that the "indifferent service" and "close" space "don't meet the expectations" set by such "expensive" tabs.

Park Place
▽ 21 | 18 | 20 | $36

5816 Mosholu Ave. (B'way), Bronx, 718-548-0977

A "popular place" in underserved Riverdale, this "quaint" "hideaway" will "warm your heart" with its "plentiful" helpings of "well-done" Continental fare and "attentive service"; if the "intimate" quarters "could use a face-lift", "the locals don't seem to mind."

Park Side ◐
24 | 19 | 21 | $43

107-01 Corona Ave. (51st Ave.), Queens, 718-271-9321;
www.parksiderestaurant.com

All "Corona swears by" this "time-warp" Italian for "quintessential" "old-world favorites" served in "generous portions" to a "packed house" "typecast" from *Goodfellas*; "modest prices" make it well "worth the journey", but "prepare to wait" while watching a game of "bocce out front."

Park Terrace Bistro Ⓜ
▽ 21 | 20 | 23 | $34

4959 Broadway (bet. Isham & 207th Sts.), 212-567-2828;
www.parkterracebistro.com

With its "soulful" French-Moroccan food, "gracious hosts" and stab at "exotic" decor, this "civilized" yet "reasonable" "outpost" feels "heaven sent" in "up-and-coming" Inwood; it's "accommodating" whether you want to "flirt with your date" or get "convivial" with the bar crowd.

Parma ◐
21 | 13 | 21 | $55

1404 Third Ave. (bet. 79th & 80th Sts.), 212-535-3520

"They treat you well" at this UES Northern Italian "haunt" starting with "top-notch" "traditional" food plus service that's "friendly to a fault" – once you're "a regular"; there are "prettier places" and prices are "not modest", but "loyal followers" insist that you "can't go wrong here."

Pars Grill House & Bar NEW
▽ 22 | 15 | 20 | $30

249 W. 26th St. (bet. 7th & 8th Aves.), 212-929-9860

"Great kebabs" lead the way to a delicious Persian excursion at this "unassuming" Chelsea newcomer "near FIT"; partisans praise the "friendly service" and "simple" but "pleasant" setting with "outdoor tables", but others parse it as "still a work in progress."

Parsonage
▽ 21 | 22 | 21 | $43

74 Arthur Kill Rd. (Clarke Ave.), Staten Island, 718-351-7879

"Staten Island's history" lives on at this "quaint" American-Continental in a "charming" "old converted" Victorian home in the "Richmond Town restoration"; expect "hands-on" service and food that's "appealing" if "not historic itself."

Pascalou
21 | 14 | 17 | $41

1308 Madison Ave. (bet. 92nd & 93rd Sts.), 212-534-7522

A Carnegie Hill "favorite" that "deserves more square footage", this "teeny" bistro boasts a "varied" selection of *magnifique* French fare served by a "dedicated" staff; despite the "tight fit", fans "keep going back" for the sizable "value."

Pasha
21 | 19 | 19 | $39

70 W. 71st St. (bet. Columbus Ave. & CPW), 212-579-8751;
www.pashanewyork.com

Like visiting "Istanbul" without airfare, this Lincoln Center–area Turk has "zesty" food, a "cheerful staff" and "lush" adornments that leave surveyors "wanting more"; "moderate prices" make this "change of pace" even more "relaxing."

Pasquale's Rigoletto

22 | 16 | 20 | $39

2311 Arthur Ave. (Crescent Ave.), Bronx, 718-365-6644
"When you want real food", this "retro" "Arthur Avenue staple" "satisfies" with "mouthwatering" "homestyle" Italian "in *abbondanza*"; the "warm" service and "lively", "authentic setting" are such "great fun" that it's easy to "fuhgeddabout" Little Italy.

Pasticcio

19 | 17 | 19 | $37

447 Third Ave. (bet. 30th & 31st Sts.), 212-679-2551; www.pasticcionyc.com
"Loved by locals" who keep it on "regular rotation", this "cozy" Murray Hill "hideaway" is a "congenial" choice for "reliable" "standard Italian" at "reasonable prices"; the "sedate" vibe is enlivened by a "great" sparkling wine selection from the in-house enoteca, Proseccheria.

PASTIS ◑

20 | 20 | 17 | $44

9 Ninth Ave. (Little W. 12th St.), 212-929-4844; www.pastisny.com
Like being "transplanted" to "Paree", Keith McNally's Meatpacking District bistro hosts a "smokin' hot" "scene" "jammed" with "upwardly mobile" "trendsters" taking in "star sightings" over "enjoyable", "decently priced" French fare; think of it as "Balthazar lite" complete with "harried staff" and "absurd waits", but you can "count on" an "energizing" time – inside or out.

Patois Ⓜ

22 | 19 | 18 | $38

255 Smith St. (bet. Degraw & Douglass Sts.), Brooklyn, 718-855-1535; www.patoisrestaurant.com
This "Smith Street pioneer" remains a Carroll Gardens "go-to" for "solid", "straightforward" French bistro food in "pleasant" "rustic" environs; the "excellent value" is also intact, as are the "functioning fireplace" and "intimate" garden that make it "romantic" in all seasons.

Patroon Ⓩ

20 | 18 | 20 | $63

160 E. 46th St. (bet. Lexington & 3rd Aves.), 212-883-7373; www.patroonrestaurant.com
Be sure to "bring your business partners" to Ken Aretsky's Midtown New American, where "solid steaks" and "classic NY" ambiance are a "reminder of the old days"; if "a little staid" for the "Rockefeller" pricing, things loosen up in the "rooftop bar"; N.B. closed weekends.

Patsy's

21 | 16 | 20 | $50

236 W. 56th St. (bet. B'way & 8th Ave.), 212-247-3491; www.patsys.com
"Frank ate there", and "Sinatra-era" "nostalgia" endures at this "down-to-earth" Carnegie Hall–area Southern Italian, a circa-'44 source of "real-deal" "Neapolitan comfort food" and "personable service"; it's "well worn" and "not so cheap", but it deservedly keeps "rolling along."

Patsy's Pizzeria

20 | 12 | 15 | $23

206 E. 60th St. (bet. 2nd & 3rd Aves.), 212-688-9707
2287-91 First Ave. (bet. 117th & 118th Sts.), 212-534-9783 ⊘
1312 Second Ave. (69th St.), 212-639-1000
509 Third Ave. (bet. 34th & 35th Sts.), 212-689-7500
67 University Pl. (bet. 10th & 11th Sts.), 212-533-3500
61 W. 74th St. (bet. Columbus Ave. & CPW), 212-579-3000
318 W. 23rd St. (bet. 8th & 9th Aves.), 646-486-7400
www.patsyspizzeriany.com
"Nonpareil" "crisp pizza" makes this mini-chain "hard to beat" as a "crowd-pleaser", even with "basic" decor and "patchy" service; cognoscenti point out that the separately owned "old-world" original in East Harlem is "the best one" – "too bad it's cash only."

Paul & Jimmy's

| 18 | 15 | 19 | $42 |

123 E. 18th St. (bet. Irving Pl. & Park Ave. S.), 212-475-9540;
www.paulandjimmys.com
It's "been around for ages", and this "family-owned" Gramercy Italian honors its "old-school" roots with "fine" "standard fare" served by a "sweet" staff; it can be counted on for a "low-key" outing.

Payard Bistro ⑤

| 24 | 21 | 19 | $51 |

1032 Lexington Ave. (bet. 73rd & 74th Sts.), 212-717-5252; www.payard.com
"Celestial" desserts are "the main attraction" at François Payard's UES patisserie/bistro, but its "high-caliber" French fare from chef Philippe Bertineau "delights" too; though it's "expensive" and inclined to be a bit "hoity-toity", any "Francophile" will "go gaga" here.

Peacock Alley NEW

| ▽ 22 | 22 | 22 | $67 |

Waldorf-Astoria, 301 Park Ave. (bet. 49th & 50th Sts.), 212-872-4920;
www.waldorf.com
A "classic reopens" with "new flair" at this "reimagined" Waldorf-Astoria showcase eatery, featuring "innovative" New American cuisine with "worldly" influences and "top" service; the "lovely", gilt-edged lobby locale offers premium "people-watching" to distract from the premium prices.

Peanut Butter & Co.

| 20 | 12 | 16 | $12 |

240 Sullivan St. (bet. Bleecker & W. 3rd Sts.), 212-677-3995;
www.ilovepeanutbutter.com
You can "indulge" "your inner child" with a "gooey treat" at this Village "throwback to sandbox days"; devoted to crafting "the ultimate peanut butter sandwich" in a variety of "genius" "combos", it's "fun for the kids", but their elders may wish all this "nostalgia" came "cheaper."

PEARL OYSTER BAR ⑤

| 26 | 14 | 19 | $41 |

18 Cornelia St. (bet. Bleecker & W. 4th Sts.), 212-691-8211;
www.pearloysterbar.com
Seafood so "fresh" you can "taste the salt air" "reels them in" to Rebecca Charles' "tiny" Village joint that pays ample tribute to the "coast of Maine" with "New England" classics like the "must-try" lobster roll; despite "speedy service", "expect to wait" for a "no-frills" berth since it's "famous" with the famished.

Pearl Room

| 22 | 21 | 21 | $47 |

8201 Third Ave. (82nd St.), Brooklyn, 718-833-6666; www.thepearlroom.com
"Why travel to Manhattan?" ask fans of this attractive Bay Ridge sea-fooder, where the "inventive", "palate-pleasing" menu and "attentive service" supply "sophistication" aplenty; youthful followers report that it's a "trendy date place" with a "busy" "bar scene."

Peasant Ⓜ

| 22 | 21 | 19 | $51 |

194 Elizabeth St. (bet. Prince & Spring Sts.), 212-965-9511;
www.peasantnyc.com
This NoLita Italian will "impress a date" with its "hearty" food and "rustic" room suffused in "candle glow"; those who feel the the Italian-language menu that a "server has to translate" "borders on preten-tious" skip it in favor of the new "downstairs wine bar."

Peep ◐

| 20 | 20 | 17 | $31 |

177 Prince St. (bet. Sullivan & Thompson Sts.), 212-254-7337;
www.peepsoho.net
A "hip scene" for "twentysomething" peeps, this "affordable" SoHo Thai tempts tongues with its "tasty" food and "awesome" specialty drinks; also adding appeal are the "mod", "pink-neon" decor and bathrooms with their "one-way mirrors" (looking out, thankfully).

Peking Duck House
22 | 16 | 18 | $36

236 E. 53rd St. (bet. 2nd & 3rd Aves.), 212-759-8260
28 Mott St. (bet. Mosco & Pell Sts.), 212-227-1810
www.pekingduckhousenyc.com
For a "surefire" "crowd-pleaser", go for this Chinese duo's "delectable duck" (complete with "tableside carving service") – however, the otherwise "ordinary" menu has some crying fowl; the Midtown location is "convenient" but "bland" while the C-town place looks "classier" but "could be more friendly."

Pellegrino's
22 | 17 | 21 | $40

138 Mulberry St. (bet. Grand & Hester Sts.), 212-226-3177
Though just a "basic Italian", this "casual" joint is "one of Little Italy's better" bets for "enjoyable" food and "pro service"; what's more, the curbside tables on Mulberry Street offer dining "with a view."

Penang
19 | 17 | 16 | $30

240 Columbus Ave. (71st St.), 212-769-3988; www.penangusa.com
1596 Second Ave. (83rd St.), 212-585-3838 ◑
This crosstown Malaysian fusion duo earns points for its "accessible", "flavorful food" enjoyed amid "lively" "tropical" environs; service may be "erratic", but for an "easy meal" "priced fairly" it "really hits home" – just remember for best results "order adventurously."

Penelope ⇗
21 | 19 | 18 | $22

159 Lexington Ave. (30th St.), 212-481-3800; www.penelopenyc.com
The "feel-good" vibe is "just what the neighborhood ordered" at this "informal" Murray Hill American, proffering "well-prepared" "home-style" food and "service with a smile" in "New England–esque" digs; predictably, "crazy waits" are standard for "delish brunch."

Pepe Giallo To Go
19 | 10 | 15 | $20

253 10th Ave. (bet. 24th & 25th Sts.), 212-242-6055

Pepe Rosso
127 Ave. C (8th St.), 212-529-7747 ⇗ **NEW**
Grand Central, lower level (42nd St. & Vanderbilt Ave.),
212-867-6054

Pepe Rosso To Go ⇗
149 Sullivan St. (bet. Houston & Prince Sts.), 212-677-4555

Pepe Verde To Go ⇗
559 Hudson St. (bet. Perry & W. 11th Sts.), 212-255-2221
www.peperossotogo.com
"Pricing is low, quality is high" at these "hole-in-the-wall" Italian "quick" stops supplying "surprisingly" "tasty" pastas and other "basic" "cheap eats"; given the "sardine" seating and "hit-or-miss" service, though, many heed the name and order "to go."

Pepolino
23 | 16 | 21 | $48

281 W. Broadway (bet. Canal & Lispenard Sts.), 212-966-9983;
www.pepolino.com
Pepped-up cognoscenti cheer this TriBeCa Tuscan as a "hidden treasure" for "primo" "rustic" cuisine served "without pretense" by "sweet" staffers in "rugged but comfortable" environs; despite an "under-the-radar" locale, it's been "discovered" and can get "loud."

Perbacco ◑⇗
24 | 16 | 20 | $37

234 E. Fourth St. (bet. Aves. A & B), 212-253-2038
Backers can't resist the "Italian tapas" at this "bohemian" East Villager, where "scrumptious" small plates paired with "spot-on" wines keep the "tight space" "crowded and loud"; it's "cash-only", but "reasonable" prices promise you won't need much.

Periyali ⌾

23 | 18 | 22 | $53

35 W. 20th St. (bet. 5th & 6th Aves.), 212-463-7890;
www.periyali.com

It "hasn't changed, and shouldn't" say supporters of this "upscale" Flatiron District standby that's "still holding strong" with "top-of-the-line Greek" cuisine; the "soothing" setting, "gracious" service and "expensive" prices make it appeal especially to "grown-ups"; N.B. a recent complete overhaul of the interior may outdate the above Decor score.

Per Lei ◐ NEW

∇ 19 | 18 | 16 | $52

1347 Second Ave. (71st St.), 212-439-9200; www.perleinyc.com

Bringing "much-needed energy" to the neighborhood, this new UES "Baraonda offshoot" hosts a "hot" "scene" backed by a "fine" Italian kitchen that keeps the "attractive" room "madly busy"; critics cite "cramped" conditions and "clueless service", but as a "hip" purlieu it has sure started out "strong."

PERRY STREET ◐

25 | 25 | 24 | $74

176 Perry St. (West St.), 212-352-1900; www.jean-georges.com

You're bound to "feel rich and thin" at Jean-Georges Vongerichten's "sleek" West Village yearling, given the "scintillating" New American menu's "refined flavors" and the "striking" "minimalist" decor that matches the Richard Meier–designed tower that houses it for "elegance" "without glitz"; with service in "a very professional groove", it's "worth the cost" to be "blown away" by this "definite winner."

PER SE

28 | 27 | 28 | $287

Time Warner Ctr., 10 Columbus Circle, 4th fl. (60th St. at B'way),
212-823-9335; www.perseny.com

In a "life-altering" "league of its own", Thomas Keller's "apex of dining" "never fails to thrill" via the "ethereal" "finesse" of its French–New American tasting menus and "incomparable" service (voted No. 1 in NYC); the Time Warner Center setting affords "spectacular" Columbus Circle and Central Park views from Adam Tihany's discreetly "opulent" space and sets the scene for "culinary bliss" that justifies the "overblown prices", so per-se-vere with the "all-time-headache" reservations routine – "you're worth it."

Persepolis

19 | 14 | 19 | $34

1407 Second Ave. (bet. 74th & 75th Sts.), 212-535-1100;
www.persepolisnyc.com

"Not your usual kebab house", this UES Iranian "will knock your socks off" with "authentic Persian" fare (including trademark "wonderful" sour cherry rice) and "prompt" service; N.B. a post-*Survey* move to new down-the-block digs may outdate the above Decor score.

Pershing Square

15 | 16 | 16 | $36

90 E. 42nd St. (Park Ave.), 212-286-9600

Favored for "breakfast with clients" and "lunch meetings", this "predictable" brasserie provides "casual" American food just south of Grand Central Station; however, some square off against the "hit-or-miss" service and "boisterous" "commuter-type bar patrons" "after 5 PM."

Pescatore ◐

19 | 15 | 18 | $38

955 Second Ave. (bet. 50th & 51st Sts.), 212-752-7151;
www.pescatorerestaurant.com

For "locals" "in the mood for fish", this "well-run" East Midtowner is a "popular" "price performer" where "surprisingly" "solid" Italian seafood is served by an "etiquette"-conscious staff; as an "alfresco" bonus, the second floor features a "lovely *terrazzo*."

Petaluma
18 | 16 | 18 | $43

1356 First Ave. (73rd St.), 212-772-8800; www.petalumanyc.com
This Yorkville stalwart owes its "staying power" to "dependable" "midpriced" takes on "standard Italian" and a "spacious" setting that's "relaxed" even when you're "with the kids"; it's also the de facto "Sotheby's cafeteria."

PETER LUGER STEAK HOUSE ⊄
28 | 14 | 19 | $68

178 Broadway (Driggs Ave.), Brooklyn, 718-387-7400; www.peterluger.com
"Devout" carnivores go on "pilgrimages" to this "venerable" Williamsburg cow "Valhalla" that's our surveyors' choice as the No. 1 steakhouse in NYC for the 23rd year running; its "matchless" "marbled beef" is of such "juicy" "perfection" that fans freely forgive the "crusty" service and "macho" "Bavarian beer hall" setting; they also say "fuhgeddabout the menu" and stick with those porterhouses, and "bring lots of cash" to cover those plastic-less "prime" prices.

Pete's Downtown Ⓜ
17 | 15 | 17 | $37

2 Water St. (Old Fulton St.), Brooklyn, 718-858-3510;
www.petesdowntown.com
You "can't beat the view" of the Brooklyn Bridge and "city skyline" from this Dumbo "waterfront" joint, though its "basic" "old-style" Italian eats attract less attention; it plays "second fiddle to the River Cafe" across the way, but then it's a "bargain" in comparison.

Pete's Tavern ◐
13 | 15 | 15 | $30

129 E. 18th St. (Irving Pl.), 212-473-7676
It's "worth stopping in" to this "vintage" 1864 Gramercy "haunt" more for its "scruffy" "charm" than its "typical" American "pub fare"; famed as a locale where O. Henry "penned", it's now a pen for "brew aficionados" enjoying a "liquid meal" and the game.

Petite Abeille
18 | 14 | 16 | $27

401 E. 20th St. (1st Ave.), 212-727-1505
466 Hudson St. (Barrow St.), 212-741-6479 ⊄
134 W. Broadway (Duane St.), 212-791-1360
44 W. 17th St. (bet. 5th & 6th Aves.), 212-604-9350
www.petiteabeille.com
A "quick", "economical" "go-to" for "legitimate" "Belgian comfort food", this "swell" quartet features "favorites" such as moules frites plus imported brews; expect "simple" settings with "Tintin comics decor" and "quirky" but "pleasant" service.

Petrarca Vino e Cucina ◐ NEW
▽ 21 | 21 | 20 | $44

34 White St. (Church St.), 212-625-2800
"Less expensive and formal" than its "across-the-street" parent, Arqua, this "hip" new TriBeCan matches "solid trattoria" food with Italian wines; given the "charming" enotecalike space and a "sincere" staff to add "character", most predict its popularity will "grow with time."

Petrossian ◐
24 | 23 | 22 | $73

182 W. 58th St. (7th Ave.), 212-245-2214; www.petrossian.com
"Let's hear it for champagne and caviar" cheer fans of this "high-end" deco "indulgence" near Carnegie Hall, whose "superlative" French-Continental cuisine, "fine service" and interior with "all that Lalique" and "Erté" make a "decadent" "treat"; sure, the à la carte prices can balloon, but the "various prix fixe" menus can help deflate the bill.

Philip Marie ◐Ⓜ
20 | 17 | 20 | $43

569 Hudson St. (W. 11th St.), 212-242-6200; www.philipmarie.com
West Villagers consider this somewhat "undiscovered" New American to be a "cozy" "charmer" serving "creative" cuisine with a "personal

touch" at a "fair price"; even more "intimate" is the wine cellar's "private room for two", an "amazing" "hideaway" for "special occasions."

Philippe ⬤ NEW | 22 | 18 | 15 | $60

33 E. 60th St. (bet. Madison & Park Aves.), 212-644-8885;
www.philippechow.com

A "hot newcomer" to East Midtown, former Mr. Chow chef Philippe Chow's namesake sticks to the "trendy" Chinese template with "tasty" food, "modern" digs and a clientele of "Euros" and "size ones" who overlook "disorganized" service and chow "pricey for what it is."

Philly Slim's Cheesesteaks | ▽ 18 | 7 | 14 | $11

789 Ninth Ave. (bet. 52nd & 53rd Sts.), 212-333-3042
106 University Pl. (bet. 12th & 13th Sts.), 212-989-8281 NEW
www.phillyslims.com

City of Brotherly Love natives marooned "north of the Turnpike" hit this "no-frills" Hell's Kitchen "take-out" joint (with a few seats) for fixes of "legit" Philly-style cheese steaks, in all their "messy, juicy" glory; N.B. a Greenwich Village branch opened post-*Survey.*

Pho Bang ⇗ | 21 | 5 | 13 | $14

157 Mott St. (bet. Broome & Grand Sts.), 212-966-3797
3 Pike St. (bet. Division St. & E. B'way), 212-233-3947
82-90 Broadway (Elmhurst Ave.), Queens, 718-205-1500
41-07 Kissena Blvd. (Main St.), Queens, 718-939-5520

Vietnamese "doesn't get more authentic" than the "comfort pho" and other "delicious" "cheap eats" at these "quick", "no-nonsense" noodlerias; foes bang the "surly service" and "total lack of decor", but how else can they keep the cost at "rock bottom"?

Phoenix Garden ⇗ | 24 | 7 | 14 | $28

242 E. 40th St. (bet. 2nd & 3rd Aves.), 212-983-6666

"There's no need to go to Chinatown" for "solid Cantonese" thanks to this "wonderful" Tudor City–area "jewel" (rated NYC's No. 1 Chinese), made extra "wallet-friendly" by a BYO policy; unfortunately, "the real thing" also includes "worn" decor and "brusque" service.

Pho Pasteur ⇗ | 20 | 5 | 14 | $15

85 Baxter St. (bet. Bayard & Canal Sts.), 212-608-3656

The name has changed (fka New Pasteur), but this Chinatown "hole-in-the-wall" still supplies "heavenly" Vietnamese at "bargain prices"; "super-fast" service makes it an "ideal jury duty" destination, though the "threadbare surroundings" are overdue for an update too.

Pho Viet Huong | 21 | 9 | 13 | $18

73 Mulberry St. (bet. Bayard & Canal Sts.), 212-233-8988

With "fabulous" pho in the forefront, this "busy" C-town Vietnamese "mainstay" is a "great value" and a "best bet for jury duty"; the service and "Saigon kitsch" decor leave "room for improvement", but then "that's not why you go here."

Piadina ⬤⇗ | ▽ 21 | 18 | 16 | $31

57 W. 10th St. (bet. 5th & 6th Aves.), 212-460-8017

"Grab a date and get cozy" at this "dark" Village hideout; it offers "good, simple" Italian "standards" that ducat-deprived romeos note are "well priced", but "watch out" because it "doesn't take plastic."

Piano Due ⊠ | 26 | 26 | 25 | $69

Equitable Center Arcade, 151 W. 51st St., 2nd fl. (bet. 6th & 7th Aves.),
212-399-9400; www.pianoduenyc.com

"Nothing's second rate" at this second-floor Midtown Italian from Michael Cetrulo (of Scalini Fedeli fame), where one is "whisked" via elevator to a "luxurious" upstairs dining room for "sublime" food, "top-notch service" and subdued "conversation"; it's "quite expensive" but truly "special", so "go now" "before it's discovered"; P.S. don't miss Sandro Chia's "landmarked" murals of Siena's famous horse race in the "gorgeous" downstairs Palio Bar.

Piccola Venezia

25 | 17 | 23 | $52

42-01 28th Ave. (42nd St.), Queens, 718-721-8470; www.piccola-venezia.com
As a "longtime favorite" "on the Queens scene", this Astoria Italian's "excellence" centers on a "never-ending menu" of "A+" "old-country" cooking served with such "warmth" that you're sure to "feel at home"; it's "showing its age" in all but the "Manhattan prices", yet "never fails to satisfy" its loyal clientele.

Piccolo Angolo Ⓜ

24 | 13 | 20 | $39

621 Hudson St. (Jane St.), 212-229-9177
It's "hard to get in" to this "small", "homey" West Village Italian, but the "huge" plates of *fantastico* food and "bargain" tabs are "so worth" the hassle; crowds "crammed" "cheek-to-jowl" can count on "over-the-top host" Renato Migliorini for plenty of "feel-good" hospitality.

PICHOLINE

26 | 24 | 25 | $83

35 W. 64th St. (bet. B'way & CPW), 212-724-8585;
www.artisanalcheese.com
"J'adore" coo enthusiasts as Terry Brennan's West Side "class act" "continues to soar" with an "exquisite" French-Med menu (featuring an "unsurpassed cheese-cart" encore), "standout" service and an atmosphere of bourgeoise "elegance" that validates the "big bucks" spent; a $38 Saturday prix fixe lunch eases the pinch, and the private rooms remain "a special treat"; N.B. a post-*Survey* redo, which added a front wine-and-cheese bar, may outdate the above Decor score.

Picket Fence Ⓜ

19 | 14 | 17 | $28

1310 Cortelyou Rd. (bet. Argyle & Rugby Rds.), Brooklyn, 718-282-6661;
www.picketfencebrooklyn.com
For picky types in "woefully underserved" Ditmas Park, this "affordable" New American "stands out" with its "wonderful" "homestyle cooking" and "family-friendly" feel; "peak times" find the modest space "overwhelmed", but the back garden more than compensates.

Picnic Market & Café

21 | 12 | 18 | $36

2665 Broadway (101st St.), 212-222-8222
Upper Westsiders are "glad to have" this deli/cafe "offshoot of Silver Moon Bakery" nearby since it's an "easygoing" "oasis" for "super" French bites; but even "spruced up", the "no-frills" environs are at odds with the "pretty prices."

Pier 2110 NEW

– | – | – | E

2110 Seventh Ave. (bet. 125th & 126th Sts.), 212-280-7437; www.pier2110.com
Spacious and splashy, this new upscale Harlem seafooder is rigged with a central raw bar, nautical accents and flat-screen TVs broadcasting ocean vistas; look for a creative, expensive surf 'n' turf menu jazzed up with soul-food staples like grits, cornbread and collard greens.

Pies-N-Thighs ⊄ NEW

– | – | – | I

351 Kent Ave. (enter on S. 5th St.), Brooklyn, 347-282-6005;
www.piesandthighs.com
Think pulled pork, collard greens and fried green tomatoes to get in the down-home mood at this new low-budget South Williamsburg soul shack; the just-folks moniker suits the unadorned digs, which offer a few counter stools, alleyway outdoor tables and seating in the amped-up, adjoining Rock Star Bar.

Pietrasanta

20 | 14 | 17 | $35

683 Ninth Ave. (47th St.), 212-265-9471

Pietrasanta to Go ☒ NEW

88 Fulton St. (Gold St.), 212-693-2600
www.pietrasantanyc.com

"Teeny" "but hospitable", this Hell's Kitchen "stalwart" "consistently" pleases "theater-bound" "pastaholics" with "solid" "traditional Italian" and "quick" service; the "squeezed" space is "showing some wear", but the "value" holds up just "fine"; N.B. the new South Street Seaport branch has a few seats but is mostly for takeout.

Pietro's ☒

22 | 13 | 21 | $60

232 E. 43rd St. (bet. 2nd & 3rd Aves.), 212-682-9760

It's "been around forever", but this Italian steakhouse near Grand Central remains "reliable" for "hearty" "old-style" food and "professional service"; the "time-warp" digs "need a makeover" to match the "expensive" tabs, but the mature regulars report that its "modest pleasures" "always feel good."

Pigalle ❶

17 | 17 | 15 | $36

Hilton Garden Inn, 790 Eighth Ave. (48th St.), 212-489-2233;
www.pigallenyc.com

Although the backdrop "won't be mistaken for" the real Pigalle, this "lively" Theater Districter does "decent" "brasserie-type" "French grub" at "fair prices"; it's "spacious" and "relaxed", but some are galled by the "noise level" and "sketchy" service at prime times.

Pig Heaven ❶

19 | 14 | 17 | $32

1540 Second Ave. (bet. 80th & 81st Sts.), 212-744-4333; www.pigheaven.biz

Beyond the "pervasive" pork, this "inviting" UES Chinese standby goes "whole hog" with a "well-rounded" lineup of "first-rate" food and "sweet" service overseen by the "friendliest owner" around; though the "kitschy" decor's a drawback, "kids just love it" and no one complains about the "reasonable" prices.

Pinch - Pizza by the Inch

21 | 10 | 18 | $18

416 Park Ave. S. (bet. 28th & 29th Sts.), 212-686-5222; www.pizzabytheinch.com

"Every inch" a "great concept", this "casual" Gramercy stop measures out its "rectangular pizzas" in "thin-crust" segments loaded with "addictive" "gourmet" toppings; fans are "pleasantly surprised" by the rest of the menu, though a few find the tab has a way of inching up.

Ping's Seafood ❶

21 | 12 | 14 | $25

22 Mott St. (bet. Bayard & Pell Sts.), 212-602-9988
83-02 Queens Blvd. (Goldsmith St.), Queens, 718-396-1238

The "excellent Cantonese" seafood and dim sum at this "busy" Chinatown-Elmhurst duo provide "authentic" "Hong Kong quality"; a "brusque" staff and "proletarian" digs are balanced by "bargain" rates.

Pink Tea Cup ❶⇪

21 | 11 | 16 | $22

42 Grove St. (bet. Bedford & Bleecker Sts.), 212-807-6755;
www.thepinkteacup.com

Villagers "jonesing" for "country cooking" "savor the flavor" of the "serious" Southern soul food at this "fixture" for "cheap", "downhome" eats; yes, it's "small" and "kind of a dive", but the "bad-for-you brunch" still draws "lines down the street."

Pinocchio Ⓜ

▽ 23 | 15 | 23 | $43

1748 First Ave. (bet. 90th & 91st Sts.), 212-828-5810

It's no lie that this "quaint" Yorkville Italian is a "local find" for "topnotch" "homestyle" food and "personal service"; however, its "narrow closet of a space" is already short on "elbow room" – so "shhh, don't tell" anyone else about it.

Pintaile's Pizza
19 | 6 | 13 | $16

26 E. 91st St. (bet. 5th & Madison Aves.), 212-722-1967
1443 York Ave. (bet. 76th & 77th Sts.), 212-717-4990
1577 York Ave. (bet. 83rd & 84th Sts.), 212-396-3479
The "wafer-thin" whole-wheat crust and "imaginative toppings" make these Eastsiders' "semi–guilt free" pizza "stand out" as "distinctively different"; there's "not much ambiance" or service on hand, so many pin their hopes on "reliable delivery."

Piola NEW
▽ 19 | 15 | 19 | $24

48 E. 12th St. (bet. B'way & University Pl.), 212-777-7781
An "appetizing variety" of "pizzas for a pittance" leads the "long menu" at this Village link in a Brazil-based Italian chain; it's a "colorful place" for a "youngish" crowd to "kick back", and the "neighborly" staff and "excellent" drinks seal the "good deal."

Pioneer Bar-B-Q ☻⇗ NEW
– | – | – | I

318 Van Brunt St. (Pioneer St.), Brooklyn, 718-701-2189;
www.pioneerbarbq.com
Boyish charm prevails at this boisterous, low-budget Red Hook BBQ joint where a cheery staff dishes out decent meats and sides washed down with local suds and single-batch bourbons; a beer garden with a horseshoe court adds to the down-home appeal.

Pio Pio
23 | 13 | 15 | $22

1746 First Ave. (bet. 90th & 91st Sts.), 212-426-5800
264 Cypress Ave. (bet. 138th & 139th Sts.), Bronx, 718-401-3300 ⇗
62-30 Woodhaven Blvd. (63rd Ave.), Queens, 718-458-0606 ⇗
84-13 Northern Blvd. (bet. 84th & 85th Sts.), Queens, 718-426-1010
"Poultry lovers with huge appetites" salute the "awesome" rotisserie chicken and "zesty" sauces at these "super-cheap" Peruvians; service "can be spotty" and the settings are "nothing fancy", but "quality" keeps the "throngs" coming.

Pipa
20 | 23 | 16 | $41

ABC Carpet & Home, 38 E. 19th St. (bet. B'way & Park Ave. S.),
212-677-2233; www.abchome.com
"Fun and funky", this Flatiron Spaniard's "cool" "chandeliered" space is bound to be "hoppin'" with twentysomethings fueling a fiesta with "enjoyable" tapas and "mind-altering sangria"; just beware of the "aloof staff" and bills that "add up quickly."

Pisticci
23 | 19 | 19 | $31

125 La Salle St. (B'way), 212-932-3500; www.pisticcinyc.com
"If you can find it", this "cheerful" "side-street" Italian near Columbia pays off with "surprisingly" "scrumptious" "rustic Italian" fare served by a "zero-attitude" crew; its pricing is "easy on student budgets", and as the "energetic crowds" attest, the "secret's out."

Pizza Gruppo
▽ 26 | 13 | 18 | $18

186 Ave. B (bet. 11th & 12th Sts.), 212-995-2100
To "elevate your standard" for pizza, check out this "little" East Villager, whose "awesome" "crisp" crusts and "delectable" toppings make for "one of the best" brick-oven pies going; it's "not much" on looks, but focus on the food and "you'll be happy."

Pizza 33 ☻
22 | 7 | 13 | $11

489 Third Ave. (33rd St.), 212-545-9191

(continued)

(continued)
Pizza 33
171 W. 23rd St. (bet. 6th & 7th Aves.), 212-337-3661
268 W. 23rd St. (8th Ave.), 212-206-0999
Mega-popular as weekend "havens" for "late-night pizza", this three-some "does the trick" with "fresh", "thin-crusted deliciousness" (though at a "steep price per slice"); it "could use a little charming up", but "in the wee hours" "do you really care?"

P.J. Clarke's ◐ | 17 | 16 | 17 | $32 |
915 Third Ave. (55th St.), 212-317-1616
P.J. Clarke's on the Hudson NEW
4 World Financial Ctr. (Vesey St.), 212-285-1500
www.pjclarkes.com
"Go for the history, stay for the burger" should be the motto of this Midtown "sentimental favorite", a circa-1884 tavern where the "old-school bar" and "solid pub fare" still "hit the spot"; the Sidecar, its upstairs adjunct, offers a "white-tablecloth" alternative, while the "huge" new Financial District spin-off services the "banker crowd."

Place, The | 22 | 23 | 22 | $46 |
310 W. Fourth St. (bet. Bank & 12th Sts.), 212-924-2711; www.theplaceny.com
Place on West 10th, The NEW
142 W. 10th St. (bet. Greenwich Ave. & 7th Ave. S.), 212-462-2880;
www.theplaceonwest10th.com
"A lovely place" for "date night", this "intimate" Villager serves "well-executed" midpriced Med–New American fare in a "sexy grotto" with candles and a fireplace that "set hearts afire"; the new 10th Street site plies the same menu but comes on more "comfortably chic" than "irresistibly romantic."

Planet Thailand ◐⇜ | 20 | 19 | 16 | $24 |
133 N. Seventh St. (bet. Bedford Ave. & Berry St.), Brooklyn, 718-599-5758;
www.planetthailand.com
Planethailand 212 ◐ NEW
30 W. 24th St. (bet. 5th & 6th Aves.), 212-727-7026; www.pt212.com
Serving a "huge menu" in a "massive" "industrial" space, this Williamsburg Thai-Japanese "rocks" with "satisfying" food "at a price that'll make you smile"; though "perfunctory", it "gets the job done" and pulls "absurd" crowds into its orbit; N.B. a Flatiron branch, with a more limited menu, opened post-*Survey*.

Ploes ◐   ▽ | 23 | 19 | 20 | $34 |
33-04 Broadway (33rd St.), Queens, 718-278-1001
With "a ton of mezes" to liven up its "well-prepared" "real Greek cooking", this "friendly" Astoria "taverna" ranks "above average" in a competitive neighborhood; the rusticated setting and "reasonable" cost are "pleasant" too.

Pó | 25 | 16 | 21 | $47 |
31 Cornelia St. (bet. Bleecker & W. 4th Sts.), 212-645-2189;
www.porestaurant.com
Still "going strong", this Village "classic" provides a "potent" package of "heavenly" Italian "delights", "charming service" and "cost-effective" tabs; scoring a seat at this "closet" full of "flying elbows" may be "a pain", but the "incredible" eating "won't let you down."

Poke ☒⊠⇜ | 25 | 12 | 18 | $35 |
343 E. 85th St. (bet. 1st & 2nd Aves.), 212-249-0569
Even in "roomier new digs", this East Side Japanese BYO is a "no-nonsense" spot for "impeccably crafted", "oh-so-fresh" sushi at a

cost "reasonable" enough that you'll forget the "cash-only" rule; but "the word is out", so prepare for "waits" and "pokey" service.

Pomodoro Rosso

| 21 | 15 | 19 | $38 |

229 Columbus Ave. (bet. 70th & 71st Sts.), 212-721-3009

Loyal locals declare this Lincoln Center–area trattoria "a definite repeat" thanks to its "generous" helpings of "delicious" "Italian comfort" food, "congenial setting" and "reasonable prices"; "they aim to please", but the "no-reservations" policy means "go early or be prepared to wait."

Pongal

| 21 | 12 | 14 | $26 |

1154 First Ave. (bet. 63rd & 64th Sts.), 212-355-4600
110 Lexington Ave. (bet. 27th & 28th Sts.), 212-696-9458
www.pongal.org

With a "well-prepared" lineup led by "some of the best dosas ever", this kosher vegetarian South Indian duo is a "wholesome" alternative at "a great price"; unfortunately, the "sketchy" service and "hole-in-the-wall" decor aren't "equally pleasing."

Pongsri Thai

| 20 | 11 | 16 | $24 |

106 Bayard St. (Baxter St.), 212-349-3132
311 Second Ave. (18th St.), 212-477-2727
244 W. 48th St. (bet. B'way & 8th Ave.), 212-582-3392
165 W. 23rd St. (bet. 6th & 7th Aves.), 212-645-8808 ◗

They "keep it real" at these Thai "standbys", where "addictive" eats are served up "fast and fresh" at "unbeatable prices"; "never mind" the "shopworn" decor, it's the "consistently" "high quality" that followers "count on."

Ponticello

| ∇ 22 | 17 | 21 | $45 |

46-11 Broadway (bet. 46th & 47th Sts.), Queens, 718-278-4514;
www.ponticelloristorante.com

A bastion of "old-world style", this "tried-and-true" Astoria Italian offers "impressive" renditions of the "classics" served by a "courteous" crew who see that "no one rushes you"; while holding "no surprises", it remains well "above the norm."

Pop Burger ◗

| 19 | 15 | 13 | $18 |

58-60 Ninth Ave. (bet. 14th & 15th Sts.), 212-414-8686;
www.popburger.com

"Hipsters" "drool in line" over the mini-burgers at this "amusingly trendy" Meatpacking District New American, pairing "cool" fast food up front with a "chill" "party scene" in the back lounge; the music may be "overpowering" and service "lacking", but nonetheless it's usually popping.

Popover Cafe

| 18 | 14 | 16 | $25 |

551 Amsterdam Ave. (bet. 86th & 87th Sts.), 212-595-8555;
www.popovercafe.com

The "fabulous" "fluffy popovers" "can't be beat" at this "shabby-chic" UWS "staple" where the "predictable" American menu suits an "unhurried" stopover; just beware of "twee" teddy-bear decor, "sporadic" service and "mobbed" weekend brunches when all the neighborhood pops over.

Porchetta ⊅ NEW

| – | – | – | M |

241 Smith St. (Douglass St.), Brooklyn, 718-237-9100

Cobble Hill's erstwhile Banania Cafe has reopened with a new moniker, a new cuisine (casual Italian) and new moose-antler light fixtures, but longtimers can breathe a sigh of relief: its wildly popular weekend brunch and affordable prices remain unchanged.

Porter House New York NEW — — — E

Time Warner Ctr., 10 Columbus Circle, 4th fl. (60th St. at B'way),
212-823-9500; www.porterhousenewyork.com
Set to open at press time, this new Time Warner Center steakhouse
from Michael Lomonaco (ex Windows on the World) will serve an
American grill menu highlighting dry-aged prime beef and an array of
seafood; Jeffrey Beers' Mission-esque design is just as cosseting as
the food, with a beckoning bar area and splendid Central Park views,
and the pricing's more palatable than that of its high-end neighbors.

Portofino Grille 17 | 19 | 18 | $43

1162 First Ave. (bet. 63rd & 64th Sts.), 212-832-4141; www.portofinogrille.com
Via its "murals" showing a "pretty arbor" and simulated "stars over-
head", this "hospitable" East Side Italian does its best to "transport you"
to Portofino itself; however, despite "friendly servers" and "big portions" of grill "favorites", fairly "ordinary" cooking dims the effect.

Portofino's ● ▽ 20 | 20 | 19 | $41

555 City Island Ave. (Cross St.), Bronx, 718-885-1220;
www.portofinocityisland.com
"Aging but respectable", this City Island Italian "overlooking the water" specializes in Italian seafood served by "attentive" staffers; it's
"somewhat pricey", but in summer there's a "delightful outdoor deck"
and come winter the "fireplace is a plus."

Positano ● 20 | 14 | 18 | $36

122 Mulberry St. (bet. Canal & Hester Sts.), 212-334-9808;
www.positanolittleitaly.com
To "avoid the tourist throngs" in Little Italy, there's always this
Southern Italian veteran that's a "good bet" for "palatable" food and
prices in a "fast-paced" setting; "traditionalists" "enjoy its typical-
ness" right down to the dated digs.

Post House 23 | 19 | 22 | $70

Lowell Hotel, 28 E. 63rd St. (bet. Madison & Park Aves.), 212-935-2888;
www.theposthouse.com
For "a civilized steak" "away from the hoi polloi", this Eastsider "more
than holds its own" with "terrific" beef and "smooth" service in an
"old-school stylish" room; a gender-neutral "business crowd" calls
its "kinder, gentler" approach "refreshing", though "an expense account helps" at meal's end.

Posto 23 | 12 | 16 | $21

310 Second Ave. (18th St.), 212-716-1200
Pizza with "personality" is the trademark of this "neat little" Gramercy
"asset", where the "cracker-thin" crust and "fresh", "creative toppings" are a "wonderful" "switch from the norm"; now that it's a hit,
"too-crowded" conditions suggest "they need to expand."

Prem-on Thai ● ▽ 20 | 17 | 17 | $34

138 W. Houston St. (bet. MacDougal & Sullivan Sts.), 212-353-2338;
www.prem-on.com
"Innovative", "upscale Thai" dishes in "camera-ready" presenta-
tions make this "hidden" Villager stand out, as do its "sleek", "modern" setup and "eager-to-please" servers; though "not as authentic"
as some, it's "moderately priced" and has the culinary "flair" to
justify return visits.

Pre:Post ●⌧M NEW — — — M

547 W. 27th St. (bet. 10th & 11th Aves.), 212-695-7270; www.prepostnyc.com
While there's plenty of nightlife on this Chelsea block, eating options are
few, hence the need for this new dusk-to-dawn American, open most

nights until 6 AM; the laid-back lair features faux log cabin booths up front and sunken cabanas in the rear, separated by an open kitchen.

Press 195
21 | 13 | 16 | $16

195 Fifth Ave. (bet. Sackett & Union Sts.), Brooklyn, 718-857-1950
40-11 Bell Blvd. (bet. 40th & 41st Aves.), Queens, 718-281-1950 NEW
www.press195.com

"Awesome panini" "elevates the sandwich" at this "informal" Park Slope cafe just joined by a Bayside sibling; "outdoor patio" seating adds to their appeal, though some wish they'd press the pace of their service.

Primavera ⏺
23 | 21 | 22 | $66

1578 First Ave. (82nd St.), 212-861-8608; www.primaveranyc.com

"Real class" endures at Nicola Civetta's "lovely" UES "oasis", where the "fabulous" Northern Italian fare is prepared with "*amore*" and paired with "personal" black-tie service in "quiet, elegant" quarters; sure, "you pay for it", but for "old-fashioned" "magic" longtime loyalists "love this place."

Prime Grill
22 | 18 | 17 | $62

60 E. 49th St. (bet. Madison & Park Aves.), 212-692-9292;
www.theprimegrill.com

Observant diners primed for "the finest" kosher beef (and "artfully" done sushi) deem this "high-end" Midtown steakhouse to be "one of the best" around; service "can be curt" and prices "steep", but the overall "polished" performance keeps it "jam-packed."

Primola
22 | 15 | 19 | $59

1226 Second Ave. (bet. 64th & 65th Sts.), 212-758-1775

A "local favorite" among "moneyed" types, this "urbane" East Side Italian provides "marvelous food", "pro service" and primo "people-watching"; for best results, you'd better "be a regular" or "look like you should be."

Provence ⏺
21 | 20 | 20 | $50

38 MacDougal St. (Prince St.), 212-475-7500; www.provence-soho.com

"So very Provençal", this SoHo standby is an "unpretentious" bistro "paradigm" serving "*magnifique*" "traditional fare" with "no drama"; though decidedly "not cutting-edge", the "relaxing" setting complete with a "quaint" "enclosed garden" is "enjoyable" "year-round."

Provence en Boite NEW
– | – | – | M

263 Smith St. (Degraw St.), Brooklyn, 718-797-0707;
www.provenceenboite.com

After several years in Bay Ridge, this Provençal bistro/pastry shop has reopened on a busy Smith Street corner; expect a mix of steak frites, fresh-baked baguettes and brunchtime *oeufs* Benedict, charmingly presented by the French chef-and-hostess owners.

Prune
24 | 15 | 19 | $47

54 E. First St. (bet. 1st & 2nd Aves.), 212-677-6221

The "crowds bear witness" to chef Gabrielle Hamilton's "wondrous" talents at this "teeny-weeny" East Village New American; given the "inventive" cuisine, "mind-bendingly tasty" brunches and "down-to-earth" service, admirers just "grin and bear" the "cramped seating" and inevitable "wait in line."

Public ⏺
23 | 25 | 20 | $52

210 Elizabeth St. (bet. Prince & Spring Sts.), 212-343-7011;
www.public-nyc.com

"Broad palates" praise this "unflaggingly" "trendy" NoLita Eclectic for "original" dishes with dashes of "Australian flair", matched with a "gorgeous" "library-themed" space; service runs from "worldly" to "haughty" and costs run high, but the net result is "uplifting."

Pukk

∇ | 22 | 20 | 21 | $19 |

71 First Ave. (bet. 4th & 5th Sts.), 212-253-2741
Vegetarians "reward" themselves with "super" meatless Thai food at this "tiny" East Village "true find"; with its "sweet staff" and "mod", "futuristic" decor ("the bathroom alone is worth a visit"), fans claim it will give you plenty of "bang" for very few bukks.

Pump Energy Food

| 19 | 5 | 14 | $13 |

Crystal Pavilion, 805 Third Ave. (50th St.), 212-421-3055 ⊠
113 E. 31st St. (bet. Lexington Ave. & Park Ave. S.), 212-213-5733
31 E. 21st St. (bet. B'way & Park Ave. S.), 212-253-7676
40 W. 55th St. (bet. 5th & 6th Aves.), 212-246-6844
112 W. 38th St. (bet. B'way & 6th Ave.), 212-764-2100
www.thepumpenergyfood.com
The "gymming set" refuels with "guiltless pleasure" at this "fast health-food" mini-chain, where "fitness-friendly meals" "pumped with flavor" "leave you feeling light" at "unbeatable prices"; given the "bare-bones" setups, though, you may want to save your energy and "order in."

Punch

| 21 | 18 | 19 | $37 |

913 Broadway (bet. 20th & 21st Sts.), 212-673-6333;
www.punchrestaurant.com
"Terrific" Eclectic eats including an "inventive", "good-value" brunch await at this "Flatiron find"; service is "friendly" and the "comfortable" setting "relaxing", though a few take jabs at the "loud" upstairs lounge.

Pure Food and Wine

| 21 | 21 | 21 | $51 |

54 Irving Pl. (bet. 17th & 18th Sts.), 212-477-1010;
www.purefoodandwine.com
"Even die-hard carnivores" are "amazed" by the "delicious", "decadent" raw vegan cuisine ("who would have thought?") and "sophisticated" organic wines at this Gramercy "innovator"; though it's also appreciated for its "gorgeous" garden, critics cite "high cost" for "plants" in "pixie portions."

Puttanesca

| 20 | 16 | 18 | $36 |

859 Ninth Ave. (56th St.), 212-581-4177; www.puttanesca.com
Located in the sweet spot "close to Lincoln Center" and "near the Theater District", this "cozy" Italian offers "tasty trattoria-style" meals at "affordable prices" served by an "eager-to-please" staff; no longer a "local secret", it gets "busy and noisy" at "peak times."

Pylos ●

| 23 | 22 | 20 | $40 |

128 E. Seventh St. (bet. Ave. A & 1st Ave.), 212-473-0220;
www.pylosrestaurant.com
They "do everything right" at this "charming" East Village Greek, from the "fantastic" regional fare and Hellenic wines to the "kind, attentive" service; the "lovely" setting features a "pottery-covered ceiling" and "lively" communal table.

Q Thai Bistro

| 22 | 19 | 20 | $38 |

108-25 Ascan Ave. (bet. Austin & Burns Sts.), Queens, 718-261-6599;
www.qbistrony.com
"Hidden away in Forest Hills", this "intimate" Thai "jewel" shines with "high-quality", "flavorful" fusion fare and "excellent" wines by the glass dispensed by a "friendly" staff; "Manhattan prices" cause critics to consider this "blessing" a bit mixed.

Quaint NEW
— | — | — | M

46-10 Skillman Ave. (bet. 46th & 47th Sts.), Queens, 917-779-9220;
www.quaintnyc.com

Set on the border of historic Sunnyside Gardens, this quaint-enough New American is helmed by an acolyte of the sustainable foods movement and offers seasonal dishes with ingredients drawn from local farms; the warm, sophisticated setting and moderate prices compensate for the no-reservations policy.

Quality Meats ●NEW
▽ 23 | 21 | 22 | $70

57 W. 58th St. (bet. 5th & 6th Aves.), 212-371-7777;
www.qualitymeatsnyc.com

Arriving like "a breath of fresh air on the stuffy Midtown scene", this "excellent" New American steakhouse lives up to its name with "exceptional" beef, "sexy", "hip" decor by au courant designers AvroKO and service that's "up to" any challenge; it's expensive, but, well, Alan Stillman's in charge.

Quartino
21 | 20 | 17 | $32

11 Bleecker St. (Elizabeth St.), 212-529-5133 ⊟
21 Peck Slip (Water St.), 212-349-4433

"Simple", "delicious" Ligurian fare in the Seaport augmented by organic vegetarian dishes and seafood in NoHo make these "rustic" Italian siblings a double "treat"; "pretty" digs and "value" prices offset the "variable" service.

Quatorze Bis
21 | 18 | 19 | $55

323 E. 79th St. (bet. 1st & 2nd Aves.), 212-535-1414

Upper Eastsiders "can't imagine life without this wonderful" stalwart's "definitive" French bistro fare, soothing setting and "attentive" service; though tabs are "stiff", longtime *copains* contend the frites alone are "worth the trip" to First Avenue.

Quattro Gatti
19 | 16 | 20 | $45

205 E. 81st St. (bet. 2nd & 3rd Aves.), 212-570-1073

"Let's hear it for the cats" yowl fans of this UES "old haunt", where the "pampering" staff delivers "delicious" Italian standards and "great" wines; though a few hiss that it's a bit "tired" and takes too much scratch, most purr "always a pleasure."

Queen
24 | 13 | 20 | $39

84 Court St. (bet. Livingston & Schermerhorn Sts.), Brooklyn,
718-596-5955

Brooklyn "lawyers, judges and politicos", who agree on little else, are in accord that this "old-time" Italian "red-sauce heaven" on Court Street is "king in King's County"; "gruff" but "reliable" service and decidedly "unpretentious" decor and prices add to the "authentic" feel.

Queen's Hideaway ⓜ╤NEW
▽ 22 | 16 | 21 | $30

222 Franklin St. (bet. Green & Huron Sts.), Brooklyn, 718-383-2355

"As much an artist as a cook", chef-owner Liza Queen rules at this Greenpoint greenhorn serving "sophisticated" Southern-accented New American fare that's both "delectable" and "reasonable"; the "lovely" staff "makes you feel like family" in the "small", "dark", "speakeasy"-like digs that open into a "relaxing" garden.

Quercy
22 | 16 | 19 | $37

242 Court St. (bet. Baltic & Kane Sts.), Brooklyn, 718-243-2151

La Lunchonette's Cobble Hill *frère* "strikes the right notes" with "flavorful", fairly priced French "comfort" food, "interesting" wines, an "inviting" setting and "at times, even a chanteuse"; with "helpful" service to boot, it's "surprising it isn't better known."

Rack & Soul NEW

▽ | 22 | 13 | 19 | $23 |

2818 Broadway (109th St.), 212-222-4800; www.rackandsoul.com
UWS 'cue-noisseurs craving "down-home" eats "welcome" this kid-friendly newcomer serving "excellent" BBQ and "quality" Southern eats; "bland" decor aside, it's a "great addition" to the scene.

Rain

| 21 | 21 | 19 | $40 |

100 W. 82nd St. (bet. Amsterdam & Columbus Aves.), 212-501-0776; www.rainrestaurant.com
"Atmospheric" and "upbeat" (read: "noisy") jungle-themed digs, "enjoyable" Pan-Asian food and "middle-class prices" ensure this Upper Westsider remains a local "mainstay"; to a few the "crowd-pleaser" formula feels overly "focus-grouped", but for most it "consistently" "hits the mark."

RAINBOW ROOM M

| 20 | 28 | 21 | VE |

GE Bldg., 30 Rockefeller Plaza, 65th fl. (enter on 49th St., bet. 5th & 6th Aves.), 212-632-5100; www.rainbowroom.com
With its "old-NY class" (à la Fred and Ginger) and "priceless" panoramic views, this 65th-floor, black-tie-preferred Rockefeller Center "institution" remains "the tops" for "special occasions" featuring "smooth" formal service and "quality" Venetian cuisine; yes, it's a monumental "splurge", but everyone should go "at least once"; N.B. unfortunately it's open to the public only for Friday and Saturday prix fixe dinner ($200) and Sunday brunch ($80).

RAO'S ☒∌⋢

| 21 | 15 | 21 | $66 |

455 E. 114th St. (Pleasant Ave.), 212-722-6709; www.raos.com
"Reservations are impossible" for mere mortals at this vintage 1896 East Harlem Southern Italian – about the only way to get in is to "befriend one of the regulars" who rent their tables by the year; "celebs, politicians" and made men savor "wonderful traditional" fare and whaddaya want service that feels more like being in a "*Sopranos* episode" than in a normal restaurant – especially since owner Frank Pellegrino actually plays a part in the series.

Raoul's ◐

| 22 | 19 | 20 | $53 |

180 Prince St. (bet. Sullivan & Thompson Sts.), 212-966-3518; www.raouls.com
"When in doubt" go with this "little bit of the old SoHo", a perpetually "cool", *très* "Parisian" French bistro where the "second-to-none" steak au poivre and such comes in "dark", "cozy", "first date"–friendly digs including an "intimate" back garden room; it's "pricey" for the genre, but most don't notice because "fun is the word" here.

Rare Bar & Grill

| 21 | 15 | 17 | $29 |

Shelburne Murray Hill Hotel, 303 Lexington Ave. (37th St.), 212-481-1999
228 Bleecker St. (bet. Carmine St. & 6th Ave.), 212-691-7273 NEW
www.rarebarandgrill.com
"Thick is an understatement" when it comes to this "cool" Murray Hill "dive" joint's "big, juicy" "upscale burgers" crowned with "every kind of topping you can imagine", so most don't mind that the "aloof" service isn't rare; if it's "too crowded", go for a "delicious cocktail" at the "rooftop bar" instead; N.B. a Village outpost opened recently.

Rectangles ◐

| 18 | 13 | 15 | $29 |

1431 First Ave. (bet. 74th & 75th Sts.), 212-744-7470; www.rectanglesrestaurant.com
Still somewhat "undiscovered" since moving to Yorkville from the East Village last year, this "real-deal" Yemenite Israeli is considered a "keeper" by those who know it; "tasty", "affordable" kosher dishes and a "pleasant" staff add spark to the otherwise "ordinary" space.

Red Café ⓂI
▽ | 22 | 16 | 20 | $34

78 Fifth Ave. (bet. Prospect & St. Marks Pls.), Brooklyn, 718-789-1100
This New American "charmer" along Park Slope's dining strip "makes the best of" its "tiny" quarters with "inviting" crimson-hued decor, "lovely" service and an "inventive" (if "limited") menu; that the "well-done" dishes "won't break the bank" seals the deal.

Red Cat
24 | 20 | 22 | $51

227 10th Ave. (bet. 23rd & 24th Sts.), 212-242-1122;
www.beanstalkrestaurants.com
The original "cat's meow" by Danny Abrams (Mermaid Inn) and Jimmy Bradley (The Harrison), this "Chelsea standout" serves "dynamic", "farmer's market–fresh" New American–Med dishes; its "Hamptons barn" look and "tip-top staff" contribute to its "wild popularity", "loud" acoustics and serious tabs aside.

Redeye Grill ⓿
20 | 18 | 19 | $51

890 Seventh Ave. (56th St.), 212-541-9000; www.redeyegrill.com
In a "noisy air hangar of a space", this New American "Shelly Fireman production" offers "seafood galore", including trademark "dancing shrimp"; a "fantastic raw bar", "speedy service" and "Carnegie Hall convenience" keep its "tourist"-heavy crowd "running up the bill."

Red Garlic ⓿
19 | 13 | 18 | $30

916 Eighth Ave. (bet. 54th & 55th Sts.), 212-489-5237
"Fresher-than-average" Thai with a "seafood focus" sets this "reasonable" Hell's Kitchener apart from others on its "crowded strip"; if you can look past the "glum" setting, it's an "excellent pre-theater option" away from the "hordes of tourists."

Regency
18 | 20 | 21 | $63

Regency Hotel, 540 Park Ave. (61st St.), 212-339-4050;
www.loewshotels.com
"You don't dine here – you breakfast" say "business" and political hobnobbers for whom this Tisch family New American on the East Side is "the place to be seen at 9 AM"; some also favor its "romantic setting" for "drinks, nibbles" and live music come nighttime when it morphs into the cabaret club Feinstein's.

Regional ⓿
18 | 15 | 16 | $34

2607 Broadway (bet. 98th & 99th Sts.), 212-666-1915
Upper Westsiders say this Italian "youngster" is a "step above the usual" for the neighborhood, citing its "hearty" regional dishes and "great wine list", all at a "modest cost"; despite gripes about the "noisy", "stark" room and "amateurish service", it's popular enough to be "packed" most of the time.

Regional Thai
18 | 14 | 16 | $27

1479 First Ave. (77th St.), 212-744-6374
208 Seventh Ave. (22nd St.), 212-807-9872
A "pleasing menu" of "Thai favorites" keeps enthusiasts "eating well" at this Chelsea-UES duo "with a tropical flair"; it's a "dependable" "great value", particularly at lunchtime, but just "don't expect fabulous."

Relish ⓿
21 | 20 | 17 | $28

225 Wythe Ave. (bet. Metropolitan Ave. & N. 3rd St.), Brooklyn, 718-963-4546;
www.relish.com
"High-end comfort food" and "classic cocktails" add polish to this "sleek", "perfectly restored" 1950s dining car in Williamsburg; with a "beautiful" outdoor garden and "innovative", "lick-the-plate good" New American cooking, anyone would relish a meal here but for the sometimes-disappointing "hipster" service.

Remi
21 21 20 $56

145 W. 53rd St. (bet. 6th & 7th Aves.), 212-581-4242; www.remi.citysearch.com
Both the "lovely", "classic" Venetian-accented Italian cuisine and "light and airy", mural-adorned space make this Midtowner "a sure bet" for "power suits", "groups" and "dates"; "pleasant" service enhances the "lively but not overwhelming" room, while prix fixe deals add further appeal.

René Pujol Ⓜ
22 19 22 $55

321 W. 51st St. (bet. 8th & 9th Aves.), 212-246-3023; www.renepujol.com
"C'est si bon" say fans of "the best French place you've probably never heard of", a "civilized" if slightly "worn" Theater District "old-timer" with "fine" "country" cooking and prix fixe perks; following its 2005 shift to an employee-owned coop model, some surveyors report "even better service."

Republic
18 14 15 $20

37 Union Sq. W. (bet. 16th & 17th Sts.), 212-627-7172; www.thinknoodles.com
"Fast" and "cheap", this Union Square "noodle bastion" draws a "young crowd" for Pan-Asian fare that's "tasty", "abundant" and "healthy"; though its "modern" sensibility wins nods, the "cavernous", "noisy" space with "cafeteria-style seating" and "robotic" service lead some to seek their sustenance elsewhere.

Re Sette
20 18 18 $53

7 W. 45th St. (bet. 5th & 6th Aves.), 212-221-7530; www.resette.com
"Above-average" Italian from the Barese region comes in "intimate", mural-bedecked digs at this Midtowner that's well-located for a "pre-theater" meal; skeptics shrug "nothing special" and note "it'll set you back", but even they tout the upstairs King's Table for private parties.

Revival
▽ 20 18 19 $34

2367 Frederick Douglass Blvd. (127th St.), 212-222-8338;
www.harlemrevival.com
Melding French-American cooking with Caribbean and Creole touches, this "hidden treasure in Harlem" offers "original", "flavorful" dishes at "moderate prices"; "great drinks", neighborhood photos and a "lovely atmosphere" make it a "breath of fresh air."

Ribot Ⓢ
▽ 19 20 19 $48

780 Third Ave. (48th St.), 212-355-3700; www.ribotnyc.com
"Bravo" say early samplers of this Midtown newcomer, citing "solid" Mediterranean cuisine, "quality wines" and a "young, attentive" staff; add in an airy, "soothing" interior and pleasing patio and you've got what could be "a winner" – although no bargain.

Rice ⊘
19 15 16 $19

115 Lexington Ave. (28th St.), 212-686-5400
227 Mott St. (bet. Prince & Spring Sts.), 212-226-5775 ☽
166 DeKalb Ave. (Cumberland St.), Brooklyn, 718-858-2700 NEW
81 Washington St. (bet. Front & York Sts.), Brooklyn, 718-222-9880
www.riceny.com
Everyone's "favorite starch" is "the main dish" with a "mix-and-match" "twist" at this Eclectic quartet; opinions on the "interesting" culinary combos range from "bland" to "the best", but all agree that the overall performance is "cost-effective."

Rice 'n' Beans
21 9 15 $22

744 Ninth Ave. (bet. 50th & 51st Sts.), 212-265-4444;
www.ricenbeansrestaurant.com
Hell's Kitchen "crowds" pile into this "phone booth"–size eatery, because the "oh-so-good" "authentic" "Brazilian home cooking" "can't

be beat for price or portion"; middling service and "no-frills" surroundings are part of the "bargain."

Rickshaw Dumpling Bar
18 10 14 $13

61 W. 23rd St. (bet. 5th & 6th Aves.), 212-924-9220; www.rickshawdumplings.com

"Tasty, fast and filling dumplings" in lots of "unusual" varieties carry the meal at this "upscale take-out" Flatiron Chinese; whether customers find the room "stylish" or "sterile", most welcome its "Mott Street–on–Main Street" convenience.

Riingo
20 20 19 $53

Alex Hotel, 205 E. 45th St. (bet. 2nd & 3rd Aves.), 212-867-4200; www.riingo.com

"Inventive" New American–Japanese cuisine from chef Marcus Samuelsson and "catchy" cocktails highlight this Midtowner's "dark", "serene" setting; some sniff that the "small portions for large prices" "don't satisfy", but the majority leaves most "impressed."

Risotteria
21 10 18 $23

270 Bleecker St. (Morton St.), 212-924-6664; www.risotteria.com

"Risotto anyone?" – the "excellent", "seemingly endless varieties" fill a "niche" at this Village Italian, which is "great for vegetarians" and also "sets the standard for gluten-free dining"; "accommodating" service and "value" pricing offset its "cramped" "college-town" feel.

RIVER CAFÉ
26 27 25 VE

1 Water St. (bet. Furman & Old Fulton Sts.), Brooklyn, 718-522-5200; www.rivercafe.com

"Bring the love of your life" and take in the "magnificent" skyline view at this "special-occasion" Dumbo destination "tucked under the Brooklyn Bridge"; its "exquisite" New American cuisine, "flower-filled" interior and "gracious" service work in "artful" harmony, but it's that "fantastic view of the harbor" (and the prix fixe tab) that will "take your breath away."

Riverdale Garden
24 20 20 $45

4576 Manhattan College Pkwy. (242nd St.), Bronx, 718-884-5232; www.riverdalegarden.com

This Bronx "hideaway" boasts a "rich", "seasonal" New American menu that makes for a "luxe night out"; despite service that can be "too casual", many relish the "hominess" of its "stoveside" dining room, as well as its "flower-filled" garden come springtime.

River Room Ⓜ NEW
▽ 22 25 18 $47

Riverbank State Park, 750 W. 145th St. (Riverside Dr.), 212-491-1500

"Spectacular" Hudson River, Palisades and GW Bridge views inspire "road trips" to this "sophisticated", glass-walled "beauty" in Harlem's Riverbank State Park; its pricey "nouveau Southern cuisine" comes spiked with Creole-Latin flavors and weekend jazz performances.

Riverview
▽ 17 25 17 $49

2-01 50th Ave. (enter at Center Blvd. & 49th Ave.), Queens, 718-392-5000; www.riverviewny.com

"Stunning views" of the Manhattan skyline uplift this "lovely" relative "newcomer" to Long Island City; though some feel the food and service have been "declining" of late, a new Italian menu and lower prices may give it new appeal.

Roberto Passon ☕
22 16 19 $42

741 Ninth Ave. (50th St.), 212-582-5599; www.robertopasson.com

"Unpretentious" yet "creative" Italian fare is the hallmark of this moderately priced Hell's Kitchen trattoria; the "rustic" room can grow downright "noisy" and the "friendly" service can turn "rushed" at prime times.

ROBERTO'S ⊠   27 | 20 | 22 | $49

603 Crescent Ave. (Hughes Ave.), Bronx, 718-733-9503
"Believe the hype" report the legion fans of Roberto Paciullo's "superb" Salerno cuisine at this Arthur Avenue–area Italian; while the "no-reservations" policy may mean "outrageous waits", it's a "far-and-away" "favorite" where savvy diners "let the chef" do the ordering.

Roc ◑   21 | 19 | 21 | $48

190-A Duane St. (Greenwich St.), 212-625-3333;
www.rocrestaurant.com
Hailing from the "old European school" of Italian dining, owner Rocco Cadolini draws "lots of regulars" to his TriBeCa "date spot" thanks to "fantastic", "upscale" food; a "welcoming" staff and "crisp" room and sidewalk tables help explain customers' roc-solid loyalty.

Rocco Ⓜ   ▽ 19 | 14 | 18 | $38

181 Thompson St. (bet. Bleecker & Houston Sts.), 212-677-0590;
www.roccorestaurant.com
This 1920s "Village classic" sets down "consistent", affordable Southern Italian food in "homey" environs; though the decor is "not much to brag about" and seating is "tight", the "amusing waiters" and "old-fashioned" food are "why you come."

Rock Center Cafe   18 | 21 | 18 | $44

Rockefeller Ctr., 20 W. 50th St. (bet. 5th & 6th Aves.), 212-332-7620;
www.restaurantassociates.com
"Festive" year-round, this Rock Center American "lunch mecca" attracts out-of-towners and "NBC celebrities" alike to savor a "ringside view" of ice skating in winter or the summertime patio; the food is "surprisingly decent" for a "tourist trap", but it's mainly the spectacle that "draws the crowd."

Rocking Horse   20 | 16 | 17 | $35

182 Eighth Ave. (bet. 19th & 20th Sts.), 212-463-9511;
www.rockinghorsecafe.com
"Colorful", "modern Mexican" cuisine and a "stylish", "noisy" crowd amps up this "Chelsea staple"; despite hit-or-miss service and tabs "a bit pricey" for the genre, the "kickin' margaritas" keep it "happening"; N.B. there's a pre-theater discount for Joyce patrons.

Rolf's   16 | 21 | 16 | $39

281 Third Ave. (22nd St.), 212-477-4750
Both "sausage cravings" and "kitsch" addictions are sated at this Gramercy Park German offering "heavy" "home cooking" as well as a string-of-Xmas-lights decorating scheme; come the holidays, the lit-up interior is "long on charm" and "worth battling the crowds" to see.

Roll-n-Roaster ◑   19 | 8 | 12 | $12

2901 Emmons Ave. (bet. E. 29th St. & Nostrand Ave.), Brooklyn,
718-769-5831; www.rollnroaster.com
"Melt-in-your-mouth" "roast beef sandwiches with the works" plus "can't-miss cheese fries" buoy this Sheepshead Bay family biz; fans forgive the "priceless" "'70s" look and "slow" service since this low-budget locale "beats a fast-food joint any day."

Room 4 Dessert ◑⊠NEW   ▽ 19 | 19 | 19 | $27

17 Cleveland Pl. (bet. Kenmare & Spring Sts.), 212-941-5405
You may decide to "skip dinner altogether" for this NoLita sweets bar where "mad-scientist" pastry chef Will Goldfarb crafts "wildly cre-

ative" yet "subtle" confections paired with wines and teas; though a few hunger for more "substance", most leave on a "sugar high."

Room Service NEW

–	–	–	M

166 Eighth Ave. (bet. 18th & 19th Sts.), 212-691-0299;
www.roomservicerestaurant.com

Designed to mimic a chic boutique hotel eatery, this lively new Chelsea Thai sports all the appropriate trappings: pumping music, white-leather banquettes and a mirrored bar area; only its modestly priced lineup of traditional dishes breaks from the tony concept.

Roppongi ●

20	15	18	$35

434 Amsterdam Ave. (81st St.), 212-362-8182;
www.ropponginyc.net

Its space is "no frills" but "quieter" than across-the-street competitor Haru, and devotees of this UWS Japanese declare its sushi "just as tasty"; "consistent" quality, "reasonable prices" and "attentive" service are other reasons it's a "dependable" choice.

ROSA MEXICANO ●

22	21	20	$47

61 Columbus Ave. (62nd St.), 212-977-7700
9 E. 18th St. (bet. B'way & 5th Ave.), 212-533-3350 NEW
1063 First Ave. (58th St.), 212-753-7407
www.rosamexicano.com

At these "extremely popular" Mexicans, "standout" fare is served by "friendly" staffers in "splashy", "lively" settings; "everyone knows" to start with the "killer" pomegranate margaritas and "unbelievable guacamole" and then sit back and take in the "noisy", "jumping" "scene" while your entrees come and "the bill grows."

Rose Water

25	19	23	$42

787 Union St. (6th Ave.), Brooklyn, 718-783-3800

Leave behind "Manhattan prices and pretensions" at this "special" Park Slope New American featuring an "ever-changing" menu of "inventive" dishes based on "top-quality" local ingredients; the "kind" staff will make you feel welcome in "cozy" but "tight" quarters.

Rossini's

23	18	23	$54

108 E. 38th St. (bet. Lexington & Park Aves.), 212-683-0135;
www.rossinisrestaurant.com

Seekers of a "nostalgic, old-NY feel" need look no further than this Murray Hill Northern Italian, where "gracious", "tuxedoed" waiters dispense "reliably" "excellent" standards; the "spacious" setting could use "updating", but devoted regulars don't seem to mind – even when they get the hefty bill.

Rothmann's

22	20	21	$66

3 E. 54th St. (bet. 5th & Madison Aves.), 212-319-5500;
www.rothmannssteakhouse.com

It "flies under the radar", but enthusiasts say this East Midtown steakhouse "should be a top-tier name" given its "excellent", seriously "expensive" cuts, "winning" wine list and "feel-like-a-king" service; no surprise its "spacious" setting hosts a "testosterone-heavy" "after-work" crowd.

Roth's Westside Steakhouse

20	17	19	$50

680 Columbus Ave. (93rd St.), 212-280-4103;
www.rothswestsidesteakhouse.com

A rare "find", this "serious" UWS steakhouse offers "solid" beef and "pleasant" service, plus "wonderful" live jazz that contributes to the "warm", "comfortable" ambiance; relatively affordable for the genre, it's a "popular" local destination.

Rouge

▽ 20 19 20 $39

107-02 70th Rd. (Austin St.), Queens, 718-793-5514

Considered a Forest Hills "must-try", this first-rate French bistro doles out all the "standards" in a "European cafe atmosphere"; "reasonable" prices and "unpretentious service" add to its "neighborhood" appeal, though authenticity-seekers wish it were a little less "Americanized."

Royal's Downtown NEW

▽ 24 23 23 $40

215 Union St. (bet. Clinton & Henry Sts.), Brooklyn, 718-923-9866; www.royalsdowntown.com

A tree-lined Carroll Gardens street seems the perfect place for this "delicious" new Med-influenced New American whose menu relies heavily on Greenmarket produce; "prompt" service and a "spacious", romantic setting complete with a "wonderful" patio help justify tabs considered "pricey" "for the area."

Royal Siam

20 12 17 $27

240 Eighth Ave. (bet. 22nd & 23rd Sts.), 212-741-1732

"The chef knows what he's doing" at this "friendly", "under-the-radar" source for "reliable", "fresh" Thai in Chelsea; the fact that it's something of a "neighborhood secret" means there's "never a line", and while the decor's "no-frills", so are the prices.

Roy's New York

24 19 21 $52

Marriott Financial Ctr., 130 Washington St. (bet. Albany & Carlisle Sts.), 212-266-6262; www.roysnewyork.com

Maybe "it's not quite Maui" but this Financial District outpost of chef Roy Yamaguchi's empire has "delectable", "creative" Hawaiian fusion fare and a staff embodying "the spirit of aloha"; despite a "generic hotel setting", "out-of-the-way location" and "high prices", for most it's a "sure thing."

RUB BBQ

19 8 15 $27

208 W. 23rd St. (bet. 7th & 8th Aves.), 212-524-4300; www.rubbbq.net

"Pretty dang good 'cue" comes out of the pit at this "friendly" low-cost "Kansas City import" in Chelsea whose hickory-fired style is rated "most authentic"; however, the "kitchen can run out" of popular choices in "later hours" and the "no-frills" space screams "church basement" – "there's the rub."

Ruby Foo's ●

19 21 17 $41

1626 Broadway (49th St.), 212-489-5600
2182 Broadway (77th St.), 212-724-6700
www.brguestrestaurants.com

"Over-the-top" "faux-Chinese" decor straight off a "Broadway set" (think "Disney does Beijing") plus "crowd-pleasing" Pan-Asian eats ensure this "loud", "festive" Times Square–UWS duo is a "sure bet" for "out-of-town guests" and "large groups"; since it's "always packed", "make a reservation."

Rue 57 ●

18 18 16 $45

60 W. 57th St. (6th Ave.), 212-307-5656; www.rue57.com

"French bistro classics" and sushi may be an "odd marriage", but it "works" for this "popular" Midtowner that's a local lunch "favorite" and also "well-situated for Carnegie Hall"; unless you want to head back to the *rue,* ignore "bothersome noise" levels and a "young actor" staff that has given it the nickname "Rude 57."

Rughetta ⊠

23 15 21 $43

347 E. 85th St. (bet. 1st & 2nd Aves.), 212-517-3118

It's "charm perfected" rave fans of this "romantic" "little local" UES Roman, where they "handle customers with the same care" as the "delicious" food; "space is tight", though, so for best results it's wise to go at off hours.

Russian Samovar ● M
17 | 16 | 16 | $47

256 W. 52nd St. (bet. B'way & 8th Ave.), 212-757-0168; www.russiansamovar.com

You "feel like you're in Russia" – or at least "Little Odessa" – at this "colorful, noisy" Theater Districter where the menu's Continental, but "Roosky" vodka and caviar "reigns"; most overlook the "Soviet service" and "tsar"-worthy prices because it's always "so much fun", especially when the "magical" live music starts.

Ruth's Chris Steak House
24 | 20 | 22 | $63

148 W. 51st St. (bet. 6th & 7th Aves.), 212-245-9600; www.ruthschris.com

"Big", "sizzling" steaks "bathed in butter" ("bring your Lipitor") are what this Times Square link of the "upscale" chophouse chain is "reliable" for; the wood-paneled setting is "pleasant" (if "mundane") and service is "nice and easy", but true to the genre it's "costly."

Sacred Chow
▽ 21 | 15 | 20 | $18

227 Sullivan St. (bet. Bleecker & W. 3rd Sts.), 212-337-0863; www.sacredchow.com

"Who knew vegetarian could be so good?" marvel converts to this "wholesome yet tasty" "hippie-chic" organic health-fooder deep in "NYU country" where everything's vegan and kosher; maybe "the chairs aren't comfy if you're over 25" – but then "most patrons aren't."

Sac's Place
21 | 15 | 17 | $27

25-41 Broadway (29th St.), Queens, 718-204-5002

Some of the "best pizza in Astoria" comes out of the "coal-fired" oven at this "cozy" Italian manned by an "accommodating" crew; its "paper-thin", "crunchy"-crusted pies are voted "insanely great", but some say "the rest" of the menu is just "so-so."

Sadie Mae's Cafe M NEW
– | – | – | I

131 Sixth Ave. (bet. Park & Sterling Pls.), Brooklyn, 718-636-4270

As funky as its name, this hard-to-resist Park Slope soul-fooder is so down-home that it lists Kool-Aid among its drinks; the more than affordable entrees come with a choice of two sides, including a mean mac 'n' cheese.

S'Agapo ●
▽ 20 | 11 | 18 | $34

34-21 34th Ave. (35th St.), Queens, 718-626-0303

The "carefully prepared" dishes at this "old-fashioned" Hellenic are considered "some of the best" in Astoria's "Little Greece"; the staff is "super-nice" and "you can't beat the prices" given the "huge portions", so most overlook the "minimal" decor ("outdoor seating is preferable").

Sahara ●
22 | 14 | 15 | $26

2337 Coney Island Ave. (bet. Aves. T & U), Brooklyn, 718-376-8594

"Soon they will need their own zip code" quip fans of this "ever-expanding" Gravesend Turk that's "always" "loud and busy" with seekers of "honest, fresh" grub priced and portioned for "value"; "don't come for romance" – service can be "abrupt" and the space verges on "cafeteria"-like – but at least the "garden is pleasant."

SAIGON GRILL ●
23 | 9 | 16 | $21

620 Amsterdam Ave. (90th St.), 212-875-9072
91-93 University Pl. (bet. 11th & 12th Sts.), 212-982-3691 NEW
www.saigongrill.com

"Cheap, fast and amazing" explains why these "excellent" Vietnamese (the UES branch, closed for remodeling, is expected to reopen this winter) have earned "institution" status despite "packed", "zero-atmosphere" setups and "abrupt" service; now the new Village branch "should create a whole new group of followers."

Sakura Café

▽ | 22 | 17 | 18 | $38

388 Fifth Ave. (bet. 6th & 7th Sts.), Brooklyn, 718-832-2970

A "tiny treasure" in Park Slope, this "sweet storefront" specializes in "traditional" Japanese home cooking, but also slices "fantastic sushi"; "value" prices, an "excellent sake selection" and a "gracious" owner compensate for service that's sometimes "on snail time."

Sala

21 | 20 | 19 | $38

344 Bowery (Great Jones St.), 212-979-6606
35 W. 19th St. (bet. 5th & 6th Aves.), 212-229-2300
www.salanyc.com

"Terrific tapas" plus "killer sangria" equal "lots of fun" at this "lively", "noisy" Spanish duo, where "warm" service and "decent prices" take the sting out of "long waits" at prime times; the "dark, sexy" NoHo original is "great for a date", while the roomier Flatiron offshoot seems to be "a must" for "after-work warriors."

Salaam Bombay

20 | 16 | 18 | $33

317 Greenwich St. (bet. Duane & Reade Sts.), 212-226-9400;
www.salaambombay.com

The "lavish" $13.95 lunch buffet "can't be beat" at this TriBeCa Indian, which also boasts "outdoor seating" ideal for "people-watching"; however, "faded" decor and "inconsistent" food and service have some wondering "who's minding" the store?

Sal Anthony's Lanza

18 | 17 | 18 | $38

168 First Ave. (bet. 10th & 11th Sts.), 212-674-7014

Sal Anthony's S.P.Q.R.

133 Mulberry St. (bet. Grand & Hester Sts.), 212-925-3120
www.salanthonys.com

"Good old-fashioned Italian" is the deal at this "friendly" Little Italy–East Village duo delivering "big portions" in "comfortable" environs; ok, maybe their "tourist-trap" tendencies are a tad "tacky", but no one argues with their "real-steal" prix fixe menus.

Sala Thai ●

20 | 13 | 17 | $28

1718 Second Ave. (bet. 89th & 90th Sts.), 212-410-5557

"Superior", "no-nonsense Thai" is what's on the plate at this "reliable" UES veteran; maybe the decor's "duller than grandma's living room", but given that the food's "fabulous", the prices "cheap" and the service "gracious", no one complains much.

Salt ⑤

23 | 19 | 20 | $41

58 MacDougal St. (bet. Houston & Prince Sts.), 212-674-4968

Salt Bar ●⑤Ⓜ

29A Clinton St. (bet. Houston & Stanton Sts.), 212-979-8471
www.saltnyc.com

"Inventive" comfort food "full of flavor" is served up in "tiny" digs at this "warm" SoHo New American featuring "intimate" (some say "cramped") communal tables and a "New England feel"; its more "animated" LES sibling focuses more on "upscale drinks and tapas."

Salute!

19 | 19 | 17 | $43

270 Madison Ave. (39th St.), 212-213-3440

This "casual" Murray Hill Northern Italian is "insanely busy at lunchtime" thanks to its "decent" thin-crust pizzas and pastas and "wonderful wines by-the-glass"; an attractive space helps justify tabs "on the pricey side", but "uneven" service can detract.

Samba-Lé ◑⊘ NEW
23 Ave. A (bet. 1st & 2nd Sts.), 212-529-2919

| – | – | – | M |

Brazilian tapas washed down with cool caipirinhas is the draw at this vibrant new East Villager where both the food and the clientele are easy on the eyes; given the live Brazilian combos on weekends, some say this one is more about scene than cuisine.

Sambuca
20 W. 72nd St. (bet. Columbus Ave. & CPW), 212-787-5656;
www.sambucanyc.com

| 19 | 15 | 18 | $36 |

Think "Carmine's without the tourists" and you've got this "friendly" UWS Italian that delivers "garlicky" ("bring the Tic Tacs"), "down-to-earth" pastas and such in "gargantuan" "family-style" portions; P.S. it also offers a gluten-free menu – "is that an oxymoron for Italian?"

Sammy's Roumanian
157 Chrystie St. (Delancey St.), 212-673-0330

| 17 | 9 | 16 | $48 |

"Ya gotta do it once, especially if you're Jewish" advise initiates of this "jovial" LES Eastern European "experience unlike any other" doling out "enough schmaltz to induce a coronary"; "do yourself a mitzvah" and "drink copious vodka" with the "damn-good chopped liver" – you'll have "a hoot of an evening" taking in the "real shtick.

San Domenico
240 Central Park S. (bet. B'way & 7th Ave.), 212-265-5959

| 22 | 22 | 23 | $73 |

"Old-world charm and hospitality" are the hallmark of this "outstanding" CPS modern Italian offering "delicate, delicious" cuisine via chef Odette Fada and "attentive but unobtrusive" service, all overseen by owner Tony May; the jackets-required policy and "deep pockets"– essential pricing don't deter its crowd of "tony" "regulars" and "special-occasion" celebrators who note that lunch is both more laid-back and less expensive.

San Luigi ⧄M NEW
311 Amsterdam Ave. (bet. 74th & 75th Sts.), 212-362-8828

| – | – | – | M |

Affordable Southern Italian pastas and raw-bar specialties, backed by a reasonably priced list of wines, explain the popularlity of this roomy new Westsider; it's a casual neighborhood spot where patrons can dine on sidewalk tables or stay inside to watch a live feed of the chefs in the kitchen transmitted via flat-screen TV.

San Pietro ⧄
18 E. 54th St. (bet. 5th & Madison Aves.), 212-753-9015; www.sanpietro.net

| 23 | 20 | 22 | $73 |

The "captains-of-finance" lunch crowd at this "top-flight" Midtown Italian is nearly as "interesting" as the "excellent" "traditional cooking"; but outsiders warn "you have to be somebody – or be with somebody" – to "be treated well", and try not to flinch when the bill arrives.

Santa Fe
73 W. 71st St. (bet. Columbus Ave. & CPW), 212-724-0822

| 18 | 14 | 17 | $37 |

"Killer margaritas" are the drink of choice at this "dependable" UWS Southwestern; though the "stark" room strikes some as "depressing", it's "family-friendly" with service that's "gracious" and food that's "fresh" – what more could you ask from a "neighborhood spot"?

Sant Ambroeus
1000 Madison Ave. (bet. 77th & 78th Sts.), 212-570-2211
259 W. Fourth St. (Perry St.), 212-604-9254
www.santambroeus.com

| 21 | 20 | 19 | $54 |

"Snazzy Euro" types find "intrinsic elegance" in this "civilized" West Village–UES Italian duo where the "delicious" "à la Milano" cuisine comes via a "caring staff"; too bad its "European style" extends to its prices; P.S. the Uptown original has a counter for "excellent gelato and espresso" to go.

Sapa ●

22	25	20	$56

43 W. 24th St. (bet. B'way & 6th Ave.), 212-929-1800;
www.sapanyc.com

The "breathtaking" decor at this "high-priced" Flatiron French-Vietnamese engenders a "Zen-like feeling" and threatens to outshine chef Patricia Yeo's "brilliant" handiwork; "warm, caring" service and the "coolest bathrooms" are other attractions.

Sapori D'Ischia Ⓜ

24	16	20	$44

55-15 37th Ave. (56th St.), Queens, 718-446-1500

"Gourmet Italian grocer by day", "upscale" eatery "by night", this "treasure hidden among warehouses" fully justifies the trip to Woodside; the "delicious" "authentic" cooking is enhanced by "gracious" service, and the "opera singers" on Thursday nights "push the experience over the top."

Sapphire Indian

20	18	18	$41

1845 Broadway (bet. 60th & 61st Sts.), 212-245-4444;
www.sapphireny.com

Convenient to Lincoln Center, this relatively "elegant" Indian "excels" on the power of its "lavish lunch buffet" that happily "has rarely increased in price" over the years; however, the pro service inspires differing reactions ("pleasant" vs. "condescending").

Sapporo East ●

21	10	16	$23

164 First Ave. (10th St.), 212-260-1330

This East Village "Japanese restaurant–meets–rock 'n' roll high school" (expect "loud AC/DC" and the like on the sound system) offers "solid" sushi and other "standards" delivered by a "swift" staff; for most "long lines" and "seedy" decor are "worth it" for such a "cheap treat."

Sarabeth's

21	17	17	$32

423 Amsterdam Ave. (bet. 80th & 81st Sts.), 212-496-6280
40 Central Park S. (bet. 5th & 6th Aves.), 212-826-5959
Chelsea Mkt., 75 Ninth Ave. (bet. 15th & 16th Sts.), 212-989-2424
1295 Madison Ave. (bet. 92nd & 93rd Sts.), 212-410-7335
Whitney Museum, 945 Madison Ave. (75th St.), 212-570-3670 Ⓜ
www.sarabeth.com

American "comfort" classics "like you wish your mother used to make" are the specialty of this "countrified" "comfort" chainlet that's especially favored for its "amazing" "breakfasts and brunches" (be sure to queue up "an hour before you think you'll be hungry"); insiders say the newer CPS location is "easier to get into."

Saravanaas Ⓜ

▽ 22	11	15	$23

81 Lexington Ave. (26th St.), 212-679-0204; www.saravanaas.com

"Spicy dosas are what we go fa'" say surveyors of this Gramercy link of a South Indian "veggie" Indian chain; it's relatively new but already "packed" with "hip, young expats" overlooking the "disinterested" service and focusing on the "scandalously cheap" bill.

Sardi's ●Ⓜ

16	21	19	$50

234 W. 44th St. (bet. B'way & 8th Ave.), 212-221-8440;
www.sardis.com

"Celeb caricatures line the walls" and "real waiters, not actors" provide the "friendly" service at this "last of the legendary eateries of Broadway"; "iffy", "expensive" Continental fare leads many to lament "it's not what it once was", but still the "trip-back-in-time" experience deserves to be had "at least once."

Sarge's Deli ◐

19 | 7 | 14 | $22

548 Third Ave. (bet. 36th & 37th Sts.), 212-679-0442; www.sargesdeli.com
"Oy vey!" – "they don't make 'em like this" "hunger-busting" "authentic 24-hour deli" in Murray Hill anymore, where regulars "double up their Lipitor" to handle the "must-try" sandwiches; maybe it's on the "seedy" side, but for most it remains a "perennial favorite" within a dying breed.

Sascha ◐ NEW

20 | 23 | 17 | $54

55-61 Gansevoort St. (bet. Greenwich & Washington Sts.), 212-989-1920; www.sascharestaurant.com
Already a Meatpacking District "haunt", this New American arrival's "tasty" bistro fare is served till late in three "gorgeous" "old NY"–chic spaces: a bakery, a casual bar/cafe and a more formal upstairs dining room; however, the post-*Survey* exit of namesake chef Sascha Lyon leaves the future unclear for this "fun addition" to the scene.

SAUL

27 | 20 | 24 | $54

140 Smith St. (bet. Bergen & Dean Sts.), Brooklyn, 718-935-9844; www.saulrestaurant.com
"You can taste chef-owner Saul Bolton's passion for food" on every plate at this Boerum Hill New American offering a "perfect combination" of "neighborhood friendliness and elegant cuisine", not to mention "solicitous, well-informed" service; even "Manhattanites don't mind" making the schlep, especially since the tabs offer "great bang for your buck."

Savann

20 | 14 | 18 | $39

414 Amsterdam Ave. (bet. 79th & 80th Sts.), 212-580-0202; www.savann.com
A "lovely neighborhood" boîte helmed by a "chef who takes pride" in his "creative, seasonal dishes" describes this "small" UWS French-Med; it's appealingly "quiet, grown-up and unflashy", leading fans to wonder why it's "not more popular."

Savoia

21 | 17 | 19 | $29

277 Smith St. (bet. Degraw & Sackett Sts.), Brooklyn, 718-797-2727
"Awesome" "brick-oven" pizzas are the signature of this Carroll Gardens "favorite" where locals find "genuine Italian warmth" in the "loving staff" and "charming" atmosphere; it's a "great place to take the kids", and happily it now accepts reservations.

Savoy

23 | 20 | 22 | $53

70 Prince St. (Crosby St.), 212-219-8570; www.savoynyc.com
"After over 15 years" this "warm, romantic" SoHo Med–New American is still pumping out "creative, fresh, seasonal" cuisine delivered by a "gracious staff" in a "charming" split-personality space (casual downstairs, more formal upstairs); chef Peter Hoffman's "respect for his ingredients" shines through in every plate.

Scaletta

21 | 18 | 23 | $50

50 W. 77th St. (bet. Columbus Ave. & CPW), 212-769-9191; www.scalettaristorante.com
"Old-fashioned" Northern Italian is the name of the game at this "quiet" UWS "hideaway", where everyone's "treated well" by "friendly" staffers; except for its prices, it's a "throwback to a different era", which suits its "older crowd" fine, though a few note the decor's getting "a bit tired."

Scalinatella ◐

25 | 17 | 21 | $73

201 E. 61st St. (3rd Ave.), 212-207-8280
The "mouthwatering Italian" food at this East Side Capri-esque vet comes in stone-walled subterranean digs that some call appealingly

"private and dark" but others "dank"; all agree the staff's "attentive", but warn that the "specials" sometimes mean you'd "better bring two credit cards" just in case.

SCALINI FEDELI ⑤

26 | 25 | 25 | $81

165 Duane St. (bet. Greenwich & Hudson Sts.), 212-528-0400; www.scalinifedeli.com

"Superb", "sophisticated" Northern Italian cuisine ("foam and all") draws applause for this "TriBeCa pleasure", whose vaulted room (the former Bouley space) is "a delight" and whose "attentive, unobtrusive" staffers win raves; over the shouts of "mama mia!" when the check comes you'll hear most diners insisting it's "worth every penny."

Scarlatto ● NEW

▽ 23 | 20 | 20 | $40

250 W. 47th St. (bet. B'way & 8th Ave.), 212-730-4535; www.scarlattonyc.com

"The clean, crisp" "*Roman Holiday*"–reminiscent decor at this new "Theater District jewel" is a fitting foil for its "fresh, clean-tasting" Northern Italian fare; "portions are excellent" and "reasonably priced", so the only bone is that service may be "erratic."

Schiller's ●

19 | 20 | 16 | $36

131 Rivington St. (Norfolk St.), 212-260-4555; www.schillersny.com

Keith McNally's "bright, festive" Eclectic "captures that French feel" while adding its own "Lower East Side flavor" (and pricing); it's an "always-packed" "hot spot" where those in-the-know "go early to beat the crowds", "long waits" and "deafening" noise; P.S. "brunch is particularly good."

Scottadito Osteria Toscana ⊅

21 | 22 | 19 | $38

788A Union St. (bet. 6th & 7th Aves.), Brooklyn, 718-636-4800; www.scottadito.com

"A Tuscan village setting" with matching "delightful rustic cuisine" featuring "organic" ingredients makes this "friendly" Italian "a great find" on Park Slope's Fifth Avenue strip; the only "downside" is its "cash-only" policy.

SEA

21 | 22 | 17 | $24

75 Second Ave. (bet. 4th & 5th Sts.), 212-228-5505
114 N. Sixth St. (Berry St.), Brooklyn, 718-384-8850 ●
www.spicenyc.net

These two "tasty" Thais are decidedly different: the "much bigger" Williamsburg branch hosts a "trendy scene" in its "funky, unusual" quarters, while the smaller, "tightly packed" East Village original is more minimal; both boast "amazing values" that give rise to "long waits."

Sea Grill ⑤

24 | 24 | 22 | $65

Rockefeller Ctr., 19 W. 49th St. (bet. 5th & 6th Aves.), 212-332-7610; www.theseagrillnyc.com

The "archetypical tourist experience" at this Rockefeller Center warhorse in winter comes with a "beautiful" view of Christmas tree and ice skaters and yearlong with "excellent" seafood produced by longtime chef Ed Brown; see, sometimes the "out-of-towners" are right!

Serafina ●

18 | 16 | 15 | $39

Dream Hotel, 210 W. 55th St. (B'way), 212-315-1700
38 E. 58th St. (bet. Madison & Park Aves.), 212-832-8888 ⑤
29 E. 61st St. (bet. Madison & Park Aves.), 212-702-9898
393 Lafayette St. (4th St.), 212-995-9595
1022 Madison Ave., 2nd fl. (79th St.), 212-734-2676
www.serafinarestaurant.com

This "casually upscale" Italian quintet supplies "surprisingly good" thin-crust pizzas to "good-looking" "Euro" types packed into "crowded, noisy" quarters; most say "*grazie*" for the "fun" scene, but not for the "rushed" service and food that's "a bit pricey for what it is."

Serendipity 3 ◐

18	19	14	$27

225 E. 60th St. (bet. 2nd & 3rd Aves.), 212-838-3531; www.serendipity3.com
Long a "NY staple", this "whimsical" East Side "dessert emporium"–cum–toy shop continues to enchant tykes and tourists with famous frozen hot chocolate and other "decadent" dishes; the only sour notes are "ludicrously" long lines and "irritable" service.

Setacci NEW

–	–	–	E

420 Hudson St. (St. Luke's Pl.), 212-675-0810
The name means 'to sift', and this Village newcomer has indeed sifted through the Italian repertoire to create a highly original menu; high ceilings, warm candlelight and well-spaced tables set a romantic mood that not even the high tabs can disturb.

Sette ◐

19	16	16	$39

191 Seventh Ave. (bet. 21st & 22nd Sts.), 212-675-5935;
www.settenyc.com
A "fun", "trendy" feel, "reasonable" prices and a "steady kitchen" that "does right by the basics" make this Chelsea Italian a "solid" "date place" and "local" standout; "popularity" has its price, however: it's often "crowded and noisy."

Sette Enoteca e Cucina

22	18	20	$40

207 Seventh Ave. (3rd St.), Brooklyn, 718-499-7767;
www.setteparkslope.com
Another "great addition to the Slope", this "charming" Southern Italian is winning friends with "*delizioso*" pizzas and dishes from a wood-burning oven; "affordable" tabs and an "open-all-year" patio make the occasional miscue from the "well-intentioned" staff easy to stomach.

Sette Mezzo ◐⊟

22	16	20	$62

969 Lexington Ave. (bet. 70th & 71st Sts.), 212-472-0400
"Year in, year out" this "chic" Italian pleases its "elite" East Side demographic with "superb" classics and "careful" service; "regulars" don't seem to mind the "too-close tables" or "sky-high" cash-only tabs, which might as well be "club membership" dues.

Seven ◐⊠

17	17	16	$39

350 Seventh Ave. (bet. 29th & 30th Sts.), 212-967-1919
This "surprising" "slice of sophistication" near Madison Square Garden hosts "noisy", "big crowds" pre- or post-game; the kicking "bar scene" may be its main draw, but "decent" New American eats, relatively "fancy" digs and "friendly" service mean it's also appealing for dinner.

718

22	19	19	$40

35-01 Ditmars Blvd. (35th St.), Queens, 718-204-5553;
www.718restaurant.com
At this "unique" Astorian, the "creative" French fare comes with Spanish accents in "lounge"-like digs; despite debate over the pricing ("affordable" vs. "expensive for the area"), it's indisputably "adventurous in such a conservative neighborhood."

71 Irving Place

19	17	16	$16

71 Irving Pl. (bet. 18th & 19th Sts.), 212-995-5252;
www.irvingfarm.com
"Bohemia comes to Irving Place" at this "destination" coffeehouse, an "anti-Starbucks" that's so "charming" it "feels like the Berkshires"; be ready for "unpredictable" service and a "perennially packed" scene – everyone from "soccer moms" to the "occasional celeb."

Sevilla ❷

| 22 | 13 | 19 | $39 |

62 Charles St. (W. 4th St.), 212-929-3189;
www.sevillarestaurantandbar.com

Declaring "it's been there forever for a reason", customers laud this 60-plus-year-old Village Spaniard for "strong, fruity sangria" and "the best paella" at fair prices; sure, the "quaint" interior is "faded" and the waiters aren't getting any younger, but for loyalists it's an ongoing "love affair" nonetheless.

Sezz Medi'

| 20 | 15 | 17 | $31 |

1260 Amsterdam Ave. (122nd St.), 212-932-2901; www.sezzmedi.com

A "real find" near Columbia, this "agreeable neighborhood" Med offers "real-deal" pizzas and other "satisfying" standards in "pleasant", "upscale" digs; just be prepared to "bump into your professors."

Sfoglia ⌧ NEW

| ▽ 22 | 21 | 20 | $48 |

1402 Lexington Ave. (92nd St.), 212-831-1402; www.sfogliarestaurant.com

It's "our new favorite" declare early visitors to this "tiny" Northern Italian, a recent import from Nantucket, that has settled in "just across from the 92nd Street Y"; given the "wonderful" rustic fare and "gracious" sensibility, it's no surprise that you must "make reservations."

Shabu-Shabu 70

| 21 | 13 | 19 | $37 |

314 E. 70th St. (bet. 1st & 2nd Aves.), 212-861-5635

There's "fun for the whole family" in "cooking your own food" at this "tucked-away" UES hot-pot (and sushi) specialist overseen by a "warm" team; the "unassuming" digs are on the "shabby-shabby" side, but most surveyors stay focused on the "tasty, affordable" offerings.

Shabu-Tatsu ❷

| ▽ 23 | 14 | 18 | $33 |

216 E. 10th St. (bet. 1st & 2nd Aves.), 212-477-2972

Best enjoyed "with a group" and a round of "Sapporo", this East Village Japanese offers a "delicious", "fun experience" of a "do-it-yourself" shabu-shabu or sukiyaki meal; "reasonable" tabs and "patient" servers who "show you what to do" make "tight" quarters easy to stomach.

Shaffer City Oyster Bar & Grill ⌧

| 21 | 15 | 19 | $48 |

5 W. 21st St. (bet. 5th & 6th Aves.), 212-255-9827; www.shaffercity.com

An "oyster lover's dream", this "friendly" Flatiron seafooder boasts a raw bar that's the "pearl of the neighborhood"; praise for "gracious" host-owner Jay Shaffer drowns out carping about "unadorned" "pub"-like quarters that don't half measure up to the size of the check.

Shake Shack

| 23 | 14 | 12 | $13 |

Madison Square Park (23rd St.), 212-889-6600; www.shakeshacknyc.com

"Spring really arrives" when Danny Meyer's seasonal (May–December), alfresco "king-of-fast-food" pavilion opens in Madison Square Park, peddling "truly amazing" burgers, dogs and shakes; despite complaints about "excruciatingly slow" service, it continues to generate "ridiculously long" lines as a "special NYC experience."

Shanghai Cuisine ⊄

| ▽ 20 | 11 | 14 | $21 |

89 Bayard St. (Mulberry St.), 212-732-8988

"Satisfying" soup dumplings that come "complete with cartoon instructions" cause "crowds" to collect at this "cash-only" Chinatown Shanghainese; given the "tight seating" and "rushed service", just plan to "come, eat and get out."

Shanghai Pavilion

| 22 | 18 | 20 | $37 |

1378 Third Ave. (bet. 78th & 79th Sts.), 212-585-3388

"Sophisticated" Shanghai savories "served with flair" distinguish this Upper Eastsider from its peers, as do the "fancy digs" and "solicitous" service; its "superior soup dumplings" are a "special treat", and short of a "trip to Chinatown", it's hard to beat the "moderate prices."

Sharz Cafe & Wine Bar — 20 | 13 | 18 | $39

435 E. 86th St. (bet. 1st & York Aves.), 212-876-7282; www.sharzcafe.com
Upper East Side locals praise this "very special" "neighborhood" Mediterranean bistro/wine bar for its "tasty" fare and "first-rate" wines ("especially by-the-glass"); "great-value" pricing compensates for its "tiny tables" and "hole-in-the-wall" setup.

Shelly's — ▽ 24 | 19 | 21 | $55

41 W. 57th St. (bet. 5th & 6th Aves.), 212-245-2422; www.shellysnewyork.com
Though it moved "across the street" recently, Shelly Fireman's "quality" steakhouse-meets–raw bar is "still convenient to Carnegie Hall" and still a "favorite"; "attentive" service and a "fun" upstairs jazz club round out the "lively" vibe, leaving prices as the only snare.

Sherwood Cafe ◑⊅ — ▽ 19 | 23 | 17 | $25

195 Smith St. (bet. Baltic & Warren Sts.), Brooklyn, 718-596-1609; www.sherwoodcafe.com
"Like eating in a Parisian thrift shop", this "funky"-"chic" Smith Street French bistro offers "tasty" classics along with a chance to browse "eclectic" "antiques"; "nice prices" and a "lovely garden" ("little beats it in summertime") make iffy service easy to forgive.

Shula's Steak House — 19 | 19 | 18 | $67

Westin NY Times Sq., 270 W. 43rd St. (bet. B'way & 8th Ave.), 212-201-2776; www.donshulas.com
Coach Don Shula's eponymous Midtown-by-way-of-Miami chain steakhouse scores points for its "solid" lineup of beef and sides in "football-size" portions; still, a "bland" hotel setting and "way expensive" prices lead surveyors to gang tackle it as "strictly for tourists and Dolphin fans."

Shun Lee Cafe ◑ — 20 | 16 | 18 | $40

43 W. 65th St. (bet. Columbus Ave. & CPW), 212-769-3888; www.shunleewest.com
"Terrific dim sum" from the "cart parade" makes this "black-and-white" West Side Chinese just the place for a "good", "quick" meal near Lincoln Center; it's a "less-expensive spin-off" of its "more formal" siblings, but some suggest the decor is beginning to get "tired."

Shun Lee Palace ◑ — 23 | 20 | 22 | $53

155 E. 55th St. (bet. Lexington & 3rd Aves.), 212-371-8844; www.shunleepalace.com
"Still going strong" after 35 years, Michael Tong's "formal" Midtown "landmark" provides "top-of-the-line" "gourmet" Chinese fare and "impeccable service" in "elegant" surroundings; repeating the phrase "holy amazing food" may help distract you when the "huge bill" arrives.

Shun Lee West ◑ — 22 | 21 | 21 | $52

43 W. 65th St. (bet. Columbus Ave. & CPW), 212-595-8895; www.shunleewest.com
A long-running "class act" near Lincoln Center, this "refined" West Side Chinese continues to transport diners to "another place and time" with "imaginative dishes", "fancy" "black-lacquered" decor and "attentive service"; no surprise it may be a "dragon your wallet."

Siam Inn — 22 | 14 | 19 | $29

854 Eighth Ave. (bet. 51st & 52nd Sts.), 212-757-4006; www.siaminn.com
"Consistently superior" Siamese fare, "fast, friendly" service and "inexpensive" prices make this Midtown Thai a "terrific pre-theater

find"; only the "sterile" setting prevents it from receiving "bravos" across the board.

Siam Square ⓜ

▽ 24 | 18 | 21 | $27

564 Kappock St. (Henry Hudson Pkwy.), Bronx, 718-432-8200; www.siamsq.com
"Fresh", "exceptionally tasty" Thai food "presented as art" make this destination "worth the trip to Riverdale"; staffers who are "friendly from the moment you walk in the door", a "pleasant atmosphere" and equally agreeable prices ensure it's "a winner."

Sipan ❶

20 | 18 | 18 | $37

702 Amsterdam Ave. (94th St.), 212-665-9929
"Start with pisco sours" and move on to the "wonderful ceviche" and other "fresh seafood" at this "surprisingly suave" yet "well-priced" UWS Peruvian; some wonder how it still "flies below the radar" – overly "dark" lighting and sometimes "slow" service may explain it.

Sip Sak

19 | 9 | 14 | $24

928 Second Ave. (bet. 49th & 50th Sts.), 212-583-1900; www.sip-sak.com
The "homey" open kitchen "cooks up miracles" in the form of falafel and multitudinous meze at this "consistent" East Midtown Turkish; "superb value" and (at last) a liquor license compensate for the "lack of decor" and issues with the owner.

Sistina ❶

24 | 16 | 20 | $67

1555 Second Ave. (bet. 80th & 81st Sts.), 212-861-7660
A meal at this "inspired" little UES Italian's "like getting beamed to Roma" thanks to "fresh", "carefully prepared" dishes, an "enormous" wine cellar and service that's all "grace and dignity"; no wonder its "mature" clientele isn't bothered by the "drab" decor or "up-there" tabs.

66

20 | 23 | 18 | $59

241 Church St. (bet. Leonard & Worth Sts.), 212-925-0202; www.jean-georges.com
Jean-Georges does "21st-century Chinese" at this "sleek" TriBeCan where Richard Meier's "chic minimalist" design is geared toward a crowd clad in "head-to-toe Barneys"; still, some say it should be deep-sixed given the "big prices" for food that's "a little ordinary."

S'mac ⓜ NEW

– | – | – | I

345 E. 12th St. (bet. 1st & 2nd Aves.), 212-358-7912; www.smacnyc.com
Comfort foodies crowd the counter of this cheap East Village one-hit wonder for 10 varieties of mac 'n' cheese that come with a choice of pasta and a bread-crumb option; the creamy results, served in a skillet, can be enjoyed at a handful of tables.

Smith & Wollensky

23 | 18 | 20 | $64

797 Third Ave. (49th St.), 212-753-1530; www.smithandwollensky.com
Beef lovers "can't go wrong" at this "old-time" mega duplex Midtown steakhouse–cum–"men's club" with a history of "big steaks, big drinks" and equally hefty tabs, as well as "no-nonsense" service; you can also "damn your cholesterol" at the "less-expensive", less-formal Wollensky's Grill next door, which also stays open later.

Smorgas Chef

18 | 14 | 17 | $30

924 Second Ave. (49th St.), 212-486-1411 ❶
53 Stone St. (William St.), 212-422-3500
283 W. 12th St. (4th St.), 212-243-7073 ❶ NEW
www.smorgaschef.com
For "Swedish delights" "just the way Inga used to make them" (including "a mean meatball"), try this trio of "small", "bright" Scandinavians

manned by an "attentive", if sometimes "slow", staff; it's pleasingly "cheap" and "very casual", but still a real "bump up from Ikea."

Snack
22 | 12 | 16 | $25

105 Thompson St. (bet. Prince & Spring Sts.), 212-925-1040
Blink and "you might miss" this "charming" SoHo Greek that packs "big, authentic" flavors into its "tiny" storefront; "annoying waits" and "sardine-like" squeezes are par for the course, but no one is arguing about the "incredibly tasty" "homestyle cooking" and "cheap" prices.

Snack Taverna
21 | 16 | 17 | $39

63 Bedford St. (Morton St.), 212-929-3499
The younger, more upscale sibling to Snack, this "friendly" "modern Greek" on a "lovely Village corner" is touted for its "mouthwatering twists" on the "classics" and all-Hellenic wine list; sure, it "can get noisy", but still most "everybody leaves happy."

Soba Nippon
▽ 20 | 14 | 17 | $35

19 W. 52nd St. (bet. 5th & 6th Aves.), 212-489-2525
"Sit at the counter" and take a "noontime trip" to Tokyo – that's pretty much the effect of this "reasonable" Midtown Japanese specializing in "serious", "satisfying" soba soups; "subdued" decor and "rushed" service are part of the journey.

Soba-ya
23 | 17 | 19 | $27

229 E. Ninth St. (bet. 2nd & 3rd Aves.), 212-533-6966
At this "tranquil" East Village shrine to "traditional Japanese soba", you can watch noodles being "made right in front of you" as you slurp away at your own "steamy, heady" bowl; dubbed a "poor man's Honmura An", it's "good and cheap" enough to generate "agonizing waits" and "crowds."

Sofrito ◑ NEW
– | – | – | M

400 E. 57th St. (bet. 1st Ave. & Sutton Pl.), 212-754-5999
Back after a two-year hiatus, restaurateur Jimmy Rodriguez has re-jiggered his former Jimmy's Downtown into this new Sutton Place Latino; the upscale Puerto Rican eats, salsa music and wall art via graffiti king De La Vega are already attracting lively mojito-drinkers, as well as the owner's sports-star following.

Solera ⊠
21 | 18 | 19 | $52

216 E. 53rd St. (bet. 2nd & 3rd Aves.), 212-644-1166;
www.solerany.com
Located in an East Midtown brownstone, this "classy", "comfortable" Spaniard is a "favorite" for "after-work drinks and a light bite to eat" or a "wonderful" multicourse prix fixe meal; a "lovely" wine list and "warm" service are other reasons to go.

Solo
▽ 24 | 22 | 21 | $69

Sony Plaza Atrium, 550 Madison Ave. (bet. 55th & 56th Sts.),
212-833-7800; www.solonyc.com
Some of the best kosher dining "short of a plane ride to Israel" can be found at this "fabulous, classy" Midtown Mediterranean whose "fancy schmancy" fare leaves many marveling "who woulda thunk it's glatt?"; just prepare for "massive sticker shock."

Sol y Sombra ◑
18 | 17 | 18 | $36

462 Amsterdam Ave. (bet. 82nd & 83rd Sts.), 212-400-4036
"Filling a need", this "lively", "well-priced" UWS Spaniard plies "interesting, varied" tapas in an "appealing" "exposed-brick" space; still, a "disappointed" minority shrugs it's "nothing to write home about."

Son Cubano ⊠

20 21 16 $42

405 W. 14th St. (bet. 9th Ave. & Washington St.), 212-366-1640;
www.soncubanonyc.com

"The scene" is everything at this "hot" Meatpacking District Cuban, where the blaring "salsa and merengue" would fit in "South Beach" but the decor's straight out of "old Havana"; fortunately, the "tropical" fare bridges the two cities' cuisines.

Song ⇄

23 18 19 $20

295 Fifth Ave. (bet. 1st & 2nd Sts.), Brooklyn, 718-965-1108

This "friendly" Thai has Park Slopers singing the praises of its "delicious, cheap" offerings – "the same menu" as its sibling Joya – served in "hip", "industrial" digs complete with "kickin' DJs"; those who find the "nonstop" music "too loud" tout the "tranquil garden."

Sorrel Ⓜ⇄ NEW

∇ 23 17 20 $40

605 Carlton Ave. (St. Marks Ave.), Brooklyn, 718-622-1190

An "almost secret" location on an out-of-the-way Prospect Heights corner sets the mood at this "friendly", "minimalist" New American bistro offering an appealing "fresh-from-the-market" menu at "value" prices; now "if only they took credit cards."

Sosa Borella

19 16 17 $37

832 Eighth Ave. (50th St.), 212-262-7774 ☾
460 Greenwich St. (bet. Desbrosses & Watts Sts.), 212-431-5093
www.sosaborella.com

"Argentinean or Italian?" ask admirers of this "delightful" TriBeCa–Theater District duo, which features an "enjoyable" "cross-cultural" "tango" of the two cuisines; the "relaxed, chic" settings and "reasonable" rates at both are appreciated.

South Shore Country Club Ⓜ NEW

∇ 21 25 23 $49

South Shore Country Club, 200 Huguenot Ave. (Arthur Kill Rd.), Staten Island, 718-356-7017; www.south-shore.com

Staten Islanders shorely appreciate this "high-end" country club dining room for its "good" if "limited" New American menu and "warm", "romantic" environs; it's "expensive", but that's par for the course for a "special-occasion" venue.

SPARKS STEAK HOUSE ⊠

25 19 21 $68

210 E. 46th St. (bet. 2nd & 3rd Aves.), 212-687-4855;
www.sparkssteakhouse.com

A "bastion of males, meat and martinis", this "legendary" Midtown moo house remains a "power scene" where "suits" relish "immense", "top-notch" steaks and "superb wines" in quintessentially "old NY" environs; it all goes down best when it's on the "expense account" and when "you're a regular" – still, people are dying to get in.

Sparky's American Food ☾⇄

∇ 18 9 13 $12

333 Lafayette St. (Bleecker St.), 212-334-3035 NEW
135A N. Fifth St. (Bedford Ave.), Brooklyn, 718-302-5151

When "hipsters" hanker for an "all-natural Happy Meal" they head to these "cheap", "guilt-free" NoHo-Williamsburg fast-fooders where the "drool-worthy" burgers and dogs are "organic" and include "veggie-friendly" options; "dumpy" decor and "sloow" counter folk are the only downsides.

Spice

20 16 16 $25

199 Eighth Ave. (bet. 19th & 20th Sts.), 212-989-1116
1411 Second Ave. (bet. 73rd & 74th Sts.), 212-988-5348

(continued)
Spice
60 University Pl. (10th St.), 212-982-3758
www.spicenyc.net
"Addicting" "fresh and fragrant Thai" keeps throngs of "younger generation" types returning to these "chic, fun" triplets; given the "amazingly" "affordable" prices, who cares about "shoulder-to-shoulder waits on the sidewalk" or the "harried" service?

SPICE MARKET ⓓ

| 22 | 26 | 19 | $57 |

403 W. 13th St. (9th Ave.), 212-675-2322; www.jean-georges.com
"Hanging lanterns and diaphanous curtains" play a role in the "spectacular", "exotic", "transporting" decor scheme at Jean-Georges Vongerichten's "spicy hot" SE Asian duplex in the Meatpacking District that serves "elevated" Thai-Malay-Vietnamese street food to a "pretty-people" clientele; portions may be as "skimpy" as the staff's "pajama"-like uniforms, but most agree that the prices, while "not cheap", represent a "relative bargain" for a fab "JGV" venture; N.B. the private rooms downstairs are spicy too.

Spicy & Tasty ⱷ

| ▽ 22 | 11 | 14 | $21 |

39-07 Prince St. (39th Ave.), Queens, 718-359-1601
Check out this "authentic", unpretentious Flushing Szechuan for its "delicious", "mouth-numbingly spicy" dishes that are "completely different" from "the usual Chinese"; "minimal English is spoken" but the dirt-cheap prices need no translation.

Spiga NEW

| ▽ 22 | 17 | 18 | $48 |

200 W. 84th St. (bet. Amsterdam Ave. & B'way), 212-362-5506
Partisans praise this "tiny" West 80s newcomer for its "lovely, inventive" Italian cuisine, "rustic" "wine cellar"–like ambiance and "accommodating" staff; still, a few find the kitchen's "ambitious" output "uneven", saying "the verdict's still out."

Spigolo

| 25 | 16 | 21 | $55 |

1561 Second Ave. (81st St.), 212-744-1100
The "secret's out" on this "tough-ticket" UES Italian that has "morphed into a full-fledged hit" under husband-and-wife team Scott and Heather Fratangelo; he turns out the "delicious" food while she turns on the "charm" in the "comfortably crowded" dining room; "expansion would be divine", but in the meantime, "call a year ahead."

Spotted Pig ⓓ

| 22 | 16 | 16 | $41 |

314 W. 11th St. (Greenwich St.), 212-620-0393; www.thespottedpig.com
They've "added space upstairs" but this "fantastic" Italian-accented West Village British gastropub is still "perma-packed" with "A-list" "hipsters" who "squeeze" in for chef April Bloomfield's cooking savored in "stylishly downscale" digs; a "great beer selection" helps make the "horrible waits" and "spot-ty" service easier to digest.

Spring Street Natural ⓓ

| 19 | 15 | 16 | $28 |

62 Spring St. (Lafayette St.), 212-966-0290; www.springstreetnatural.com
Revisit "California circa 1972" via this NoLita standby offering "fresh", "tasty", "value"-priced veggie fare, plus fish and fowl dishes befitting its "non-militant" philosophy; its "huge space" means tables are easy to come by, but be ready for "slow" service.

SRIPRAPHAI ⱷ

| 27 | 14 | 17 | $22 |

64-13 39th Ave. (bet. 64th & 65th Sts.), Queens, 718-899-9599
Voted NYC's No. 1 Thai, this Woodsider's "out-of-this-world", "real-deal" dishes "awaken taste buds" with "fiery hot" flavors that lead aficionados to jump "on the 7 train"; a "lovely garden", "smiling ser-

vice" and super-"cheap" checks mitigate the "cafeterialike" setup and cash-only rule.

Stage Deli ◐

| 19 | 9 | 13 | $27 |

834 Seventh Ave. (bet. 53rd & 54th Sts.), 212-245-7850; www.stagedeli.com
"Fress, bubbala, fress" – but you'll need to "open your mouth real wide" to fit in the "classic" sandwiches at this "old-time" Midtown deli; just prepare for service so "rude" "they treat even NYers as if they were tourists"; N.B. this is where Midwesterners come to learn which is the bagel and which is the lox.

Staghorn Steakhouse ⑤NEW

| – | – | – | E |

315 W. 36th St. (bet. 8th & 9th Aves.), 212-239-4390; www.staghornsteakhouse.com
On an out-of-the-way block in the Garment District, this spacious, if spare, new steakhouse puts out pricey porterhouses and other carnivore delights along with à la carte sides; oenophiles are happy to discover a stairway alcove that doubles as a glass-enclosed wine cellar.

Stamatis ◐

| 21 | 11 | 17 | $30 |

31-14 Broadway (bet. 31st & 32nd Sts.), Queens, 718-204-8964
29-12 23rd Ave. (bet. 29th & 31st Sts.), Queens, 718-932-8596
Find Hellenic "fish heaven" at these Astoria "staples" that are separately owned but offer much the same "hearty portions", "kitschy" decor and "family atmosphere" reminiscent of a "visit to your Greek relatives down the block"; "reasonable" prices are yet another hook.

Stanton Social ◐

| 24 | 25 | 20 | $49 |

99 Stanton St. (bet. Ludlow & Orchard Sts.), 212-995-0099; www.thestantonsocial.com
"Fun" is the word on this "groovy, gorgeous" LES Eclectic, where the globe-spanning menu of "little bites" hits the spot but can add up "In a big way"; "young", "fabulous" crowds create a "scene" that's "loud as a rock concert", so instead of talking, just "graze" and gaze.

Steak Frites ◐

| 17 | 15 | 15 | $40 |

9 E. 16th St. (bet. 5th Ave. & Union Sq. W.), 212-463-7101
You almost "expect Edith Piaf" to appear at this "cozy, cramped" Union Square French bistro/steakhouse that's "good for its namesake" dish and other "standards"; "reasonable" pricing is a plus, but "spacey" service and "run-down" decor are beginning to take a toll.

Stella del Mare ⑤

| ▽ 21 | 18 | 22 | $54 |

346 Lexington Ave. (bet. 39th & 40th Sts.), 212-687-4425; www.stelladelmareny.com
"Elegant European-style service" elevates the "fine" fin fare at this "pleasant", if "unexciting", Murray Hill Italian, where the fish is "filleted tableside" and a "charming piano bar" is part of the scenery; "they make you feel very special", though naturally, pampering has its price.

Stone Park Café Ⓜ

| 24 | 20 | 21 | $44 |

324 Fifth Ave. (3rd St.), Brooklyn, 718-369-0082; www.stoneparkcafe.com
It's "Brooklyn at its best" dote devotees of this "delightful" Park Slope New American that pairs "sophisticated cuisine" with a "casual" ambiance; "reasonable" prices and "attentive" service mean some "never want to leave", though others flee "roaring" acoustics at peak hours.

Strip House ◐

| 25 | 22 | 21 | $66 |

13 E. 12th St. (bet. 5th Ave. & University Pl.), 212-328-0000; www.theglaziergroup.com
Yes, the name "has a double-meaning" at Peter and Penny Glazier's "sexy" Village steakhouse where the "red-hot retro" decor features

photos of "old-time strippers" that threaten to "distract" diners from the "top-notch" beef; it's predictably "pricey", but the "warm" service and all-around "superb dining experiences" are well "worth the price of admission."

Suba

20 | 25 | 19 | $51

109 Ludlow St. (bet. Delancey & Rivington Sts.), 212-982-5714; www.subanyc.com

"Still thriving" as a "trendy" Lower East Side destination, this "very cool" Spaniard is most noted for its "romantic" "moat"-ringed "grotto" dining room where diners feel as if they're "floating on water"; "by the way, the food's good" too, though it's "not the main attraction."

Sueños

23 | 19 | 19 | $44

311 W. 17th St. (bet. 8th & 9th Aves.), 212-243-1333; www.suenosnyc.com

"Dreamy indeed", chef-owner Sue Torres' "upscale" Chelsea Mexican continues to "capture the best" of south-of-the-border cooking and "jazzes it up several notches"; "bright", "hot-colored" decor and "pro service" are additional attractions.

Sugiyama ●🅳🅼

28 | 20 | 27 | $94

251 W. 55th St. (bet. B'way & 8th Ave.), 212-956-0670; www.sugiyama-nyc.com

At Nao Sugiyama's "superb-in-every-way" Midtown Japanese, aficionados advise going with the "oh-my-god" "modern kaiseki" menu and "place yourself in the hands of the master"; "serene" surroundings and "excellent" servers are part of the package, but just expect to "spend a lot."

Sumile 🅢🅼

▽ 22 | 20 | 21 | $64

154 W. 13th St. (bet. 6th Ave. & 7th Ave. S.), 212-989-7699; www.sumile.com

Chef Josh DeChellis "actually makes fusion work" at this "soothing" French-influenced Village Japanese where "lovingly prepared and presented" small plates come in "Zen-like" surroundings; still, short-funded skeptics shrug "small dishes, big prices."

Superfine 🅼

18 | 19 | 16 | $29

126 Front St. (bet. Jay & Pearl Sts.), Brooklyn, 718-243-9005

This "favorite neighborhood hangout" in "cool", "warehouse"-like Dumbo digs plies "tasty", "bargain"-priced Med eats, but its true "charm" is its "funky" "honky-tonk" feel abetted by a "free pool" table and a "great bar"; most think it lives up to its name even if the "friendly" service is less than swift.

Supper ●🌢

23 | 19 | 16 | $33

156 E. Second St. (bet. Aves. A & B), 212-477-7600; www.supperrestaurant.com

"Fabulous", "inexpensive" Northern Italian cooking keeps the "crowds" coming to this "no-reservations", no-plastic East Villager where the "rustic" decor features socially active "communal tables"; given the "incredible pastas" and ebullient atmosphere, most accept "long waits" and "lacking" service as part of the bargain.

Surya

23 | 16 | 20 | $37

302 Bleecker St. (bet. Grove St. & 7th Ave. S.), 212-807-7770; www.suryany.com

They "take their food seriously" at this "pleasant" Bleecker Street Indian, whose "fresh, subtle", "rich and spicy" fare elevates it a clear "cut above" other "curry crowd" competitors; "attentive" service and a pleasant backyard are other reasons locals "never tire of this place."

Sushi Ann ⊠
∇ 25 | 17 | 21 | $60

38 E. 51st St. (bet. Madison & Park Aves.), 212-755-1780; www.sushiann.com
"Super-fresh sushi" is sliced and rolled in "spare but pleasant" environs at this "traditional Japanese" in East Midtown; overseen by a "courteous" crew, it's a "pricey-but-worthy indulgence" per insiders who "just say 'omakase'" and are always "delighted."

Sushiden
23 | 16 | 20 | $57

19 E. 49th St. (bet. 5th & Madison Aves.), 212-758-2700
123 W. 49th St. (bet. 6th & 7th Aves.), 212-398-2800 ⊠
www.sushiden.com
A "safe choice" for a "business" meal, this "old-fashioned" crosstown Japanese duo's "silky smooth sushi" is "beautifully served" by a kimono-clad staff; some claim it's "overpriced", but few flinch given the "amazing" variety and "top-notch" quality.

Sushi Hana ◐
20 | 18 | 17 | $36

466 Amsterdam Ave. (bet. 82nd & 83rd Sts.), 212-874-0369
1501 Second Ave. (78th St.), 212-327-0582
"Swimmingly fresh" sushi cements the "mainstay" status of this "reliable" Japanese twosome, where an easy "neighborhood" vibe lures "dates and families alike"; following a "face-lift" last year, the East Side branch sports a "trendier" look.

SUSHI OF GARI Ⓜ
27 | 11 | 19 | $70

402 E. 78th St. (bet. 1st & York Aves.), 212-517-5340
"Wow" – the "creativity is unsurpassable" at chef Gari Sugio's UES Japanese, where the staff "guides you through an amazing assortment" of "life-altering" sushi; the space is "bare-bones" with "tables on top of each other" and you'll need a "bank loan" before leaving, but "concentrate on the food" and all else will be forgotten.

SushiSamba ◐
22 | 20 | 17 | $47

245 Park Ave. S. (bet. 19th & 20th Sts.), 212-475-9377
87 Seventh Ave. S. (Barrow St.), 212-691-7885
www.sushisamba.com
It "feels like a party in Miami" at these "vibrant" fusionfests where "young, hip" types generate "abundant energy" and "noise" while downing "killer drinks" and "tasty" "sushi with a Latin twist"; P.S. check out the West Village branch's "fun rooftop."

SUSHI SEKI ◐⊠
27 | 14 | 20 | $57

1143 First Ave. (bet. 62nd & 63rd Sts.), 212-371-0238
Sushi "masterpieces" as "delectable as they are beautiful" make this "late-night" (till 3 AM) East Side Japanese a "dangerous habit"; no, it "isn't cheap", and the setup's "rather plain", but nonetheless cognoscenti cheer "*kanpai!*" and join the "line out the door."

Sushi Sen-nin
25 | 15 | 20 | $53

30 E. 33rd St. (bet. Madison Ave. & Park Ave. S.), 212-889-2208
1420 Third Ave. (bet. 80th & 81st Sts.), 212-249-4992 ⊠
www.sushisennin.com
"Exceptional slices" of "sparkling"-fresh fish in "creative" combos add up to "amazingly good" sushi at these East Side Japanese siblings; longtime Murray Hill dwellers declare "thank goodness" a "pretty" new branch has replaced the original 34th Street location.

Sushiya
21 | 14 | 20 | $32

28 W. 56th St. (bet. 5th & 6th Aves.), 212-247-5760
"Abundant portions" of "fresh", "solid" sushi at a "reasonable price" make this "friendly" Midtown Japanese "the kind of place you want to

visit weekly"; it's a "neighborhood favorite", though its ratings show many are less impressed by its "low-key" (some say "spartan") setup.

SUSHI YASUDA ⊠

| 28 | 22 | 24 | $75 |

204 E. 43rd St. (bet. 2nd & 3rd Aves.), 212-972-1001; www.sushiyasuda.com
"Prepare to be wowed" at this "sublime" Grand Central–area "temple" that is once again voted the No. 1 Japanese in NYC thanks to chef Naomichi Yasuda's "amazingly fresh" "traditional" preparations that will "redefine your idea of sushi"; the "elegant", "serene" light-wood setting and "attentive but not overbearing" service create a "Zen-like ambiance" that helps you cope with the "breathtaking prices."

Sushi Zen ⊠

| 25 | 20 | 21 | $55 |

108 W. 44th St. (bet. B'way & 6th Ave.), 212-302-0707; www.sushizen-ny.com
Specializing in "pristine"-quality sushi, this "simple", "lovely" Theater District Japanese wins extra points for its "creative" combos and "fine sakes"; insiders say the "chef's omakase" is "among the best" going, but "hopefully someone else is picking up the tab."

Swagat Indian Cuisine

| 23 | 12 | 19 | $25 |

411A Amsterdam Ave. (bet. 79th & 80th Sts.), 212-362-1400
"What a gem!" rave reviewers of this "small, hospitable" UWS Indian, where "friendly" staffers serve "delicious, authentic dishes" at "reasonable" rates; as for the "tiny" quarters, one diner's "cozy" is another's "cramped" and "claustrophobic."

Sweet Melissa

| 23 | 16 | 18 | $16 |

276 Court St. (bet. Butler & Douglass Sts.), Brooklyn, 718-855-3410
175 Seventh Ave. (bet. 1st & 2nd Sts.), Brooklyn, 718-502-9153 NEW
www.sweetmelissapatisserie.com
For dessert lovers, this "adorable nook" in Cobble Hill is "a little slice of heaven"; there are also sandwiches and salads, and its "fun high tea" is even more of a "delight" when taken in the "beautiful garden"; N.B. though the SoHo branch closed recently, it has been replaced by a brand-new outlet in Park Slope.

Sweet-n-Tart Cafe ●⊘⊅

| 20 | 11 | 14 | $18 |

136-11 38th Ave. (Main St.), Queens, 718-661-3380; www.sweetntart.com
"Hip young Asians" and other lovers of "innovative", "delicious" dim sum, "exotic" fresh fruit drinks and "a whole lot of everything else" "crowd" into this "authentic, inexpensive" Flushing Chinese; when it comes to the "unusual" desserts, regulars urge "be adventuresome."

Swifty's ●

| 17 | 18 | 17 | $60 |

1007 Lexington Ave. (bet. 72nd & 73rd Sts.), 212-535-6000; www.swiftysny.com
The "swells" of the UES convene at this "clubby, genteel" Traditional American for "surprisingly good" "upscale classics" with "warm" service – if you're "a regular"; critics dismiss it as "cliquish" and wonder "don't Wasps have taste buds" too?

Sylvia's

| 16 | 12 | 16 | $29 |

328 Lenox Ave. (bet. 126th & 127th Sts.), 212-996-0660;
www.sylviassoulfood.com
There's "nothing like soul food to brighten up your day", and the menu at this down-home Harlem "classic" is "filled with temptations"; but while some say the "first-rate" experience has them "smiling for days after", others report "the zest has gone" and declare it "a total tourist trap."

Symposium

| 20 | 13 | 20 | $24 |

544 W. 113th St. (bet. Amsterdam Ave. & B'way), 212-865-1011
"Still the same as it was 30 years ago", this "friendly", "no-frills" Columbia-area "fixture" offers "good, solid" Greek classics delivered

by an "easygoing" staff; its a "favorite" of both students and locals, partly because it offers "amazing value."

TABLA
25 | 25 | 24 | $62

11 Madison Ave. (25th St.), 212-889-0667; www.tablany.com

This Madison Square Park–adjacent, Indian-accented New American once again receives "thunderous applause" for Floyd Cardoz's cuisine that's at once "daring, subtle, exotic and comforting", and served by an "attentive" but "unobtrusive" staff; whether in the "beautiful" mezzanine dining room or on the ground floor in the "more casual and reasonably priced" Bread Bar, it "never fails to dazzle."

Table d'Hôte
20 | 16 | 19 | $45

44 E. 92nd St. (bet. Madison & Park Aves.), 212-348-8125

Exuding "charm" and offering "darn good" "classic bistro fare", this Upper East Side French can also be counted on for "bargain" prix fixe deals that allow you to "dine very well without mortgaging the apartment"; its "tiny" dining room is either "intimate" or "skimpy", depending on your attitude.

Table XII ▣
▽ 21 | 20 | 21 | $53

Lombardy Hotel, 109 E. 56th St. (Park Ave.), 212-750-5656; www.tablexii.com

Early discoverers of this pricey Midtown Italian yearling "almost hate to let the cat out of the bag" given its "wonderful" "classics" via chef John Scotto (of Fresco by Scotto renown); its "elegant, blessedly quiet" hotel digs, "gracious" staff and "unabashedly old-fashioned" sensibility have most diners declaring it a "winner."

Taboon
23 | 20 | 21 | $47

773 10th Ave. (52nd St.), 212-713-0271

It's "the bread, the bread, the bread" that keeps carbophiles "coming back" to this midpriced Hell's Kitchen Med–Middle Eastern, though the rest of the "impeccably fresh", "creatively prepared" offerings are "outstanding" too; an "airy", "inviting" space and "gracious" staff are other reasons it's a "boon to the neighborhood."

Taci's Beyti
▽ 22 | 11 | 18 | $24

1955 Coney Island Ave. (bet. Ave. P & Kings Hwy.), Brooklyn, 718-627-5750

Regulars happily overlook the "plastic plants and fluorescent lights" at this "modest" Midwood Turkish-Mediterranean and focus instead on the "tasty, well-prepared" food; "inexpensive" prices and a BYO policy that "really keeps the costs down" help explain why "locals love it."

Taco Chulo
▽ 24 | 20 | 20 | $20

318 Grand St. (bet. Havemeyer St. & Marcy Ave.), Brooklyn, 718-302-2485; www.tacochulo.com

"Now this is what Mexican should be" enthuse aficionados of the "delicious" dishes employing "fresh, organic ingredients" at this "first-rate" Williamsburg yearling; a "super-nice staff" and "cool vibe" seal the deal; P.S. check out its "fantastic brunch."

Taka ⓜ
▽ 23 | 9 | 19 | $43

61 Grove St. (bet. Bleecker St. & 7th Ave. S.), 212-242-3699

West Villagers praise this Japanese's "consistently delicious" sushi and "lovely" service, but not its "hole-in-the-wall" decor; maybe it "lost a bit of its luster" with the departure of its namesake chef, but regulars report it's "still above the norm" – and suggest you take a chance on the "early-bird special."

Takahachi

22 14 21 $36

85 Ave. A (bet. 5th & 6th Sts.), 212-505-6524 ◑
145 Duane St. (bet. Church St. & W. B'way), 212-571-1830
www.takahachi.net

These "unassuming" TriBeCa–East Village Japanese siblings make up for "nothing-to-write-home-about" interiors with "quick, super-friendly" service as well as generous portions of "creative" sushi; insiders suggest ordering "whatever is on" the "divine specials" list.

Taksim

20 10 17 $24

1030 Second Ave. (bet. 54th & 55th Sts.), 212-421-3004; www.taksim.us

"It's just a storefront" in East Midtown, but this "small", "cramped" Turk has a loyal fan base because its "extremely fresh" fare is "sooo good and sooo cheap"; it's "always bustling", so it's no wonder the "cheerful" service is sometimes "rushed."

Tamarind ◑

24 22 22 $50

41-43 E. 22nd St. (bet. B'way & Park Ave. S.), 212-674-7400;
www.tamarinde22.com

"Everything – but everything – is incredibly delicious" at this "stylish" Flatiron "modern Indian" whose "brilliant" cuisine is rated a "big notch above" the competition; "premium prices" come with the territory, but there's always the "bargain" prix fixe lunch or next-door tearoom.

Tang Pavilion

21 17 19 $35

65 W. 55th St. (bet. 5th & 6th Aves.), 212-956-6888

"Upscale Shanghainese" plus "quick, attentive" service and "reasonable prices" have made this Midtown Chinese a local "favorite"; better still, the delivery is so "fast" some say it "defies the laws of physics."

Tanoreen Ⓜ

▽ 25 11 18 $26

7704 Third Ave. (bet. 77th & 78th Sts.), Brooklyn, 718-748-5600;
www.tanoreen.com

"Delicious with a capital 'D'" is how devotees describe this Bay Ridge Med–Middle Eastern's "unparalleled" "homestyle" cooking ("especially the meze"); "gracious" attention from chef-owner Rawia Bishara and "just-right prices" make the "stark" "storefront setting" easy to overlook.

TAO ◑

22 27 18 $55

42 E. 58th St. (bet. Madison & Park Aves.), 212-888-2288;
www.taorestaurant.com

"Killer crowds" of "sexy" "young" things gather nightly in this "club-like" Midtown Pan-Asian's "soaring, spectacular" space centered around a "gigantic Buddha"; fans say the kitchen's "intricate, interesting" (and "pricey") output is "wonderful", but they admit it's often "over-shadowed by" the "noisy bar scene" and staff's "major attitude."

Taormina

▽ 22 19 20 $42

147 Mulberry St. (bet. Grand & Hester Sts.), 212-219-1007

"Old-world waiters" staff this longtime Italian "staple" whose "well-prepared" "red-sauce" "classics" are enjoyed amid "typical Little Italy" atmosphere; it's a "dependable" choice for the "designer sweat-suit" crowd, "especially in summer" when "you can sit at a sidewalk table."

Tarallucci e Vino

▽ 21 18 18 $33

15 E. 18th St. (bet. B'way & 5th Ave.), 212-228-5400 **NEW**
163 First Ave. (10th St.), 212-388-1190 ◑

The Flatiron's "newest not-so-secret local hangout" is this "sweet-heart" of an Italian eatery/wine bar, a "fancier incarnation" of the East Village original, offering "interesting" vinos and a "versatile", "affordable" menu including "memorable" small plates; its "rustic" "charm" is winning fans, even though the "enthusiastic" service "needs work."

Tartine ∌   22 | 13 | 16 | $27
253 W. 11th St. (4th St.), 212-229-2611
"Unlimited patience" is a must for those who brave "looong lines" and "seriously cramped seating" at this West Village provider of "outstanding French bistro fare at terrific prices"; a BYO policy that "keeps the cost down" and "fun" weekend brunch are other reasons it's "popular."

Taste   22 | 16 | 19 | $50
1413 Third Ave. (80th St.), 212-717-9798; www.elizabar.com
"Casual" cafe by day, "quiet", "slightly upscale" restaurant by night, Eli Zabar's UES New American presents "creative" cuisine that's like "bounty on the plate" given the "wonderfully fresh" ingredients; the "quality is unsurpassed", but of course it comes "at a price."

TASTING ROOM ☒ Ⓜ   27 | 15 | 26 | $63
264 Elizabeth St. (bet. Houston & Prince Sts.), 212-358-7831 NEW
72 E. First St. (bet. 1st & 2nd Aves.), 212-358-7831
www.thetastingroomnyc.com
Having outgrown its East Village home, this much-revered New American has opened a NoLita annex where chef Colin Alevras offers a daily changing menu that's now presented more conventionally, giving equal time to main courses with less emphasis on small plates (its all-American wine list remains as lengthy as ever); the new space is considerably larger than the cramped original, which has morphed into a casual wine bar/cafe.

Taverna Kyclades   24 | 13 | 19 | $31
33-07 Ditmars Blvd. (bet. 33rd & 35th Sts.), Queens, 718-545-8666;
www.tavernakyclades.com
"Stick to the" "incredibly fresh", "expertly prepared" seafood and "you can't go wrong" at this "casual", "friendly" "marine-themed" Astoria Greek; just "prepare for long waits" because it's "small" and "popular" and "doesn't accept reservations."

TAVERN ON THE GREEN   14 | 24 | 16 | $61
Central Park W. (bet. 66th & 67th Sts.), 212-873-3200;
www.tavernonthegreen.com
It's "a tourist trap, but who cares" when you can revel in "the magic of Central Park" at this West Side "landmark"; "everyone should go once" to experience the "spectacular" setting and "gorgeous" decor that's "like being inside a Fabergé egg", but just "don't expect much" from the "uninspiring" Traditional American fare; P.S. it's "great for private parties."

Tea & Sympathy   20 | 16 | 17 | $24
108 Greenwich Ave. (bet. 12th & 13th Sts.), 212-807-8329;
www.teaandsympathynewyork.com
"Terrific" afternoon tea and "jolly good" British offerings come in "tiny", "snug" quarters at this West Village "slice of the U.K."; some grumble about staff betraying "little sympathy", but for most it "warms the heart" all the same.

Tea Box ☒   ▽ 20 | 18 | 16 | $29
Takashimaya, 693 Fifth Ave. (bet. 54th & 55th Sts.), 212-350-0180
At this "Zen-like respite" in a tony Fifth Avenue department store, everything on the "light" "Japanese-ish" menu is "beautiful and delicious" – especially the "sublime" afternoon tea; its "calm", "peaceful" atmosphere makes it a "wonderful place" for "tired shoppers" to "rejuvenate."

TELEPAN NEW
25 20 23 $67

72 W. 69th St. (bet. Columbus Ave. & CPW), 212-580-4300;
www.telepan-ny.com
Upper Westsiders have a "new star" to cheer in ex–JUdson Grill chef
Bill Telepan's "civilized" New American near Lincoln Center; expect
an "innovative but unfussy" menu (including "mid courses along with
starters and mains") served in a "minimal", "Prada-green" setting
complete with a "charming bar area" – it's "expensive", but given the
"quality", open seats are rare.

Telly's Taverna ◐
22 14 18 $36

28-13 23rd Ave. (bet. 28th & 29th Sts.), Queens, 718-728-9056
For "expert versions of traditional Greek favorites", this "busy" "old
standby" in Astoria is a good option; however, regulars warn "don't go
for the decor", just focus on the "always-fresh" seafood, and "sit out
back in summertime."

Tempo
24 22 23 $48

256 Fifth Ave. (bet. Carroll St. & Garfield Pl.), Brooklyn, 718-636-2020;
www.tempobrooklyn.com
A somewhat "unsung hero", this "smart", "upscale" Park Slope Med
offers "amazing dining experiences" via "innovative", "wonderfully
prepared" cuisine and a "terrific" wine list, a "stylish" setting and
"outstanding" service; "Brooklyn prices" save the day.

Tenzan
23 15 20 $32

285 Columbus Ave. (73rd St.), 212-580-7300 ◐
7116 18th Ave. (71st St.), Brooklyn, 718-621-3238
The "secret's out" on the "super-fresh, super-reasonable" sushi
sliced and rolled at these "great little" UWS and Borough Park
"joints", and now they "always seem to be crowded"; luckily they also
offer "excellent, fast" takeout and delivery.

Teodora
20 14 18 $48

141 E. 57th St. (bet. Lexington & 3rd Aves.), 212-826-7101;
www.teodoranyc.com
Despite its location on "busy 57th Street", this Midtown "hideaway"
boasts "a wonderful neighborhood feel"; insiders choose the "civilized", "more spacious" upper level over the "cramped" downstairs
but report that the "delicious pastas" and other Northern Italian classics served on both levels justify the "serious" tabs.

Teresa's
18 10 14 $19

103 First Ave. (bet. 6th & 7th Sts.), 212-228-0604
80 Montague St. (Hicks St.), Brooklyn, 718-797-3996
"Cheap, filling and tasty" is the consensus on this East Village–Brooklyn
Heights Polish coffee shop duo doling out "hearty" "standards" in
"diner-ish" digs; the brunch is a "Sunday morning tradition", but,
unfortunately, so is the "slow service."

Terrace in the Sky Ⓜ
22 25 22 $64

400 W. 119th St. (bet. Amsterdam Ave. & Morningside Dr.), 212-666-9490;
www.terraceinthesky.com
With "a gorgeous" rooftop setting high above Morningside Heights, this
"elegant" French-Med is all "stunning views" and "harp serenades";
fortunately the food and service are just as "lovely" – but beware,
"some guy decides to propose" almost every night.

Tevere
▽ 22 18 19 $57

155 E. 84th St. (bet. Lexington & 3rd Aves.), 212-744-0210; www.teverenyc.com
When a "romantic kosher restaurant" is in order, this "pricey" UES
Italian fills the bill with "solid", "enjoyable" cuisine served by a "de-

lightful" "pro" staff; expect to "pay top dollar" for the experience, and, given the "small" space, be sure to "reserve in advance."

Thai Pavilion

▽ 23 | 14 | 22 | $21

37-10 30th Ave. (37th St.), Queens, 718-777-5546;
www.thaipavilionny.com
"Authentic as can be", this Astoria Thai may be the "best in the neighborhood" and is made even more palatable by its prices and "friendly" staff; given such overall "value", most take the de minimus decor in stride.

Thai Son

▽ 22 | 11 | 16 | $14

89 Baxter St. (Canal St.), 212-732-2822
Don't let the name fool you – this "friendly" Chinatowner serves Vietnamese food, including "wonderful, big, hearty bowls" of pho noodle soup; maybe the decor's "cheesy" and the "prompt" service "brusque", but with prices this low all is forgiven.

Thalassa

23 | 24 | 21 | $61

179 Franklin St. (bet. Greenwich & Hudson Sts.), 212-941-7661;
www.thalassanyc.com
"Dazzlingly fresh seafood" prepared with "sparkling flavors" is the calling card of this "chic", "beautiful" TriBeCa Hellenic manned by a "pro" crew; "close your eyes, and you're in the Greek isles" – and keep them shut when the bill comes, because the per-pound pricing "adds up."

Thalia ◗

20 | 21 | 19 | $47

828 Eighth Ave. (50th St.), 212-399-4444; www.restaurantthalia.com
Thanks to its "Theater District convenience" and "appealing" New American menu that "should appeal to everyone", this "swank", "airy" Hell's Kitchen "standby" is just the place to dine "before curtain time"; praise also goes to the "excellent", "reasonable" weekend brunch.

Thomas Beisl ◗

18 | 17 | 18 | $37

25 Lafayette Ave. (Ashland Pl.), Brooklyn, 718-222-5800
Indulging "BAM-goers" with "deliciously rich" "Austrian classics" at the "right price", this Fort Greene Viennese also provides "attentive" service and an outdoor beer garden with a "*gemütlich*" vibe; now if only they'd open a Manhattan branch.

Thor ◗

21 | 22 | 19 | $61

The Hotel on Rivington, 107 Rivington St. (bet. Essex & Ludlow Sts.),
212-796-8040; www.hotelonrivington.com
The post-*Survey* departure of chef Kurt Gutenbrunner (Wallsé, Blaue Gans) places the Food rating for this "super-cool" LES New American in question; though the tide of "beautiful people" flowing into its "trendy, upscale" space shows no sign of ebbing, a few wags whisper "the early '90s called and wants its decor back."

360 Ⓜ⇗

23 | 15 | 19 | $38

360 Van Brunt St. (bet. Sullivan & Wolcott Sts.), Brooklyn, 718-246-0360;
www.360brooklyn.com
Folks "looking for culinary adventure" in "deepest Red Hook" turn to this New French "pioneer" where the menu changes daily depending on "what's fresh and available"; "amazing" organic wines and a "$25 prix fixe deal" compensate for a "cranky owner."

Tía Pol

23 | 15 | 18 | $37

205 10th Ave. (bet. 22nd & 23rd Sts.), 212-675-8805; www.tiapol.com
It's "Barcelona on 10th Avenue" at this "lively", "relaxed" Chelsea Spaniard whose roster of "outstanding", "affordable" tapas has won it an ardent following; as it's a "sliver" of a place, waits are "super-

long" – so come at odd hours because "the early bird catches the marinated anchovies" here.

Tides ⓜ
▽ 23 | 22 | 23 | $37

102 Norfolk St. (bet. Delancey & Rivington Sts.), 212-254-8855
"Imagine a trendy", "gorgeous" "seafood shack", and you've got this LES yearling whose "ace lobster roll" and other "exquisite" offerings are "packed into a pint-size space"; "super-friendly" service and "reasonable prices" have most making multiple "return visits."

Tierras Colombianas ⊘
20 | 11 | 17 | $21

33-01 Broadway (33rd St.), Queens, 718-956-3012
82-18 Roosevelt Ave. (82nd St.), Queens, 718-426-8868
It helps to "bring cash", a big "appetite" and "basic Spanish skills" to get the most out of this "loud, fun" Astoria–Jackson Heights Colombian twosome; besides getting "huge, delicious" portions at "dirt-cheap prices", you should expect "rough-around-the-edges" decor – and oh yeah, bring "Alka-Seltzer" too.

Tigerland ⓜ NEW
▽ 22 | 20 | 22 | $33

85 Ave. A (bet. 5th & 6th Sts.), 212-477-9887
Surveyors who've discovered this East Village Vietnamese-Thai new-comer say the food "sparkles", the crimson-walled space is "chic yet cozy" and the staff "friendly"; however, some say this tiger still needs to earn its stripes.

Tintol ❶ NEW
▽ 19 | 16 | 17 | $43

155 W. 46th St. (bet. 6th & 7th Aves.), 212-354-3838; www.tintol.net
"Delicious" tapas and wines by the glass served in "simple", rela-tively "tourist"-free environs make this midpriced Theater District Portuguese yearling "useful" to have around; despite grumbling over "service issues" and the fact that "those small plates really add up", for most people it's a "new favorite."

Tiramisu ❶
18 | 15 | 17 | $33

1410 Third Ave. (80th St.), 212-988-9780
This "noisy", "family-friendly" UES Italian is "always busy" with seek-ers of "fine" brick-oven pizzas and other classics ("don't forget the namesake dessert"); it's a "no-brainer when you don't want to cook", but the less-impressed dismiss it as "McItalian."

Tocqueville
26 | 23 | 25 | $68

1 E. 15th St. (bet. 5th Ave. & Union Sq. W.), 212-647-1515;
www.tocquevillerestaurant.com
Its new digs just down the block are "airy" and "elegant" and the "food is as outstanding as ever" at Marco Moreira's contemporary French-American off Union Square; it's "worth the splurge" given its "Greenmarket-friendly" menu, "attentive, polished" service and "re-fined" setting; P.S. "run, run" for the "bargain" $25 prix fixe lunch.

Todai NEW
– | – | – | M

6 E. 32nd St. (bet. 5th & Madison Aves.), 212-725-1333; www.todai.com
One big fish (Minado, a regionally based Japanese restaurant chain) just got swallowed by an even bigger one (the international Todai chain), but little else has changed at this 600-seat Murray Hill buffet hall; plans are underway to add a hibachi grill and yakitori station to the already long all-you-can-eat smorgasbord of raw and cooked offerings.

Tokyo Pop NEW
▽ 22 | 20 | 21 | $32

2728 Broadway (bet. 104th & 105th Sts.), 212-932-1000
Locals give a thumbs-up to this "hip" new Japanese for filling the neighborhood's "dire need" for a "great sushi place"; toss in "won-

derful" bento boxes and "value" prices and it's no surprise that it has plenty of well-wishers.

Tommaso's
∇ 25 | 18 | 22 | $47

1464 86th St. (bet. 14th & 15th Aves.), Brooklyn, 718-236-9883
"One of the best in Brooklyn – and thus the world" proclaim proud patrons of this Bensonhurst Italian standby supplying "excellent" "old-world" cuisine, a "terrific wine list" and opera (sometimes performed by "great host" and owner Thomas Verdillo); less-than-lovely decor is the *o solo* minus.

TOMOE SUSHI ⊠
27 | 8 | 17 | $39

172 Thompson St. (bet. Bleecker & Houston Sts.), 212-777-9346
Come "rain, snow or heat", there's "always a line of drooling patrons" in front of this no-reservations, no-decor Village Japanese famed for "stellar" "jumbo-size" sushi at "rock-bottom prices"; the fish is "tender and melty" enough to make some sniff "Nobu-schmobu", so "hire someone to wait on line for you."

Tomo Sushi & Sake Bar ◑
18 | 14 | 17 | $25

2850 Broadway (bet. 110th & 111th Sts.), 212-665-2916
"Tasty", "predictable" sushi "at college prices" is the general take on this Morningside Japanese; although all should try to "ignore" the "nothing-special" decor and "rushed" service, Columbia types ought to pay special attention to the "good discounts for students."

Tom's ⊠⇄
18 | 16 | 24 | $14

782 Washington Ave. (Sterling Pl.), Brooklyn, 718-636-9738
At this "venerable" 1930s-era Prospect Heights coffee shop, "free cookies" make Saturday breakfast waits almost enjoyable; once you've nabbed a coveted "cracking booth", service is "super-fast" and the food, including some of the city's last real egg creams, "filling and flavorful" – but hey, "why no Sunday brunch?"

Tony Luke's
– | – | – | I

576 Ninth Ave. (bet. 41st & 42nd Sts.), 212-967-3055;
www.tonylukesnyc.com
After a redo and expansion (bye-bye "fallout-shelter lighting and linoleum floors"), this Times Square offshoot of the South Philly institution is back in business with its "heaven-on-a-roll" cheese steaks and "succulent roast pork sandwiches" dispensed in publike digs.

Tony's Di Napoli
19 | 14 | 17 | $34

1606 Second Ave. (83rd St.), 212-861-8686
147 W. 43rd St. (bet. B'way & 6th Ave.), 212-221-0100 ◑
www.tonysnyc.com
"Garlicky", "gigantic", "family-style" servings of "basic" Italian are the draw at these "Carmine's rivals"; tabs are "affordable", but you'll need to brush up on your "sign language" if you want to talk over the "din."

Topaz Thai
20 | 10 | 16 | $25

127 W. 56th St. (bet. 6th & 7th Aves.), 212-957-8020
"Jam-packed" at lunch and "pre-theater", this "tiny" yet "tantalizing" Thai near Carnegie Hall supplies "delicious" food at "low-budget" prices; on the downside, given that its "no-frills" space can be a "squeeze" and service is often "rushed", it's "not a place to linger."

Top of the Tower
∇ 15 | 24 | 18 | $54

Beekman Tower, 3 Mitchell Pl., 26th fl. (1st Ave.), 212-980-4796;
www.affinia.com
Back after a hiatus, this U.N.-area American atop the Beekman Tower Hotel is now serving dinner from a prix fixe–only menu at

$45 or $60 a pop; given the kitchen's middling performance and the "can't-be-beat" "panoramic" views, some prefer to go "just for a cocktail or dessert."

Tosca Café ◐ 20 | 23 | 19 | $29

4038 E. Tremont Ave. (bet. Miles & Sampson Aves.), Bronx, 718-239-3300; www.toscanyc.com

"Worth the trip to the Boogie Down", this Throgs Neck Italian has a "hip" "Manhattan" feel that extends to its "cool" "martini lounge" and "sidewalk seating"; "simple" food that's a "treat" and staffers who are "easy on the eyes" help explain why it's "always crowded."

Tossed 19 | 7 | 10 | $14

295 Park Ave. S. (bet. 22nd & 23rd Sts.), 212-674-6700
30 Rockefeller Plaza Concourse (bet. 49th & 50th Sts.), 212-218-2525 [S]
www.tossed.com

Lettuce lovers "make mom proud" by "eating their veggies" at this "popular" "custom salad" chain offering enough "toss-in" options "to make your head spin"; wilting some surveyors' enthusiasm are "pokey" service and prices deemed "too costly" for "an everyday lunch."

Totonno's Pizzeria Napolitano 22 | 10 | 14 | $21

462 Second Ave. (26th St.), 212-213-8800
1544 Second Ave. (bet. 80th & 81st Sts.), 212-327-2800
1524 Neptune Ave. (bet. W. 15th & 16th Sts.), Brooklyn, 718-372-8606 [M]
www.totonnos.com

"Divine" "classic" pizza is the deal at this cross-boro threesome, so never mind the "not-so-hot" decor and "lackluster" service; "proud Brooklynites" point out that for true "charred" and "bubbling" bliss, "you need" to head to the Coney Island original.

Tour ◐ NEW – | – | – | E

102 Eighth Ave. (15th St.), 212-242-7773; www.tourrestaurantnyc.com

Globe-trotters are drawn to this new Chelsea spot (the former Diner 24) offering a round-the-world mix of Eclectic eats on an almost round-the-clock schedule (it's open 24 hours Thursday–Sunday, and until midnight the rest of the week); no surprise, it's targeted toward the post-clubbing crowd.

Tournesol ◐ 23 | 16 | 20 | $36

50-12 Vernon Blvd. (bet. 50th & 51st Aves.), Queens, 718-472-4355

Those in "need of a dose of Paris" without having to fly make the pilgrimage to this "tiny" Long Island City French bistro; its "flavorful" and "affordable" dishes served with a side of "charm" make the "very tight" seating easy to digest.

Town 24 | 25 | 22 | $71

Chambers Hotel, 15 W. 56th St. (bet. 5th & 6th Aves.), 212-582-4445; www.townnyc.com

"Swank" and "energizing", Geoffrey Zakarian's Midtown New American is home to "posh" decor and patrons alike, as well as cuisine that "looks almost too good to eat" – but "you're glad you did"; for a "luxurious" night out that feels like "the most important party in town", this is "as good as it gets" (with prices that are nearly "as high as it gets").

Trata Estiatorio 21 | 16 | 19 | $52

1331 Second Ave. (bet. 70th & 71st Sts.), 212-535-3800; www.trata.com

The seafood "couldn't be fresher" at this Eastsider where the "traditional" Hellenic specialties are "indeed special" and, when eaten on the outdoor patio, "almost make you feel as if you're in the Greek" isles; "hang onto your wallet", though, because the prices are "out of sight."

Trattoria Alba ◐

| 20 | 18 | 21 | $42 |

233 E. 34th St. (bet. 2nd & 3rd Aves.), 212-689-3200; www.trattoriaalba.com
A "mature", "loyal" clientele patronizes this "old-fashioned" Murray Hill Italian proffering a "tried-and-true" menu; pleasantly "quiet", "dark" surroundings, "friendly, competent" service and "reasonable" bills are the secret to its long success.

Trattoria Dell'Arte ◐

| 22 | 19 | 20 | $53 |

900 Seventh Ave. (bet. 56th & 57th Sts.), 212-245-9800;
www.trattoriadellarte.com
Known for its "special" antipasto bar and "plaster body-part" decorations ("meet me by the nose"), this "lively" Midtown Italian facing Carnegie Hall affords ample "people-watching" to go with its "terrific" food; "chaos reigns", but "what fun."

TRATTORIA L'INCONTRO Ⓜ

| 27 | 20 | 24 | $47 |

21-76 31st St. (Ditmars Blvd.), Queens, 718-721-3532;
www.trattorialincontro.com
Chef-owner Rocco Sacramone's "all over making sure everything's just right" at this "top-notch" Astoria Italian where "personable" waiters recite a "mile-long list" of specials "like a Shakespeare soliloquy"; iffy "faux Tuscan" decor aside, it's "well worth the trip to Ditmars."

Trattoria Pesce & Pasta

| 18 | 13 | 18 | $31 |

262 Bleecker St. (bet. 6th Ave. & 7th Ave. S.), 212-645-2993 ◐
625 Columbus Ave. (bet. 90th & 91st Sts.), 212-579-7970
1079 First Ave. (59th St.), 212-888-7884 ◐
1562 Third Ave. (bet. 87th & 88th Sts.), 212-987-4696 ◐
www.pescepasta.com
"The name tells it all" when it comes to these pleasingly "reliable" Italian eateries specializing in "basic", "well-made" seafood and pasta; though "nothing spectacular", they satisfy with "casual" atmosphere, "laid-back" service and "very reasonable" prices.

Trattoria Romana

| 24 | 14 | 20 | $39 |

1476 Hylan Blvd. (Benton Ave.), Staten Island, 718-980-3113;
www.trattoriaromana.com
There's "always a line" at Staten Island's "premier" Italian, and "for a good reason" – "generous portions" of "consistently fine" classics at a modest price; "excellent" service makes the "tight" seating easy to take, and to avoid "long waits", "go during the week."

tre dici Ⓢ

| ▽ 22 | 19 | 20 | $44 |

128 W. 26th St. (bet. 6th & 7th Aves.), 212-243-8183
Though off "on a deserted Chelsea block", this "delightful" "little" Italian yearling is winning local hearts with its "well-prepared", "creative" cooking and "friendly" attitude; regulars "hesitate to tell" how "wonderful" it is lest they "never be able to get a table again."

Trestle on Tenth Ⓜ NEW

| – | – | – | M |

242 10th Ave. (24th St.), 212-645-5659; www.trestleontenth.com
Hearty, herbal flavors infuse everything from the cordials to the cuisine at this Swiss-influenced Chelsea New American with a pretty walled back garden; a knowledgeable staff, uncommon beer-and-wine selection and fair prices augment the convivial, neighborly atmosphere.

Triangolo ◐

| 21 | 15 | 21 | $38 |

345 E. 83rd St. (bet. 1st & 2nd Aves.), 212-472-4488;
www.triangolorestaurant.com
"Easy to miss" given its "tiny shoebox" dimensions, this UES Italian is worth seeking out for "simple" but "tasty" pastas and such delivered

by a "couldn't-be-nicer" crew; "now that it takes credit cards" (AmEx only), it's "even better."

Tribeca Grill
22 | 20 | 21 | $56

375 Greenwich St. (Franklin St.), 212-941-3900; www.tribecagrill.com
Still "busy", "vibrant" and "noisy" "after all these years", this "exposed-brick" New American grill from Drew Nieporent and Robert De Niro has become TriBeCa's "classic"; "well-prepared" food, "just-right" service and a "what-movie-did-I-see-him-in?" clientele keep it humming despite a sense that it's "not quite what it once was."

Trinity Place NEW
– | – | – | M

115 Broadway (enter on Cedar St., bet. B'way & Trinity Pl.), 212-964-0939; www.trinityplacenyc.com
Behind a 35-ton door lies this new Financial District arrival, a long, meandering space set in a vintage former bank vault featuring a noisy front barroom that yields to a clubby rear dining area; the Eclectic pub grub menu is tailored to appeal to young business types.

Trio ⊠
21 | 18 | 21 | $46

167 E. 33rd St. (bet. Lexington & 3rd Aves.), 212-685-1001; www.triorestaurant.citysearch.com
Valued as a "charming" "local treasure", this "old-world" Murray Hill Mediterranean may be NYC's sole source of "standout" Croatian dishes; a trio of assets, namely its "pleasant setting", "polite" service and "live piano", make it a "keeper."

Triomphe
24 | 22 | 22 | $62

Iroquois Hotel, 49 W. 44th St. (bet. 5th & 6th Aves.), 212-453-4233; www.triomphe-newyork.com
"Hidden" in Midtown's Iroquois Hotel, this "wonderful" little New French "lives up to its name" with "triumphant" cuisine, "dimly lit, romantic" quarters and "attentive" service; it's the place to go "when you want a quiet, mature", "refined" meal, assuming you're not on a budget.

Tropica ⊠
21 | 18 | 19 | $49

MetLife Bldg., 200 Park Ave. (enter on 45th St., bet. Lexington & Vanderbilt Aves.), 212-867-6767; www.tropicany.com
Given its "convenient" Grand Central location and "tasty" seafood, it's no wonder this Key West–style spot is a "standby" for "expense-account" and "pre-train" diners; maybe it's "not that exciting" and a bit "pricey", but it "consistently delivers", even at 17 years old.

Tsampa ◑
∇ 19 | 17 | 18 | $24

212 E. Ninth St. (bet. 2nd & 3rd Aves.), 212-614-3226
"Good for a change of pace", this East Village Tibetan puts out "healthful" home cooking in "peaceful" environs; "very affordable" tabs make meals here all the more "serene", even if service is a little "too meditative."

Tse Yang
24 | 22 | 23 | $57

34 E. 51st St. (bet. Madison & Park Aves.), 212-688-5447; www.tseyang.citysearch.com
"Exceptional" "gourmet" Chinese fare "fit for an emperor" and priced accordingly sums up this "upscale" East Midtowner; "big with the business crowd", it's particularly appreciated for its "superb" Peking duck, as well as its "dreamy" decor and "deluxe" service.

Tuk Tuk
19 | 15 | 18 | $21

49-06 Vernon Blvd. (bet. 49th & 50th Aves.), Queens, 718-472-5597
The Brooklyn original has closed, but this Long Island City Thai-Vietnamese yearling continues to turn out "delicious" dishes "not

dumbed-down for the American palate" (i.e. "super-spicy"); what it lacks in atmosphere, it makes up for in "value."

Turkish Cuisine ●   21 | 15 | 20 | $30

631 Ninth Ave. (bet. 44th & 45th Sts.), 212-397-9650
To "linger over" kebabs and Istanbul-worthy coffee, try this "homey" "mom-and-pop" Hell's Kitchen Turk where the "tasty appetizers" alone can make a meal; maybe it "isn't pretty", but it's a "delicious" "bargain" with "gracious service" and a "decent backyard" dining area to boot.

Turkish Kitchen   23 | 18 | 19 | $39

386 Third Ave. (bet. 27th & 28th Sts.), 212-679-6633;
www.turkishkitchen.com
The "flame"-colored decor at this "upscale" East Side Turk may have you "seeing red", but mouthwatering "spreads and breads" and "to-die-for kebabs" will fly your taste buds right to "the Bosporus"; "delightful" Sunday brunch is touted as a "terrific deal", so naturally there's "always a line."

Turks & Frogs NEW   ▽ 22 | 23 | 24 | $36

458 Greenwich St. (bet. Debrosses & Watts Sts.), 212-966-4774
A "welcome addition to TriBeCa", this "tasteful" Turk tenders a "wonderful", well-priced menu of meze and classic dishes; the long room includes a "delightful" front wine bar and small lounge in back, plus a cellar that's designed for private parties.

Turkuaz ●   19 | 20 | 18 | $34

2637 Broadway (100th St.), 212-665-9541; www.turkuazrestaurant.com
"Fun" "under-the-tent dining" and a "costumed staff" are part of the appeal of this theatrical UWS Turk; everything is "reasonably priced" and the food is "tasty" enough, but it's really the "exotic belly dancing" that sets the mood.

Turquoise   22 | 18 | 22 | $49

240 E. 81st St. (bet. 2nd & 3rd Aves.), 212-988-8222
This UES "fish find" has won a sparkling reputation for its "fresh, simply prepared" Mediterranean-accented seafood, genuine "hospitality" and "pleasant" "oceanic" environs; the "extra spark" brought by the "kooky", "flirty" owner is a "major draw."

Tuscany Grill   22 | 19 | 19 | $45

8620 Third Ave. (bet. 86th & 87th Sts.), Brooklyn, 718-921-5633
Long a "local favorite", this "small", "romantic" Bay Ridge Northern Italian is known for "richly flavorful" food that's "always on the money"; its "cozy" quarters are often "packed" with patrons, which occasionally overwhelms the otherwise "accommodating" staff.

12th St. Bar & Grill   21 | 19 | 20 | $36

1123 Eighth Ave. (bet. 11th & 12th Sts.), Brooklyn, 718-965-9526
Considered a "model of a good neighborhood bistro", this "casual" Park Slope New American has been a "go-to favorite" for over 10 years thanks to "dependable" grill fare at "decent prices"; if it's "not the most exciting place", at least it "won't disappoint."

24 Prince NEW   ▽ 18 | 17 | 15 | $34

24 Prince St. (bet. Elizabeth & Mott Sts.), 212-226-8624;
www.24prince.com
"Cozy quarters" and "reasonable prices" lure locals to this new NoLita American featuring a "comfort food deluxe" menu that's "unchallenging but solid" (e.g. the "popular" mac 'n' cheese rolls); don't mind the "inattentive", "easily distracted" staff.

21 CLUB ☒

22 | 24 | 24 | $69

21 W. 52nd St. (bet. 5th & 6th Aves.), 212-582-7200; www.21club.com
"You can feel the history" at this "essential" Midtown American, a "legendary" former speakeasy that still attracts "captains of industry" with its solid "traditional" menu, "gracious" service and "old-money", "country-club" airs; for maximum enjoyment, bring a "large wallet", "wear a jacket and tie" (it's required) and request a "tour of the hidden wine cellar downstairs"; P.S. there are also plenty of private party rooms.

26 Seats Ⓜ

23 | 16 | 19 | $37

168 Ave. B (bet. 10th & 11th Sts.), 212-677-4787; www.26seats.com
"'Cozy' is an understatement" at this beyond-"intimate" East Villager with exactly that many seats arranged in a "hippie pad" setting; the "terrific, inexpensive" French cooking "makes up for being unable to move" – this "great find has, alas, been found."

Two Boots

18 | 10 | 13 | $14

37 Ave. A (bet. 2nd & 3rd Sts.), no phone
42 Ave. A (3rd St.), 212-254-1919 ◑
74 Bleecker St. (B'way), 212-777-1033 ◑
Grand Central, lower level (42nd St. & Vanderbilt Ave.), 212-557-7992
30 Rockefeller Plaza, downstairs (bet. 49th & 50th Sts.), 212-332-8800
201 W. 11th St. (7th Ave. S.), 212-633-9096 ◑
514 Second St. (bet. 7th & 8th Aves.), Brooklyn, 718-499-3253
www.twoboots.com
"Pizza gone Mardi Gras" is the theme at this "groovy" chain best known for its "zesty" cornmeal-crust pies with "inventive names"; the "atmosphere is zip", unless you count the "*Romper Room* vibe", which is especially true of the "kid-filled", separately managed Brooklyn outlet.

212 ◑

17 | 17 | 16 | $45

133 E. 65th St. (bet. Lexington & Park Aves.), 212-249-6565;
www.212restaurant.com
It helps to be "young, beautiful and European" at this New American near Bloomie's that's "loud at lunch" and "wild at dinner" (credit the "fantastic" vodka list); maybe the food is "average" and the service "rude", but "somehow the show still goes on" here.

202 Cafe

21 | 17 | 18 | $32

Chelsea Mkt., 75 Ninth Ave. (bet. 15th & 16th Sts.), 646-638-1173
"Two favorite pursuits – shopping and eating" – meet at this Chelsea Market Mediterranean–cum–Nicole Farhi boutique where "surprisingly good" grub and garb are served simultaneously; some say the setup's "strange", but at least the food's "priced more reasonably than the clothes."

2 West

▽ 21 | 23 | 24 | $59

Ritz-Carlton Battery Park, 2 West St. (Battery Pl.), 917-790-2525;
www.ritzcarlton.com
"Uncrowded and underappreciated", this Financial District steakhouse offers the chance to rub elbows with "out-of-town big shots" staying at the Ritz; the "pricey" preparations are "beautifully presented" by a "classy" staff, and it's especially good for "business gatherings."

Ubol's Kitchen

▽ 22 | 10 | 18 | $23

24-42 Steinway St. (bet. Astoria Blvd. & 25th Ave.), Queens, 718-545-2874
You'd never know it from its looks, but this Astoria Thai "storefront" produces "consistently delicious" food, and "when you request it", it's blazingly hot; given its "hole-in-the-wall" quarters, locals like the "fast delivery."

Umberto's Clam House ❶   19 | 14 | 17 | $35

178 Mulberry St. (Broome St.), 212-343-2053; www.umbertosclamhouse.com
2356 Arthur Ave. (186th St.), Bronx, 718-220-2526;
www.umbertosclamhousebronx.com
"Go for the clams, baby" say fans of this "Little Italy must" that pulls
a "loyal" (and "touristy") following into its "nothing-fancy" digs for
surprisingly good "back-to-basics" Italian fare; outta-boro boosters
claim the "Bronx edition" is "better", but that's like debating the merits
of the Yankees and the Mets.

Una Pizza Napoletana Ⓜ⌀   24 | 10 | 12 | $25

349 E. 12th St. (bet. 1st & 2nd Aves.), 212-477-9950; www.unapizza.com
Pizza is a minimalist "art form" at this elemental East Village joint
whose "limited", no-slices menu has but "four options", each priced
at $16.95 (their hours depend on when they "run out of fresh dough");
realists remind "it's pizza, guys", but even they admit these pies
are amazingly good.

Uncle Jack's Steakhouse   24 | 19 | 22 | $65

440 Ninth Ave. (bet. 34th & 35th Sts.), 212-244-0005
39-40 Bell Blvd. (40th Ave.), Queens, 718-229-1100
www.unclejacks.com
Though "very traditional", these Garment District–Bayside steakhouses
produce "top-shelf dining experiences"; their "power-player"/
"expense-account" fans favor them for "big" slabs of meat, "stiff
drinks", "terrific" "old-school" service and "classy" environs, not for
their hefty bills.

Uncle Nick's   20 | 11 | 16 | $32

747 Ninth Ave. (bet. 50th & 51st Sts.), 212-245-7992
"Always busy", this "noisy-as-hell" Midtown Greek is home to perpetual "crowds" who attest to its "satisfying grilled fish, meze" and
the like, as well as its "outstanding value"; forget the "seedy" decor
and "desultory" service – just "ask for the flaming cheese."

Union Smith Café NEW   ▽ 18 | 17 | 18 | $26

305 Smith St. (Union St.), Brooklyn, 718-643-3293
"Could be pricier, but it's not" is the word on this "friendly" Carroll
Gardens New American, a "favorite new addition" to the Smith Street
scene thanks to its "solid" cooking and "casual, comfortable" vibe;
its "really nice outdoor dining space" makes it especially "pleasant"
in warmer months.

UNION SQUARE CAFE   27 | 22 | 26 | $63

21 E. 16th St. (bet. 5th Ave. & Union Sq. W.), 212-243-4020;
www.unionsquarecafe.com
The "granddaddy of Danny Meyer–ville" is this Union Square "classic"
that remains at the "top of every NYer's list" thanks to its "winning formula" of Michael Romano's "exemplary" New American cuisine, a
"wonderful" wine list, "warm" decor and "welcoming" staffers who
"make the experience unforgettable"; getting a reservation may be
the only hard part in what's otherwise a "truly happy experience."

Uno Chicago Grill ❶   14 | 12 | 13 | $22

432 Columbus Ave. (81st St.), 212-595-4700
220 E. 86th St. (bet. 2nd & 3rd Aves.), 212-472-5656
391 Sixth Ave. (bet. 8th St. & Waverly Pl.), 212-242-5230
South Street Seaport, Pier 17, 89 South St. (Fulton St.), 212-791-7999
55 Third Ave. (bet. 10th & 11th Sts.), 212-995-9668
9201 Fourth Ave. (92nd St.), Brooklyn, 718-748-8667
39-02 Bell Blvd. (39th Ave.), Queens, 718-279-4900

(continued)

Uno Chicago Grill

107-16 70th Rd. (bet. Austin St. & Queens Blvd.), Queens,
718-793-6700
37-11 35th Ave. (38th St.), Queens, 718-706-8800
www.unos.com

These low-budget outposts of "suburbia" deliver Chicago-style "deep-dish pizza" and "huge portions" of "run-of-the-mill" American food via a staff that "ranges from fantastic to demented"; skeptics ask "you made it in NYC, and you're eating here?"

Ureña NEW
25 | 12 | 21 | $62

37 E. 28th St. (bet. Madison Ave. & Park Ave. S.), 212-213-2328;
www.urena-nyc.com

Chef Alex Ureña is a "genius", "wowing diners" at this Gramercy "nouvelle" Spaniard with his "adventuresome" cuisine; however, such "clever food" comes at "high prices", and it's near-unanimous that the decor here "needs major help" – "kill" those "bright lights" already.

Uskudar
20 | 10 | 18 | $34

1405 Second Ave. (bet. 73rd & 74th Sts.), 212-988-2641

"Consistent" "homestyle" Turkish cuisine and a "welcoming" staff make this UES "hole-in-the-wall" "worth a try"; it may be "tiny and cramped" and its offerings "predictable", but the overall "quality" and "good-deal" prices mean it's "nearly always full."

Utsav
21 | 19 | 18 | $38

1185 Sixth Ave., 2nd fl. (enter on 46th St., bet. 6th & 7th Aves.),
212-575-2525; www.utsavny.com

"Handy to the Theater District", this "upscale" Indian's "quality" kitchen and "spacious" dining room make it a "pleasant respite" from the usual – "if you can find it"; the $15.95 lunch buffet is a "wonderful" way to sample its "exotic" oeuvre.

Uva ◗
20 | 21 | 20 | $37

1486 Second Ave. (bet. 77th & 78th Sts.), 212-472-4552

A "favorite" for "more than just pasta", this "affordable" UES Italian has an "extensive wine list" and "knowledgeable" staffers to help navigate it; the "cozy" setting includes a "romantic" garden, though its "noisy" "twentysomething" scene dampens any seductive aspirations.

Valbella ⊠ NEW
▽ 25 | 24 | 26 | $75

421 W. 13th St. (bet. 9th Ave. & Washington St.), 212-645-7777;
www.valbellany.com

Spun off from an esteemed Greenwich, CT, parent, this "top-notch" new Northern Italian is a "welcome addition" to the Meatpacking District thanks to its *bella* food, "impeccable service" and "sleek" decor; just know that "sticker shock" is part of the "fine-dining" experience here.

V&T ◗
18 | 8 | 13 | $20

1024 Amsterdam Ave. (bet. 110th & 111th Sts.), 212-666-8051

It's the "old-school" vibe and "cheap, tasty" pizzas and pastas that make this Morningside Heights Italian a Columbia student "standby"; "aging" decor and "cranky" service only add to its "cruddy charm."

Vatan ⓜ
20 | 20 | 22 | $34

409 Third Ave. (29th St.), 212-689-5666; www.vatanny.com

"Sit back, relax and pig out" is the routine at this all-you-can-eat Gramercy Indian where "attentive" staffers proffer an "endless supply" of vegetarian dishes for $22.95; capping off the "transporting" experience, the place resembles a "storybook Indian village."

Veniero's ◉

| 23 | 13 | 13 | $15 |

342 E. 11th St. (bet. 1st & 2nd Aves.), 212-674-7070; www.venierospastry.com
"Loosen your belt" before hitting this circa-1894 East Village Italian "pastry palace" where fans say the "divine cannoli" and "dizzying array" of other sweets are like "bites of heaven"; sour notes are "abrupt" service and lines so "long" that wags claim "people from opening day" are still on queue.

Vento ◉

| 18 | 18 | 17 | $47 |

675 Hudson St. (14th St.), 212-699-2400; www.brguestrestaurants.com
Despite "consistently good" food and a warm ambiance, Steve Hanson's "lively" Meatpacking District Italian isn't up to his normally high standards; still, it's a "place to be seen" with "outdoor seats" that are "perfect" for "watching the scene."

Vera Cruz ◉

| 17 | 13 | 15 | $23 |

195 Bedford Ave. (bet. N. 6th & 7th Sts.), Brooklyn, 718-599-7914
Drawing a "lively" crowd craving "slushy" margaritas and "large portions" of "better-than-average" "staples", this "no-attitude" Williamsburg Mexican is best enjoyed in the "lush candlelit garden"; service can be "slow" and the decor's "showing its age", but it's generally "reliable" and inexpensive.

VERITAS

| 27 | 22 | 25 | $85 |

43 E. 20th St. (bet. B'way & Park Ave. S.), 212-353-3700; www.veritas-nyc.com
"Serious" oenophiles swoon for Scott Bryan's Flatiron New American that's "famous" for a wine list the "size of *War and Peace*" along with a "drool"-worthy $72 prix fixe–only menu; although it offers "nothing but winners", the "understated room" and "personal service" make it feel almost as if it's "still undiscovered."

Vermicelli

| 20 | 16 | 17 | $29 |

1492 Second Ave. (bet. 77th & 78th Sts.), 212-288-8868;
www.vermicellirestaurant.com
It "sounds Italian" but "tastes Vietnamese" explain initiates of this Yorkville "local favorite" that's appreciated for its "savory" flavors and "bargain" box lunches; "grouchy" service garners grumbles, but not enough to outweigh the "excellent value."

Veselka

| 18 | 11 | 13 | $19 |

144 Second Ave. (9th St.), 212-228-9682 ◉
First Park, 75 E. First St. (1st Ave.), 347-907-3317 ⊘ NEW
www.veselka.com
For a "borscht fix" 24/7, try this popular East Village Ukrainian diner dispensing "delicious" "bubbe's-in-the-kitchen" classics in "huge portions"; service is "with a scowl" and decor at a minimum, but the "hip" clientele doesn't mind, given the "low prices"; N.B. have your pierogi alfresco at the new kiosk with 10 outdoor tables adjacent to the F station in First Park.

Vespa

| 19 | 18 | 18 | $37 |

1625 Second Ave. (bet. 84th & 85th Sts.), 212-472-2050; www.barvespa.com
A backyard garden that's a "perfect summer hideaway" makes this "cozy" UES Italian ideal "for couples"; its "casual-chic" interior and moderate prices are "pleasant" too, but some still find "nothing to write home about" here.

Via Brasil

| 20 | 16 | 19 | $38 |

34 W. 46th St. (bet. 5th & 6th Aves.), 212-997-1158;
www.viabrasilrestaurant.com
The next best thing to "having dinner in São Paulo", this "festive" Theater District Brazilian hosts a "nonstop" beeffest fueled by "high-

octane caipirinhas" and live music; "accommodating" service and "decent" prices further enhance the "satisfying" experience.

Via Emilia ☒⊄ — — — 1

47 E. 21st St. (bet. B'way & Park Ave. S.), 212-505-3072
Reopened a few blocks from its previous home, this Flatiron Italian offers the same inexpensive Emilia-Romagna–focused menu as before, plus a spacious, more stylish setting with a long bar and a front lounge.

Viand 16 7 16 $19

2130 Broadway (75th St.), 212-877-2888; www.viandnyc.com ●
300 E. 86th St. (2nd Ave.), 212-879-9425 ●
673 Madison Ave. (bet. 61st & 62nd Sts.), 212-751-6622 ⊄
1011 Madison Ave. (78th St.), 212-249-8250
"Fresh-carved turkey sandwiches" are the claim to fame of this "consistent", low-budget coffee shop quartet whose "large selection" of diner "staples" are served all day by "quick" "old NY"–style staffers; seating is "sardine"-worthy, but the "crowds" keep coming.

Via Oreto 21 15 19 $46

1121-23 First Ave. (bet. 61st & 62nd Sts.), 212-308-0828
It's "the best neighborhood place for blocks" claim locals with a taste for this "family-run" UES Italian doling out "homey", "mama"-style cooking; its overall "warm", "charming" style wins hearts, though "wallet-shrinking" tabs are less endearing.

Via Quadronno 22 14 16 $39

25 E. 73rd St. (bet. 5th & Madison Aves.), 212-650-9880;
www.viaquadronno.com
Think "Milano" "just off Madison" and you've got this "excellent" Italian source for panini, coffee and other "authentic" tastes "usually found only with a plane ticket"; no wonder its "shoebox" digs are "crowded" with "Euros" willing to overlook the "high prices."

ViceVersa ☒ 23 21 22 $52

325 W. 51st St. (bet. 8th & 9th Aves.), 212-399-9291;
www.viceversarestaurant.com
You'll make "the curtain without feeling rushed" at this "classy" West 50s Northern Italian where even those "without tickets" applaud the "never-goes-wrong" menu served in "low-key" quarters "overlooking a garden"; its "friendly, attentive staff" is clearly valued by patrons – and vice versa – with lunch being a special value.

Vico ●⊄ 20 15 18 $55

1302 Madison Ave. (bet. 92nd & 93rd Sts.), 212-876-2222
The Italian vico-tuals "never disappoint" at this Carnegie Hill "gathering spot" that's "packed" with "regulars"; "smiling" staffers who "know your name" are one reason it's deemed a "club worth joining", but even the "Park Avenue set" calls it "pricey" and dis the "no credit card" rule.

Victor's Cafe ● 21 19 19 $46

236 W. 52nd St. (bet. B'way & 8th Ave.), 212-586-7714; www.victorscafe.com
Revolucionarios revel in the "crave-inducing" Cuban fare and "fantastic energy" at this "little slice of Havana"; dissidents declare it "overpriced", but the masses counter that this "old standby" is a "good alternative" to the usual Theater District suspects.

VietCafé 20 19 17 $32

345 Greenwich St. (bet. Harrison & Jay Sts.), 212-431-5888;
www.viet-cafe.com
It's hard "saying nyet" to the "delightful" Viet food at this "excellent addition" to TriBeCa's "Greenwich Street lineup"; "cool, arty" decor

and "friendly" service also contribute to the overall "value", though "small portions" and "uncomfortable" seating are minuses.

View, The 16 | 26 | 19 | $61

Marriott Marquis Hotel, 1535 Broadway, 47th fl. (bet. 45th & 46th Sts.), 212-704-8900; www.nymarriottmarquis.com

"The name says it all" at this "revolving" 47th-floor Times Square surf 'n' turfer, which is "top of the heap" for "fabulous, romantic" vistas "from sunset to snowstorm"; "pricey" tabs are no surprise given its "touristy" tendencies, and remember: "it's called The View, not The Food."

Villa Berulia 21 | 17 | 22 | $50

107 E. 34th St. (bet. Lexington & Park Aves.), 212-689-1970; www.villaberulia.com

"How lucky" Murray Hill is to have this "dependable" Northern Italian "oldie", where "charming servers" deliver "nice-sized portions" of "the basics"; maybe the decor "could be more modern" and the tab less modern, but it's still great as a "romantic" place to "linger and *mangia*."

Village 19 | 19 | 18 | $42

62 W. Ninth St. (bet. 5th & 6th Aves.), 212-505-3355; www.villagerestaurant.com

Just the "right mix" of "tasty", modestly priced French–New American cuisine and "skylight"-enhanced "bistro-ish" ambiance ensure this "nifty" Villager remains a "crowd-pleaser"; "noise" from the "happening" front bar and sometimes-"spotty" service can irk, but for most, "reasonable" tabs mean all's forgiven.

Villa Mosconi Ⓢ 19 | 15 | 21 | $44

69 MacDougal St. (bet. Bleecker & Houston Sts.), 212-673-0390; www.villamosconi.com

"They greet you like an old friend" at this "old-line" Greenwich Village Italian serving "delicious" "red-sauce" basics with "family pride"; "loyal" longtimers appreciate that "no one rushes you" here and add that it "hasn't changed in years – and that's a compliment."

Vincent's ◐ 21 | 13 | 18 | $33

119 Mott St. (Hester St.), 212-226-8133; www.originalvincents.com

"Endless pasta" and red sauce "spiced to your taste" come "with a side of Pacino" at this "legendary" Little Italy centenarian; addicts who "need a dose" without the "touristy" "right-outta-the-*Sopranos*" "scene" "might want to buy a bottle of the sauce to take home."

Virgil's Real Barbecue ◐ 20 | 13 | 16 | $32

152 W. 44th St. (bet. B'way & 6th Ave.), 212-921-9494; www.virgilsbbq.com

"Cholesterol be damned", tourists and locals shout "yee-haw" and "strap on the feed bag" for the "best Southern north of the Mason-Dixon" at this "hopping" Times Square "BBQ joint"; despite the "frat house"–meets–"Wild West" vibe, fans heed the "cattle call."

Vittorio Cucina Ⓜ ▽ 21 | 17 | 19 | $44

308-310 Bleecker St. (bet. Grove St. & 7th Ave. S.), 212-463-0730; www.vittoriocri.com

Diners feel like "extended family" at this "lovely" Village Italian with a rotating menu of "interesting regional specialties" including trademark "not-to-be-missed" "Parmesan wheel pasta"; "vibrant paintings", a "pretty backyard" and moderate prices boost its "date-spot" appeal.

Vivolo 19 | 17 | 19 | $46

140 E. 74th St. (bet. Lexington & Park Aves.), 212-737-3533

Like going "back in time", this "quaint" East Side "hideaway" is championed by "older" types for its "reliable" Italian classics, "pleasant" service and "bargain" early-bird deal; "beautiful" fireplaces and dim lighting lend its "mahogany-paneled" duplex space a "romantic" air.

Vong
23 | 23 | 21 | $61

200 E. 54th St. (3rd Ave.), 212-486-9592; www.jean-georges.com
"A must" for spice lovers, Jean-Georges Vongerichten's "stylish" Midtown French-Thai offers the "winning combination" of cuisine that's an "epicurean delight", "impeccable" service and "golden-splendor" decor; since such "splash" comes with a "high" price tag, frugal foodies go for the lunch and pre-theater prix fixe "steals."

Vynl ●
19 | 21 | 17 | $24

754 Ninth Ave. (51st St.), 212-974-2003; www.vynl-nyc.com
As "groovy" as its name, this "retro" Hell's Kitchen diner still doles out "heaping portions" of "inexpensive" New American–Thai comfort fare, but now in "bigger, better" digs; service "with a smile" and "kitschy" bathrooms – "shrines" to Elvis, Cher, Dolly and Nelly – add to the "funky charm."

Waldy's Wood Fired Pizza
20 | 10 | 15 | $17

800 Sixth Ave. (bet. 27th & 28th Sts.), 212-213-5042; www.waldyspizza.com
"Imaginative" gourmet pies with "thin, fire-seared crusts" and a "fresh herb" bar elevate Waldy Malouf's popular Chelsea pizza parlor to a slice "above the usual"; however, given the "minimal" ambiance and service, many say "takeout is advisable."

WALLSÉ ●
26 | 22 | 24 | $66

344 W. 11th St. (Washington St.), 212-352-2300; www.wallse.com
"Vienna never had it this good" gush groupies of Kurt Gutenbrunner's "elegant" West Village Austrian, where the "incredible" updated classics are matched with "beautiful" wines and "expert" service; an evening in this "modern" space, accessorized with Julian Schnabel paintings, "will cost you", but to most it's "worth every pfenning."

Water Club
21 | 25 | 21 | $60

East River at 30th St. (enter on 23rd St.), 212-683-3333; www.thewaterclub.com
"Until your ship comes in", this "serene" East River barge's "tremendous" views will do for a "glamorous", "romantic" evening; the Traditional American fare and service are "high-quality" too, but "gazing at the river" is the "real delight" that justifies the "pricey" tabs.

Waterfront Ale House
19 | 13 | 17 | $23

540 Second Ave. (30th St.), 212-696-4104
155 Atlantic Ave. (bet. Clinton & Henry Sts.), Brooklyn, 718-522-3794
www.waterfrontalehouse.com
These "eclectic" saloons pour "superlative" microbrews, but it's the "surprisingly gourmet" pub grub and "polite" service that give them "flair"; they're as "rustic" and "cramped" as the competition, but "perfect" nonetheless for "unwinding" and "hoisting a cold one."

Water's Edge ⌧
21 | 24 | 20 | $61

East River & 44th Dr. (Vernon Blvd.), Queens, 718-482-0033;
www.watersedgenyc.com
This LIC New American "could coast" on its "unparalleled view" of the Manhattan skyline alone, but happily the "scrumptious" seafood is "worth writing home about" too; it's a good thing the "dreamy" river taxi to and from Midtown is free because you'll need "plenty of cash" here.

wd-50 ●
22 | 19 | 23 | $75

50 Clinton St. (bet. Rivington & Stanton Sts.), 212-477-2900; www.wd-50.com
The "culinary wilds" of Wylie Dufresne's LES American-Eclectic are "awe-inspiring" to devotees, "maddeningly" "eccentric" to doubters

and "memorable" to all; the service is "exceptional" and the atmosphere is "fun" and "low-key", but you may need "your Foucault textbook" to "interpret the menu" – and a fat wallet to pay for it.

West Bank Cafe ☻
19 | 15 | 18 | $41

Manhattan Plaza, 407 W. 42nd St. (bet. 9th & 10th Aves.), 212-695-6909; www.westbankcafe.com

Thanks to a new chef, this "casual" Theater District "standby" "has grown into its own" with "improved" New American food and a "friendly" staff; maybe the decor "doesn't bring down the house", but "gorgeous" flowers and ample "actor" sightings distract.

Westville
22 | 12 | 18 | $22

210 W. 10th St. (bet. Bleecker & W. 4th Sts.), 212-741-7971

"Terrific" "market vegetable dishes" and other "cheap", "wholesome comfort" choices make the perfect "cure" for a "home-cooking" jones at this "quirky" American in the West Village; surveyors' only bone to pick is that its "mini-space" is too "busy", producing "lines" and "tight squeezes."

Whole Foods Café
19 | 10 | 10 | $15

Time Warner Ctr., 10 Columbus Circle, downstairs (60th St. at B'way), 212-823-9600
4 Union Square S. (bet. B'way & University Pl.), 212-673-5388
www.wholefoods.com

The "best thing to happen to NYC" since the "automat", these self-serve "cafeterias" set inside the city's "crème de la crème" grocery stores couldn't be more "convenient" for pre-shopping pit stops, in which customers pick from an array of "fresh, bountiful" Eclectic prepared foods, go through the check-out line and then try to nab a "tough-to-find" cafe table; while this strikes many as a "wholesome paradise", the "per-pound prices add up", and "oh, those lines."

Whym NEW
20 | 20 | 19 | $43

889 Ninth Ave. (bet. 57th & 58th Sts.), 212-315-0088; www.whymnyc.com

A "real comer" in Hell's Kitchen, this "casual-chic", "super-friendly" New American proffers affordable, "no-gimmicks" "comfort food with a twist"; its "mod" digs are "minimalist" in style but maximalist in "noise."

'wichcraft
21 | 11 | 15 | $18

Bryant Park, Sixth Ave. (bet. 40th & 42nd Sts.), 212-780-0577 NEW
Equinox, 106 Crosby St. (Prince St.), 212-780-0577 NEW
60 E. Eighth St. (Mercer St.), 212-780-0577 NEW
555 Fifth Ave. (46th St.), 212-780-0577 NEW
397 Greenwich St. (Beach St.), 212-780-0577
Terminal Warehouse, 224 12th Ave. (bet. 27th & 28th Sts.), 212-780-0577
www.wichcraftnyc.com

"Bewitching" sandwiches "impeccably crafted" are the midday stars at this proliferating mini-chain from Craft's Tom Colicchio, serving "inspired" breakfasts and lunches ideal for those "on the run"; "premium" prices elicit grumbles, but to most it's an "amazing" "value" considering the "quality", pedigree and convenience.

Wicker Park NEW
– | – | – | M

1469 Third Ave. (83rd St.), 212-734-5600

This new UES Continental-American evokes an old NY pub with its long mahogany bar and mosaic tile floors (inherited from the former tenant, the long-running Martell's); the menu includes such novelties as filet mignon sliders.

Wild Ginger ☻

| 19 | 17 | 18 | $26 |

51 Grove St. (bet. Bleecker St. & 7th Ave. S.), 212-367-7200;
www.wildginger-ny.com
The "cheesy yellow sign outside" gives no hint of the "cool loungey vibe" within this West Village Thai "bamboo wonderland"; "caring" service and "lovely", "spicy-to-taste" food at "cheap" rates have locals calling it an outright "treasure trove."

Willie's Steak House ☻

| ▽ 22 | 16 | 20 | $27 |

1832 Westchester Ave. (bet. Taylor & Thieriot Aves.), Bronx, 718-822-9697;
www.williessteakhouse.com
At this "friendly" Bronx steakhouse, "intergenerational diners" gorge on economical slabs of beef and Latino dishes that are as "spirited" as the "great Latin jazz" performances on Wednesdays and Saturdays; "what it lacks in decor", it "makes up for in lively ambiance and service."

Wo Hop ☻⇗

| 20 | 5 | 13 | $16 |

17 Mott St. (Canal St.), 212-267-2536
A "great equalizer" where "cops dine with investment bankers", this 24/7 Chinatown "dowager's" "authentic" Cantonese food "satisfies even the skeptical Taoist"; it costs little more than "the price of a cup of coffee", so "brusque" service and "dumpy" decor are really beside the point.

Wolfgang's Steakhouse

| 25 | 20 | 20 | $69 |

409 Greenwich St. (bet. Beach & Hubert Sts.), 212-925-0350 **NEW**
4 Park Ave. (33rd St.), 212-889-3369
www.wolfgangssteakhouse.com
This Murray Hill steakhouse's "mouthwatering" meat comes via "pushy", "old-school" waiters in a "pleasing" (though "noisy") setting boosted by a "stunning vaulted ceiling"; yes, prices are "outrageous" and "waits" aren't unusual "even with reservations", but there's always the new (post-*Survey*) TriBeCa offshoot that's more spacious, if less atmospheric.

Wollensky's Grill ☻

| 22 | 16 | 19 | $51 |

201 E. 49th St. (3rd Ave.), 212-753-0444;
www.smithandwollensky.com
Expect the "same great steak" as its parent's but "without the pomp" – as well as "without the wait and price" – at this "casual", often "noisy" East Midtown offshoot of Smith & Wollensky; the "friendly" atmosphere, "old-school" waiters and late-night hours gratify "up-and-coming suits" gathering to "discuss their newest venture", be it business or romance.

Wondee Siam

| 22 | 7 | 16 | $21 |

792 Ninth Ave. (bet. 52nd & 53rd Sts.), 212-459-9057 ⇗
813 Ninth Ave. (bet. 53rd & 54th Sts.), 917-286-1726
With Thai food "this good" and "responsive service" to boot, it's no surprise these "dirt-cheap" Hell's Kitcheners "stand out" despite "hole-in-the-wall" digs; "if you like spicy", "ask for 'Thai style'", and if decor matters, "do takeout."

Won Jo ☻

| 21 | 13 | 16 | $31 |

23 W. 32nd St. (bet. B'way & 5th Ave.), 212-695-5815;
www.wonjokoreanrestaurant.com
"Wood-burning grills" enhance the "terrific" do-it-yourself barbecue at this 24/7 Garment District Korean, where "good prices" make up for "gracious" but "frantic" service and "smoky" atmosphere; you'd better like the food since you're the cook.

Woo Lae Oak

| 23 | 22 | 19 | $48 |

148 Mercer St. (bet. Houston & Prince Sts.), 212-925-8200;
www.woolaeoaksoho.com

"Grill-it-yourself" BBQ is the main attraction at this "hip" Korean, but the "Zen-chic atmosphere" is what makes it a "refreshing alternative" to "diner-style" K-towners; meanwhile, "very hot" (and "attentive") staffers distract from the "SoHo prices."

Wu Liang Ye

| 22 | 11 | 16 | $29 |

215 E. 86th St. (bet. 2nd & 3rd Aves.), 212-534-8899
338 Lexington Ave. (bet. 39th & 40th Sts.), 212-370-9648
36 W. 48th St. (bet. 5th & 6th Aves.), 212-398-2308

"Spicy means spicy" at this "efficient" Szechuan trio, but most agree the "tongue burn is worth it" given such "superb ingredients" and "authentic", "tangy" flavors; atoning for the "drab decor" and "cranky" staff are "eminently reasonable" tabs.

Xing

| 20 | 22 | 18 | $39 |

785 Ninth Ave. (52nd St.), 646-289-3010; www.xingrestaurant.com

For a "taste of the future" try this "friendly" Hell's Kitchen Asian fusion "find" offering a mix of affordable "nouveau" cooking and "retro swing music"; the bamboo-adorned main room, "sleek" Plexiglas bar and back "red-velvet dungeon" set an overall "soothing" scene.

X.o. ∌

| 19 | 9 | 12 | $16 |

148 Hester St. (bet. Bowery & Elizabeth St.), 212-965-8645
96 Walker St. (bet. Centre & Lafayette Sts.), 212-343-8339

These "crammed", "trendy" Hong Kong–style Chinatown cafes keep the "young Asian crowd" and others coming with their "taste-of-everything" offerings; really "cheap" prices ensure customers are "happy", though uneven service does not.

Xunta ❶

| 20 | 13 | 14 | $28 |

174 First Ave. (bet. 10th & 11th Sts.), 212-614-0620; www.xuntatapas.com

It's "anything but a siesta" at this "inexpensive" East Village Spaniard, where young types ready to "party" love the "strong" sangria and "delectable" tapas; sure, the seating "over barrels" is "uncomfortable", but live flamenco gives this "dive" a "festive" feel.

Yakitori Totto ❶

| ▽ 25 | 19 | 20 | $44 |

251 W. 55th St., 2nd fl. (bet. B'way & 8th Ave.), 212-245-4555

"Thumbs-up" for this "small", "modern" Midtown Japanese and its "super-authentic" yakitori (grilled skewers) like "little nuggets of divinity"; it's "pricey" and "there's always a wait" despite the "hidden" second-floor location, but most marvel "what's not to love?"

Yama

| 24 | 11 | 16 | $37 |

38-40 Carmine St. (bet. Bedford & Bleecker Sts.), 212-989-9330 Ⓢ
308 E. 49th St. (bet. 1st & 2nd Aves.), 212-355-3370 Ⓢ **NEW**
122 E. 17th St. (Irving Pl.), 212-475-0969 Ⓢ
92 W. Houston St. (bet. La Guardia Pl. & Thompson St.), 212-674-0935 ❶Ⓜ
www.yamarestaurant.com

"Gargantuan" "slabs" of "melt-in-your-mouth" sushi at "fair prices" add up to "long waits" at this "noisy" Japanese quartet; "low-rent" digs and "rushed" service don't deter the "insane crowds", so "be patient" or choose one of the Village branches (which take reservations).

York Grill

| 23 | 20 | 22 | $47 |

1690 York Ave. (bet. 88th & 89th Sts.), 212-772-0261

"Mature" Eastsiders happily travel "off the beaten path" to this "clubby" Yorkville New American, where the offerings are "surprisingly fine" and service "cordial"; ok, maybe the menu "could use updating", but for most customers "consistency is a good thing."

Yuca Bar ⭑ | 21 | 15 | 16 | $27 |

111 Ave. A (7th St.), 212-982-9533; www.yucabarnyc.com
Revelers "go for the sangria" and end up "staying for the tapas" at this "kickin'" Pan-Latin in the East Village, a zip code where "flavorful" meals don't come this "amazingly cheap" anymore; "sticky" tables and "slap-dash" service don't dampen the "party" vibe.

Yuka | 22 | 11 | 18 | $27 |

1557 Second Ave. (bet. 80th & 81st Sts.), 212-772-9675
"Beware the buttons flying" as patrons partake of the "$18 all-you-can-eat" sushi deal at this "perpetually jam-packed" Yorkville Japanese; while the "closet"-like digs and "rushed" service are no surprise, the mystery is "how do they" provide such "quality" "so cheap"?

Yuki Sushi ⭑ | 21 | 14 | 19 | $31 |

656 Amsterdam Ave. (92nd St.), 212-787-8200
"Well-priced", "inventive" sushi – whoever "thought to add peanuts to the avocado roll" was "brilliant" – brings "big crowds" to this "tiny", "friendly" UWS Japanese; those turned off by "pedestrian" environs opt for "speedy" delivery.

Yura & Co. | 20 | 11 | 14 | $24 |

1292 Madison Ave. (92nd St.), 212-860-8060
1645 Third Ave. (92nd St.), 212-860-8060
1659 Third Ave. (93rd St.), 212-860-8060
Even "picky diners" are satisfied by the "haute luncheonette" fare and "irresistible" pastries at these consistently "overrun" UES American bakery/cafes; those put off by "slow" service or "stroller"-packed setups "bring it home" instead.

Yuva NEW | ▽ 21 | 18 | 20 | $41 |

230 E. 58th St. (bet. 2nd & 3rd Aves.), 212-339-0090
This "promising" East Midtown newcomer balances "superb" traditional Northern Indian with "gentle" innovation", and serves it in a stylish old-meets-new space; if early reports bear out, "58th Street's Indian Row" has gained "another subcontinental winner."

Zabar's Cafe ⊘ | 18 | 5 | 9 | $15 |

2245 Broadway (80th St.), 212-787-2000; www.zabars.com
Holy blintzes, it's a "food lover's heaven" at this white Formica adjunct to the city's most renowned gourmet market, where "can't-be-beat" deli fare comes with a side of real West Side – "offensive" service and "elusive seating."

Zarela | 20 | 16 | 17 | $41 |

953 Second Ave. (bet. 50th & 51st Sts.), 212-644-6740; www.zarela.com
At Zarela Martinez's "jovial" bi-level Midtown "cantina", it's "Cinqo de Mayo every day" downstairs, but "clubby" and "quieter" upstairs; both floors feature "knockout margaritas", "sophisticated" Mexican cuisine and "welcoming" service, but may also need a little "sprucing up."

Zaytoons | 22 | 13 | 16 | $17 |

472 Myrtle Ave. (bet. Hall St. & Washington Ave.), Brooklyn, 718-623-5522
283 Smith St. (Sackett St.), Brooklyn, 718-875-1880
www.zaytoonsrestaurant.com
Offering a "delightful" "range of Middle Eastern" "home cooking", these BYO Brooklynites are "reliable" for a "hearty meal" that's also a "great deal"; given their minimal cost, it's easy to overlook "uneven" service and "lacking" decor.

Za Za ◑
19 | 15 | 18 | $36

1207 First Ave. (bet. 65th & 66th Sts.), 212-772-9997; www.zazanyc.com
"Trusty" from the "simple, unpretentious" Tuscan dishes to the "kind" staff, this "affordable" Italian is a perennial Eastsider's "go-to local"; maybe the "small" interior's just "average"-looking, but the "fabulous" garden recalls "Italy itself."

Zebú Grill
21 | 16 | 20 | $36

305 E. 92nd St. (bet. 1st & 2nd Aves.), 212-426-7500; www.zebugrill.com
"Bold flavors" help make this "low-profile" UES Brazilian a "comforting" "find", especially for meat eaters drawn to the "tasty" specialty churrasco; "cozy" quarters, "solicitous" service, "reasonable prices" and "super caipirinhas" keep the customers happy.

Zen Palate
19 | 16 | 17 | $26

663 Ninth Ave. (46th St.), 212-582-1669
34 Union Sq. E. (16th St.), 212-614-9291
www.zenpalate.com
"Nirvana for non-carnivores", this vegetarian twosome works "wonders" by convincingly turning tofu, tempeh and the like into quite "palatable" "faux meats"; holdouts call it "kind of bland", but most are "won over" by an "affordable" way to dine as a "herbivore."

Zerza ◑
▽ 20 | 20 | 18 | $34

304 E. Sixth St. (bet. 1st & 2nd Aves.), 212-529-8250; www.zerza.com
An "authentic Moroccan" on "Indian Row", this East Village stand-in for "Marrakech" supplies "flavorful" food via a "friendly but unskilled" crew; set in an atmospheric duplex, its "upstairs is quieter than the main floor" where the "hookahs" and the "belly dancers" hold court.

Zeytin
19 | 18 | 17 | $36

519 Columbus Ave. (85th St.), 212-579-1145
Thanks to "surefire" "authentic" food and a "comfy setting", this UWS Turk is about as close as you're likely to get to "being in Istanbul"; add "polite" (if sometimes "disorganized") service and it "fits the bill" for "unpretentious" dining "at a fair price."

Zip Burger ◑ NEW
– | – | – | I

300½ E. 52nd St. (bet. 1st & 2nd Aves.), 212-308-1308;
www.zipburger.com
Gleaming tile and chrome set the zippy tone at this new UES burger duplex offering veggie, salmon and turkey variations in addition to the classic beef versions; fans like its 'build-your-own-burger' approach, allowing you to put together your choice of bun, patty, topping, sauce and cheese.

Zócalo
20 | 16 | 17 | $38

174 E. 82nd St. (bet. Lexington & 3rd Aves.), 212-717-7772
Grand Central, lower level (42nd St. & Vanderbilt Ave.), 212-687-5666
www.zocalonyc.com
The "winning combination" of "zesty" "upscale Mexican" and "wicked margaritas" keeps 'em "happy" at this "bustling" East Side and Grand Central pair; while the decor isn't exciting, the eating is so "easy" and "satisfying", "who cares?"

Zoë
20 | 19 | 19 | $47

90 Prince St. (bet. B'way & Mercer St.), 212-966-6722;
www.zoerestaurant.com
A favored "drop-in" after "browsing the SoHo shops", this "busy" New American "stalwart" "still works" for "creative" cooking and "smiling" service; attractions like the open kitchen's "show" and a "scrumptious" brunch explain why it's "enduring" so well.

Zona Rosa ⓢ

19	17	18	$43

40 W. 56th St. (bet. 5th & 6th Aves.), 212-247-2800;
www.zonarosarestaurant.com

"Not your usual taco", this midpriced Midtown Mexican's "fine"
"nontraditional" offerings are a "treat" "for adults" especially when
backed up by primo margaritas; though some grumble it's in the
"overpriced" zone, most consider it a "keeper."

Zum Schneider ⊅

18	17	16	$25

107 Ave. C (7th St.), 212-598-1098; www.zumschneider.com

"It's always Oktoberfest" in Alphabet City at this "German beer hall"
"done right", where "boisterous" folk at "communal tables" wash
down "authentic" food with brew "by the liter"; "service is spotty",
but that hardly spoils the "cheapish" good cheer.

Zum Stammtisch

22	19	20	$33

69-46 Myrtle Ave. (bet. 70th St. & 69th Pl.), Queens, 718-386-3014;
www.zumstammtisch.com

This Glendale German "perennial" "still holds up" with "zaftig" portions of "awesome", "stick-to-your-ribs" "comfort food" and "efficient" service in a "dark", "old-world" setting; it doesn't miss a
"cliché", but for "real-deal" "*gemütlichkeit*" "this is the place."

Zutto

21	17	19	$38

62 Greenwich Ave. (bet. 7th Ave. S. & W. 11th St.), 212-367-7204
77 Hudson St. (Harrison St.), 212-233-3287
www.sushizutto.com

For a "spur-of-the-moment" "fish fix", these "neighborhood" Japanese
"standbys" supply "tasty, fresh" sushi in "simple", "serene" settings;
some sigh "ho hum", but given "competent" performance and "fair
prices", "what's not to like?"

Indexes

CUISINES
LOCATIONS
SPECIAL FEATURES

CUISINES

Afghan
Afghan Kebab/18/multi. loc.

African
Les Enfants Terribles/19/LES

American (New)
Above/18/W 40s
Aesop's Tables/22/Staten Is
Alma Grill/–/E 40s
Annisa/27/G Vill
applewood/25/Park Slope
Arabelle/23/E 60s
Aspen/18/Flatiron
Aureole/27/E 60s
Bar Americain/23/W 50s
barmarché/18/NoLita
Battery Gardens/18/Financial Dist
Beacon/22/W 50s
BG/19/W 50s
Bistro Ten 18/19/W 100s
Bliss/21/Sunnyside
BLT Prime/24/Gramercy
Blue Hill/26/G Vill
Blue Ribbon/25/multi. loc.
Blue Ribbon Bakery/23/G Vill
Boathouse/16/E 70s
Bouchon Bakery/23/W 60s
Bridge Cafe/21/Financial Dist
Bruckner B&G/22/Bronx
Bull Run/19/Financial Dist
Butter/19/E Vill
Café Botanica/21/W 50s
Cafe Condesa/–/W Vill
Café Opaline/19/E 50s
Cafe S.F.A./17/E 40s
Café St. Bart's/16/E 50s
CamaJe/21/G Vill
Candela/18/Union Sq
Caviar Russe/26/E 50s
Chestnut/23/Carroll Gdns
Chop't Creative/21/multi. loc.
Cibo/20/E 40s
Cité/21/W 50s
Cité Grill/20/W 50s
Clinton St. Baking/24/LES
Cocotte/21/Park Slope
Compass/22/W 70s
Cornelia St. Cafe/18/G Vill
Country/23/Gramercy
Craft/26/Flatiron

Craftbar/21/Flatiron
Cub Room/17/SoHo
davidburke/donatella/25/E 60s
David Burke/Bloom./19/E 50s
Deborah/22/G Vill
Devin Tavern/–/TriBeCa
Diner/22/Williamsburg
District/19/W 40s
dominic/21/TriBeCa
Downtown Atlantic/20/Boerum Hill
Dressler/–/Williamsburg
Duane Park Cafe/23/TriBeCa
Dublin 6/–/W Vill
DuMont/23/Williamsburg
Eatery/19/W 50s
Eleven Madison/26/Gramercy
elmo/16/Chelsea
Essex/19/LES
Etats-Unis/25/E 80s
Farm on Adderley/–/Ditmas Pk
Fillip's/21/Chelsea
Five Front/21/DUMBO
Five Points/22/NoHo
Fives/23/W 50s
Food Bar/17/Chelsea
44/20/W 40s
44 & X Hell's Kit./21/W 40s
Fred's at Barneys/20/E 60s
Freemans/21/LES
Garden Cafe/27/Prospect Hts
Gilt/–/E 50s
Giorgio's/Gramercy/23/Flatiron
good/20/W Vill
Gotham B&G/27/G Vill
Gramercy Tavern/28/Flatiron
Gramercy 24/17/Gramercy
Grocery, The/27/Carroll Gdns
Harrison, The/24/TriBeCa
Hearth/25/E Vill
Henry's End/25/Brooklyn Hts
HQ/22/SoHo
Ici/22/Ft Greene
Inside/22/G Vill
Isabella's/19/W 70s
Jane/21/G Vill
Josephina/18/W 60s
Jovia/–/E 60s
Kings' Carriage Hse./21/E 80s
Kitchen 22/20/Flatiron
Knickerbocker B&G/20/G Vill

Lenox Room/*19/E 70s*
Lever House/*22/E 50s*
Little Bistro/*20/Cobble Hill*
Little D Eatery/*24/Park Slope*
Little Giant/*23/LES*
Little Owl/*–/W Vill*
Maggie Brown/*19/Clinton Hill*
Magnolia/*18/Park Slope*
March/*26/E 50s*
Mark's/*22/E 70s*
Mas/*26/G Vill*
Mercer Kitchen/*21/SoHo*
Metrazur/*19/E 40s*
Modern, The/*25/W 50s*
Momofuku Ssäm Bar/*–/E Vill*
Monkey Bar/*19/E 50s*
Morgan, The/*–/Murray Hill*
My Most Favorite/*18/W 40s*
New Leaf/*20/Washington Hts.*
NoHo Star/*17/NoHo*
Norma's/*25/W 50s*
North Square/*23/G Vill*
Oceana/*26/E 50s*
One/*18/Meatpacking*
One if by Land/*23/G Vill*
101/*20/multi. loc.*
Orchard, The/*25/LES*
Ouest/*25/W 80s*
Pair of 8's/*21/W 80s*
Park Ave. Cafe/*23/E 60s*
Patroon/*20/E 40s*
Peacock Alley/*22/E 40s*
Perry Street/*25/W Vill*
per se/*28/W 60s*
Philip Marie/*20/W Vill*
Picket Fence/*19/Ditmas Pk*
Place, The/*22/multi. loc.*
Pop Burger/*19/Meatpacking*
Pre:Post/*–/Chelsea*
Prune/*24/E Vill*
Quaint/*–/Sunnyside*
Quality Meats/*23/W 50s*
Queen's Hideaway/*22/Greenpt*
Red Café/*22/Park Slope*
Red Cat/*24/Chelsea*
Redeye Grill/*20/W 50s*
Regency/*18/E 60s*
Relish/*21/Williamsburg*
Riingo/*20/E 40s*
River Café/*26/DUMBO*
Riverdale Garden/*24/Bronx*
Rose Water/*25/Park Slope*
Royal's Downtown/*24/Carroll Gdns*

Salt/*23/multi. loc.*
Sascha/*20/Meatpacking*
Saul/*27/Boerum Hill*
Savoy/*23/SoHo*
Seven/*17/Chelsea*
Sorrel/*23/Prospect Hts*
South Shore Club/*21/Staten Is*
Stone Park Café/*24/Park Slope*
Tabla/*25/Gramercy*
Taste/*22/E 80s*
Tasting Room/*27/multi. loc.*
Telepan/*25/W 60s*
Thalia/*20/W 50s*
Thor/*21/LES*
Tocqueville/*26/Union Sq*
Tossed/*19/multi. loc.*
Town/*24/W 50s*
Trestle on Tenth/*–/Chelsea*
Tribeca Grill/*22/TriBeCa*
12th St. B&G/*21/Park Slope*
212/*17/E 60s*
Union Smith Café/*18/Carroll Gdns*
Union Sq. Cafe/*27/Union Sq*
Veritas/*27/Flatiron*
Village/*19/G Vill*
Vynl/*19/W 50s*
Water's Edge/*21/LIC*
wd-50/*22/LES*
West Bank Cafe/*19/W 40s*
Whym/*20/W 50s*
York Grill/*23/E 80s*
Zoë/*20/SoHo*

American (Traditional)
Alexandra/*22/W Vill*
Algonquin/*16/W 40s*
Alias/*22/LES*
Alice's Tea Cup/*19/multi. loc.*
American Grill/*19/Staten Is*
Angus McIndoe/*17/W 40s*
Annie's/*18/E 70s*
Bamn!/*–/E Vill*
Barking Dog/*16/multi. loc.*
Bayard's/*24/Financial Dist*
Big John/*–/LES*
Brooklyn Diner/*16/W 50s*
Brouwers/Stone St./*–/Financial Dist*
Bryant Park/*16/W 40s*
Bubby's/*18/multi. loc.*
Burgers/Cupcakes/*–/Garment Dist*
Cafeteria/*18/Chelsea*
Chadwick's/*22/Bay Ridge*
Chat 'n Chew/*17/Union Sq*

Coffee Shop/15/Union Sq
Comfort Diner/16/multi. loc.
Cookshop/23/Chelsea
Corner Bistro/23/W Vill
Dirty Bird to-go/17/W Vill
E.A.T./19/E 80s
EJ's Luncheonette/16/multi. loc.
Elaine's/12/E 80s
Elephant & Castle/17/G Vill
ESPN Zone/12/W 40s
Fairway Cafe/19/W 70s
Fetch/17/E 90s
41 Greenwich/18/G Vill
Fraunces Tavern/16/Financial Dist
Friend of a Farmer/18/Gramercy
Good Enough to Eat/20/W 80s
Grand Tier/18/W 60s
Hard Rock Cafe/13/W 40s
Heartland Brew./14/multi. loc.
HK/17/Garment Dist
Home/21/G Vill
Houston's/20/multi. loc.
Hudson Cafeteria/19/W 50s
Jackson Hole/16/multi. loc.
Jerry's/18/SoHo
Joe Allen/17/W 40s
KitchenBar/–/Park Slope
Lodge/16/Williamsburg
Lorenzo's/23/Staten Is
Mama's Food /21/E Vill
Mayrose/16/Flatiron
Melba's/19/Harlem
Odeon/18/TriBeCa
O'Neals'/16/W 60s
Parsonage/21/Staten Is
Penelope/21/Murray Hill
Pershing Square/15/E 40s
Popover Cafe/18/W 80s
Revival/20/Harlem
Rock Center Cafe/18/W 50s
Sarabeth's/21/multi. loc.
S'mac/–/E Vill
Swifty's/17/E 70s
Tavern on Green/14/W 60s
Top of the Tower/15/E 40s
24 Prince/18/NoLita
21 Club/22/W 50s
Uno Chicago/14/multi. loc.
Water Club/21/Murray Hill
Westville/22/W Vill
Wicker Park/–/E 80s
Yura & Co./20/E 90s

Argentinean
Azul Bistro/21/LES
Buenos Aires/19/E Vill
Cambalache/21/E 60s
Chimichurri Grill/22/W 40s
Futura/19/Park Slope
Hacienda Argentina/20/E 70s
Industria Argentina/20/TriBeCa
Novecento/20/SoHo
Pampa/22/W 90s
Sosa Borella/19/multi. loc.

Asian
Aja/20/E 50s
Asia de Cuba/23/Murray Hill
Bright Food Shop/20/Chelsea
China Grill/22/W 50s
Chino's/20/Gramercy
Citrus B&G/20/W 70s
East Buffet/19/Flushing
Hispaniola/20/Washington Hts.

Asian Fusion
Buddakan/23/Chelsea
Buddha Bar/18/Meatpacking
Chow Bar/21/W Vill
Nana/20/Park Slope
Xing/20/W 50s

Australian
Bondi Road/–/LES

Austrian
Blaue Gans/21/TriBeCa
Café Sabarsky/21/E 80s
Danube/26/TriBeCa
Thomas Beisl/18/Ft Greene
Wallsé/26/W Vill

Bakeries
Amy's Bread/23/multi. loc.
Blue Ribbon Bakery/23/G Vill
Bouchon Bakery/23/W 60s
City Bakery/21/Flatiron
Clinton St. Baking/24/LES
Columbus Bakery/18/multi. loc.
La Bergamote/23/Chelsea
La Flor Bakery/24/Woodside
Le Pain Quotidien/20/multi. loc.
Mother's Bake Shop/21/Bronx
Once Upon a Tart/22/SoHo
Pies-N-Thighs/–/Williamsburg
Provence en Boite/–/Carroll Gdns
Yura & Co./20/E 90s

Barbecue

Blue Smoke/*21/Gramercy*
Brother Jimmy's/*16/multi. loc.*
Daisy May's/*23/W 40s*
Dallas BBQ/*15/multi. loc.*
Dinosaur BBQ/*22/Harlem*
Pioneer Bar-B-Q/*–/Red Hook*
Rack & Soul/*22/W 100s*
RUB BBQ/*19/Chelsea*
Virgil's Real BBQ/*20/W 40s*

Belgian

Café de Bruxelles/*21/W Vill*
Le Pain Quotidien/*20/multi. loc.*
Markt/*19/Meatpacking*
Petite Abeille/*18/multi. loc.*

Brazilian

Buzina Pop/*–/E 70s*
Cafe Colonial/*19/NoLita*
Carne Vale/*–/E Vill*
Casa/*20/W Vill*
Churrascaria/*22/multi. loc.*
Circus/*19/E 60s*
Coffee Shop/*15/Union Sq*
Green Field Churra./*19/Corona*
Malagueta/*27/Astoria*
Rice 'n' Beans/*21/W 50s*
Samba-Lé/*–/E Vill*
Via Brasil/*20/W 40s*
Zebú Grill/*21/E 90s*

British

A Salt & Battery/*19/W Vill*
ChipShop/Curry/*20/multi. loc.*
Spotted Pig/*22/W Vill*
Tea & Sympathy/*20/W Vill*

Burmese

Mingala Burmese/*20/multi. loc.*

Cajun

Delta Grill/*19/W 40s*
Great Jones Cafe/*20/NoHo*
Jacques-Imo's/*16/multi. loc.*
Mara's Homemade/*19/E Vill*
107 West/*17/multi. loc.*

Californian

Michael's/*21/W 50s*

Caribbean

A/*22/W 100s*
Brawta Caribbean/*20/Boerum Hill*

Don Pedro's/*21/E 90s*
Ideya/*21/SoHo*
Ivo & Lulu/*23/SoHo*
Mo-Bay/*21/multi. loc.*

Caviar

Caviar Russe/*26/E 50s*
Petrossian/*24/W 50s*

Cheese Steaks

Carl's Steaks/*22/multi. loc.*
99 Miles to Philly/*19/E Vill*
Philly Slim's/*18/multi. loc.*
Tony Luke's/*–/W 40s*

Chinese

(* dim sum specialist)
Au Mandarin/*19/Financial Dist*
Big Wong/*22/Ctown*
Café Evergreen*/*19/E 60s*
Chef Ho's/*20/E 80s*
Chiam/*21/E 40s*
Chinatown Brasserie*/*21/NoHo*
Chin Chin/*22/E 40s*
Dim Sum Go Go*/*20/Ctown*
Dumpling Man/*19/E Vill*
East Manor*/*18/Flushing*
Empire Szechuan/*15/multi. loc.*
Evergreen Shanghai*/*19/multi. loc.*
Excellent Dumpling*/*20/Ctown*
Flor de Mayo/*20/multi. loc.*
Friendhouse/*20/E Vill*
Fuleen Seafood/*23/Ctown*
Ginger/*20/Harlem*
Golden Unicorn*/*20/Ctown*
Goodies/*19/Ctown*
Grand Sichuan/*22/multi. loc.*
HSF*/*18/Ctown*
Hunan Park/*19/W 70s*
Ivy's Cafe/*19/W 70s*
Jing Fong*/*19/Ctown*
Joe's/*22/multi. loc.*
Kam Chueh/*23/Ctown*
King Yum/*17/Fresh Meadows*
Liberty View/*20/Financial Dist*
Lili's Noodle/*17/multi. loc.*
Mandarin Court*/*22/Ctown*
Mee Noodle Shop/*18/multi. loc.*
Mr. Chow/*22/E 50s*
Mr. Chow Tribeca/*–/TriBeCa*
Mr. K's/*24/E 50s*
Mr. Tang/*20/multi. loc.*
New Bo-Ky/*22/Ctown*

New Green Bo/*22/Ctown*
Nice*/*20/Ctown*
NoHo Star/*17/NoHo*
Ollie's/*16/multi. loc.*
Oriental Garden*/*24/Ctown*
Our Place/*21/multi. loc.*
Peking Duck/*22/multi. loc.*
Philippe/*22/E 60s*
Phoenix Garden/*24/E 40s*
Pig Heaven/*19/E 80s*
Ping's Seafood*/*21/multi. loc.*
Rickshaw Dumpling/*18/Flatiron*
Shanghai Cuisine/*20/Ctown*
Shanghai Pavilion/*22/E 70s*
Shun Lee Cafe*/*20/W 60s*
Shun Lee Palace/*23/E 50s*
Shun Lee West/*22/W 60s*
66/*20/TriBeCa*
Spicy & Tasty/*22/Flushing*
Sweet-n-Tart*/*20/Flushing*
Tang Pavilion/*21/W 50s*
Tse Yang/*24/E 50s*
Wo Hop/*20/Ctown*
Wu Liang Ye/*22/multi. loc.*
X.O.*/*19/Ctown*

Coffeehouses
Ferrara/*22/Little Italy*
French Roast/*15/multi. loc.*
Le Pain Quotidien/*20/multi. loc.*
Omonia Cafe/*18/multi. loc.*
Once Upon a Tart/*22/SoHo*
71 Irving Pl./*19/Gramercy*

Coffee Shops/Diners
Brooklyn Diner/*16/W 50s*
Burger Heaven/*16/multi. loc.*
Chat 'n Chew/*17/Union Sq*
Clinton St. Baking/*24/LES*
Comfort Diner/*16/multi. loc.*
Diner/*22/Williamsburg*
Edison Cafe/*14/W 40s*
EJ's Luncheonette/*16/multi. loc.*
Empire Diner/*15/Chelsea*
Googie's/*14/E 70s*
Jerry's/*18/SoHo*
Junior's/*18/multi. loc.*
La Taza de Oro/*18/Chelsea*
Mayrose/*16/Flatiron*
Teresa's/*18/multi. loc.*
Tom's/*18/Prospect Hts*
Veselka/*18/E Vill*
Viand/*16/multi. loc.*

Colombian
Tierras/*20/multi. loc.*

Continental
Battery Gardens/*18/Financial Dist*
Café Pierre/*20/E 60s*
Cebu/*23/Bay Ridge*
Four Seasons/*26/E 50s*
Gin Lane/*–/Chelsea*
Grand Tier/*18/W 60s*
Jack's Lux. Oyster/*24/E Vill*
Lake Club/*20/Staten Is*
Park Place/*21/Bronx*
Parsonage/*21/Staten Is*
Petrossian/*24/W 50s*
Russian Samovar/*17/W 50s*
Sardi's/*16/W 40s*
Wicker Park/*–/E 80s*

Creole
Delta Grill/*19/W 40s*
Jacques-Imo's/*16/multi. loc.*
Mara's Homemade/*19/E Vill*

Cuban
Asia de Cuba/*23/Murray Hill*
Azucar/*19/W 50s*
Cafecito/*22/E Vill*
Cafe Con Leche/*17/multi. loc.*
Café Habana/*22/NoLita*
Cuba/*21/G Vill*
Cuba Cafe/*18/Chelsea*
Cubana Café/*19/multi. loc.*
Havana Alma/*21/W Vill*
Havana Central/*18/multi. loc.*
Havana Chelsea/*19/Chelsea*
Son Cubano/*20/Meatpacking*
Victor's Cafe/*21/W 50s*

Delis
Artie's Deli/*18/W 80s*
Barney Greengrass/*23/W 80s*
Ben's Kosher Deli/*18/multi. loc.*
Carnegie Deli/*21/W 50s*
Ess-a-Bagel/*23/multi. loc.*
Katz's Deli/*23/LES*
Liebman's/*19/Bronx*
Mill Basin Deli/*21/Mill Basin*
Picnic Market/*21/W 100s*
Sarge's Deli/*19/Murray Hill*
Stage Deli/*19/W 50s*
Zabar's Cafe/*18/W 80s*

Dessert
Café Sabarsky/*21/E 80s*
ChikaLicious/*25/E Vill*
Chocolate Room/*24/Park Slope*

davidburke/donatella/*25/E 60s*
Ferrara/*22/Little Italy*
Junior's/*18/multi. loc.*
La Bergamote/*23/Chelsea*
Lady Mendl's/*21/Gramercy*
La Flor Bakery/*24/Woodside*
Max Brenner/*–/Union Sq*
My Most Favorite/*18/W 40s*
Omonia Cafe/*18/multi. loc.*
Once Upon a Tart/*22/SoHo*
Payard Bistro/*24/E 70s*
Room 4 Dessert/*19/NoLita*
Serendipity 3/*18/E 60s*
Sweet Melissa/*23/multi. loc.*
Veniero's/*23/E Vill*

Dominican
Cafe Con Leche/*17/multi. loc.*
El Malecon/*21/multi. loc.*
Hispaniola/*20/Washington Hts.*

Eastern European
Sammy's Roumanian/*17/LES*

Eclectic
Bamn!/*–/E Vill*
Bouley, Upstairs/*25/TriBeCa*
B. Smith's/*18/W 40s*
Carol's Cafe/*23/Staten Is*
Chubo/*21/LES*
Colors/*21/E Vill*
Delegates Dining Rm./*17/E 40s*
East Buffet/*19/Flushing*
East of Eighth/*16/Chelsea*
5 Ninth/*20/Meatpacking*
Good Fork/*25/Red Hook*
Harry's/*–/Financial Dist*
Hudson Cafeteria/*19/W 50s*
Josephina/*18/W 60s*
Josie's/*19/multi. loc.*
La Flor Bakery/*24/Woodside*
Little D Eatery/*24/Park Slope*
Maggie Brown/*19/Clinton Hill*
Monkey Town/*19/Williamsburg*
Nook/*21/W 50s*
Public/*23/NoLita*
Punch/*21/Flatiron*
Rice/*19/multi. loc.*
Schiller's/*19/LES*
Stanton Social/*24/LES*
Tour/*–/Chelsea*
Trinity Place/*–/Financial Dist*
wd-50/*22/LES*
Whole Foods/*19/multi. loc.*

Egyptian
Casa La Femme/*19/E 50s*

Ethiopian
Awash Ethiopian/*22/multi. loc.*
Ethiopian Rest./*17/E 80s*
Ghenet/*21/NoLita*
Meskerem/*19/multi. loc.*

European
A.O.C. Bedford/*23/G Vill*
August/*22/W Vill*
Bette/*19/Chelsea*
Employees Only/*17/W Vill*
Knife + Fork/*–/E Vill*

Filipino
Cendrillon/*22/SoHo*
Kuma Inn/*23/LES*

French
A/*22/W 100s*
Arabelle/*23/E 60s*
Asiate/*23/W 60s*
Barbès/*21/Murray Hill*
Bayard's/*24/Financial Dist*
Bouchon Bakery/*23/W 60s*
Bouillabaisse 126/*22/Carroll Gdns*
Bouterin/*19/E 50s*
Breeze/*21/W 40s*
Brick Cafe/*20/Astoria*
Bruno Jamais/*21/E 80s*
Buzina Pop/*–/E 70s*
Café Boulud/*28/E 70s*
Café des Artistes/*22/W 60s*
Café du Soleil/*20/W 100s*
Cafe Gitane/*19/NoLita*
Café Pierre/*20/E 60s*
Chanterelle/*27/TriBeCa*
Cocotte/*21/Park Slope*
Danal/*21/E Vill*
Darna/*21/W 80s*
Degustation/*25/E Vill*
Demarchelier/*17/E 80s*
Django/*21/E 40s*
Fillip's/*21/Chelsea*
Fives/*23/W 50s*
Fleur de Sel/*25/Flatiron*
44/*20/W 40s*
Gribouille/*–/Williamsburg*
Ici/*22/Ft Greene*
Indochine/*21/E Vill*
Ivo & Lulu/*23/SoHo*
Jack's Lux. Oyster/*24/E Vill*

Jolie/21/Boerum Hill
Kitchen Club/20/NoLita
La Baraka/21/Little Neck
La Bergamote/23/Chelsea
La Boîte en Bois/21/W 60s
La Grenouille/27/E 50s
La Mirabelle/21/W 80s
Le Cirque/24/E 50s
L'Ecole/25/SoHo
Le Colonial/19/E 50s
Le Grainne Café/20/Chelsea
Le Perigord/24/E 50s
Le Refuge Inn/26/Bronx
Le Rivage/20/W 40s
Les Enfants Terribles/19/LES
Mark's/22/E 70s
Mercer Kitchen/21/SoHo
Métisse/19/W 100s
Modern, The/25/W 50s
Montrachet/25/TriBeCa
Once Upon a Tart/22/SoHo
Park Terrace/21/Washington Hts.
per se/28/W 60s
Petrossian/24/W 50s
Picholine/26/W 60s
Picnic Market/21/W 100s
René Pujol/22/W 50s
Revival/20/Harlem
Sapa/22/Flatiron
Terrace in the Sky/22/W 100s
26 Seats/23/E Vill
Vong/23/E 50s

French (Bistro)

Alouette/19/W 90s
A.O.C./19/W Vill
Bandol Bistro/17/E 70s
BarTabac/18/Boerum Hill
Belleville/18/Park Slope
Bistro Cassis/21/W 70s
Bistro Citron/–/W 80s
Bistro du Nord/18/E 90s
Bistro Les Amis/20/SoHo
Bistro Le Steak/18/E 70s
Bistro 61/19/E 60s
Cafe Joul/18/E 50s
Cafe Loup/19/G Vill
Cafe Luluc/19/Cobble Hill
Cafe Luxembourg/19/W 70s
Cafe Un Deux/16/W 40s
CamaJe/21/G Vill
Capsouto Frères/23/TriBeCa
Casimir/19/E Vill

Chelsea Bistro/20/Chelsea
Chez Jacqueline/18/G Vill
Chez Josephine/20/W 40s
Chez Napoléon/19/W 50s
Chez Oskar/19/Ft Greene
Cornelia St. Cafe/18/G Vill
Cosette/19/Murray Hill
Country Café/20/SoHo
db Bistro Moderne/25/W 40s
Deux Amis/19/E 50s
Félix/17/SoHo
Flea Mkt. Cafe/19/E Vill
Florent/19/Meatpacking
French Roast/15/multi. loc.
Gascogne/23/Chelsea
Gavroche/19/W Vill
Jack/17/G Vill
Jarnac/21/W Vill
Jean Claude/22/SoHo
JoJo/24/E 60s
Jubilee/22/E 50s
La Bonne Soupe/18/W 50s
La Goulue/19/E 60s
La Lunchonette/21/Chelsea
La Mangeoire/19/E 50s
La Mediterranée/18/E 50s
Landmarc/23/TriBeCa
La Petite Auberge/19/Gramercy
La Ripaille/19/W Vill
Le Bilboquet/20/E 60s
Le Boeuf/Mode/21/E 80s
Le Gamin/19/multi. loc.
Le Gigot/25/G Vill
Le Jardin Bistro/20/NoLita
Le Madeleine/20/W 40s
Le Père Pinard/19/LES
Le Refuge/21/E 80s
Le Sans Souci/22/Astoria
Les Halles/20/multi. loc.
Le Singe Vert/19/Chelsea
Le Tableau/23/E Vill
Le Veau d'Or/21/E 60s
L'Express/17/Flatiron
Loulou/22/Ft Greene
Lucien/21/E Vill
Madison Bistro/19/Murray Hill
Mon Petit Cafe/18/E 60s
Montparnasse/20/E 50s
Moutarde/18/Park Slope
Nice Matin/20/W 70s
Odeon/18/TriBeCa
Paradou/19/Meatpacking
Paris Commune/19/W Vill

Paris Match/*18/E 60s*
Park Bistro/*20/Gramercy*
Pascalou/*21/E 90s*
Pastis/*20/Meatpacking*
Patois/*22/Carroll Gdns*
Payard Bistro/*24/E 70s*
Provence/*21/SoHo*
Provence en Boite/*–/Carroll Gdns*
Quatorze Bis/*21/E 70s*
Quercy/*22/Cobble Hill*
Raoul's/*22/SoHo*
Rouge/*20/Forest Hills*
Sherwood Cafe/*19/Boerum Hill*
Steak Frites/*17/Union Sq*
Table d'Hôte/*20/E 90s*
Tartine/*22/W Vill*
Tournesol/*23/LIC*
Village/*19/G Vill*

French (Brasserie)
Aix Brasserie/*21/W 80s*
Artisanal/*23/Murray Hill*
Balthazar/*23/SoHo*
Brasserie/*19/E 50s*
Brasserie 8½/*21/W 50s*
Brasserie Julien/*17/E 80s*
Brasserie LCB/*23/W 50s*
Brasserie Ruhlmann/*19/W 50s*
Café d'Alsace/*22/E 80s*
Café Gray/*25/W 60s*
Cercle Rouge/*15/TriBeCa*
Cité Grill/*20/W 50s*
Jacques/*19/multi. loc.*
L'Absinthe/*22/E 60s*
Le Marais/*21/W 40s*
Le Monde/*17/W 100s*
Maison/*22/W 50s*
Marseille/*20/W 40s*
Orsay/*17/E 70s*
Pershing Square/*15/E 40s*
Pigalle/*17/W 40s*
Rue 57/*18/W 50s*

French (New)
Alain Ducasse/*27/W 50s*
Bouley/*28/TriBeCa*
Carlyle/*22/E 70s*
Daniel/*28/E 60s*
Elephant, The/*21/E Vill*
Jean Georges/*28/W 60s*
L'Atelier/Joël Robuchon/*–/E 50s*
Le Bernardin/*28/W 50s*
Pascalou/*21/E 90s*
Savann/*20/W 70s*

718/*22/Astoria*
360/*23/Red Hook*
Tocqueville/*26/Union Sq*
Triomphe/*24/W 40s*

German
Blaue Gans/*21/TriBeCa*
Hallo Berlin/*18/W 40s*
Heidelberg/*17/E 80s*
Killmeyer Bavarian/*19/Staten Is*
Nurnberger Bierhaus/*19/Staten Is*
Rolf's/*16/Gramercy*
Zum Schneider/*18/E Vill*
Zum Stammtisch/*22/Glendale*

Greek
Agnanti/*24/multi. loc.*
Ammos/*22/multi. loc.*
Avra/*23/E 40s*
Cafe Bar/*19/Astoria*
Cávo/*19/Astoria*
Demetris/*24/Astoria*
Eliá/*25/Bay Ridge*
Elias Corner/*21/Astoria*
En Plo/*22/W 70s*
Ethos/*21/Murray Hill*
Greek Kitchen/*20/W 50s*
Ithaka/*20/E 80s*
Kellari Taverna/*21/W 40s*
Kyma/*18/W 40s*
Meltemi/*19/E 50s*
Metsovo/*18/W 70s*
Milos/*26/W 50s*
Molyvos/*22/W 50s*
Omonia Cafe/*18/multi. loc.*
Onera/*25/W 70s*
Parea/*–/Gramercy*
Periyali/*23/Flatiron*
Ploes/*23/Astoria*
Pylos/*23/E Vill*
S'Agapo/*20/Astoria*
Snack/*22/SoHo*
Snack/*21/W Vill*
Stamatis/*21/Astoria*
Symposium/*20/W 100s*
Taverna Kyclades/*24/Astoria*
Telly's Taverna/*22/Astoria*
Thalassa/*23/TriBeCa*
Trata Estiatorio/*21/E 70s*
Uncle Nick's/*20/W 50s*

Hamburgers
Better Burger/*15/multi. loc.*
Big Nick's Burger/*18/W 70s*

Blue 9 Burger/*19/E Vill*
Burger Heaven/*16/multi. loc.*
burger joint/Parker M./*24/W 50s*
Burger Joint/*20/Gramercy*
Burgers/Cupcakes/*–/Garment Dist*
Corner Bistro/*23/W Vill*
Cozy Soup/Burger/*18/G Vill*
db Bistro Moderne/*25/W 40s*
DuMont/*23/Williamsburg*
goodburger/*18/E 40s*
Hard Rock Cafe/*13/W 40s*
Island Burgers/*21/W 50s*
Jackson Hole/*16/multi. loc.*
J.G. Melon/*21/E 70s*
New York Burger/*17/Flatiron*
P.J. Clarke's/*17/multi. loc.*
Pop Burger/*19/Meatpacking*
Rare B&G/*21/multi. loc.*
Shake Shack/*23/Flatiron*
Sparky's American/*18/multi. loc.*
Zip Burger/*–/E 50s*

Hawaii Regional
Roy's NY/*24/Financial Dist*

Health Food
Blue/Green/*20/multi. loc.*
Candle Cafe/*22/E 70s*
Candle 79/*24/E 70s*
Energy Kitchen/*17/multi. loc.*
Pump Energy Food/*19/multi. loc.*
Sacred Chow/*21/G Vill*
Spring St. Natural/*19/NoLita*
Whole Foods/*19/multi. loc.*

Hot Dogs
F & B/*18/multi. loc.*
Gray's Papaya/*20/multi. loc.*
Papaya King/*20/multi. loc.*
Sparky's American/*18/multi. loc.*

Ice Cream Parlors
Emack & Bolio's/*25/multi. loc.*
L & B Spumoni/*23/Bensonhurst*
Serendipity 3/*18/E 60s*

Indian
Adä/*24/E 50s*
Amma/*23/E 50s*
Angon on Sixth/*21/E Vill*
Baluchi's/*18/multi. loc.*
Banjara/*22/E Vill*
Bay Leaf/*19/W 50s*
Bombay Palace/*20/W 50s*

Bombay Talkie/*20/Chelsea*
Brick Lane Curry/*22/E Vill*
Bukhara Grill/*21/E 40s*
Cafe Spice/*18/multi. loc.*
Chennai Garden/*21/Gramercy*
ChipShop/Curry/*20/Park Slope*
Chola/*24/E 50s*
Copper Chimney/*20/Gramercy*
Curry Leaf/*19/multi. loc.*
Dakshin Indian/*22/E 80s*
Dawat/*23/E 50s*
Delhi Palace/*21/Jackson Hts*
dévi/*24/Flatiron*
Diwan/*21/E 40s*
Hampton Chutney/*21/multi. loc.*
Haveli/*20/E Vill*
Indus Valley/*23/W 100s*
Jackson Diner/*22/Jackson Hts*
Jewel of India/*21/W 40s*
Kati Roll Co./*22/multi. loc.*
Leela Lounge/*26/G Vill*
Mint/*23/E 50s*
Mughlai/*20/W 70s*
Pongal/*21/multi. loc.*
Salaam Bombay/*20/TriBeCa*
Sapphire Indian/*20/W 60s*
Saravanaas/*22/Gramercy*
Surya/*23/W Vill*
Swagat Indian/*23/W 70s*
Tamarind/*24/Flatiron*
Utsav/*21/W 40s*
Vatan/*20/Gramercy*
Yuva/*21/E 50s*

Irish
Moran's Chelsea/*18/Chelsea*
Neary's/*15/E 50s*

Israeli
Azuri Cafe/*24/W 50s*
Miriam/*22/Park Slope*
Rectangles/*18/E 70s*

Italian
(N=Northern; S=Southern)
Abboccato/*23/W 50s*
Acappella (N)/*24/TriBeCa*
Acqua Pazza/*21/W 50s*
Adrienne's Pizza/*24/Financial Dist*
Agata & Valentina (S)/*18/E 70s*
Al Di La (N)/*26/Park Slope*
Aleo/*19/Flatiron*
Al Forno Pizza/*19/E 70s*

Alfredo of Rome (S)/*19/W 40s*
Aliseo Osteria/*21/Prospect Hts*
Alto/*25/E 50s*
Ama (S)/*22/SoHo*
Amarone/*19/W 40s*
Amici Amore/*20/Astoria*
Amorina/*22/Prospect Hts*
Angelina's/*22/Staten Is*
Angelo's/Mulberry (S)/*23/Little Italy*
Anthony's (S)/*20/Park Slope*
Antica Venezia/*23/W Vill*
Antonucci/*22/E 80s*
ápizz/*24/LES*
Aquaterra/*20/E 50s*
Areo/*25/Bay Ridge*
Arezzo (N)/*22/Flatiron*
Arqua (N)/*24/TriBeCa*
Arté Café/*17/W 70s*
Arturo's Pizzeria/*21/G Vill*
Aurora (N)/*25/Williamsburg*
A Voce/*24/Gramercy*
Babbo/*27/G Vill*
Baci & Abbracci/*–/Williamsburg*
Baldoria/*21/W 40s*
Bamonte's/*22/Williamsburg*
Baraonda/*19/E 70s*
Barbetta (N)/*20/W 40s*
Barbone/*–/E Vill*
Barbuto/*21/W Vill*
Barolo/*18/SoHo*
Bar Pitti/*22/G Vill*
Basilica/*20/W 40s*
Basso Est/*23/LES*
Basta Pasta/*21/Flatiron*
Becco/*21/W 40s*
Beccofino/*24/Bronx*
Bella Blu (N)/*19/E 70s*
Bella Via/*21/LIC*
Bellavitae/*22/G Vill*
Bello/*19/W 50s*
Beppe (N)/*23/Flatiron*
Bettola/*21/W 70s*
Bianca (N)/*23/NoHo*
Bice (N)/*20/E 50s*
Biricchino (N)/*18/Chelsea*
Bocca/*19/Staten Is*
Bocca Lupo/*–/Cobble Hill*
Bocelli/*24/Staten Is*
Bond 45/*18/W 40s*
Boom (S)/*20/SoHo*
Borgo Antico/*17/G Vill*
Bottega del Vino/*22/E 50s*
Bottino (N)/*18/Chelsea*

Bravo Gianni (N)/*22/E 60s*
Bread Tribeca/*19/TriBeCa*
Bricco/*19/W 50s*
Brick Cafe/*20/Astoria*
Brio/*19/E 60s*
Cacio e Pepe (S)/*22/E Vill*
Café Fiorello/*20/W 60s*
Caffe Bondi (S)/*23/Staten Is*
Caffe Buon Gusto/*17/multi. loc.*
Caffe Cielo (N)/*19/W 50s*
Caffe Grazie/*18/E 80s*
Caffe Linda/*19/E 40s*
Caffé/Green/*21/Bayside*
Campagnola/*24/E 70s*
Canaletto (N)/*21/E 60s*
Cara Mia/*19/W 40s*
Carbone (S)/*–/Garment Dist*
Carino (S)/*20/E 80s*
Carmine's (S)/*20/multi. loc.*
Cascina/*18/W 40s*
Celeste (S)/*24/W 80s*
Cellini (N)/*21/E 50s*
Centolire (N)/*20/E 80s*
'Cesca (S)/*23/W 70s*
Chianti/*22/Bay Ridge*
Cibo (N)/*20/E 40s*
Cipriani Dolci/*19/E 40s*
Cipriani Dwntn/*20/SoHo*
Coco Pazzo (N)/*22/E 70s*
Col Legno (N)/*19/E Vill*
Coppola's/*19/multi. loc.*
Cortina (N)/*19/E 70s*
Crispo (N)/*22/W Vill*
Cucina di Pesce/*17/E Vill*
Da Andrea (N)/*23/W Vill*
Da Antonio/*20/E 50s*
Da Ciro/*21/Murray Hill*
Da Filippo (N)/*21/E 60s*
Da Nico/*20/Little Italy*
Da Noi (N)/*23/Staten Is*
Da Silvano (N)/*20/G Vill*
Da Tommaso (N)/*20/W 50s*
Da Umberto (N)/*24/Chelsea*
DeGrezia/*23/E 50s*
Del Posto/*23/Chelsea*
Destino/*17/E 50s*
Divino (N)/*19/E 80s*
dominic/*21/TriBeCa*
Dominick's/*22/Bronx*
Don Giovanni/*18/multi. loc.*
Don Peppe/*24/Ozone Pk*
Due (N)/*21/E 70s*
Ecco/*22/TriBeCa*

Cuisines

Elaine's/*12/E 80s*
Elio's/*23/E 80s*
English is Italian/*18/E 40s*
Ennio & Michael/*19/G Vill*
Enzo's/*24/Bronx*
Erminia (S)/*25/E 80s*
Esca (S)/*24/W 40s*
etcetera etcetera/*22/W 40s*
Falai/*24/LES*
F & J Pine/*22/Bronx*
Felidia/*25/E 50s*
Ferdinando's (S)/*22/Carroll Gdns*
Fiamma Osteria/*25/SoHo*
50 Carmine (N)/*20/G Vill*
F.illi Ponte/*22/TriBeCa*
Finestra/*18/E 70s*
Fino/*20/multi. loc.*
Fiorentino's (S)/*21/Gravesend*
Firenze (N)/*20/E 80s*
Fragole/*23/Carroll Gdns*
Frank/*23/E Vill*
Frankies Spuntino/*23/multi. loc.*
Frank's/*20/Chelsea*
Franny's/*23/Prospect Hts*
Fred's at Barneys (N)/*20/E 60s*
Fresco by Scotto (N)/*22/E 50s*
Fresco on the Go (N)/*20/E 50s*
Futura/*19/Park Slope*
Gabriel's (N)/*22/W 60s*
Gargiulo's (S)/*21/Coney Is*
Gennaro/*24/W 90s*
Giambelli/*20/E 50s*
Gigino/*21/multi. loc.*
Gino/*19/E 60s*
Giorgione/*21/SoHo*
Girasole/*21/E 80s*
Gnocco Caffe (N)/*23/E Vill*
Gonzo/*22/G Vill*
Googie's/*14/E 70s*
Grace's Trattoria/*18/E 70s*
Gradisca/*20/G Vill*
Grifone (N)/*23/E 40s*
Grotta Azzurra (S)/*17/Little Italy*
Gusto/*21/G Vill*
Hearth (N)/*25/E Vill*
I Coppi (N)/*22/E Vill*
Il Bagatto/*22/E Vill*
Il Bastardo (N)/*18/Chelsea*
Il Buco/*25/NoHo*
Il Cantinori (N)/*22/G Vill*
Il Corallo/*22/SoHo*
Il Cortile/*23/Little Italy*
Il Fornaio/*23/Little Italy*

Il Gattopardo (S)/*23/W 50s*
Il Giglio (N)/*26/TriBeCa*
Il Mattone/*20/TriBeCa*
Il Mulino/*27/G Vill*
Il Nido (N)/*23/E 50s*
Il Palazzo/*21/Little Italy*
Il Postino/*23/E 40s*
Il Riccio (S)/*20/E 70s*
Il Tinello (N)/*24/W 50s*
Il Vagabondo/*18/E 60s*
'ino/*24/G Vill*
'inoteca/*23/LES*
Intermezzo/*19/Chelsea*
I Tre Merli (N)/*18/multi. loc.*
I Trulli/*23/Gramercy*
John's of 12th St./*19/E Vill*
Jovia/*–/E 60s*
La Bottega/*17/Chelsea*
La Cantina Toscana (N)/*24/E 60s*
La Focaccia/*19/W Vill*
La Giara/*20/Murray Hill*
La Gioconda/*21/E 50s*
La Grolla (N)/*20/W 70s*
La Lanterna/*19/G Vill*
La Locanda Vini/*21/W 40s*
Lamarca (S)/*18/Gramercy*
La Masseria (S)/*22/W 40s*
La Mela/*18/Little Italy*
La Pizza Fresca/*22/Flatiron*
La Rivista/*19/W 40s*
Lattanzi (S)/*22/W 40s*
Lavagna/*24/E Vill*
La Vela (N)/*18/W 70s*
La Villa Pizzeria/*21/multi. loc.*
La Vineria/*21/W 50s*
Le Zie 2000 (N)/*21/Chelsea*
Lil' Frankie Pizza/*22/E Vill*
L'Impero/*26/E 40s*
Lisca (N)/*19/W 90s*
Little Charlie's (S)/*22/NoLita*
Locanda Vini/Olii (N)/*23/Clinton Hill*
Luca/*20/E 80s*
Luna Piena/*18/E 50s*
Lupa/*25/G Vill*
Lusardi's (N)/*23/E 70s*
Luxia/*19/W 40s*
Macelleria (N)/*19/Meatpacking*
Madison's/*20/Bronx*
Malatesta (N)/*21/W Vill*
Manducatis/*22/LIC*
Manetta's/*22/LIC*
Mangiarini/*19/E 80s*
Marco Polo/*21/Carroll Gdns*

Maremma (N)/19/W Vill
Maria Pia/21/W 50s
Marinella/23/G Vill
Mario's (S)/22/Bronx
Maruzzella/21/E 70s
Maurizio Trattoria (N)/20/G Vill
Max/23/E Vill
Max SoHa (S)/22/W 100s
Mediterraneo/19/E 60s
Mezzaluna/19/E 70s
Mezzogiorno (N)/20/SoHo
Minetta Tavern (N)/18/G Vill
Monte's/19/G Vill
Nanni (N)/23/E 40s
Naples 45 (S)/17/E 40s
Nello (N)/18/E 60s
Nick's/22/multi. loc.
Nicola's/22/E 80s
Nino's (N)/21/multi. loc.
Nocello (N)/21/W 50s
Nonna/17/W 80s
Noodle Pudding/25/Brooklyn Hts
Novitá (N)/23/Gramercy
One 83 (N)/19/E 80s
101/20/multi. loc.
Orso (N)/22/W 40s
Osso Buco/17/multi. loc.
Osteria al Doge (N)/20/W 40s
Osteria del Circo (N)/22/W 50s
Osteria del Sole (S)/21/W Vill
Osteria Gelsi (S)/24/Garment Dist
Osteria Laguna/22/E 40s
Otto/21/G Vill
Palà (S)/21/LES
Panino'teca 275/24/Carroll Gdns
Paola's/22/E 80s
Paper Moon (N)/20/E 50s
Pappardella/19/W 70s
Park Side/24/Corona
Parma (N)/21/E 70s
Pasquale's Rigoletto/22/Bronx
Pasticcio/19/Murray Hill
Patsy's (S)/21/W 50s
Paul & Jimmy's/18/Gramercy
Peasant/22/NoLita
Pellegrino's/22/Little Italy
Pepe...To Go/19/multi. loc.
Pepolino (N)/23/TriBeCa
Perbacco/24/E Vill
Per Lei/19/E 70s
Pescatore/19/E 50s
Petaluma/18/E 70s
Pete's Downtown/17/DUMBO

Petrarca.Vino/21/TriBeCa
Piadina/21/G Vill
Piano Due/26/W 50s
Piccola Venezia/25/Astoria
Piccolo Angolo/24/W Vill
Pietrasanta/20/multi. loc.
Pietro's/22/E 40s
Pinocchio/23/E 90s
Piola/19/G Vill
Pisticci/23/W 100s
Pó/25/G Vill
Pomodoro Rosso/21/W 70s
Ponticello/22/Astoria
Porchetta/–/Cobble Hill
Portofino Grille/17/E 60s
Portofino's/20/Bronx
Positano (S)/20/Little Italy
Primavera (N)/23/E 80s
Primola/22/E 60s
Puttanesca/20/W 50s
Quartino (N)/21/multi. loc.
Quattro Gatti/19/E 80s
Queen/24/Brooklyn Hts
Rainbow Room (N)/20/W 40s
Rao's (S)/21/Harlem
Regional/18/W 90s
Remi/21/W 50s
Re Sette/20/W 40s
Risotteria/21/G Vill
Riverview/17/LIC
Roberto Passon/22/W 50s
Roberto's/27/Bronx
Roc/21/TriBeCa
Rocco (S)/19/G Vill
Rossini's (N)/23/Murray Hill
Rughetta (S)/23/E 80s
Sac's Place/21/Astoria
Sal Anthony's/18/multi. loc.
Salute! (N)/19/Murray Hill
Sambuca/19/W 70s
San Domenico/22/W 50s
San Luigi (S)/–/W 70s
San Pietro/23/E 50s
Sant Ambroeus (N)/21/multi. loc.
Sapori D'Ischia/24/Woodside
Savoia/21/Carroll Gdns
Scaletta (N)/21/W 70s
Scalinatella/25/E 60s
Scalini Fedeli (N)/26/TriBeCa
Scarlatto (N)/23/W 40s
Scottadito (N)/21/Park Slope
Serafina/18/multi. loc.
Setacci/–/W Vill

Sette/19/Chelsea
Sette Enoteca (S)/22/Park Slope
Sette Mezzo/22/E 70s
Sfoglia (N)/22/E 90s
Sistina (N)/24/E 80s
Sosa Borella/19/multi. loc.
Spiga/22/W 80s
Spigolo/25/E 80s
Stella del Mare (N)/21/Murray Hill
Supper (N)/23/E Vill
Table XII/21/E 50s
Taormina/22/Little Italy
Tarallucci e Vino/21/multi. loc.
Teodora (N)/20/E 50s
Tevere/22/E 80s
Tiramisu/18/E 80s
Tommaso's/25/Bensonhurst
Tony's Di Napoli (S)/19/multi. loc.
Tosca Café/20/Bronx
Tratt. Alba/20/Murray Hill
Tratt. Dell'Arte/22/W 50s
Tratt. L'incontro/27/Astoria
Tratt. Pesce/18/multi. loc.
Tratt. Romana/24/Staten Is
tre dici/22/Chelsea
Triangolo/21/E 80s
Tuscany Grill (N)/22/Bay Ridge
Umberto's/19/multi. loc.
Uva/20/E 70s
Valbella (N)/25/Meatpacking
V&T/18/W 100s
Veniero's/23/E Vill
Vento/18/Meatpacking
Vespa/19/E 80s
Via Emilia (N)/–/Flatiron
Via Oreto/21/E 60s
Via Quadronno (N)/22/E 70s
ViceVersa (N)/23/W 50s
Vico/20/E 90s
Villa Berulia (N)/21/Murray Hill
Villa Mosconi/19/G Vill
Vincent's/21/Little Italy
Vittorio Cucina/21/W Vill
Vivolo/19/E 70s
Za Za (N)/19/E 60s

Jamaican
Aki/26/G Vill
Maroons/21/Chelsea
Negril/21/multi. loc.

Japanese
(* sushi specialist)
Aburiya Kinnosuke/25/E 40s
Aji Sushi*/21/Murray Hill

Aki/26/G Vill
Aki Sushi*/18/multi. loc.
Anzu*/–/Chelsea
Aquamarine/–/Murray Hill
Asiate/23/W 60s
Bar Masa*/23/W 60s
Blue Ribbon Sushi*/26/multi. loc.
Bond Street*/25/NoHo
Butai/20/Gramercy
Chanto/–/G Vill
Chiyono/21/E Vill
Cube 63/24/multi. loc.
Dae Dong/19/multi. loc.
Donguri/26/E 80s
EN Japanese/21/W Vill
Friendhouse*/20/E Vill
Fushimi*/25/Staten Is
Gari*/26/W 70s
Geisha/22/E 60s
Gyu-Kaku/23/E Vill
Hakata Grill/20/W 40s
Haru*/21/multi. loc.
Hasaki*/24/E Vill
Hatsuhana*/24/E 40s
Hedeh*/24/NoHo
Honmura An/26/SoHo
Ichiro*/21/E 80s
Inagiku*/23/E 40s
Iron Sushi*/20/multi. loc.
Ivy's Cafe*/19/W 70s
Japonais/–/Gramercy
Japonica*/22/G Vill
Jewel Bako*/26/E Vill
Kai/25/E 60s
Kanoyama*/27/E Vill
Katsu-Hama/24/E 40s
Kitchen Club/20/NoLita
Kodama*/20/W 40s
Koi*/23/W 40s
Korea Palace*/20/E 50s
Ko Sushi*/20/multi. loc.
Kuruma Zushi*/28/E 40s
Lan*/23/E Vill
Le Miu*/24/E Vill
Masa*/27/W 60s
Matsuri/23/Chelsea
Megu/25/TriBeCa
Megu Midtown/–/E 40s
Menchanko-tei/19/multi. loc.
Mishima*/23/Murray Hill
Mizu Sushi*/24/Flatiron
Momofuku Noodle/22/E Vill
Momoya*/22/Chelsea

Monster Sushi*/18/multi. loc.
Morimoto/23/Chelsea
Nëo Sushi*/23/W 80s
Ninja/18/TriBeCa
Nippon*/22/E 50s
Nobu*/27/TriBeCa
Nobu 57*/26/W 50s
Nooch/15/Chelsea
Omen/24/SoHo
Ono*/20/Meatpacking
Osaka*/25/Cobble Hill
Ota-Ya*/21/E 80s
Paris Match*/18/E 60s
Planet Thailand/20/multi. loc.
Poke*/25/E 80s
Riingo/20/E 40s
Roppongi*/20/W 80s
Rue 57*/18/W 50s
Sakura Café*/22/Park Slope
Sapporo East*/21/E Vill
Shabu-Shabu 70*/21/E 70s
Shabu-Tatsu/23/E Vill
Soba Nippon/20/W 50s
Soba-ya/23/E Vill
Sugiyama/28/W 50s
Sumile/22/G Vill
Sushi Ann*/25/E 50s
Sushiden*/23/multi. loc.
Sushi Hana*/20/multi. loc.
Sushi of Gari*/27/E 70s
SushiSamba*/22/multi. loc.
Sushi Seki*/27/E 60s
Sushi Sen-nin*/25/multi. loc.
Sushiya*/21/W 50s
Sushi Yasuda*/28/E 40s
Sushi Zen*/25/W 40s
Taka*/23/W Vill
Takahachi*/22/multi. loc.
Tea Box/20/E 50s
Tenzan*/23/multi. loc.
Todai/–/Murray Hill
Tokyo Pop*/22/W 100s
Tomoe Sushi*/27/G Vill
Tomo Sushi*/18/W 100s
Yakitori Totto/25/W 50s
Yama*/24/multi. loc.
Yuka*/22/E 80s
Yuki Sushi*/21/W 90s
Zutto*/21/multi. loc.

Jewish

Artie's Deli*/18/W 80s
Carnegie Deli*/22/W 50s
Edison Cafe/14/W 40s
Lattanzi/22/W 40s

Mo Pitkin's/17/E Vill
Sammy's Roumanian/17/LES

Korean

(* barbecue specialist)
Bann/22/W 50s
Bonjoo/–/E Vill
Cho Dang Gol*/22/Garment Dist
Dae Dong*/19/multi. loc.
Do Hwa*/21/G Vill
Dok Suni's/21/E Vill
Franchia/24/Murray Hill
Gahm Mi Oak/23/Garment Dist
Hangawi/24/Murray Hill
Kang Suh*/21/Garment Dist
Korea Palace*/20/E 50s
Kori/21/TriBeCa
Kum Gang San*/22/multi. loc.
Mandoo Bar/19/Garment Dist
Mill Korean/19/W 100s
Momofuku Ssäm Bar/–/E Vill
Won Jo*/21/Garment Dist
Woo Lae Oak*/23/SoHo

Kosher

Abigael's/20/Garment Dist
Azuri Cafe/24/W 50s
Ben's Kosher Deli/18/multi. loc.
Chennai Garden/21/Gramercy
Darna/21/W 80s
Le Marais/21/W 40s
Levana/21/W 60s
Liebman's/19/Bronx
Mill Basin Deli/21/Mill Basin
My Most Favorite/18/W 40s
Park East Grill/20/E 80s
Pongal/21/multi. loc.
Prime Grill/22/E 40s
Rectangles/18/E 70s
Sacred Chow/21/G Vill
Solo/24/E 50s
Tevere/22/E 80s

Lebanese

Al Bustan/21/E 50s

Malaysian

Fatty Crab/21/W Vill
Nyonya/23/multi. loc.
Penang/19/multi. loc.

Mediterranean

Aesop's Tables/22/Staten Is
Aleo/19/Flatiron

Alta/*22/G Vill*
Amaranth/*19/E 60s*
Barbounia/*20/Flatiron*
Beast/*19/Prospect Hts*
Bello Sguardo/*19/W 70s*
Bouterin/*19/E 50s*
Cafe Bar/*19/Astoria*
Café Botanica/*21/W 50s*
Cafe Centro/*19/E 40s*
Café du Soleil/*20/W 100s*
Café Opaline/*19/E 50s*
Cafe Ronda/*19/W 70s*
Café Soleil/*–/E 50s*
Convivium Osteria/*25/Park Slope*
Cru/*25/G Vill*
Danal/*21/E Vill*
Dani/*20/SoHo*
Dee's Pizza/*22/Forest Hills*
Django/*21/E 40s*
Dona/*24/E 50s*
Epices du Traiteur/*20/W 70s*
Extra Virgin/*22/W Vill*
Fig & Olive/*19/E 60s*
Five Points/*22/NoHo*
Frederick's Madison/*19/E 60s*
Il Buco/*25/NoHo*
In Tent/*–/NoLita*
Isabella's/*19/W 70s*
KitchenBar/*–/Park Slope*
Levana/*21/W 60s*
Little Owl/*–/W Vill*
Loft/*18/W 80s*
Mangia/*20/multi. loc.*
Marseille/*20/W 40s*
Miriam/*22/Park Slope*
My Moon/*18/Williamsburg*
Nice Matin/*20/W 70s*
Nick & Toni's/*17/W 60s*
Nisos/*18/Chelsea*
Olea/*22/Ft Greene*
Olives/*23/Union Sq*
Park, The/*15/Chelsea*
Picholine/*26/W 60s*
Place, The/*22/multi. loc.*
Red Cat/*24/Chelsea*
Ribot/*19/E 40s*
Savann/*20/W 70s*
Savoy/*23/SoHo*
Sezz Medi'/*20/W 100s*
Sharz Cafe/*20/E 80s*
Solo/*24/E 50s*
Superfine/*18/DUMBO*
Taboon/*23/W 50s*

Taci's Beyti/*22/Midwood*
Tanoreen/*25/Bay Ridge*
Tempo/*24/Park Slope*
Terrace in the Sky/*22/W 100s*
Trio/*21/Murray Hill*
202 Cafe/*21/Chelsea*

Mexican

Alamo, The/*18/E 40s*
Alma/*20/Carroll Gdns*
Blockhead Burrito/*17/multi. loc.*
Bonita/*22/Williamsburg*
Bright Food Shop/*20/Chelsea*
Café Frida/*20/W 70s*
Café Habana/*22/NoLita*
Centrico/*18/TriBeCa*
Chipotle/*18/multi. loc.*
Cosmic Cantina/*19/E Vill*
Crema/*23/Chelsea*
Diablo Royale/*18/W Vill*
Dos Caminos/*20/multi. loc.*
El Centro/*17/W 50s*
El Parador Cafe/*22/Murray Hill*
El Paso Taqueria/*23/multi. loc.*
Gabriela's/*–/W 90s*
Hell's Kitchen/*24/W 40s*
Itzocan/*24/multi. loc.*
Ixta/*20/Gramercy*
La Esquina/*21/NoLita*
La Flor Bakery/*24/Woodside*
La Palapa/*20/multi. loc.*
Lucy Latin Kit./*22/Flatiron*
Lupe's East LA Kit./*18/SoHo*
Mamá Mexico/*19/multi. loc.*
Maya/*23/E 60s*
Maz Mezcal/*21/E 80s*
Mercadito/*23/multi. loc.*
Mexicana Mama/*25/multi. loc.*
Mexican Radio/*18/NoLita*
Mi Cocina/*22/W Vill*
Pampano/*24/E 40s*
Rocking Horse/*20/Chelsea*
Rosa Mexicano/*22/multi. loc.*
Sueños/*23/Chelsea*
Taco Chulo/*24/Williamsburg*
Vera Cruz/*17/Williamsburg*
Zarela/*20/E 50s*
Zócalo/*20/multi. loc.*
Zona Rosa/*19/W 50s*

Middle Eastern

Mamlouk/*22/E Vill*
Moustache/*22/multi. loc.*

Olive Vine Cafe/*17/Park Slope*
Taboon/*23/W 50s*
Tanoreen/*25/Bay Ridge*
Zaytoons/*22/multi. loc.*

Moroccan
Barbès/*21/Murray Hill*
Cafe Gitane/*19/NoLita*
Cafe Mogador/*22/E Vill*
Darna/*21/W 80s*
Park Terrace/*21/Washington Hts.*
Zerza/*20/E Vill*

Noodle Shops
Bao Noodles/*20/Gramercy*
Great NY Noodle/*22/Ctown*
Honmura An/*26/SoHo*
Kelley & Ping/*16/multi. loc.*
Lili's Noodle/*17/multi. loc.*
Mee Noodle Shop/*18/multi. loc.*
Menchanko-tei/*19/multi. loc.*
Momofuku Noodle/*22/E Vill*
New Bo-Ky/*22/Ctown*
Nooch/*15/Chelsea*
Noodle Bar/*21/G Vill*
Pho Bang/*21/multi. loc.*
Republic/*18/Union Sq*
Soba Nippon/*20/W 50s*
Soba-ya/*23/E Vill*
Thai Son/*22/Ctown*

North African
Country Café/*20/SoHo*
Nomad/*–/E Vill*

Nuevo Latino
Beso/*20/Park Slope*
Cabana/*20/multi. loc.*
Calle Ocho/*22/W 80s*
Citrus B&G/*20/W 70s*
Esperanto/*21/E Vill*
Luz/*24/Ft Greene*
Novo/*21/SoHo*
Paladar/*20/LES*

Pan-Asian
Abigael's/*20/Garment Dist*
bluechili/*19/W 50s*
Cendrillon/*22/SoHo*
Chance/*21/Boerum Hill*
Kelley & Ping/*16/multi. loc.*
Mai/*23/Boerum Hill*
Noodle Bar/*21/G Vill*
O.G./*23/E Vill*

Rain/*21/W 80s*
Republic/*18/Union Sq*
Ruby Foo's/*19/multi. loc.*
Tao/*22/E 50s*

Pan-Latin
Boca Chica/*19/E Vill*
Bogota Latin/*20/Park Slope*
Mo Pitkin's/*17/E Vill*
Willie's/*22/Bronx*
Yuca Bar/*21/E Vill*

Persian/Iranian
Pars Grill House/*22/Chelsea*
Persepolis/*19/E 70s*

Peruvian
Coco Roco/*20/Park Slope*
Flor de Mayo/*20/multi. loc.*
Lima's Taste/*22/W Vill*
Mancora/*22/multi. loc.*
Pio Pio/*23/multi. loc.*
Sipan/*20/W 90s*

Pizza
Adrienne's Pizza/*24/Financial Dist*
Al Forno Pizza/*19/E 70s*
Amorina/*22/Prospect Hts*
Angelo's Pizza/*21/multi. loc.*
Anthony's/*20/Park Slope*
ápizz/*24/LES*
Arturo's Pizzeria/*21/G Vill*
Baci & Abbracci/*–/Williamsburg*
Bella Blu/*19/E 70s*
Bella Via/*21/LIC*
Bettola/*21/W 70s*
Café Fiorello/*20/W 60s*
Carbone/*–/Garment Dist*
Cascina/*18/W 40s*
Coals/*25/Bronx*
Col Legno/*19/E Vill*
Dee's Pizza/*22/Forest Hills*
Denino's/*24/Staten Is*
Di Fara/*26/Midwood*
Don Giovanni/*18/multi. loc.*
Fornino/*22/Williamsburg*
Franny's/*23/Prospect Hts*
Gonzo/*22/G Vill*
Grimaldi's/*26/DUMBO*
Il Mattone/*20/TriBeCa*
Joe's Pizza/*23/multi. loc.*
John's Pizzeria/*22/multi. loc.*
La Bottega/*17/Chelsea*
L & B Spumoni/*23/Bensonhurst*

La Pizza Fresca/*22/Flatiron*
La Villa Pizzeria/*21/multi. loc.*
La Vineria/*21/W 50s*
Lil' Frankie Pizza/*22/E Vill*
Lombardi's/*24/NoLita*
Mediterraneo/*19/E 60s*
Mezzaluna/*19/E 70s*
Naples 45/*17/E 40s*
Nick's/*22/multi. loc.*
Otto/*21/G Vill*
Palà/*21/LES*
Patsy's Pizzeria/*20/multi. loc.*
Pinch - Pizza/*21/Gramercy*
Pintaile's Pizza/*19/multi. loc.*
Pizza Gruppo/*26/E Vill*
Pizza 33/*22/multi. loc.*
Posto/*23/Gramercy*
Sac's Place/*21/Astoria*
Savoia/*21/Carroll Gdns*
Sette Enoteca/*22/Park Slope*
Sezz Medi'/*20/W 100s*
Tiramisu/*18/E 80s*
Totonno Pizza/*22/multi. loc.*
Two Boots/*18/multi. loc.*
Una Pizza/*24/E Vill*
Uno Chicago/*14/multi. loc.*
V&T/*18/W 100s*
Waldy's Pizza/*20/Chelsea*

Polish

Teresa's/*18/multi. loc.*

Portuguese

Alfama/*21/W Vill*
Luzia's/*18/W 80s*
Tintol/*19/W 40s*

Pub Food

J.G. Melon/*21/E 70s*
Neary's/*15/E 50s*
O'Neals'/*16/W 60s*
Pete's Tavern/*13/Gramercy*
P.J. Clarke's/*17/multi. loc.*
Trinity Place/*–/Financial Dist*
Waterfront Ale/*19/multi. loc.*

Puerto Rican

La Taza de Oro/*18/Chelsea*
Sofrito/*–/E 50s*

Russian

FireBird/*21/W 40s*

Sandwiches

Amy's Bread/*23/multi. loc.*
Artie's Deli/*18/W 80s*

Barney Greengrass/*23/W 80s*
Bouchon Bakery/*23/W 60s*
Bread/*19/NoLita*
Brennan & Carr/*20/Sheepshead Bay*
Chop't Creative/*21/multi. loc.*
Cosí/*16/multi. loc.*
Dishes/*22/E 40s*
DuMont/*23/Williamsburg*
E.A.T./*19/E 80s*
Ess-a-Bagel/*23/multi. loc.*
Hale & Hearty Soup/*19/multi. loc.*
Katz's Deli/*23/LES*
Le Pain Quotidien/*20/multi. loc.*
Liebman's/*19/Bronx*
Nicky's Viet./*23/multi. loc.*
Panino'teca 275/*24/Carroll Gdns*
Peanut Butter & Co./*20/G Vill*
Press 195/*21/multi. loc.*
Roll-n-Roaster/*19/Sheepshead Bay*
Sarge's Deli/*19/Murray Hill*
Stage Deli/*19/W 50s*
Sweet Melissa/*23/multi. loc.*
Tossed/*19/multi. loc.*
'wichcraft/*21/multi. loc.*
Zabar's Cafe/*18/W 80s*

Scandinavian

AQ Cafe/*22/Murray Hill*
Aquavit/*25/E 50s*
Smorgas Chef/*18/multi. loc.*

Seafood

Acqua Pazza/*21/W 50s*
Ammos/*22/multi. loc.*
Aquagrill/*26/SoHo*
Atlantic Grill/*22/E 70s*
Avra/*23/E 40s*
BLT Fish/*23/Flatiron*
Blue Fin/*22/W 40s*
Blue Water/*23/Financial Dist*
Bond 45/*18/W 40s*
Bouillabaisse 126/*22/Carroll Gdns*
Brooklyn Fish Camp/*22/Park Slope*
Christos/*23/Astoria*
City Crab/*17/Flatiron*
City Hall/*21/TriBeCa*
City Lobster/*17/W 40s*
Ditch Plains/*17/G Vill*
Docks Oyster Bar/*19/multi. loc.*
Elias Corner/*21/Astoria*
En Plo/*22/W 70s*
Esca/*24/W 40s*
Fish/*19/G Vill*
Foley's Fish/*20/W 40s*

Francisco's Centro/*21/Chelsea*
fresh/*23/TriBeCa*
Fuleen Seafood/*23/Ctown*
Gramercy 24/*17/Gramercy*
Grill Room/*18/Financial Dist*
Harbour Lights/*16/Seaport*
Ithaka/*20/E 80s*
Jack's Lux. Oyster/*24/E Vill*
Kam Chueh/*23/Ctown*
Kellari Taverna/*21/W 40s*
Lake Club/*20/Staten Is*
Le Bernardin/*28/W 50s*
Little Charlie's/*22/NoLita*
Lobster Box/*19/Bronx*
London Lennie's/*21/Rego Pk*
Lure Fishbar/*–/SoHo*
Marina Cafe/*20/Staten Is*
Mary's Fish Camp/*24/W Vill*
McCormick & Schmick/*19/W 50s*
Meltemi/*19/E 50s*
Mermaid Inn/*23/E Vill*
Milos/*26/W 50s*
Minnow/*20/Park Slope*
Moran's Chelsea/*18/Chelsea*
Neptune Room/*22/W 80s*
Oceana/*26/E 50s*
Ocean Grill/*23/W 70s*
Oriental Garden/*24/Ctown*
Oyster Bar/*21/E 40s*
Pampano/*24/E 40s*
Pearl Oyster/*26/G Vill*
Pearl Room/*22/Bay Ridge*
Pescatore/*19/E 50s*
Pier 2110/*–/Harlem*
Ping's Seafood/*21/multi. loc.*
Portofino's/*20/Bronx*
Redeye Grill/*20/W 50s*
Red Garlic/*19/W 50s*
Sea Grill/*24/W 40s*
Shaffer City/*21/Flatiron*
Shelly's/*24/W 50s*
Sipan/*20/W 90s*
Stamatis/*21/Astoria*
Stella del Mare/*21/Murray Hill*
Taverna Kyclades/*24/Astoria*
Telly's Taverna/*22/Astoria*
Thalassa/*23/TriBeCa*
Tides/*23/LES*
Todai/*–/Murray Hill*
Trata Estiatorio/*21/E 70s*
Tratt. Pesce/*18/multi. loc.*
Tropica/*21/E 40s*
Turquoise/*22/E 80s*
Umberto's/*19/multi. loc.*

View, The/*16/W 40s*
Water's Edge/*21/LIC*

Small Plates
(See also Spanish tapas specialist)
Alta (Med)/*22/G Vill*
Beast (Med)/*19/Prospect Hts*
Bellavitae (Italian)/*22/G Vill*
Bello Sguardo (Med)/*19/W 70s*
Beyoglu (Turkish)/*21/E 80s*
Bocca Lupo (Italian)/*–/Cobble Hill*
Butai (Japanese)/*20/Gramercy*
Chino's (Asian)/*20/Gramercy*
Degustation (French/Spanish)/*25/ E Vill*
EN Japanese (Japanese)/*21/W Vill*
Frankies Spuntino (Italian)/*23/ multi. loc.*
'inoteca (Italian)/*23/LES*
Kuma Inn (SE Asian)/*23/LES*
Little D Eatery (Eclectic)/*24/Park Slope*
Mercadito (Mexican)/*23/multi. loc.*
Momofuku Ssäm Bar (Korean)/*–/ E Vill*
Novo (Nuevo Latino)/*21/SoHo*
One (American)/*18/Meatpacking*
Perbacco (Italian)/*24/E Vill*
Samba-Lé (Brazilian)/*–/E Vill*
Stanton Social (Eclectic)/*24/LES*
Sumile (Japanese)/*22/G Vill*
Tarallucci e Vino (Italian)/*21/multi. loc.*
Turks & Frogs (Turkish)/*22/TriBeCa*
Uncle Nick's (Greek)/*20/W 50s*

Soul Food
Amy Ruth's/*22/Harlem*
Billie's Black/*–/Harlem*
Charles' Southern/*23/Harlem*
Londel's/*22/Harlem*
Miss Mamie's/Maude's/*22/Harlem*
Mo-Bay/*21/multi. loc.*
Pier 2110/*–/Harlem*
Pies-N-Thighs/*–/Williamsburg*
Pink Tea Cup/*21/W Vill*
Sadie Mae's Cafe/*–/Park Slope*
Sylvia's/*16/Harlem*

Soup
Cozy Soup/Burger/*18/G Vill*
Hale & Hearty Soup/*19/multi. loc.*

South African
Madiba/*18/Ft Greene*

South American
Cafe Ronda/19/W 70s
Camino Sur/23/Garment Dist
Don Pedro's/21/E 90s
Empanada Mama/21/W 50s

Southeast Asian
Cafe Asean/20/G Vill
Spice Market/22/Meatpacking

Southern
Amy Ruth's/22/Harlem
B. Smith's/18/W 40s
Charles' Southern/23/Harlem
Great Jones Cafe/20/NoHo
Ida Mae/22/Garment Dist
Jezebel/19/W 40s
Kitchenette/20/multi. loc.
Londel's/22/Harlem
Maroons/21/Chelsea
Miss Mamie's/Maude's/22/Harlem
Old Devil Moon/19/E Vill
Pink Tea Cup/21/W Vill
Rack & Soul/22/W 100s
River Room/22/Harlem

Southwestern
Agave/19/W Vill
Canyon Road/20/E 70s
Cilantro/17/multi. loc.
Cowgirl/16/W Vill
Los Dos Molinos/18/Gramercy
Mesa Grill/24/Flatiron
Miracle Grill/18/multi. loc.
Santa Fe/18/W 70s

Spanish
(* tapas specialist)
Alcala*/22/E 40s
Azafran*/21/TriBeCa
Barça 18*/19/Flatiron
Bolo/23/Flatiron
Boqueria*/–/Flatiron
Cafe Español/19/G Vill
Casa Mono/25/Gramercy
Degustation/25/E Vill
El Charro Español/23/G Vill
El Cid*/22/Chelsea
El Faro/21/W Vill
El Pote/22/Murray Hill
El Quijote/19/Chelsea
Euzkadi/20/E Vill
Flor de Sol*/21/TriBeCa
Francisco's Centro/21/Chelsea

La Paella*/20/E Vill
Las Ramblas*/19/G Vill
Marbella*/19/Murray Hill
Ñ*/19/SoHo
Oliva*/21/LES
Pipa*/20/Flatiron
Sala*/21/multi. loc.
Sevilla/22/W Vill
Solera*/21/E 50s
Sol y Sombra*/18/W 80s
Suba/20/LES
Tía Pol*/23/Chelsea
Tintol*/19/W 40s
Ureña/25/Gramercy
Xunta*/20/E Vill

Steakhouses
AJ Maxwell's/–/W 40s
Alonso's/–/Chelsea
Angelo & Maxie's/21/Flatiron
Austin's/23/Bay Ridge
Ben & Jack's/24/E 40s
Ben Benson's/23/W 50s
Bistro Le Steak/18/E 70s
Blair Perrone/21/E 40s
BLT Prime/24/Gramercy
BLT Steak/24/E 50s
Bobby Van's/22/multi. loc.
Bond 45/18/W 40s
Bull & Bear/20/E 40s
Cambalache/21/E 60s
Capital Grille/23/E 40s
Carne/18/W 100s
Carne Vale/–/E Vill
Chimichurri Grill/22/W 40s
Christos/23/Astoria
Churrascaria/22/multi. loc.
City Hall/21/TriBeCa
Craftsteak/24/Chelsea
Del Frisco's/25/W 40s
Delmonico's/22/Financial Dist
Dylan Prime/24/TriBeCa
Embers/21/Bay Ridge
Erawan/23/Bayside
Fairway Cafe/19/W 70s
Frankie & Johnnie/21/multi. loc.
Frank's/20/Chelsea
Gallagher's/21/W 50s
Green Field Churra./19/Corona
Grill Room/18/Financial Dist
Hacienda Argentina/20/E 70s
Harry's/–/Financial Dist
Il Bastardo/18/Chelsea

Industria Argentina/20/TriBeCa
Jake's/24/Bronx
Keens/24/Garment Dist
Knickerbocker B&G/20/G.Vill
Le Marais/21/W 40s
Les Halles/20/multi. loc.
Macelleria/19/Meatpacking
Maloney & Porcelli/22/E 50s
MarkJoseph/25/Financial Dist
Michael Jordan's/20/E 40s
Monkey Bar/19/E 50s
Moran's Chelsea/18/Chelsea
Morton's/23/E 40s
Nick & Stef's/21/Garment Dist
Novecento/20/SoHo
Old Homestead/23/Meatpacking
Outback/15/multi. loc.
Palm/24/multi. loc.
Pampa/22/W 90s
Park East Grill/20/E 80s
Patroon/20/E 40s
Peter Luger/28/Williamsburg
Pietro's/22/E 40s
Porter House NY/–/W 60s
Post House/23/E 60s
Prime Grill/22/E 40s
Quality Meats/23/W 50s
Rothmann's/22/E 50s
Roth's Westside/20/W 90s
Ruth's Chris/24/W 50s
Shelly's/24/W 50s
Shula's/19/W 40s
Smith & Wollensky/23/E 40s
Sparks/25/E 40s
Staghorn/–/Garment Dist
Steak Frites/17/Union Sq
Strip House/25/G Vill
2 West/21/Financial Dist
Uncle Jack's/24/multi. loc.
Via Brasil/20/W 40s
View, The/16/W 40s
Willie's/22/Bronx
Wolfgang's/25/multi. loc.
Wollensky's/22/E 40s

Tex-Mex
Burritoville/17/multi. loc.
Mary Ann's/15/multi. loc.
107 West/17/multi. loc.

Thai
Bann Thai/21/Forest Hills
Breeze/21/W 40s

Elephant, The/21/E Vill
Erawan/23/Bayside
Friendhouse/20/E Vill
Highline/20/Meatpacking
Holy Basil/22/E Vill
Isle/19/G Vill
Jaiya Thai/21/Gramercy
Jasmine/20/E 80s
Joya/25/Cobble Hill
Kin Khao/21/SoHo
Kittichai/23/SoHo
Klong/21/E Vill
Kuma Inn/23/LES
Land/22/W 80s
Lemongrass Grill/17/multi. loc.
Long Tan/20/Park Slope
Nooch/15/Chelsea
Pam Real Thai/24/W 40s
Peep/20/SoHo
Planet Thailand/20/multi. loc.
Pongsri Thai/20/multi. loc.
Prem-on Thai/20/G Vill
Pukk/22/E Vill
Q Thai Bistro/22/Forest Hills
Red Garlic/19/W 50s
Regional Thai/18/multi. loc.
Room Service/–/Chelsea
Royal Siam/20/Chelsea
Sala Thai/20/E 80s
SEA/21/multi. loc.
Siam Inn/22/W 50s
Siam Square/24/Bronx
Song/23/Park Slope
Spice/20/multi. loc.
Sripraphai/27/Woodside
Thai Pavilion/23/Astoria
Tigerland/22/E Vill
Topaz Thai/20/W 50s
Tuk Tuk/19/LIC
Ubol's Kitchen/22/Astoria
Vong/23/E 50s
Vynl/19/W 50s
Wild Ginger/19/W Vill
Wondee Siam/22/W 50s

Tibetan
Tsampa/19/E Vill

Tunisian
Epices du Traiteur/20/W 70s

Turkish
Akdeniz/21/W 40s
Ali Baba/22/Murray Hill

Bereket/20/LES
Beyoglu/21/E 80s
Dervish Turkish/19/W 40s
Kapadokya/20/Brooklyn Hts
Meze/–/Bay Ridge
Pasha/21/W 70s
Sahara/22/Gravesend
Sip Sak/19/E 40s
Taci's Beyti/22/Midwood
Taksim/20/E 50s
Turkish Cuisine/21/W 40s
Turkish Kitchen/23/Gramercy
Turks & Frogs/22/TriBeCa
Turkuaz/19/W 100s
Uskudar/20/E 70s
Zeytin/19/W 80s

Ukrainian
Veselka/18/E Vill

Vegetarian
(* vegan)
Angelica Kit.*/20/E Vill
Blossom*/24/Chelsea
Blue/Green*/20/multi. loc.
Candle Cafe*/22/E 70s
Candle 79*/24/E 70s
Chennai Garden/21/Gramercy
Counter/22/E Vill
Franchia/24/Murray Hill
Gobo*/22/multi. loc.
Hangawi/24/Murray Hill
JivamukTea*/–/G Vill
Pongal/21/multi. loc.
Pukk/22/E Vill
Pure Food & Wine*/21/Gramercy
Quartino/21/multi. loc.

Sacred Chow*/21/G Vill
Saravanaas/22/Gramercy
Spring St. Natural/19/NoLita
Vatan/20/Gramercy
Zen Palate/19/multi. loc.

Venezuelan
Caracas/23/E Vill
Flor's Kitchen/19/multi. loc.

Vietnamese
Anh/21/Gramercy
Bao Noodles/20/Gramercy
Bao 111/22/E Vill
Boi/22/E 40s
Doyers Viet./21/Ctown
Indochine/21/E Vill
Le Colonial/19/E 50s
Miss Saigon/18/E 80s
Nam/23/TriBeCa
New Bo-Ky/22/Ctown
Nha Trang/22/Ctown
Nicky's Viet./23/multi. loc.
O Mai/24/Chelsea
Pho Bang/21/multi. loc.
Pho Pasteur/20/Ctown
Pho Viet Huong/21/Ctown
Saigon Grill/23/multi. loc.
Sapa/22/Flatiron
Thai Son/22/Ctown
Tigerland/22/E Vill
Tuk Tuk/19/LIC
Vermicelli/20/E 70s
VietCafé/20/TriBeCa

Yemenite
Rectangles/18/E 70s

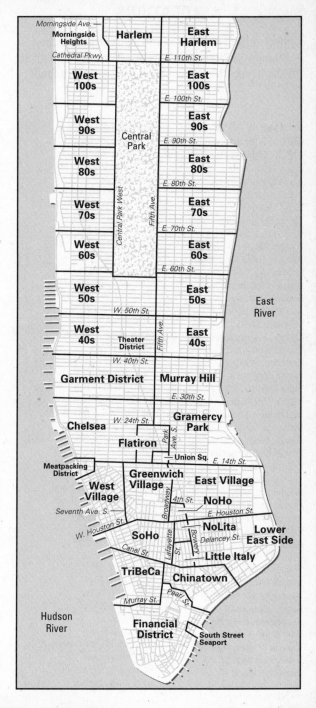

Morningside Ave. —
Morningside Heights
Cathedral Pkwy.

Harlem

East Harlem

E. 110th St.

West 100s

East 100s

E. 100th St.

West 90s

East 90s

E. 90th St.

Central Park

West 80s

East 80s

E. 80th St.

Central Park West

Fifth Ave.

West 70s

East 70s

E. 70th St.

West 60s

East 60s

E. 60th St.

West 50s

East 50s

East River

W. 50th St.

West 40s

Theater District

Fifth Ave.

East 40s

W. 40th St.

Garment District

Murray Hill

E. 30th St.

W. 24th St.

Chelsea

Gramercy Park

Flatiron

Park Ave. S.

Union Sq. E. 14th St.

Meatpacking District

Greenwich Village

East Village

West Village

Broadway

4th St.

NoHo

Seventh Ave. S. —

E. Houston St.

W. Houston St.

NoLita

SoHo

Lafayette St.

Bowery

Delancey St.

Lower East Side

Canal St.

Little Italy

TriBeCa

Chinatown

Pearl St.

Murray St.

Hudson River

Financial District

South Street Seaport

LOCATIONS

(Restaurant name followed by its street location.
A=Avenue, s=Street, e.g. 1A/116s=First Ave. at 116th St.;
3A/82-3s=Third Ave. between 82nd & 83rd Sts.)

MANHATTAN

Chelsea
(24th to 30th Sts., west of 5th;
14th to 24th Sts., west of 6th)
Alonso's *20s/7-8A*
Amy's Bread *9A/15-6s*
Anzu *10A/22-3s*
Bette *23s/9-10A*
Better Burger *8A/19s*
Biricchino *29s/8A*
Blossom *9A/21-2s*
Bombay Talkie *9A/21-2s*
Bottino *10A/24-5s*
Bright Food Shop *8A/21s*
Buddakan *9A/16s*
Burritoville *23s/7-8A*
Cafeteria *7A/17s*
Chelsea Bistro *23s/8-9A*
Cookshop *10A/20s*
Craftsteak *10A/15-6s*
Crema *17s/6-7A*
Cuba Cafe *8A/20-1s*
Dallas BBQ *8A/23s*
Da Umberto *17s/6-7A*
Del Posto *10A/16s*
Don Giovanni *10A/22-3s*
East of Eighth *23s/7-8A*
El Cid *15s/8-9A*
elmo *7A/19-20s*
El Quijote *23s/7-8A*
Empire Diner *10A/22s*
Energy Kitchen *17s/8-9A*
F & B *23s/7-8A*
Fillip's *7A/21-2s*
Food Bar *8A/17-8s*
Francisco's Centro *23s/6-7A*
Frank's *16s/9-10A*
Gascogne *8A/17-8s*
Gin Lane *14s/8-9A*
Grand Sichuan *9A/24s*
Hale & Hearty Soup *9A/15-6s*
Havana Chelsea *8A/19-20s*
Il Bastardo *7A/21-2s*
Intermezzo *8A/20-1s*

La Bergamote *9A/20s*
La Bottega *9A/17s*
La Lunchonette *10A/18s*
La Taza de Oro *8A/14-5s*
Le Gamin *15s/7-8A*
Le Grainne Café *9A/21s*
Le Singe Vert *7A/19-20s*
Le Zie 2000 *7A/20-1s*
Maroons *16s/7-8A*
Mary Ann's *8A/16s*
Matsuri *16s/9A*
Momoya *7A/21s*
Monster Sushi *23s/6-7A*
Moran's Chelsea *10A/19s*
Morimoto *10A/16s*
Negril *23s/8-9A*
Nisos *8A/19s*
Nooch *8A/17s*
O Mai *9A/19-20s*
Park, The *10A/17-8s*
Pars Grill House *26s/7-8A*
Patsy's Pizzeria *23s/8-9A*
Pepe...To Go *10A/24-5s*
Pizza 33 *multi. loc.*
Pongsri Thai *23s/6-7A*
Pre:Post *27s/10-1A*
Red Cat *10A/23-4s*
Regional Thai *7A/22s*
Rocking Horse *8A/19-20s*
Room Service *8A/18-9s*
Royal Siam *8A/22-3s*
RUB BBQ *23s/7-8A*
Sarabeth's *9A/15-6s*
Sette *7A/21-2s*
Seven *7A/29-30s*
Spice *8A/19-20s*
Sueños *17s/8-9A*
Tía Pol *10A/22-3s*
Tour *8A/15s*
tre dici *26s/6-7A*
Trestle on Tenth *10A/24s*
202 Cafe *9A/15-6s*
Waldy's Pizza *6A/27-8s*
'wichcraft *12A/27-8s*

Chinatown
(Canal to Pearl Sts.,
west of Bway)
Big Wong *Mott/Bayard-Canal*
Dim Sum Go Go *E. Bway/Chatham*
Doyers Viet. *Doyers/Chatham*
Evergreen Shanghai *Mott/Bayard*
Excellent Dumpling *Lafayette/Canal*
Fuleen Seafood *Division/Bowery*
Golden Unicorn *E. Bway/Catherine*
Goodies *E. Bway/Catherine-Oliver*
Grand Sichuan *Canal/Bowery*
Great NY Noodle *Bowery/Bayard*
HSF *Bowery/Bayard-Canal*
Jing Fong *Elizabeth/Bayard-Canal*
Joe's *multi. loc.*
Kam Chueh *Bowery/Bayard-Canal*
Mandarin Court *Mott/Bayard-Canal*
Mr. Tang *Mott/Bayard*
New Bo-Ky *Bayard/Mott-Mulberry*
New Green Bo *Bayard/Elizabeth*
Nha Trang *multi. loc.*
Nice *E. Bway/Catherine-Mkt.*
Oriental Garden *Elizabeth/Bayard*
Peking Duck *Mott/Pell-Mosco*
Pho Bang *Pike/Division-E. Bway*
Pho Pasteur *Baxter/Bayard-Canal*
Pho Viet Huong *Mulberry/Bayard*
Ping's Seafood *Mott/Bayard-Pell*
Pongsri Thai *Bayard/Baxter*
Shanghai Cuisine *Bayard/Mulberry*
Thai Son *Baxter/Canal*
Wo Hop *Mott/Canal*
X.O. *multi. loc.*

East 40s
Aburiya Kinnosuke *45s/2-3A*
Alamo, The *48s/1-2A*
Alcala *46s/1-2A*
Alma Grill *48s/Lex-3A*
Ammos *Vanderbilt/44-5s*
Avra *48s/Lex-3A*
Ben & Jack's *44s/2-3A*
Blair Perrone *2A/47-8s*
Bobby Van's *Park/46s*
Boi *44s/2-3s*
Brother Jimmy's *42s/Vanderbilt*
Bukhara Grill *49s/2-3A*
Bull & Bear *Lex/49s*
Burger Heaven *multi. loc.*
Cafe Centro *Park/45s-Vanderbilt*
Cafe S.F.A. *5A/49-50s*
Cafe Spice *42s/Vanderbilt*

Caffe Linda *49s/Lex-3A*
Capital Grille *42s/Lex-3A*
Chiam *48s/Lex-3A*
Chin Chin *49s/2-3A*
Chipotle *44s/Lex-3A*
Cibo *2A/41s*
Cipriani Dolci *42s/Vanderbilt*
Comfort Diner *45s/2-3A*
Delegates Dining Rm. *1A/45s*
Dishes *multi. loc.*
Diwan *48s/Lex-3A*
Django *Lex/46s*
Docks Oyster Bar *3A/40s*
Energy Kitchen *2A/41s*
English is Italian *3A/40s*
goodburger *2A/43s*
Grifone *46s/2-3A*
Hale & Hearty Soup *multi. loc.*
Haru *Park/48s*
Hatsuhana *multi. loc.*
Il Postino *49s/1-2A*
Inagiku *49s/Lex-Park*
Jacques-Imo's *42s/Vanderbilt*
Junior's *42s/Vanderbilt*
Katsu-Hama *47s/5A-Mad*
Kuruma Zushi *47s/5A-Mad*
L'Impero *Tudor City/42-3s*
Mamá Mexico *49s/2-3A*
Mangia *48s/5A-Mad*
Mee Noodle Shop *2A/49s*
Megu Midtown *1A/47s*
Menchanko-tei *45s/Lex-3A*
Metrazur *42s/Park*
Michael Jordan's *42s/Vanderbilt*
Morton's *5A/45s*
Nanni *46s/Lex-3A*
Naples 45 *Park/45s*
Nino's *2A/47-8s*
Osteria Laguna *42s/2-3A*
Oyster Bar *42s/Vanderbilt*
Palm *2A/44-5s*
Pampano *49s/2-3A*
Patroon *46s/Lex-3A*
Peacock Alley *Park/49-50s*
Pepe...To Go *42s/Vanderbilt*
Pershing Square *42s/Park*
Phoenix Garden *40s/2-3A*
Pietro's *43s/2-3A*
Prime Grill *49s/Mad-Park*
Ribot *3A/48s*
Riingo *45s/2-3A*
Sip Sak *2A/49-50s*
Smith & Wollensky *3A/49s*

Smorgas Chef *2A/49s*
Sparks *46s/2-3A*
Sushiden *49s/5A-Mad*
Sushi Yasuda *43s/2-3A*
Top of the Tower *1A/49s*
Tropica *45s/Lex-Vanderbilt*
Two Boots *42s/Lex*
'wichcraft *5A/46s*
Wollensky's *49s/3A*
Yama *49s/1-2A*
Zócalo *42s/Vanderbilt*

East 50s

Adä *58s/2-3A*
Aja *1A/58s*
Al Bustan *3A/50-1s*
Alto *53s/5A-Mad*
Amma *51s/2-3A*
Angelo's Pizza *2A/55s*
Aquaterra *56s/2-3A*
Aquavit *55s/Mad-Park*
Baluchi's *53s/2-3A*
Bice *54s/5A-Mad*
Blockhead Burrito *2A/50-1s*
BLT Steak *57s/Lex-Park*
Bobby Van's *54s/Lex-Park*
Bottega del Vino *59s/5A-Mad*
Bouterin *59s/1A-Sutton*
Brasserie *53s/Lex-Park*
Burger Heaven *multi. loc.*
Burritoville *3A/52s*
Cafe Joul *1A/58-9s*
Café Opaline *Mad/56-7s*
Café Soleil *2A/53-4s*
Café St. Bart's *50s/Park*
Caffe Buon Gusto *2A/53-4s*
Casa La Femme *1A/58-9s*
Caviar Russe *Mad/54-5s*
Cellini *54s/Mad-Park*
Chipotle *52s/Lex-3A*
Chola *58s/2-3A*
Chop't Creative *multi. loc.*
Columbus Bakery *1A/52-3s*
Cosí *56s/Mad-Park*
Da Antonio *55s/Lex-3A*
David Burke/Bloom. *59s/Lex-3A*
Dawat *58s/2-3A*
DeGrezia *50s/2-3A*
Destino *1A/50s*
Deux Amis *51s/1-2A*
Dona *52s/2-3A*
Dos Caminos *3A/50s*
Energy Kitchen *2A/57-8s*

Ess-a-Bagel *3A/50-1s*
F & B *52s/Lex-3A*
Felidia *58s/2-3A*
Four Seasons *52s/Lex-Park*
Fresco by Scotto *52s/Mad-Park*
Fresco on the Go *52s/Mad-Park*
Giambelli *50s/Mad-Park*
Gilt *Mad/50-1s*
Grand Sichuan *2A/55-6s*
Houston's *54s/3A*
Il Nido *53s/2-3A*
Jubilee *54s/1-2A*
Korea Palace *54s/Lex-Park*
La Gioconda *53s/2-3A*
La Grenouille *52s/5A-Mad*
La Mangeoire *2A/53-4s*
La Mediterranée *2A/50-1s*
L'Atelier/Joël Robuchon *57s/Mad*
Le Cirque *58s/Lex-3A*
Le Colonial *57s/Lex-3A*
Le Perigord *52s/FDR-1A*
Lever House *53s/Mad-Park*
Luna Piena *53s/2-3A*
Maloney & Porcelli *50s/Mad-Park*
March *58s/1A-Sutton*
Meltemi *1A/51s*
Mint *50s/Lex-3A*
Monkey Bar *54s/Mad-Park*
Montparnasse *51s/2-3A*
Mr. Chow *57s/1-2A*
Mr. K's *Lex/51s*
Neary's *57s/1A*
Nippon *52s/Lex-3A*
Oceana *54s/Mad-Park*
Our Place *55s/Lex-3A*
Outback *56s/2-3A*
Paper Moon *58s/Mad-Park*
Peking Duck *53s/2-3A*
Pescatore *2A/50-1s*
P.J. Clarke's *3A/55s*
Pump Energy Food *3A/50s*
Rosa Mexicano *1A/58s*
Rothmann's *54s/5A-Mad*
San Pietro *54s/5A-Mad*
Serafina *58s/Mad-Park*
Shun Lee Palace *55s/Lex-3A*
Sofrito *57s/1A-Sutton*
Solera *53s/2-3A*
Solo *Mad/55-6s*
Sushi Ann *51s/Mad-Park*
Table XII *56s/Park*
Taksim *2A/54-5s*
Tao *58s/Mad-Park*

Tea Box *5A/54-5s*
Teodora *57s/Lex-3A*
Tratt. Pesce *1A/59s*
Tse Yang *51s/Mad-Park*
Vong *54s/3A*
Yuva *58s/2-3A*
Zarela *2A/50-1s*
Zip Burger *52s/1-2A*

East 60s

Alice's Tea Cup *64s/Lex*
Amaranth *62s/5A-Mad*
Arabelle *64s/Mad*
Aureole *61s/Mad-Park*
Baluchi's *1A/63s*
Bistro 61 *1A/61s*
Bravo Gianni *63s/2-3A*
Brio *61s/Lex*
Burger Heaven *Lex/62s*
Cabana *3A/60-1s*
Café Evergreen *1A/69-70s*
Café Pierre *61s/5A*
Cambalache *64s/1A-York*
Canaletto *60s/2-3A*
Circus *61s/Lex-Park*
Da Filippo *2A/69-70s*
Daniel *65s/Mad-Park*
davidburke/donatella *61s/Lex-Park*
Fig & Olive *Lex/62-3s*
Frederick's Madison *Mad/65-6s*
Fred's at Barneys *Mad/60s*
Geisha *61s/Mad-Park*
Gino *Lex/60-1s*
Hale & Hearty Soup *Lex/64-5s*
Il Vagabondo *62s/1-2A*
Jackson Hole *64s/2-3A*
John's Pizzeria *64s/1A-York*
JoJo *64s/Lex-3A*
Jovia *62s/Lex-Park*
Kai *Mad/68-9s*
L'Absinthe *67s/2-3A*
La Cantina Toscana *1A/60-1s*
La Goulue *Mad/64-5s*
Le Bilboquet *63s/Mad-Park*
Le Pain Quotidien *Lex/63-4s*
Le Veau d'Or *60s/Lex-Park*
Maya *1A/64-5s*
Mediterraneo *2A/66s*
Mon Petit Cafe *Lex/62s*
Nello *Mad/62-3s*
Paris Match *65s/Mad-Park*
Park Ave. Cafe *63s/Lex-Park*
Patsy's Pizzeria *multi. loc.*

Philippe *60s/Mad-Park*
Pongal *1A/63-4s*
Portofino Grille *1A/63-4s*
Post House *63s/Mad-Park*
Primola *2A/64-5s*
Regency *Park/61s*
Scalinatella *61s/3A*
Serafina *61s/Mad-Park*
Serendipity 3 *60s/2-3A*
Sushi Seki *1A/62-3s*
212 *65s/Lex-Park*
Viand *Mad/61-2s*
Via Oreto *1A/61-2s*
Za Za *1A/65-6s*

East 70s

Afghan Kebab *2A/70-1s*
Agata & Valentina *1A/79s*
Aki Sushi *York/75-6s*
Al Forno Pizza *2A/77-8s*
Annie's *3A/78-9s*
Atlantic Grill *3A/76-7s*
Bandol Bistro *78s/Lex-3A*
Baraonda *2A/75s*
Barking Dog *York/77s*
Bella Blu *Lex/70-1s*
Bistro Le Steak *3A/75s*
Blue/Green *74s/2-3A*
Boathouse *72s/CPD*
Brother Jimmy's *2A/77-8s*
Burritoville *2A/77-8s*
Buzina Pop *Lex/73s*
Café Boulud *76s/5A-Mad*
Caffe Buon Gusto *77s/2-3A*
Campagnola *1A/73-4s*
Candle Cafe *3A/74-5s*
Candle 79 *79s/Lex-3A*
Canyon Road *1A/76-7s*
Carlyle *76/Mad*
Cilantro *1A/71s*
Coco Pazzo *74s/5A-Mad*
Cortina *2A/75-6s*
Dallas BBQ *3A/72-3s*
Due *3A/79-80s*
EJ's Luncheonette *3A/73s*
Finestra *York/73s*
Googie's *2A/78s*
Grace's Trattoria *71s/2-3A*
Hacienda Argentina *75s/1-2A*
Haru *3A/76s*
Il Riccio *79s/Lex-3A*
Iron Sushi *78s/1-2A*
J.G. Melon *3A/74s*

Ko Sushi *2A/70s*
Lenox Room *3A/73-4s*
Le Pain Quotidien *77s/2-3A*
Lusardi's *2A/77-8s*
Mark's *77s/Mad*
Maruzzella *1A/77-8s*
Mary Ann's *2A/78-9s*
Mezzaluna *3A/74-5s*
Mingala Burmese *2A/72-3s*
Nino's *1A/72-3s*
Orsay *Lex/75s*
Parma *3A/79-80s*
Payard Bistro *Lex/73-4s*
Per Lei *2A/71s*
Persepolis *2A/74-5s*
Petaluma *1A/73s*
Pintaile's Pizza *York/76-7s*
Quatorze Bis *79s/1-2A*
Rectangles *1A/74-5s*
Regional Thai *1A/77s*
Sant Ambroeus *Mad/77-8s*
Sarabeth's *Mad/75s*
Serafina *Mad/79s*
Sette Mezzo *Lex/70-1s*
Shabu-Shabu 70 *70s/1-2A*
Shanghai Pavilion *3A/78-9s*
Spice *2A/73-4s*
Sushi Hana *2A/78s*
Sushi of Gari *78s/1A-York*
Swifty's *Lex/72-3s*
Trata Estiatorio *2A/70-1s*
Uskudar *2A/73-4s*
Uva *2A/77-8s*
Vermicelli *2A/77-8s*
Viand *Mad/78s*
Via Quadronno *73s/5A-Mad*
Vivolo *74s/Lex-Park*

East 80s

Antonucci *81s/Lex-3A*
Baluchi's *multi. loc.*
Better Burger *2A/84s*
Beyoglu *3A/81s*
Blockhead Burrito *2A/81-2s*
Brasserie Julien *3A/80-1s*
Bruno Jamais *81s/Mad*
Burger Heaven *3A/86-7s*
Café d'Alsace *2A/88s*
Café Sabarsky *5A/86s*
Caffe Grazie *84s/5A-Mad*
Carino *2A/88-9s*
Centolire *Mad/85-6s*
Chef Ho's *2A/89-90s*

Cilantro *2A/88-9s*
Dakshin Indian *1A/88-9s*
Demarchelier *86s/Mad-Park*
Divino *2A/80-1s*
Donguri *83s/1-2A*
E.A.T. *Mad/80-1s*
Elaine's *2A/88-9s*
Elio's *2A/84-5s*
Emack & Bolio's *1A/81-2s*
Erminia *83s/2-3A*
Etats-Unis *81s/2-3A*
Ethiopian Rest. *York/83-4s*
Firenze *2A/82-3s*
Girasole *82s/Lex-3A*
Gobo *3A/81s*
Heidelberg *2A/85-6s*
Ichiro *2A/87-8s*
Ithaka *86s/1-2A*
Jackson Hole *2A/83-4s*
Jacques *85s/2-3A*
Jasmine *2A/84s*
Kings' Carriage Hse. *82s/2-3A*
Ko Sushi *York/85s*
Le Boeuf/Mode *81s/E. End-York*
Le Pain Quotidien *Mad/84-5s*
Le Refuge *82s/Lex-3A*
Lili's Noodle *3A/84-5s*
Luca *1A/88-9s*
Mangiarini *2A/82-3s*
Maz Mezcal *86s/1-2A*
Miss Saigon *3A/80-1s*
Nicola's *84s/Lex*
One 83 *1A/83-4s*
Ota-Ya *2A/81-2s*
Our Place *3A/82s*
Paola's *84s/2-3A*
Papaya King *86s/3A*
Park East Grill *2A/81-2s*
Penang *2A/83s*
Pig Heaven *2A/80-1s*
Pintaile's Pizza *York/83-4s*
Poke *85s/1-2A*
Primavera *1A/82s*
Quattro Gatti *81s/2-3A*
Rughetta *85s/1-2A*
Sala Thai *2A/89-90s*
Sharz Cafe *86s/1A-York*
Sistina *2A/80-1s*
Spigolo *2A/81s*
Sushi Sen-nin *3A/80-1s*
Taste *3A/80s*
Tevere *84s/Lex-3A*
Tiramisu *3A/80s*

Tony's Di Napoli *2A/83s*
Totonno Pizza *2A/80-1s*
Tratt. Pesce *3A/87-8s*
Triangolo *83s/1-2A*
Turquoise *81s/2-3A*
Uno Chicago *86s/2-3A*
Vespa *2A/84-5s*
Viand *86s/2A*
Wicker Park *3A/83s*
Wu Liang Ye *86s/2-3A*
York Grill *York/88-9s*
Yuka *2A/80-1s*
Zócalo *82s/Lex-3A*

East 90s & 100s
(90th to 110th Sts.)
Barking Dog *3A/94s*
Bistro du Nord *Mad/93s*
Brother Jimmy's *3A/93s*
Don Pedro's *2A/96s*
El Paso Taqueria *multi. loc.*
Fetch *3A/92-3s*
Itzocan *Lex/101s*
Jackson Hole *Mad/91s*
Nick's *2A/94s*
Osso Buco *3A/93s*
Pascalou *Mad/92-3s*
Pinocchio *1A/90-1s*
Pintaile's Pizza *91s/5A-Mad*
Pio Pio *1A/90-1s*
Sarabeth's *Mad/92-3s*
Sfoglia *Lex/92s*
Table d'Hôte *92s/Mad-Park*
Vico *Mad/92-3s*
Yura & Co. *multi. loc.*
Zebú Grill *92s/1-2A*

East Village
(14th to Houston Sts.,
east of Bway)
Angelica Kit. *12s/1-2A*
Angon on Sixth *6s/1-2A*
Awash Ethiopian *6s/1-2A*
Baluchi's *2A/6s*
Bamn! *St. Marks/2-3A*
Banjara *1A/6s*
Bao 111 *Ave. C/7-8s*
Barbone *Ave. B/11-2s*
Blue 9 Burger *3A/12-3s*
Boca Chica *1A/1s*
Bonjoo *1A/6-7s*
Brick Lane Curry *6s/2A*
Buenos Aires *6s/Aves. A-B*

Burritoville *2A/8-9s*
Butter *Lafayette/Astor-4s*
Cacio e Pepe *2A/11-2s*
Cafecito *Ave. C/11-2s*
Cafe Mogador *St. Marks/Ave. A-1A*
Caracas *multi. loc.*
Carne Vale *Ave. B/3-4s*
Casimir *Ave. B/6-7s*
ChikaLicious *10s/1-2A*
Chipotle *St. Marks/2-3A*
Chiyono *6s/1-2A*
Col Legno *9s/2-3A*
Colors *Lafayette/Astor-4s*
Cosmic Cantina *3A/12-3s*
Counter *1A/6-7s*
Cucina di Pesce *4s/Bowery-2A*
Dallas BBQ *2A/St. Marks*
Danal *10s/3-4A*
Degustation *5s/2-3A*
Dok Suni's *1A/7s-St. Marks*
Dumpling Man *St. Marks/Ave. A-1A*
Elephant, The *1s/1-2A*
Esperanto *Ave. C/9s*
Euzkadi *4s/1-2A*
Flea Mkt. Cafe *Ave. A/9s-St. Marks*
Flor's Kitchen *1A/9-10s*
Frank *2A/5-6s*
Friendhouse *multi. loc.*
Gnocco Caffe *10s/Aves. A-B*
Grand Sichuan *St. Marks/2-3A*
Gyu-Kaku *Cooper/Astor-4s*
Hasaki *9s/2-3A*
Haveli *2A/5-6s*
Hearth *12s/1A*
Holy Basil *2A/9-10s*
I Coppi *9s/Ave. A-1A*
Il Bagatto *2s/Aves. A-B*
Indochine *Lafayette/Astor-4s*
Itzocan *9s/Ave. A-1A*
Jack's Lux. Oyster *2A/5-6s*
Jewel Bako *5s/2-3A*
John's of 12th St. *12s/2A*
Kanoyama *2A/11s*
Kelley & Ping *Bowery/2s*
Klong *St. Marks/2-3A*
Knife + Fork *4s/1-2A*
Lan *3A/10-1s*
La Paella *9s/2-3A*
La Palapa *St. Marks/1-2A*
Lavagna *5s/Aves. A-B*
Le Gamin *5s/Aves. A-B*
Le Miu *Ave. A/6-7s*
Le Tableau *5s/Aves. A-B*
Lil' Frankie Pizza *1A/1-2s*

Lucien *1A/1s*
Mama's Food *3s/Aves. A-B*
Mamlouk *4s/Aves. A-B*
Mancora *1A/6s*
Mara's Homemade *6s/1-2A*
Mary Ann's *2A/5s*
Max *Ave. B/3-4s*
Mercadito *Ave. B/11-2s*
Mermaid Inn *2A/5-6s*
Mingala Burmese *7s/2-3A*
Momofuku Noodle *1A/10-1s*
Momofuku Ssäm Bar *2A/13s*
Mo Pitkin's *Ave. A/2-3s*
Moustache *10s/Ave. A-1A*
Nicky's Viet. *2s/Ave. A*
99 Miles to Philly *3A/12-3s*
Nomad *2A/4s*
O.G. *6s/Aves. A-B*
Old Devil Moon *12s/Aves. A-B*
Pepe...To Go *Ave. C/8s*
Perbacco *4s/Aves. A-B*
Pizza Gruppo *Ave. B/11-2s*
Prune *1s/1-2A*
Pukk *1A/4-5s*
Pylos *7s/Ave. A-1A*
Sal Anthony's *1A/10-1s*
Samba-Lé *Ave. A/1-2s*
Sapporo East *1A/10s*
SEA *2A/4-5s*
Shabu-Tatsu *10s/1-2A*
S'mac *12s/1-2A*
Soba-ya *9s/2-3A*
Supper *2s/Aves. A-B*
Takahachi *Ave. A/5-6s*
Tarallucci e Vino *1A/10s*
Tasting Room *1s/1-2A*
Teresa's *1A/6-7s*
Tigerland *Ave. A/5-6s*
Tsampa *9s/2-3A*
26 Seats *Ave. B/10-1s*
Two Boots *multi. loc.*
Una Pizza *12s/1-2A*
Uno Chicago *3A/10-1s*
Veniero's *11s/1-2A*
Veselka *multi. loc.*
Xunta *1A/10-1s*
Yuca Bar *Ave. A/7s*
Zerza *6s/1-2A*
Zum Schneider *Ave. C/7s*

Financial District
(South of Murray St.)
Adrienne's Pizza *Pearl/Coenties*
Au Mandarin *Vesey/West*

Battery Gardens *Battery Pk.*
Bayard's *Hanover/Pearl-Stone*
Blue Water *Union Sq. W./16s*
Bobby Van's *Broad/Exchange*
Bridge Cafe *Water/Dover*
Brouwers/Stone St. *Stone/Pearl*
Bull Run *William/Pine*
Burritoville *Water/Broad*
Chipotle *Bway/Whitehall*
Cosí *Vesey/West*
Delmonico's *Beaver/William*
Fino *Wall/Pearl*
Fraunces Tavern *Pearl/Broad*
Gigino *Battery/West*
Grill Room *Liberty/West*
Hale & Hearty Soup *Broad/Beaver*
Harry's *multi. loc.*
Lemongrass Grill *William/Maiden*
Les Halles *John/Bway-Nassau*
Liberty View *S. End/3 Pl.-Thames*
Lili's Noodle *North End/Vesey*
Mangia *Wall/Nassau-William*
MarkJoseph *Water/Peck Slip*
P.J. Clarke's *World Fin./Vesey*
Roy's NY *Wash./Albany-Carlisle*
Smorgas Chef *Stone/William*
Trinity Place *Cedar/Bway-Trinity*
2 West *West/Battery*

Flatiron District
(14th to 24th Sts.,
6th Ave. to Park Ave. S.,
excluding Union Sq.)
Aleo *20s/5A*
Angelo & Maxie's *Park/19s*
Arezzo *22s/5-6A*
Aspen *22s/5-6A*
Barbounia *Park/20s*
Barça 18 *Park/18-9s*
Basta Pasta *17s/5-6A*
Beppe *22s/Bway-Park*
BLT Fish *17s/5-6A*
Bolo *22s/Bway-Park*
Boqueria *29s/5-6A*
Chipotle *6A/21-2s*
City Bakery *18s/5-6A*
City Crab *Park/19s*
Comfort Diner *23s/5-6A*
Cosí *multi. loc.*
Craft *19s/Bway-Park*
Craftbar *Bway/19-20s*
dévi *18s/Bway-5A*
Fleur de Sel *20s/Bway-5A*

Giorgio's/Gramercy *21s/Bway-Park*
Gramercy Tavern *20s/Bway-Park*
Haru *Park/18s*
Kitchen 22 *22s/Bway-Park*
La Pizza Fresca *20s/Bway-Park*
Le Pain Quotidien *19s/Bway-Park*
L'Express *Park/20s*
Lucy Latin Kit. *18s/Bway-Park*
Mangia *23s/5-6A*
Mayrose *Bway/21s*
Mesa Grill *5A/15-6s*
Mizu Sushi *20s/Bway-Park*
New York Burger *multi. loc.*
Outback *23s/5-6A*
Periyali *20s/5-6A*
Petite Abeille *17s/5-6A*
Pipa *19s/Bway-Park*
Planet Thailand *24s/5-6A*
Pump Energy Food *21s/Bway-Park*
Punch *Bway/20-1s*
Rickshaw Dumpling *23s/5-6A*
Rosa Mexicano *18s/Bway-5A*
Sala *19s/5-6A*
Sapa *24s/Bway-6A*
Shaffer City *21s/5-6A*
Shake Shack *Mad Sq./23s*
SushiSamba *Park/19-20s*
Tamarind *22s/Bway-Park*
Tarallucci e Vino *18s/Bway-5A*
Tossed *Park/22-3s*
Veritas *20s/Bway-Park*
Via Emilia *21s/Bway-Park*

Garment District
(30th to 40th Sts., west of 5th)
Abigael's *Bway/38-9s*
Aki Sushi *36s/Bway-7A*
Ben's Kosher Deli *38s/7-8A*
Burgers/Cupcakes *9A/35-6s*
Burritoville *39s/9A*
Camino Sur *37s/8-9A*
Carbone *38s/8-9A*
Chipotle *34s/8A*
Cho Dang Gol *35s/5-6A*
Cosí *7A/36-7s*
Dae Dong *32s/Bway-5A*
Frankie & Johnnie *37s/5-6A*
Gahm Mi Oak *32s/Bway-5A*
Gray's Papaya *8A/37s*
Hale & Hearty Soup *7A/35s*
Heartland Brew. *5A/34s*
HK *9A/39s*
Ida Mae *38s/Bway-6A*

Kang Suh *Bway/32s*
Keens *36s/5-6A*
Kum Gang San *32s/Bway-5A*
Mandoo Bar *32s/Bway-5A*
Nick & Stef's *33s/7-8A*
Osteria Gelsi *9A/38s*
Pump Energy Food *38s/Bway-6A*
Staghorn *36s/8-9A*
Uncle Jack's *9A/34-5s*
Won Jo *32s/Bway-5A*

Gramercy Park
(24th to 30th Sts., east of 5th;
14th to 24th Sts., east of Park)
Aki Sushi *27s/Lex-Park*
Anh *3A/26-7s*
A Voce *Mad/26s*
Baluchi's *29s/Lex-Park*
Bao Noodles *2A/22-3s*
BLT Prime *22s/Lex-Park*
Blue Smoke *27s/Lex-Park*
Burger Joint *3A/19-20s*
Butai *18s/Irving-Park*
Casa Mono *Irving/17s*
Chennai Garden *27s/Lex-Park*
Chino's *3A/16-7s*
Copper Chimney *28s/Lex-Park*
Coppola's *3A/27-8s*
Country *Mad/29s*
Curry Leaf *Lex/27s*
Dos Caminos *Park/26-7s*
Eleven Madison *Mad/24s*
Ess-a-Bagel *1A/21s*
Friend of a Farmer *Irving/18-9s*
Gramercy 24 *3A/24s*
Houston's *Park/27s*
I Trulli *27s/Lex-Park*
Ixta *29s/Mad-Park*
Jaiya Thai *3A/28s*
Japonais *18s/Irving-Park*
Lady Mendl's *Irving/17-8s*
Lamarca *22s/3A*
La Petite Auberge *Lex/27-8s*
Les Halles *Park/28-9s*
Los Dos Molinos *18s/Irving-Park*
Novitá *22s/Lex-Park*
Parea *20s/Bway-Park*
Park Bistro *Park/28-9s*
Paul & Jimmy's *18s/Irving-Park*
Pete's Tavern *18s/Irving*
Petite Abeille *20s/1A*
Pinch - Pizza *Park/28-9s*
Pongal *Lex/27-8s*

Pongsri Thai *2A/18s*
Posto *2A/18s*
Pure Food & Wine *Irving/17-8s*
Rice *Lex/28s*
Rolf's *3A/22s*
Saravanaas *Lex/26s*
71 Irving Pl. *Irving/18-9s*
Tabla *Mad/25s*
Totonno Pizza *2A/26s*
Turkish Kitchen *3A/27-8s*
Ureña *28s/Mad-Park*
Vatan *3A/29s*
Yama *17s/Irving*

Greenwich Village

(Houston to 14th Sts., west of
Bway, east of 7th Ave. S.,
excluding NoHo)

Aki *4s/Barrow-Jones*
Alta *10s/5-6A*
Amy's Bread *Blkr./Carmine-Leroy*
Annisa *Barrow/7A-4s*
A.O.C. Bedford *Bedford/Downing*
Arturo's Pizzeria *Houston/Thompson*
Babbo *Waverly/MacDougal-6A*
Bar Pitti *6A/Blkr.-Houston*
Bellavitae *Minetta/MacDougal-6A*
Blue Hill *Wash. Pl./MacDougal-6A*
Blue Ribbon Bakery *Downing/*
  Bedford
Borgo Antico *13s/5A-Uni.*
Cafe Asean *10s/Greenwich A-6A*
Cafe Español *multi. loc.*
Cafe Loup *13s/6-7A*
Cafe Spice *Uni./10-1s*
CamaJe *MacDougal/Blkr.-Houston*
Chanto *7A/Charles-10s*
Chez Jacqueline *MacDougal/Blkr.*
Chipotle *8s/Bway-Uni.*
Cornelia St. Cafe *Cornelia/Blkr.-4s*
Cosí *multi. loc.*
Cozy Soup/Burger *Bway/Astor*
Cru *5A/9s*
Cuba *Thompson/Blkr.-3s*
Cubana Café *Thompson/Prince*
Da Silvano *6A/Blkr.-Houston*
Deborah *Carmine/Bedford-Blkr.*
Ditch Plains *Bedford/Downing*
Do Hwa *Carmine/Bedford-7A*
El Charro Español *Charles/7A*
Elephant & Castle *Greenwich A/7A*
Empire Szechuan *multi. loc.*
Ennio & Michael *La Guardia/Blkr.-3s*

50 Carmine *Carmine/Bedford-Blkr.*
Fish *Blkr./Jones*
Flor's Kitchen *Waverly/6-7A*
41 Greenwich *Greenwich A/Charles*
French Roast *11s/6A*
Gobo *6A/8s-Waverly*
Gonzo *13s/6-7A*
Gotham B&G *12s/5A-Uni.*
Gradisca *13s/6-7A*
Gray's Papaya *6A/8s*
Gusto *Greenwich A/Perry*
Home *Cornelia/Blkr.-4s*
Il Cantinori *10s/Bway-Uni.*
Il Mulino *3s/Sullivan-Thompson*
'ino *Bedford/Downing-6A*
Inside *Jones/Blkr.-4s*
Isle *Blkr./Jones-7A*
Jack *Uni./11s*
Jane *Houston/La Guardia-Thompson*
Japonica *Uni./12s*
JivamukTea *Bway/13s*
Joe's Pizza *Carmine/Blkr.-6A*
John's Pizzeria *Blkr./6-7A*
Kati Roll Co. *MacDougal/Blkr.-3s*
Knickerbocker B&G *Uni./8-9s*
La Lanterna *MacDougal/3-4s*
La Palapa *6A/Wash. Pl.-4s*
Las Ramblas *4s/Cornelia-Jones*
Leela Lounge *3s/Bway-Mercer*
Le Gamin *Houston/MacDougal*
Le Gigot *Cornelia/Blkr.-4s*
Lemongrass Grill *13s/5A-Uni.*
Le Pain Quotidien *5A/8s*
Lupa *Thompson/Blkr.-Houston*
Marinella *Carmine/Bedford*
Mas *Downing/Bedford-Varick*
Maurizio Trattoria *13s/5-6A*
Meskerem *MacDougal/Blkr.-3s*
Mexicana Mama *12s/Bway-Uni.*
Minetta Tavern *MacDougal/Blkr.-3s*
Monte's *MacDougal/Blkr.-3s*
Negril *3s/La Guardia-Thompson*
Noodle Bar *Carmine/Bedford-Blkr.*
North Square *Waverly/MacDougal*
One if by Land *Barrow/7A-4s*
Osso Buco *Uni./11-2s*
Otto *5A/8s*
Patsy's Pizzeria *Uni./10-1s*
Peanut Butter & Co. *Sullivan/Blkr.*
Pearl Oyster *Cornelia/Blkr.-4s*
Philly Slim's *Uni./12-3s*
Piadina *10s/5-6A*
Piola *12s/Bway-Uni.*

Place, The *10s/Greenwich A-7A*
Pó *Cornelia/Blkr.-4s*
Prem-on Thai *Houston/MacDougal*
Rare B&G *Blkr./Carmine-6A*
Risotteria *Blkr./Morton*
Rocco *Thompson/Blkr.-Houston*
Sacred Chow *Sullivan/Blkr.-3s*
Saigon Grill *Uni./11-2s*
Spice *Uni./10s*
Strip House *12s/5A-Uni.*
Sumile *13s/6-7A*
SushiSamba *7A/Barrow*
Tomoe Sushi *Thompson/Blkr.*
Tratt. Pesce *Blkr./6-7A*
Uno Chicago *6A/8s-Waverly*
Village *9s/5-6A*
Villa Mosconi *MacDougal/Blkr.*
'wichcraft *8s/Mercer*
Yama *multi. loc.*
Zutto *Greenwich A/7A-11s*

Harlem/East Harlem
(110th to 157th Sts.,
excluding Columbia U. area)
Amy Ruth's *116s/Lenox-7A*
Billie's Black *119s/Douglass*
Charles' Southern *Douglass/151s*
Dinosaur BBQ *131s/12A*
Ginger *5A/116s*
Londel's *Douglass/139-40s*
Melba's *114s/Douglass*
Miss Mamie's/Maude's *multi. loc.*
Mo-Bay *125s/5A-Lenox*
Papaya King *125s/Lenox-7A*
Patsy's Pizzeria *1A/117-8s*
Pier 2110 *7A/125-6s*
Rao's *114s/Pleasant*
Revival *Douglass/127s*
River Room *145s/Riverside*
Sylvia's *Lenox/126-7s*

Little Italy
(Canal to Kenmare Sts.,
Bowery to Lafayette St.)
Angelo's/Mulberry *Mulberry/Grand*
Da Nico *Mulberry/Broome-Grand*
Ferrara *Grand/Mott-Mulberry*
Grotta Azzurra *Broome/Mulberry*
Il Cortile *Mulberry/Canal-Hester*
Il Fornaio *Mulberry/Grand-Hester*
Il Palazzo *Mulberry/Grand-Hester*
La Mela *Mulberry/Broome-Grand*
Nyonya *Grand/Mott-Mulberry*

Pellegrino's *Mulberry/Grand-Hester*
Pho Bang *Mott/Broome-Grand*
Positano *Mulberry/Canal-Hester*
Sal Anthony's *Mulberry/Grand*
Taormina *Mulberry/Grand-Hester*
Umberto's *Mulberry/Broome*
Vincent's *Mott/Hester*

Lower East Side
(Houston to Canal Sts.,
east of Bowery)
Alias *Clinton/Riving.*
ápizz *Eldridge/Riving.-Stanton*
Azul Bistro *Stanton/Suffolk*
Basso Est *Orchard/Houston*
Bereket *Houston/Orchard*
Big John *Orchard/Houston-Stanton*
Bondi Road *Riving./Clinton-Suffolk*
Chubo *Clinton/Houston-Stanton*
Clinton St. Baking *Clinton/Houston*
Cube 63 *Clinton/Riving.-Stanton*
Essex *Essex/Riving.*
Falai *Clinton/Riving.*
Frankies Spuntino *Clinton/Houston*
Freemans *Riving./Bowery-Chrystie*
'inoteca *Riving./Ludlow*
Katz's Deli *Houston/Ludlow*
Kuma Inn *Ludlow/Delancey-Riving.*
Le Père Pinard *Ludlow/Houston*
Les Enfants Terribles *Canal/Ludlow*
Little Giant *Orchard/Broome*
Oliva *Houston/Allen*
Orchard, The *Orchard/Riving.*
Palà *Allen/Stanton*
Paladar *Ludlow/Houston-Stanton*
Salt *Clinton/Houston-Stanton*
Sammy's Roumanian *Chrystie/
    Delancey*
Schiller's *Riving./Norfolk*
Stanton Social *Stanton/Ludlow*
Suba *Ludlow/Delancey-Riving.*
Thor *Riving./Essex-Ludlow*
Tides *Norfolk/Delancey-Riving.*
wd-50 *Clinton/Riving.-Stanton*

Meatpacking District
(Gansevoort to 15th Sts.,
west of 9th Ave.)
Buddha Bar *Little W. 12s/9A-Wash.*
5 Ninth *9A/Gansevoort-Little W. 12s*
Florent *Gansevoort/Greenwich s*
Highline *Wash./Little W. 12s*
Macelleria *Gansevoort/Greenwich s*

Markt *14s/9A*
Old Homestead *9A/14-5s*
One *Little W. 12s/9A*
Ono *9A/13s*
Paradou *Little W. 12s/Greenwich s*
Pastis *9A/Little W. 12s*
Pop Burger *9A/14-5s*
Sascha *Gansevoort/Greenwich s*
Son Cubano *14s/9A-Wash.*
Spice Market *13s/9A*
Valbella *13s/9A-Wash.*
Vento *Hudson/14s*

Murray Hill

(30th to 40th Sts., east of 5th)
Aji Sushi *3A/34-5s*
Ali Baba *34s/2-3A*
AQ Cafe *Park/37-8s*
Aquamarine *2A/38-9s*
Artisanal *32s/Mad-Park*
Asia de Cuba *Mad/37-8s*
Barbès *36s/5A-Mad*
Barking Dog *34s/Lex-3A*
Better Burger *3A/37s*
Blockhead Burrito *3A/33-4s*
Carl's Steaks *3A/34s*
Cosette *33s/Lex-3A*
Da Ciro *Lex/33-4s*
El Parador Cafe *34s/1-2A*
El Pote *2A/38-9s*
Ethos *3A/33-4s*
Evergreen Shanghai *38s/5A-Mad*
Fino *36s/5A-Mad*
Franchia *Park/34-5s*
Grand Sichuan *Lex/33-4s*
Hangawi *32s/5A-Mad*
Iron Sushi *3A/30-1s*
Jackson Hole *3A/35s*
Josie's *3A/37s*
La Giara *3A/33-4s*
Lemongrass Grill *34s/Lex-3A*
Madison Bistro *Mad/37-8s*
Marbella *33s/Lex-3A*
Mee Noodle Shop *2A/30-31s*
Mishima *Lex/30-1s*
Morgan, The *Mad/36-7s*
Pasticcio *3A/30-1s*
Patsy's Pizzeria *3A/34-5s*
Penelope *Lex/30s*
Pizza 33 *3A/33s*
Pump Energy Food *31s/Lex-Park*
Rare B&G *Lex/37s*
Rossini's *38s/Lex-Park*

Salute! *Mad/39s*
Sarge's Deli *3A/36-7s*
Stella del Mare *Lex/39-40s*
Sushi Sen-nin *33s/Mad-Park*
Todai *32s/5A-Mad*
Tratt. Alba *34s/2-3A*
Trio *33s/Lex-3A*
Villa Berulia *34s/Lex-Park*
Water Club *E. River/23s*
Waterfront Ale *2A/30s*
Wolfgang's *Park/33s*
Wu Liang Ye *Lex/39-40s*

NoHo

(Houston to 4th Sts.,
Bowery to Bway)
Bianca *Blkr./Bowery-Elizabeth*
Bond Street *Bond/Bway-Lafayette*
Chinatown Brasserie *Lafayette/Gr. Jones*
Five Points *Gr. Jones/Bowery*
Great Jones Cafe *Gr. Jones/Bowery*
Hedeh *Gr. Jones/Bowery-Lafayette*
Il Buco *Bond/Bowery-Lafayette*
NoHo Star *Lafayette/Blkr.*
Quartino *Blkr./Elizabeth*
Sala *Bowery/Gr. Jones*
Serafina *Lafayette/4s*
Sparky's American *Lafayette/Blkr.*
Two Boots *Blkr./Bway*

NoLita

(Houston to Kenmare Sts.,
Bowery to Lafayette St.)
barmarché *Spring/Elizabeth*
Blue/Green *Mott/Houston-Prince*
Bread *Spring/Elizabeth-Mott*
Cafe Colonial *Elizabeth/Houston*
Cafe Gitane *Mott/Prince*
Café Habana *Prince/Elizabeth*
Ghenet *Mulberry/Houston-Prince*
In Tent *Mott/Prince-Spring*
Jacques *Prince/Elizabeth-Mott*
Kitchen Club *Prince/Mott*
La Esquina *Kenmare/Lafayette*
Le Jardin Bistro *Cleveland/Kenmare*
Little Charlie's *Kenmare/Bowery*
Lombardi's *Spring/Mott-Mulberry*
Mexican Radio *Cleveland/Kenmare*
Peasant *Elizabeth/Prince-Spring*
Public *Elizabeth/Prince-Spring*
Rice *Mott/Prince-Spring*
Room 4 Dessert *Cleveland/Kenmare*

Spring St. Natural *Spring/Lafayette*
Tasting Room *Elizabeth/Houston*
24 Prince *Prince/Elizabeth-Mott*

SoHo
(Canal to Houston Sts.,
west of Lafayette St.)
Ama *MacDougal/King-Prince*
Aquagrill *Spring/6A*
Balthazar *Spring/Bway-Crosby*
Baluchi's *Spring/Sullivan-Thompson*
Barolo *W. Bway/Broome-Spring*
Bistro Les Amis *Spring/Thompson*
Blue Ribbon *Sullivan/Prince-Spring*
Blue Ribbon Sushi *Sullivan/Prince*
Boom *Spring/W. Bway-Wooster*
Cendrillon *Mercer/Broome-Grand*
Chipotle *Varick/Houston-King*
Cipriani Dwntn *W. Bway/Broome*
Country Café *Thompson/Broome*
Cub Room *Sullivan/Prince*
Dani *Hudson/Charlton*
Dos Caminos *W. Bway/Houston*
Emack & Bolio's *Houston/W. Bway*
Félix *W. Bway/Grand*
Fiamma Osteria *Spring/6A-Sullivan*
Giorgione *multi. loc.*
Hampton Chutney *Prince/Crosby*
Honmura An *Mercer/Houston-Prince*
HQ *Thompson/Prince-Spring*
Ideya *W. Bway/Broome-Grand*
Il Corallo *Prince/Sullivan-Thompson*
I Tre Merli *W. Bway/Houston-Prince*
Ivo & Lulu *Broome/6A-Varick*
Jean Claude *Sullivan/Prince*
Jerry's *Prince/Greene-Mercer*
Kelley & Ping *Greene/Prince*
Kin Khao *Spring/Thompson-W. Bway*
Kittichai *Thompson/Broome-Spring*
L'Ecole *Bway/Grand*
Le Pain Quotidien *Grand/Greene*
Lupe's East LA Kit. *6A/Watts*
Lure Fishbar *Mercer/Prince*
Mercer Kitchen *Prince/Mercer*
Mezzogiorno *Spring/Sullivan*
Ñ *Crosby/Broome-Grand*
Novecento *W. Bway/Broome-Grand*
Novo *Hudson/Dominick-Spring*
Omen *Thompson/Prince-Spring*
Once Upon a Tart *Sullivan/Prince*
Peep *Prince/Sullivan-Thompson*
Pepe...To Go *Sullivan/Prince*
Provence *MacDougal/Prince*

Raoul's *Prince/Sullivan-Thompson*
Salt *MacDougal/Houston-Prince*
Savoy *Prince/Crosby*
Snack *Thompson/Prince-Spring*
'wichcraft *Crosby/Prince*
Woo Lae Oak *Mercer/Prince*
Zoë *Prince/Bway-Mercer*

South Street Seaport
Cabana *Pier 17/Fulton*
Harbour Lights *Pier 17/Fulton*
Heartland Brew. *South/Fulton*
Pietrasanta *Fulton/Gold*
Quartino *Peck Slip/Water*
Uno Chicago *Pier 17/Fulton*

TriBeCa
(Canal to Murray Sts.,
west of Bway)
Acappella *Hudson/Chambers*
Arqua *Church/White*
Azafran *Warren/Greenwich s*
Baluchi's *Greenwich s/Warren*
Blaue Gans *Duane/Church-W. Bway*
Bouley *W. Bway/Duane*
Bouley, Upstairs *W. Bway/Duane*
Bread Tribeca *Church/Walker*
Bubby's *Hudson/Moore*
Burritoville *Chambers/Church*
Capsouto Frères *Wash./Watts*
Carl's Steaks *Chambers/Bway*
Centrico *W. Bway/Franklin*
Cercle Rouge *W. Bway/Beach-White*
Chanterelle *Harrison/Hudson*
Churrascaria *W. Bway/Franklin*
City Hall *Duane/Church-W. Bway*
Danube *Hudson/Duane-Reade*
Devin Tavern *Greenwich s/Franklin*
dominic *Greenwich s/Harrison-Jay*
Duane Park Cafe *Duane/Hudson*
Dylan Prime *Laight/Greenwich s*
Ecco *Chambers/Church-W. Bway*
F.illi Ponte *Desbrosses/West*
Flor de Sol *Greenwich s/Franklin*
fresh *Reade/Church-W. Bway*
Gigino *Greenwich s/Duane-Reade*
Harrison, The *Greenwich s/Harrison*
Il Giglio *Warren/Greenwich s*
Il Mattone *Greenwich s/Hubert*
Industria Argentina *Greenwich s/
    Duane-Jay*
Kitchenette *Chambers/Greenwich s*
Kori *Church/Franklin-Leonard*

Landmarc *W. Bway/Leonard-Worth*
Mary Ann's *W. Bway/Chambers*
Megu *Thomas/Church-W. Bway*
Montrachet *W. Bway/Walker-White*
Mr. Chow Tribeca *Hudson/Moore*
Nam *Reade/W. Bway*
Ninja *Hudson/Duane-Reade*
Nobu *multi. loc.*
Odeon *W. Bway/Duane-Thomas*
Pepolino *W. Bway/Canal-Lispenard*
Petite Abeille *W. Bway/Duane*
Petrarca Vino *White/Church*
Roc *Duane/Greenwich s*
Salaam Bombay *Greenwich s/*
   Duane-Reade
Scalini Fedeli *Duane/Greenwich s*
66 *Church/Leonard-Worth*
Sosa Borella *Greenwich s/Watts*
Takahachi *Duane/Church-W. Bway*
Thalassa *Franklin/Greenwich s*
Tribeca Grill *Greenwich s/Franklin*
Turks & Frogs *Greenwich s/Watts*
VietCafé *Greenwich s/Harrison-Jay*
'wichcraft *Greenwich s/Beach*
Wolfgang's *Greenwich s/Beach*
Zutto *Hudson/Harrison*

Union Square
(14th to 17th Sts.,
5th Ave. to Union Sq. E.)
Candela *16s/Irving-Park*
Chat 'n Chew *16s/5A-Union Sq. W.*
Chop't Creative *17s/Bway-5A*
Coffee Shop *Union Sq. W./16s*
Havana Central *17s/Bway-5A*
Heartland Brew. *Union Sq. W./16-7s*
Max Brenner *Bway/13-4s*
Olives *Park/17s*
Republic *Union Sq. W./16-7s*
Steak Frites *16s/5A-Union Sq. W.*
Tocqueville *15s/5A-Union Sq. W.*
Union Sq. Cafe *16s/5A-Union Sq. W.*
Whole Foods *Union Sq. S./Bway-Uni.*
Zen Palate *Union Sq. E./16s*

Washington Hts./Inwood
(North of W. 157th St.)
Dallas BBQ *Bway/166s*
El Malecon *Bway/175s*
Empire Szechuan *Bway/170-71s*
Hispaniola *181s/Cabrini*
New Leaf *Corbin/190s*
107 West *187s/Ft. Wash.-Pinehurst*
Park Terrace *Bway/Isham-207s*

West 40s
Above *42s/7-8A*
AJ Maxwell's *48s/5-6A*
Akdeniz *46s/5-6A*
Alfredo of Rome *49s/5-6A*
Algonquin *44s/5-6A*
Amarone *9A/47-8s*
Amy's Bread *9A/46-7s*
Angus McIndoe *44s/Bway-8A*
Baldoria *49s/Bway-8A*
Barbetta *46s/8-9A*
Basilica *9A/46-7s*
Becco *46s/8-9A*
Better Burger *9A/42-3s*
Blue Fin *Bway/47s*
Bond 45 *45s/6-7A*
Breeze *9A/45-6s*
Bryant Park *40s/5-6A*
B. Smith's *46s/8-9A*
Burritoville *9A/44s*
Cafe Un Deux *44s/Bway-6A*
Cara Mia *9A/45-6s*
Carmine's *44s/Bway-8A*
Cascina *9A/45-6s*
Chez Josephine *42s/9-10A*
Chimichurri Grill *9A/43-4s*
Chipotle *42s/5-6A*
Churrascaria *49s/8-9A*
City Lobster *49s/6-7A*
Cosí *42s/5-6A*
Daisy May's *11A/46s*
Dallas BBQ *42s/7-8A*
db Bistro Moderne *44s/5-6A*
Del Frisco's *6A/49s*
Delta Grill *9A/48s*
Dervish Turkish *47s/6-7A*
District *46s/6-7A*
Don Giovanni *44s/8-9A*
Edison Cafe *47s/Bway-8A*
Energy Kitchen *47s/9-10A*
Esca *43s/9A*
ESPN Zone *Bway/42s*
etcetera etcetera *44s/8-9A*
FireBird *46s/8-9A*
Foley's Fish *7A/47-8s*
44 *44s/5-6A*
44 & X Hell's Kit. *10A/44s*
Frankie & Johnnie *45s/Bway-8A*
Hakata Grill *48s/Bway-8A*
Hale & Hearty Soup *42s/5-6A*
Hallo Berlin *10A/44-5s*
Hard Rock Cafe *Bway/43s*
Haru *43s/Bway-8A*

Havana Central *46s/6-7A*
Heartland Brew. *43s/Bway-6A*
Hell's Kitchen *9A/46-7s*
Jewel of India *44s/5-6A*
Jezebel *9A/45s*
Joe Allen *46s/8-9A*
John's Pizzeria *44s/Bway-8A*
Junior's *45s/Bway-8A*
Kati Roll Co. *46s/6-7A*
Kellari Taverna *44s/5-6A*
Kodama *45s/8-9A*
Koi *40s/5-6A*
Kyma *46s/8A*
La Locanda Vini *9A/49-50s*
La Masseria *48s/Bway-8A*
La Rivista *46s/8-9A*
Lattanzi *46s/8-9A*
Le Madeleine *43s/9-10A*
Le Marais *46s/6-7A*
Le Rivage *46s/8-9A*
Luxia *48s/8-9A*
Marseille *9A/44s*
Meskerem *47s/9-10A*
Monster Sushi *46s/5-6A*
My Most Favorite *45s/Bway-6A*
Ollie's *44s/Bway-8A*
Orso *46s/8-9A*
Osteria al Doge *44s/Bway-6A*
Pam Real Thai *multi. loc.*
Pietrasanta *9A/47s*
Pigalle *8A/48s*
Pongsri Thai *48s/Bway-8A*
Rainbow Room *49s/5-6A*
Re Sette *45s/5-6A*
Ruby Foo's *Bway/49s*
Sardi's *44s/Bway-8A*
Scarlatto *47s/Bway-8A*
Sea Grill *49s/5-6A*
Shula's *43s/Bway-8A*
Sushiden *49s/6-7A*
Sushi Zen *44s/Bway-6A*
Tintol *46s/6-7A*
Tony Luke's *9A/41-2s*
Tony's Di Napoli *43s/Bway-6A*
Tossed *Rock Plz./49-50s*
Triomphe *44s/5-6A*
Turkish Cuisine *9A/44-5s*
Two Boots *Rock Plz./49-50s*
Utsav *46s/6-7A*
Via Brasil *46s/5-6A*
View, The *Bway/45-6s*
Virgil's Real BBQ *44s/Bway-6A*
West Bank Cafe *42s/9-10A*

'wichcraft *6A/40-2s*
Wu Liang Ye *48s/5-6A*
Zen Palate *9A/46s*

West 50s
Abboccato *55s/6-7A*
Acqua Pazza *52s/5-6A*
Afghan Kebab *9A/51-2s*
Aki Sushi *52s/8-9A*
Alain Ducasse *58s/6-7A*
Angelo's Pizza *multi. loc.*
Azucar *8A/55-6s*
Azuri Cafe *51s/9-10A*
Baluchi's *56s/Bway-8A*
Bann *50s/8-9A*
Bar Americain *52s/6-7A*
Bay Leaf *56s/5-6A*
Beacon *56s/5-6A*
Bello *9A/56s*
Ben Benson's *52s/6-7A*
BG *5A/57-8s*
Blockhead Burrito *50s/8-9A*
bluechili *51s/Bway-8A*
Bobby Van's *50s/6-7A*
Bombay Palace *52s/5-6A*
Brasserie 8½ *57s/5-6A*
Brasserie LCB *55s/5-6A*
Brasserie Ruhlmann *50s/5-6A*
Bricco *56s/8-9A*
Brooklyn Diner *57s/Bway-7A*
burger joint/Parker M. *56s/6-7A*
Café Botanica *CPS/6-7A*
Cafe Spice *55s/5-6A*
Caffe Cielo *8A/52-3s*
Carnegie Deli *7A/55s*
Chez Napoléon *50s/8-9A*
China Grill *53s/5-6A*
Cité *51s/6-7A*
Cité Grill *51s/6-7A*
Cosí *Bway/51s*
Da Tommaso *8A/53-4s*
Eatery *9A/53s*
El Centro *9A/54s*
Empanada Mama *9A/51-2s*
Fives *5A/55s*
Gallagher's *52s/Bway-8A*
Grand Sichuan *9A/50-1s*
Greek Kitchen *10A/58s*
Hale & Hearty Soup *56s/5-6A*
Heartland Brew. *6A/51s*
Hudson Cafeteria *58s/8-9A*
Il Gattopardo *54s/5-6A*
Il Tinello *56s/5-6A*

Island Burgers *9A/51-2s*
Joe's *56s/5-6A*
La Bonne Soupe *55s/5-6A*
La Vineria *55s/5-6A*
Le Bernardin *51s/6-7A*
Le Pain Quotidien *7A/58s*
Lili's Noodle *7A/56-7s*
Maison *7A/53-4s*
Mangia *57s/5-6A*
Maria Pia *51s/8-9A*
McCormick & Schmick *52s/6-7A*
Mee Noodle Shop *9A/53s*
Menchanko-tei *55s/5-6A*
Michael's *55s/5-6A*
Milos *55s/6-7A*
Modern, The *53s/5-6A*
Molyvos *7A/55-6s*
Nino's *58s/6-7A*
Nobu 57 *57s/5-6A*
Nocello *55s/Bway-8A*
Nook *9A/50s*
Norma's *57s/6-7A*
Osteria del Circo *55s/6-7A*
Palm *50s/Bway-8A*
Patsy's *56s/Bway-8A*
Petrossian *58s/7A*
Philly Slim's *9A/52-3s*
Piano Due *51s/6-7A*
Pump Energy Food *55s/5-6A*
Puttanesca *9A/56s*
Quality Meats *58s/5-6A*
Redeye Grill *7A/56s*
Red Garlic *8A/54-5s*
Remi *53s/6-7A*
René Pujol *51s/8-9A*
Rice 'n' Beans *9A/50-1s*
Roberto Passon *9A/50s*
Rock Center Cafe *50s/5-6A*
Rue 57 *57s/6A*
Russian Samovar *52s/Bway-8A*
Ruth's Chris *51s/6-7A*
San Domenico *CPS/Bway-7A*
Sarabeth's *CPS/5-6A*
Serafina *55s/Bway*
Shelly's *57s/5-6A*
Siam Inn *8A/51-2s*
Soba Nippon *52s/5-6A*
Sosa Borella *8A/50s*
Stage Deli *7A/53-4s*
Sugiyama *55s/Bway-8A*
Sushiya *56s/5-6A*
Taboon *10A/52s*

Tang Pavilion *55s/5-6A*
Thalia *8A/50s*
Topaz Thai *56s/6-7A*
Town *56s/5-6A*
Tratt. Dell'Arte *7A/56-7s*
21 Club *52s/5-6A*
Uncle Nick's *9A/50-1s*
ViceVersa *51s/8-9A*
Victor's Cafe *52s/Bway-8A*
Vynl *9A/51s*
Whole Foods *60s/Bway*
Whym *9A/57-8s*
Wondee Siam *multi. loc.*
Xing *9A/52s*
Yakitori Totto *55s/Bway-8A*
Zona Rosa *56s/5-6A*

West 60s
Asiate *60s/Bway*
Bar Masa *60s/Bway*
Bouchon Bakery *60s/Bway*
Café des Artistes *67s/Col.-CPW*
Café Fiorello *Bway/63-4s*
Café Gray *60s/Bway*
Empire Szechuan *Col./68-9s*
Gabriel's *60s/Bway-Col.*
Grand Tier *Lincoln Ctr./63-5s*
Hale & Hearty Soup *Rock Plz./49s*
Jean Georges *CPW/60-1s*
Josephina *Bway/63-4s*
La Boîte en Bois *68s/Col.-CPW*
Le Pain Quotidien *65s/Bway-CPW*
Levana *69s/Bway-Col.*
Masa *60s/Bway*
Nick & Toni's *67s/Bway-Col.*
Ollie's *Bway/67-8s*
O'Neals' *64s/Bway-CPW*
per se *60s/Bway*
Picholine *64s/Bway-CPW*
Porter House NY *60s/Bway*
Rosa Mexicano *Col./62s*
Sapphire Indian *Bway/60-1s*
Shun Lee Cafe *65s/Col.-CPW*
Shun Lee West *65s/Col.-CPW*
Tavern on Green *CPW/66-7s*
Telepan *69s/Col.-CPW*

West 70s
Alice's Tea Cup *73s/Amst.-Col.*
Arté Café *73s/Amst.-Col.*
Bello Sguardo *Amst./79-80s*
Bettola *Amst./79-80s*

Big Nick's Burger *multi. loc.*
Bistro Cassis *Col./70-1s*
Burritoville *72s/Amst.-Col.*
Café Frida *Col./77-8s*
Cafe Luxembourg *70s/Amst.-W. End*
Cafe Ronda *Col./71-2s*
'Cesca *75s/Amst.*
Citrus B&G *Amst./75s*
Compass *70s/Amst.-W. End*
Coppola's *W. 79s/Amst.-Bway*
Cosí *Bway/76s*
Dallas BBQ *72s/Col.-CPW*
Emack & Bolio's *Amst./78-9s*
Empire Szechuan *72s/Bway-W. End*
En Plo *77s/Col.*
Epices du Traiteur *70s/Col.*
Fairway Cafe *Bway/74s*
Gari *Col./77-8s*
Gray's Papaya *Bway/72s*
Hunan Park *Col./70-1s*
Isabella's *Col./77s*
Ivy's Cafe *72s/Bway-Col.*
Jacques-Imo's *Col./77s*
Josie's *Amst./74s*
La Grolla *Amst./79-80s*
La Vela *Amst./77-8s*
Le Pain Quotidien *72s/Col.-CPW*
Metsovo *70s/Col.-CPW*
Mughlai *Col./75s*
Nice Matin *79s/Amst.*
Ocean Grill *Col./78-9s*
Onera *79s/Amst.-Bway*
Pappardella *Col./75s*
Pasha *71s/Col.-CPW*
Patsy's Pizzeria *74s/Col.-CPW*
Penang *Col./71s*
Pomodoro Rosso *Col./70-1s*
Ruby Foo's *Bway/77s*
Sambuca *72s/Col.-CPW*
San Luigi *Amst./74-5s*
Santa Fe *71s/Col.-CPW*
Savann *Amst./79-80s*
Scaletta *77s/Col.-CPW*
Swagat Indian *Amst./79-80s*
Tenzan *Col./73s*
Viand *Bway/75s*

West 80s

Aix Brasserie *Bway/88s*
Artie's Deli *Bway/82-3s*
Barney Greengrass *Amst./86-7s*
Bistro Citron *Col./82-3s*
Brother Jimmy's *Amst./80-1s*

Cafe Con Leche *Amst./80-1s*
Calle Ocho *Col./81-2s*
Celeste *Amst./84-5s*
Columbus Bakery *Col./82-3s*
Darna *Col./89s*
Docks Oyster Bar *Bway/89-90s*
EJ's Luncheonette *Amst./81-2s*
Flor de Mayo *Amst./83-4s*
French Roast *Bway/85s*
Good Enough to Eat *Amst./83-4s*
Hampton Chutney *Amst./82-3s*
Haru *Amst./80-1s*
Jackson Hole *Col./85s*
La Mirabelle *86s/Amst.-Col.*
Land *Amst./81-2s*
Le Pain Quotidien *Amst./84s*
Loft *Col./84-5s*
Luzia's *Amst./80-1s*
Nëo Sushi *Bway/83s*
Neptune Room *Amst./84-5s*
Nonna *Col./85s*
Ollie's *Bway/84s*
Ouest *Bway/83-4s*
Pair of 8's *Amst./87-8s*
Popover Cafe *Amst./86-7s*
Rain *82s/Amst.-Col.*
Roppongi *Amst./81s*
Sarabeth's *Amst./80-1s*
Sol y Sombra *Amst./82-3s*
Spiga *84s/Amst.-Bway*
Sushi Hana *Amst./82-3s*
Uno Chicago *Col./81s*
Zabar's Cafe *Bway/80s*
Zeytin *Col./85s*

West 90s

Alouette *Bway/97-8s*
Cafe Con Leche *Amst./95-6s*
Carmine's *Bway/90-1s*
El Malecon *Amst./97-8s*
Gabriela's *Col./93-4s*
Gennaro *Amst./92-3s*
Lemongrass Grill *Bway/94-5s*
Lisca *Amst./92-3s*
Mary Ann's *Bway/90-1s*
Pampa *Amst./97-8s*
Regional *Bway/98-9s*
Roth's Westside *Col./93s*
Saigon Grill *Amst./90s*
Sipan *Amst./94s*
Tratt. Pesce *Col./90-1s*
Yuki Sushi *Amst./92s*

West 100s
(See also Harlem/
East Harlem)
A *Col./106-7s*
Awash Ethiopian *Amst./106-7s*
Bistro Ten 18 *Amst./110s*
Café du Soleil *Bway/104s*
Carne *Bway/105s*
Empire Szechuan *Bway/100s*
Flor de Mayo *Bway/101s*
Indus Valley *Bway/100s*
Kitchenette *Amst./122-3s*
Le Monde *Bway/112-3s*
Mamá Mexico *Bway/102s*
Max SoHa *Amst./123s*
Métisse *105s/Amst.-Bway*
Mill Korean *Bway/112-3s*
Ollie's *Bway/116s*
107 West *Bway/107-8s*
Picnic Market *Bway/101s*
Pisticci *La Salle/Bway*
Rack & Soul *Bway/109s*
Sezz Medi' *Amst./122s*
Symposium *113s/Amst.-Bway*
Terrace in the Sky *119s/Amst.*
Tokyo Pop *Bway/104-5s*
Tomo Sushi *Bway/110-1s*
Turkuaz *Bway/100s*
V&T *Amst./110-1s*

West Village
(Houston to 14th Sts.,
west of 7th Ave. S., excluding
Meatpacking District)
Agave *7A/Charles-10s*
Alexandra *Hudson/Barrow-Morton*
Alfama *Hudson/Perry*
Antica Venezia *West/10s*
A.O.C. *Blkr./Grove*
A Salt & Battery *Greenwich A/12-3s*
August *Blkr.-Charles-10s*
Barbuto *Wash./Jane-12s*
Burritoville *Blkr./7A*
Cafe Condesa *10s/7A-4s*
Café de Bruxelles *Greenwich A/13s*
Casa *Bedford/Commerce*
Chow Bar *4s/10s*
Corner Bistro *4s/Jane*
Cowgirl *Hudson/10s*
Crispo *14s/7-8A*
Da Andrea *Hudson/Perry-11s*
Diablo Royale *10s/Blkr.-4s*
Dirty Bird to-go *14s/7-8A*

Dublin 6 *Hudson/Bank-11s*
El Faro *Greenwich s/Horatio*
Emack & Bolio's *7A/13-4s*
Employees Only *Hudson/10s*
Energy Kitchen *Christopher/Blkr.-7A*
EN Japanese *Hudson/Leroy*
Extra Virgin *4s/Charles-Perry*
Fatty Crab *Hudson/Gansevoort*
Gavroche *14s/7-8A*
good *Greenwich A/Bank-12s*
Havana Alma *Christopher/Bedford*
I Tre Merli *10s/4s*
Jarnac *12s/Greenwich s*
La Focaccia *Bank/4s*
La Ripaille *Hudson/Bethune-12s*
Le Gamin *Hudson/Charles-10s*
Lima's Taste *Christopher/Bedford*
Little Owl *Bedford/Grove*
Malatesta *Wash./Christopher*
Maremma *10s/Blkr.-Hudson*
Mary's Fish Camp *Charles/4s*
Mercadito *7A/Grove*
Mexicana Mama *Hudson/10s*
Mi Cocina *Jane/Hudson*
Miracle Grill *Blkr./Bank-11s*
Monster Sushi *Hudson/Charles*
Moustache *Bedford/Barrow-Grove*
Osteria del Sole *4s/Perry*
Papaya King *14s/7A*
Paris Commune *Bank/Greenwich s*
Pepe...To Go *Hudson/Perry-11s*
Perry Street *Perry/West*
Petite Abeille *Hudson/Barrow*
Philip Marie *Hudson/11s*
Piccolo Angolo *Hudson/Jane*
Pink Tea Cup *Grove/Bedford-Blkr.*
Place, The *4s/Bank-12s*
Sant Ambroeus *4s/Perry*
Setacci *Hudson/St. Luke's*
Sevilla *Charles/4s*
Smorgas Chef *12s/4s*
Snack *Bedford/Morton*
Spotted Pig *11s/Greenwich s*
Surya *Blkr./Grove-7A*
Taka *Grove/Blkr.-7A*
Tartine *11s/4s*
Tea & Sympathy *Greenwich A/12-3s*
Two Boots *11s/7A*
Vittorio Cucina *Blkr./Grove-7A*
Wallsé *11s/Wash.*
Westville *10s/Blkr.-4s*
Wild Ginger *Grove/Blkr.-7A*

BRONX

Beccofino *Mosholu/Fieldston*
Bruckner B&G *Bruckner/3A*
Coals *Eastchester/Morris Park*
Dominick's *Arthur/Crescent-187s*
El Malecon *Bway/231s*
Enzo's *multi. loc.*
F & J Pine *Bronxdale/Morris*
Jake's *Bway/242s*
Le Refuge Inn *City Is./Beach-Cross*
Liebman's *235s/Johnson*
Lobster Box *City Is./Belden*
Madison's *Riverdale/259s*
Mario's *Arthur/184-6s*

Mother's Bake Shop *235/Oxford*
Park Place *Mosholu/Bway*
Pasquale's Rigoletto *Arthur/ Crescent*
Pio Pio *Cypress/138-9s*
Portofino's *City Is./Cross*
Riverdale Garden *Manhtn Coll./242s*
Roberto's *Crescent/Hughes*
Siam Square *Kappock/Henry Hudson*
Tosca Café *Tremont/Miles-Sampson*
Umberto's *Arthur/186s*
Willie's *Westchester/Taylor-Thieriot*

BROOKLYN

Bay Ridge
Agnanti *5A/78s*
Areo *3A/84-5s*
Austin's *5A/90s*
Baluchi's *3A/84s*
Cebu *3A/88s*
Chadwick's *3A/89s*
Chianti *3A/86s*
Eliá *3A/86-7s*
Embers *3A/95-6s*
Meze *3A/72s*
Mr. Tang *3A/76s*
Omonia Cafe *3A/76-7s*
101 *4A/100-1s*
Pearl Room *3A/82s*
Tanoreen *3A/77-8s*
Tuscany Grill *3A/86-7s*
Uno Chicago *4A/92s*

Bensonhurst
L & B Spumoni *86s/10-1s*
Tommaso's *86s/14-5A*

Boerum Hill
BarTabac *Smith/Dean*
Brawta Caribbean *Atlantic/Hoyt*
Chance *Smith/Butler*
Downtown Atlantic *Atlantic/Bond*
Jolie *Atlantic/Hoyt-Smith*
Mai *Atlantic/Nevins-3A*
Nicky's Viet. *Atlantic/Hoyt-Smith*
Saul *Smith/Bergen-Dean*
Sherwood Cafe *Smith/Baltic*

Borough Park
Tenzan *18A/71s*

Brighton Beach
Mr. Tang *Coney Is./Ave. X*

Brooklyn Heights
Caffe Buon Gusto *Montague/ Clinton-Henry*
Chipotle *Montague/Court*
ChipShop/Curry *Atlantic/Clinton*
Curry Leaf *Remsen/Clinton-Court*
Hale & Hearty Soup *Court/Remsen*
Henry's End *Henry/Cranberry*
Kapadokya *Montague/Clinton-Henry*
Noodle Pudding *Henry/Cranberry*
Queen *Court/Livingston-Schermer.*
Teresa's *Montague/Hicks*
Waterfront Ale *Atlantic/Clinton*

Carroll Gardens
Alma *Col./Degraw*
Bouillabaisse 126 *Union/Col.-Hicks*
Chestnut *Smith/Degraw-Sackett*
Cubana Café *Smith/Degraw*
Ferdinando's *Union/Col.-Hicks*
Fragole *Court/Carroll-1 Pl.*
Frankies Spuntino *Court/4 Pl.*
Grocery, The *Smith/Sackett-Union*
Marco Polo *Court/Union*
Panino'teca 275 *Smith/Degraw*
Patois *Smith/Degraw-Douglass*
Provence en Boite *Smith/Degraw*
Royal's Downtown *Union/Clinton*
Savoia *Smith/Degraw-Sackett*
Union Smith Café *Smith/Union*
Zaytoons *Smith/Sackett*

Clinton Hill
Locanda Vini/Olii *Gates/Cambridge*
Maggie Brown *Myrtle/Wash.*

Cobble Hill
Bocca Lupo *Henry/Warren*
Cafe Luluc *Smith/Baltic*

Cube 63 *Court/Baltic-Warren*
Joya *Court/Warren*
Lemongrass Grill *Court/Dean*
Little Bistro *Court/Pacific*
Mancora *Smith/Warren-Wyckoff*
Osaka *Court/Degraw-Kane*
Porchetta *Smith/Douglass*
Quercy *Court/Baltic-Kane*
Sweet Melissa *Court/Butler*

Coney Island
Gargiulo's *15s/Mermaid-Surf*
Totonno Pizza *Neptune/15-6s*

Ditmas Park
Farm on Adderley *Cortelyou/*
    Stratford-Westminster
Picket Fence *Cortelyou/Argyle*

Downtown
Dallas BBQ *Livingston/Hoyt-Smith*
Junior's *Flatbush/DeKalb*

Dumbo
Blue/Green *Jay/John-Plymouth*
Bubby's *Main/Plymouth-Water*
Five Front *Front/Old Fulton*
Grimaldi's *Old Fulton/Front-Water*
Pete's Downtown *Water/Old Fulton*
Rice *Wash./Front-York*
River Café *Water/Furman-Old Fulton*
Superfine *Front/Jay-Pearl*

Dyker Heights
Outback *86s/15A*

Fort Greene
Chez Oskar *DeKalb/Adelphi*
Ici *DeKalb/Clermont-Vanderbilt*
Loulou *DeKalb/Adelphi-Clermont*
Luz *Vanderbilt/Myrtle-Willoughby*
Madiba *DeKalb/Carlton*
Mo-Bay *DeKalb/Ashland-St. Felix*
Olea *Lafayette/Adelphi*
Rice *DeKalb/Cumberland*
Thomas Beisl *Lafayette/Ashland*
Zaytoons *Myrtle/Hall-Wash.*

Gravesend
Fiorentino's *Ave. U/McDonald-West*
Sahara *Coney Is./Aves. T-U*

Greenpoint
Queen's Hideaway *Franklin/Green*

Midwood
Di Fara *Ave. J/15s*
Taci's Beyti *Coney Is./Ave. P-Kings*

Mill Basin
La Villa Pizzeria *Ave. U/66-7s*
Mill Basin Deli *Ave. T/59s*

Park Slope
Al Di La *5A/Carroll*
Anthony's *7A/14-5s*
applewood *11s/7-8A*
Belleville *5A/5s*
Beso *5A/Union*
Blue Ribbon *5A/1s-Garfield*
Blue Ribbon Sushi *5A/1s-Garfield*
Bogota Latin *5A/Lincoln-St. Johns*
Brooklyn Fish Camp *5A/Degraw*
ChipShop/Curry *5A/6-7s*
Chocolate Room *5A/St. Marks*
Coco Roco *5A/6-7s*
Cocotte *5A/4s*
Convivium Osteria *5A/Bergen*
Futura *9s/4-5A*
Joe's Pizza *7A/Carroll-Garfield*
KitchenBar *6A/20s*
La Villa Pizzeria *5A/1s-Garfield*
Lemongrass Grill *7A/Berkeley*
Little D Eatery *7A/14-5s*
Long Tan *5A/Berkeley-Union*
Magnolia *6A/12s*
Minnow *9s/6-7A*
Miracle Grill *7A/4s*
Miriam *5A/Prospect*
Moutarde *5A/Carroll*
Nana *5A/Lincoln-St. Johns*
Olive Vine Cafe *multi. loc.*
Press 195 *5A/Sackett-Union*
Red Café *5A/Prospect-St. Marks*
Rose Water *Union/6A*
Sadie Mae's Cafe *6A/Park-Sterling*
Sakura Café *5A/6-7s*
Scottadito *Union/6-7A*
Sette Enoteca *7A/3s*
Song *5A/1-2s*
Stone Park Café *5A/3s*
Sweet Melissa *7A/1-2s*
Tempo *5A/Carroll-Garfield*
12th St. B&G *8A/11-2s*
Two Boots *2s/7-8A*

Prospect Heights
Aliseo Osteria *Vanderbilt/Park*
Amorina *Vanderbilt/Prospect*
Beast *Bergen/Vanderbilt*
Franny's *Flatbush/Prospect-St. Marks*
Garden Cafe *Vanderbilt/Prospect*

Le Gamin *Vanderbilt/Bergen-Dean*
Sorrel *Carlton/St. Marks*
Tom's *Wash./Sterling*

Red Hook
Good Fork *Van Brunt/Coffey*
Pioneer Bar-B-Q *Van Brunt/Pioneer*
360 *Van Brunt/Sullivan-Wolcott*

Sheepshead Bay
Brennan & Carr *Nostrand/Ave. U*
Roll-n-Roaster *Emmons/29s*

Sunset Park
Nyonya *8A/54s*

Williamsburg
Aurora *Grand/Wythe*
Baci & Abbracci *Grand/Bedford*

Bamonte's *Withers/Lorimer-Union*
Bonita *Bedford/S. 2-3s*
Diner *Bway/Berry*
Dressler *Bway/Bedford-Driggs*
DuMont *multi. loc.*
Fornino *Bedford/N. 7s*
Gribouille *Hope/Roebling*
Lodge *Grand/Havemeyer*
Monkey Town *N. 3s/Kent-Wythe*
My Moon *N. 10s/Bedford-Driggs*
Peter Luger *Bway/Driggs*
Pies-N-Thighs *Kent/S. 5s*
Planet Thailand *N. 7s/Bedford-Berry*
Relish *Wythe/Metro.-N. 3s*
SEA *N. 6s/Berry*
Sparky's American *N. 5s/Bedford*
Taco Chulo *Grand/Havemeyer-Marcy*
Vera Cruz *Bedford/N. 6-7s*

QUEENS

Astoria
Agnanti *Ditmars/19s*
Amici Amore *Newtown/30s*
Ammos *Steinway/20A-20R*
Brick Cafe *33s/31A*
Cafe Bar *36s/34A*
Cávo *31A/42-3s*
Christos *23A/41s*
Demetris *Bway/32-3s*
Elias Corner *31s/24A*
Emack & Bolio's *31s/Ditmars-21A*
Le Sans Souci *Bway/44-5s*
Malagueta *36A/28s*
Omonia Cafe *Bway/33s*
Piccola Venezia *28A/42s*
Ploes *Bway/33s*
Ponticello *Bway/46-7s*
Sac's Place *Bway/29s*
S'Agapo *34A/35s*
718 *Ditmars/35s*
Stamatis *multi. loc.*
Taverna Kyclades *Ditmars/33-5s*
Telly's Taverna *23A/28-9s*
Thai Pavilion *30A/37s*
Tierras *Bway/33s*
Tratt. L'incontro *31s/Ditmars*
Ubol's Kitchen *Steinway/Astoria-25A*
Uno Chicago *35A/38s*

Bayside
Ben's Kosher Deli *26A/211s*
Caffé/Green *Cross Is./Clearview*
Dae Dong *Northern/220s*

Erawan *multi. loc.*
Jackson Hole *Bell/35A*
Outback *Bell/26A*
Press 195 *Bell/40-1A*
Uncle Jack's *Bell/40A*
Uno Chicago *Bell/39A*

Corona
Green Field Churra. *Northern/108s*
Park Side *Corona/51A*

Elmhurst
Outback *Queens/56A*
Pho Bang *Bway/Elmhurst*
Ping's Seafood *Queens/Goldsmith*

Flushing
East Buffet *Main/Maple*
East Manor *Kissena/Laburnum*
Joe's *37A/Main-Union*
Kum Gang San *Northern/Union*
Phở Bang *Kissena/Main*
Spicy & Tasty *Prince/39A*
Sweet-n-Tart *38s/Main*

Forest Hills
Bann Thai *Austin/Yellowstone*
Cabana *70R/Austin-Queens*
Dee's Pizza *Metro./74A*
Nick's *Ascan/Austin-Burns*
Q Thai Bistro *Ascan/Austin-Burns*
Rouge *70R/Austin*
Uno Chicago *70R/Austin-Queens*

Fresh Meadows
King Yum *Union/181s*

Glendale
Zum Stammtisch *Myrtle/69 Pl.-70s*

Howard Beach
La Villa Pizzeria *153A/82-3s*

Jackson Heights
Afghan Kebab *37A/74-5s*
Delhi Palace *74s/37A-37R*
Jackson Diner *74s/Roosevelt-37R*
Jackson Hole *Astoria/70s*
Pio Pio *Northern/84-5s*
Tierras *Roosevelt/82s*

Little Neck
La Baraka *Northern/Little Neck*

Long Island City
Bella Via *Vernon/48A*
Manducatis *Jackson/47A*

Manetta's *Jackson/49A*
Riverview *49A/Center*
Tournesol *Vernon/50-1A*
Tuk Tuk *Vernon/49-50A*
Water's Edge *E. River/44 Dr.*

Ozone Park
Don Peppe *Lefferts/149A*

Rego Park
London Lennie's *Woodhaven/Fleet*
Pio Pio *Woodhaven/63A*

Sunnyside
Bliss *Skillman/46s*
Quaint *Skillman/46-7s*

Woodside
La Flor Bakery *Roosevelt/53s*
Sapori D'Ischia *37A/56s*
Sripraphai *39A/64-5s*

STATEN ISLAND

Aesop's Tables *Bay/Maryland*
American Grill *Victory/Clove*
Angelina's *Jefferson/Annadale*
Bocca *Hylan/Bath*
Bocelli *Hylan/Clove-Old Town*
Caffe Bondi *Hylan/Dongan Hills*
Carol's Cafe *Richmond/Four Corners*
Da Noi *Victory/Westshore*
Denino's *Port Richmond/Hooker*
Fushimi *Richmond/Lincoln*
Killmeyer Bavarian *Arthur Kill/
   Sharrotts*

Lake Club *Clove/Victory*
Lorenzo's *South/SI Expwy*
Marina Cafe *Mansion/Hillside*
Nurnberger Bierhaus *Castleton/
   Davis*
101 *Richmond/Amboy*
Parsonage *Arthur Kill/Clarke*
South Shore Club *Huguenot/Arthur
   Kill*
Tratt. Romana *Hylan/Benton*

SPECIAL FEATURES

(Indexes list the best in each category. Multi-location restaurants' features may vary by branch.)

Breakfast

(See also Hotel Dining)
Annie's
Balthazar
Barney Greengrass
Brasserie
Bubby's
Cafe Colonial
Cafe Con Leche
Cafe Luxembourg
Cafe Mogador
Café Sabarsky
Carnegie Deli
City Bakery
City Hall
E.A.T.
EJ's Luncheonette
Florent
Giorgione
Good Enough to Eat
Googie's
HK
Katz's Deli
Kitchenette
Le Pain Quotidien
Mayrose
Michael's
Naples 45
Nice Matin
NoHo Star
Pastis
Payard Bistro
Penelope
Pershing Square
Rue 57
Sant Ambroeus
Sarabeth's
Tartine
Taste
Teresa's
Veselka

Brunch

Aix Brasserie
Annie's
A.O.C.
applewood
Aquagrill
Aquavit
Arté Café
Artisanal
Balthazar
Beacon
Beso
Billie's Black
Blue Ribbon Bakery
Blue Water
Bubby's
Café Botanica
Cafe Con Leche
Café de Bruxelles
Café des Artistes
Cafe Luxembourg
Cafe Mogador
Cafe Ronda
Cafeteria
Cafe Un Deux
Caffe Cielo
Capsouto Frères
Carlyle
Carmine's
Cebu
Celeste
Chez Oskar
Clinton St. Baking
Cocotte
Cornelia St. Cafe
Danal
davidburke/donatella
Delta Grill
Diner
Eatery
Elephant & Castle
Eleven Madison
elmo
Essex
Extra Virgin
Félix
Five Points
41 Greenwich
Friend of a Farmer
Gascogne
good
Good Enough to Eat
Googie's
Great Jones Cafe

Home
HQ
Isabella's
Jackson Diner
Jane
Jean Georges
Jerry's
JoJo
Le Gigot
Le Grainne Café
Les Halles
L'Express
Lupe's East LA Kit.
Luzia's
Maggie Brown
Mark's
Mayrose
Mesa Grill
Minnow
Miracle Grill
Miriam
Miss Mamie's/Maude's
Mon Petit Cafe
Nice Matin
Norma's
Ocean Grill
Odeon
Olea
One
Ouest
Paris Commune
Pastis
Patois
Penelope
Petrossian
Pietrasanta
Pink Tea Cup
Pipa
Popover Cafe
Porchetta
Provence
Prune
Public
Punch
Rainbow Room
River Café
Riverdale Garden
Rocking Horse
Rose Water
Sarabeth's
Schiller's
Sette Enoteca
718
Spotted Pig

Spring St. Natural
Stanton Social
Stone Park Café
Sylvia's
Taco Chulo
Tartine
Taste
Teresa's
Thalia
Tribeca Grill
Turkish Kitchen
Wallsé
Water Club
Zoë

Buffet Served
(Check availability)
Above
Aquavit
Arabelle
Bay Leaf
Beacon
Bombay Palace
Brick Lane Curry
Bruckner B&G
Bukhara Grill
Bull Run
Café Botanica
Carlyle
Charles' Southern
Chennai Garden
Chola
Churrascaria
City Bakery
Copper Chimney
Curry Leaf
Dakshin Indian
Darna
Delegates Dining Rm.
Delhi Palace
Diwan
Docks Oyster Bar
East Buffet
East Manor
Fives
Foley's Fish
Green Field Churra.
Hudson Cafeteria
Jackson Diner
Jewel of India
Kittichai
La Baraka
Malatesta

Mangia
Mary Ann's
Rainbow Room
Roy's NY
Salaam Bombay
Sapphire Indian
Sette Enoteca
Surya
SushiSamba
Todai
Turkish Kitchen
Turkuaz
2 West
Utsav
View, The
Water Club
Yuva

BYO
A
Afghan Kebab
Angelica Kit.
A.O.C. Bedford
Aureole
Bereket
Blossom
Bouillabaisse 126
Brawta Caribbean
Cocotte
Comfort Diner
Cube 63
Dallas BBQ
Di Fara
Django
East Buffet
Fairway Cafe
Falai
Flor de Mayo
Franchia
Fuleen Seafood
goodburger
Goodies
Hampton Chutney
Havana Chelsea
Island Burgers
Ivo & Lulu
Joe's
Kitchen 22
La Mangeoire
La Taza de Oro
Mandarin Court
Metrazur
Nino's

Noodle Bar
Nook
Olive Vine Cafe
Peking Duck
Philly Slim's
Pho Bang
Phoenix Garden
Pó
Poke
Red Cat
Revival
Riverdale Garden
Russian Samovar
Sadie Mae's Cafe
Sfoglia
Sweet Melissa
Taci's Beyti
Taksim
Tanoreen
Tartine
Wo Hop
Wondee Siam
Yura & Co.
Zaytoons

Celebrations
Beacon
BLT Fish
BLT Prime
Bond 45
Bouley
Café Botanica
Café des Artistes
Café Gray
'Cesca
Daniel
FireBird
Four Seasons
Fresco by Scotto
Gotham B&G
La Grenouille
Le Bernardin
Le Cirque
Lobster Box
Mark's
Mas
Matsuri
Megu
Mercer Kitchen
Modern, The
Molyvos
Nobu 57
Odeon

Special Features

Olives
One if by Land
Ouest
Palm
Park Ave. Cafe
Peter Luger
Petrossian
Provence
Rainbow Room
Raoul's
Redeye Grill
River Café
River Room
Rock Center Cafe
Rolf's
Rosa Mexicano
Ruby Foo's
San Domenico
Sea Grill
Tavern on Green
Terrace in the Sky
Tratt. Dell'Arte
View, The
Water Club
Water's Edge

Celebrity Chefs

Julieta Ballesteros
  Crema
Dan Barber
  Blue Hill
Lidia Bastianich
  Del Posto
  Felidia
Mario Batali
  Babbo
  Casa Mono
  Del Posto
  Esca
  Lupa
  Otto
April Bloomfield
  Spotted Pig
David Bouley
  Bouley
  Bouley, Upstairs
  Danube
Daniel Boulud
  Café Boulud
  Daniel
  db Bistro Moderne
Anthony Bourdain
  Les Halles
Jimmy Bradley
  Harrison, The
  Red Cat

Terrance Brennan
  Artisanal
  Picholine
Scott Bryan
  Veritas
David Burke
  davidburke/donatella
  David Burke/Bloom.
Marco Canora
  Hearth
Floyd Cardoz
  Tabla
Andrew Carmellini
  A Voce
Cesare Casella
  Maremma
Michael Cetrulo
  Piano Due
  Scalini Fedeli
Ian Chalermkittichai
  Kittichai
Rebecca Charles
  Pearl Oyster
Tom Colicchio
  Craft
  Craftbar
  Craftsteak
  'wichcraft
Scott Conant
  Alto
  L'Impero
Alain Ducasse
  Alain Ducasse
Wylie Dufresne
  wd-50
Todd English
  English is Italian
  Olives
Odette Fada
  San Domenico
Bobby Flay
  Bar Americain
  Bolo
  Mesa Grill
Shea Gallante
  Cru
Kurt Gutenbrunner
  Blaue Gans
  Café Sabarsky/Fledermaus
  Wallsé
Gabrielle Hamilton
  Prune

Peter Hoffman
   Savoy
Sara Jenkins
   Bread Tribeca
Thomas Keller
   Bouchon Bakery
   per se
Gabriel Kreuther
   Modern, The
Gray Kunz
   Café Gray
Anita Lo
   Annisa
Michael Lomonaco
   Porter House NY
Pino Luongo
   Centolire
Waldy Malouf
   Beacon
Zarela Martinez
   Zarela
Hemant Mathur
   dévi
Nobu Matsuhisa
   Nobu
   Nobu 57
Henry Meer
   City Hall
Marco Moreira
   Tocqueville
Masaharu Morimoto
   Morimoto
Eberhard Müller
   Bayard's
Marc Murphy
   Ditch Plains
   Landmarc
Wayne Nish
   March
Tadashi Ono
   Matsuri
Charlie Palmer
   Aureole
   Metrazur
David Pasternack
   Esca
François Payard
   In Tent
   Payard Bistro
Zak Pelaccio
   Fatty Crab
   5 Ninth

Don Pintabona
   Dani
John Policastro
   Garden Cafe
Alfred Portale
   Gotham B&G
Jean-Jacques Rachou
   Brasserie LCB
Carl Redding
   Amy Ruth's
Mary Redding
   Brooklyn Fish Camp
   Mary's Fish Camp
Cyril Renaud
   Fleur de Sel
Eric Ripert
   Barça 18
   Le Bernardin
Joël Robuchon
   L'Atelier/Joël Robuchon
Michael Romano
   Union Sq. Cafe
Marcus Samuelsson
   Aquavit
Aarón Sanchez
   Centrico
   Paladar
Suvir Saran
   dévi
Pierre Schaedelin
   Le Cirque
Mark Strausman
   Coco Pazzo
Noriyuki Sugie
   Asiate
Gari Sugio
   Gari
   Sushi of Gari
Nao Sugiyama
   Sugiyama
Masayoshi Takayama
   Bar Masa
   Masa
Bill Telepan
   Telepan
Sue Torres
   Sueños
Laurent Tourondel
   BLT Fish
   BLT Prime
   BLT Steak
   Brasserie Ruhlmann
Alex Ureña
   Ureña
Tom Valenti
   Ouest

Special Features

Jean-Georges Vongerichten
  Jean Georges
  JoJo
  Mercer Kitchen
  Perry Street
  66
  Spice Market
  Vong
David Waltuck
  Chanterelle
David Walzog
  Strip House
Jonathan Waxman
  Barbuto
Naomichi Yasuda
  Sushi Yasuda
Patricia Yeo
  Sapa
Geoffrey Zakarian
  Country
  Country, Café at
  Town
Galen Zamarra
  Mas

Cheese Trays

Above
Acqua Pazza
Agnanti
Alain Ducasse
Alexandra
Alfama
Aliseo Osteria
Alto
Ama
Amici Amore
Amorina
A.O.C.
A.O.C. Bedford
applewood
Arabelle
Artisanal
Babbo
Bar Americain
BLT Steak
Brasserie LCB
Bruno Jamais
Bryant Park
Cacio e Pepe
Café Boulud
Café Gray
Cafe Joul

Cafe Luxembourg
Café Pierre
Cafe Un Deux
Caffé/Green
CamaJe
Capsouto Frères
Carlyle
Centolire
Cercle Rouge
Chanterelle
Chelsea Bistro
Chestnut
Chez Jacqueline
Chez Napoléon
Chubo
Cité
Cocotte
Convivium Osteria
Country
Craft
Cru
Daniel
Demarchelier
Deux Amis
Django
Eleven Madison
Etats-Unis
Felidia
Fillip's
Flea Mkt. Cafe
41 Greenwich
Garden Cafe
Gramercy Tavern
I Trulli
Jean Georges
Kitchen Club
La Grenouille
La Lanterna
La Mangeoire
Le Gigot
Le Père Pinard
Lever House
Lucien
Lusardi's
Macelleria
Maison
Mark's
Mas
Mercer Kitchen
Métisse
Michael's
Mon Petit Cafe
Montparnasse

Morgan, The
Moutarde
Nice Matin
Nino's
Nocello
Nonna
Novitá
Olives
One if by Land
Onera
Orsay
Osteria Laguna
Otto
Panino'teca 275
Paradou
Park Bistro
Pascalou
Pastis
Peacock Alley
per se
Petrarca Vino
Picholine
Picnic Market
Pigalle
Quercy
Riverdale Garden
Room 4 Dessert
Rughetta
San Domenico
Savoy
Scalini Fedeli
Spigolo
Stone Park Café
Swifty's
Table XII
Taste
Tasting Room
Telepan
Tempo
Thalia
Tocqueville
Tournesol
Town
Triomphe
2 West
Village
Wallsé
Water's Edge

Chef's Table

Abigael's
Alain Ducasse
Aquavit

Bao 111
Barbuto
Brasserie Julien
Café Gray
Col Legno
Country
Cub Room
Daniel
Il Buco
Maloney & Porcelli
Megu
Olives
Park Ave. Cafe
Patroon
Remi
Smith & Wollensky
Valbella

Child-Friendly

(See also Theme places;
* children's menu available)
Alice's Tea Cup*
Amy Ruth's*
Annie's
Antica Venezia
Artie's Deli*
Barking Dog
Beccofino
Beso
Blue Smoke*
Boathouse*
Brennan & Carr
Bubby's*
Cafe Un Deux
Carmine's
Chat 'n Chew*
Columbus Bakery
Comfort Diner*
Cowgirl*
Dallas BBQ*
Da Nico*
EJ's Luncheonette*
Fetch
Friend of a Farmer*
Gargiulo's
Good Enough to Eat*
Googie's*
Hard Rock Cafe*
Jackson Hole*
Junior's*
L & B Spumoni*
London Lennie's*
Miss Mamie's/Maude's

Nice
Nick's
Peanut Butter & Co.
Pig Heaven
Rack & Soul*
Rock Center Cafe*
Rossini's
Sammy's Roumanian
Sarabeth's
Savoia
Serendipity 3
Shake Shack
Sylvia's*
Tavern on Green*
Tony's Di Napoli
Two Boots*
View, The*
Virgil's Real BBQ*
Whole Foods
Zum Stammtisch*

Commuter Oases
Grand Central
  Ammos
  Bobby Van's
  Brother Jimmy's
  Burger Heaven
  Cafe Centro
  Cafe Spice
  Capital Grille
  Cipriani Dolci
  Dishes
  Django
  Docks Oyster Bar
  English is Italian
  Hale & Hearty Soup
  Hatsuhana
  Jacques-Imo's
  Junior's
  Menchanko-tei
  Metrazur
  Michael Jordan's
  Morton's
  Nanni
  Oyster Bar
  Patroon
  Pepe...To Go
  Pershing Square
  Sushi Yasuda
  Tropica
  Two Boots
  Zócalo
Penn Station
  Burgers/Cupcakes
  Camino Sur

Carbone
Chipotle
Gray's Papaya
Nick & Stef's
Staghorn
Uncle Jack's
Port Authority
  Above
  Angus McIndoe
  Better Burger
  Chez Josephine
  Chimichurri Grill
  Dallas BBQ
  Don Giovanni
  Esca
  ESPN Zone
  etcetera etcetera
  John's Pizzeria
  Le Madeleine
  Marseille
  Shula's
  Tony Luke's
  West Bank Cafe

Cool Loos
Bette
Brasserie
Butter
Compass
ESPN Zone
44
Matsuri
Megu
Morimoto
Nooch
Ono
Paradou
Pastis
Peep
P.J. Clarke's
Prem-on Thai
Pukk
Sapa
Schiller's
SEA
Tao
wd-50

Critic-Proof
(Gets lots of business
despite so-so food)
Algonquin
Barking Dog

Better Burger
Boathouse
Brooklyn Diner
Brother Jimmy's
Bryant Park
Burger Heaven
Café St. Bart's
Cafe Un Deux
Cercle Rouge
Coffee Shop
Comfort Diner
Cosí
Cowgirl
Dallas BBQ
East of Eighth
Edison Cafe
EJ's Luncheonette
Elaine's
elmo
Empire Diner
Empire Szechuan
ESPN Zone
Fraunces Tavern
French Roast
Googie's
Harbour Lights
Hard Rock Cafe
Heartland Brew.
Jackson Hole
Jacques-Imo's
Kelley & Ping
Mary Ann's
Mayrose
Nooch
Ollie's
O'Neals'
Outback
Park, The
Pershing Square
Pete's Tavern
Rolf's
Sardi's
Sylvia's
Tavern on Green
Uno Chicago
Viand
View, The

Dancing
Cávo
Rainbow Room
Tavern on Green

Entertainment
(Call for days and times of
performances)
Alfama (fado/jazz)
Algonquin (cabaret)
Blue Fin (jazz)
Blue Smoke (jazz)
Blue Water (jazz)
Café Pierre (piano/singer)
Chez Josephine (piano)
Cornelia St. Cafe (varies)
Delta Grill (jazz/blues/zydeco)
FireBird (harp/piano)
Flor de Sol (Spanish bands)
Ideya (salsa)
Knickerbocker B&G (jazz)
La Lanterna (jazz)
La Lunchonette (accordion/
    singer)
Londel's (jazz)
Madiba (South African bands)
Monkey Bar (piano)
Mo Pitkin's (varies)
Ñ (flamenco)
Rainbow Room (orchestra)
River Café (piano)
Russian Samovar (Russian)
Son Cubano (Cuban bands)
Sylvia's (blues/gospel/jazz)
Tavern on Green (DJ/piano)
Tommaso's (piano/singers/opera)

Fireplaces
Adä
Agave
Amici Amore
Aquaterra
Aspen
Bayard's
Beppe
Bistro Ten 18
Caffé/Green
Cebu
Chelsea Bistro
Col Legno
Cornelia St. Cafe
Cub Room
Cucina di Pesce
Danal
Darna
Dee's Pizza
Delta Grill
Frankie & Johnnie

Friend of a Farmer
Hacienda Argentina
Harbour Lights
Ici
I Trulli
Jovia
Jubilee
Keens
Lady Mendl's
La Grenouille
Lake Club
La Lanterna
La Petite Auberge
La Ripaille
Lattanzi
Lobster Box
Lorenzo's
Loulou
Manducatis
March
Marco Polo
Metsovo
Moran's Chelsea
One if by Land
Paola's
Park, The
Patois
Pearl Room
per se
Piccola Venezia
Place, The
Portofino Grille
Public
Quality Meats
Quartino
René Pujol
Riverdale Garden
Royal's Downtown
Santa Fe
Saravanaas
Savoy
Shaffer City
Sherwood Cafe
Telepan
Terrace in the Sky
Tony's Di Napoli
Triomphe
Turks & Frogs
21 Club
Uncle Jack's
Vittorio Cucina
Vivolo
Water Club

Water's Edge
wd-50

Game in Season

Aesop's Tables
Alain Ducasse
Alfama
Alto
Aquavit
Babbo
Barbetta
Bayard's
Beacon
Beppe
Blue Hill
Borgo Antico
Café d'Alsace
Café des Artistes
Café Gray
'Cesca
Compass
Cookshop
Craft
Cru
Daniel
Da Umberto
dévi
Felidia
Fleur de Sel
Four Seasons
Gascogne
Girasole
Harrison, The
Hearth
Henry's End
I Coppi
Il Mulino
I Trulli
Jean Georges
La Grenouille
La Lunchonette
L'Atelier/Joël Robuchon
Le Perigord
Les Halles
Levana
Lusardi's
Madiba
March
Mas
Nino's
Olives
Osteria del Circo
Ouest

Peasant
Piccola Venezia
Picholine
Primavera
Quality Meats
River Café
Saul
Scalini Fedeli
Tamarind
Tocqueville
Town
Tratt. L'incontro

Gracious Hosts

Amici Amore, *Dino & Gianni Redzic*
Angelina's, *Angelina Malerba*
Angus McIndoe, *Angus McIndoe*
Barbetta, *Laura Maioglio*
Bricco, *Nino Cituogno*
Chanterelle, *Karen Waltuck*
Chez Josephine, *Jean-Claude Baker*
Chin Chin, *James Chin*
Danube, *Walter Kranjc*
davidburke/donatella, *Donatella Arpaia*
Degustation, *Grace & Jack Lamb*
Deux Amis, *Bucky Yahiaoui*
Dona, *Donatella Arpaia*
Due, *Ernesto Cavalli*
Eliá, *Christina & Pete Lekkas*
Four Seasons, *Julian Niccolini, Alex von Bidder*
Fresco by Scotto, *Marion Scotto*
Garden Cafe, *Camille Policastro*
Jean Georges, *P. Vongerichten*
Jewel Bako, *Grace & Jack Lamb*
Kitchen Club, *Marja Samsom*
La Baraka, *Lucette Sonigo*
La Grenouille, *Charles Masson*
La Mirabelle, *Annick Le Douaron*
Le Cirque, *Sirio Maccioni*
Lenox Room, *Tony Fortuna*
Le Perigord, *Georges Briguet*
Le Zie 2000, *Claudio Bonotto*
Loulou, *Christine & William Snell*
Luca, *Luca Marcato*
Montrachet, *Bruce Yung*
Neary's, *Jimmy Neary*
Nino's, *Nino Selimaj*
Paola's, *Paola Marracino*
Piccolo Angolo, *R. Migliorini*

Pig Heaven, *Nancy Lee*
Primavera, *Nicola Civetta*
Rao's, *Frank Pellegrino*
San Domenico, *Tony May*
San Pietro, *Gerardo Bruno*
Shaffer City, *Jay Shaffer*
Sistina, *Giuseppe Bruno*
Tamarind, *Avtar & Gary Walia*
Tasting Room, *Renée Alevras*
Tocqueville, *Jo-Ann Makovitzky*
Tommaso's, *Thomas Verdillo*
Tratt. L'incontro, *Rocco Sacramone*
Tratt. Romana, *V. Asoli, A. Lobianco*
Union Sq. Cafe, *Danny Meyer*

Historic Places

(Year opened; * building)
1762 Fraunces Tavern
1767 One if by Land*
1794 Bridge Cafe*
1812 Heartland Brew.*
1827 Delmonico's
1834 Lady Mendl's*
1835 Five Front*
1835 Savoy*
1836 MarkJoseph*
1851 Bayard's*
1853 Morgan, The*
1855 Parsonage*
1860 Comfort Diner*
1860 fresh*
1863 City Hall*
1864 Pete's Tavern
1867 Le Refuge Inn*
1868 Old Homestead
1868 P.J. Clarke's*
1870 Downtown Atlantic*
1870 Tavern on Green*
1875 Ecco*
1875 Harry's*
1875 Vivolo*
1879 Serafina*
1880 Café St. Bart's*
1880 Veniero's*
1885 Keens
1887 Peter Luger
1888 Katz's Deli
1890 John's of 12th St.*
1891 Cowgirl*
1892 Ferrara
1896 Rao's

1897 Carol's Cafe*
1899 Carnegie Deli*
1900 Bamonte's
1900 Le Rivage*
1900 Sarabeth's*
1902 Algonquin
1902 Angelo's/Mulberry
1902 Cornelia St. Cafe*
1904 Chocolate Room*
1904 Ferdinando's
1904 Sal Anthony's*
1904 Trinity Place*
1904 Vincent's
1906 Barbetta
1907 Gargiulo's*
1908 Barney Greengrass
1910 Wolfgang's*
1912 Frank's
1913 Oyster Bar*
1917 Café des Artistes
1918 Monte's*
1919 Caffé/Green*
1919 Mario's
1920 Junior's*
1921 Sardi's
1922 Rocco
1922 Tosca Café
1924 Totonno Pizza
1925 Daniel*
1925 El Charro Español
1926 Frankie & Johnnie
1926 Little Charlie's
1926 Palm
1927 Diner*
1927 El Faro
1927 Gallagher's
1927 L'Impero*
1929 Eleven Madison*
1929 Empire Diner*
1929 John's Pizzeria
1929 21 Club
1930 Carlyle
1930 El Quijote
1931 Café Pierre
1932 Pietro's
1933 New Leaf*
1933 Patsy's Pizzeria
1934 Papaya King
1934 Rainbow Room
1936 Monkey Bar*
1936 Tom's
1937 Denino's
1937 Le Veau d'Or

1937 Minetta Tavern
1938 Brennan & Carr
1938 Bright Food Shop*
1938 Heidelberg
1938 Stage Deli
1938 Wo Hop
1939 L & B Spumoni
1941 Sevilla
1943 Burger Heaven
1944 Patsy's
1945 Gino
1945 V&T
1946 Lobster Box
1947 Delegates Dining Rm.
1950 Junior's
1950 Paul & Jimmy's
1952 Lever House*
1953 King Yum
1953 Liebman's
1954 Mother's Bake Shop
1954 Pink Tea Cup
1954 Serendipity 3
1954 Veselka
1957 Arturo's Pizzeria
1957 Giambelli
1957 La Taza de Oro
1957 Moran's Chelsea

Hotel Dining

Afinia Dumont
   Barking Dog
Alex Hotel
   Riingo
Algonquin Hotel
   Algonquin
Beekman Tower
   Top of the Tower
Blakely Hotel
   Abboccato
Bryant Park Hotel
   Koi
Carlton Hotel
   Country
   Country, Café at
Carlyle Hotel
   Carlyle
Chambers Hotel
   Town
City Club Hotel
   db Bistro Moderne
Club Quarters Hotel
   Bull Run
Dream Hotel
   Serafina

Edison Hotel
  Edison Cafe
Elysée Hotel
  Monkey Bar
Embassy Suites
  Lili's Noodle
Four Seasons Hotel
  L'Atelier/Joël Robuchon
Gansevoort Hotel
  Ono
Helmsley Middletowne
  Diwan
Hilton Garden Inn
  Lorenzo's
  Pigalle
Hilton Times Sq.
  Above
Hotel on Rivington, The
  Thor
Hudson Hotel
  Hudson Cafeteria
Inn at Irving Pl.
  Lady Mendl's
Iroquois Hotel
  Triomphe
Jumeirah Essex House
  Alain Ducasse
  Café Botanica
Le Parker Meridien
  burger joint
  Norma's
Le Refuge Inn
  Le Refuge Inn
Lombardy Hotel
  Table XII
Lowell Hotel
  Post House
Mandarin Oriental Hotel
  Asiate
Marcel Hotel
  Gramercy 24
Maritime Hotel
  La Bottega
  Matsuri
Mark Hotel
  Mark's
Marriott Financial Ctr.
  Roy's NY
Marriott Marquis Hotel
  View, The
Mercer Hotel
  Mercer Kitchen
Morgans Hotel
  Asia de Cuba

Muse Hotel
  District
NY Palace Hotel
  Gilt
Peninsula Hotel
  Fives
Pickwick Arms
  Montparnasse
Pierre Hotel
  Café Pierre
Plaza Athénée Hotel
  Arabelle
Radisson Lexington Hotel
  Alma Grill
Regency Hotel
  Regency
Renaissance NY Hotel
  Foley's Fish
Ritz-Carlton Battery Park
  2 West
Royalton Hotel
  44
San Carlos Hotel
  Mint
Shelburne Murray Hill Hotel
  Rare B&G
60 Thompson
  Kittichai
Surrey Hotel
  Café Boulud
Trump Int'l Hotel
  Jean Georges
Waldorf-Astoria
  Bull & Bear
  Inagiku
  Peacock Alley
Washington Square Hotel
  North Square
Westin NY Times Sq.
  Shula's
W Times Sq.
  Blue Fin
W Union Sq.
  Olives

Jacket Required
(* Tie also required)
Alain Ducasse
Aureole
Café Pierre
Carlyle
Daniel
Danube

Delegates Dining Rm.
Four Seasons
Jean Georges
La Grenouille*
Le Bernardin
Le Cirque
Modern, The
per se
Rainbow Room*
River Café
San Domenico
21 Club*

Jury Duty
(Near Foley Sq.)
Acappella
Arqua
Big Wong
Blaue Gans
Bouley
Bread Tribeca
Carl's Steaks
City Hall
Dim Sum Go Go
Doyers Viet.
Duane Park Cafe
Ecco
Evergreen Shanghai
Excellent Dumpling
fresh
Fuleen Seafood
Golden Unicorn
Goodies
Great NY Noodle
HSF
Jing Fong
Joe's
Kam Chueh
Kapadokya
Kori
Mandarin Court
Mary Ann's
Nam
New Bo-Ky
New Green Bo
Nha Trang
Nice
Odeon
Oriental Garden
Peking Duck
Petite Abeille
Petrarca Vino

Pho Pasteur
Pho Viet Huong
Ping's Seafood
Pongsri Thai
Shanghai Cuisine
Takahachi
Wo Hop

Late Dining
(Besides most diners and
delis; weekday closing hour)
Arturo's Pizzeria (1 AM)
Aspen (varies)
Balthazar (1 AM)
Bamn! (24 hrs.)
Bao 111 (2 AM)
Baraonda (1 AM)
BarTabac (varies)
Bereket (24 hrs.)
Big Nick's Burger (varies)
Blue Ribbon (varies)
Blue Ribbon Sushi (varies)
Bonjoo (2 AM)
Brennan & Carr (1 AM)
Bruno Jamais (1 AM)
Buzina Pop (1 AM)
Café Fiorello (1 AM)
Café Soleil (1 AM)
Cafeteria (24 hrs.)
Carnegie Deli (3:30 AM)
Cávo (2 AM)
Cebu (3 AM)
Cercle Rouge (varies)
Chez Josephine (1 AM)
Coffee Shop (varies)
Corner Bistro (3:30 AM)
Cosí (1 AM)
Cosmic Cantina (5 AM)
Cozy Soup/Burger (24 hrs.)
Dallas BBQ (varies)
Demetris (1 AM)
Ditch Plains (2 AM)
DuMont (2 AM)
Elaine's (2 AM)
El Malecon (varies)
Empire Diner (24 hrs.)
Empire Szechuan (varies)
Employees Only (4 AM)
Florent (24 hrs.)
Frank (1 AM)
French Roast (24 hrs.)
Fuleen Seafood (3 AM)
Gahm Mi Oak (24 hrs.)

Gray's Papaya (24 hrs.)
Great NY Noodle (4 AM)
Grotta Azzurra (1 AM)
Havana Central (1 AM)
HK (1 AM)
'ino (2 AM)
'inoteca (3 AM)
I Tre Merli (varies)
Jack (2 AM)
Jackson Hole (varies)
J.G. Melon (2:30 AM)
Joe's Pizza (varies)
Kam Chueh (3 AM)
Kang Suh (24 hrs.)
Kati Roll Co. (varies)
Knickerbocker B&G (1 AM)
Kum Gang San (24 hrs.)
La Bottega (varies)
La Lanterna (3 AM)
La Mela (2 AM)
Landmarc (2 AM)
Las Ramblas (1 AM)
L'Express (24 hrs.)
Lil' Frankie Pizza (2 AM)
Little Charlie's (1 AM)
Macelleria (1 AM)
Maison (24 hrs.)
Mas (4 AM)
Ñ (1:30 AM)
Neary's (1:30 AM)
Odeon (1 AM)
Ollie's (varies)
Omen (1 AM)
Omonia Cafe (4 AM)
One (varies)
Pastis (1 AM)
Ping's Seafood (varies)
Pioneer Bar-B-Q (2 AM)
P.J. Clarke's (varies)
Planet Thailand (varies)
Pop Burger (4 AM)
Pre:Post (4 AM)
Raoul's (1 AM)
Roll-n-Roaster (1 AM)
Sahara (2 AM)
Sarge's Deli (24 hrs.)
Sascha (1 AM)
Schiller's (1 AM)
Spotted Pig (2 AM)
Stage Deli (2 AM)
Stamatis (1 AM)
Stanton Social (3 AM)
SushiSamba (varies)

Sushi Seki (3 AM)
Tour (6 AM)
Two Boots (varies)
212 (1 AM)
Umberto's (varies)
Uno Chicago (varies)
Uva (2 AM)
Veselka (varies)
Viand (varies)
Vincent's (1:30 AM)
West Bank Cafe (1 AM)
Wo Hop (24 hrs.)
Wollensky's (2 AM)
Won Jo (24 hrs.)

Meet for a Drink
(Most top hotels and the
following standouts)
Alamo, The
Algonquin
Amaranth
Artisanal
Aspen
Atlantic Grill
Aurora
Balthazar
Bandol Bistro
Barbounia
Barça 18
Bar Masa
Beast
Blue Fin
Boathouse
Bond Street
Boqueria
Brick Cafe
Brouwers/Stone St.
Bryant Park
Buddakan
Buddha Bar
Bull & Bear
Buzina Pop
Café Gray
Cafe Luxembourg
City Hall
Compass
Country, Café at
Daniel
Demarchelier
Ditch Plains
Django
Dos Caminos
Dressler

Four Seasons
Freemans
Geisha
Gotham B&G
Gramercy Tavern
Harry's
HK
Houston's
Il Bastardo
'inoteca
Jean Georges
Keens
Kellari Taverna
Koi
Le Cirque
Le Colonial
Lenox Room
L'Impero
Luz
Maloney & Porcelli
Marbella
Mark's
Matsuri
Michael Jordan's
Modern, The
Mo Pitkin's
Nobu 57
Odeon
One
O'Neals'
Ouest
Paper Moon
Parea
Park, The
Pastis
Piano Due
Pies-N-Thighs
Quaint
Room Service
Sala
Samba-Lé
Sapa
Spice Market
Stanton Social
Stone Park Café
Tao
Thor
Top of the Tower
Town
212
Vera Cruz
Wollensky's

Natural/Organic
(Specializing in organic, local
ingredients)
A
Alexandra
Angelica Kit.
applewood
Better Burger
Big Nick's Burger
Blossom
Blue Hill
Café St. Bart's
Candle Cafe
Candle 79
Chennai Garden
Chestnut
Cho Dang Gol
Chop't Creative
City Bakery
Clinton St. Baking
Cosmic Cantina
Counter
Craft
Fornino
41 Greenwich
Frankies Spuntino
Franny's
Ginger
Gobo
Grocery, The
Ivo & Lulu
Josephina
Josie's
Luxia
Mas
New Leaf
New York Burger
Once Upon a Tart
Peacock Alley
Picnic Market
Popover Cafe
Pure Food & Wine
Quartino
Sacred Chow
Saul
Savoy
Scottadito
Sparky's American
Spring St. Natural
Superfine
Tasting Room
360
Tocqueville

Tsampa
Whole Foods
Zebú Grill
Zen Palate

Noteworthy Newcomers (222)

(Name, cuisine; * not open at press time, but looks promising)

Agata & Valentina, *Italian*
AJ Maxwell's, *Steakhouse*
Alia*, *Mediterranean*
Allen & Delancey*, *American*
Alma Grill, *American*
Alonso's, *Steakhouse*
Anthony's, *Italian*
Antonucci, *Italian*
Anzu, *Japanese*
Aquamarine, *Japanese*
Aquaterra, *Italian*
Artemis*, *Greek*
Aspen, *American*
A Voce, *Italian*
Baci & Abbracci, *Italian*
Bamn!, *American*
Barbone, *Italian*
Barbounia, *Mediterranean*
Barça 18, *Spanish*
Bar Martignetti*, *French*
Beccofino, *Italian*
BG, *American*
Big John, *American*
Billie's Black, *Soul Food*
Bistro Citron, *French*
Blair Perrone, *Steakhouse*
Blaue Gans, *Austrian*
Blossom, *Vegan*
BLT Market*, *American*
Blue/Green, *Vegan*
Bocca Lupo, *Italian*
Bondi Road, *Australian*
Bonjoo, *Korean*
Boqueria, *Spanish*
Bouchon Bakery, *Sandwiches*
Brasserie Ruhlmann, *French*
Brgr*, *Hamburgers*
Brouwers/Stone St., *American*
Buddakan, *Asian Fusion*
Buddha Bar, *Asian Fusion*
Buenos Aires, *Argentinean*
Burgers/Cupcakes, *American*
Buzina Pop, *Brazilian/French*

Cafe Condesa, *American*
Café d'Alsace, *French*
Café Largo*, *Mediterranean*
Café Soleil, *Mediterranean*
Camino Sur, *South American*
Carbone, *Italian*
Carne Vale, *Brazilian*
Centro Vinoteca*, *Italian*
Cercle Rouge, *French*
Chanto, *Japanese*
Chat Noir*, *French*
Chinatown Brasserie, *Chinese*
Chiyono, *Japanese*
Cluny*, *American*
Colors, *Eclectic*
Comix*, *American*
Cookshop, *American*
Country, *American*
Craftsteak, *Steakhouse*
Crema, *Mexican*
Dani, *Mediterranean*
David Burke/Bloom., *American*
Degustation, *French/Spanish*
Del Posto, *Italian*
Destino, *Italian*
Devin Tavern, *American*
Dirty Bird to-go, *American*
Ditch Plains, *Seafood*
Dona, *Mediterranean*
Dressler, *American*
Dublin 6, *American*
El Centro, *Mexican*
Eleven B*, *Italian*
E.U., The*, *Gastropub*
Farm on Adderley, *American*
Fatty Crab, *Malaysian*
Fette Sau*, *BBQ*
15 East*, *Japanese*
Fillip's, *American/French*
Fireside*, *Tapas*
FR.OG*, *French*
Funky Diner*, *American*
Futura, *Argentinean/Italian*
Gilt, *American*
Ginger, *Chinese*
Gin Lane, *Continental*
Goblin Market*, *American*
goodburger, *Hamburgers*
Good Fork, *Eclectic*
Gordon Ramsay/London*, *Mod. European*
Graffiti Bistro*, *Eclectic*
Grayz Bar & Lounge*, *American*

Gribouille, *French*
Harry Cipriani*, *Italian*
Harry's, *Eclectic/Steakhouse*
Hawaiian Tropic Zone*, *American*
Hill Country*, *BBQ*
HQ, *American*
Hudson River Cafe*, *Seafood*
I-Chin*, *Chinese*
Il Brigante*, *Italian*
Il Lunetta*, *Mediterranean*
Industria Argentina, *Argentinean*
In Tent, *Mediterranean*
Jack, *French*
Japonais, *Japanese*
JivamukTea, *Vegan*
Johnny Utah's*, *Southwestern*
Jovia, *American/Italian*
Kampuchea Noodle*, *SE Asian*
Karen's*, *Eclectic*
Kellari Taverna, *Greek*
KitchenBar, *American/Med*
Klee Brasserie*, *European*
Knife + Fork, *Modern European*
Kobe Club*, *Steakhouse*
Kyotofu*, *Japanese/Desserts*
La Moelle*, *French/Steakhouse*
Las Ramblas, *Spanish*
L'Atelier/Joël Robuchon, *French*
Le Cirque, *French*
Leela Lounge, *Indian*
Le Miu, *Japanese*
Little Bistro, *American*
Little D Eatery, *Eclectic*
Little Owl, *American/Med*
Loft, *Mediterranean*
Lonesome Dove*, *Southwestern*
Mai, *Pan-Asian*
Mai House*, *Vietnamese*
Marbella, *Spanish*
Marshall Stack*, *Eclectic*
Masala Garden*, *Indian*
Max Brenner, *Dessert*
Metro Marché*, *French*
Meze, *Turkish*
Mint, *Indian*
Moment*, *American*
Momofuku Ssäm Bar, *Korean*
Monkey Town, *Eclectic*
Morandi*, *Italian*
Morgan, The, *American*
Morimoto, *Japanese*
Mumbo Gumbo*, *Cajun/BBQ*
My Moon, *Mediterranean*

Nelson Blue*, *New Zealand*
99 Miles to Philly, *Cheese Steaks*
Nizza*, *Mediterranean*
Nomad, *North African*
Noodle Bar, *Pan-Asian*
Novo, *Nuevo Latino*
Nurnberger Bierhaus, *German*
Olea, *Mediterranean*
Orchard, The, *American*
Ovelia*, *Greek*
Pair of 8's, *American*
Palà, *Italian*
Parea, *Greek*
Park Chinois*, *Chinese*
Pars Grill House, *Persian/Iranian*
Peacock Alley, *American*
Pera*, *Turkish/Med*
Per Lei, *Italian*
Petite Crevette*, *Seafood*
Petrarca Vino, *Italian*
Philippe, *Chinese*
Pier 2110, *Seafood/Soul Food*
Pies-N-Thighs, *Bakery/Soul Food*
Pioneer Bar-B-Q, *Barbecue*
p*ong*, *Desserts*
Porchetta, *Italian*
Porter House NY, *Steakhouse*
Pre:Post, *American*
Prosecco*, *Italian*
Quaint, *American*
Quality Meats, *American/ Steakhouse*
Rack & Soul, *Barbecue/Southern*
River Room, *Southern*
Room 4 Dessert, *Dessert*
Room Service, *Thai*
Rosanjin*, *Japanese*
Royal's Downtown, *American*
Russian Tea Room*, *Continental*
Sadie Mae's Cafe, *Soul Food*
Samba-Lé, *Brazilian*
Sascha, *American*
Scarlatto, *Italian*
Setacci, *Italian*
7 Square*, *American*
Sfoglia, *Italian*
S'mac, *American*
Sofrito, *Puerto Rican*
Sorrel, *American*
Spiga, *Italian*
Staghorn, *Steakhouse*
Stella Maris*, *Mod. European*
STK*, *Steakhouse*

Telepan, *American*
Tigerland, *Thai/Vietnamese*
Tini Ristorante*, *Italian*
Tintol, *Portuguese/Spanish*
Todai, *Japanese*
Tokyo Pop, *Japanese*
Tour, *Eclectic*
Trestle on Tenth, *American*
Trinity Place, *Eclectic*
24 Prince, *American*
Union Smith Café, *American*
Ureña, *Spanish*
Valbella, *Italian*
Waverly Inn*, *American*
Whym, *American*
Wicker Park, *Continental*
Yuva, *Indian*
Zip Burger, *Hamburgers*

Noteworthy Closings (102)

A&B Lobster King
Amuse
Assaggio
Babu
Banania Cafe
Bayou
Bellini
Belluno
Bill Hong's
Biltmore Room
Bistro du Vent
Bistro St. Mark's
Bivio
Black Pearl
Blue Star
Bolzano's
Bruculino
Cafe Trevi
Canton
Casa Mia
Caviar & Banana
Chez Michallet
coast
Cyclo
da Giacomo
Della Rovere
D'or Ahn
East Lake
Eemo
El Rancho
Fontana di Trevi
14 Wall Street

French Quarter
Frère Jacques
Grilled Cheese
Hue
Ian
Il Menestrello
Il Monello
Jean-Luc
Jewel Bako Makimono
Josephs Citarella
Julian's
Khyber Grill
Kitchen/Cocktails
Kitchen 82
Komegashi
Le Pescadou
Les Moules
Le Zinc
Lo Scalco
Magnifico
Mainland
Manhattan Grille
Manhattan Ocean
McHales
Meet
Metropol
Minado
MJ Grill
Monsoon
Océo
Onju
Osteria Stella
Pace
Parish & Co.
Park Avalon
Pearson's BBQ
Petrosino
Plate NYC
Raga
Raymond's Cafe
Rib
River
Sabor
Sandia
Scopa
Second Ave Deli
Secretes
71 Clinton Fresh
Shaan
shore
Shorty's Half Shell
Silverleaf Tavern
Smoked

Soho Cantina
Soju
SQC
Sultan
Sushi Rose
Taku
Tennessee Mtn.
343
Tre Pomodori
Ulrika's
Uovo
Vela
Viva Mar Cafe
V Steakhouse
Yellow Fin
Yujin
Yumcha

Outdoor Dining

(G=garden; P=patio;
S=sidewalk; T=terrace)
Aesop's Tables (G)
Aleo (G)
Alma (T)
A.O.C. (G)
Aquagrill (T)
Barbetta (G)
Barolo (G)
Bar Pitti (S)
Battery Gardens (G, P, T)
Blue Hill (G, P)
Blue Water (T)
Boathouse (T)
Bottino (G)
Bryant Park (G)
Cabana (T)
Cacio e Pepe (G, S)
Cafe Centro (S)
Café Fiorello (S)
Café St. Bart's (T)
Cávo (G, P)
Coffee Shop (S)
Convivium Osteria (G)
Da Nico (G, S)
Da Silvano (S)
East of Eighth (G)
Employees Only (G)
Esca (P)
Five Front (G)
Fragole (G)
Gascogne (G)
Gavroche (G)
Gigino (P, S)

Gnocco Caffe (G)
Grocery, The (G)
Harbour Lights (T)
Home (G)
I Coppi (G)
Il Gattopardo (P)
Il Palazzo (S)
Isabella's (S)
I Trulli (G)
Jolie (G)
La Bottega (T)
Lake Club (G)
La Lanterna (G)
L & B Spumoni (G, P)
Lattanzi (G, T)
Le Jardin Bistro (G)
Le Refuge (G)
L'Impero (P)
Long Tan (G)
Loulou (G)
Luxia (G)
March (G, T)
Marina Cafe (T)
Markt (S)
New Leaf (P)
Ocean Grill (S)
One (S)
Ono (G, S)
Osaka (G)
Pampano (T)
Panino'teca 275 (G)
Paradou (G)
Park, The (G)
Pastis (T)
Patois (G)
Pete's Tavern (S)
Portofino's (T)
Pure Food & Wine (G)
Relish (G)
Ribot (T)
River Café (G)
Riverdale Garden (G)
Riverview (P)
Rock Center Cafe (T)
Sahara (G)
Sea Grill (G)
Sherwood Cafe (G, P)
Sripraphai (G)
Surya (G)
Sweet Melissa (G)
Tartine (S)
Tavern on Green (G)
Terrace in the Sky (T)

Vento (S)
ViceVersa (G)
Vittorio Cucina (G)
Water Club (P)
Water's Edge (P)
Wollensky's (S)
Zum Schneider (S)

People-Watching
Alto
Angus McIndoe
Asia de Cuba
Aspen
A Voce
Babbo
Balthazar
Barbuto
Bar Pitti
Bayard's
Ben Benson's
Bette
Bice
Blue Water
Boqueria
Cafe Gitane
Cafe Luxembourg
Cipriani Dwntn
Coco Pazzo
Da Silvano
Elaine's
Elio's
Employees Only
Five Points
Four Seasons
Freemans
Fresco by Scotto
Gabriel's
Great Jones Cafe
Il Cantinori
Indochine
Jean Georges
Joe Allen
Koi
La Esquina
La Grenouille
Le Bernardin
Le Cirque
Lever House
Long Tan
Matsuri
Mercer Kitchen
Michael's
Mr. Chow

Nam
Nobu
Nobu 57
Odeon
Ono
Orchard, The
Pastis
Peacock Alley
Per Lei
Perry Street
per se
Pre:Post
Provence en Boite
Public
Rao's
Regency
Sardi's
Sascha
Schiller's
Smith & Wollensky
Spice Market
Spotted Pig
Stanton Social
Thor
21 Club
212
wd-50
Yuca Bar
Zum Schneider

Power Scenes
Bar Americain
Bayard's
Ben Benson's
BLT Prime
Bobby Van's
Carlyle
City Hall
Coco Pazzo
Daniel
Delmonico's
Del Posto
Elio's
44
Four Seasons
Fresco by Scotto
Gallagher's
Gilt
Gotham B&G
Harry's
Jean Georges
Keens
La Grenouille

Le Bernardin
Le Cirque
Lever House
Michael's
Nobu
Nobu 57
Peter Luger
Rao's
Regency
Smith & Wollensky
Sparks
21 Club

Private Rooms/Parties
(Call for capacity)
Alain Ducasse
Arabelle
Barbetta
Battery Gardens
Bayard's
Beacon
Ben & Jack's
BLT Fish
BLT Prime
BLT Steak
Blue Hill
Blue Smoke
Blue Water
Buddakan
Café Gray
Capital Grille
Cellini
Centolire
City Hall
Compass
Daniel
Danube
Del Frisco's
Delmonico's
Eleven Madison
English is Italian
EN Japanese
ESPN Zone
Felidia
Fiamma Osteria
F.illi Ponte
FireBird
Four Seasons
Fresco by Scotto
Gabriel's
Geisha
Gramercy Tavern
Il Buco

Il Cortile
'inoteca
Jean Georges
Jezebel
Keens
La Grenouille
Le Bernardin
Le Perigord
Lever House
Le Zie 2000
L'Impero
Maloney & Porcelli
March
Matsuri
Megu
Michael's
Mi Cocina
Milos
Modern, The
Moran's Chelsea
Mr. Chow
Mr. K's
Nobu
Nobu 57
Oceana
Park, The
Park Ave. Cafe
Periyali
per se
Picholine
Redeye Grill
Remi
Re Sette
Riingo
River Café
Rock Center Cafe
Sambuca
Shun Lee Palace
Solo
Sparks
Spice Market
Tabla
Tao
Tavern on Green
Terrace in the Sky
Thalassa
Tocqueville
Tribeca Grill
21 Club
212
Vento
Water Club
Water's Edge

Pubs/Microbreweries

(See Zagat NYC Nightlife)

Angus McIndoe
Chadwick's
ChipShop/Curry
Corner Bistro
Heartland Brew.
Jackson Hole
J.G. Melon
Joe Allen
Killmeyer Bavarian
Moran's Chelsea
Neary's
O'Neals'
Pete's Tavern
P.J. Clarke's
Spotted Pig
Wollensky's

Quick Bites

Amorina
Amy's Bread
A Salt & Battery
Azuri Cafe
Bamn!
Bereket
Better Burger
Blue 9 Burger
Brennan & Carr
Burritoville
Caracas
Carl's Steaks
ChipShop/Curry
Chop't Creative
City Bakery
Coals
Columbus Bakery
Cosí
Cosmic Cantina
Cozy Soup/Burger
Daisy May's
David Burke/Bloom.
Dishes
Dumpling Man
Ess-a-Bagel
F & B
Fresco on the Go
goodburger
Good Enough to Eat
Gray's Papaya
Hale & Hearty Soup
Hampton Chutney
'ino

Island Burgers
Joe's Pizza
Kati Roll Co.
La Esquina
Morgan, The
Nicky's Viet.
99 Miles to Philly
Noodle Bar
Once Upon a Tart
Papaya King
Peanut Butter & Co.
Philly Slim's
Press 195
Pump Energy Food
Rice 'n' Beans
Rickshaw Dumpling
Risotteria
Shake Shack
Tony Luke's
Tossed
Two Boots
Westville
Whole Foods
'wichcraft
Zabar's Cafe
Zip Burger

Quiet Conversation

Alto
Arabelle
Asiate
Café Botanica
Café Pierre
Chanterelle
Fleur de Sel
Gribouille
Il Gattopardo
Jean Georges
Kai
Kings' Carriage Hse.
Knife + Fork
La Grenouille
Le Bernardin
March
Mark's
Masa
Mr. K's
Peacock Alley
per se
Petrarca Vino
Petrossian
Picholine
Pier 2110

Provence en Boite
Room 4 Dessert
Sfoglia
Sorrel
Terrace in the Sky
Tocqueville
Tsampa

Raw Bars
Angus McIndoe
Aquagrill
Artisanal
Atlantic Grill
Avra
Baldoria
Balthazar
Bar Americain
Ben & Jack's
BLT Fish
bluechili
Blue Fin
Blue Ribbon
Blue Smoke
Blue Water
Bond 45
Brooklyn Fish Camp
Brouwers/Stone St.
Café Soleil
Caviar Russe
City Crab
City Hall
City Lobster
Craftsteak
Docks Oyster Bar
East Buffet
En Plo
Fish
Giorgione
Gramercy 24
Harbour Lights
Jack's Lux. Oyster
Le Singe Vert
Little Charlie's
London Lennie's
Lure Fishbar
Markt
McCormick & Schmick
Mercer Kitchen
Mermaid Inn
Milos
Minnow
Neptune Room
Ocean Grill

Old Homestead
Olea
Oyster Bar
Pearl Oyster
Sapa
Shaffer City
Shelly's
Shula's
Thalia
Tides
Trata Estiatorio
Tropica
Umberto's
Uncle Jack's
Water Club
Water's Edge

Romantic Places
Aix Brasserie
Alain Ducasse
Aleo
Algonquin
Alma
Alta
Amici Amore
Asiate
Aureole
Balthazar
Barbetta
Barolo
Battery Gardens
Blue Hill
Blue Ribbon Bakery
Boathouse
Bottino
Bouley
Bouterin
Café des Artistes
Café Pierre
Caffé/Green
CamaJe
Candela
Capsouto Frères
Casa La Femme
Caviar Russe
Chanterelle
Chelsea Bistro
Chez Josephine
Cipriani Dwntn
Convivium Osteria
Country
Country Café
Danal

Daniel
Danube
davidburke/donatella
Erminia
FireBird
Firenze
Five Front
Fleur de Sel
Flor de Sol
Four Seasons
Frankies Spuntino
Futura
Garden Cafe
Gascogne
Geisha
Gigino
Grocery, The
Harbour Lights
I Coppi
Il Buco
I Trulli
Jack
Jack's Lux. Oyster
Jezebel
JoJo
Jolie
Jovia
Kings' Carriage Hse.
Kitchen Club
L'Absinthe
Lady Mendl's
La Grenouille
La Lanterna
La Ripaille
Las Ramblas
Le Gigot
Le Refuge
Le Refuge Inn
L'Impero
March
Maria Pia
Mark's
Mas
Metsovo
Mr. K's
Nino's
Oliva
One if by Land
Pam Real Thai
Paola's
Pasha
Patois
Periyali

Petrossian
Philip Marie
Piano Due
Piccola Venezia
Pinocchio
Place, The
Portofino Grille
Primavera
Provence
Quercy
Rainbow Room
Raoul's
René Pujol
River Café
Riverview
Roc
Room 4 Dessert
Royal's Downtown
Sacred Chow
Sakura Café
Savoy
Scalini Fedeli
Sistina
Spice Market
Suba
Teodora
Terrace in the Sky
Tocqueville
Top of the Tower
Town
Uva
View, The
Water Club
Water's Edge

Senior Appeal
Arabelle
Artie's Deli
Aureole
Baldoria
Bamonte's
Barbetta
Barney Greengrass
Borgo Antico
Bouterin
Café Botanica
Café des Artistes
Caffé/Green
Campagnola
Capsouto Frères
Chadwick's
Chez Napoléon
Dawat

Del Posto
Embers
Felidia
Fetch
Gallagher's
Grifone
Il Nido
Il Tinello
Jean Georges
La Bonne Soupe
La Goulue
La Mangeoire
La Petite Auberge
Lattanzi
Le Boeuf/Mode
Le Marais
Le Perigord
Levana
Lusardi's
MarkJoseph
Mark's
Mr. K's
Nicola's
Nippon
Park Ave. Cafe
Paul & Jimmy's
Piccola Venezia
Pietro's
Ponticello
Primola
Quattro Gatti
Rao's
René Pujol
River Café
Rossini's
Rughetta
Sal Anthony's
San Pietro
Sardi's
Saul
Scaletta
Shun Lee West
Tavern on Green
Teresa's

Singles Scenes

Angelo & Maxie's
Asia de Cuba
Aspen
Atlantic Grill
Balthazar
Baraonda
Barça 18

Blue Fin
Blue Ribbon
Blue Water
Boca Chica
Brasserie 8½
Brother Jimmy's
Bryant Park
Buddakan
Buddha Bar
Butter
Cabana
Canyon Road
Cercle Rouge
Chinatown Brasserie
Cité Grill
Citrus B&G
Coffee Shop
Dos Caminos
East of Eighth
Elephant, The
elmo
Employees Only
Essex
Félix
Flor de Sol
Freemans
Heartland Brew.
Houston's
Hudson Cafeteria
Ideya
'inoteca
Isabella's
Jane
Japonais
Joya
Koi
La Esquina
La Goulue
Maloney & Porcelli
Markt
Mesa Grill
Monkey Bar
Mo Pitkin's
One
Otto
Pam Real Thai
Pastis
Peep
Pete's Tavern
Pipa
Pre:Post
Punch
Ruby Foo's

Sascha
Schiller's
Spice Market
Suba
SushiSamba
Tao
Thor
Tribeca Grill
Xunta
Zarela

Sleepers
(Good to excellent food,
but little known)
Aburiya Kinnosuke
Alcala
Alexandra
Amorina
Antica Venezia
AQ Cafe
Azuri Cafe
Bann
Beccofino
Bocelli
Bruckner B&G
Caffe Bondi
Camino Sur
Charles' Southern
Coals
Craftsteak
Crema
Degustation
Dona
Franchia
Fushimi
Good Fork
Hedeh
HQ
Kam Chueh
Kuma Inn
Kuruma Zushi
La Cantina Toscana
Le Cirque
Leela Lounge
Le Miu
Le Sans Souci
Lima's Taste
Little Charlie's
Little D Eatery
Londel's
Lorenzo's
Luz
Mai

Malagueta
Mint
Nippon
Olea
Pars Grill House
Peacock Alley
Ploes
Quality Meats
Queen's Hideaway
Rack & Soul
Red Café
River Room
Royal's Downtown
Sakura Café
Saravanaas
Scarlatto
Sfoglia
Shelly's
Siam Square
Sorrel
Taci's Beyti
Taco Chulo
Taka
Tevere
Thai Pavilion
Tides
Tigerland
Tokyo Pop
Tommaso's
tre dici
Turks & Frogs
Willie's

Sunday Best Bets
(See also Hotel Dining)
Aquagrill
Aquavit
Artisanal
Balthazar
Bar Americain
Blue Hill
Blue Ribbon
Blue Water
Bouley
Café de Bruxelles
Café des Artistes
Chez Oskar
Coco Pazzo
davidburke/donatella
Demarchelier
Five Points
Gotham B&G

Gramercy Tavern
La Mediterranée
Le Père Pinard
Lupa
Luxia
Mesa Grill
Mi Cocina
Moran's Chelsea
Odeon
Onera
Ouest
Our Place
Peter Luger
Piccolo Angolo
Picholine
Prune
River Café
Solo
Tavern on Green
Tratt. Dell'Arte
Tribeca Grill
Union Sq. Cafe
Water Club
Zoë

Tasting Menus

($ minimum)
Alain Ducasse (235)
Alto (115)
Amma (50)
Anh (25)
Annisa (68)
applewood (55)
Aquavit (105)
Asiate (95)
Aureole (89)
Babbo (70)
Barbuto (50)
Beppe (60)
Blue Hill (68)
Bond Street (80)
Café Boulud (125)
Caviar Russe (95)
Chanterelle (125)
Chestnut (60)
Chiam (40)
Chubo (56)
Country (85)
Cru (110)
Daniel (155)
Danube (85)
davidburke/donatella (85)
Del Posto (120)

dévi (60)
Django (75)
dominic (55)
Dona (75)
Donguri (85)
Eleven Madison (90)
EN Japanese (50)
Esca (75)
Fillip's (59)
FireBird (110)
Fleur de Sel (86)
Four Seasons (135)
Frederick's Madison (65)
fresh (75)
Gilt (145)
Gramercy Tavern (98)
Grocery, The (75)
Hasaki (50)
Hearth (75)
Honmura An (75)
Il Buco (85)
Inagiku (58)
'inoteca (34)
Jack's Lux. Oyster (50)
Jean Georges (125)
Jewel Bako (95)
JoJo (65)
Kai (150)
Kittichai (50)
Knife + Fork (45)
La Grenouille (120)
La Mangeoire (51)
L'Atelier/Joël Robuchon (160)
Le Bernardin (130)
Le Cirque (135)
Le Miu (55)
Le Perigord (75)
Le Tableau (50)
Lever House (115)
L'Impero (110)
March (78)
Maremma (49)
Mas (95)
Masa (350)
Modern, The (125)
Montrachet (85)
Morimoto (120)
Nippon (50)
Nobu (80)
Oceana (110)
Olives (72)
One if by Land (95)
Onera (75)

Park Terrace (50)
Payard Bistro (72)
Peacock Alley (95)
Peking Duck (30)
per se (210)
Petrossian (62)
Philip Marie (90)
Piano Due (80)
Picholine (120)
Pó (48)
Pure Food & Wine (59)
River Café (102)
Roppongi (60)
Rose Water (48)
San Domenico (75)
Scalini Fedeli (90)
Setacci (65)
66 (66)
Solera (75)
Solo (85)
Spigolo (65)
Suba (55)
Sueños (50)
Sugiyama (52)
Sumile (65)
SushiSamba (70)
Sushi Zen (50)
Tabla (79)
Taka (60)
Takahachi (30, 45)
Telepan (59)
Terrace in the Sky (100)
Tocqueville (75)
Triomphe (75)
21 Club (85)
View, The (75)
Vong (70)
Wallsé (75)
Water's Edge (75)
wd-50 (105)
West Bank Cafe (45)

Tea Service

Alice's Tea Cup
Bette
BG
Café Opaline
Café Pierre
Cafe S.F.A.
Danal
Franchia

Kai
Kings' Carriage Hse.
Lady Mendl's
Mark's
Morgan, The
North Square
Payard Bistro
Sant Ambroeus
Sarabeth's
Sweet Melissa
Tea & Sympathy
Tea Box
202 Cafe

Theme Restaurants

Brooklyn Diner
Cowgirl
ESPN Zone
Hard Rock Cafe
Ninja
Shula's

Transporting Experiences

Asiate
Balthazar
Bayard's
Boathouse
Buddakan
Buddha Bar
Café des Artistes
Chez Josephine
FireBird
Fraunces Tavern
Il Buco
Jezebel
Keens
La Grenouille
Le Colonial
Masa
Matsuri
Megu
Ninja
One if by Land
per se
Rainbow Room
Rao's
Suba
Tao
Tavern on Green
Vatan
Water's Edge

Special Features

Trendy
Angus McIndoe
Aspen
A Voce
Balthazar
Bar Americain
Barbounia
Barça 18
Bar Pitti
Bette
Blaue Gans
Blue Ribbon
Blue Ribbon Sushi
Blue Water
Bondi Road
Bond Street
Boqueria
Buddakan
Buddha Bar
Butter
Casa Mono
Cercle Rouge
'Cesca
Chinatown Brasserie
Cookshop
Country
davidburke/donatella
db Bistro Moderne
Diner
Dos Caminos
elmo
Employees Only
EN Japanese
Fatty Crab
5 Ninth
Franny's
Freemans
Geisha
Gilt
Gin Lane
Gonzo
Gramercy Tavern
Grocery, The
Harrison, The
Hearth
Highline
'inoteca
Jack's Lux. Oyster
Japonais
Jewel Bako
Joya

Koi
La Bottega
La Esquina
Landmarc
Lever House
L'Impero
Lure Fishbar
Marseille
Matsuri
Megu
Mermaid Inn
Modern, The
Morimoto
Nobu
Nobu 57
Odeon
Olives
One
Ono
Otto
Ouest
Paradou
Park, The
Pastis
Pearl Oyster
Peep
Perry Street
Planet Thailand
Pop Burger
Pre:Post
Red Cat
Sascha
Schiller's
SEA
Shake Shack
Spice Market
Spotted Pig
Stanton Social
Suba
SushiSamba
Thor
Vento
wd-50

Views
Above
Alma
Asiate
Battery Gardens
BG
Boathouse

Bryant Park
Bubby's (Dumbo)
Café Botanica
Café Gray
Cafe S.F.A.
Caffé/Green
Cipriani Dolci
Craftsteak
Delegates Dining Rm.
F.illi Ponte
Foley's Fish
Gigino
Grill Room
Harbour Lights
Heartland Brew.
Hispaniola
Lake Club
Liberty View
Lobster Box
Marina Cafe
Metrazur
Michael Jordan's
per se
Pete's Downtown
P.J. Clarke's (Financial Dist.)
Porter House NY
Portofino's
Rainbow Room
River Café
River Room
Riverview
Rock Center Cafe
Sarabeth's (CPS)
Sea Grill
Tavern on Green
Terrace in the Sky
Top of the Tower
View, The
Water Club
Water's Edge

Visitors on Expense Account
Alain Ducasse
Bouley
Carlyle
Chanterelle
Craft
Craftsteak
Daniel

Del Frisco's
Four Seasons
Harry's
Il Mulino
Jean Georges
Kuruma Zushi
Le Cirque
Masa
Megu
Milos
Nobu 57
One if by Land
per se
Petrossian

Waterside
Alma
Battery Gardens
Boathouse
Cabana
Grimaldi's
Harbour Lights
Lake Club
Lobster Box
Marina Cafe
Pete's Downtown
Portofino's
River Café
Riverview
Water Club
Water's Edge

Winning Wine Lists
Aix Brasserie
Alain Ducasse
Alfama
Alto
Annisa
Aquavit
Artisanal
Asiate
Aureole
A Voce
Babbo
Balthazar
Barbetta
Barolo
Bayard's
Becco
Bella Blu

Ben Benson's
BLT Steak
Blue Fin
Blue Hill
Blue Ribbon
Blue Water
Bottega del Vino
Bouley
Café Boulud
Cafe Centro
Café Gray
Capital Grille
Capsouto Frères
Casa Mono
'Cesca
Chanterelle
Chiam
Churrascaria
Cité
City Hall
Compass
Convivium Osteria
Counter
Country
Craft
Cru
Da Filippo
Daniel
Danube
db Bistro Moderne
DeGrezia
Del Frisco's
Del Posto
Eleven Madison
Felidia
Fiamma Osteria
F.illi Ponte
Fleur de Sel
Frankies Spuntino
Fresco by Scotto
Gabriel's
Gotham B&G
Gramercy Tavern
Harrison, The
Hearth
Il Buco
'ino
'inoteca
I Trulli
Jean Georges

Landmarc
La Pizza Fresca
Lavagna
Le Bernardin
Le Cirque
Le Madeleine
Le Perigord
L'Impero
Lupa
Lusardi's
Maloney & Porcelli
March
Mas
Megu
Michael Jordan's
Michael's
Milos
Modern, The
Montparnasse
Montrachet
Nice Matin
Nick & Stef's
Oceana
Olives
One if by Land
Onera
Orsay
Osteria del Circo
Otto
Ouest
Park Ave. Cafe
per se
Picholine
Post House
Raoul's
René Pujol
Rose Water
Rothmann's
Ruth's Chris
San Domenico
San Pietro
Scalini Fedeli
Sea Grill
Sette Enoteca
Shaffer City
Sharz Cafe
Smith & Wollensky
Solera
Sparks
Strip House

Supper
Tabla
Tasting Room
360
Tocqueville
Tommaso's
Town
Tribeca Grill
Tse Yang

21 Club
Union Sq. Cafe
Uva
Veritas
Wallsé
Water Club
West Bank Cafe
Zoë

Wine Vintage Chart

This chart, based on the 0 to 30 scale used throughout our *Survey,* is designed to help you select wine. The ratings (prepared by **Howard Stravitz,** a law professor at the U. of South Carolina) reflect both the quality of the vintage and the wine's readiness for consumption. We do not include 1987, 1991–1993 vintages because they are not especially recommended. A dash indicates that a wine is either past its peak or too young to rate.

	'86	'88	'89	'90	'94	'95	'96	'97	'98	'99	'00	'01	'02	'03	'04	'05
WHITES																
French:																
Alsace	–	–	26	26	25	24	24	23	26	24	26	27	25	22	24	25
Burgundy	25	–	23	22	–	28	27	24	23	26	25	24	27	23	25	26
Loire Valley	–	–	–	–	–	–	–	–	–	24	25	26	23	24	25	
Champagne	25	24	26	29	–	26	27	24	23	24	24	22	26	–	–	–
Sauternes	28	29	25	28	–	21	23	25	23	24	24	28	25	26	21	26
German	–	25	26	27	24	23	26	25	26	23	21	29	27	25	26	26
Austrian:																
Grüner Velt./ Riesling	–	–	–	–	25	21	28	28	27	22	23	24	26	26	26	–
California (Napa, Sonoma, Mendocino):																
Chardonnay	–	–	–	–	–	–	–	–	–	24	23	26	26	27	28	29
Sauvignon Blanc/Sémillon	–	–	–	–	–	–	–	–	–	–	–	27	28	26	27	26
REDS																
French:																
Bordeaux	25	23	25	29	22	26	25	23	25	24	29	26	24	25	23	27
Burgundy	–	–	24	26	–	26	27	26	22	27	22	24	27	24	24	25
Rhône	–	26	28	28	24	26	22	24	27	26	27	26	–	25	24	–
Beaujolais	–	–	–	–	–	–	–	–	–	–	24	–	23	27	23	28
California (Napa, Sonoma, Mendocino):																
Cab./Merlot	–	–	–	28	29	27	25	28	23	26	22	27	26	25	24	24
Pinot Noir	–	–	–	–	–	–	–	24	23	24	23	27	28	26	23	–
Zinfandel	–	–	–	–	–	–	–	–	–	–	25	23	27	22	–	–
Oregon:																
Pinot Noir	–	–	–	–	–	–	–	–	–	–	26	27	24	25	–	–
Italian:																
Tuscany	–	–	–	25	22	24	20	29	24	27	24	26	20	–	–	–
Piedmont	–	–	27	27	–	23	26	27	26	25	28	27	20	–	–	–
Spanish:																
Rioja	–	–	–	26	26	24	25	22	25	24	27	20	24	25		
Ribera del Duero/Priorat	–	–	–	26	26	27	25	24	25	24	27	20	24	26	–	
Australian:																
Shiraz/Cab.	–	–	–	–	24	26	23	26	28	24	24	27	27	25	26	–

ZAGATMAP

Manhattan Subway Map

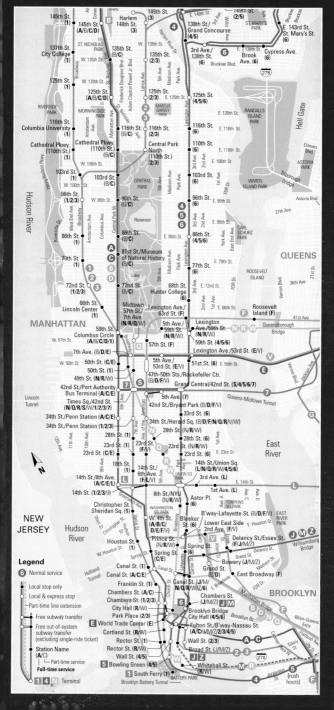

New Yorkers' Favorite Restaurants

Map coordinates follow each name. Sections A–H lie south of 34th Street (see adjacent map). Sections I–P lie north of 34th Street (see reverse side of map).

1. Gramercy Tavern (B-4)
2. Union Square Cafe (B-4)
3. Le Bernardin (O-3)
4. Babbo (C-3)
5. Peter Luger (E-7)
6. Bouley (F-4)
7. Gotham Bar & Grill (C-4)
8. Daniel (M-4)
9. Jean Georges (N-3)
10. Blue Water Grill (B-4)
11. Nobu (F-3)
12. Eleven Madison Park (B-4)
13. per se (N-3)
14. Rosa Mexicano (B-4, N-3, N-6)
15. Balthazar (E-4)
16. Modern, The (O-4)
17. Chanterelle (F-3)
18. Tabla (B-4)
19. Atlantic Grill (L-5)
20. Four Seasons (O-5)
21. Aquavit (N-4)
22. Artisanal (A-4)
23. davidburke & donatella (N-5)
24. Café des Artistes (M-3)
25. Aquagrill (E-3)
26. Aureole (N-4)
27. Spice Market (C-2)
28. Il Mulino (D-4)
29. Café Boulud (L-4)
30. Carmine's (K-2, P-3)
31. Ouest (K-2)
32. Picholine (N-3)
33. Palm (O-3, P-5)
34. Saigon Grill (C-4, K-2)
35. L'Impero (P-6)
36. Craft (B-4)
37. Lupa (D-4)
38. Blue Ribbon (E-3, G-7)
39. Café Gray (N-3)
40. Blue Hill (D-3)
41. One if by Land (D-3)
42. Blue Smoke (A-4)
43. Pastis (C-2)
44. Sparks (O-5)
45. Asia de Cuba (P-4)
46. Del Frisco's (O-4)
47. Tao (N-4)
48. Mesa Grill (C-4)
49. Felidia (N-5)
50. Becco (O-3)

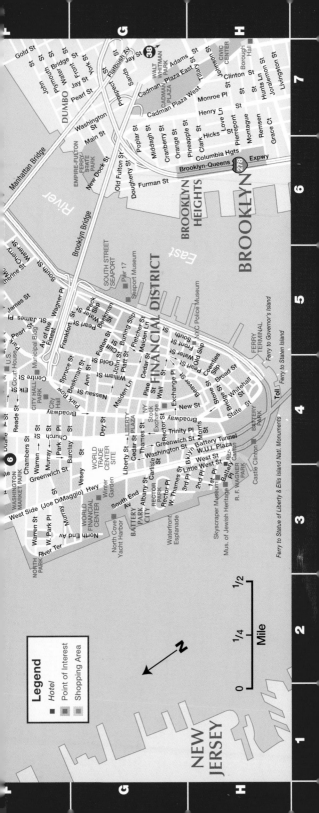